Law & Gospel

*How to Read and
Apply the Bible*

Law & Gospel

How to Read and Apply the Bible

CARL FERDINAND WILHELM WALTHER

General Editor
Charles P. Schaum

Assistant Editors
John P. Hellwege Jr.
Thomas E. Manteufel

Translated by
Christian C. Tiews

CONCORDIA PUBLISHING HOUSE • SAINT LOUIS

Copyright © 2010 Concordia Publishing House
3558 S. Jefferson Ave., St. Louis, MO 63118-3968
1-800-325-3040 • www.cph.org

Manufactured in the United States of America

Library of Congress Cataloging-in-Publication Data

Walther, C. F. W. (Carl Ferdinand Wilhelm), 1811–1887.
    [Rechte Unterscheidung von Gesetz und Evangelium. English]
    Law and Gospel : how to read and apply the Bible / Carl Ferdinand Wilhelm Walther ; translated by Christian C. Tiews ; general editor, Charles P. Schaum ; assistant editors, John P. Hellwege, Jr., Thomas E. Manteufel.
        p. cm.
    Includes indexes.
    ISBN 978-0-7586-1688-3
    1. Law and Gospel. I. Tiews, Christian C. II. Schaum, Charles P. III. Hellwege, John P. IV. Manteufel, Thomas. V. Title.
    BT79.W3413 2010
    241'.2—dc22   2009043391

1 2 3 4 5 6 7 8 9 10   19 18 17 16 15 14 13 12 11 10

❖ Contents ❖

❖ ABBREVIATIONS ❖

AC   Augsburg Confession

AE   *Luther's Works: American Edition.* Volumes 1–30: Edited by Jaroslav Pelikan. St. Louis: Concordia, 1955–76. Volumes 31–55: Edited by Helmut Lehmann. Philadelphia/Minneapolis: Muhlenberg/Fortress, 1957–86.

ANF   *The Ante-Nicene Fathers: Translations of the Writings of the Fathers down to A.D. 325.* Edited by Alexander Roberts and James Donaldson. Revised by A. Cleveland Coxe. 10 vols. Buffalo: Christian Literature Publishing Co., 1885–96. Reprint, Peabody, MA: Hendrickson, 1994.

Ap   Apology of the Augsburg Confession

Concordia   *Concordia: The Lutheran Confessions,* second edition. Edited by Paul McCain, et al. St. Louis: Concordia, 2006.

Ep   Epitome of the Formula of Concord

FC   Formula of Concord

Halle Ed.   See W[1]

LC   Large Catechism

LCMS   The Lutheran Church—Missouri Synod

LSB   *Lutheran Service Book*

Müller   *Die symbolischen Bücher der evangelisch-lutherischen Kirche,* eleventh edition. Edited by Johann T. Müller. Gütersloh: Bertelsmann, 1912.

NPNF[1]   *A Select Library of the Christian Church: Nicene and Post-Nicene Fathers: Second Series.* Edited by Philip Schaff. 14 vols. New York, 1886–89. Reprint, Peabody, MA: Hendrickson, 1994.

NPNF[2]   *A Select Library of the Christian Church: Nicene and Post-Nicene Fathers: Second Series.* Edited by Philip Schaff and Henry Wace. 14 vols. New York, 1890–1900. Reprint, Peabody, MA: Hendrickson, 1994.

PL	*Patrologiae cursus completus: Series Latina.* Edited by J.-P. Migne. 221 vols. in 223. Paris: Garnier Fratres, 1844–64.
SA	Smalcald Articles
SC	Small Catechism
SD	Solid Declaration of the Formula of Concord
St. Louis Ed.	See W²
Tr	Treatise on the Power and Primacy of the Pope
Triglot Concordia	*Triglot Concordia: The Symbolical Books of the Ev.-Lutheran Church.* Edited by G. Friedrich Bente and William H. T. Dau. St. Louis: Concordia, 1921.
W¹	*D. Martin Luthers sowol in Deutscher als Lateinischer Sprache verfertigte und aus der letztern in die erstere übersetzte Sämmtliche Schriften.* Edited by Johann G. Walch. 24 vols. Halle: Gebauer, 1740–53.
W²	*Dr. Martin Luthers Sämmtliche Schriften.* Edited by Albrecht F. Hoppe. 23 vols. St. Louis: Concordia, 1880–1910.
WA	*D. Martin Luthers Werke: Kritische Gesamtausgabe.* 73 vols. in 85. Weimar: Hermann Böhlau, 1883–.
WA DB	*D. Martin Luthers Werke: Deutsche Bibel.* 12 vols. in 15. Weimar: Hermann Böhlau, 1906–.

❖ FOREWORD ❖

There is little doubt that *Law and Gospel* is the most influential and utilized work bearing the name of C. F. W. Walther. Yet it is the result of a rather curious pedigree—Walther never saw the work in print.

Law and Gospel was a series of Friday evening lectures given by Walther between September 12, 1884, and November 6, 1885. As W. H. T. Dau correctly noted, there is a difference between the lecture style and its more informal use of side comments, gestures, vocalizations, etc., and the more formal, structured style of a text prepared for publication. The German text was the transcription of stenographic notes prepared by Theodore Claus, edited by Ludwig Fürbringer, which appeared in 1897, ten years after Walther's death. This was published in 1901. Students of *Law and Gospel* have always wondered whether Walther would have permitted the publication of the lectures in the form presented.

Four English renditions followed: (1) Dau, in 1929; (2) Walter C. Pieper's condensation of Dau under the title *God's No and God's Yes* in 1973; (3) Herbert J. A Bouman's "considerable abridgment and condensation of the original . . . dictated by the publisher's space limitations" for the collection of Walther's writings produced in 1981; and (4) the present translation, which omits some of Dau's language and editorial choices and makes Walther sound more like Walther than a British academician.

Walther is often criticized as being a "citation theologian." A glance at *Law and Gospel* and almost any other work by Walther other than sermons would seem to support this view. Walther readily acknowledged that it was true, and he made no apology for it. He was content to sit at the feet of or stand on the shoulders of those who defended biblical teaching. Walther always began with proof from the Word of God (*Beweis aus Gottes Wort*). Then followed the witness of the Church in its official confessions (*Zeugnisse der Kirche in ihren öffentlichen Bekenntnissen*). Then followed the witness of the Church in the private writings of its teachers (*Zeugnisse der Kirche in den Privatschriften ihrer Lehrer*).

Of the teachers of the Church, no one outranks Martin Luther. Walther was convinced that a knowledge of Luther was necessary for both pastors and laity in the Church. The production of the St. Louis edition, a genuine people's edition, was promoted by Walther for that purpose. The magazine *Der Lutheraner*, presided over by Walther from its beginning in 1844 until his death, carried the motto: "Gottes Wort und Luthers Lehr, vergehet nun und nimmermehr" ("God's Word and Luther's teaching, endures now and evermore").

There is a reason why the series of lectures was also known as "Lutherstunden" ("Luther Hours"). The copious citations from Luther's writings are an indication of the thorough knowledge of Luther in the mind and thought of Walther and of his determination to let Luther speak to and enrich the thought and life of his students.

Throughout the lectures, Walther speaks as a pastor to the future pastors of the Church. This is of the utmost significance to understanding the import of what Walther is doing in these lectures. Walther is often thought of as a theologian, professor, seminary president, synodical president, author, leader among Lutherans, etc. What is frequently overlooked is that he was first and foremost a pastor. From 1841 until his death in 1887, at the same time he accomplished all the things associated with the above titles, he was the pastor of the St. Louis joint congregation—first, Trinity, then also Holy Cross, Zion, and Immanuel. While each of the four locations had its own resident pastor, Walther was the pastor, and he regularly preached in the four churches on a rotating basis. Thus much of Walther's preaching was not of the "special occasion" variety nor in the role of guest, but as the called pastor of the flock.

In this role, Walther was a liturgical preacher; the texts he chose for preaching were the historic pericopes. In the tradition of such preaching, Walther did not consider it strange to preach frequently on the same text. In fact, there are fifteen printed sermons for Christmas Day on Luke 2:1–14, delivered between 1843 and 1873. Although Walther occasionally preached from a free text, he normally preached on either the Epistle or the Gospel for the day.

Walther's preaching served as a model for the pastors in preparation. What Walther developed in the lecture series is what he modeled in the pulpit—a pastor caring for the sheep entrusted to his care.

May this new edition of Walther's classic lectures enable pastors, future pastors, and the laity of the Church to learn from a genuine pastor how to properly distinguish between Law and Gospel.

William J. Schmelder
Professor Emeritus
Concordia Seminary, St. Louis, Missouri

❖ PREFACE ❖

WALTHER'S TEXT

In 1878 Carl Ferdinand Wilhelm Walther presented a lecture series based on thirteen theses about Law and Gospel. The lectures proved to be so popular that Walther decided to present a second, expanded, lecture series in 1884–85 based on twenty-five theses. These second lectures form the central message of this book.

Walther did not arrange for his notes to be published. After he died in 1887, however, Walther's colleagues and students wanted to preserve what they had been taught for the sake of future generations. In close collaboration with Concordia Publishing House, they published many of Walther's "literary remains." These were his papers, sermons, and other writings that he left behind but never published in his lifetime. In 1893, Concordia printed notes from the first lecture series in German as *Gesetz und Evangelium*, which is translated as *Law and Gospel*. Yet many students remembered his second lectures to be twice as long as the first. One attendee of that second series, Pastor Theodor Claus of Elkhart, Indiana, is the reason for the existence of this book. His fairly accurate shorthand notes of the second series of lectures were transcribed and reviewed by Professor Ludwig Fürbringer of Concordia Seminary. (Fürbringer later served as the seminary's president.) Concordia Publishing House printed this very literal account of Walther's lectures in 1897, reprinted in 1901, again in German, as *Die Rechte Unterscheidung von Gesetz und Evangelium* (*The Proper Distinction Between Law and Gospel*).

In 1929 Concordia published William H. T. Dau's English translation of Walther's second lecture series as *The Proper Distinction Between Law and Gospel*. Dau's book, based on the German text, is the English standard, and it forms a substantial part of this edition. However, Dau's work is not a literal translation, because he thought that presenting class notes, which were sometimes rough, without additional explanation would not be helpful. Therefore, Dau changed Walther's style and some of the content. Despite this intervention, Dau's translation has been the most popular of Walther's works.

WALTHER'S STYLE

Walther presented his evening lectures before a group of seminary students ranging in age from about eighteen to twenty-two. Walther's lectures were both informative and entertaining, delivered in a rapid-fire manner with subtle jokes and the occasional off-color remark. At times, Walther liked to role-play to illustrate his point. He spoke in a very conversational way. Dau wanted the written lectures to become a loftier, literary work. Therefore, he made three general decisions. First, Dau changed or deleted Walther's language when he felt that it was necessary.[1] Second, Dau used a flowing, literary British style that was common in the academic writing of that era. Third, Dau introduced extensive editorial changes and additions within the main text of the lectures in order to help the reader.

Walther's oral delivery of the lectures was at times probably choppy, but it came across to the listeners as edgy and powerful. Walther typically spoke from memory, and he tended to express thoughts as they came to him. This edition of *Law and Gospel* brings the reader closer to the original German text, and thus to Walther's actual lectures, letting the reader "hear" Walther's presentations in English as German hearers would have understood them. It trusts that Walther's original style will be more engaging for today's readers.

Many of Dau's helpful corrections remain, but we have chosen the original Walther text where Dau might not have. We have avoided inserting editorial matter into the body text. Footnotes include information that explains significant editorial decisions.

Although his lectures had an extemporaneous quality, Walther took a very detailed approach and put a lot of work into his preparation. Where he found errors in his first series of lectures, Walther fixed them in the second series. He was never afraid to admit and fix his mistakes. He also tried to teach this attitude of humility to his students. Walther thought and lived like a parish pastor and made that a central part of being a professor. His lectures speak to pastors, yet their intent is to be an advocate on behalf of the salvation of the laypeople. Walther knew that a pastor's most important calling is to distinguish Law and Gospel as he brings the Word of God to the souls in his care, so that in the hour of death and on the Last Day they can say, "I shall not die, but I shall live, and recount the deeds of the LORD" (Psalm 118:17).

---

1   Sometimes Dau did not agree with Walther's phrasing of theological terms. Dau also disliked the parts where Walther became a little too rough in his language. William Dallmann reports on this human side of Walther in Dallmann's autobiography, *My Life* (St. Louis: Concordia, 1945).

❖ ACKNOWLEDGMENTS ❖

Concordia Publishing House offers warm thanks to the following people and organizations whose contributions have significantly enriched this book for the benefit of the Church:

The Rev. Dr. Martin R. Noland provided insights into the history and the theological method of C. F. W. Walther in several publications. He also provided information regarding the intellectual history and context of the nineteenth century.

The Rev. Marvin A. Huggins, interim director of Concordia Historical Institute, and the staff of the institute provided valuable information that helped to improve the LCMS maps and other aspects of this volume. Mrs. Laura Marrs helped to provide photographs from the institute's collection used in this edition.

Mr. Dennis Rathert, archivist of Historic Trinity Lutheran Church in the Soulard neighborhood of St. Louis, generously provided additional photographs and documents.

Mr. Keith Lenharth, archivist of Holy Cross Lutheran Church, on Miami Street and Ohio Avenue west of Concordia Publishing House, generously provided additional photographs. Holy Cross continues to serve as an important part of the worship life at Concordia.

The United States Library of Congress has made available on its American Memory Web pages the following resource used in this book: Compton, Richard J. *Pictorial St. Louis, the great metropolis of the Mississippi valley; a topographical survey drawn in perspective A.D. 1875, by Camille N. Dry; designed & edited by Rich. J. Compton.* St. Louis: Compton & Co., 1876.

❖ USER'S GUIDE ❖

Boldface type represents emphasis in the German text called "separated type" (*Sperrdruck*). English typesetting conventions caused much of this emphasis to be lost in the Dau edition. When **boldface type** appears in a quotation, this indicates that Walther emphasized this material from another author.

Italic type is used for foreign words, technical terms, and additional points of emphasis.

Direct citations appear between quotation marks or are set in block quotes.

Square brackets [ ] contain words added by an editor for the sake of clarity.

Angle brackets < > include wording from an alternate translation, used in citations from *Concordia*.

Scripture citations come from the English Standard Version except where Walther makes a specific point using Luther's German translation of the Bible (identified in the margin note by the word "Luther" after the Bible reference). In such instances, the text is an English translation from the 1901 German edition of Walther's lectures.

Boldface margin notes indicate the start of a lecture, identify topics, and provide references to Scripture, the Book of Concord, and Luther's writings. Prior editions of *Law and Gospel* divided the text into thirty-nine chapters, one for each lecture. This edition divides the text into an introduction and twenty-five theses.

Footnotes contain the German and Latin words that Walther spoke, information about sources that Walther used, and other helpful facts about people or situations mentioned in the lectures. Where Walther used a Greek word or phrase to indicate his level of education and that expected of his students, this has been replaced entirely with English. Where Walther used Greek to indicate an important New Testament word, the Greek has been retained using letters recognizable to English readers.

Editor's notes provide useful information at the beginning of each thesis to help unlock Walther's presentation for the reader and make it more applicable to the reader's life.

Sperrdruck

Thesis number

Thesis

Annotation by the editor

margin note

identifies text from Luther Bible

< > Wording from alternate translation

Start of new lecture

date of delivery

Footnotes with technical terms

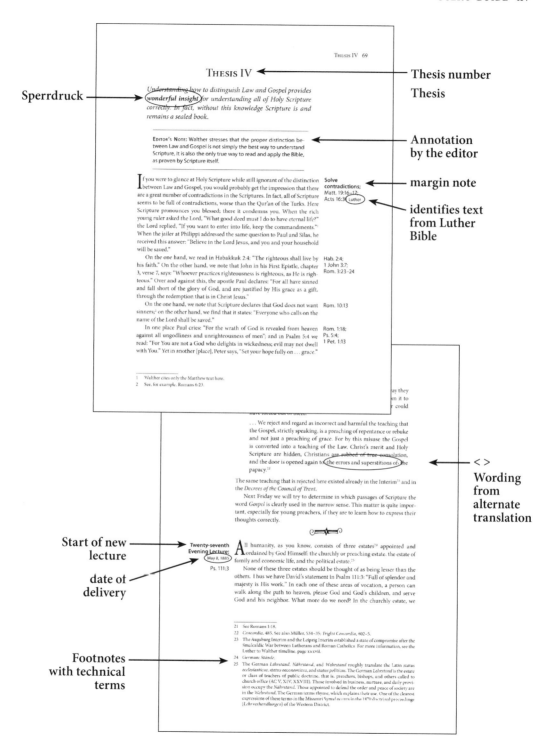

THESIS IV   69

THESIS IV

Understanding how to distinguish Law and Gospel provides ***wonderful insight*** *for understanding all of Holy Scripture correctly. In fact, without this knowledge Scripture is and remains a sealed book.*

EDITOR'S NOTE: Walther stresses that the proper distinction between Law and Gospel is not simply the best way to understand Scripture, it is also the only true way to read and apply the Bible, as proven by Scripture itself.

If you were to glance at Holy Scripture while still ignorant of the distinction between Law and Gospel, you would probably get the impression that there are a great number of contradictions in the Scriptures. In fact, all of Scripture seems to be full of contradictions, worse than the Qur'an of the Turks. Here Scripture pronounces you blessed; there it condemns you. When the rich young ruler asked the Lord, "What good deed must I do to have eternal life?" the Lord replied, "If you want to enter into life, keep the commandments." When the jailer at Philippi addressed the same question to Paul and Silas, he received this answer: "Believe in the Lord Jesus, and you and your household will be saved."

Solve contradictions; Matt. 19:16–17; Acts 16:31 *Luther*

On the one hand, we read in Habakkuk 2:4: "The righteous shall live by his faith." On the other hand, we note that John in his First Epistle, chapter 3, verse 7, says: "Whoever practices righteousness is righteous, as He is righteous." Over and against this, the apostle Paul declares: "For all have sinned and fall short of the glory of God, and are justified by His grace as a gift, through the redemption that is in Christ Jesus."

Hab. 2:4; 1 John 3:7; Rom. 3:23–24

On the one hand, we note that Scripture declares that God does not want sinners;[2] on the other hand, we find that it states: "Everyone who calls on the name of the Lord shall be saved."

Rom. 10:13

In one place Paul cries: "For the wrath of God is revealed from heaven against all ungodliness and unrighteousness of men"; and in Psalm 5:4 we read: "For You are not a God who delights in wickedness; evil may not dwell with You." Yet in another [place], Peter says, "Set your hope fully on … grace."

Rom. 1:18; Ps. 5:4; 1 Pet. 1:13

1   Walther cites only the Matthew text here.
2   See, for example, Romans 6:23.

... ay they ... m it to ... r could have forced out of them.

… We reject and regard as incorrect and harmful the teaching that the Gospel, strictly speaking, is a preaching of repentance or rebuke and not just a preaching of grace. For by this misuse the Gospel is converted into a teaching of the Law. Christ's merit and Holy Scripture are hidden, Christians are robbed of true consolation, and the door is opened again to the errors and superstitions of the papacy.[22]

The same teaching that is rejected here existed already in the *Interim*[23] and in the *Decrees of the Council of Trent.*

Next Friday we will try to determine in which passages of Scripture the word *Gospel* is clearly used in the narrow sense. This matter is quite important, especially for young preachers, if they are to learn how to express their thoughts correctly.

Twenty-seventh Evening Lecture: *May 8, 1885*

Ps. 111:3

All humanity, as you know, consists of three estates[24] appointed and ordained by God Himself: the churchly or preaching estate, the estate of family and economic life, and the political estate.[25]

None of these three estates should be thought of as being lesser than the others. Thus we have David's statement in Psalm 111:3: "Full of splendor and majesty is His work." In each one of these areas of vocation, a person can walk along the path to heaven, please God and God's children, and serve God and his neighbor. What more do we need? In the churchly estate, we

21   See Romans 1:18.
22   *Concordia,* 485. See also Müller, 534–35; *Triglot Concordia,* 802–5.
23   The Augsburg Interim and the Leipzig Interim established a state of compromise after the Smalcaldic War between Lutherans and Roman Catholics. For more information, see the Luther to Walther timeline, page xxxvii.
24   German: *Stände.*
25   The German *Lehrstand, Nährstand,* and *Wehrstand* roughly translate the Latin *status ecclesiasticus, status oeconomicus,* and *status politicus.* The German *Lehrstand* is the estate or class of teachers of public doctrine, that is, preachers, bishops, and others called to church office (AC V, XIV, XXVIII). Those involved in business, nurture, and daily provision occupy the *Nährstand.* Those appointed to defend the order and peace of society are in the *Wehrstand.* The German terms rhyme, which explains their use. One of the clearest expressions of these terms in the Missouri Synod occurs in the 1879 doctrinal proceedings (*Lehrverhandlungen*) of the Western District.

WALTHER'S
PLACE IN
LUTHERAN
HISTORY

This portrait of C. F. W. Walther was made in the 1840s. It became the most well-known image of Walther. His signature and a handwritten portion of 1 Peter 2:9 often accompanied an engraved version of this image. See, for example, Ludwig Fürbringer, *Eighty Eventful Years* (St. Louis: Concordia, 1944), 70. Image courtesy of Concordia Historical Institute.

❖ THE LIFE OF C. F. W. WALTHER ❖

It probably came as little surprise that Carl Ferdinand Wilhelm Walther became a pastor, though at his birth no one could have predicted the tremendous role that he would play in the history of American Christianity.[1] Born on October 25, 1811, to Gottlob Heinrich Wilhelm and Johanna Wilhelmina Walther, Ferdinand (as he was known) became part of a family of Lutheran preachers. His great-grandfather Moritz Heinrich Walther, grandfather Adolph Heinrich Walther, and father all served as pastors in Saxony. Ferdinand and his older brother, Otto, also entered the ministry.

Ferdinand was reared in a traditional German Lutheran pastor's home in the parsonage at the church in Langenchursdorf, where his father served until his death in 1841. German society was very class conscious at that time and remains so today. The family occupied an upper-middle-class position in the community, not because of wealth but because of the education that German pastors received. Likewise, Ferdinand was reared in the knowledge and respect of the Bible as God's Word, and he was educated concerning God's grace. One well-known account from his childhood relates that at age three he memorized a poem for Christmas:

> Jesus, Thy blood and righteousness
> My beauty are, my glorious dress,
> Wherein before my God I'll stand
> When I shall reach the heavenly land.[2]

His father was so impressed by this memory work that he gave Ferdinand a three-penny piece. This left an indelible mark on the young boy, who determined that if knowing this text was worth so much to his father, it must contain a very important truth.

It was common in the early 1800s to leave home to attend school, even for what we would now call grade school, and Ferdinand was no exception. First, he attended a boys' school in Hohenstein, about ten kilometers northeast of Zwickau. Walther's uncle was the schoolmaster. At age ten, Ferdinand was sent to a Latin school in Schneeberg, some twenty kilometers southeast of Zwickau. Walther's brother-in-law was the vice-rector. Unfortunately, Rationalism and theological liberalism were broadly accepted in the German lands of that time, and even as a child, Ferdinand was instructed that the

---

1   For a fuller account of the life of C. F. W. Walther, see Martin Günther, *Dr. C. F. W. Walther: Lebensbild* (St. Louis: Concordia, 1890), and August R. Suelflow, *Servant of the Word: The Life and Ministry of C. F. W. Walther* (St. Louis: Concordia, 2000).

2   Suelflow, *Servant of the Word*, 15. This poem was part of a hymn written by Count Nikolaus Ludwig von Zinzendorf, who was first a Lutheran Pietist, then a Moravian bishop. See also the entry for Zinzendorf in the Index of Persons and Groups, page 501.

Bible could not be trusted and that Christianity was nothing but simple moralistic teachings. This led Ferdinand to turn his attention away from theology, and when he graduated from Schneeberg, he planned on studying music. However, Ferdinand's father offered to give him a *Thaler*[3] a week to help with expenses if he studied theology. Also, his older brother, Otto, who had just finished his second year of studying theology at the University of Leipzig, gave him a biography of Pastor Jean Frédéric Oberlin.[4] This book in particular motivated Ferdinand with its example of piety and humble service.

Thus Ferdinand started at the University of Leipzig as a theology student, and he quickly joined a small group of students known as the "Holy Club," of which Otto was already a member. While most of Leipzig's professors were thoroughgoing rationalists, the Holy Club was made up of students who were seeking something more certain, and they soon fell into a form of strict Pietism that believed one must go through great personal struggles in order to be saved. This threw Walther into great spiritual torments as he wondered if he truly was saved. This experience later contributed to Walther's keen insights on how Christians need to distinguish Law and Gospel.

Ferdinand found the solace of the Gospel from three different sources. First, he frequented the home of Friedrich W. Barthel in Leipzig. In the Barthel home, he was reminded time and again of his redemption through Christ. Mrs. Barthel also told her young visitor that she regularly prayed for solace for him. Still looking for comfort, Ferdinand wrote to a noted Lutheran pastor in Dresden, Martin Stephan. Walther later recorded that, before opening Stephan's reply, he prayed that God would keep him from more misleading comfort, but when he opened the letter, he was overjoyed at the words of Gospel that Stephan wrote. Thus began one of the most influential relationships in Ferdinand's life. The third source of consolation came in the unusual form of illness during the winter of 1831–32. He was forced to take a semester off to recuperate at his parents' parsonage, and Ferdinand busied himself with reading his father's collection of Luther's writings. During this time, Ferdinand became convinced of the scriptural soundness of Luther's theology and especially of the reformer's emphasis on the Gospel.

After completing his university education, Ferdinand could not qualify to be called as a pastor until he had completed two examinations, with a mandatory two-year interim between the tests. His father feared that Ferdinand's conservative views of the Bible and the Lutheran Confessions would cause problems with the examining committees. However, his fears proved unfounded because Ferdinand successfully completed the examinations

---

3   At the time of Walther's lectures, the *Thaler* (origin of *dollar*; sounds like *taller*) was worth three German marks. A *Thaler* from about 1825 would be approximately $30–$50 today.

4   Oberlin (1740–1826) was known for his works of Christian mercy in eastern France.

and received a call to serve as pastor in Bräunsdorf, Saxony, not far from his father's church. He was ordained on January 15, 1837.

Walther's time in Bräunsdorf was difficult because he found himself squarely in the middle of the battle between the rationalists and the conservatives in Saxony. His superintendent[5] and the schoolteacher in Bräunsdorf were rationalists, and Walther butted heads with them often. Because of the rationalist teachings that had held sway, upon his arrival Walther found the general state of the parish in terms of biblical, Christian training to be rather poor. The spiritual care of the people had been lacking, and he worked to correct this. However, when he attempted to order conservative, Bible-based books for the school, both the schoolteacher and the superintendent attempted to stop the purchase. But Count Detlef von Einsiedel stepped in. As patron of the territory, and a conservative ally, Einsiedel donated the books to the school. He also reminded the schoolteacher and the superintendent that the pastor had the right to choose the textbooks and that disputes were to be settled by the district school inspector. Despite this outcome, Walther's struggles continued.

Walther remained in close contact with an informal group of confessional Lutherans, sometimes called Old Lutherans, headed by Pastor Stephan, who was something of a lightning rod in the struggles of the German Lutheran churches. Many of the church leaders in Saxony did not like or trust Stephan, but for others who had been comforted in the Gospel, such as Otto and Ferdinand Walther, Stephan was a hero of the faith. Once, when a prominent churchman urged Ferdinand Walther to distance himself from Stephan, he replied: "Shall I forsake a man who, by God's grace, has saved my soul?"[6]

Lurking behind many of the concerns of the confessional Lutherans were the events in Prussia, a neighboring German state. In 1817, on the three-hundredth anniversary of the start of the Reformation, the king of Prussia, Frederick William III, decreed that the Lutheran and Reformed churches were to be merged into a new union church, which is often called the Prussian Union. This edict greatly offended many Lutherans who still treasured their identity kindled by Luther in 1517. The king was forcing them into church fellowship with a group with whom they had obvious and long-standing theological disagreements. While this union held sway only in Prussia, the conservative Lutherans in Saxony were worried that they, too, might be forced into such a merger. Although since 1697 the rulers of Saxony had been Roman Catholic, they had supported the Lutheran church in the territory as a matter of politics and had left its administration to church officials. Now, at a time

---

5   In the German Lutheran churches of this time period, a *Superintendent* would have been similar to a district president in the LCMS.

6   Suelflow, *Servant of the Word*, 53.

when Lutheran identity in all of the German lands had been so undermined by Rationalism, many church leaders were inclined to the type of union that had occurred in Prussia.

Because of concerns about the theological weakening of the church and the attempts by church leaders to enforce Rationalism, confessional Lutherans in Saxony, including the Walther brothers, were uneasy about the future of true Lutheranism in Germany. This fear was compounded when charges of fraudulent administration and sexual misconduct were brought against Stephan and he was suspended from his pastoral office. Stephan began disputing expenses and answering official hearings and inquiries. The charges produced few conclusive findings; at least one woman retracted her claims.

These actions against Stephan encouraged the long-held belief by Walther and others that they were targets of persecution. Believing that true Lutheranism was doomed in Germany, the group led by Stephan, which had already been discussing emigration, sped up the process. The actions of the emigrant company made the authorities suspicious, yet the suspicion of the authorities only accelerated the emigrants' activities and strengthened their resolve. After considering Australia and various parts of the United States, the group settled on Missouri as the proper destination. They established the goal to set up a colony of German-speaking Lutherans in Missouri outside of St. Louis. In this new community they could worship in purity and raise their children in the faith. About seven hundred people booked passage on five ships sailing from Bremerhaven to New Orleans in November 1838. During the passage, Stephan was elected bishop of the group and a document was written for "Stephan's Investiture." Those on the other ships, including the Walther brothers, signed this document upon reaching New Orleans. The immigrants settled temporarily in St. Louis while looking for land on which to establish their new community. Although rules created before leaving Germany called for a communal system of ownership, Stephan lived better than the rest, paying his expenses out of the common treasury as he had been accustomed to doing as a member of the territorial church in Saxony. The group eventually purchased 4,475 acres in Perry County, Missouri (south of St. Louis), along the banks of the Mississippi River. Stephan and an initial group of settlers moved to the property on April 26, 1839, while the others stayed in St. Louis until the settlement was prepared for their arrival.

However, a series of revelations dramatically changed the situation for those who remained in St. Louis. Following a May 5, 1839, service in which Pastor G. H. Löber preached, two women independently confessed to him that they had had adulterous relations with Stephan, further claiming that he had seduced them. These confessions were shared with the other pastors among those who had remained in St. Louis. This was compounded by the fact that Stephan had left his wife behind in Germany. Not only was the immigrants' trust in Stephan rocked, but the men also realized that he was no longer fit for a position of authority within the church. The church leaders also began to look more critically at Stephan's leadership and even the orthodoxy of his teachings. After discussing the matter, it was decided that one pastor would have to go to Perry County and share this news with the rest of the immigrants. Perhaps because he was the youngest, this task fell to Ferdinand Walther.

Even as Stephan was upset that Walther had arrived without his permission, Walther shared his news with the rest of the immigrants. By May 30, most of those who had remained in St. Louis had traveled to Perry County to attend a "council" that accused Stephan of sexual immorality, mismanagement, and teaching false doctrine. Stephan refused to meet with the council, claiming it had no authority. The council removed Stephan from office and excommunicated him. Allowed to take a few possessions, Stephan was ferried across the river and deposited in Illinois. He continued to act as an independent pastor in the area of Red Bud, Illinois, until his death in 1846.

It is difficult to overestimate the effect of these events on Ferdinand Walther and the rest of the immigrants. After all, Stephan was not only their spiritual leader, but he also was the civil leader and organizer of the group. In fact, they had left Germany to create an ecclesiastically organized settlement based on the authority the immigrants had vested in Stephan. Thus the group was left questioning the legitimacy of their presence in North America. If they had embarked on this quest to establish a bastion of the true church, they now had to question if they were even a church at all. These questions hit Walther and the other pastors especially hard because they had left the churches to which they were properly called, and they did not actually have calls to serve this group of immigrants.

These concerns, as well as the hardships of creating a self-sufficient settlement, led to two trying years for the immigrants. They struggled to clear the land, and they suffered from sickness and death, which was compounded by the spiritual uncertainty with which they lived. The distrust of Stephan was transferred to the remaining clergy, and for a period of time the churches held their congregational meetings without the presence of a pastor. The Saxons adopted a Parish Order (*Parochialordnung*) that established a church council in each congregation composed of the pastor as "teaching elder" and ordained lay "ruling elders." Both pastors and lay elders were to be treated with respect, but in a qualified sense. Because of Stephan's misconduct and coarse sins, pastors in particular were limited in the kinds of pastoral care they could give. For example, pastors were not permitted to visit any member of their congregations without another person present. At the time, Ferdinand Walther was twenty-eight and a bachelor. Several other pastors were bachelors in their thirties. Most were married within a few years.

Pastors were limited in their authority to the preaching and teaching of the Word of God. Lay elders were given financial and civil authority within the group. The lay elders could perform all official acts of Word and Sacrament in an emergency, and no church discipline could occur without the agreement of the lay elders or the assembled congregation. The church council acted on behalf of the lay members of the congregation, whose assembly retained supreme authority as the highest court in the congregation.[7] Even with the new Parish Order, some immigrants returned to Germany, though most either could not afford passage or did not want to return. Eventually the colony managed to stabilize in external matters, building houses and schools and establishing farms. In December 1839, the group opened a log cabin college and seminary to train future pastors.[8]

The turning point for the group came when an attorney, Franz Adolph Marbach (who may have helped write the Parish Order),[9] challenged Ferdinand Walther to a debate over the question "Are we a church or not?" In preparation for the debate, Walther plunged himself into study of the Bible and Luther's writings, eventually crafting eight theses. The debate was held on April 15 and 21, 1841, in the colony's newly formed town of Altenburg. In what has come to be known as the Altenburg Theses, Walther argued that the Church, properly understood, is made up of all believers in Christ and that a local church is a place in which God's Word is proclaimed and the Sacraments are administered, even if that body is heterodox. Based upon this reasoning, Walther then argued that even if the immigrants had strayed both in their decision to emigrate and in their doctrine, they remained Church. Therefore, being Church, this group possessed the right to call pastors and administer the Sacraments and had a duty to seek doctrinal purity.

Walther clearly won the debate, as even Marbach conceded. The outcome of the debate reassured the immigrants that they were truly Church, could trust God's grace, and could move forward in their new land with hope and

---

7   Copies of this Parish Order still exist in the published minutes of the Buffalo Synod: *Fünfter Synodal-Brief von der Synode der aus Preußen ausgewanderten evangelisch-lutherischen Kirche, versammelt zu Buffalo, N.Y. von 23. Juni bis 5. Juli 1856.* (Buffalo: Druck von Friedrich Reinecke, Eck von Main- und Geneseestr., 1856), 49–52. It appears that the original documents were lost.

8   More than a seminary, the college, also a parish school, enrolled four female students.

9   Portions of the Parish Order that describe the rights of a congregation and its administration by the pastor are similar to language in the German legal tradition regarding a privately held corporation classified as a *societas* or *Gesellschaft*. As the lawyer for the emigration company (*Auswanderungsgesellschaft*), Marbach typically described the company's situation in legal terms. He also applied German corporate law to the Church in his book *Ein Wort über den Rechtscharakter der Actiengesellschaft* (Leipzig: Teubner, 1844).

unity. Even twenty-five years later, Pastor Georg Schieferdecker described the effects of Walther's explanations in monumental terms:

> With convincing clarity it was explained that despite all the aberrations we still had the LORD Christ; His word, His true Sacraments, and the Office of the Keys were held among us that the LORD had here His people, His Church. More was not needed to free the consciences that were severely distressed and to restore the greatly depressed faith in the hearts of many and to call them from death to life. It was the Easter day of our hard-pressed churches. Like a child dead in the faith, [they saw] again the LORD, and in light of His grace and the power of His resurrection, [they were] filled with joy and hope.[10]

Shortly before the debate, Otto Walther, who had been pastor of Trinity congregation in St. Louis, passed away, leaving a widow and an infant son. The congregation had extended a call to his younger brother. However, Ferdinand did not immediately accept the call, both because of weakness from an illness and because he wanted to await the outcome of the debate to ensure the congregation was duly able to offer such a call. Now, with the matter firmly settled and with his health recovering, Ferdinand Walther, the strong defender of biblical theology, returned to St. Louis and accepted the call. Although the youngest pastor to emigrate, Walther was considered the group's theological leader even as he took his place as senior Lutheran pastor of the St. Louis area. In the years that followed, Walther would take on other roles and responsibilities, but the office of pastor was to be his constant calling for the rest of his life.

As if these events were not enough to make the year 1841 monumental for Ferdinand Walther, on August 10 he proposed marriage via a letter to Christiane Emilie Bünger, a member of the Perry County group and the older sister of Agnes, his late brother's widow. Ferdinand and Emilie Walther were wed on September 21, thus beginning a long and happy marriage blessed with six children, though only four survived to adulthood. Professor Ludwig Fürbringer, the son of Agnes and her second husband, Ottomar Fürbringer, noted that Walther often expressed his thankfulness that his "good wife took care of all externals and, above all, took the very best care of him."[11] Walther proved to be a caring father and, eventually, grandfather. He demonstrated great care and encouragement for his children, even in their adult years.[12]

---

10 Günther, *Dr. C. F. W. Walther*, 46.

11 Ludwig Fürbringer, *Eighty Eventful Years* (St. Louis: Concordia, 1944), 87.

12 Walther even had pet names for his daughters, calling Magdalena "Lenchen" ("Little Lena") and Julie "Julchen." In much the same way he had nicknames for his grandchildren: Theodore was "Thodo," Ferdinand was "Nand," Emilie was "Milie," and Emma was "Emmchen." However, he appears to have called his two sons, Ferdinand and Constantin,

When he took over the spiritual leadership of the St. Louis congregation, the congregation lacked a building, a constitution, and even a name. In 1842, the church members, while thankful for the Christian hospitality of Christ Episcopal Church, were ready to build. The cornerstone was laid in June at the property on Third and Lombard, and the building was officially dedicated on December 4, 1842. Concerning the name, Walther required that it not be named after a man, that it should contain a statement of faith, and that it should not be open to mockery. As a result, the congregation settled on the name "Trinity." In spring 1843, the members of Trinity adopted a constitution, which was based on Walther's key themes of remaining true to the Bible and to the Lutheran Confessions. Virtually all congregational constitutions in the LCMS are based on this document, and it greatly influenced the structure of the Synod itself.

On September 7, 1844, Walther launched a venture that would have a wider impact on U.S. Lutheranism than he could have anticipated: the publication of the church newspaper *Der Lutheraner* (*The Lutheran*). Intended as a voice for biblical theology and Lutheran teachings for the scattered Germans in the American West, this publication found its way into the hands of confessional Lutherans scattered across North America who had no previous awareness of the group in Missouri. Key individuals who received *Der Lutheraner* and soon entered into correspondence with Walther included Dr. Wilhelm Sihler of Pomeroy, Ohio; Rev. Friedrich Conrad Dietrich Wyneken of Fort Wayne, Indiana; and Rev. F. August Crämer of Frankenmuth, Michigan. These pastors were dissatisfied with the lax conditions in many American, English-speaking Lutheran church bodies. They all became leaders in the formation and development of what would become the LCMS.

Pastors Sihler and Crämer were among those recruited in Germany by Pastor J. K. Wilhelm Löhe to be sent to North America to fill the need for solidly Lutheran pastors for the German emigrants. Löhe also established a practical seminary in Fort Wayne for the preparation of additional men for the pastoral ministry. Thanks to *Der Lutheraner*, a number of the "Löhe men" came into contact with the Saxons who had emigrated to St. Louis and Perry County. The first real fruits of Walther's publishing efforts, beyond strengthening the faith of individual Christians, were found when a contingent of Löhe men, including Sihler, visited St. Louis to meet with Walther and others in September 1845. Walther received the men warmly, and soon there were discussions about the creation of a union of orthodox Lutheran congregations. Thus within one year of its launch, *Der Lutheraner* already was bringing confessional Lutherans in North America closer to one another.

---

by their given names. Sometimes his relationship with Constantin, whose business ventures cost Walther, could be strained. Suelflow, *Servant of the Word*, 236.

In 1846, Walther invited the Löhe men to attend a special meeting at Trinity to discuss the formation of a synod. The visitors presented a plan, but were surprised by its strong rejection by the members of Trinity. The concern came from the Saxons' bitter pain following the events with Stephan; therefore, they insisted that the synod be an advisory body only. Nonetheless, the members of Trinity voted on June 18 to send Walther to a July meeting in Fort Wayne to discuss further the formation of a synod. At this meeting, the group considered a constitution proposed by Walther; based on this preliminary draft, the final synodical constitution was crafted.

Representatives met again in April 1847 in Chicago to form the synod. Twelve pastors and twenty congregations agreed to create *Die deutsche evangelisch-lutherische Synode von Missouri, Ohio, und anderen Staaten* ("The German Evangelical Lutheran Synod of Missouri, Ohio, and other States," the church body now known as The Lutheran Church—Missouri Synod). At this meeting, Walther was elected the first president of this new church body, a post he held until 1850. He also offered *Der Lutheraner* to the new organization, making it the official communication piece of the Missouri Synod until it ended publication in 1974. Discussions were also held about taking over both the Saxon log cabin college in Altenburg and the practical seminary in Fort Wayne, which Löhe had offered to the new church body.

During this period, Walther's work at Trinity and his outreach to German-speaking people in St. Louis grew greatly. Trinity formed several daughter congregations in the St. Louis region, the first being Immanuel in North St. Louis in 1847, followed by Holy Cross in South St. Louis in 1858 and Zion in 1860. What was unique about these daughter congregations is that they were not truly independent. Along with Trinity, they formed a "composite union congregation"[13] that extended throughout the city. Walther was the head pastor, yet another pastor was called to each daughter church. This arrangement was maintained until shortly after Walther's death, at which time, after a brief period of bitterness, each of the four congregations re-constituted itself as an independent congregation.

Even as Walther was in the midst of forming the Synod, he remained a pastor and was forced to deal with some great struggles in this role. Without a doubt, one of the most trying occasions came in early 1849. St. Louis was in the opening throes of a cholera epidemic that would eventually claim 8,444 lives out of a population of 63,000. In the midst of the epidemic, on May 17, a fire destroyed 640 buildings, as well as 27 steamships. Although the fire claimed

---

13   German: *Gesamtgemeinde*. The word *gesamt* refers to joining distinct congregations into a larger whole without merging them. The English word that best describes that union is "composite." Note also that the Immanuel congregation in North St. Louis, now an ELCA congregation, is not the Immanuel congregation in Olivette, Missouri. Zion, now located at 2100 N. 21st Street, is still a member of the LCMS, as are Trinity and Holy Cross.

only three lives, the economic effects on the city were monumental because most of the business district was destroyed. As a good pastor, Walther worked to comfort his people and the city's residents with the Gospel. Following the Chicago fire of 1871, which burned much of that city, Walther received a number of requests for the sermon he delivered following the St. Louis fire to be published for the comfort of the people of Chicago.

As if all of this was not enough for Walther to worry about, in December 1849 the seminary was moved from the log cabin in Altenburg to St. Louis, with Trinity as its sponsoring congregation. At this time the school was char- tered as Concordia College, and Walther was called as the first professor and the head of the seminary. Martin Stephan Jr., the son of the disgraced Stephan and a student of Walther, designed the building that housed Concordia College until 1882. When the new seminary building was completed on the Jefferson Avenue property that had belonged to Trinity in June 1850, the Walther family moved into housing in the building.[14] In his capacity as semi- nary professor, Walther would give the series of lectures that make up this volume.[15] From 1849 to 1850 and from 1864 to 1878, Walther served as semi- nary professor and president, president of the Missouri Synod, and editor of *Der Lutheraner* and, later, of *Lehre und Wehre*.[16] However, throughout all of these duties, he insisted on remaining first and foremost a pastor and contin- ued to serve as head pastor of the "composite union congregation" of St. Louis and pastor at Trinity Lutheran Church.

Furthering his emphasis on theological leadership, and in addition to his professorship at the seminary, in January 1855 Walther published the first edition of the academic monthly *Lehre und Wehre*. In a statement in *Der Lutheraner*, Walther addressed the concerns that many conservative Lutherans had about academic Rationalism by emphasizing that *Lehre und Wehre* was not to be a "friend of the church but a servant of the church."[17] This new publication served as an academic voice of confessional Lutheranism whereas *Der Lutheraner* became more popular in nature.

These publishing efforts served not only those within the fellowship of the Missouri Synod but also reached out to other U.S. confessional Lutherans. Like most church leaders, Walther desired the unity of all Christian churches; however, he also believed that true unity could come only from unity in doc- trine because Christians are united by the work of the Holy Spirit through a

---

14   The land originally had been planned as the cemetery for the "composite union con- gregation," but that was moved from the area of Holy Cross congregation to the present Concordia Cemetery near the intersection of Bates and Morganford in South St. Louis.

15   The lectures were delivered from September 12, 1884, through November 6, 1885.

16   The title, which in English means "doctrine and defense," may have been influenced by a quotation from Luther printed in the May 3, 1845, edition of *Der Lutheraner*.

17   Günther, *Dr. C. F. W. Walther*, 95.

right understanding of God's Word. To facilitate this unity, in the January 1856 edition of *Lehre und Wehre*, Walther called for free conferences of Lutherans to discuss the Augsburg Confession and to find true doctrinal unity. These were not to be meetings of official representatives of church bodies; rather, they were to be gatherings of theologians. This call was successful, and on October 1–7, 1856, the first conference was held in Columbus, Ohio. It was followed in 1857 by a conference in Pittsburgh; an 1858 gathering in Cleveland, Ohio; and a fourth conference in Fort Wayne, Indiana. An indication of the important role played by Walther is the cancellation of a fifth gathering that had been planned for Cleveland in June 1860. Because Walther and another key leader, F. W. Lehmann, were unable to attend, the conference was not held.

Along with the rest of the country, the start of the Civil War in 1861 rocked Walther. Fearing for the safety of his family, he sent them to the country, though he remained in St. Louis with his congregation and seminary. Because of the various state draft rules, the preparatory college, which had been part of Concordia Seminary since its inception, was separated from the seminary and moved to Fort Wayne, Indiana, while the practical seminary was moved to St. Louis and housed with the theoretical, or academic, seminary. Toward the end of the Civil War, Walther served a second term as president of the Missouri Synod (1864–78).

From the beginning, Walther and the Missouri Synod considered printing and publishing to be vital aspects of spreading the Gospel in North America. In fact, *Der Lutheraner* predated the formation of the Missouri Synod. In 1847, Trinity printed a German hymnal, which would become the basis for all German-language hymnals in the Missouri Synod. After the synod worked with three printers in succession, in 1867, some members of Trinity put printing equipment in the seminary and petitioned the 1869 synodical convention to create a publishing house. The request was granted, and a building for the new printing house was added to the St. Louis seminary campus. In 1870, Walther unofficially named the publishing house "our Concordia Press."[18] He used this name because the printing office and the press operated as a part of Concordia Seminary, while the retail side of the business, a separate entity until 1872, was handled through the bookstore of Martin C. Barthel near Trinity. Barthel became the general manager of the synodical press in 1874. Regardless of the name's origin, in 1878 the synodical convention officially

---

18   Bruce A. Cameron, *The Word of the Lord Endures Forever* (St. Louis: Concordia, 1994), 7. For more details, see Edmund Seuel, "Publication Activity of the Missouri Synod," in *Ebenezer*, ed. W. H. T. Dau (St. Louis: Concordia, 1922), 289–306.

gave the printing house the name "Lutheran Concordia Publishing."[19] In 1890, the press incorporated separately as Concordia Publishing House.

Following the Civil War, Lutherans renewed their efforts to create an organic unity among synods. Walther, as Missouri Synod president, again contributed to the cause, but instead of free conferences, the discussions were carried out in colloquies of official representatives of the Missouri Synod and one other synod to discuss doctrine with the goal of attaining church fellowship. Under Walther's leadership, colloquies were held between 1866 and 1872 with the Buffalo Synod, the Iowa Synod, the Ohio Synod, the Wisconsin Synod, the Illinois Synod, the Minnesota Synod, and the English Conference. These efforts culminated in 1872 with the creation of the Evangelical Lutheran Synodical Conference comprised of the Missouri, Ohio, Wisconsin, Norwegian, Illinois, and Minnesota Synods. Through this conference, the member synods were in fellowship with one another and pledged to work toward the unity of all Lutheran church bodies in North America. As seemed to happen so often at these events, at the founding meeting Walther was elected president of the Synodical Conference.

While the Missouri Synod's work at this time was done only in German, this did not mean Walther was opposed to the use of English in Lutheran churches. This became apparent in 1872 when Walther had a free conference with English-speaking Lutherans in Missouri who hoped to join the Missouri Synod, though at this time the Synod was technically the *German* Evangelical Lutheran Synod of Missouri, Ohio, and Other States. Walther believed the Missouri Synod had a particular mission to reach out to those in the United States who spoke German. Therefore, he urged those who spoke English to form their own English Evangelical Lutheran Conference of Missouri, which was from the beginning in fellowship with the Missouri Synod.[20]

The Missouri Synod began to experience its biggest schism to date in 1877, following Walther's presentation to the Western District of the Missouri Synod of an essay on predestination. In this essay, Walther explained that God's eternal election is based purely on His grace and that it is not produced in any way by men. Although it had little effect on the Synod at first, in 1879 Professor F. A. Schmidt of the Norwegian Synod, who was also at Concordia Seminary, took issue with Walther's statements, arguing that Walther's view was really a form of Calvinism. This resulted in a bitter controversy within the Synodical Conference. Ultimately the disagreement settled down when the Joint Synod of Ohio and the Norwegian Synod both withdrew from the Synodical Conference in the early 1880s. A few Missouri

---

19   German: *Lutherischer Concordia-Verlag.*

20   The English Conference, which became the English Synod, joined the Missouri Synod in 1911 as the English District, the synod's first nongeographic district.

Synod congregations, pastors, and professors, including F. W. Stellhorn, also left the Missouri Synod.

Although the events marking the controversy would become quite bitter, it was a bitterness that no one wanted. For example, enough mutual goodwill still existed in 1878 that the seminary of the Joint Synod of Ohio granted Walther an honorary Doctor of Divinity degree. This was actually the second such degree that Walther was offered. The University of Göttingen in Germany had offered Walther an honorary degree in 1855 after he published the first edition of *Kirche und Amt* (*Church and Ministry*).[21] Walther declined that earlier honor, but he accepted the second degree because he was in fellowship with the Joint Synod of Ohio at the time. From this point forward, Walther was generally known as Professor Doctor Walther.

In 1878, Walther stepped down as president of the Missouri Synod. However, his service to the church was far from over. He continued to serve as head pastor in St. Louis, as well as seminary president and professor. Under his tenure, the seminary continued to grow. In 1875 the seminary experienced growing pains as the practical seminary was transferred to Springfield, Illinois, from its common home with the theoretical seminary in St. Louis. Because of continued growth at the St. Louis seminary, a new building was dedicated in 1883 on Jefferson Avenue in South St. Louis, near Concordia Publishing House and Holy Cross Lutheran Church. That building housed the seminary until 1926, when the seminary moved to Clayton, Missouri.

Walther's time in this world was growing short. In summer 1885, after forty-four years of marriage, Walther's beloved Emilie became gravely ill. In a letter to his son-in-law Stephanus Keyl, Walther noted that "there would be no harder blow for me than if in my last days my wonderful helpmeet, who has always been standing at my side, would be lost."[22] Despite his prayers to the contrary, Walther did hand Emilie into the arms of Jesus on August 23, 1885. Her constant love, support, and encouragement had been an important support for Walther throughout his life, and he deeply grieved her passing.

By January 1887, Walther was facing his own battles with weakening health. He remained sick in bed until his death. Thus he was unable to be present at the convention of the Missouri Synod that began on May 4. On the evening of May 6, Pastor K. Georg Stöckhardt visited Walther to conduct Evening Prayer. Knowing that Walther was at death's door, he asked if Walther was prepared to die firm in the confidence of the Gospel of Jesus Christ that he had preached throughout his life. Walther answered with a loud "Ja!" ("Yes!"). The following afternoon, May 7, 1887, Walther died in that

---

21 A translation of the third edition of the German text was made by J. T. Mueller (St. Louis: Concordia, 1987).

22 Suelflow, *Servant of the Word*, 257.

faith, confident to the end that his Lord and Savior had won his salvation and that he was being received into the Church Triumphant.

It is difficult to account fully for the changes that occurred throughout Walther's lifetime. Born in rationalist Germany, he became one of the great Christian historical figures in North America. He left his homeland and security to follow a church leader who ultimately would be forced out in disgrace. Walther would become the group's theological leader, influencing confessional Lutheran doctrine and practice even to the current day. In 1847, when Walther helped to found the Missouri Synod, the church body included 19 pastors, 30 congregations, and 4,099 baptized members; at the time of his death forty years later, this church body had grown to 931 pastors, 678 member congregations, 746 affiliated congregations, 544 preaching stations, and 459,376 baptized members.[23]

The interior of Historic Trinity Church on the corner of Eighth and Soulard in St. Louis has changed little since it was rebuilt after a devastating tornado in 1896. Although the floral details painted on the walls and ceiling and the large painted image behind the altar (nicknamed "the Eye of God") no longer exist, the baptismal font is now located in the church's narthex. The pulpit survived the tornado and is used today by Walther's successors. Image courtesy of Concordia Historical Institute.

---

23 Suelflow, *Servant of the Word*, 143.

FROM MARTIN LUTHER
❖ TO C. F. W. WALTHER ❖

A TIMELINE

January 17, 1463	Prince-Elector Frederick (Friedrich) III, "the Wise," born.
	Frederick, of House Wettin in Electoral Saxony, succeeded his father, Ernst, and reigned from 1486 until his death in 1525. He was a reformist prince, first, in a political sense, then as Luther's protector. The Ernestine Wettins established the University of Jena, supported the Gnesio-Lutherans ("Genuine Lutherans"), and married leading Protestant royalty. Their descendants include the British royal family.
October 28, 1466 or 1469	Desiderius Erasmus of Rotterdam born.
	Erasmus was a prominent scholar who supported a number of Luther's reforms but differed with Luther on the freedom of the will, the number and nature of the sacraments, and the authority of Scripture. He died in 1536.
November 10, 1483	Martin Luther born.
	Luther saw the limits and fallibility of human reason and came to hold Scripture not just as an important authority but as the sole authority in determining each person's relationship with God. Luther rejected papal authority when it demanded belief of doctrines not found in Scripture. This included a rejection of the Roman sacramental system and its ideas of justification, sin, and grace; the worship of the saints; prayer for the dead; and other false teachings. Luther also abolished the special status of the clergy as a "spiritual" estate above the laity.
December 3, 1483	Nikolaus von Amsdorf born.
	Amsdorf supported Luther throughout his career. He became an important member of the Gnesio-Lutheran ("Genuine Lutheran") party at the University of Jena, a group that was opposed to Melanchthon. He died in 1565.
January 1, 1484	Swiss reformer Ulrich (Huldrych) Zwingli born.
	Zwingli's background in classical literature led him to state that God works immediately with the believer on the basis of predestination and that the sacraments and even Scripture are only symbols, external things that prepare the way for the Holy Spirit. He died in battle in 1531.

June 24, 1485	Johann Bugenhagen born.
	Bugenhagen became a leader in the Reformation and served as pastor of the Wittenberg city church. Bugenhagen took the Reformation to Low German-speaking areas, as well as to Denmark, which at the time was united with Norway. He died in 1558.
November 11, 1491	Martin Bucer born.
	Bucer tried to unify German Protestants. He worked with reformers in Strassburg who had been influenced by Zwingli. He held many beliefs in common with Luther but differed on aspects of unworthy Communion and the matter of a "double" predestination to heaven and to hell. He helped achieve the 1536 Wittenberg Concord. After 1548 he was Regius Professor of Divinity at Cambridge, where he helped revise the *Book of Common Prayer* until his death in 1551.
February 20, 1494	Johann Agricola born.
	Agricola studied under Luther at Wittenberg and served as his secretary at the Leipzig Disputation. He and Luther disagreed sharply over whether Christians are still under the Law, a conflict that became known as the Antinomian Controversy. His participation in the writing of the Augsburg Interim made him an outcast among Protestants. He died in 1566.
February 16, 1497	Philip Melanchthon born.
	Melanchthon was one of the youngest early leaders of the Reformation. In a 1519 disputation, at the age of twenty-two, his defense against John Eck, a passionate opponent of Luther and defender of the pope, showed Melanchthon's commitment to the sole authority of Scripture. The high point of his career was the drafting of the Augsburg Confession and its Apology (or Defense). Some of his positions on the Lord's Supper displeased Luther. He opposed the Augsburg Interim but wrote the softened Leipzig Interim.
January 29, 1499	Birth of Katharina von Bora.
	Katharina was a nun who later converted to Lutheranism and married Luther in 1525. Luther relied on her skills to manage his household. She died in Torgau while escaping plague in Wittenberg in 1552.
July 10, 1509	John Calvin (French name: Jean Cauvin) born in Noyon, France.
	Calvin received a Doctor of Law degree from the University of Orleans in 1532 and was openly Protestant by 1533. He fled Paris and settled first in Basel, Switzerland, then in Geneva, where he and Guillaume Farel advanced the Reformation from 1536 to 1538. After being expelled from Geneva, Calvin served a French Protestant (Huguenot) community in Strassburg until his return to Geneva in 1541. His theology, born of his legal training, provides much of the basis of the Reformed tradition. He died in 1564.

October 31, 1517	Luther sends his *Disputation on the Explanation of the Virtues of Indulgences* (the Ninety-Five Theses) to Bishop Albrecht of Mainz. Luther may have nailed a copy of his document to the church door in Wittenberg. Whether mailed or nailed, the theses are posted and spark the Protestant Reformation.
April 26, 1518	During the Augustinian Order's general chapter meeting, the Heidelberg Disputation takes place. This helps establish Luther's "theology of the cross."
June 28, 1519	Charles V, ruler of Spain, Austria, and the Netherlands, is elected to succeed his grandfather, Maximillian I, as Holy Roman emperor. This causes France to oppose Charles and his family, the Hapsburgs.
July 4, 1519	The name "Lutheran" is first used for those who strictly follow the writings of Luther. The name "Protestant" would arise later.
July 16, 1519	The Leipzig Debate between Luther and John Eck ends. The two debated the fundamental tenets of Lutheranism and the Roman Church.
February 24, 1520	Pope Leo X crowns Charles V, now king of Germany, as emperor of the Holy Roman Empire.
June 15, 1520	Pope Leo X issues the papal bull *Exsurge Domine* condemning Luther as a heretic.
January 3, 1521	Pope Leo X excommunicates Luther.
January 28, 1521	The Imperial Congress opens in Worms.
	The Imperial Congress of the Holy Roman Empire was called as needed in different locations until it was established in permanent session at Regensburg (1663–1806). Often referred to as *Reichstag* or *Diet*, these German and Latin words mean an "imperial congress" or "parliament." This imperial congress was convened in part to question Luther on his writings.
April 18, 1521	At the Diet of Worms, Luther refuses to recant his writings. He refuses because no one offers a rebuttal to them based on the clear evidence of Scripture.
May 25, 1521	Charles V issues the Edict of Worms, condemning the Reformation and placing Luther under the "greater ban" that deprives him of all rights as a citizen.
November 9, 1522	Martin Chemnitz born.
	Chemnitz was a student of Melanchthon, but he held with Luther's confession of the Lord's Supper against Melanchthon. Chemnitz did use Melanchthon's humanistic methods of teaching and of studying both Scripture and doctrine throughout his career. He assisted in writing the Formula of Concord and penned other important theological works. He died in 1586.

April 20, 1529	The Second Diet of Speyer revokes earlier concessions given to the Evangelical princes. The name "Protestant" comes from the protest signed by those princes.
April 23, 1529	Luther publishes his German Catechism, called the Large Catechism.
May 16, 1529	Luther publishes the Small Catechism. With the Augsburg Confession, this forms the widest consensus among Lutherans.
October 1–3, 1529	At the Marburg Colloquy, Lutherans, Zwinglians, and others meet to settle disputes over the doctrine of the Lord's Supper. This attempt fails. Luther writes the Articles of Marburg that outline points of agreement and disagreement.
June 20, 1530–November 19, 1530	The Diet of Augsburg tries to combat the growing religious schism. It later adjourns, renewing the Edict of Worms and prohibiting ecclesiastical innovations.
June 25, 1530	The leaders of the Reformation present the Augsburg Confession to Emperor Charles V. The Confession is the fundamental explanation of Lutheran doctrine.
August 5, 1530	Romanists present the Confutation of the Augsburg Confession.
September 22, 1530	Melanchthon's Apology of the Augsburg Confession is rejected by the Diet of Augsburg, including Charles V.
February 26, 1531	David Chytraeus born. Chytraeus played an important role in the writing of the Formula of Concord. His death in 1600 closed the confession-making era for Lutherans.
March 28, 1531	The Smalcaldic League, named for the town of Schmalkalden, forms as a defensive alliance of Lutheran nobility.
March 30, 1533	Henry VIII of England promulgates the Act of Supremacy, breaking with the Roman Church in order to divorce his wife, Catherine of Aragon.
July 11, 1533	Pope Clement VII excommunicates Henry VIII.
August 15, 1534	Ignatius of Loyola founds the Society of Jesus (the Jesuits). This group plays a preeminent role in the Counter-Reformation and the shaping of Lutheran orthodoxy.
May 26, 1536	Martin Bucer convinces the Lutherans and the Swiss Protestants to sign the Wittenberg Concord concerning the Lord's Supper. That does not, however, end the dispute between the Lutherans and other Protestants.
October 30, 1536	At the Diet of Copenhagen, Christian III decrees Lutheranism the state religion of Denmark and Norway. Johann Bugenhagen writes the church orders (the rules for the administration of the church and the celebration of the Divine Service).

January 31, 1537	Luther departs for Schmalkalden with the Smalcald Articles. He shows signs of becoming more distant from Melanchthon. At Schmalkalden, Melanchthon presents the Treatise on the Power and Primacy of the Pope.
May 22, 1542	Pope Paul III calls the Council of Trent.
December 13, 1545	The first session of the Council of Trent opens.
February 18, 1546	Luther dies.
July 15, 1546–May 24, 1547	The Smalcaldic War begins with the Lutheran Moritz of Ducal Saxony invading Electoral Saxony for political gain. Elector John Frederick defeats Moritz but loses the war. The war ends with Charles V disbanding the Smalcaldic League. Electoral Saxony goes to Moritz and the Albertine branch of House Wettin. The Albertine Wettins converted to Catholicism in 1697 in order to receive the Polish crown. They married leading Catholic royalty and reigned in Saxony, including Walther's birthplace, until 1918.
May 15, 1548	The Augsburg Interim creates a temporary truce between Catholics and Protestants. Lutheran princes oppose it on religious grounds. Catholic princes oppose it on political grounds because it enhances Hapsburg power.
December 22, 1548	The Leipzig Interim, based on a document by Melanchthon written at Zella, is adopted under pressure from Moritz. The interim compromised several Lutheran doctrines. This inflamed the Adiaphoristic Controversy and helped the Gnesio-Lutherans ("Genuine Lutherans") rally around Amsdorf in Jena. Article X of the Formula of Concord settled the matter, stating that *adiaphora* (rites and ceremonies that Scripture neither commands nor prohibits) lose their provisional neutrality in the case of persecution, creating a "state of confession," a state of civil disobedience known in Latin as a *status confessionis*.
September 25, 1555	Holy Roman Emperor Ferdinand I issues the Peace of Augsburg, establishing Lutheranism as a legitimate religion in Germany.
April 19, 1560	Melanchthon dies.
January 26, 1564	The Council of Trent releases its conclusions in the *Canons and Decrees of the Council of Trent*, making a clear distinction between Roman Catholicism and Protestantism and affirming Roman doctrinal innovations.
August 24, 1572	The St. Bartholomew's Day Massacre begins with events surrounding the wedding of Henri of Navarre (the future Henri IV of France) and Margaret of Valois. For the next two days, thousands of Huguenots are killed throughout France, most likely on the orders of Catherine de' Médici, the queen mother.

June 7, 1576	Jacob Andreae (1528–90), Chemnitz, Chytraeus, Nicholas Selnecker (1532–92), and others complete the Torgau Book based on the Swabian-Saxon Concord and the Maulbronn Formula. Andreae condenses it into the Epitome of the Formula of Concord. The Torgau Book is revised into the Bergen Book, the basis of the Solid Declaration of the Formula of Concord.
August 21, 1577	Lutherans sign the Formula of Concord at Gotha. It confesses Scripture as the only rule of faith and engages doctrinal controversies that arose since the 1530s.
June 25, 1580	Fifty years after the presentation of the Augsburg Confession, the *Book of Concord* is made available to the public.
July 24, 1580	Frederick II of Denmark and Norway bans the Formula of Concord from his kingdom, likely because of his ties with Elizabeth I of England, who opposes it. Many Lutherans do not sign the Formula of Concord because of regional politics.
March 20, 1593	Through the Decree of Uppsala, Sweden adopts the Augsburg Confession.
April 30, 1598	Henri IV issues the Edict of Nantes, which gives many religious and civil freedoms to the Huguenots.
Winter 1618	Division over the election of Ferdinand II as Holy Roman emperor prompts Bohemia to offer its crown to Prince-Elector Frederick V of the Palatinate. This triggers the start of the Thirty Years' War. Lutheran Electoral Saxony initially supports Catholic Emperor Ferdinand II against Calvinist Elector Frederick V.
November 13, 1618	Opening of the Synod of Dordrecht (Dort), which affirms the Calvinist doctrinal positions identified by the acronym TULIP: **t**otal depravity of man, **u**nconditional election, **l**imited atonement, **i**rresistible grace, and the **p**erseverance of the saints.
February 20, 1620	Rasmus Jensen dies at Port Churchill, Hudson Bay, Canada, the first Lutheran pastor to serve in North America.
November 8, 1620	Initially successful, the largely Calvinist opposition to Ferdinand II declines after the Battle of White Mountain. Frederick V loses everything. His lands and title go to Maximillian of Bavaria. Forced re-catholicization causes major population shifts. Brandenburg, recently Calvinized, remains a northern haven for Protestants, especially Calvinists, fleeing the south.
April 21, 1623	Dutch Remonstrants, including Anabaptist Mennonites, adopt the Dordrecht Confession. The Remonstrants, also called Arminians after Dutch theologian Jacobus Arminius, take the position opposite Calvin's TULIP and strongly influence Methodism through the Wesley brothers.
August 6, 1623	Imperial general Tilly defeats Christian of Braunschweig (English: Brunswick), and the Protestant revolt collapses. James I of England pressures Frederick V, his son-in-law, to extricate himself from the war.

March 6, 1629	Emboldened by the Protestant collapse, Ferdinand II issues the Edict of Restitution that restores the full provisions of the 1555 Peace of Augsburg, notably the elimination of Protestantism in Catholic-held lands. The edict also declares that only Lutherans following the Augsburg Confession are legitimate.
May 22, 1629	The Treaty of Lübeck ends the Danish phase of the war fought since 1621. Wallenstein, who crushed the Danish forces but failed to take Denmark, turns to the rest of northern Germany. Wallenstein directly profits from the defeated territories, making enemies on both sides.
1630–35	The Swedish phase of the war sees the dismissal of Wallenstein, the death of Tilly, the loss of half the empire to the Swedes, the recall of Wallenstein, the death of Gustavus Adolphus II at the Battle of Lützen (1632), the assassination of Wallenstein, and the Treaty of Prague (1635) that stabilizes matters within the Holy Roman Empire.
January 13, 1635	Philipp Jakob Spener born.
	Spener became one of the leading voices in Pietism, a movement that included many German Lutherans. Reacting to the Thirty Years' War, this movement showed a mistrust of authority and institutional churches, turning toward faith as truth in action and the personal religious experience of the individual. Spener, also the godfather of Nikolaus Ludwig von Zinzendorf, died in 1705.
1636–48	The French, who had subsidized Protestant forces, directly intervene in the war in order to weaken the Hapsburgs. They meet with great loss. Cardinal Mazarin enters negotiations to end the war in 1644. The negotiations are centered in Osnabrück in Westphalia. Subsequent defeats of imperial forces leave Austria as the only territory under direct Hapsburg control. A series of treaties establishes the Peace of Westphalia in 1648.
March 1, 1638	The first Swedish settlers in North America land in modern-day Delaware. The settlers soon establish the first Lutheran congregation.
February 15, 1643	Johan Campanius arrives in North America with the governor of New Sweden, Johan Printz. Campanius serves as a pastor to German and Swedish settlers and as a missionary to the Delaware Indians, for whom he translates Luther's Small Catechism.
September 4, 1645	The first Lutheran church building in North America is dedicated near Essington, Pennsylvania.
October 24, 1648	The Treaty of Münster, part of a series of treaties known as the Peace of Westphalia, is signed, granting Calvinists equal status with Lutherans and Catholics in the Holy Roman Empire and establishing the political order that would last until the empire fell to Napoleon in 1806.
December 6, 1664	The oldest congregation that is now a member of the LCMS, St. Matthew's in New York City, is chartered.

October 22, 1685	Louis XIV revokes the Edict of Nantes. Many of the Huguenots depart for England and the Low Countries.
March 26, 1700	Count Nikolaus Ludwig von Zinzendorf born. In 1722, Zinzendorf allowed persecuted members of the Moravian or Bohemian Brethren to build the Herrnhut community on part of his Berthelsdorf estate. He supported the printing of many pietistic books and tracts and the sending of missionaries through connections with the Danish crown. He broke with the Lutheran Church and was consecrated as a Moravian bishop in 1737. Zinzendorf still presented himself as a Lutheran in his bid for unionism. He died in 1760.
1700–1730	Late Lutheran orthodoxy enters a period of decline. David Hollaz was the leading orthodox Lutheran theologian of the time, but his son and grandson became Pietists. Valentin Ernst Löscher was the last great voice of Lutheran orthodoxy, warning against the inroads being made by English and French Rationalism as well as the rise of Pietism. With his death, no prominent confessional Lutheran voices would be heard until that of Claus Harms in 1817.
September 7, 1711	Henry Melchior Muhlenberg born. Muhlenberg, associated with the University of Halle, helped to organize the Pennsylvania Ministerium. He also helped many established Lutherans find an identity apart from the general Reformed tendencies in the British Colonies. He warned against the activity of Zinzendorf. He died in 1787.
1730	The University of Halle is the leading voice of pietistic Lutheranism. The university's professors help create the bias against orthodox Lutheran theology that claims it is contrary to mission. Among the Pietists, missionary voices are heard in professors such as August Hermann Francke and Johann Jakob Rambach. Yet Halle, long controlled by Brandenburg and Prussia, later becomes a center for Rationalism. The Halle faculty stood in tension with the Wittenberg faculty throughout much of this century. After the Congress of Vienna in 1815, the Prussians gained control of the territory around Wittenberg. Prussian King Frederick William III conveniently "merged" the University of Wittenberg with that of Halle, thereby taking control of Wittenberg's large, formerly Lutheran endowments for his church union project.
March 12, 1734	After being banished by Roman Catholic authorities in Salzburg, Austria, a group of Lutheran immigrants arrives in Savannah, Georgia.
August 26, 1748	The Pennsylvania Ministerium is organized, becoming the first Lutheran synod in North America.

1750–1817	German Rationalism enters its dominant Enlightenment phase with the Pantheistic Controversy and discussions regarding the source of language and reason. Great voices include Christian Wolff, Gottfried Leibniz, and Immanuel Kant. Yet an emotionalist reaction also emerges in the *Sturm und Drang* period (1760–90) led by Johann Georg Hamann.
	Hamann would influence Johann Gottfried Herder and Johann Wolfgang von Goethe, helping to lay the foundation for the era of philosophy known as Romanticism in the nineteenth century. This era would shape historical-critical methods of interpretation. Walther spoke out strongly against Romanticism.
August 13, 1777	Martin Stephan born in Moravia.
	Raised as an orphan, Stephan was supported by Lutherans. He emerged from a mixture of Pietism and the confessional awakening of the nineteenth century to lead a Saxon immigrant group to North America. He was deposed from his position of leadership in 1839 and died in 1846.
May 25, 1778	Claus Harms born.
	Harms was the father of the confessional Lutheran revival in the nineteenth century.
May 13, 1810	Friedrich Conrad Dietrich Wyneken born.
	Wyneken was the first of the Missouri Synod founders to arrive in North America. He served as the second president of the LCMS (1850–64). His description of the state of German Lutherans in North America moved J. K. Wilhelm Löhe to train and send emergency missionaries.
October 25, 1811	Carl Ferdinand Wilhelm Walther born.
	Walther served as the first president of Concordia Seminary (1849–87) and the LCMS (1847–50). He later served as the third incumbent president of the Synod (1864–78).
September 27, 1817	Frederick William III of Prussia creates the Prussian Union, ordering the joint communion of the Lutheran Church and the Reformed Church.
October 31, 1817	Harms issues his Ninety-five Theses in protest of Rationalism and the Prussian Union.
	Even as a pastor in Kiel, Harms' theses helped great scholars and theologians such as Franz Delitzsch, Gottlieb C. A. von Harless, Johann W. F. Höfling, J. K. Wilhelm Löhe, Johann G. Scheibel, August Vilmar, and others find a voice for confessional Lutheranism. Every confessional Lutheran church body today developed from the confessional awakening sparked by Harms.

April 5, 1819	Heinrich Christian Schwan born.
	Schwan served as the fourth president of the LCMS (1878–99). He is credited with popularizing the Christmas tree in the United States. He also laid the groundwork for the questions and answers in the Missouri Synod's edition of Luther's Small Catechism.
January 23, 1831	Johann A. Hügli born.
	Hügli organized eight congregations in and near Detroit, Michigan; was one of the founders of the school for the deaf in Detroit; and served as president of the LCMS Northern District. With Ottomar Fürbringer and Walther, he helped to shape the way in which the early Missouri Synod interpreted the Bible.
February 25, 1835	Adolf Hönecke born.
	Hönecke studied at Halle and came to North America under the auspices of the Berlin Missionary Society. He was a leading figure in the Wisconsin Synod as pastor, professor of theology, editor, and author.
June 8, 1838	Approximately 250 Lutheran immigrants, led by August Kavel, leave Germany for Australia. They land in Southern Australia seven months later and name their settlement Klemzig, near present-day Adelaide.
November 3–18, 1838	The Saxon immigrants led by Stephan leave Bremen, Germany, on the ships *Johann Georg* and *Copernicus*. Later, the *Republik*, *Olbers*, and *Amalia* also depart. The *Amalia* is lost at sea; all aboard perish. On January 14, 1839, Stephan is confirmed as bishop of the Saxon immigrants.
May 30, 1839	The Saxons depose Stephan in Perry County, Missouri, on charges of immorality, maladministration, and false doctrine.
June 10, 1839	Otto Hermann Walther, older brother of Ferdinand Walther, is installed as pastor of Trinity Church, St. Louis, Missouri.
	Otto married Agnes Bünger, whose older sister Emilie married Ferdinand. Otto died in 1840, leaving a widow and infant son. Agnes then married Ottomar Fürbringer.
February 8, 1841	Trinity Church in St. Louis calls Ferdinand Walther to succeed Otto. He delays acceptance until after the Altenburg Debate.
April 15, 1841	The Altenburg Debate on church and ministry begins between Walther and Franz Adolf Marbach.
	Marbach had influenced the Parochial Order of 1839–40 that governed the Saxons under a presbytery of ordained clergy and ordained lay elders. This incited strong criticism from J. A. Grabau and the Buffalo Synod. Walther's argument that the Saxons comprised a valid church prevailed.
December 4, 1842	The Saxon immigrants dedicate the building of Trinity Church, St. Louis.

February 13, 1843	Philip Andreas von Rohr born in Buffalo, New York. He would serve as president of the Wisconsin Synod.
September 1, 1844	Walther publishes the first issue of *Der Lutheraner*, calling scattered Lutherans to unite around Scripture and the Confessions.
April 4, 1845	Theodor F. D. Kliefoth ordains Friedrich A. Crämer in Schwerin, Germany, before Crämer leaves for missionary work in Michigan, where he establishes the Frankenmuth Colony. Crämer would help found the Missouri Synod after leaving the Michigan Synod.
September 18, 1845	In Cleveland, nine members of the Ohio Synod, including Dr. Wilhelm Sihler and Christian A. T. Selle, sign the *Document of Separation* stating their reasons for resigning from the synod. The reasons include a "careless" confessionalism within Ohio. Most of the signers join the Missouri Synod. Some would join the Iowa Synod a decade later.
July 6, 1846	Friedrich Brunn and twenty-six families leave the territorial church of Nassau.
	They suffered persecution until greater toleration was granted after the 1848 socialist revolution. Brunn and Walther began to correspond. They met in 1860, and Brunn established a pre-seminary in Steeden that sent Walther 235 pastoral candidates over twenty years.
August 2, 1846	The "emergency pastors" sent by Löhe found the German Theological Seminary in Fort Wayne, Indiana.
	The Missouri Synod officially chartered this "practical" seminary in Indiana on January 21, 1850.
April 26, 1847	The German Evangelical Lutheran Synod of Missouri, Ohio, and Other States (today's LCMS) is organized in Chicago.
August 12, 1849	The Altenburg (Perry County), Missouri, congregation of Trinity donates the log cabin school founded in 1839 to the Missouri Synod, provided it be moved to St. Louis. Trinity Church in St. Louis helps to secure that move.
November 8, 1849	The cornerstone of Concordia College, St. Louis, is laid.
	A successor to the log cabin school, it became a classical *Gymnasium* that offered high school and seminary instruction for boys. It was chartered in Missouri as Concordia College on February 23, 1853, the name under which Concordia Seminary still grants degrees.
December 8, 1849	The Wisconsin Synod is organized as the First German Evangelical Lutheran Synod of Wisconsin.
June 27, 1852	Franz August Otto Pieper born.
	Pieper became the second president of Concordia Seminary (1887–1931) and the fifth president of the LCMS (1899–1911).

August 24, 1854	The Evangelical Lutheran Synod of Iowa and Other States is organized. Tension between the Missouri and Iowa Synods serves as background for Walther's Law and Gospel lectures.
January 1, 1855	Walther publishes the first edition of *Lehre und Wehre*.
April 22, 1859	Johann Friedrich Pfotenhauer born. He became the sixth president of the LCMS (1911–35).
November 13, 1867	The Missouri and Iowa Synods hold a colloquy in Milwaukee, Wisconsin, to define the term "open question." The colloquy eventually agrees that open questions are theological questions not answered in the Bible.
September 11, 1869	The Missouri Synod establishes its own press under the Articles of Association of Concordia College. It would be incorporated in 1890 as Concordia Publishing House.
January 2, 1872	Löhe dies. Missionaries that he sent to North America became the founders of the Missouri and Iowa Synods.
May 4, 1876	Wyneken dies.
August 1, 1876	*The Evangelical Lutheran Free Church* is printed and circulated by K. Georg Stöckhardt. He is sentenced to six months in prison but is able to take a call to Holy Cross in St. Louis to avoid incarceration.
1876–77	Matters that had been building for almost a decade move rapidly in Saxony. Dissenting Lutheran pastors and congregations form the Evangelical Lutheran Free Church in Saxony and Other States, the "Other States" being added in 1877 because of rapid growth.
November 16, 1881	Those who left the Missouri Synod after the Election Controversy hold their first organizational meeting in Blue Island, Illinois.
May 21, 1882	The first issue of *The Lutheran Witness* is printed. This continues to be an official publication of the LCMS.
March 19, 1884	John William Behnken born. He became the seventh president of the LCMS (1935–62).
May 7, 1887	Walther dies.

MAPS

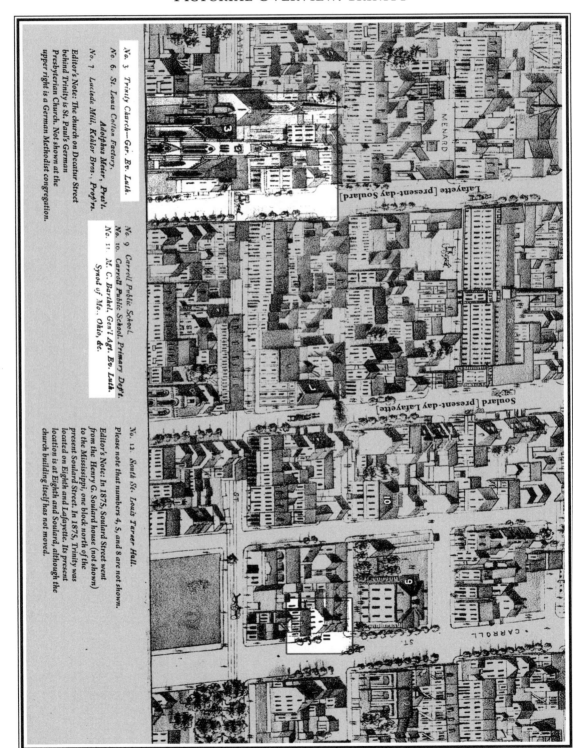

No. 3. Trinity Church—Ger. Ev. Luth.

No. 6. St. Louis Cotton Factory.

Adolphus Meier, Pres't.

No. 7. Laclede Mill, Kehlor Bros., Prop'rs.

Editor's Note: The church on Decatur Street behind Trinity is St. Paul's German Presbyterian Church. Not shown at the upper right is a German Methodist congregation.

No. 9. Carroll Public School.

No. 10. Carroll Public School, Primary Dep't.

No. 11. M. C. Barthel, Gen'l Ag't. Ev. Luth. Synod of Mo., Ohio, &c.

No. 12. South St. Louis Turner Hall.

Please note that numbers 4, 5, and 8 are not shown.

Editor's Note: In 1875, Soulard Street went from the Henry G. Soulard house (not shown) to the Mississippi, one block north of the present Soulard Street. In 1875, Trinity was located on Eighth and Lafayette. Its present location is at Eighth and Soulard, although the church building itself has not moved.

№1 Ad. Hinnecke .   № 4 . Prof. C.F.W. Walther .   № 7 Lutheran Printing House .
„ 2 Church of the Holy Cross (Ger. Ev. Luth)   „ 5 . Printing Office   Editor's note: This represents the older
„ 3 Concordia College. Ev. Luth.   „ 6 . E.F.W. Meier   seminary building that was replaced in
Rev. Prof. C.F.W. Walther Prest   1883. Today, the site is a paved lot.

MAP OF ST. LOUIS, CIRCA 1875

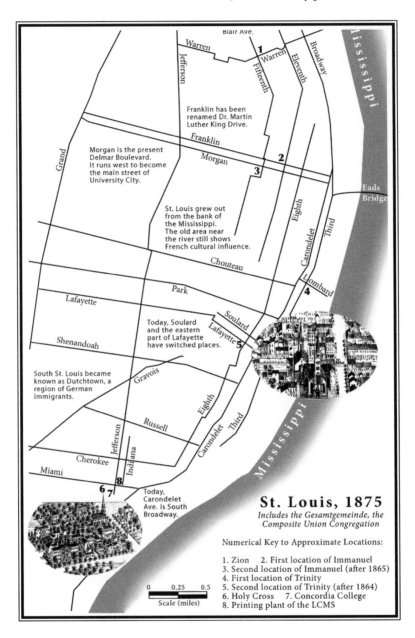

Blair Ave.

Warren

Jefferson

Warren

Eleventh

Broadway

Blair Ave.

1

Mississippi

Franklin has been
renamed Dr. Martin
Luther King Drive.

Franklin

Morgan is the present
Delmar Boulevard.
It runs west to become
the main street of
University City.

Morgan

Grand

2

3

Eads
Bridge

St. Louis grew out
from the bank of
the Mississippi. The
old area near
the river still shows
French cultural influence.

Eighth

Carondelet

Third

Chouteau

Park

Lombard

Lafayette

4

Shenandoah

Today, Soulard
and the eastern
part of Lafayette
have switched places.

Soulard

Lafayette

5

South St. Louis became
known as Dutchtown, a
region of German
immigrants.

Gravois

Eighth

Russell

Jefferson

Indiana

Carondelet

Third

Mississippi

Cherokee

Miami

8

6 **7**

Today,
Carondelet
Ave. is South
Broadway.

Mississippi

St. Louis, 1875
*Includes the Gesamtgemeinde, the
Composite Union Congregation*

Numerical Key to Approximate Locations:

1. Zion   2. First location of Immanuel
3. Second location of Immanuel (after 1865)
4. First location of Trinity
5. Second location of Trinity (after 1864)
6. Holy Cross   7. Concordia College
8. Printing plant of the LCMS

0   0.25   0.5
Scale (miles)

MAP OF SAXONY, CIRCA 1866

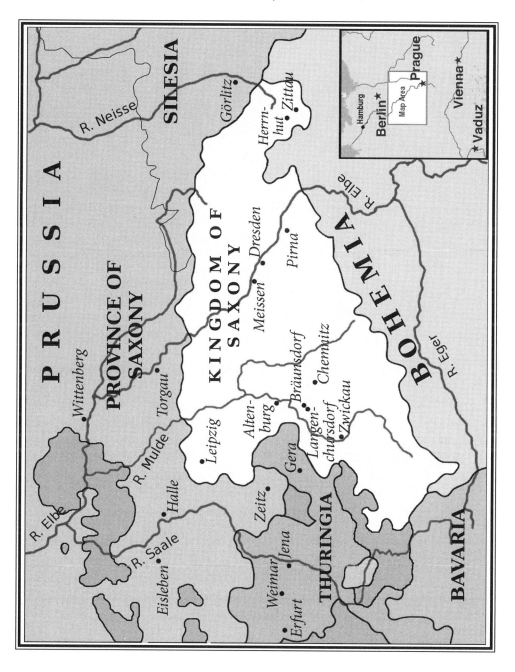

Maps of the Missouri Synod, circa 1870–90

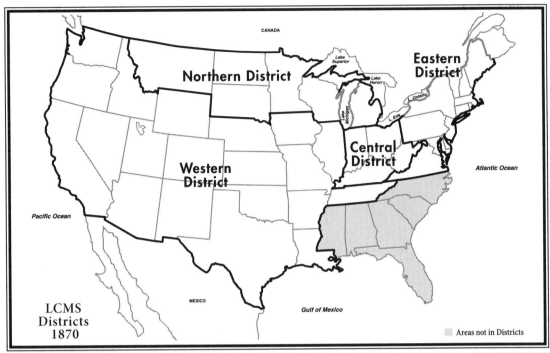

Northern District

Eastern District

Central District

Western District

Atlantic Ocean

Pacific Ocean

CANADA

Lake Superior

Lake Huron

Lake Michigan

L. Erie

Ontario

MEXICO

Gulf of Mexico

LCMS Districts 1870

Areas not in Districts

Canada District

Northwestern District

Iowa Dist.

IL Dist.

N. Dist.

Central District

Eastern District

Western District

Atlantic Ocean

Pacific Ocean

CANADA

Lake Superior

Lake Huron

Lake Michigan

L. Erie

Ontario

MEXICO

Gulf of Mexico

LCMS Districts 1880

Areas not in Districts

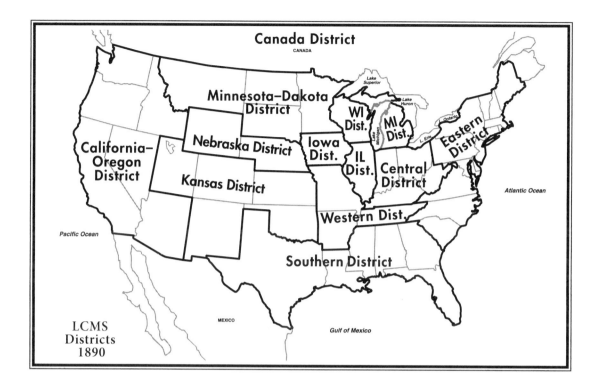

Canada District
CANADA

Minnesota–Dakota District

WI Dist.

MI Dist.

Eastern District

California–Oregon District

Nebraska District

Iowa Dist.

IL Dist.

Central District

Kansas District

Western Dist.

Southern District

Atlantic Ocean

Pacific Ocean

MEXICO

Gulf of Mexico

Lake Superior

Lake Huron

Lake Michigan

Ontario

L. Erie

LCMS
Districts
1890

In 1849, both actual and anticipated growth of the LCMS touched off a debate on the challenges faced especially by the president of the Synod in performing his office. A five-year process resulted in the adoption of the "New Constitution" in 1854 that established a "General Synod" and, at the time, four "District Synods": the Western District, Northern District, Central District, and Eastern District. Those districts remained virtually unchanged until 1874. Meanwhile, the size of the LCMS general convention grew to the point where, in 1872, the General Synod that had consisted of clergy and lay delegates from every congregation became the "General Delegate-Synod" made up of elected delegates representing groups of pastors and congregations in electoral circuits. Beginning in 1874 and occurring frequently thereafter, growth demanded the creation of more districts. The maps on these pages depict that growth.

Fueled by waves of German immigration, the LCMS experienced tremendous growth at the same time that Walther and his colleagues were following in the footsteps of Claus Harms and other confessional leaders of the nineteenth-century Lutheran awakening. The unflinching, countercultural devotion to Scripture, Law and Gospel, Luther, and historic, orthodox Lutheranism helped the LCMS stand out on an intellectual and cultural landscape that had turned its back on inerrant Scripture even before Walther was born. God's Word never returns empty. Walther and his colleagues proclaimed that Word in all its clarity, to the glory of God and to the growth and blessing of the Church.

These maps are designed to illustrate for the reader the dynamic process of creating new districts. The maps reflect the actual state of the LCMS approximate to the times indicated.

C. F. W. Walther's study included many Lutheran books from the sixteenth century to the nineteenth. When Walther quoted Luther, Chemnitz, Gerhard, and others, one could be sure that he had first read their writings. Walther told his students that they should always look up the facts before speaking or writing about a topic. In his lectures, Walther allowed his students to challenge him to produce his sources. See William Dallmann, *My Life* (St. Louis: Concordia, 1945), 30. Image courtesy of Concordia Historical Institute.

An Overview of Law & Gospel

Law & Gospel
❖ in Christian Theology ❖

A Timeline

L aw and Gospel are foundational for the message of all of Scripture. For example, when Adam and Eve fell into sin, they violated the Law God had given them and were condemned. Yet God gave the Gospel promise of a Savior who would save humanity from sin, death, and the devil (Genesis 3:15). The theme of Law and Gospel runs throughout the history of Israel in terms of human sin and God's judgment, yet God continually promises and reveals His grace. The central and dual message of the prophets is judgment and salvation, which is Law and Gospel.

Law and Gospel do not always appear in Scripture with such overt labels; the palette of language in the Scriptures is multicolored with rich hues. Passages alternate topics that commonly illustrate the broader themes of Law and Gospel. These topics can include fallen creation and new creation, darkness and light, death and life, wandering and Promised Land, exile and return, ignorance and wisdom, demon possession and the kingdom of God, sickness and healing, lost and found, guilt and righteousness, flesh and spirit, fear and joy, hunger and feast, Babylon and the new Jerusalem, or many others. But the common element is God's restoration of fallen humanity through His Son.

In Exodus 33:12, Moses asks God to show him His ways. God responds with a self-confession or creed in Exodus 34:6–7, the elements of which are Law and Gospel. This passage is drawn from the earlier explanation of the First Commandment (Exodus 20:5–6; compare the numerous cross-references to this wording throughout the Old Testament). This is the text Luther includes in "The Close of the Commandments" in the Small Catechism, which bridges the catechumen from understanding the Law to understanding the Gospel taught in the Apostles' Creed.

In Mark 1:14–15, we see the Gospel connected with the kingdom of God drawing near as Jesus' ministry in Galilee approaches its apex. Jesus accents the fulfillment of the season; God's kingdom shall break forth in a new and glorious way. Similarly, Jesus gives the promise of His Father that the disciples shall be clothed with power from on high in order to be His witnesses to the world (Luke 24:44–49). In preparing the disciples, however, Jesus points to Scripture—to the Torah, the Prophets, and the Writings—that the central witness of Him from Adam, Abraham, and Moses onward should be preached to the nations for the forgiveness of sin. Here again we see Law and

Gospel, but bound with Christ Himself, His kingdom, and His message of salvation. This seemingly "foolish" message is the wisdom that Paul preaches (1 Corinthians 1:18–25).

The following timeline will illustrate how the Law and Gospel themes of Scripture persisted in the ancient and medieval Church and how Luther brought them back to full clarity.[1] It will help the reader appreciate the broad and deep heritage that contributed to Walther's efforts to explain Scripture as Law and Gospel.

---

1   See also the research of Victor Hasler, *Gesetz und Evangelium in der alten Kirche bis Origenes, eine auslegungsgeschichtliche Untersuchung* (Zurich: Gotthelf, 1953); Hans-Martin Barth, "Gesetz und Evangelium," in *Theologische Realenzyklopädie* XIII (Berlin: de Gruyter, 1984), 126–42.

AD 48–56	Paul writes the Epistle to the Galatians at the beginning of this period and the Epistle to the Romans at the end. In addition to the Gospel according to Matthew, Paul's Epistles provide much of the biblical grounding for the discernment of Law and Gospel. Major passages include Romans 2:14–15; 16:25–26; and Galatians 3:12.
	Most important is the conviction that the content of the scriptural testimony is Jesus Christ Himself. Jesus affirms this: "The Scriptures . . . bear witness about Me" (John 5:39). The message of the Scriptures is the Good News of God's work to reconcile the fallen world to Himself through the life, death, and resurrection of Jesus. The Holy Spirit breathed the Scriptures in a manner that leads one to find, as Luther commonly said, "that which promotes Christ" (German: *was Christum treibet*) in every passage of every canonical book in contrast with fallible human reason. See WA DB 7:384; WA 3:492; 4:379; 39/1:47; and other places.
ca. 96	The *First Epistle of Clement to the Corinthians* points to faith in the blood of Christ as true repentance even for the Gentiles, pointing also to the preaching of Noah and the saving work of God beyond the covenant with Abraham (ANF 1:7).
ca. 100	The *Epistle of Barnabas* speaks of old and new covenants to argue against a resurgence of Jewish nationalism in the late first and early second centuries after the destruction of Jerusalem. This early Christian writing views Law and Gospel in the biblical context of sin and grace to argue that faith, not works, is the mark of the new covenant (ANF 1:39).
ca. 109	Ignatius of Antioch stresses continuity between the true prophets and the apostles in chapter 5 of his *Epistle to the Philadelphians* (ANF 1:82). He identifies the Gospel proclamation with this unbroken line of true believers, whereas the false prophets and false teachers do not have the Gospel of Christ.

144   The Roman Church excommunicates Marcion, who forms his own church in competition with Christianity. Influenced by Gnostic false doctrine, Marcion teaches that the Old Testament "God" of the Jews is an evil deity who created the world and established the Law. He likewise teaches that the New Testament "God" is a hidden deity of spirit, Gospel, and love revealed in a Christ who never took on human flesh but only appeared to be human.

Marcion is the first historical figure whose documents arranging the New Testament books of Scripture into a canon, a collection of authorized documents, have survived. Yet 2 Peter 3:15–16 suggests that a collection of Paul's letters was known already in the first century AD. Marcion's action does not create the canon; rather, it urges the Church to reaffirm the true canon of Scripture pointed to by Christ (Luke 24:44) and the apostles.

165   Justin Martyr speaks of an old Law and a new Law in the sense of an old covenant and a new covenant. Although he picks this up from biblical language about Law and Gospel in terms of sin and grace, he links the verses to ideas of an old covenant for the Jews alone that is inferior to the new covenant for all people. He speaks of them both as Law, a kind of divine philosophy. In that we see elements of both Law and Gospel. In Justin's writings faith is not a work, yet faith and works remain connected (ANF 1:199–202).

177–202   Irenaeus of Lyon refers to the Gospel as the message about Christ taught from God by the apostles and published in Scripture (ANF 1:414). Irenaeus believes that truth comes from God alone; departing from that truth is sin. True knowledge of God comes only through the Word (ANF 1:463). This independent truth also forms the basis of humanity's reaction to it, namely, knowledge of sin, grace in Christ, and forgiveness (ANF 1:450).

Irenaeus rejects those who scoff at the old covenant and the Jews. He sees God at work in His promises of forgiveness throughout the Old Testament (ANF 1:463ff.). Irenaeus teaches a clear, two-covenant theology with Christ as the point of unity (ANF 1:495ff.). The old covenant points the way to Christ, while the new reveals His actuality, person, and work.

ca. 200   Tertullian writes extensively against Marcion. He also writes about consulting "Scripture and apostolic law" in his *Elucidations* (ANF 3:94). In *An Answer to the Jews*, Tertullian clearly sees the Gospel in Old Testament prophets such as Isaiah (ANF 3:151–73).

His writing *Against Marcion* (ANF 3:237–654) defends against the Marcionites by appealing to the unity of God, the excellence of creation and its witness to God, and Christ as the revealer of the Creator. He focuses on the unity of Scripture by pointing to the unified witness concerning Christ in the Old Testament and New Testament. He argues that one must alter Paul's doctrine in order to create Marcion's false understanding of Law and Gospel (ANF 3:453).

As with Irenaeus, we see a strong appeal to Scripture, an awareness of Law and Gospel, and the focus on Christ as preeminent and true for all eternity.

248 Cyprian of Carthage writes three books of testimonies against the Jews in which he engages the issue of old Law and new Law. He points to the loss of a Jewish homeland as evidence against the old order and in favor of the new in Christ. He appears to equate Christian faith with a positive attribute credited to believers even as the Jews' rejection of the fulfillment of the Law in Christ is a negative mark against them (ANF 5:507ff.).

Cyprian tends to look at a Gospel-Law dynamic, yet he does come back to the theme of Baptism and God's forgiveness of sin, adding a final note of Gospel (ANF 5:556). One sees a free movement between Law and Gospel as Cyprian exhorts his readers to avoid falling away. We also remember that this is the era of the great persecutions under Roman Emperors Septimius Severus and Decius.

ca. 380 Tyconius was a layman who was excommunicated by the breakaway Donatist Christians. Nevertheless, he refused to join the catholic Christians who adhered to the Nicene Creed. About this time he writes *The Book of Rules*, which becomes the first text specifically on hermeneutics, the topic of biblical interpretation. (This book would become part of the Western Christian tradition through the treatise *On Christian Doctrine* by Augustine of Hippo.)

Tyconius openly uses the principle that Scripture interprets Scripture. He makes extensive use of the prophetic books and the Epistles of Paul. He considers some ways in which reason might engage grammar to gain a better understanding of Scripture. He used this approach to suggest that the Church, the Body of the Lord, can contain both good and evil members.

Of his seven rules, the third rule, "Concerning the Promise and the Law," engages us here (NPNF[1] 2:568ff.). Tyconius uses this rule to sort out apparent contradictions between unconditional and conditional covenant statements. To those on the "right side" of the Church the unconditional covenant of the Gospel applies because (Tyconius says) they have the Holy Spirit and do of their free will what God wants. The Law, however, applies to the "left side" of the Church and shows them that they cannot be saved unless they flee to God's mercy.

Tyconius believes sin is spread like a cold; the Donatists were intent on avoiding this disease. He believes that God gives good works as rewards for faith, but he also believes that faith is something that people create as a work, contrary to Scripture (NPNF[1] 2:569). Augustine sees that the rules of Tyconius confuse Law and Gospel with respect to faith, even though they help one to better understand how clear passages in Scripture illuminate more obscure ones.

ca. 386–98 John Chrysostom's comments on 2 Corinthians 3:6 are similar to those of Augustine below. Later interpreters see "letter" as literalistic interpretation and "Spirit" as typological or allegorical interpretation. Chrysostom writes:

> In the Law, he that has sin is punished. Here, he that has sins comes and is baptized and is made righteous, and being made righteous, he lives, being delivered from the death of sin. The Law, if it lay hold of a murderer, puts him to death. The Gospel, if it lay hold on a murderer, enlightens and gives him life. (NPNF[1] 12:307)

397–415	Augustine of Hippo writes the first three chapters, called "books," of *On Christian Doctrine*, wherein he devotes a portion to engaging the seven rules of interpretation formulated by Tyconius. He seeks to use the positive aspects of the seven rules in a way that is true to Scripture.

In *A Treatise on the Spirit and the Letter*, Augustine writes of the Law of Moses compared to the new Law/grace (NPNF[1] 5:95). Righteousness is the gift of God, and faith, not works, justifies (NPNF[1] 5:104–5). In *On Nature and Grace*, written against Pelagius, Augustine points to the fallen nature of man needing grace with no merit of its own; Christ is the fulfillment of the Law and only the grace that He offers is sufficient to save (NPNF[1] 5:121–22). The Law threatens while the Gospel does not.

Augustine first teaches that the human will is free to choose the good and improve. He later changes his position to say that the human will is bound and cannot choose the good without God's grace. Augustine finally concludes that there must be some who are predestined to heaven and others to hell. In his work we see a progenitor of Luther's confession of Law and Gospel, yet we also find an ancestor of Calvin's thought.

412–444   Cyril, archbishop of Alexandria, confuses Law and Gospel. He speaks of a "Gospel law" that follows Christ's supernatural joining with our human flesh and His submission to the old "natural" Law and all its punitive requirements. We may thus walk in the way of Christ and bear witness to the Gospel by living out the Gospel law.

529   Canon 21 of the Second Council of Orange affirms Augustine's position in *On Nature and Grace* that demonstrates the total depravity of human nature in light of the cross. The justification of the sinner before God comes from Christ alone. Christ fulfilled the Law in order to seek and save the lost. The canon draws on Galatians 2:21; Matthew 5:17; and Luke 19:10.

ca. 590   Pope Gregory I (d. AD 600) lifts the allegorical, moral, and heavenly meanings over the literal in order to protect the validity of scriptural application (Epistle 5; NPNF[2] 12:75b). As the Roman Empire fades into history and new languages and peoples coalesce out of barbaric chaos, allegory helps bridge cross-cultural divides. Later theologians locate the teaching authority of the Church with the allegorical. They wander from a Law and Gospel understanding of the text, which is a watershed event in the history of biblical interpretation.

1090–1153   Bernard of Clairvaux writes about the effects of Law and Gospel in a manner that echoes Scripture and the early Church Fathers:

> Let [your works] confess Him in two ways, let them be clad, as it were, in a double robe of confession. That is: confession of your own sins, and of the praise of God. . . . Let the humility of confession of your imperfection supply what is lacking in your daily life. For that imperfection is not hidden from God's eyes. If He has commanded that His precepts should be diligently kept (Psalm 119:4) it is in order that, seeing our constant imperfection and our inability to fulfill the duty that we ought to do, we may fly to His mercy, and say, "Your steadfast love is better than life" (Psalm 63:3a). And not being able to appear clad in innocence or righteousness, we may at least be covered in the robe of confession. (*The Life and Works of St. Bernard of Clairvaux: The Advent and Christmas Sermons* [London: John Hodges, 1889–96], 354, 357)

twelfth century

The *Glossa Ordinaria*, attributed to the ninth-century monk and scholar Walafrid Strabo of Fulda, came together as a standard work from a number of independent traditions during the twelfth century. It contains traditions of interpretation from the Church Fathers in the late Roman period, from the ninth-century rebirth of monastic learning under Charlemagne, and from the development of Scholasticism in the cathedral schools that would give rise to Europe's great universities. Texts in the *Glossa* express Law and Gospel in two primary ways. One focus engages doing things that are good versus doing evil. This is connected with the presence or absence of the revealed Law (see PL 114:476). In the Middle Ages, the Law began to have increasing value as a means of knowing about the created world and about how people know things in relation to God. That is reflected still in the modern Roman Catholic approach to good and evil. They speak of a natural law of good and evil and a natural relationship to God apart from revealed Law and Gospel. They reject that man is completely fallen and affirm a "divine spark" that must be present in order for man to know the natural law in his heart.

In the *Glossa* there remains also a focus on God as the sole source of grace. From faith, righteousness and life arise, but the Law does not come from faith (PL 114:575). With this approach, one cannot live solely on the basis of works without falling into despair. This element of the long tradition in the Church helps to produce Luther's understanding of Law and Gospel. This focus within the greater Western tradition is older than the development of Law as a theory of knowledge among the Scholastics. It reaches all the way back to Paul's Epistles and to the words of Christ Himself.

1266–73

In his *Summa theologica*, Thomas Aquinas retains the "law" language of Augustine but changes the definitions. Both "old" and "new" law come under the general definition of Law and what it does. Especially in part II.I, Question 106, Thomas divides the Gospel into the grace of the Holy Spirit and the teachings of faith. He writes that grace is bestowed, and it alone justifies, yet it does not confirm people instantly into a sinless state. Therefore, grace requires statutes of faith to guide people onward in a state of grace.

1300–1500

Scholastic theology takes facets of the Law into specialized directions. One is of the absolute and ordinate power of God, where God chooses to work through means that He ordains. Outside of the means, for example, we are not permitted to speculate on the absolute power of God to save. That forms part of Luther's definitions of the hidden and revealed God and the two kinds of righteousness. For example, under the old Law, circumcision was the mode of salvation; under the new Law, Baptism is the mode of salvation.

Toward the end of this period we have diverging groups of theologians. Luther will build on the foundations laid by John Wycliffe, John Hus, John of Wessel, and others who believe the Gospel is knowledge of redemption, a knowledge that ranks higher than the Decalogue. On the other hand, among Gabriel Biel and others, Gospel is basically Law plus the infusion of the gift of grace. This growing rift will pave the way for the Reformation.

1517–46   Luther says that both the Old and New Testaments contain Law and Gospel. Yet the Old Testament has the Gospel in a hidden manner, while it is fully revealed in Christ in the New Testament. The meanings of Law and Gospel are finally made clear in the New Testament.

The fall has caused God's undivided Word to speak Law and Gospel, even as the Smalcald Articles clearly show (Part III, Article I; *Concordia*, 270–71). There Luther rejects medieval philosophical errors that confused Law and Gospel. These errors include the idea that man's reason and nature have remained whole and uncorrupted after the fall; that mankind has free will to do good and resist evil; that one can love God and neighbor, as well as keep the Ten Commandments, by his natural powers alone; and that doing one's best wins grace from God. These false statements rest on the claim that the image of God and the dignity of man prove that people and creation cannot be wholly corrupt, allowing mankind to have a positive relationship with God outside of revealed Law and Gospel. This philosophy has no support in Scripture.

Luther discerns a difference between the Ten Commandments and the ceremonial law that governed Old Testament worship along with the political law that governed the Israelites. The latter two have passed away in Christ, who is the end of the Law. Yet the Ten Commandments remain written in the hearts of all as natural law, even if the Sinai Covenant is only for the Jews.

Luther states that human sin blinds us to knowing the true reality of God and creation. We can know that things are happening, but we cannot discover ultimate root causes or ends. Moreover, God hides Himself, His absolute will, even as He governs creation. The Gospel and the loving God are revealed only in God's Means of Grace.

1521   Philip Melanchthon writes the first edition of his *Loci Communes*. Much of what he writes reflects Luther's influence. He points out how philosophy caused the Church to depart from the biblical doctrines of sin, grace, and human will.

Melanchthon sees that the Church Fathers mingled too much philosophy with the concept of God's Law. He sees the discussion of eternal predestination precisely in this context. Melanchthon's position challenges ethical models of predestination as a confusion of Law and Gospel.

Melanchthon sees natural law as something that can mirror what one finds in the Ten Commandments, yet Melanchthon sees the Ten Commandments as revealed moral Law from God. He enters into an extended discussion against Scholastic philosophy, dealing with both divinely revealed Law and human laws.

Concerning the Gospel, Melanchthon begins by pointing out that it alone is the source of grace. All Scripture consists of Law and Gospel. The Law, as the servant of death, points out the malady, while the Gospel provides the cure. Like Luther, Melanchthon sees words of Law and Gospel throughout Scripture. Melanchthon makes very clear the necessary movement from Law to Gospel. The Gospel is what God promises and does; it follows sin to bring justification and sanctification to the otherwise condemned sinner.

Melanchthon decries as heresy the Scholastic teaching of Christ as a second Moses; this Scholastic position flows, of course, from understanding the Law as a description of human reality. Melanchthon sees the proper work of the Law as the revelation of sin, even as the proper work of the Gospel is giving comfort to the conscience.

1545–59   Melanchthon's Latin editions of his *Loci* enter a third period of revision. They still owe much to Luther's thought as they relate to his teaching of Law and Gospel. The locus on the Gospel does not change significantly between the second and third revisions.

Melanchthon draws on Luther's two kinds of righteousness, pointing to external civil works as well as to the human desire to disobey the conscience. He speaks of sin and the fall as clouding the conscience and changing the context of the Law's promises, similar to Luther's position in the Smalcald Articles. Melanchthon retains his classifications concerning the revealed and natural law and the issues of definition over against the Scholastics. Like his 1521 *Loci*, he retains the major distinction of Law and Gospel under the locus of the Gospel.

1549–59   Melanchthon's German editions of his *Loci* in the 1550s reflect changes in his approach to theology and natural philosophy in the latter 1540s. He moves away from the earlier translations of Georg Spalatin and Justus Jonas.

The context is a world where being Protestant can have devastating political consequences and Roman Catholics are saying that Lutherans advocate faith without its subsequent results in the world. Melanchthon has to work with both church and political leaders. He responds to an extraordinary complex and stressful situation by using Scholastic categories to show blessing and benefit, to speak to the ethical dimension of faith and works, and to place Lutheran thought in the greater world of ideas. Luther, as a condemned man since the Diet of Worms in 1521, was ironically freed from the shackles of using a conventional approach.

Melanchthon's presentation of the Gospel changes as a result of all this. He includes not only the primary promise of the Lord Jesus Christ and the gifts in the Means of Grace but also the secondary promise of temporal blessing that he unfolds in four major causes of blessing for Church and world. While seeking to give answers to tangible current issues, his language takes on patterns and arguments that are reminiscent of Scholastic theology and its confusion of Law and Gospel.

1553–91   Martin Chemnitz studies and lectures on Melanchthon's *Loci Communes*. After Chemnitz's death, his notes are gathered and published by Polycarp Leyser as *Loci Theologici* (*Theological Topics*). Chemnitz preserves the *Loci* of Melanchthon and, in a nonconfrontational manner, adds a level of precision and definition.

One great contribution by Chemnitz is his recourse to Scripture to clarify the senses and use of Law and Gospel. This helps to explain how the Church Fathers understood these categories. He traces Law and Gospel from the Septuagint through Christ and the apostolic use in the New Testament. Chemnitz finds a number of errors in the treatment of Law and Gospel in the Church Fathers.

Chemnitz states that human reason can deal with the Law to some extent, but the Gospel is entirely foreign to it unless revealed. This follows Scripture and Luther. Chemnitz also follows Luther regarding the term *Law*. He notes the differences in "the promises," the phrase that Melanchthon often used for the Gospel. Chemnitz's treatment of Law and Gospel becomes standard for Lutheran orthodoxy and for Walther. Whereas Melanchthon depended heavily on philosophical definitions, Chemnitz is far more a biblical theologian, and he shows how Lutheran dogmatics flows from biblical theology.

1559   John Calvin prints the final version of his *Institutes of the Christian Religion*. There he draws from the language of earlier Church Fathers to use the term "divine Law" for the free covenant of God made with Abraham, as well as for the complete system of moral, ceremonial, and civil law given to Moses. He sees the first use of the moral Law as a mirror revealing sin. His second use is a curb for the ungodly. His third use contains two parts: the Law as a means to know God's plans and dispositions, and the Law as a means to urge and humble the flesh.

Calvin believes that the Law can teach grace. Yet the Law also thunders its commands. This idea comes from Scholastic theology, which sees the Law more as something to describe God, the world, and religion. It is a philosophical approach that uses the idea of "Law" as a kind of science. Calvin sees the Law driving people simultaneously to despair in themselves and to God's pardon, where he finds the Gospel.

Calvin's understanding of Law and Gospel differs greatly from Luther and the Lutherans. He is much more an heir of medieval philosophy than is Luther. His three uses of the Law differ from the three uses of the Law described in the Formula of Concord (*Concordia*, 552–61). Calvin mingles Law and Gospel by making Law an overarching principle of knowledge.

1610   Johann Gerhard publishes his *Loci Theologici* (*Theological Commonplaces*). He gives a greater role to etymology and also returns to definitions from classical authors as well as the biblical witness. His work builds on that of Chemnitz. Gerhard goes to a far greater depth of study than anyone before him (and probably everyone after him).

A trend from Melanchthon to Gerhard shows Law and Gospel moving from an early place in the Lutheran ordering of topics to a later place, becoming part of the discussion regarding the Means of Grace. Orthodox Lutheranism puts a great distance between the principles of knowledge created before the fall, as given in the early placement of the locus of creation, and the present state of human affairs that occurs after the topics of sin, Christ, grace, and conversion. This movement follows on the Lutheran principle of *sola scriptura* ("by Scripture alone"), and it finds its roots in Luther and the Formula of Concord, though it grows more fully after Chemnitz and especially Gerhard. Thus Law and Gospel are comprehended primarily in connection with Scripture.

1687   The trend mentioned above has an interesting side effect. Among orthodox Lutherans, the discussion of natural law touches on the doctrines of creation, the image of God, man, sin, and the revealed Word. By the time of Johann Wilhelm Baier, we do not see a specific locus on natural law, yet in books about biblical interpretation Lutherans still have to engage the issue of the natural faculties of man and their role in biblical interpretation.

Thus the issue of natural law has not gone away; rather, it becomes something that tends to have differing applications. This will affect strongly the understanding of Law and Gospel in light of philosophy as Pietism (ca. 1650–1750) gives way to full-blown Rationalism. This sets the stage for Walther's lectures.

1738   With the publication of *Hermeneutical Institutes* and *Ethics*, Johann Jakob Rambach presents the position of supranaturalist Pietism and its debt to English philosophers concerning the role of "common sense." When one follows one's "heart," Rambach and others assume that the human mind, especially the Christian in union with the Holy Spirit, will live a sanctified life.

In this model, truth only becomes "true" when it generates an effect. One's faith only becomes "true" when it is acted out in love. It forms part of the tradition brought to the United States by many Lutherans.

1878–85   Walther relies heavily on Scripture and Luther to confront popular, yet false, ideas about Law and Gospel that were the result of Rationalism and Pietism.

Many American Lutherans tended to adhere to the position that Christian truth depends on ethics in view of faith. This approach came from Pietists in Germany and Scandinavia as well as from Rationalist German professors. The German academic interpretation of Scripture according to its totality severed divine truth from any particular Bible passage, helping to boil down the message of salvation in Christ to mere ethics. Many Americans also were guided by ideas from England, where people, according to "common sense," were considered to be basically good, and religion tapped into that goodness to help guide the American "city on a hill."

Walther argues extensively against Pietist and Rationalist views in the lectures on Law and Gospel because a number of advocates for these positions use the theology of eternal predestination in a way that says, "If I love God and am doing right, then I know I have faith because only faith can produce such a life." They go from effect to root cause in a manner similar to scientific reasoning. Walther realizes that biblical, Christian faith does not work like that. Such thinking not only ignores the biblical doctrine of sin, but it also crowds out Scripture itself as a necessary Means of Grace in favor of human works.

Walther's message about Law and Gospel, which has a voice in every age of the Church, nevertheless remains foreign to popular American religiosity and human philosophy. Therefore, one must work hard, as Walther himself says, to study, understand, and practice the proper distinction between Law and Gospel.

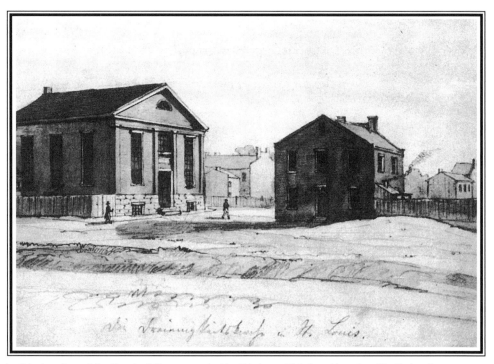

In this drawing of the first building occupied by Trinity at Third and Lombard in St. Louis, Walther's parsonage appears to the right, across the street. He moved from the parsonage to the Jefferson campus of Concordia College after the buildings were erected in 1850. Handwritten at the bottom of the drawing is the German name of Trinity congregation: "Die Dreieinigkeitskirche in St. Louis." See also the map of St. Louis in the front of the book. Image courtesy of Historic Trinity Church.

Law & Gospel in
❖ Walther's Teaching ❖

Setting: Baier Auditorium

It is Friday, September 12, 1884, and the auditorium of Concordia Seminary in St. Louis, Missouri, is slowly filling with students. The new building, with its loud, clear bell, was dedicated just last year.[1] Professor Doctor Walther has served as president since 1849, before the seminary was incorporated in 1853.[2] His colleague, Professor Pieper, will succeed Walther as president.

The official name of the school is Concordia College. The building stands on Jefferson Avenue, just south and west of the Synod's press plant on the corner of Indiana and Miami. The business office of the press is a part of the seminary, and the press is called Lutheran Concordia Publishing. The seminary campus is immediately southeast of Holy Cross Church, where Pastor Stöckhardt serves. He, like Walther, came here from Germany to avoid government interference in religious matters. Because he has a degree from the University of Leipzig, Stöckhardt is also a part-time professor of biblical theology.[3] He and Walther, together with the editors of the St. Louis edition of Luther's writings, will shape how the Missouri Synod reads and applies the Bible for many years to come.

The three-year "theoretical" program is in good hands with the six pastors who serve as full-time or part-time faculty.[4] Before ministerial candidates

---

1 See the photo of Concordia Seminary, page lxxviii. See also the maps in the front of the book.

2 In 1839, the "log cabin school" was established as a parish school and seminary of Trinity congregation in Altenburg, Missouri. The school was transferred to Trinity congregation in St. Louis in 1849. It has been incorporated as Concordia College since February 23, 1853. In 1846, J. K. Wilhelm Löhe backed the founding of a "practical" preacher's seminary in Fort Wayne, Indiana. That was incorporated as the German Theological Seminary of the German Evangelical Lutheran Synod of Missouri, Ohio, and Other States on January 21, 1850. The practical seminary was joined with the theoretical program of Concordia College in 1861. In 1875, the general delegate-synod of the LCMS provided for the relocation of the practical seminary to Springfield, Illinois, which happened in 1876. In 1926, Concordia College relocated to Clayton, Missouri. In 1976, the practical seminary returned to Fort Wayne. For a time, both seminaries were known as Concordia Theological Seminary. Today, Concordia College does business as Concordia Seminary, while Concordia Theological Seminary is located in Fort Wayne. In the last thirty years, both seminaries have developed programs that are both academic and practical in focus.

3 Stöckhardt received a licentiate, the general equivalent of a Doctor of Theology degree, from Leipzig because the Erlangen faculty, where Stöckhardt had studied, considered his firm confession of biblical theology to be "unscientific" (*unwissenschaftlich*).

4 See the photograph of the seminary faculty from 1887 to 1892 on page 354. See also the illustration of the seminary faculty around 1880 that includes Martin Günther, J. M. Gottlieb Schaller, C. F. W. Walther, and C. H. Rudolph Lange, page 68.

started at seminary, they spent six years in preparatory schools, learning classical Latin, classical Greek, biblical Hebrew, German, English, and sometimes French and Spanish. By studying these languages in addition to logic, rhetoric, mathematics, history, and other subjects, the sons of farmers, merchants, and tradesmen will receive an education similar to the rich. Even if they do not become pastors, some will become university instructors, diplomats, medical doctors, or lawyers.

The auditorium is named for Johann Wilhelm Baier, the Lutheran theologian in the early 1700s whose Latin *Compendium of Positive Theology*, edited by Doctor Walther, serves the students as an important textbook. Baier's book teaches students about the categories and classes of words used to speak about the doctrines that the Bible teaches. Walther's lectures on Baier's *Compendium* are wonderful to hear. Walther's oral exams, however, are feared. One has to memorize whole sections of Baier in Latin, and Walther knows almost the whole thing by heart.

See, here comes the good Doctor! He always walks with a spring in his step. Unlike some of his colleagues, he has remained quite thin and seems always full of energy. Walther still dresses as he did when he began teaching forty years ago: frock coat, white shirt, and parricide collar.[5] Yet the students admire his unique style.[6] Walther is carrying his notes with him, about six pages of outline for each of these lectures that he gives on Friday evenings. Here Walther is somewhat more relaxed than in the regular lectures, yet his eyes look right into you.[7] Students have been up since 5:30 this morning, so Walther keeps things interesting. They know not to speak as casually in the pulpit as he does here! There will be no sleepers this evening, though the hiss and glow of the gas lamps can make one tired.

Walther knows which books he needs when he gets to the right place in his outline. Still, you should hear what the man can quote from memory! If he had his way, the students would all be able to draw on Scripture and the Book of Concord at any time. Pastors need to be ready at all times. Now Walther is taking his place behind the desk and sitting in that high-backed chair from which he thunders with his strong voice!

---

5   See the photo of the aged Walther, standing, page 8.

6   These reflections on Walther's mannerisms have been gleaned from letters and other publications by those who knew and worked with or studied under Walther, including William Dallmann, who served as president of the English Evangelical Lutheran Synod of Missouri and Other States, as well as a tireless missionary, pastor, and first vice president of the LCMS. He had power of attorney to sign for Walther as an administrative assistant. Ludwig Fürbringer succeeded Franz Pieper as president of Concordia Seminary. He was also a part of Walther's extended family. W. H. T. Dau served as a professor at Concordia and as president of Valparaiso University.

7   See the Walther portrait, page xviii.

BROAD CONTEXT OF WALTHER'S LECTURES

The immediate, physical setting of Walther's lectures in the Baier Auditorium serves as an important context for learning about Walther's lectures. Yet one must also understand what people were thinking about and talking about at that time—the intellectual setting. Walther makes many passing references to people, events, and attitudes in his lectures. By considering this context briefly, one can gain a deeper understanding of the lectures and how they connect with modern reading and application of the Bible.

Europeans of the 1800s had few religious options open to them. It was difficult to maintain historic confessional religious positions—whether Lutheran, Reformed, or even Roman Catholic. The change in European society between 1650 and 1750 reduced those who adhered to historic confessional beliefs to small groups of people. The situation was so bad that, by 1817, the king of Prussia decreed a union between Lutheran and Reformed churches. His edict technically "united" these different confessional groups into one church body, the Union Church or Evangelical Christian Church. Those congregations or individuals who chose to retain their unique confessional positions were persecuted. Additionally, the intellectual elite criticized and suppressed Roman Catholics and other Christians. Open atheism and secularism began to be acceptable in society.

PIETISM (1650–1750 AND TO THE PRESENT)

To avoid persecution, on the one hand, and atheism, on the other, a person might try to be religious in the sense of individual faith and a moral life. This attitude generally coincided with a movement called Pietism that arose among Protestants, but especially among Lutherans.[8] Such an approach generally parted ways with the historic, corporate emphasis in the teaching and piety of the Church because it was based partly on the new model of a reasoning individual: "I think, therefore, I am." In Christian hymnody, for example, older hymns tend to speak of "we" having sinned, needing salvation, having been saved, and so on. Hymns that come from the era of Pietism tend to speak of "I" having sinned, needing salvation, having been saved, and so on.

Many European believers embraced Pietism because this movement included a diverse understanding of personal faith in different circumstances. The movement developed after the Thirty Years' War (1618–48) as a reaction to the connection between the territorial churches and the political powers that had brought so much suffering to Europe. These institutions and leaders seemed entirely opposite of the description of Jesus found in Scripture. There,

---

8   In some European countries with significant Roman Catholic populations, a similar movement called Quietism met with opposition and suppression by the papacy.

He heals the sick, makes the infirm whole again, casts out demons, and brings the kingdom of God into the midst of people. He also chastises the Pharisees, the sanctimonious establishment that knows its dogmas and yet does not follow them and has blood on its hands, including the blood of Jesus and of Stephen. That contrast in war-ravaged Europe helped to motivate believers to seek a new way of personal devotion.

Pietism tried to find an identity apart from worldly institutions, yet it became just as institutionalized and political as those it opposed. Pietism found a home at the new University of Halle under the direction of Philipp Jakob Spener and August Hermann Francke, both of whom were Lutheran pastors. Johann Jakob Rambach, the great preacher and scholar, also joined their ranks. Spener, Francke, and Rambach still influence Lutheranism today; certainly Walther and others in the early Missouri Synod knew their writings. Yet Reformed theology also influenced those at Halle,[9] preparing them for the king of Prussia's announcement in 1817 of the forced merger of Lutherans and Reformed—known as the Prussian Union.[10] Because of its subjectivity and flexibility, Pietism was capable of forging ties between Lutherans and Reformed that the clear definitions in the historic confessions of both churches would mutually exclude.

Pietists embraced the understanding of natural law and human reason that was radiating out from its origins in England and France. These "works-oriented" Christians, including those at the University of Halle, received financial support from wealthy patrons eager to see new worldviews dominate religion, politics, and society.[11] These perspectives also began to dominate mission activity.

In Pietism, as Walther says in his lectures, the focus drifted from what a Christian is according to categories defined in Scripture to what a Christian does. That shift reflects the way the modern scientific method recognizes a root cause by the careful observation of the effects. The problem with that

---

9   Perhaps the most prominent among the Reformed professors at Halle and Berlin was Friedrich D. E. Schleiermacher, who in many respects defined the modern approaches to biblical interpretation and church history. He was influential in the development of higher criticism.

10 The University of Halle was young, progressive, and political in nature. The elector of Brandenburg, who later became king of Prussia, founded the University of Halle in 1694. Its faculty was often at odds with the more traditional Lutheran faculty at the University of Wittenberg. Its pietistic scholars helped the king to foster a unified, civil religion in Prussia. In 1815, at the expense of Saxony, the Congress of Vienna granted Prussia more territory, including the town of Wittenberg. In 1817, as part of the union program, the Prussian king closed the University of Wittenberg, which was now under his control. In what was technically a merger, the king seized the sizable endowments donated by three centuries of Lutherans and transferred everything to the University of Halle.

11 See, for example, the entry for Nikolaus Ludwig von Zinzendorf in the Index of Persons and Groups, page 501.

approach, however, is sin. We read in John 7:43 that Jesus' ministry brought division among the people. Romans 16:17; 1 Corinthians 11:18; Galatians 5:20; and Jude 19 speak or warn about divisions in the Church. The creeds of the Church were developed in order to answer division and heresy with Scripture. Modern expectations of evidence require the unity in Christ (John 17:11) to become a visible unity within the visible Church. During the last two thousand years, that sort of unity has remained fleeting and elusive. Therefore, Pietism puts less trust in the institutional church and more in the private, small-group study of Scripture. Although today's small-group Bible studies may have nothing to do with Pietism, that method of Bible study originated with the development of Pietism.

Pietism's primary focus on works stands in tension with Scripture's teaching about the hidden and visible Church. It introduces the possibility that the meaning of Scripture depends not only on God but also on human experience. Pietism also remains challenged by the divine mandate that stands behind Holy Baptism, the Holy Supper, and Holy Absolution. The mandate and institution of Christ in Matthew 28:19–20; Matthew 26:26–29, its parallels, and 1 Corinthians 11:23–26; and John 20:21–23 establish a reality whose truth precedes the ability to measure it. Luther defends the scriptural doctrines of the Lord's Supper and infant Baptism by pointing to the nature of the Sacrament that is established by the Word according to the authority of Christ.[12] Luther's approach is one of faith in prior truth, while Pietism depends on faith together with observation. A side effect of Pietism was a tremendous drop in the number of people who received the Lord's Supper. This offers an example of how differences in approach are connected with changes in practice.

Within Pietism there were royalists who were reacting to the carnage of the Napoleonic era (1799–1815). The movement also included Norwegians who adopted a modern democratic constitution on May 17, 1814. The movement even included Germans who supported the 1848 socialist revolutions. Pietism was subjective and adaptable to communities that interpret the Bible according to their needs. Many different pietistic viewpoints came with immigrants to the United States, and most viewpoints had some kind of representation in the early Missouri Synod. Walther took issue with Pietism precisely because of its subjective interpretation of Scripture and its focus on works as the measure of salvation. By pointing to the proper distinction between Law and Gospel, Walther helped draw differing people with differing points of view toward a common biblical understanding that helped to define an emerging identity within the Missouri Synod.

---

12 See Luther's defense of infant Baptism and the Lord's Supper in LC IV and V (*Concordia*, 428–34).

RATIONALISM (1700–1830 AND TO THE PRESENT)

Rationalism is the application of modern methods of evidence to the individual person as a thinking entity. Its roots go back to the Renaissance and Reformation eras, but it began to grow significantly after 1650. By 1700, European philosophy was using a method of evidence that focuses on effects or results and thus traces a number of possible causes. This method had been gaining ground since Copernicus published *On the Revolutions of the Celestial Spheres* in 1543. Rationalism calls into question the idea that the universe has a place for everything and that God has put everything in its place. This method looks at a situation and eliminates all but the one thing without which the event could not take place—the necessary cause of the effect. It is like Sherlock Holmes solving a mystery, eliminating all false leads until the one thing left, however unlikely, is the cause that produces the culprit.

Rationalism is concerned about the things you can observe as well as the thoughts you can think. By using the modern method of finding causes from their effects in a series of observations or controlled experiments, one compiles a library of knowledge. One uses that knowledge in the present to predict the future. Rationalism finds a ready application in the sciences, yet the Achilles' heel of this method is the belief that somehow we can sift through all the necessary evidence.[13] This approach, born in leading European universities, creates a problem with anything that involves God. Using this understanding of cause and effect, natural philosophers concluded that to know nature is to experience it; to know God is to experience Him. Philosophers concluded that we cannot state things as fact if they lie outside our experience.

The subtle, unspoken rule in Rationalism is that human observation runs the show by determining the context. Major philosophers have long rejected the objective ability to know about spiritual things. The result is that we either cannot know God or that we can know God only through our own intellect and experience.[14] Using this worldview, any kind of religious teaching that goes beyond scientific observation cannot be known for certain and must be interpreted as a metaphor for the individual or the community. Creation, miracles, the resurrection of Christ, and the Last Day become hidden in doubt. Thus Rationalism runs contrary to Scripture (1 Corinthians 15).

Rationalism was all about the intellect. Reason was considered self-defining, self-critical, and aimed toward the goal of general human improvement when well guided. The downfall of this approach, however, was that no one could find a good theory about how reason comes into being. Additionally,

---

13   See John W. Klotz, *Genes, Genesis, and Evolution* (St. Louis: Concordia, 1970), 1–24.

14   Consider the writings of René Descartes (1596–1650), Immanuel Kant (1724–1804), and Friedrich Schleiermacher (1768–1834).

all logic and no emotion makes for a dull life. As a result, a growing reaction against Rationalism and the Enlightenment emerged after 1760.[15] By about 1830, this settled into the period of Romanticism,[16] in which reason, coupled with emotion and intuition, formed a model of general human advancement. With the theory of evolution popularized after 1859 by Charles Darwin, everything was supposed to get better. The descendants of Rationalism were supposed to fix everything.

Rationalism and its descendants proved to be a broken reed. The Great War (1914–19) all but erased the world order that had existed in Europe until that time. The Second World War continued the fighting left over from the first. In the nineteenth century, philosophers expressed doubt that people were rational, and this theory, especially in the form of "God is dead" Nihilism, reached a climax in the twentieth century. More recently, the community as the seat of interpretation has eclipsed the idea of the reasoning individual.[17]

Pietism looked to individual belief in God. Rationalism took that further to mean individual piety *without* God. The New World became a magnet for Europeans who had had enough of narrow, established lives and were willing to suffer great risk for the hope of a life in which they could live their faith free of a socially intrusive, bureaucratic state. North America was, however, a place in which freedom *of* religion mingled with freedom *from* religion. Pietism and Rationalism existed side by side. The strictness of the Puritans yielded to the Half-Way Covenant in 1662. The first Great Awakening, similar to Pietism and Methodism, arose between 1700 and 1750. A Rationalist "Christianity" then dominated the revolutionary period. A second Great Awakening after 1801 saw the explosive spread of Baptists and Methodists, which diminished the traditional Anglican, Presbyterian, Reformed, and Lutheran churches. In the eastern United States, Lutherans and Reformed mixed freely, often through language and culture, as they were woven into the fabric of a new nation.

---

15 This was the period of "seething and longing" (German: *Sturm und Drang*).

16 Romanticism is a movement in both art and philosophy that adopts an idealized goal for humanity and finds elements of that ideal world in the present. Therefore, it ignores obvious, measurable flaws in today's society if they can be sold as necessary sacrifices for a brighter tomorrow. This kind of thinking underlies abortion, euthanasia, world wars, Soviet ethnic cleansing, Nazi concentration camps, and racial segregation and mistreatment in the United States and elsewhere. This stands contrary to God's command to love one's neighbor (Leviticus 19:18; Matthew 19:19; 22:39; Mark 12:31; Romans 13:9; Galatians 5:14; and James 2:8).

17 So-called postmodernism is merely the newest offspring of the motley family tree of ideas and philosophies that has arisen from Rationalism. Although some criticize the cruelty of religion and the blood that has been spilled in the name of God, it is Rationalism whose death toll rose to disastrous heights during the twentieth century and in whose name the unborn and aged are being put to death today.

REVIVALISM

As just noted, Pietism helped to fuel waves of Christian revivalism in the United States. The first and second Great Awakenings were connected with a new style of sermons and the way people practiced their faith. Instead of using arguments based on logic and doctrine, people began to put emotional involvement at the center of their religious experience. Preachers who embraced revivalism, with its unique style of preaching, came to be known as "new lights," while those who retained more traditional approaches were called "old lights." Among the laity, people studied the Bible at home in small groups while downplaying the defining role of public worship.

During Walther's lifetime, a revival meeting happened over several days to even a week or more. It was a series of worship services designed to gain new converts and to energize Christians in faith, life, worship, and mission. When there was a strong focus on gaining converts, tents or a space that was not usually associated with a church was used.

A traveling preacher, perhaps one with an established reputation, would deliver a revival sermon or a series of sermons. Most of these sermons were intended to produce a visible response from the audience, either to make a decision to follow Jesus or to repent from past sins and renew that commitment. A prominent part of the sermon included a sort of "altar call" in which people were invited to the anxious bench. There, they became the focus of the preacher's sermon, which usually described hell in all its terror and then offered them the hope of salvation. Others would pray with those on the anxious bench, and the result was often a very emotional moment of "conversion" and acceptance, accompanied by the singing, praying, and praise of the audience. Revivalism was becoming the American form of religion.

Walther strongly objected to revivals. He saw in them a way in which man was trying to control the Holy Spirit. These meetings contradicted John 3:8, which teaches about the work of the Spirit through the Means of Grace. Walther also viewed revivals as a form of works-righteousness. Finally, he perceived revival meetings as an opportunity for a kind of psychological manipulation. Having experienced Martin Stephan's influence, Walther had firsthand knowledge of how dangerous the clergy can be if they build their message on emotion and the ability to turn people's hearts in an irrational, highly emotional setting.

SUMMARY

Walther's lectures on Law and Gospel keep Pietism, Rationalism, and revivalism in mind as they engage important aspects of our salvation. The content of these lectures touches directly on how God works to save us through Scripture as a Means of Grace. Walther knows that hope in the resurrection is a fact established by God. It is not our work of belief. God's unchanging truth remains central to all Christian hope in this world and to life with God in the next.

Walther repeatedly comments in his lectures about two general problems among Christians. The first problem is a "dead" adherence to the truth. Luther calls this a mere historical faith.[18] This sort of approach suggests that the knowledge of Bible facts or doctrine can save. Luther and others observe that even Satan knows who Jesus Christ is, but that does him no good. The fact that Christ went the sad road to the cross for us, suffered the pain of hell on our behalf, and gives us forgiveness through His Means of Grace today should move us beyond mere historical knowledge. Faith is either living or it is dead, and the Gospel creates living faith because it is where the Holy Spirit works in Word and Sacrament.

The other error happens when a Christian takes his or her faith experience or individual, subjective knowledge and tries to make that knowledge a part of the objective faith (doctrine) that all believe. Walther gives a number of examples of this error.[19] He sees parallels for this error among Romanists, Rationalists, and Pietists. Walther criticizes this approach as being doomed to failure. God's Law condemns all human efforts to achieve salvation. God's Gospel, however, offers immediate assurance of salvation. Anything that tries either to remove something from or to add something to Scripture changes the Gospel message and destroys the certainty of salvation.

IMMEDIATE CONTEXT OF WALTHER'S LECTURES: THE ELECTION CONTROVERSY (1872–1928)

Having reviewed the major intellectual movements of Walther's day, it is important to understand one other aspect of the historical setting for Walther's lectures. His presentations on Law and Gospel engage ideas found in a large number of documents that reflect the doctrinal struggles of the Missouri Synod at that time. The Election Controversy, also known as the Predestinarian Controversy, had its beginnings in 1872 and addressed the issue of whether a person's salvation rests ultimately on his free decision. It was far more than a dispute between Walther and Gottfried Fritschel of the Iowa Synod.[20] Animosity between the Missouri and Iowa Synods existed

---

18 See AE 34:110; WA 39/1:46; 37:45.

19 See, for example, various discussions in Theses IX, X, XIII, and XVII.

20 The best description of the matter exists in Walther's article "Ist es wirklich lutherische Lehre: daß die Seligkeit des Menschen im letzten Grunde auf des Menschen freier, eigener Entscheidung beruhe?" *Lehre und Wehre* (July–December 1872).

already in the early 1850s[21] and encompassed much more than just eternal election to grace.

Walther addressed the Election Controversy specifically in the 1877 *Proceedings* of the Western District of the Missouri Synod and later in the 1882 *Proceedings* of the Synodical Conference, among other sources. He wanted to show that proper discernment of Law and Gospel does not merely show a Christian how to find this or that meaning in Scripture. It shows a Christian how to read Scripture, how to weigh age-old questions of faith in light of Scripture, and how to be certain of salvation in Christ Jesus—the particular matter disputed in the Election Controversy.

SCRIPTURE, THEOLOGY, AND PHILOSOPHY

Although the concerns about eternal predestination to grace were the most obvious point of dispute, the Election Controversy was at its core a struggle about whether and how Scripture can remain a true Means of Grace. From its beginnings, the Missouri Synod—and Walther in particular—had been sparring with the theological faculty at the Friedrich-Alexander-University in Erlangen. This group had taken traditional Lutheran language and connected it with new philosophies and ideas to make Lutheranism amenable to modern thought.[22] The Erlangen faculty did not represent the more conservative, biblical position that helped shape the Missouri Synod.

Many theologians, such as those who were members of the Erlangen faculty, were influenced by Pietism and Rationalism. Philosophers and churchmen began to focus on the inner aspects of human life and the importance of the individual. At the same time, rationalist thinkers began to redefine how human beings are capable of knowing their world: "I think, therefore, I am." As described in the section on Rationalism, this approach has tremendous difficulty evaluating anything that involves God—especially election to grace. Using the modern understanding of cause and effect, people either cannot know God or they think they can know God only through the world of their own intellect and experience. The result is that religion turns into ethics.

PIETISM AND ETHICS IN VIEW OF FAITH

Professors Heinrich Schmid and Gottfried Thomasius of the University of Erlangen advanced the idea that God saves people in view of their faith, their

---

21   An important source is Pastor Carl A. W. Röbbelen's 1855 tract *Wie stehen wir zu Herrn Pfarrer Löhe*, wherein he gives an account of how events unfolded with Johannes A. Deindörfer and Georg M. Großmann, who, with Michael Schüller and Conrad Sigmund Fritschel, helped form the Iowa Synod in 1854.

22   Claude Welch, *Protestant Thought in the Nineteenth Century: Volume 1* (New Haven, CT: Yale University Press, 1972), 192–93, 218–27.

ethics, and their conduct. This was but another round in the ancient discussion of whether human lives are predetermined or whether we have free will. The term "in view of faith"[23] tries to steer between a universe that is totally predetermined and one of total freedom without getting snared in the problem of evil. Walther knew this quite well, so he added many Lutheran orthodox citations on conversion and election to his edition of Johann Wilhelm Baier's *Compendium of Positive Theology* in order to forestall modern criticisms of faith, ethics, and the purpose of the Christian life and a relationship with God.[24]

Walther was quite aware of Luther's dealings with "in view of faith" language and its relationship to the doctrine of election. The meaning among Lutherans achieved its classical form during the controversy regarding conversion and predestination at the end of the sixteenth century. Many orthodox Lutherans, including Johann Gerhard, use "in view of faith" language,[25] yet they use it in the sense of something that flows from the prior act of God reaching out to a lost world through Word and Sacrament. The later use among Lutherans in Germany and the United States focuses more on faith in action as the deciding factor instead of the eternal will of God. Teachings about faith and election begin to change with the rise of Pietism and continue on that path throughout the Rationalist period.

ELECTION AND BAPTISM

H. U. Sverdrup's edition of Luther's Small Catechism helps to frame the issue of election. For Sverdrup, Holy Baptism is the backdrop for either remaining in one's baptismal covenant or falling away from it. Yet Baptism takes a back seat of sorts to one's conduct and will. Sverdrup emphasizes the godly life of a Christian over Scripture as proof of a loving relationship with God. This undermines the Bible's comforting message about election in Christ. Sverdrup would not speak against Baptism, but he would speak of one's conduct as the real indicator of whether Baptism was effective.[26]

If people see one's conduct as the real measure of faith, people can draw conclusions from that outlook that can undermine their salvation. In the matter of election, both Sverdrup and Georg Fritschel of the Iowa Synod take an almost dualistic approach to good and evil with respect to conduct. It is as if God and Satan use the Last Day to claim, respectively, good and bad people

---

23 Latin: *intuitu fidei.*

24 Johann Wilhelm Baier, *Compendium Theologiae Positivae*, ed. C. F. W. Walther (St. Louis: Concordia, 1879), 2:37–45.

25 Latin: *intuitu fidei.* See Johann Gerhard, *Loci Theologici, Locus de electione*, § 161.

26 H. U. Sverdrup, *Explanation of Luther's Small Catechism Based on Dr. Erick Pontoppidan*, trans. E. G. Lund (Minneapolis: Augsburg, 1900), 25, 30, 74, 109–11.

and take these people to their respective eternal dwellings based on conduct.[27] The focus on conduct can lead to a dualistic view of God and Satan as co-equal causes of good and evil, each content to allow the other his due, as it were.

Yet God tells us that "all have sinned and fall short of the glory of God" (Romans 3:23). If the devil is to "claim his own," using this line of reasoning, the devil would have to take us all if the matter were decided by conduct and not grace alone. Pietists have a focus on conduct as the key to eternal outcomes. The result is not only election in view of one's conduct but also a change in the way that Pietism understands and applies the Law. In the context of Pietism, the Law becomes less condemning. Sverdrup writes about whether we can "perfectly keep [the Law]," as opposed to whether we can keep it at all. Therefore, there is a failure to distinguish Law and Gospel in matters of salvation and election, which Walther addresses directly in his lectures.

For Pietists, Baptism became a door into the covenant, but the measure of keeping the covenant was one's conduct. With such a heavy emphasis on works, Baptism and the preaching of the Gospel become only a doorway or an invitation to Christ, an invitation to believe and accept grace. That becomes more and more like the emphasis of revivalism. With the blending of Pietism and revivalism in American religious culture, many began to see Baptism and preaching the Gospel as acts that do not fully bring God and the believer into a state of reconciliation. This emerged as a strong theme in Scandinavian-American theology. Walther took an unrelenting stance against it because he saw it as undermining the Means of Grace. One result was the rise of the Anti-Missourian Brotherhood among Norwegian Lutherans in North America.

Yet among Norwegian Lutherans there was a great struggle over how to view the Means of Grace, conversion, faith, and predestination. The Election Controversy tore apart church bodies, congregations, and families.[28] When the human element becomes the key element, that development rejects the "by grace alone" of the Reformation.

SUMMARY: CERTAINTY OF SALVATION

The issue in the Election Controversy comes down to what humans can know of themselves and of God. Walther engages what it means when God works doctrine into the heart. In 1855, Walther stated that he wanted to use Pietism as a kind of bridge back to orthodox Lutheranism.[29] Walther

---

27 Compare Georg J. Fritschel, *Die Schriftlehre von der Gnadenwahl* (Chicago: Wartburg, 1906), 41–45, 111–13.

28 The reason Walther spoke against Sverdrup's approach and so many Norwegian and Scandinavian Lutherans in North America struggled with this approach is that the truth-in-action emphasis conflicts with Luther's two kinds of righteousness.

29 See, for example, the article "Lutherisch-theologische Pfarrers Bibliothek" in *Lehre und Wehre* (1855–58).

then developed an approach that understands how the way people thought about their world and their place in it changed during the period of Lutheran orthodoxy (from about 1580 to about 1700). Walther does not like becoming wrapped up in debates over what kind of cause something is or how much philosophical hairsplitting one can do. Walther is a pastor. He knows how philosophy can help. He knows how philosophy can harm. He also knows that laypeople are not going to devote their time to philosophy. They have their own vocations and lives with which to glorify God.

Keeping this in mind, Walther knows that one cannot simply throw seventeenth-century technical terms at nineteenth-century people. Doing so only invites confusion. During the nineteenth century, some German theologians were taking advantage of that confusion to connect old words with new ideas to make the new ideas sound as though they had been used for centuries. Pietism used a vocabulary that connected with both the older era and the modern world. The disagreements with the Erlangen theologians and the Norwegian Lutheran tradition occurred partly because the bridge formed by Pietism and its vocabulary that Walther envisioned was threatened by the Election Controversy. Some of the language that Walther wanted to use ceased to lead from Pietism to Lutheran orthodoxy; it became a one-way bridge to Rationalism.

That is why Walther's tone in the lectures on Law and Gospel is so strident and sometimes bitter. It is not a matter of ego. Walther knew that Lutheran pastors must speak the absolutely true, infallible Word of God when they baptize, absolve, commune, and bury Christians. What happens there is the confession of God's work to call Christians from a toilsome and troubled life in this world to an eternally blessed one in the next. To bring doubt to the working of God and to give any credit to humans does great injury to faith—an act not lightly overlooked on the Last Day.

The final two themes that Walther passed along to his students were the proper distinction between Law and Gospel and the inspiration of Scripture. Yet these were some of the first topics that he stressed as a pastor, teacher, and Lutheran leader. Similar themes on the doctrine of justification, on salvation by grace through faith alone, on the limits of human reason, and on the Word of God already appear in the 1844–45 inaugural year of *Der Lutheraner*. In 1855, Walther dealt with such themes in the pages of *Lehre und Wehre*, the periodical of Concordia Seminary. Concern for the proper interpretation of Scripture pervaded Walther's ministry. Through him and others, this concern became a cornerstone of the Missouri Synod and remains a cornerstone for the entire, historic tradition of the Evangelical Lutheran Church.

From 1883 to 1926, this building in South St. Louis housed Concordia Seminary. The institution was started in 1839 by Trinity congregation in Altenburg, Missouri. It operated as both a parish school and a school for pastors at this Perry County location until 1849, when it was transferred to the auspices of Trinity congregation in St. Louis. The first home of the official "Concordia College" was built in 1850 and demolished in 1882. After the school moved to Clayton in 1926, the building shown here was demolished. The clocks in the seminary tower shown here are now located in the belfry of Holy Cross. Today, a parking lot occupies the site. Image courtesy of Concordia Historical Institute.

WALTHER'S
THESES ON
LAW & GOSPEL

❖ LAW & GOSPEL THESES ❖

[BASIC CONCEPTS][1]

Thesis I

The doctrinal contents of all Holy Scripture, both of the Old and the New Testament, consist of two doctrines that differ fundamentally from each other. These two doctrines are Law and Gospel.

Thesis II

If you wish to be an orthodox teacher, you must present all the articles of faith in accordance with Scripture, yet [you] must also rightly **distinguish** *Law and Gospel.*

Thesis III

To rightly distinguish Law and Gospel is the most difficult and highest Christian art—and for theologians in particular. It is taught only by the Holy Spirit in combination with experience.

Thesis IV

Understanding how to distinguish Law and Gospel provides **wonderful insight** *for understanding all of Holy Scripture correctly. In fact, without this knowledge Scripture is and remains a sealed book.*

[TWENTY-ONE WAYS TO CONFUSE LAW AND GOSPEL][2]

[Improperly Making Christ a Lawgiver][3]

Thesis V

The most common way people mingle Law and Gospel—and one that is also the easiest to detect because it is so crude—is prevalent among Papists, Socinians, and Rationalists. These people turn Christ into a kind of new Moses or Lawgiver. This transforms the Gospel into a doctrine of meritorious works. Furthermore, some people—like the Papists—condemn and anathematize those who teach that the Gospel is the message of the free grace of God in Christ.

---

1   The first four theses are the basis for all the others. This is a natural division that Walther made in the body of his lectures by stating these first theses positively.

2   Walther enumerates twenty-one ways to confuse Law and Gospel. He states these remaining theses negatively.

3   To avoid the possible confusion of saying, "Thesis VI, second; Thesis VII, third;" and so on, Walther's additional numbering scheme has been replaced with bracketed subheadings.

[Incorrect Preaching]

Thesis VI

You are not rightly distinguishing Law and Gospel in the Word of God if you do not preach the Law in its full sternness and the Gospel in its full sweetness. Similarly, do not mingle Gospel elements with the Law or Law elements with the Gospel.

Thesis VII

You are not rightly distinguishing Law and Gospel in the Word of God if you first preach the Gospel and then the Law, or first sanctification and then justification, or first faith and then repentance, or first good works and then grace.

Thesis VIII

You are not rightly distinguishing Law and Gospel in the Word of God if you preach the Law to those who are already in terror on account of their sins or the Gospel to those who are living securely in their sins.

[Wrongly Directing People toward Salvation by Works]

Thesis IX

You are not rightly distinguishing Law and Gospel in the Word of God if you point sinners who have been struck down and terrified by the Law toward their own prayers and struggles with God and tell them that they have to work their way into a state of grace. That is, do not tell them to keep on praying and struggling until they would feel that God has received them into grace. Rather, point them toward the Word and the Sacraments.

Thesis X

You are not rightly distinguishing Law and Gospel in the Word of God if you preach that "dead" faith can justify and save in the sight of God—while that believer is still living in mortal sins. In the same way, do not preach that faith justifies and saves those unrepentant people because of the love and renewal it produces in them.

[Improper Understanding of Contrition]

Thesis XI

You are not rightly distinguishing Law and Gospel in the Word of God if you only want to comfort those with the Gospel who are contrite because they love God. You also need to comfort people with the Gospel who are only contrite because they fear His wrath and punishment.

Thesis XII

You are not rightly distinguishing Law and Gospel in the Word of God if you teach that the reason our sins are forgiven is because we both believe and are contrite.

[Improper Understanding of Faith]

Thesis XIII

You are not rightly distinguishing Law and Gospel in the Word of God if you explain faith by demanding that people are able to make themselves believe or at least can collaborate toward that end. Rather, preach faith into people's hearts by laying the Gospel promises before them.

Thesis XIV

You are not rightly distinguishing Law and Gospel in the Word of God if you demand that faith is a condition for justification and salvation. It would be wrong to preach that people are righteous in the sight of God and are saved not only by *their faith, but also* on account of *their faith,* for the sake of *their faith, or* in view of *their faith.*

[Improper Understanding of Conversion and Repentance]

Thesis XV

You are not rightly distinguishing Law and Gospel in the Word of God if you turn the Gospel into a preaching of repentance.

Thesis XVI

You are not rightly distinguishing Law and Gospel in the Word of God if you claim that people are truly converted when they get rid of certain vices and, instead, engage in certain works of piety and virtuous practices.

[Improper Presentation of New Obedience]

Thesis XVII

You are not rightly distinguishing Law and Gospel in the Word of God if you describe believers in a way that is not always realistic—both with regard to the strength of their faith and to the feeling and fruitfulness of their faith.

[Improper Understanding of the Sinful Human Condition]

Thesis XVIII

You are not rightly distinguishing Law and Gospel in the Word of God if you describe the universal corruption of mankind so as to create the impression that even true believers are still under the spell of ruling sins and sin deliberately.

Thesis XIX

You are not rightly distinguishing Law and Gospel in the Word of God if you preach about certain sins as if they were not damnable but only venial.

[Improper Understanding of Church, Word, and Sacrament]

Thesis XX

You are not rightly distinguishing Law and Gospel in the Word of God if a person's salvation is made to depend on his association with the visible orthodox Church and if you claim that salvation is denied to every person erring in any article of faith.

Thesis XXI

You are not rightly distinguishing Law and Gospel in the Word of God if you teach that the Sacraments save ex opere operato, *that is, merely by their outward performance.*

[False Understanding of Conversion and Human Will]

Thesis XXII

*You are not rightly distinguishing Law and Gospel in the Word of God if a false distinction is made between a person's being awakened and being converted; moreover, when a person's **inability** to believe is mistaken for not being **permitted** to believe.*

[Improper Uses of the Law]

Thesis XXIII

You are not rightly distinguishing Law and Gospel in the Word of God if you use the demands, threats, or promises of the Law to try and force the unregenerate to put away their sins and engage in good works and thus become godly; and then, on the other hand, if you use the commands of the Law—rather than the admonitions of the Gospel—to urge the regenerate to do good.

[Improperly Preaching on the Unforgivable Sin]

Thesis XXIV

You are not rightly distinguishing Law and Gospel in the Word of God if you claim the unforgivable sin against the Holy Spirit cannot be forgiven because of its magnitude.

[Failing to Let the Gospel Predominate]

Thesis XXV

You are not rightly distinguishing Law and Gospel in the Word of God if you do not allow the Gospel to predominate in your teaching.

WALTHER'S
LECTURES ON
LAW & GOSPEL

Image and signature from Martin Günther, *Dr. C. F. W. Walther: Lebensbild* (St. Louis: Concordia, 1890).

❖ INTRODUCTION ❖

MY DEAR FRIENDS: —

**First
Evening Lecture:**
Sept. 12, 1884

2 Cor. 4:13;
Acts 4:20

If you are to become efficient teachers in our churches and schools, there is no doubt that you need extremely detailed knowledge of every doctrine of the Christian revelation. However, that is not all. What you need to know as well is how to **apply** these doctrines correctly. Not only must you have a clear understanding of these doctrines, but they must also enter deeply into your heart,[1] so they can reveal their divine, heavenly power. All these doctrines must be so precious, so valuable, so dear to you that you cannot but profess with a glowing heart in the words of Paul: "We also believe, and so we also speak," and in the words of all the apostles: "For we cannot but speak of what we have seen and heard." Although you indeed have not seen these things with your physical eyes or heard them with your physical ears (as the apostles did), you ought to experience them with the eyes and ears of your spirit.

While in our dogmatics lectures my goal is to ground you in every doctrine and make you certain of them, I have designed these Friday evening lectures to make you truly practical theologians.[2] I wish to talk the Christian doctrine into your very heart, enabling you to come forward as living witnesses with a demonstration of the Spirit and of power. I do not want you to be standing in your pulpits like lifeless statues, but to speak with confidence and cheerful courage, offering help where help is needed.

Now, of all doctrines, the first and foremost is the doctrine of justification. However, immediately following upon it—and almost equally as important—is the doctrine of **how to distinguish between Law and Gospel**. Let us now focus on this distinction between Law and the Gospel—a task to which we want to apply ourselves diligently.

Luther says that the man who possesses the skill of distinguishing Law and Gospel is foremost among his peers and should be regarded as a doctor of theology. But I would not have you believe that *I* regard myself to be foremost among my peers or that you should regard *me* as a doctor of theology. It would be a great mistake if you were to believe that. While I admit that people sometimes do address me by that burdensome title of "Doctor of Theology," I would prefer to remain a humble disciple and sit at the feet of our Dr. Luther, just as he learned the teachings from the apostles and prophets.

---

1   This translation uses the singular *heart* throughout in the manner of the Rite of Confession. (Cf. *LSB*, p. 151: ". . . with our whole heart.")

2   Walther emphasizes theology as both the things that a pastor and his congregation need to know about God and His plan for us as well as the things that a pastor needs to do on behalf of his congregation. See also "theology" in the Glossary, page 487.

As often as you attend these lectures, I want you to come breathing a silent prayer in your heart that God may grant us His Holy Spirit abundantly, that you would profitably hear, and that I would effectively teach. Let us then take up our task, trusting firmly that God would bless our souls and the souls of those whom we are to rescue.

When we compare Holy Scripture with other writings, we notice that no book seems to be as full of contradictions as the Bible. And this seems to be true not only in minor points but also even in its main point, namely, regarding the doctrine of how we may come to God and are saved.

For instance, in one passage, the Bible offers forgiveness to all sinners, yet in another passage forgiveness of sins is withheld from all sinners. Or, in still another passage, life everlasting is offered freely to all people, but in yet another, people are directed to do something themselves in order to be saved. This riddle can be solved when we consider that there are two entirely different doctrines in Scripture: the doctrine of the Law and the doctrine of the Gospel.

Thesis I

The doctrinal contents of all Holy Scripture, both of the Old and the New Testament, consist of two doctrines that differ fundamentally from each other. These two doctrines are Law and Gospel.

Editor's Note: In this thesis, Walther shows that the Law and the Gospel share some characteristics but also have important differences, which make it necessary to distinguish the two. He uses extensive quotations from Scripture and Luther to define the doctrines and to show agreement from Scripture through Luther's time to Walther's era and even to the present day.

It is not my intent to give a systematic treatment of the doctrine of Law and Gospel in these lectures. Rather, my aim is to show you how easily we can inflict great damage on our hearers when we mingle Law and Gospel—despite their fundamental differences—and thus defeat the purpose of both doctrines. But you cannot begin to appreciate this point until you grasp the differences between Law and Gospel.

The difference between Law and Gospel is not that the Gospel is a divine doctrine and that the Law is a human doctrine, resting on the reason of man. Not at all. Whatever of either doctrine is contained in the Scriptures—*all* of it is the Word of the living God Himself.

Nor is this the difference: that only the Gospel is necessary and not the Law—as if the latter were a mere afterthought that could be done away with if necessary. No, both doctrines are equally necessary for us humans. Without the Law, we cannot understand the Gospel; and without the Gospel, the Law is of no benefit to us.

Nor can we permit this uninformed distinction: that the Law is the teaching of the Old Testament, while the Gospel is the teaching of the New Testament. By no means. There is Gospel content in the Old Testament and Law content in the New Testament. Moreover, in the New Testament, the Lord opened the seal of the Law by purging Jewish rules from it.[1]

---

1   In the 1865 doctrinal proceedings (*Lehrverhandlungen*) of the Northern District, Pastor F. A. Ahner asserted that the Old Testament is Law and the New Testament is Gospel. This position was corrected in 1867 by the theses on biblical interpretation in the *Proceedings* of the Northern District. The 1867 theses defined Missouri Synod biblical interpretation for at least seventy years. For a synopsis of the subdivision of the general Missouri Synod into smaller district-synods (German: *Distriktsynode*, a synod defined by geographic bounds),

Nor do Law and Gospel differ regarding their final aim, as though the purpose of the Gospel were salvation, while the purpose of the Law were condemnation. No, the purpose of both is the salvation of humankind—except that ever since the fall, the Law has not been capable of leading us to salvation. It can only prepare us for the Gospel. Furthermore, it is only through the Gospel that we are able to fulfill the Law to a certain extent.

Nor is the difference between Law and Gospel that they somehow contradict each other. No, there are no contradictions in Scripture. Law and Gospel are distinct from each other, yet they coexist in the most perfect harmony.

Nor is the difference between the two that only one of these doctrines is meant for Christians, while the other is not. Even for Christians the Law still retains its significance. Indeed, when a person ceases to employ either of these two doctrines, he is no longer a true Christian.

Rather, the true points of difference between Law and Gospel are as follows:

1. They differ as to how they were revealed to humans.
2. They differ regarding their **contents**.
3. They differ regarding the **promises** held out by each doctrine.
4. They differ regarding their threats.
5. They differ regarding the function and the effect of either doctrine.
6. They differ regarding the persons to whom each of them is to be preached.

Any other differences can be grouped under one of these six headings. Now, let us use Scripture to prove these claims.

First difference   First, Law and Gospel differ as to how they were revealed to us. The Law was created along with humans and was written on our heart. While the fall has caused what was written on our heart to become dull, God's writing has not been completely erased. So when the Law is preached to even the most ungodly persons, their conscience will tell them: "That is true." Yet when the Gospel is preached to them, their conscience does not react the same. In fact, the preaching of the Gospel might even make them angry. The most immoral persons admit that they ought to do what is written in the Law. Why is that? Because the Law is written on their heart.

Now, when we preach the Gospel, we are dealing with a different situation. The Gospel proclaims and reveals nothing but free acts of divine grace, though they are not at all self-evident. God did not have to do what He did according to the Gospel. He was not forced to act, as if He could not choose to act otherwise, should He wish to remain a righteous and loving God.

---

see the article "Lutheran Church—Missouri Synod, Districts of The," in *Lutheran Cyclopedia* (St. Louis: Concordia, 1975), 493. See also the maps in the front of the book.

No, even if He had allowed all men to go to the devil, God would still have remained eternal Love.

Romans 2:14–15 reads as follows:

> For when Gentiles, who do not have the law, by nature do what the law requires, they are a law to themselves, even though they do not have the law. They show that the work of the law is written on their hearts, while their conscience also bears witness, and their conflicting thoughts accuse or even excuse them.

Rom. 2:14–15

Here we have the apostle's [Paul's] testimony that even blind unbelievers bear the moral Law in their heart and conscience. No supernatural revelation was needed to inform them of the moral Law. The Ten Commandments were given only for the purpose of bringing out in bold letters the dulled script of the original Law that had been written on mankind's heart.

On the other hand, we have from the same apostle—and in the same Epistle—this statement concerning the Gospel, namely, Romans 16:25–26:

> Now to Him who is able to strengthen you according to my gospel and the preaching of Jesus Christ, according to the revelation of the **mystery** that was kept secret for long ages but has now been disclosed and through the prophetic writings has been made known to all nations, according to the command of the eternal God, to bring about the obedience of faith.

Rom. 16:25–26

In clear terms the apostle testifies here that—since the beginning of the world—it has been impossible to discover the Gospel. It became known only through an act of the Holy Spirit, who inspired sanctified[2] men to write His message.

Please note this important distinction! Every religion contains portions of the Law. In fact, some unbelievers, by their knowledge of the Law, have advanced so far that they realize that their souls need to be cleansed, that their thoughts and desires need to be purified. But only in the Christian religion will you find the Gospel. Other religions do not contain even a speck of it.

Had the Law not been written on the human heart, no one would listen to the preaching of the Law. Rather, everybody would turn away from it and say, "That is too cruel; nobody is able to keep Commandments such as these." But, my friends, do not hesitate to preach the Law! People may despise it, yet they do so only with their mouths, because the things you say when preaching

---

2   Walther includes "sanctified" on the basis of the 1865 and 1867 *Proceedings* of the Northern District, in addition to other documents. The early Missouri Synod was clear that God shaped the lives of the biblical holy authors ("*die heilige Schreiber*") to make them—and no others—His perfect tools for the unique task of divine inspiration. He breathed His words through them onto the pages of Scripture.

the Law are the same things that their own conscience preaches to them every day. Nor could we convert anyone by preaching the Gospel to them, unless we preached the Law to them first. It would be impossible to convert anyone if the Law had not already been written on his heart. Of course, here I am talking about God, about how He has **revealed** Himself, and about how He has devised His own order of salvation. Needless to say, God was able to save all men by a mere act of His will.[3]

Second difference   The second point of difference between Law and Gospel is indicated by the particular contents of each. The Law tells us what to do. No such instruction is contained in the Gospel. Rather, the Gospel reveals to us only what God is doing. The Law speaks about our works, whereas the Gospel speaks about the great works of God. In the Law we hear the tenfold summons: "You shall." Beyond that, the Law has nothing to say to us. The Gospel, on the other hand, makes no demands whatsoever.

What if someone says, "But the Gospel demands faith!" Well, just picture someone who is hungry. You tell him: "Come, sit down at my table and eat." That hungry person would hardly reply, "Who are *you* to boss me around?" No, he would understand and accept your words as a kind invitation. That is exactly what the Gospel is—a kind invitation to partake of heavenly blessings.

Gal. 3:12   Galatians 3:12: "But the law is not of faith, rather 'The one who does them shall live by them.'" This is an exceedingly important passage. The Law has nothing to say about forgiveness or about grace. The Law does not say: "If you are contrite, if you begin to make amends, the remainder of your sins will be forgiven." Not a word of this is found in the Law. The Law issues only commands and demands. The Gospel, on the other hand, only offers. The Gospel does not take anything. It gives.

John 1:17   Accordingly, we read in John 1:17: "For the law was given through Moses; grace and truth came through Jesus Christ." The Gospel contains nothing but grace and truth. How important this is! When we read the Law, when we think about it, when we measure our conduct against its teaching, we are terrified by the multitude of demands it makes upon us. If that were all we ever heard, we would be hurled into despair and would be lost. But God be praised! There is still another doctrine: the Gospel. And to that we cling.

Third difference   Third, Law and Gospel differ by the *promises* held out by each doctrine. What the Law promises is just as great a blessing as what the Gospel promises, namely, everlasting life and salvation. But there is a huge difference: All the promises of the Law are made on certain conditions, namely, that we fulfill the Law perfectly. Accordingly, the greater the promises of the Law, the more

---

3   The Dau edition adds: "But He has not *revealed* to us that He intends to do so, and the definite order of salvation which He has appointed for us does not indicate any intention of this kind."

disheartening they are. The Law offers us that food, but not close enough for us to reach it. The Law offers us salvation in about the same manner as refreshments were offered to Tantalus in the hell of the pagan Greeks.[4] Indeed, it says to us, "I will quench the thirst of your soul and satisfy your hunger." But the Law is not able to accomplish this because it always adds: "All this you will have, but only if you do what I command."

How different is the lovely, sweet, and comforting language of the Gospel! It promises us the grace of God and salvation—without any condition whatsoever. It is a promise of free grace. And it asks nothing of us but this: "Take what I give, and you will have it." This is not a condition, but rather a kind invitation.

Leviticus 18:5 reads: "You shall therefore keep My statutes and My rules; if a person does them, he shall live by them." This means that only the person who **keeps the Law**, and no one else, will be saved by the Law.

Lev. 18:5

When [questioned] by the self-righteous scribe in Luke 10:26[–28], Christ raises the counterquestion: "What is written in the Law? How do you read it?" The scribe answers correctly: "You shall love the Lord your God with all your heart and with all your soul and with all your strength and with all your mind, and your neighbor as yourself." And then Christ says to him: "Do this, and you will live." On this particular occasion the Lord testifies that, were salvation to come by way of the Law, the only way to obtain salvation would be to keep the Law perfectly. But even if people were to do the will of God and were to receive salvation as a reward for their merit, that, too, would be thanks only to the goodness of God. But those "strings" attached to the Law hurl us into despair.

Luke 10:26–28

When the Lord wished to instruct the disciples as to what they should preach, He said, "Go into all the world and proclaim the gospel to the whole creation. Whoever believes and is baptized will be saved" (Mark 16:15–16). Thus no condition whatsoever is attached to the Gospel; it is solely a promise of grace. Furthermore, we read in Romans 3:22–24: "For there is no distinction: for all have sinned and fall short of the glory of God, and are justified by His grace as a gift, through the redemption that is in Christ Jesus."

Mark 16:15–16;
Rom. 3:22–24

Ephesians 2:8–9 states: "For by grace you have been saved, through faith. And this is not your own doing; it is the gift of God, not a result of works, so that no one may boast." Unconditional promises of grace and salvation—that

Eph. 2:8–9

---

4   In Greek mythology, King Tantalus angered the gods. He then killed his son Pelops and made a stew of him for the gods. Because of this and other atrocities, his spirit dwells in Tarterus, the deepest realm of Hades. Tantalus stands forever thirsty in water that he cannot reach, forever hungry below a fruit tree that he cannot reach, with a great stone always over his head. Walther drew on classical Greek and Latin literature because he was educated in the classical humanist tradition of the *Gymnasium*. The Missouri Synod largely retained this tradition until the late 1930s.

is what we find in the Gospel. What a precious difference! When the Law lays us low, we can cheerfully walk upright again because there is another doctrine beyond the Law that makes no demands of us whatsoever. If we were to ask Christ, "What is expected of me so that I may be saved?" He would answer: "Certainly not works! I have already accomplished all the works that had to be done. You need not drink one drop of the cup I had to drink."

And if you would only reflect on this, my dear friends, you, too, would jump for joy that these glad tidings have been brought to you as well. But anyone who continues to despair—despite this message—anyone who keeps on brooding and says, "I am a despicable person; there is no forgiveness for me," does nothing less than reject the Gospel. This person rejects Christ. And even if I had committed the most dreadful sins and had to say like Paul, "I am the foremost sinner,"[5] even if I had committed the sin of Judas or the sin of Cain,[6] nevertheless I need to receive the Gospel because it demands nothing of me.

Fourth difference   The fourth difference between Law and Gospel relates to threats. The Gospel does not contain any threats whatsoever—only words of consolation. Whenever you come across a threat in Scripture, you may be assured that the passage is Law. Anyone who realizes this comforting truth is truly blessed! The Holy Spirit produces this knowledge in every believer. In fact, no one can have this knowledge without the Holy Spirit. If the Holy Spirit does not work this knowledge in people, they remain unbelievers.

However, do not incorrectly assume that the Gospel makes people secure just because it has no threats to hurl at them. No, the Gospel removes believers' desire to sin. The Law, on the other hand, is nothing but threats. Just as Abraham sent Hagar into the desert with a loaf of bread and a jug of water,[7] in the same way the Law hands us, too, a piece of bread and then thrusts us into the desert.

Deut. 27:26   In Deuteronomy 27:26 God says through Moses: "'Cursed be anyone who does not confirm the words of this law by doing them.' And all the people shall say, 'Amen.'" Indeed, we humans are invited by the Law to pronounce a curse upon ourselves. Only people engulfed by hellish darkness can believe that they have a grip on the Law.

1 Tim. 1:15   In contrast, the Gospel proceeds in an entirely different fashion. Paul says in 1 Timothy 1:15: "The saying is trustworthy and deserving of full acceptance, that Christ Jesus came into the world to save sinners, of whom I am the foremost." Therefore, even the foremost of sinners is not threatened but hears only the sweetest promise.

---

5   See 1 Timothy 1:15.

6   That is, betrayal and fratricide.

7   See Genesis 21:8–21.

Luke 4:16–21 records the following:

Luke 4:16–21

And [Jesus] came to Nazareth, where He had been brought up. And as was His custom, He went to the synagogue on the Sabbath day, and He stood up to read. And the scroll of the prophet Isaiah was given to Him. He unrolled the scroll and found the place where it was written, "The Spirit of the Lord is upon me, because He has anointed me to proclaim good news to the poor. He has sent me to proclaim liberty to the captives and recovering of sight to the blind, to set at liberty those who are oppressed, to proclaim the year of the Lord's favor." And He rolled up the scroll and gave it back to the attendant and sat down. And the eyes of all in the synagogue were fixed on Him. And He began to say to them, "Today this Scripture has been fulfilled in your hearing."

On this occasion the Lord announced the contents of His doctrine—the Gospel. This is what He means: "I have not come to bring a new Law, but to proclaim the Gospel." His sermon is overflowing with comfort and salvation for sinners. Blessed is the person who realizes this! May God help us all to this effect!

My Friends: —

Second Evening Lecture: Sept. 19, 1884

A person may pretend to be a Christian though in reality he is not. As long as he is in this condition, he is quite content with his knowledge of the mere outlines of Christian doctrine. Everything beyond that, he says, is for pastors and theologians. To understand as clearly as possible everything that God has revealed—all of that is irrelevant for non-Christians. However, the moment someone becomes a Christian, there arises in him a keen desire for the doctrine of Christ. If they have not yet been converted, at the moment of their conversion even the most uncultured peasants are suddenly awakened and begin to reflect on God and heaven, salvation and damnation, etc. They start to wonder about the deepest problems of human life.

Just take the Jews who flocked to Christ—or the apostles. All those people heard Christ with great joy and were astonished because He preached with authority—in contrast to the scribes. But the majority of those hearers never advanced beyond a certain feeling of delight and admiration. The apostles, too, were uneducated people, but they acted differently. They did not stop where the rest stopped but posed all kinds of questions to Christ. After hearing one of His parables, they said, "Explain to us the parable" (Matthew 13:36). The conduct of the Bereans who searched the Scriptures daily (Acts 17:11) was similar. It is, therefore, quite true what the **Apology** says: "Men

Matt. 13:36; Acts 17:11; Ap XII (VI) 32

of good conscience are crying for the truth and proper instruction from the Word of God. Even death is not as bitter to them as when they find themselves in doubt regarding this matter or that. Accordingly, they must seek where they can find instruction" (Müller, p. 191).[8]

Striving to obtain truth and divine assurance is a necessary requirement even of an ordinary Christian. However, with a theologian this is even more so the case. A theologian who does not have the greatest interest in Christian doctrines would be unthinkable. Even someone with only a budding faith in his heart regards even the smallest point as of great importance. To such a one every doctrine is as precious as gold, silver, or gems. God grant that this may be true for you too! If it is, you will not come in a self-satisfied manner to these lectures but will ask over and over, "What is truth?"—not in the spirit of Pilate but like Mary, who sat at Jesus' feet and listened raptly to every word He spoke.[9] Then, too, every one of these lectures will be of great blessing to you, even though the instrument through which the truth is to be conveyed to you is inferior.[10]

Now, the first matter that you need to consider is the differences between these two doctrines. We have already reviewed four of these differences. Let us move on to the fifth one.

Fifth difference; Effects of the Law

The fifth difference between Law and Gospel regards the *effects* of these two doctrines. What are the effects of preaching the Law? There are three. In the first place, while the Law tells us what to do, it does not give us the strength to carry out its commands. Rather, the Law prompts in us an unwillingness to keep the Law. True, some do treat the Law as if it were a rule in arithmetic. But, for the most part, once the Law forces its way into a person's heart, that heart tends to strain with all its might *against* God—with that person becoming furious at God for demanding such impossible things of him. In fact, such people will even curse God in their heart. They would slay God if they could. They would thrust God from His throne if that were possible. The effect of preaching the Law, then, is to increase people's lust for sinning.

In the second place, while the Law uncovers a person's sins, it offers him no help to free himself from sin and thus hurls him into despair.

Here is the third difference: On the one hand, the Law does indeed produce feelings of contrition by conjuring up the terrors of hell, death, and of the wrath of God. But it has not one drop of comfort to offer the sinner. Consequently, if the Law is the only teaching that is applied to people, they

---

8   See also *Triglot Concordia*, 290; *Concordia*, 176. Walther uses the German version of the Apology; see the appendix, "Walther's Book of Concord," pages 467–68. For more information on the Apology of the Augsburg Confession, see *Concordia*, 69–72.

9   See Luke 10:38–42.

10   Walther refers to himself as the "inferior instrument."

must despair, die, and perish in their sins. Ever since the fall, this is the only effect the Law can produce in people. Romans 7:7–9 makes this clear:

> I would not have known what it is to covet if the law had not said, "You shall not covet." But sin, seizing an opportunity through the commandment, produced in me all kinds of covetousness. For apart from the law, sin lies dead. I was once alive apart from the law, but when the commandment came, sin came alive and I died.

Rom. 7:7–9

Pagans do not realize that the evil lusts deep down in our heart are actually sin. The greatest moralists have said, "It is not *my* fault that I sin; *I* cannot help it; I cannot prevent myself from sinning." But divine Law shouts: "You shall not covet! You shall not lust!" In fact, we are told that we must get rid of even the lust resulting from original sin!

When a person gives no thought to the Law, sin moves about freely throughout his heart and he does not realize he is sinning. Ask worldly people about this matter, and they will look up in surprise and state: "We have done no evil. We have killed no one. We have not committed adultery. We have not been thieves," etc. They do not notice at all that sin is a constant visitor. But when the Law strikes them like a bolt of lightning, they recognize what great sinners they are, what horribly ungodly thoughts they are harboring. This is what the apostle means when he says, "Sin came alive" when the Law arrived. The Law uncovers sin, but it offers us no comfort. If we had only the Law—the kind of Law we have today—and nothing else, we would have to perish forever and go to hell. The punishing effects and the curse of the divine Law will not be felt until we are in hell—for the Law must be fulfilled; it must preserve its divine authority.

Take 2 Corinthians 3:6, where we read: "The letter kills." The apostle calls the Law "the letter" because God inscribed it in the form of letters on stone tablets. Even pagans have observed that the Law produces an effect opposite to that which it commands. The statement of the immoral poet Ovid is well-known: "We strive after the forbidden thing and always lust after those things that are denied us."[11] Ovid himself was a swine, and so he says bluntly, "See, this is what I do: I always do things that others regard as forbidden."

2 Cor. 3:6

When the Israelites were given the Ten Commandments at Mount Sinai, they all trembled. Their behavior revealed the condition of their heart. On that occasion, God intended to point out for all time to come: "Behold, this is the effect of the Law!" Accordingly, when the rich young man came to Christ, asking how he might be saved, and was so utterly blind that he did not perceive his sinful corruption at all, we are told: "He went away sorrowful"

Matt. 19:22;
Acts 24:25

---

11   Latin: *Nitimur in vetitum, semper cupimusque negata.* This is from Ovid's *Amores* (III.4.17). Throughout the centuries, many authors have used this as a catchphrase. One sees widespread citation in the nineteenth century.

(Matthew 19:22). Christ knew it was too early to apply the Gospel to this young man because He first had to convince him that he was utterly incapable of fulfilling the Law. Again, when Paul preached to Felix, the governor, concerning righteousness, temperance, and the judgment to come, we read that Felix trembled and answered, "Go away for the present. When I get an opportunity I will summon you" (Acts 24:25).

Acts 2:37–38   But the governor never did call for Paul again; he wanted to be rid of the thunder and lightning of the Law. Similarly, when Peter preached the Law to his hearers at Pentecost, we are told [that] "they were cut to their heart." They asked him and the rest of the apostles: "Brothers, what shall we do" in order to be saved? Then Peter said to them: "Repent and be baptized every one of you in the name of Jesus Christ for the forgiveness of your sins, and you will receive the gift of the Holy Spirit" (Acts 2:38).

Fifth difference;   The effects of the Gospel are of an entirely different nature. In the first
Effects   place, while the Gospel demands faith, at the same time it also offers and
of the Gospel   gives us faith. When we preach to people: "Believe in the Lord Jesus Christ!" God gives them faith through our preaching. We preach faith, and any person not willfully resisting obtains faith. It is indeed not the mere physical sound of the spoken Word that produces this effect, but rather the *contents* of the Word.

The second effect of the Gospel is that it does not rebuke sinners at all, but rather takes all terror, all fear, all anguish from them, filling them with peace and joy in the Holy Spirit. At the return of the prodigal son, the father does not mention the son's horrible, unspeakable conduct with a single word. He says nothing—nothing whatsoever—about it. Rather, the father embraces the prodigal, kisses him, and prepares a splendid feast for him.[12] This is a glorious parable that demonstrates the effect of the Gospel. It removes all unrest and fills us with a blessed, heavenly peace.

In the third place, the Gospel does not require people to furnish anything good—neither a good heart nor a good disposition nor an improvement of their condition, neither piousness nor love—whether toward God or men. The Gospel issues no orders. Rather, it changes people. It plants love into their heart and makes them capable of all good works. It demands nothing, but gives all. Should not this fact make us leap for joy?

Acts 16:30–31   These effects of the Gospel are exhibited in Acts 16, in the case of the jailer in Philippi. He asks Paul and Silas: "Sirs, what must I do to be saved?" and receives this answer: "Believe in the Lord Jesus, and you will be saved, you and your household."

Acts 16:34   The jailer does not reply to the apostles: "How should I go about this?" No. He promptly believes, for the apostles' words have spoken faith into the man's

---

12   See Luke 15:11–32.

heart. As such, immediately "he rejoiced along with his entire household that he had believed in God." Note that the Gospel bestows the very faith that it urges. But this urging for faith is not like a demand of the Law. Rather, it is an urging of love.

Romans 1:16: "For I am not ashamed of the gospel, for it is the power of God for salvation to everyone who believes." This is a glorious thing. Can there be anything more glorious, more beautiful, more blessed, more precious than what the Gospel gives, namely, eternal salvation? *Rom. 1:16*

Ephesians 2:8–10: "For by grace you have been saved through faith. And this is not your own doing; it is the gift of God, not a result of works, so that no one may boast. For we are His workmanship, created in Christ Jesus for good works, which God prepared beforehand, that we should walk in them." Here we have a brief description of the effects of the Gospel. *Eph. 2:8–10*

The Gospel does not say, "You must do good works." Rather, it fashions us into human beings, into creatures who cannot help but serve God and fellow human beings. Without a doubt, a precious effect!

Galatians 3:2: "Let me ask you only this: Did you receive the Spirit by works of the law or by hearing with faith?" They probably answered something like: "Hearing faith preached gave us a new heart, for prior to that we could do no good. We have now been made into new creatures." You do not need to tell the sun to shine. By the same token, it would be just as useless to say to one of these new creatures, "You *must* do this or that." *Gal. 3:2*

Finally, there is a sixth difference between Law and Gospel, relating to the *persons* to whom either doctrine is to be preached. In other words, there is a difference in the objects, that is, the people, to whom Law and Gospel must be applied.[13] The persons on whom either doctrine is to work are completely different—just as the goals of each doctrine are different. Preach the Law to "secure" sinners, yet preach the Gospel to alarmed sinners. While at other times *both* doctrines must indeed be preached, at *this* point the question is: To whom must I preach the Law rather than the Gospel, and vice versa? **Sixth difference**

In 1 Timothy 1:8–10, Paul writes:

> Now we know that the law is good, if one uses it lawfully, understanding this, that the law is not laid down for the just but for the lawless and disobedient, for the ungodly and sinners, for the unholy and profane, for those who strike their fathers and mothers, for murderers, the sexually immoral, men who practice homosexuality, enslavers, liars, perjurers, and whatever else is contrary to sound doctrine. *1 Tim. 1:8–10*

---

13 Walther intends the theological meaning of *object* as the passive recipient of an action or cause. God is the only *subject*, the mover and shaker, in this passage. Walther's use of *objects* refers to people whom God moves with the Gospel.

To all persons who fit this bill, then, preach **only** the Law—and not one drop of the Gospel. As long as people are at ease in their sins, as long as they are unwilling to quit some particular sin—in this situation you must preach only the Law, which curses and condemns them. However, the moment they are frightened about their condition, administer the Gospel to them promptly, for from that moment on they can no longer be classified as secure sinners. Conversely, as long as the devil still keeps you in bondage with even one **individual** sin, you are not yet a proper object upon which the Gospel can operate. In this situation, as pastors, you should preach only the Law to such a person.

Isa. 61:1–3

The Spirit of the Lord God is upon me, because the Lord has anointed me to bring good news to the poor; He has sent me to bind up the brokenhearted, to proclaim liberty to the captives, and the opening of the prison to those who are bound; to proclaim the year of the Lord's favor, and the day of vengeance of our God; to comfort all who mourn; to grant to those who mourn in Zion—to give them a beautiful headdress instead of ashes, the oil of gladness instead of mourning, the garment of praise instead of a faint spirit.

The "day of vengeance of our God" is the judgment that God will execute on hell and the devil, as Christ explained. Can there be a more glorious message than this? The devil has horribly disfigured the human race and hurled mankind into deep distress. Christ avenged this and proclaimed to the devil: "I have conquered over you. Therefore, mankind, created in the image of God, will not be lost. I have procured salvation for them." Only those who absolutely refuse to be saved will perish, for God coerces no one in this matter.

Now—I repeat—to such poor, sad-hearted sinners not a word of the Law must be preached. Woe to the preacher who would continue to preach the Law to a starved sinner! On the contrary, to such a person the preacher must say, "Please come! There is still room! No matter how great a sinner you are, there is still room for you. Even if you were a Judas or a Cain, there is still room. Oh, do, do come to Jesus!" Persons of this kind are proper objects on whom the Gospel is to work.

Let me now cite to you a passage from Luther's *Sermon on the Distinction between Law and Gospel*. He writes:

W² 9:802f.;
Matt. 22:39 Luther

By the term "Law" nothing else is to be understood than a word of God that is a command, that enjoins upon us what to do and what to avoid, that requires from us some work of obedience. This is easily understood when we look only at the form of speech in which God expresses a certain word of His,[14] but it is very difficult in the exe-

---

14   Latin: *in causa formali.*

cution.[15] Now, there are many kinds of laws or commandments that refer to works that God requires of each person individually, according to his natural disposition, his standing in society, his office, and according to the particular season and other circumstances that have a bearing on the doing of such works. Therefore, the Commandments tell each man what tasks God has laid on him and what He requires of him, in keeping with his natural disposition and his office. For instance, a wife must tend her children and let the master of the house do the governing, etc. That is the task required of her. A servant is to obey his master and do all other things that are proper for a servant to do. In like manner a maidservant has a law to govern her conduct. However, the universal law that pertains to all of us is this, [Matthew] 22:39: "Love your neighbor as yourself." Give him advice and aid in any emergency; if he is hungry, feed him; if he is naked, clothe him; and so on. This is rightly distinguishing Law and Gospel. Law is anything that refers to what we are to do. On the other hand, the Gospel, or the Creed, is any doctrine or word of God that does not require works from us and does not command us to do something but bids us simply to accept as a gift the gracious forgiveness of our sins and the everlasting bliss offered us. In accepting these gifts, we surely are not doing anything; we merely receive what is given and presented to us by the Word, such as when God gives you a promise such as this: I give you this or that, etc. For instance, in Holy Baptism, which I have not ordained and which is not my work, but the word and work of God, He says to me, "Come here. I baptize you and wash off all your sins. Accept this gift, and it shall be yours." Now, when you are thus baptized, what else do you do than receive and accept a gracious gift?

. . . The difference, then, between Law and Gospel is this: The Law makes demands of things that we are to do; it insists on works that we are to perform in the service of God and our fellow human beings. In the Gospel, however, we are summoned to a distribution of rich alms that we are to receive and take: the loving-kindness of God and eternal salvation. Here is an easy way of illustrating the difference between the two: In offering us help and salvation as a gift and donation of God, the Gospel bids us to hold the sack open and have something given to us. The Law, however, gives nothing. It only takes and demands things from us. Now, these two, giving and taking, are surely far apart. For when something is given to me, I am not contributing anything toward that. I only receive and take; I have something given

---

15 Latin: *in causa finali.*

to me. Again, when in my profession I carry out commands, likewise when I advise and assist my fellow man, I receive nothing but give to another whom I am serving. Thus Law and Gospel are distinguished as to their formal statements:[16] the one promises; the other commands. The Gospel gives and bids us to take; the Law demands and says, "This you are to do."

We note that Luther does not develop this doctrine scientifically but proclaims it like a prophet. That is why he had such a great impact. If he had written a scientific treatise in Latin on this subject with headings A. a. *α*. א. b. *α*. א. c. *α*. א. B. a., etc., systematically presented, the people would have marveled and said, "That man is a great scholar." But if he had done it that way, he would not have had the impact he did.

In the writings of the Church Fathers we can barely find anything concerning the distinction between Law and Gospel.[17]

Third Evening Lecture: Sept. 26, 1884

False doctrine vs. pure doctrine 1 Cor. 2:14

MY FRIENDS: —

Christ Himself describes the way to heaven as a narrow path. The path of pure doctrine is just as narrow. For pure doctrine is nothing less than a teaching on how to get to heaven.

It is easy to lose your way when you are taking a narrow and rarely traveled path through a dense forest. Without intending to do so and without being aware of it, you might make a wrong turn to the right or left. It is just as easy to lose the narrow way of pure doctrine, which likewise is traveled by few people and leads through a dense forest of false teachings. You may land either in the bog of fanaticism or in the ravine of rationalism. This cannot be taken lightly. False doctrine is poison to the soul. If people at a large banquet drink from wine glasses to which arsenic has been added, they can drink physical death from their wine glasses. In the same way, an entire audience can be subject to spiritual and eternal death when they listen to a sermon to which the poison of false doctrine has been added. People can be deprived of their souls' salvation by a single false comfort or a single false rebuke administered to them. [And this is a]ll the more [true because of] the fact that we are all by nature more attracted to the glaring and glittering light of human

---

16   Latin: *in causa formali.*

17   When Walther delivered this lecture, he had recently given an essay on "how reprehensible it is" to base doctrine on the writings of the Church Fathers, however treasured and valuable these writings might be. One will not find much in the Church Fathers under a category called "Law and Gospel." One will, however, find a great deal under "old Law/new Law," "old covenant/new covenant," "Law/Promise," and "Law of Moses/Law of Love." See the Law and Gospel timeline, pages lv–lxiii.

reason than to God's truth. For "the natural person does not accept the things of the Spirit of God, for they are folly to him, and he is not able to understand them because they are spiritually discerned" (1 Corinthians 2:14).

Thus you can gather how foolish it is—in fact, how terribly deceived so many people obviously are—when they ridicule pure doctrine and say to us, "Enough already with your 'Pure doctrine, pure doctrine'! That can lead only to dead orthodoxy. Focus on pure living instead. That way you will plant the seeds of righteous Christianity." That would be like saying to a farmer, "Stop fretting about good seed! Be concerned about good fruit instead."

On the contrary, if you are concerned about good fruit, you will also be concerned about good seed. In the same way, if you are concerned about pure doctrine, you will at the same time also be concerned about genuine Christianity and a sincere Christian life.

Spreading false doctrine is like sowing weeds. The enemy does this. This in turn produces offspring of wickedness.

On the other hand, pure doctrine is like wheat seed; from it spring the children of the kingdom, who even in this present life belong in the kingdom of Jesus Christ and in the life to come will be received into the kingdom of glory. May God even now instill in your heart a great fear—even a real hatred—of false doctrine! May He graciously give you a holy desire for the pure, saving truth revealed by God Himself! That is the chief goal of these evening lectures.

Let us move on with our study. Even tonight we cannot take leave of our thesis so quickly. We have indeed observed the differences between Law and Gospel. By hearing two testimonies of Luther on the subject we have also been strengthened in our conviction that what we have heard about these differences is true. Now, let me give you a practical example of how these two doctrines must be proclaimed—without mingling the one with the other. To this end, let me submit a passage from Luther's exposition of chapters 6, 7, and 8 of the Gospel of John, written between 1530 and 1532.[18]

There is a general tendency among young people to value the beautiful language and style of an author more than the content of his writings. That is a dangerous tendency. You must always have a greater regard for the *what* than for the *how* of a treatise.[19] The Law must be preached in all its severity so the hearer will understand: "This sermon moves those still secure in their sins toward salvation." Yet you need to preach the Gospel in such a way that the hearer will understand: "This sermon applies only to those who have been struck by the Law and who are in need of comfort." Those are the key elements of a sermon.

---

18   Before getting to Luther, however, Walther offers a few more thoughts.

19   Walther adds the Latin for "what" and "how": *quid* and *quomodo*.

W² 8:81
(cf. AE 23:270);
John 7:37

On the words of Christ in John 7:37 ("If anyone thirsts, let him come to Me and drink"), **Luther** offers this comment (St. Louis Ed. 8:81): "These are the two subjects on which we preach. The Law produces thirst; it leads the hearer to hell and kills him. The Gospel, however, refreshes him and leads him to heaven." Luther speaks of this difference not only when explaining passages in which the terms "Law" and "Gospel" occur but also wherever he has an opportunity to preach these "two subjects."

The Law tells us what to do and charges us with not having done it, no matter how holy we are. Thus the Law makes us uncertain; it chases us about and thus makes us thirsty. Now, when Christ invites those who thirst, He means those who have been crushed under the hammer blows of the Law. These persons Christ invites directly to come to Him; of course, indirectly He invites *all* people. A person who is thirsting like this only needs to drink—and receive the consolation of the Gospel. When a person is really thirsty and is handed even a small glass of water, how greatly refreshed he feels! But when a person is not thirsty, you can hand him one glass of water after another—it will do him no good; it will not refresh him.

W² 8:81–82
(cf. AE 23:270–71)

[The Law] says, "You shall not kill." Its whole urging is directed toward what I am to do. It says, "You shall love the Lord your God with all your heart and your neighbor as yourself. You shall not commit adultery or swear or steal." And then it says, "Make sure that you have lived or live according to My commandments." When you reach this point, you will find that you do not love God with your whole heart as you should, and you will be forced to confess: "O my God, I have not done what I should; I have not kept the Law, for neither did I love You with all my heart today nor will I do so tomorrow. I make the same confession year after year, admitting that I have failed to do this or that." There seems to be no end to this confessing.

When will your soul ever find rest and be fully assured of divine grace? You will always be in doubt; tomorrow you will repeat the same confession you made today; the general confession will always apply to you. Now, where will your conscience find rest and a foothold because you assuredly know how God is disposed toward you? Your heart cannot tell you, even though you may be doing good works to the utmost of your ability. For the Law remains in force with its command: "You shall love the Lord your God and man with all your whole heart." You say, "But I am not doing it." And the Law replies, "You *must* do it." Thus the Law puts you in anguish. You have to become thirsty and terrified; you have to tremble. Then you exclaim, "What should I do for God to lift His gracious countenance upon me? They say I will obtain

God's grace, but only if I **keep** the Ten Commandments and have good works and many merits to show for [it]!"

But that will never happen. I am not keeping the Ten Commandments. Therefore, no grace is extended to me. The result is that man can find no rest trusting in his good works. He wants to have a good conscience. He yearns for a good, cheerful, peaceful conscience and for real comfort. He thirsts for contentment. That is what we mean by "thirst." That thirst will continue until Christ comes and asks: "Would you like to be at ease? Would you like to have rest and a good conscience? I would advise you to come to Me. Forget Moses, and ignore your own works. There is a difference between Me and Moses. The thirst that is plaguing you comes from Moses. He has done his job. He has scared you and made you thirsty. Now try Me. Come to Me. Believe in Me. Listen to **My** teaching. I am a different Preacher; I will give you to drink and refresh you."

Anyone who has not been put through this experience reverberates without meaning,[20] like a noisy gong or a clanging cymbal.[21] But if a preacher has experienced this personally, he can really speak **from** the heart. What he says will go **into** the heart of his hearers. It is by mere coincidence if someone is awakened from sin and converted by a preacher who is himself unconverted.

Accordingly, when he is getting ready to deliver his sermon, the preacher must draw up a battle plan in order to win his hearers for the kingdom of God. Otherwise, the hearers may say of his sermon only, "Oh, that was nice!" and that will be all. They will leave the church with empty hearts.

If any of you are well versed in this art, I mean, if any of you can rightly make this distinction, he would deserve to be called a doctor of theology. For Law and Gospel must be distinguished from each other. The role of the Law is to terrify men, to drive them crazy and to despair—especially rude and vulgar people—until they realize they **can** do **neither** what the Law demands nor achieve God's favor. That will make them despair of themselves. For they can never accomplish that goal—to obtain God's favor by their own efforts—and keep the Law. I recall when Dr. Staupitz said to me on a certain occasion: "More than a thousand times I have lied to God, promising that I would become godly. But I never did what I promised. I will never again resolve to become godly, for I see that I cannot carry out my resolution. I want to quit lying to God." That was also my experience under the papacy: I was very anxious to become godly, but how long did it

W² 8:82
(cf. AE 23:271)

---

20 Latin: *sine mente sonans.*
21 See 1 Corinthians 13:1.

last? Until I had finished reading the Mass. An hour later I was more evil than before. This state of affairs goes on and on until a person becomes quite weary and is forced to say, "I have had it up to *here* with being godly according to Moses and the Law. I am going to follow another Preacher, who says to me, 'Come to Me, if you labor and are heavy laden, and I will give you rest.'"

Let this phrase, "Come to Me," be soothing to your ears.

W² 8:82–83
(cf. AE 23:271–73)

This Preacher does not teach that you **can** love God or that you **must** act and live a certain way. Rather, He tells you how to be godly in God's eyes and how to be saved, **despite the fact** that you **cannot** do as you should. This kind of preaching is wholly different from the teaching of the Law of Moses, which deals only with works. The Law says, "You shall not sin. . . . Go and be godly. . . . Do this, do that . . . ." But Christ says, "Accept the fact that you are not godly. But I have been godly in your stead."[22]

. . . **These two sermons must be preached simultaneously and urged on the listeners.** You should not stick to one doctrine; for all the Law does is make people thirsty, and it does this only to terrify people's hearts. But only the Gospel satisfies people, makes them cheerful, revives them, and comforts their conscience. To prevent the Gospel from producing only lazy, frigid Christians who think that good works are not necessary, the Law says to the old Adam: "Do not sin; be godly; avoid that; do this; etc." And when our conscience feels these blows and realizes that the Law is not mere smoke and mirrors, we humans become terror-stricken. This is when we need to hear the teaching of the Gospel, namely, whenever we sin. Hear Christ, our teacher, who says to you, "Come, I will not let you die of thirst. Come, quench your thirst." If these facts had been preached to me, Dr. Luther, back when I was young, it would have spared my body much grief, and I would not have become a monk.

But now—even though these truths are being preached—the people of this godless world despise them. For they did not have to endure the sweat bath that I and others had to while we were under the papacy. Not feeling the agony of their conscience, these people despise the Gospel. They have never felt the pangs of thirst; therefore, they start all manner of sects and fanatical doings. This saying is true: "He who has not tasted bitter things does not remember sweet things."[23] He

---

22   The Dau text includes the following sentence from this Luther citation: "Take from Me what I give thee—thy sins are forgiven thee (*remissa sunt tibi peccata*)."

23   Latin: *Dulcia non meminit, qui non gustavit amara.*

who has never been thirsty has no taste for a cool drink. Thirst is a good waiter, and hunger is a good cook. But where there is no thirst, even the best drink is not enjoyed.

The doctrine of the Law, then, was given for this purpose: that a person would be stuck in a sweat bath of anguish and sorrow under the teaching of the Law. Without the sweat of the Law, men become fat and comfortable and lose all desire for the Gospel. If you meet such people, pass them by. We are not preaching to them. This preaching is for the thirsty. To them we bring the message: "Let them come to Me; I will give them cool water to drink and will refresh them."

Luther states that "Law *and* Gospel must be proclaimed, and the two must not be mingled." A pastor who is not focused in his preaching preaches himself rather than Christ. But anyone preaching himself preaches people into hell, even when they say of his preaching: "Ah, that was beautiful! That man is an orator!" Even a true, righteous preacher is tempted by vain thoughts that spring from his sinful flesh. But as soon as he notices this, he will cast these cursed thoughts of vanity aside and will cry to God to rid him of them. He enters his pulpit a humble man. People can tell whether his preaching comes from the heart or not. **Preach Christ, not self!**

Of course, you cannot preach like a Luther. Yet you still need to consider: "How can I preach the Law to the secure and, at the same time, the Gospel to crushed sinners?" Every sermon must contain both doctrines. As soon as one of them is missing, the other is wrong. For any sermon is wrong that does not present all that is necessary for a person's salvation. Do not think that you have done rightly if you generically preach Law in one part of your sermon and Gospel in the other. No. A topical division of this kind is worthless. Both doctrines may even be contained in one sentence. But everyone in your audience must have the impression: "He is preaching to me!" Even the most comforting and cheerful sermon must contain the Law as well.

Let me cite a passage from Luther's exposition of Psalm 23:3 (St. Louis Ed. 5:275): "He restores my soul." What Luther is saying is: "Inasmuch as the Lord, our God, has a twofold Word—namely, Law and Gospel—by the words 'He restores my soul,' the psalmist indicates quite clearly that he is not speaking of the Law but of the Gospel." W² 5:275 (cf. AE 12:164); Ps. 23:3

Any statements in the Bible that contain threats of punishment pertain to the Law. However, words that comfort, words that speak of giving and offering something—these belong to the Gospel. Yet you will not find a single Gospel reading from which you could not preach both Law and Gospel.

Luther proceeds:

W² 5:275
(cf. AE 12:164);
Deut. 27:26; Rom.
3:20; 4:15 Luther

The Law cannot restore the soul, for it is a word that makes demands upon us and *commands* us to love God with our whole heart, etc., and our neighbor as ourselves. The Law condemns every person who fails to do this and pronounces this sentence upon him: "Cursed is every one who does not do all that is written in the book of the Law." Now, it is certain that no person on earth can do this. Therefore, in due time the Law approaches the sinner, filling his soul with sadness and fear. If no relief is provided from its blows, it continues its onslaught, forcing the sinner into despair and eternal damnation. Therefore, St. Paul says (Romans 3:20), "Through the law comes only knowledge of sin." Again, "The Law works nothing but wrath" (Romans 4:15).

The Gospel, however, is a blessed word; it makes no demands on us but only proclaims everything that is good, namely, that God has given His only Son for us poor sinners. This good news also includes that He is to be our Shepherd, seeking us starving and scattered sheep, giving His life for us, redeeming us from sin, everlasting death, and the power of the devil.

At this point we might raise the question as to why the Law leads people into the horrible sin of despair. That is merely a coincidental feature. In and of itself, the Law, too, is good.

Let me follow up with a passage from Luther's *Commentary on Galatians*. Regarding Galatians 2:13–14, Luther says:

W² 9:157–58
(cf. AE 26:113–14)

Accordingly, when your conscience is terrified by the Law and you are wrestling with the judgment of God, do not consult your reason or the Law. Rather, take your stand solely on the grace of God and His word of consolation. Cling to this, and act as if you had never heard a word of the Law. Enter into that darkness (Exodus 20:21) where neither the Law nor human reason give their light, but only the dark word of faith. Here the believer relies with certainty on being saved in Christ—without the Law and regardless of it.

Thus the Gospel—without and regardless of the "light" of the Law and reason—leads us into the "darkness" of faith, where Law and reason exercise no authority. We must indeed hear the Law as well, but only in its proper place and at the proper time. When Moses was on the mountain, speaking face-to-face with God, he did not have the Law; he did not legislate and administer the Law. But once he had come down from the mountain, he became a legislator and governed the people with the Law. In this manner, our consciences are to be exempt from the Law, while our bodies are to obey the Law.

... Therefore, anyone who understands how to rightly distinguish the Gospel from the Law should thank God and realize that he is a theologian. Needless to say, however, in times of tribulation[24] I do not know how to do this as efficiently as I should.

W² 9:159–60
(cf. AE 26:115–16)

You should distinguish both teachings in such a manner that you place the Gospel in heaven and the Law on earth. In this way, we can call the righteousness that the Gospel proclaims a *heavenly and divine* righteousness, while the righteousness that the Law proclaims is an earthly and human righteousness.

Be careful to distinguish the righteousness of the Gospel from the righteousness of the Law with the same great care as when God separated heaven from earth, light from darkness, day from night. One of these doctrines is like the light of day; the other, like the darkness of night. If only God could let us separate them even further!

Therefore, when you are speaking of faith and conscience, leave out the Law; it must remain on earth. However, when you are dealing with human works, light the lamp of works or the righteousness of the Law at night. Thus the sun and the immeasurable light of the Gospel and of grace should shine during the day, whereas the lamp of the Law should shine at night. A conscience that has been thrown into terror because it has felt the sting of its sin should argue like this: "I am now engaged in earthly tasks. This is where you should let the donkey labor, slave, and carry the burden that is laid upon it." That is to say, "Let the body with its members be subject to the Law." But when you ascend to heaven, leave the donkey and its burden on earth. For the conscience has nothing to do with the Law, its works, and the righteousness of this earth. Thus the donkey stays in the valley, while the conscience, with Isaac, goes up onto the mountain[25]—ignoring the Law and its works, keeping an eye only on the forgiveness of sin, on nothing but the righteousness that is exhibited and given to us in Christ.

... We need to know this point of doctrine, that is, the distinction between Law and Gospel, because it contains the sum of all Christian teaching. Let everyone who would work diligently toward true piety strive with the greatest of care to learn how to make this distinction—not only in speech but also in truth[26] and in experience, that is, in

W² 9.161–62
(cf. AE 26:117)

---

24 German: *Anfechtung.* Here and subsequently, this means to be plunged into deep fear, like that of losing one's life. It assumes that your opponent is out to get you, and you are helpless to stop him.

25 See Genesis 22:1–14.

26 Latin: *affectu.*

heart and conscience. It is easy enough to make that distinction in words. But when you are struggling with sin, you will realize that the Gospel is a rare guest in a person's conscience, whereas the Law is a familiar and daily companion.

For, by nature, human reason understands the Law. Therefore, when your conscience is terrified by sin—which the Law points out and magnifies—you should speak like this: There is a time to die, and there is a time to live. There is a time to hear the Law, and there is a time to ignore the Law. There is a time to hear the Gospel—and a time to pretend that you are ignorant of the Gospel.

At that moment, let the Law be gone and let the Gospel come; for now is not the time to hear the Law but the Gospel. You have not done anything good. On the contrary, you have committed serious sins. I admit that, but I have the forgiveness of sins through Christ, for whose sake all my sins have been forgiven.

On the other hand, when your conscience is not engaged in this conflict; when you have to discharge the ordinary functions of your office; when you must act as a minister of the Word, a magistrate, a husband, a teacher, a student, etc.—that is not the season to hear the Gospel but the Law. Because those are the times when you are to perform the duties of your vocation, etc.

Our own righteousness serves us for this life, but the righteousness that the Gospel brings us is a heavenly righteousness. At a later point in time we will hear that Law and Gospel must be kept distinct not only in our sermons but also, above all, in our own heart.

Fourth Evening Lecture:
Oct. 3, 1884

If a theologian is asked to yield and make concessions so that peace may at last be established in the Church, yet if he refuses to budge on even a single point of doctrine—to human reason this looks like excessive stubbornness, even like downright evil intent. This is why such theologians are rarely loved or praised during their lifetime. On the contrary, they are scolded as disturbers of the peace or even as destroyers of the kingdom of God. They are regarded as men worthy of contempt. But at the end of the day it becomes clear that the very determined, unfailing tenacity of these theologians as they cling to the pure teaching of the divine Word by no means tears down the Church. On the contrary, it is this very attitude that—even amid the greatest dissension—builds up the Church and ultimately brings about genuine peace. Therefore, woe to the Church if it has no men of this stripe—men who would stand watch on the ramparts of Zion, sounding the alarm whenever a foe threatens to rush the walls, men who would rally to the banner of Jesus Christ, ready for a holy war![27]

Imagine what would have happened if Athanasius had made a slight concession regarding the doctrine of the deity of Christ.[28] What if he had compromised with the Arians[29] and had put his conscience at ease? After all, the Arians *did* declare that they, too, believed that Christ is God—just not from eternity. They had added that little caveat: "There was a time when He did not exist,"[30] meaning, He had *become* God. Yet they added: "Nevertheless, He is to be worshiped, for He is God." What would have happened if they had made a concession? If Athanasius had yielded back then, the Church would have crashed from the one Rock on which it was founded, which is none other than Jesus Christ.

Similarly, imagine what would have happened if Augustine had made even a slight concession regarding the doctrine of free will, if he had denied the total incapacity of man for all matters spiritual.[31] He, too, could have made a compromise with the Pelagians and put his conscience at ease since the Pelagians *did* declare: "Yes, indeed, without the aid of God's grace no one can be saved." But by "the grace of God" they meant the divine *gift* that is imparted to every person. What would have happened if Augustine had yielded back then? The Church would have lost the core of the Gospel. There would have been nothing left of it but the empty, hollow shell of the Gospel. If Augustine had yielded, the Church would have had the Gospel in name only.

For the doctrine of the Gospel—namely, that man is made righteous in the sight of God and is saved by nothing but the pure grace of God through the merits of Jesus Christ—that is, as everybody knows, the most important doctrine, the marrow and substance of Christian teaching. If this doctrine is not proclaimed, there is no Christ, no Gospel, no salvation. There people perish, and, according to this false teaching, the Son of God would have come into the world in vain.

---

27 Walther strikes a note that may have considerable cultural dissonance today. One could try to soften it by pointing to the arms and armor "of the Spirit" (see Ephesians 6:10–20) and not to physical bloodshed. Yet before the First World War, society had a more positive view of warfare.

28 Athanasius (ca. 293–373) held strongly to the formula that Christ was of the same substance (*homooúsios*) with the Father. The First Council of Constantinople (381) officially adopted the term.

29 See the Index of Persons and Groups, page 489.

30 Walther used Greek in his lecture and these words and phrases appear as Greek in the editions of Claus/Fürbringer and Dau. Greek words have been included rarely in this edition, and then usually in a transliterated form.

31 Augustine originally taught the freedom of the will, but, after diligent study of Paul's Epistles and while serving as a pastor and bishop, he publicly rejected this position as false. See also the Law and Gospel timeline, page lviii.

Finally, imagine what would have happened if Luther had made a slight concession regarding the doctrine of the Holy Supper. What if, at the Marburg Colloquy,[32] he had compromised with Zwingli and put his conscience at ease, since the Zwinglians *did* declare: "We, too, believe that the body and blood of Christ are somehow present in the Lord's Supper—just not in the presence of Christ's human substance, since God does not provide such exalted, incomprehensible things for us to believe." By claiming this, Zwingli turned Christianity in its entirety into a questionable matter, and even Melanchthon, who was usually greatly inclined to make concessions, declared that Zwingli had relapsed into paganism. Had Luther yielded, the Church even back then would have become prey to rationalism, which places man's reason above the clear Word of God.

Let us, therefore, bless all the faithful champions who have fought for every point of Christian doctrine, unconcerned about the favor of men and disregarding their threats. Their worldly disgrace, though it often was great, has not been borne in vain. People cursed them, but they continued to bear their testimony until death, and now they wear the crown of glory and enjoy the blissful communion of Christ, of all the angels and the elect.[33] Their labor and fierce battling has not been in vain. For even now, some 1,500 years or—in the latter case—some several centuries later, the Church is reaping what these faithful champions sowed.

Let us then, my friends, likewise hold fast the treasure of pure doctrine. Do not consider it strange if on that account you must bear reproach just as they did. Consider that the word of Sirach 4:33, "Even unto death fight for justice, and God will overthrow your enemies for you," will come true in our case as well.[34] Let this be your slogan: "Fight to the death on behalf of the truth, and the Lord will fight for you!"

Let us move on to a thesis that tells us that since the two doctrines of Scripture—Law and Gospel—are so different from each other, we must keep them distinct in our preaching as well.

32　At the urging of Landgrave Philip of Hesse, a colloquy, or conference, of theologians met at Marburg in 1529 in hopes of uniting the various reformers. See also Ulrich Zwingli in the Index of Persons and Groups, page 501.

33　See Revelation 2:10; 7:13–17.

34　Luther's translation of the Bible usually contains the apocryphal writings, among which is the book known as Ecclesiasticus or Wisdom of Jesus Son of Sirach—or simply as Sirach. Luther did not include the apocryphal writings because they are God's Word but as helpful writings of pious men. Some of these writings are important for understanding the Book of Revelation and are even cited in the New Testament.

THESIS II

*If you wish to be an orthodox teacher, you must present all the articles of faith in accordance with Scripture, yet [you] must also rightly **distinguish** Law and Gospel.*

EDITOR'S NOTE: In this thesis, Walther shows that errors in one doctrine can change other doctrines because everything taught in Scripture is interconnected. Since Law and Gospel are the two chief doctrines of Scripture, distinguishing them rightly is most important.

Walther takes aim at historical-critical thought and its effects on the doctrines of Christ, Law, and Gospel. Walther targets Karl F. A. Kahnis and his book *Lutheran Dogmatics Presented in a Historical-Genetic Manner*.[1] Christoph Luthardt and others used the formula: "interpretation according to Scripture as a whole."[2] Franz Pieper, in the first volume of his *Christian Dogmatics*, speaks strongly against this approach.[3] Timotheus Stiemke spoke against academic bias in the 1894 Eastern District *Proceedings*.[4] Walther sets himself against anyone who would gainsay the Word of God based on sinful human reason and thus rob Christians of their salvation.

This thesis is composed of two parts. The first part states a prerequisite of orthodox teachers, namely, that they must present all the articles of faith in accordance with Scripture. In our day, this is an unheard-of demand. Even among so-called believers, people act as if they were shocked when they hear

True doctrine from God

---

1   *Die lutherische Dogmatik historisch-genetisch dargestellt* (Leipzig: Dörffling & Francke, 1861). For more information on Kahnis and the other theologians mentioned in this thesis and its annotations, see the Index of Persons and Groups.

2   German: *dem Schriftganzen nach*.

3   Franz Pieper, *Christian Dogmatics* (St. Louis: Concordia, 1950), 1:129–90, 232–306.

4   Timotheus Stiemke speaks against this citation from Christoph E. Luthardt, *Kompendium der Dogmatik*, 2nd ed. (Leipzig: Dörffling & Francke, 1866), 237, 239. See *Verhandlungen der zweiunddreißigsten Jahresversammlung des Östlichen Districts* (St. Louis: Concordia, 1894), 23. In the *Proceedings* of the Synodical Conference (1886), the Eastern District (1894), and in *Lehre und Wehre* (1895), professor Augustus Graebner of Concordia Seminary, Stiemke, and G. Gößwein respectively showed historical-critical methods to be entirely incompatible with the Christian faith. An English translation and commentary on the work of Graebner and Stiemke exists in Charles Schaum, "Biblical Hermeneutics in the Early Missouri Synod" (Master of Sacred Theology thesis, Concordia Seminary, 2008), 93–94, 109–12, 159.

someone say, "I have found the truth; I am certain concerning every doctrine of revelation." Such a claim is considered highly arrogant. Young students in particular dare not make such a claim. In Germany they are told, "Whatever you do, do not believe that you have already found the truth! Keep on studying until you have reached the goal!" But they never let you reach the goal, even if someone were to say, "I have completed my studies on this matter." This attitude is regarded with deep suspicion.

There are people who find delight not in eating and drinking or in hoarding wealth or in leading a life of ease, but in quenching their thirst for knowledge. Needless to say, we cannot approve of this tendency either. Yet when they warn their students to "never speak of the Christian doctrine in terms of finality!" our professors are doing exactly the same thing as those people who yearn for knowledge. It would seem they are afraid that someone might speak with finality on an article of faith. They are like Sisyphus in Hades.[5] These professors keep on pushing their stone uphill, only to have it roll back down on them. This is why Kahnis, who had once been a faithful Lutheran, sought to justify himself in the preface of his miserable *Dogmatics*, citing the Latin proverb: "One day is the teacher of the next."[6] What he really meant to say was: "A year ago I believed this and that. But then other thoughts came to me, and I found other doctrines."

What a horrible idea! No, the Word of God demands that we should keep it pure and pristine, so that we would be able to say, as we step down from the pulpit, "I preached God's Word correctly, so that I would be able to swear on it. And even if an angel came down, I would be able to state: 'I preached correct doctrine.'" This is why Luther says—though it is a bit of a paradox—that when a preacher steps down from the pulpit, he should not pray the Lord's Prayer. He should pray it *before* his sermon. If he preaches pure doctrine, there will be no need to pray, "Forgive me my trespasses," after his sermon. Rather, he should be able to say, "I proclaimed the pure truth." But in our day and age, many people have become so skeptical that they regard anyone as something of a lunatic who makes that claim.

Jer. 23:28   In the Word of God, there is a passage in which the Lord says, "Let him who has My word speak My word faithfully. What has straw in common with wheat? declares the LORD" (Jeremiah 23:28). Our sermons, then, are to contain only wheat—and no straw.

---

5   Sisyphus was the mythical first king of Corinth. He was very clever and known for trickery, betrayal, and murder. His punishment in Tarterus was to roll a great stone up a hill, but the stone would always roll back down before it reached the top. Thus the clever criminal had to perform meaningless drudgery forever.

6   Latin: *Dies diem docet*. See the editor's note, page 33.

In Galatians 5:9 the apostle Paul warns the Galatians: "A little leaven leavens the whole lump." What he is saying is this: "A single false teaching spoils the entire doctrine." Even Moses says in Deuteronomy 4:2: "You shall not add to the word that I command you, nor take from it, that you may keep the commandments of the LORD your God that I command you," while John concludes the last book of the Bible with the same words.[7]

As such, it is a wicked teaching to say, "No one will ever be able to give a scriptural presentation of the articles of faith." Especially when students hear a statement such as this, it is as if some hellish poison were injected into their heart. For after a statement such as that, they will no longer show any passion to get to the bottom of the truth, to have a clear understanding of the truth.

But suppose you could truthfully say, "There was no false teaching in my sermon." Nevertheless your entire sermon may have been wrong. Can that be true? The second part of our thesis states: "If you wish to be an orthodox teacher, you must also rightly **distinguish** Law and Gospel."

That is the litmus test of a proper sermon. The value of a sermon depends not only on whether every statement in it is taken from the Word of God and on whether it is in agreement with the same but also on whether Law and Gospel have been rightly distinguished. If the same building materials are provided to two different architects, sometimes one will construct a magnificent building, while the other, using the same materials, will make a mess of it. Because he is dim-witted, the latter may want to begin with the roof, or place all the windows in one room, or stack layers of stone or brick in such a way that the wall will be crooked. One house will be out of plumb and such a bungled piece of work that it will collapse, while the other will stand firm and be a habitable and pleasant place to live. In like manner, two different sermons might contain all the various doctrines—and while the one sermon may be a glorious and precious piece of work, the other may be wrong throughout.

Note this well. When you hear some enthusiast[8] preach, you may say, "Well, he *did* preach the truth . . ." and yet you do not feel satisfied. Here is the key for unlocking this mystery: that particular preacher did not rightly distinguish Law and Gospel, and thus everything went wrong. He preached the truth of the Law where he should have preached the truth of the Gospel, and he offered Gospel truth where he should have presented the Law. Now, anyone following such a preacher will go astray; they will not arrive at the sure foundation of the divine truth; they will not attain the assurance of grace and salvation. This frequently happens when students give sermons. You will hear comforting remarks such as "It is all by grace," only to be followed

Gal. 5:9;
Deut. 4:2

Scripture teaches
Law and Gospel

---

7   See Revelation 22:18–19.
8   German: *Schwärmer*. For more information on Luther's use of this term, see the Glossary, page 486.

by "We must do good works," which are then followed by statements such as "With our works we cannot gain salvation." There is no order in such sermons. Nobody understands them—least of all the person who needs one of these two doctrines most.

Law and Gospel must be properly distinguished. Be careful to follow this rule when you write your sermons. Perhaps, for once, the words seemingly flowed into your pen. But I would advise you to read your sermon over and see whether you have rightly distinguished Law and Gospel. If not, your sermon is wrong—even though it contains no false doctrine.

Now let us look at some Bible texts that testify to the truths just stated.

2 Tim. 2:15   Second Timothy 2:15 reads as follows: "Do your best to present yourself to God as one approved, a worker who has no need to be ashamed, rightly handling the word of truth." [The Greek word][9] in this text that is rendered with "rightly handling" is apparently used in a metaphorical sense. It is taken either from the action of priests handling the sacrificial offerings or from the activities of the head of a family when he distributes food and drink to the members of his household. The latter meaning seems to be the correct one. However, many of our theologians hold to the former.

Luke 12:42   In Luke 12:42 the Lord says, "Who then is the faithful and wise manager, whom his master will set over his household, to give them their portion of food at the proper time?" Here, two things are required of a good manager. In the first place, he must at the proper time provide the servants in his house and the children with everything they need. In the second place, he must give to each individual his due portion—exactly what he or she needs. If a manager were to do no more than haul out of his pantry and cellar all that is in them and place it in a big pile, he would not be acting wisely; the children would probably grab large portions, and the rest might not get anything. He must give to each the right quantity, according to the amount of work he or she has done. If children are at the table with adults, he would be foolish to set meat and wine before children and milk and light food before adults.

But how difficult it is to realize that these very mistakes are often made in sermons! A preacher must not dump all doctrines in a heap before his hearers, just as they pop into his mind, but he must precut for each of his hearers a portion such as they need. He needs to be like a pharmacist, who must give the right medicine to the sick to treat the *particular* ailment with which they are afflicted. In the same way a preacher must give to each hearer his due; he must see to it that secure, carefree, and willful sinners hear the thunderings of the Law, while contrite sinners need to hear the sweet voice of the Savior's grace. That is what it means to give to each hearer his due.

In Ezekiel 13:18–22, where God condemns false prophetesses, we read:

---

9   Greek: *orthotomein.*

Thus says the Lord God: Woe to the women who sew magic bands upon all wrists, and make veils for the heads of persons of every stature, in the hunt for souls![10] Will you hunt down souls belonging to My people and keep your own souls alive? You have profaned Me among My people for handfuls of barley and for pieces of bread, putting to death souls who should not die and keeping alive souls who should not live, by your lying to My people, who listen to lies. Therefore thus says the Lord God: Behold, I am against your magic bands with which you hunt the souls like birds, and I will tear them from your arms, and I will let the souls whom you hunt go free, the souls like birds. Your veils also I will tear off and deliver My people out of your hand, and they shall be no more in your hand as prey, and you shall know that I am the Lord. Because you have disheartened the righteous falsely, although I have not grieved him, and you have encouraged the wicked, that he should not turn from his evil way to save his life.

Ezek. 13:18–22

Here you see how the preacher is cursed who knows that his congregation needs an application of the Law, yet for a piece of bread he keeps silent. Woe to everyone who pampers secure sinners with soft pillows and cushions! These preachers lull to sleep with the Gospel those who ought to be awakened from their sleep by the Law. It is a wrong application of the Gospel to preach it to people who are not afraid of sinning. On the other hand, it is even more horrible if a pastor is a legalistic teacher, refusing to preach the Gospel to his congregation because he says, "These people will just misuse it anyway." Should poor sinners therefore be deprived of the Gospel? Let the wicked perish! On the other hand, the children of God should know how near at hand help is and how easily it can be obtained. But anyone withholding the Gospel from those in need of consolation fails to distinguish Law and Gospel. Woe, and again woe, to such people!

Zechariah relates the following in chapter 11, verse 7: "And I tended the flock doomed to slaughter, for the sake of these miserable sheep. And I took two staffs, one I named Favor; the other I named Woe.[11] And I tended the sheep."

Zech. 11:7 Luther

---

10 The exact context of "bands" and "veils," as well as their translation, remains largely unknown because the passage of time has not preserved the knowledge of these magical rites and their origin. It remains clear in these verses, however, that God condemns all women who pretend to have access to divine power and who use magic rites to manipulate people, even to the point of life and death. This passage directly applies to modern Wiccans. Walther applies it to false pastors, putting them on the same level as practitioners of the occult. See Horace D. Hummel, *Ezekiel 1–20*, Concordia Commentary (St. Louis: Concordia), 359–61, 374–77.

11 Since ancient times, the exact renderings of these words have been disputed. The English Standard Version translates the Hebrew as *Favor* and *Union*. Walther and Luther use *Sanft* ("soft, mild, gentle," thus "Favor") and *Weh* ("Woe"). Compare the Vulgate's "grace

A real spiritual shepherd has two staffs or rods. The "Favor" rod is the Gospel, and the "Woe" rod is the Law. He must be well-informed as to whom he needs to apply either one staff or the other. The Messiah—who is the speaker in this passage—says that He used the "Woe" rod against the flock of slaughter, that is, against sheep that were to be slaughtered and not led to the pasture. The "doomed flock" represents poor sinners. Among them He uses the comforting staff and rod of the Gospel. Most preachers make the mistake of hurling the "Woe" rod at the sheep, while using the "Favor" rod on the wicked. (By the way, Luther's translation of this passage is unsurpassed. If only the people who want to revise Luther's Bible would mind their own business!)

Nature teaches that certain materials must not be mixed together if they are to retain their beneficial powers. There are certain substances that are, by themselves, medicinal, but when they are mixed, they turn into poison. This is what happens when you mingle Law and Gospel. Just look at the colors: when you combine yellow and blue, you get neither yellow nor blue but green. In like manner, you get a third substance[12] when you mingle Law and Gospel in a sermon. This new substance is entirely foreign to either original substance and causes both of them to lose their power.

In his *Sermon on the Distinction between Law and Gospel* (St. Louis Ed. 9:799f.), Luther writes:

W² 9:799–800   It is therefore a matter of utmost necessity that these two kinds of God's Word be well and properly distinguished. Where this is not done, neither the Law nor the Gospel can be understood, and the consciences of men must perish with blindness and error. The Law has its goal fixed beyond which it cannot go or accomplish anything, namely, until the point is reached where Christ comes in. It must terrify the impenitent with threats of the wrath and displeasure of God. Likewise, the Gospel has its particular function and task, that is, to proclaim forgiveness of sin to sorrowing souls. These two may not be mingled, nor the one substituted for the other, if doctrine is not to be falsified. For while Law and Gospel are indeed equally God's Word, they are not the same doctrine.

You may correctly state what the Law says and what the Gospel says. But when you frame your statement so as to combine both, you produce poison for souls. Remember: while Law and Gospel are both God's Word, they are different kinds of doctrine.

---

and [binding] cord" and the Septuagint's "beauty and allotment." The Hebrew can mean "beauty/favor" (cf. Psalm 90) and "bonds/woe."

12   Latin: *tertium genus*.

A person who does not understand this difference—the true difference—has nothing whatsoever to offer people. But even merely knowing or memorizing this difference does not prove helpful, for you can learn the facts of this difference in a few hours when preparing for an examination. Rather, this knowledge must be reinforced by experience. Until that happens, a person will not understand that the distinction between these two doctrines is a glorious one.

In the beginning of the sermon we just mentioned, Luther says:

> This is what St. Paul means: Among Christians, both preachers and hearers must adopt and teach a proper distinction between Law and Gospel, between works and faith. Accordingly, St. Paul commends this distinction to Timothy when he urges him in 2 Timothy 2:15 to rightly distinguish the word of truth, etc. This distinction between Law and Gospel is the supreme skill among Christians. Each and every one of those who glory in being Christians or who have adopted this faith can and should understand this art. For wherever there is a deficiency in this respect, it is impossible to distinguish a Christian from a Gentile or a Jew. That is how important this distinction is. For this reason St. Paul so forcefully insists that these two doctrines, Law and Gospel, be well and properly distinguished among Christians. Both the Law—or the Ten Commandments—and the Gospel are indeed God's Word. The latter was given by God in the beginning, in Paradise; the former, on Mount Sinai.[13] But the matter of decisive importance is this: that these two words be properly distinguished and not mingled. Otherwise, the true meaning of neither will be known or retained. If we imagine that we have both, we will find that we possess neither.

W² 9:804–5

---

13 See Genesis 3:15; Exodus 20:1–17.

I t is a glorious and marvelous arrangement—one that surpasses all under-standing—that God governs the kingdoms of this world, not by immediate action but through the agency of human beings who, in addition to all their other shortcomings, are far too short-sighted and far too feeble for this task. As such, it is all the more marvelous that even in His kingdom of grace, God plants, manages, extends, and sustains His kingdom not directly, but by means of men who are altogether unfit for this task. This is proof of God's loving-kindness, love for humanity, and wisdom, which no human intellect can understand. For who can measure the greatness of God's love, revealed in the fact that He desires not only to save this apostate world[14] but also even to employ human beings—that is, sinners—for this task? Who can plumb the depths of the wisdom of God, who knows how to accomplish the work of saving people by—of all things—using other people who are quite unfit and unqualified for this work? And who can understand that He has previously gloriously pursued, and still is pursuing, this work?

My dear friends, what a huge thing—not only to marvel but also to rejoice in the fact that God wants to use also you as tools of His grace. Just stop and consider: if at this place you could learn how to prolong the life of those entrusted to your care by fifty years, or even to raise the dead to a new lease on life, how great and glorious your calling would appear—not only to you but also to all people! Imagine in what great demand you would be and how you would be honored as extraordinary men! What a treasure people would think you are! And yet all of that would be as nothing compared with the exaltation and glory of the calling for which you are to be trained here. Your job is not to prolong this poor, earthly life of those entrusted to your care, but to bring to them the life that is the sum of all bliss, the life eternal, without end. Your job is not to raise those entrusted to your care from earthly death to live once more in this poor earthly life, but to pluck them out of their spiritual and eternal death and usher them into heaven.

Ps. 144:3   Oh, if you would seriously consider what a great honor God means to confer on you, you would get down on your knees every day, every hour; you would prostrate yourselves in the dust and exclaim with the psalmist: "O LORD, what is man that You regard him, or the son of man that You think of him?" (Psalm 144:3). At the same time, you would have an incentive to surrender yourselves to our merciful God every day and every hour, saying, "Lord, here I am with my body and soul and all my strength. I am willing

---

14   Walther affirms that humanity has committed apostasy, the deliberate rejection of the faith that it once had. God created human beings to be very good, without sin and without death. Adam and Eve rejected their blessed gift for the total darkness and corruption of sin. God then proclaimed to them the Gospel of salvation (Genesis 3:15), and from Cain onward, people have rejected the Gospel, as the violence and corruption of his descendants shows. Unbelief is not simply ignorance; it is participation in collective apostasy.

to apply myself fully in Your service." How gladly you would be prepared to make every sacrifice in the interest of your calling and allow yourselves to be fashioned into tools of God!

However, the matter of utmost importance for you is that, before you teach others, you first obtain a very thorough and vital knowledge for yourselves of the things that God by His prophets and apostles has revealed for the salvation of men. Let us, then, cheerfully proceed as we consider our highly important subject.

To begin with, let me submit two testimonies from **Johann Gerhard**. To be fair, he cannot claim the same depth of experience with the same divine rhetoric that was granted only to Luther. However, Gerhard *did* study Luther thoroughly, and he gave a systematic presentation of Luther's teaching. In Topic 14 regarding the Gospel, paragraph 55, Gerhard says, "The distinction between Law and Gospel is to be maintained **everywhere**."[15] Note well: *at every point*. There is not a single doctrine that does not also call upon us to rightly distinguish Law and Gospel.

Gerhard continues: "This distinction must be observed in two areas: First, in the article of justification, since we are not justified by the Law because of the corruption and weakness of our flesh, which is certainly, though accidentally,[16] incapacitated for this task. See Romans 8:3." The Law does not belong to the doctrine of justification. That is a most important point! We cannot be saved by the Law. Accordingly, God provides another means for us by which we can be saved.

Everything hinges on whether or not we accept this joyful message—the Gospel. If you remove from the Bible the doctrine of justification, Scripture would sink to the level of any other book of morals. "But now the righteousness of God has been manifested apart from the law" (Romans 3:21)—it is revealed in the Gospel, "for it is the power of God for salvation to everyone who believes" (Romans 1:16).[17]

Rom. 1:16; 3:21

To return to Gerhard:

> For this reason men should be exhorted, even urged, to perform good works according to the norm of the Law. These works, however, must not be brought into the most high sanctuary where our justification in the sight of God occurs. For at that point there is ceaseless conflict

---

15   Taken from Johann Gerhard, *Loci Theologici* (Berlin: Gustav Schlawitz, 1863–65). The Latin word *locus* (singular of *loci*) means "topic" or "commonplace." It is a way of collecting theology into an outline of topics. Concordia is publishing an English translation of this series under the title *Theological Commonplaces*.

16   Gerhard uses *accident* in the philosophical sense of something that does not exist in itself (a *nature*) but that exists as a part of such a nature.

17   These verses are part of the discussion in Gerhard's *Loci Theologici*. Walther often takes the words of Gerhard, Luther, and other Lutheran Fathers and makes them his own.

between doing and believing, between grace and works, between Law and Gospel.[18]

Woe to us if we proclaim the Gospel and mingle the Law with it! But that is exactly what we are doing when we proclaim the Gospel and go beyond simply saying, "Accept this message!"[19] That would be twisting it into Law. The Gospel demands nothing of us; it says only, "Come, eat and drink." What the Gospel offers to us is the Lord's Supper. Here is where most preachers make their mistake. They are afraid that by preaching the Gospel too clearly, it will be *their* fault if people lapse into sin. They imagine that the Gospel is food for the carnal-minded.[20]

True enough, to many the Gospel does become the smell of death unto death, but that is not the fault of the Gospel. That happens only because men do not accept—do not believe—the Gospel. Faith is not merely thinking, "I believe." Your whole heart must be seized by the Gospel and come to rest in it. When that happens, you are transformed and cannot help but love and serve God.

While people need to be most urgently warned even after they have become believers, these admonitions must not be brought into the most high sanctuary where God justifies the sinner. The Law must first discharge its function so those who hear it may accept the Gospel with a hungering and thirsting soul, drinking their fill. As soon as a person becomes a poor sinner, as soon as he is aware of the fact that he cannot be saved by his own effort, even before a spark of love has been kindled in him, Christ says: "That is exactly the way I want you! Come to Me just as you are. I will help you; I will lift off you the burden that is oppressing you. Instead, I will lay on you an easy yoke and a light burden."

The main thing to tell a person when you explain how to become righteous is to announce to him the free grace of God, concealing nothing, saying none other than what God says in the Gospel. Build a fence around Mount Sinai, but not around Golgotha, because at Golgotha all God's wrath was appeased.[21]

---

18 The word order follows both Gerhard's Latin and Walther's German, which has been translated here.

19 Decision theology existed among those opposing Walther, both in the Iowa Synod and among Norwegian-American Lutherans using the Sverdrup/Pontoppidan version of Luther's Small Catechism. Walther rejects this theology as a mingling of Law and Gospel. See the section "Election and Baptism," pages lxxv–lxxvi.

20 Here and subsequently, *carnal* means both the things of this fleshly, tangible world and the temptations of the sinful flesh.

21 Mount Sinai was a stopping point for the children of Israel after their exodus from Egypt. On this mountain, God gave the Ten Commandments—the Law—to Moses. Golgotha, a hill outside Jerusalem's walls, was the site of Jesus' crucifixion. Thus it is the "mountain" associated with the Gospel message that Jesus' death saves us.

Now, the Lord has given two "keys" to the Church—and via the Church to all preachers as well: the key for binding and the key for loosing. The key for binding locks heaven; the key for loosing opens it. The preacher holds in his hand these two wonderful keys, for the Church bestows them on him when it confers on him the Office of the Ministry.

Moving on, Gerhard explains that the distinction between Law and Gospel must be observed: "Second: Using the Keys of the Church. Do not proclaim forgiveness of sins to impenitent and secure sinners." That would be a horrible mingling of Law and Gospel. It would be like stuffing food into the mouth of a person who is already filled to the point of vomiting. Rather, what this person needs is "the wrath of God from the Law." Because "there will be tribulation and distress for every human being who does evil" (Romans 2:9). "The law is . . . laid down for . . . the lawless and disobedient, for the ungodly and sinners, for the unholy" (1 Timothy 1:9), whom it crushes under the weight of its damning accusations. But to contrite hearts administer not the threats of the Law but the oil of consolation from the Gospel! As such, Isaiah 66:1 states: "What is the house that you would build for Me, and what is the place of My rest?" And verse 2 goes on to say: "But this is the one to whom I will look: he who is humble and contrite in spirit and trembles at My word." Matthew 11:5 reads: "And the Gospel is preached to the poor."[22]

Rom. 2:9;
1 Tim. 1:9;
Isa. 66:1–2 ESV;
Matt. 11:5 Luther

If I know that a person is not in a condition to have the Gospel preached to him, I must not proclaim it to that person. However, when I speak in public, the situation is different. There I must take into consideration chiefly the elect children of God. Still, I must preach the Law even there. In fact, a sermon that does not contain any Law is worthless. In every gathering of people there are always some impenitent persons who must be shocked out of their sleep of sin. And if anyone, upon being warned, promptly responds: "Nonsense! That does not concern me"—that demonstrates that his heart has not yet been crushed.

In another place in paragraph 52, **Gerhard** writes:

> There are several reasons why we must accurately define this distinction between Law and Gospel and strictly adhere to it. (1) There are many instances from Church history that show that the pure teaching of the article of justification has not been preserved. In fact, the article of justification cannot be preserved at all if people neglect to distinguish between these two doctrines.

Woe to those who inject poison into the doctrine of justification, polluting the well that God has dug for man's salvation! Whoever takes this doctrine

---

22 The Luther version and others like it take "good news" as the technical use of "the Gospel," which is what Walther intends as well.

away from people robs them of everything, for that person would be ripping out of Christianity its very heart, which ceases to beat after this attack. This in turn kicks away the ladder reaching to heaven, which destroys any hope of salvation.

Gerhard continues: "(2) The blessings of Christ are considerably hidden when the doctrine of the Gospel is not separated from the Law by definite boundary lines." By mingling Law and Gospel, we hide the blessings of Christ and rob Christ of all His honor. In this way we attribute to humans some role toward their own salvation and thus strip away Christ completely. God created us without our cooperation, and in the same way He wants to save us—without our cooperation. We should thank Him for creating us with a hope of life everlasting. In the same way, He alone wants to save us. Woe to anyone who says that we must contribute something toward our own salvation! They deprive Christ of His entire merit. For Jesus is the Savior, not an *Associate* Savior, such as these preachers claim they are. Jesus achieved our salvation completely.

That is why we [Missouri Lutherans] are so determined in the predestination controversy,[23] for the main point in this controversy is that we insist on keeping Law and Gospel separate, while our opponents keep on mingling these two doctrines with each other. When they hear us say, "Out of pure mercy, God has elected us to the praise of His grace," or "God wants for Himself the exclusive glory of saving us," etc., they say: "That is a horrible doctrine! If that were true, God would be partial. No," they say, "He must have seen something in certain people that prompted Him to elect this or that **particular** person. And when He sees something good in a person, He elects him." If that were so, man would really be the principal cause of his salvation. In that case a person could say, "Thank God, I have done my share toward salvation." However, when we arrive in our heavenly home, this is what we will really say: "If it had been up to me, I would never have found salvation; and even supposing I had found it by myself, I would have lost it again. You, [O God,] came and drew me to Your Word—partly by tribulation, partly by anguish of heart, partly by sickness, etc. All these things You used as means to bring me into heaven, even though I was always striving for hell." When we are over on the other side, we will see—and marvel—that, in reality, there was not a single hour when God did not work in us to save us, yet there was also not a single hour when we wanted to be saved. Indeed, we are forced to say to God, "You alone have redeemed me; You alone sanctify me." Truly, as sure as there is a living God in heaven, I can contribute nothing toward my salvation. That is the point we are discussing in this controversy.

---

23   German: *Gnadenwahlstreit*, also known as the Election Controversy. See also the discussion beginning on page lxxiii.

Gerhard finally says: "(3) Mingling Law and Gospel can only confuse consciences, because if the gracious promises of the Gospel are falsified, there is no true, reliable, and abiding comfort for consciences that are alarmed and terrified." Mingling Law and Gospel makes consciences uneasy. No matter how comforting the preaching is that people hear, it is of no help to them if there is a sting to it. The honey of the Gospel may taste good at first, but if the sting of the Law is part of the equation, everything is spoiled. Your conscience cannot come to rest if you are not able to say, "According to His grace, God will receive me." If the preacher says to you, "Come, everything is now ready—provided you do this and this and this," you are lost. For in that case you would have to ask yourself, "Have I done everything God desires?" and you will find no help.

A godly Lutheran theologian once described students of theology this way: "When they get to college, they know everything. In their second year of study, they become aware of some things that they do not know. At the end of their last year of study, they are convinced that they know nothing at all." The lesson that the old theologian wished to convey is obvious: the worst delusion is to think that you have made tremendous progress in the acquisition of knowledge. As such, a sure sign that that person's knowledge must be very superficial is if he presumes to know a lot about his field.

Sixth Evening Lecture: Oct. 24, 1884

There is no doubt that what that old theologian said is quite right. It agrees perfectly with the statement of the apostle in 1 Corinthians 8:2: "If anyone imagines that he knows something, he does not yet know as he ought to know." Accordingly, all the great pedagogues and teachers of the past have warned their students, saying, "Do not study many different things, but much of one thing."[24] Everything depends not on how much we know, but on **how well** we know it. The more progress a person makes in his particular field, the more rapidly he becomes convinced that he is still lacking many things. He does not adopt the slogan of our times: "Oh, how gloriously much we know!"[25] Rather, he will repeat the confession of the great philosopher Aristotle: "Alas, how great is our ignorance!"[26] The more truly learned a person is, the humbler he will become, for he knows how much he is still

1 Cor. 8:2

---

24 Latin: *Non multa, sed multum.*

25 Latin: *Quantum est, quod scimus.*

26 Latin: *Quantum est, quod nescimus.* The Latin phrase is a catchall for similar sayings from Aristotle (*Metaphysics* ii.c.1), Pliny (*Historia naturalis* ii.c.32), Tertullian (*Adversus Haereticos* iv), Augustine (*Sermo* xxvii), Petrarch, Nicholas of Cusa, Hugo Grotius, Blaise Pascal, and many others.

lacking, within what narrow boundaries his knowledge is confined, and how much still remains to be explored.

W² 14:397

Now, if this observation applies to every kind of knowledge, to every faculty, it applies especially to the field of theology. Here is where the well-known saying of the apostle Paul applies, which he did not speak regarding genuine knowledge but concerning that conceited knowledge mentioned above. That is why **Luther** has this word of warning for every lazy student: "Study! Keep on reading!²⁷ You cannot read too much in Scripture, for what you read you cannot too fully comprehend. What you comprehend you cannot teach too well, and what you teach well you cannot put into practice too well. Believe the guy who is in the know."²⁸

It is very difficult to obtain true understanding and genuine knowledge in theology. But the greatest difficulty occurs in the doctrine that we are discussing in these evening lectures. The third thesis—now before us—provides an excellent opportunity for making this point clear.

---

27 Latin: *Attende lectioni.*

28 Latin: *Experto crede Ruperto* ("Believe Rupert, who is the expert"). The use of "Rupert" in this proverb is a slang phrase for "guy" that is similar to the modern use of "John Q. Public." Here it refers to Luther, who uses this slang phrase, popular among monks, also in his letters; cf. W² 21b:2085. Because some translators avoid translating Latin slang into English slang, translations of this phrase vary. The complete citation is in Ewald Plass, *What Luther Says* (St. Louis: Concordia, 1959), 1110.

Thesis III

To rightly distinguish Law and Gospel is the most difficult and highest Christian art—and for theologians in particular. It is taught only by the Holy Spirit in combination with experience.

Editor's Note: Walther cautions that head knowledge is not enough. Practical knowledge is also essential for understanding and applying Scripture. Walther gives examples from Scripture to show how the Holy Spirit guides this practical knowledge. Walther cites Luther and offers his own thoughts to show how all Christians, great and small, need the Spirit's guidance.

Knowledge vs. application

Some of you might be thinking: "Can this thesis really be true? I have now heard five lectures on this subject, and it is perfectly clear to me. This is supposed to be the most difficult skill there is? I understood it a long time ago."

If this is the case, my dear friends, you are greatly mistaken. Please keep in mind that this thesis does not mean that the doctrine of Law and Gospel is so difficult that it cannot be learned without the aid of the Holy Spirit. In fact, it is easy—easy enough for children to learn. Every child can understand this doctrine. It is contained in every catechism. It is not solid food but milk. It is like your ABCs. It belongs to the basics of Christianity, because without this doctrine no one can be a Christian. Even a small child soon learns these facts: "The First Chief Part of the catechism deals with the Ten Commandments; the Second Chief Part deals with the Creed. We are first told what to do; next, that a person need only believe to be saved." In other words, the child observes that the Second Chief Part does not make demands like the First Chief Part does.

Yet this doctrine of the distinction of Law and Gospel is entirely different from the doctrine by which the three persons in the Godhead are distinct from one another . . . or the doctrine of predestination with its many inscrutable mysteries . . . or the doctrine of the communication of the divine attributes to the human nature of Christ. These doctrines exceed the grasp of children and cannot be understood by them. But the doctrine of Law and Gospel is different. You know it now too. You know the doctrine of Law and Gospel.

But here we are studying the *application* and the *use* of this doctrine. The practical application of this doctrine presents difficulties that no one can overcome by reasonable reflection. Only the Holy Spirit, in the school of experience, can teach people how to deal with this doctrine. The difficulties of mastering this skill are something a pastor has to deal with not only as a Christian individual but also as a preacher.

In the first place, then, the proper distinction between Law and Gospel is a difficult and great skill for the pastor as a Christian individual. Indeed, the proper distinction between Law and Gospel is the greatest skill that *any* person can learn.

Ps. 51:10–11   Psalm 51:10–11: "Create in me a clean heart, O God, and renew a right spirit within me. Cast me not away from Your presence, and take not Your Holy Spirit from me." Here David is praying to God to receive a right spirit. This is because after his horrible fall—the shedding of innocent blood and the sin of adultery—David had lost his assurance of divine grace.[1] Absolution was indeed pronounced to him when he had come to a penitent knowledge of his sin, but we do not hear that he was cheerful after that. On the contrary, many of his psalms plainly show that he was still in very great misery and affliction. When the messenger of God approached him with the declaration: "The Lord has removed your sin," his heart sighed: "I do not think so. . . . That is not possible; my sin has been too great." We even see him flooding his bed with tears (Psalm 6:6), walking about like a bent and broken man, his body drying up like grass in the drought of summer. This exalted royal prophet knew the doctrine of Law and Gospel full well. All his psalms are full of references to the distinction between the two. But when he fell into sin himself, he lacked the practical ability to apply his knowledge. He cried, "Renew a right spirit within me."

You see, it is a characteristic of Christians to regard the Scriptures as the true, infallible Word of God. When they are in need of comfort themselves, they find none. They cry for mercy; they fall on their knees; they plead to God. God made David taste the bitterness of sin. As such, we notice that, after his fall, David is generally more often sad than joyful and that one misfortune after another happens to him.

God permitted these misfortunes to afflict David to keep him from falling into yet another sin—not because He had not forgiven his sin. It was God's love and mercy that prompted Him to act like this. Of course, someone still dead in sin would probably think: "Why was David so foolish as to torture himself with a sin that had been forgiven by God?" People reasoning this way turn the Gospel into a pillow for their carnal minds to rest upon. They keep on living in sin, imagining they will end up in heaven anyway. This kind of Gospel is a gospel for the flesh.

---

1   See 2 Samuel 11:1–12:25.

Luke 5:8: "Depart from me, for I am a sinful man, O Lord." Is this not an amazing event? Here the Lord comes to the disciple He had named *Petros*, "the Rock," and tells him and his fellow fishermen to drop their nets in deep water after their unsuccessful night on the lake. Peter does so, though he most likely expects that he will not catch anything anyway. But, look! They catch such a huge amount of fish that their nets tear. Now Peter is seized with fear. He reflects on the fact that "the man who just spoke to me must be almighty God Himself. He must be my Maker. Then someday He must be my Judge as well!" He falls down at Jesus' feet and says, "Depart from me, for I am a sinful man, O Lord." He expects the Lord to say to him, "Look at the multitude of sins you have committed. You are worthy of everlasting death and damnation."

Where does all of Peter's fear come from? Why did he not thank Jesus when he fell down at His feet? It is because his many sins had passed before his mind's eye, and in that condition it was impossible for him to express cheerful gratitude. Instead, he had to drop to his knees, trembling and crying to his Lord and Savior, saying those awful words, "Depart from me, O Lord." The devil had robbed him of all comfort and whispered to him that he must speak to Jesus in this way. Peter could not help but think that the Lord would smash him to pieces.

The problem? [Peter] was not able to distinguish Law and Gospel. If he *had* been able to, he could have approached Jesus cheerfully, remembering that He had forgiven all his sins. Many times in his later years he probably said to himself, "Peter, what a fool you were on that occasion. Instead of saying what you said to Jesus, you *should* have said, 'O Lord, abide by me, for I am a sinful man.'" That is exactly what [Peter] did on a later occasion when he fell into another sin. Then he was filled with unspeakable joy when Jesus gave him that look full of compassion [Luke 22 (especially verse 61)].

First John 3:19–20: "By this we shall know that we are of the truth and reassure our heart before Him; for whenever our heart condemns us, God is greater than our heart, and He knows everything." When our heart does not condemn us, it is easy to distinguish Law and Gospel. That is the state of a Christian. But Christians may also end up in a situation in which their heart condemns them. Do what they will, they cannot silence the accusing voice within. It calls to them again and again, reminding them of their former sins. The remembrance of some long-forgotten sin may suddenly start up in them, and they are seized with a terrible fright. Now, if in that moment people can rightly distinguish Law and Gospel, they will fall at Jesus' feet and take comfort in His merit. That, however, is not easy. People who are spiritually dead regard it as foolish to torment themselves with former sins. They become

Luke 5:8

1 John 3:19–20

increasingly indifferent toward all sins. Christians, however, feel their sins and also the witness of their conscience against them.

But in the end, when Christians have learned to apply the proper distinction between Law and Gospel in the real world, they join St. John in saying, "God is greater than my heart. He has rendered a different verdict on people who sin, and that applies to me as well." Yet how difficult this is to do! Blessed are you if you have learned this difficult art. But even if you have learned it, do not think you are experts at it. You will always be no more than beginners at this art. There will be days when you will not be able to distinguish Law and Gospel. When the Law condemns you, you must immediately grab hold of the Gospel.

Since the days of the apostles there has not been a more glorious teacher of this skill than Luther. Yet even he confesses that he was often defeated when trying to apply it in the real world. Even though he led a decent life and was not guilty of coarse sins, the devil often irritated him, tormenting him by pointing at Luther's **spiritual** sins. Completely perplexed, Luther would often come to his confessor, Bugenhagen, with his worries, kneeling before him to receive Absolution, whereupon he would depart rejoicing.[2]

Luther writes (St. Louis Ed. 9:806f.):

W² 9:806-7   God has given us His Word in these two forms: Law and Gospel. The one is from Him as well as the other. And to both He has attached a distinct order: the Law requires of everyone perfect righteousness, while the Gospel presents for free the righteousness demanded by the Law to those who do not have it (that is, to all people).

Now, then, whoever has not satisfied the demands of the Law and is captive under sin and the power of death, let him turn to the Gospel. Let him believe what is preached concerning Christ, that is, that He is truly the precious Lamb of God that takes away the sin of the world, that He has reconciled man with His Father in heaven and by pure grace—freely and without cost—gives to all who believe in this [Gospel] everlasting righteousness, everlasting life, and bliss. Let him cling solely to this message. Let him call upon Christ, pleading with Him for grace and forgiveness of sin. And since this great gift is obtained by faith alone, let him firmly believe the message, and he will receive according to his faith.

---

2   Johann Bugenhagen (1485–1558), the pastor of St. Mary's Church in Wittenberg, was Luther's pastor, to whom the reformer continued to make confession until the end of his life. As opposed to rejecting the practice of private confession and Absolution, Luther supported the view that Absolution is a sacrament because it offers the forgiveness of sins and was instituted by Christ (see John 20:22–23).

This is the proper distinction, and, truly, it is of the utmost importance that it is perceived correctly. Oh yes, we can readily make the distinction in words and preach about it, **but to put it to use and reduce it to practice, that is a great skill and not easily attained.** Papists and fanatics do not understand it at all.[3] I observe in my own case, and in that of others who know how to talk about this distinction in the very best fashion, how difficult it is. To talk about the Law as being a different word and doctrine from the Gospel—that is a common achievement, easily accomplished. But to apply the distinction in our practical experience and to make this skill operative, that is labor and sorrow.

Again, *Luther* writes (St. Louis Ed. 9:808f.):

This distinction must be observed all the more when the Law wants to force us to abandon Christ and the gift of His Gospel. In that emergency we must abandon the Law and say: "Dear Law, if I have not done the works I should have done, do them yourself. I will not, for your sake, allow myself to be plagued to death, taken captive, and kept under your yoke and thus forget the Gospel. Whether I have sinned, done wrong, or failed in any duty, let that be your concern, O Law. Away with you, and leave my heart alone. I have no room for you in my heart. But if you require me to lead a godly life here on earth, that I will gladly do. If, however, like a burglar, you want to climb in where you do not belong, causing me to lose what has been given me, I would rather not know you at all than abandon my gift."

W² 9:808

Like two hostile forces, Law and Gospel sometimes clash with each other in a person's conscience. The Gospel says to you, "You have been received into God's grace," while the Law says to you, "Do not believe it. Just look at your past life. How many and how serious are your sins! Examine the lustful thoughts and desires that you have harbored in your mind." On occasions such as this it is difficult to distinguish Law and Gospel. When this happens to you, you must say, "Away with you, Law! All your demands have been fully met, and you have nothing to demand of me. There is One who has already paid my debt." People dead in their trespasses and sins do not feel this tension. They are soon through with the Law. But the difficulty is quite real to people who have been converted. They may go to the opposite extreme and come close to despair.

---

3   Luther's main opponents included, on the one hand, those who supported the pope and set the pope's words over Scripture. On the other hand, he also was opposed by "fanatics" (German: *Schwärmer*; Latin: *fanatici*) who threw out all kinds of historic doctrine to suit their particular interpretation of Scripture. Early leaders among the fanatics were Thomas Münzer and Luther's former colleague at Wittenberg, Andreas Bodenstein von Carlstadt.

Luther says (St. Louis Ed. 9:802):

W² 9:802

Place any person who is well versed in this skill of distinguishing Law and Gospel at the top and call him a doctor of Holy Scripture, for without the Holy Spirit it is impossible to master this distinction. That is my personal experience. Moreover, I observe in the case of other people how difficult it is to distinguish the teaching of the Law from that of the Gospel. The Holy Spirit is needed as a schoolmaster and instructor in this task; otherwise, no man on earth will be able to understand or learn it. That is the reason why no pope, no false Christian, no fanatic can distinguish these two from each other, especially regarding the material cause and the object.[4]

What Luther is saying is this: "It is not difficult to say what the contents of Law and Gospel are, nor at what persons they are aiming. But it is difficult to say whether a particular statement is part of the Law or part of the Gospel, or, in real life, who needs to hear the Law and who needs to hear the Gospel." And it is the most difficult thing for theologians themselves to distinguish these things.

In his Table Talk, **Luther** says (Halle Ed. 22:665):

W¹ 22:665

There is not a man on earth who knows how to properly distinguish Law and Gospel. When we hear about it in a sermon, we imagine that we know how to do it, but we are greatly mistaken. Only the Holy Spirit knows this art. There have been times when I, too, imagine that I understand it because I have been writing so much about it for such a long time; but believe me, at the end of the day I realize that I have widely missed the mark. Accordingly, only God the Holy Spirit can be regarded as the master instructor in this art.[5]

Note that even Luther—a man who had written many books on this subject for many years—made this confession! We are always more inclined to give ear to the Law than to the Gospel.

In his commentary on Psalm 131 (St. Louis Ed. 4:2077), **Luther** writes:

W² 4:2077

There are some who imagine that they understand these matters quite well. But beware of such an overconfident thought, and remember that you must remain students of the Word. Satan is such a clever swindler that he can easily erase the difference [between Law and Gospel] and make the Law force itself into the place of the Gospel, and vice versa.

---

4   Latin: *in causa materiali et in objecto.* See under "cause" in the Glossary, pages 475–76. See also the explanation of *object*: page 21 n. 13.

5   This citation is from the Halle or first Walch edition. It was not included in the St. Louis Edition (W²).

How often do people in their final agony suffer from a stricken conscience and seize a few sayings that they suppose to be Gospel, though
in reality they are Law. Thus they forfeit the consolation of the Gospel.
For instance, just take the statement in Matthew 19:17: "If you would
enter life, keep the commandments of God." Likewise, this one in
Matthew 7:21: "Not everyone who says to Me, 'Lord, Lord,' will enter
the kingdom of heaven."

Matt. 7:21;
19:17 Luther

The devil approaches poor Christians who are in anguish of death and in
their last hour seeks to pluck them away from the Gospel. When Christians
are departing into eternity, they reflect on whether they are worthy. They
may review a multitude of texts and stumble upon one like this: "If you would
enter life, keep the Commandments," not considering that is also Law. Then
their heart tells them: "You are not fit; you cannot be saved." They cannot
distinguish between Law and Gospel.

Therefore, it is good for you to learn this skill while you are still young.
Do not think: "I am thoroughly grounded in this doctrine, and when I am in
the throes of death, I will simply cling to what I have been taught." If only that
were within our power! Because the devil will throw you into such confusion
that you will not be able to escape from your impossible situation.

Nor must you think: "Oh, I am still young." Does not God frequently
snatch people away in the flower of their youth to impress on others how
necessary it is for everyone to consider that they, too, must die?

Luther continues:

Bible verses such as these often lead the hearts of believers astray,
so they cannot think of anything but what they *have* done and what
they *should* have done. That is, they think about what God requires
and forbids. When these hearts focus their gaze upon these things,
they forget all that Christ has done and what God has promised to do
through Christ. Therefore, no one should be so overconfident as to
imagine that he has sharpened this skill to perfection.

W² 4:2077–78

You will recall that what we are discussing now is how a preacher should
distinguish Law and Gospel as a Christian individual. Of course, he *must* first
be a Christian; otherwise, he should not be a preacher. For anyone who has
not succeeded in knowing and practicing this distinction is still a heathen or
a Jew. The *forma*, the essence, of a Christian—that which makes a person a
Christian—is that he knows how to seek his salvation in Christ and thus to
escape the Law.

Thus **Luther** (St. Louis Ed. 9:161): "In your tribulations[6] you will realize
that the Gospel is a rare guest in people's conscience, while the Law is a

W² 9:161
(cf. AE 26:117)

---

6   German: *Anfechtung.*

familiar and daily companion. For by nature the human mind understands the Law." And unless a person learns this by experience, he will not learn it at all. If you are Christians, you will admit that you are far more often troubled and worried than comforted. When you feel the comfort of the Gospel in your heart, those are the gleams of light by day. Of course, there may also be days when there is not one glimpse of light. But always keep this thought in mind: For such poor sinners as I am, the Gospel—the sweet Gospel—has been provided. I have forgiveness of sins through Christ.

W² 9:161–62
(cf. AE 26:117)

When your conscience is terrified by sin, which is demonstrated and magnified by the Law, that is when you should say: "There is a time to die, and there is a time to live; there is a time to hear the Law, and there is a time to ignore the Law; there is a time to hear the Gospel, and there is a time to ignore the Gospel. Right now let the Law be gone, and let the Gospel come; for this is not the time to hear the Law, but the Gospel. So you have not done any good; on the contrary, you have committed serious sins? I admit that, but I have forgiveness of sins through Christ, for whose sake all my sins have been forgiven. However, while the conscience is not engaged in this conflict, or while I have to discharge the ordinary functions of my office—say, as a minister of the Word, a magistrate, a husband, a teacher, a student, etc.— that is not the time to hear the Gospel, but the Law. At such a time you are to perform the duties of your profession," etc.[7]

Accordingly, when you are called upon to do what is right in public, that is not the time to hear the Gospel but the Law, and to remember your calling or profession. Whenever your relation to God is not under review, you must act in accordance with the Law, yet not like a slave but like a child.

---

7   Walther quoted this previously, but now he slightly alters the punctuation and style because of his oral delivery.

Two weeks ago I shared with you Luther's statement that, without illumination by the Holy Spirit, no one can properly distinguish Law and Gospel and that Luther declared himself to be nothing but a feeble beginner in this exalted and glorious art. By no means was it my intention to depress or discourage you.

Seventh Evening Lecture: Nov. 7, 1894

What I had attempted to do was to cure of their flagrant self-conceit those listeners who somehow imagine that distinguishing Law and Gospel is quite an easy task. At the same time, I also wanted to relieve those who may be thinking: "Well, if even Luther could not acquire this art, how can *I* ever learn it?" Just consider that it is by the teaching of the Holy Spirit and through genuine Christian experience that the proper distinction between Law and Gospel can be learned. Then you can easily understand how it is quite possible that a person might be a graduate of the most illustrious schools you could ever think of, yet not have acquired this art. You must not think that the difficulties discussed in this matter relate only to poorly gifted students of theology. This is also true for those who are highly talented and well educated. As a matter of fact, the more talented and the more knowledgeable a person is, the more easily he could be tempted to self-esteem and self-reliance, and the more he would be apt to take matters easy. Accordingly, he would never understand the proper connection and the proper distinction of these doctrines.

Human wisdom vs. divine wisdom

Chrysostom, you remember, was a great scholar and an excellent orator. His given name was John, but because of his oratorical gifts he was called "the golden-mouthed one," thus "Chrysostom." Apparently he had the gift of being able to do with his audience whatever he pleased. He was just as able to make them glad or sad, exult or wail, weep and sob—according to his pleasure. And yet, all in all, this good fellow accomplished little because he was poor at distinguishing Law and Gospel, frequently confusing one doctrine with the other—a very dangerous habit.[8]

Andreas Osiander is another example. Here was a scholar with a keen intellect, an orator without peer. At first he was able to distinguish Law and Gospel superbly. The draft that he sketched for the Augsburg Confession[9] is proof of this. But that was his status only as long as he was pleased to be Luther's student. You see, he became proud of his splendid gifts and great knowledge, and before long he was totally blind in his judgment of himself. As a result, he started to mingle Law and Gospel in the most horrible way. He taught that people become righteous in the sight of God not by the righteousness that Christ by His bitter suffering and death has acquired for them, but by the indwelling of Christ's divine righteousness. Oh, do beware of such horrible examples!

---

8   Walther may be right, but see also the Law and Gospel timeline, page lvii.

9   For more information about the Augsburg Confession, see *Concordia*, 21–26.

Now, since a person under the teaching of the Holy Spirit learns to rightly distinguish Law and Gospel, it follows that genuine Christians are ideally prepared to share with others what they have experienced in their own lives. This is true even if these Christians are ever so feeble otherwise—as long as they have properly experienced the force of the Law and the consolation of the Gospel, that is, the power of faith. Accordingly, sometimes pastors who are among the poorest intellectually turn out to be the best preachers. There is no doubt that in ages past many a poor, simple presbyter[10] of no renown, called to a small rural parish, was able to distinguish Law and Gospel better than Chrysostom, the great orator in the metropolis of Constantinople; better than the philosophically trained Clement of Alexandria; better than that universal scholar Origen.

We can observe the same phenomenon at the time of the Reformation. A simple pastor such as Cordatus,[11] a very close friend of Luther's, unquestionably distinguished Law and Gospel a thousand times better than Melanchthon, even though the latter was called "Teacher of All Germany."[12] Cordatus's reputation is not diminished by the fact that Melanchthon ridiculed him by calling him *Quadratus*, "Blockhead," because he had unmasked Melanchthon when the latter had begun to err in the doctrine regarding man's free will.[13]

Accordingly, though it is a difficult achievement to distinguish Law and Gospel, you will learn this skill best when you have attained the love of the Lord Jesus and have experienced the power of Law and Gospel.

This evening we will consider that also for **theologians** the proper distinction between Law and Gospel is the highest and most difficult **skill**, and that everything else that a theologian must know is of less value than this skill.

2 Tim. 2:15   Second Timothy 2:15: "Do your best to present yourself to God as one approved, a worker who has no need to be ashamed, rightly handling the word of truth." The apostle's warning to Timothy to "**do your best**" indicates

---

10 In the Greek-speaking early Church, a presbyter ("elder") was the equivalent of a local pastor.

11 Conrad Cordatus (1476–1546). See the Index of Persons and Groups, page 491.

12 Latin: *Praeceptor totius Germaniae*. This title for Melanchthon, usually with the *totius* omitted, appeared with greater frequency at the end of the eighteenth century. It flourished after A. H. Niemeyer's 1817 essay "Philipp Melanchthon als Praeceptor Germaniae." It arose from statements made by Luther and Desiderius Erasmus (of Rotterdam) and was attributed to Melanchthon's students, who offered it as a form of praise for their teacher.

13 The Latin *Quadratus*, "square one," is a term of ridicule. Walther translates it with the slang term *der Vierschrötiger*, which likewise means "blockhead." Walther is referring to a letter by Melanchthon in which the latter shows his irritation over the judgments of "blockhead" Cordatus, who stands among Melanchthon's opponents who supposedly hate humanistic studies (*odio literarum*). See *Corpus Reformatorum* 3:187

that rightly distinguishing Law and Gospel is a great and difficult art—does it not?

Luke 12:42–44: "Who then is the faithful and wise manager, whom his master will set over his household, to give them their portion of food at the proper time? Blessed is that servant whom his master will find so doing when he comes. Truly, I say to you, he will set him over all his possessions."

Luke 12:42–44

What the Lord in this text terms a great achievement is not the mere recital of the Word of God—or, to stick to the simile, the distribution of some food to every member of the household—but this: That to everyone should be given his proper portion at the proper time, that each one is treated as his or her spiritual condition requires. This must be done at the proper time. Only a poor manager would give his servants something to eat right now, and then let a long time pass before he gives them something more. Likewise, he would be a poor manager if he were unconcerned about the quantity of food he had to provide and when it was the proper time to serve it. The lesson conveyed by this simile is this: A preacher must be well versed in the skill of ministering to each in season exactly what he needs—either Law or Gospel.

Second Corinthians 2:16: "Who is sufficient for these things?" and 2 Corinthians 3:4–6: "Such is the confidence that we have through Christ toward God. Not that we are sufficient in ourselves to claim anything as coming from us, but our sufficiency is from God, who has made us competent to be ministers of a new covenant, not of the letter but of the Spirit. For the letter kills, but the Spirit gives life."

2 Cor. 2:16; 3:4–6

The apostle assumes that only through the work of God can a person receive this great and difficult skill. By the term *letter* the apostle means the Law; by *spirit,* the Gospel. Here we have a clear testimony that *both* must be preached side by side. No one has the ability to do this by nature. God must bestow it upon him. For this reason that person must be divorced from the spirit of the world. No one still dragging around the spirit of the world can ever properly learn how to make this distinction. For the Spirit of God does not live in a heart in which the spirit of the world still claims a place. That is why the world cannot receive the Spirit.

Accordingly, anyone desiring to become a real tried-and-true pastor[14] must first become a Christian. He could possibly present every dogma correctly, but that is not enough. He must also understand how to give to each soul in his audience the very thing it needs. This is possible if the preacher is able to investigate precisely the condition of each soul. To be sure, that is very difficult—just as the diagnosis is the most difficult part of a doctor's skill. It is

---

14 Walther says: *ein rechter dókimos.* The Greek word *dókimos* means "approved, tested," which, within the context, Walther relates to being a pastor. The Dau text expands this to: "a servant approved to the Lord."

not enough to use the quick and sharp Word of God. With this sharp sword, you may very easily kill souls if you do not give them what they need.

Accordingly, a pastor must be able to distinguish whether he is facing a hypocrite or a true Christian; whether this is a person still spiritually dead or one who has already been awakened from his sleep of sin; whether this is a person tempted by the devil and his own flesh or a person who has been given over to the rule of the devil because of his evil intent. As such, an inexperienced pastor would readily think a hypocrite to be a true Christian, etc.

Preach in such a way that people in the congregation would think: "He means *me*. Sure enough, he has described me—a hypocrite—exactly as I am." On the other hand, you, the preacher, would have to describe a person afflicted with temptation so plainly that this victim of tribulation would have to admit: "That is my condition, without a doubt." Conversely, when listening to the preacher, a penitent person would think: "That comfort is meant for *me*; I need to embrace it." At the same time, an alarmed soul must be led to think: "Oh, what a joyous message. He means me!" Yes, the impenitent, too, must be made to acknowledge: "That pastor has me down to a *T*."

Accordingly, a preacher must understand how to depict accurately the inward condition of every one of his hearers. But a mere objective presentation of the various doctrines is still not enough. Some pastors might be orthodox and might have understood pure doctrine, yet sometimes they are not in personal communion with God. They have not yet settled their account with God and have not yet attained assurance that their debt of sins has been paid. How can such people prepare a Christian sermon? Here is where the saying popular with the pagans applies: "True oratory is a matter of the heart."[15] Indeed, the distinction between Law and Gospel is properly learned only in the school of the Holy Spirit—in tribulation.

That is why people love to read Luther's sermons. Initially his sermons might not grab you. But when people overcome their initial dislike, perhaps because their pastor might have called a book of Luther's sermons a "precious book," eventually they like the sermons so much that they cannot get enough. It is indeed a delight to read Luther's sermons. You recognize your own personal situation on every page.

At first his sermons shock, stun, and stupefy you. At first Luther hurls you into the depths, but once that is over, he says, "Do you believe this?" and you reply, "Yes." Then Luther says, "Very well, come on back up." Luther's sermons are full of thunder and lightning, but this is immediately followed by the soft breeze of the Holy Spirit in the Gospel. It is impossible for the reader to resist; you cannot help admitting that this is good, nourishing bread—the proper daily food for your soul. Luther does not take a long, winding road.

---

15   Latin: *Pectus facit disertum.*

He does not teach endlessly on how to get out of the depths. As soon as he has made you see that you are a poor sinner, he says to you, "Quit despairing; the grace of Christ is greater than the sins of the whole world." Luther preaches Law and Gospel side by side—making the Law look even more terrible in order to emphasize the rich comfort of the Gospel. That is what you need to learn from our dear Father Luther. That will make people listen to you. That will pique their interest. They will understand that you want to lift them out of complete ruin at this very hour, so they can leave church rejoicing.

But a preacher must exercise great care, lest he say something wrong. **Care in preaching** Again and again he must go over his sermon and consider whether everything is watertight, making sure there is nothing in the sermon that would be contrary to either Law or Gospel. For instance, it would be incorrect to say, "If a person is afraid of dying, he is not a child of God." That would be a great lie. True, it is correct to say that Christians are not afraid to appear before God, but they still dread becoming prey to decay and decomposition in the grave, etc. A statement of that kind must be immediately deleted from a sermon.

Again, young ministers who are eager to achieve results and accom- **Speaking to the worldly** plish something (and how wonderful it is when they are so ambitious!) love to speak before worldly people about the blessed state of being a Christian. However, they frequently overdo it by saying, "Oh, those poor worldly people! They are without any joy or peace or rest!" The problem is, that is not true at all. When worldly people hear a statement such as that, they think: "What a simpleton that preacher is. What does he know about us? Of course we experience joy." That preacher must express himself differently. He must admit that worldly people do have their delights and enjoyments, but at the same time he must remind them that they frequently also have thoughts such as: "What if Christians are speaking the truth? If they are right, what will my fate be?" Amid all their partying, the thought of death suddenly looms like a ghost and turns their joy to bitterness. If the preacher addresses them in this way, he forces them to acknowledge: "That preacher has a point. He is telling it like it is."

Again, if you were to portray Christians as exceedingly happy people **Christian happiness** completely without worry or trouble of any kind—once again, you would not be painting a true picture. In reality, Christians suffer from far greater anxiety, worry, and tribulation than do worldly people.

Yet, despite all this, Christians are far happier than worldly people. If God were to come to them that very night and demand their souls from them, they would say, "Praise God! My race is run; I will soon be with my Savior." On the other hand, amid their tribulations they think: "Surely, it will not be long before I can go home to my Father in heaven, and all the misery and woe of this earth will be long gone and forgotten." While Christians are weeping, the angels are rejoicing over them. And while Christians are in anguish of soul and a state of terror, God harbors the most heartfelt thoughts of love for them, saying, "You are My beloved children." These are only a few instances that serve to illustrate the danger of overstepping your boundaries in your sermons, even when you have the best of intentions.

Attacks of sin   Another point you should bear in mind when writing your sermons is not to say anything that might be misunderstood. For instance, the following statement could be misunderstood: "Anyone sinning deliberately and knowingly will fall from grace." For even true Christians occasionally sin with intent and knowledge, namely, when sin **attacks** them deep inside or externally.

Such sins are called hasty sins. Some people are hot-tempered, even though they are otherwise kindhearted. Something crosses their path, and they suddenly boil over with angry words. This is when the Spirit of God rebukes them: "Look what a miserable creature you are!" and then they ask God's forgiveness. To be fair, in any case,[16] a Christian who sins intentionally most certainly grieves the Holy Spirit. The Holy Spirit does not want to take part in that activity. This is why you must tell the people: "You are walking on dangerous ground. The Holy Spirit will withdraw from you, and instead of making progress in your Christianity, you will be thrown back. If you do not repent and remain genuinely penitent, this sin may be your ruin."

Faith and works   This statement, too, could be misunderstood: "Good works are not necessary. Only faith is necessary." Rather, it would be correct to say, "Good works are not necessary to obtain salvation." But I cannot remain on the road to heaven if I am not doing any good works. Besides, God has certainly commanded good works. He wills us to do good works.

The harm of sin; Rom. 8:1   The following statement, too, could be misunderstood: "Sin does not harm a Christian." True, a sin committed because of the weakness of the flesh does not immediately put you on God's blacklist. Nevertheless, it **does harm** you. "There is therefore now no **condemnation** for those who are in Christ Jesus," says Paul [Romans 8:1]. But he does not say, "There is nothing sinful in them." In a nutshell, you cannot be too careful in your preaching.

The unforgivable sin   Likewise, it is also wrong not to explain some points at greater length. For instance, when he was still in secondary school, Aegidius Hunnius on a certain occasion heard this statement in a worship service: "However, there is one sin that cannot be forgiven. That is the sin against the Holy Spirit." Like a dagger, that statement plunged into the young student's heart. He promptly

---

16   Walther means: "Whatever may be the case, this one thing is always certain." The original meaning of *allemal* is "always," but it also includes "in any case," to mean everything continuing on in the same path or everything coming to the same result. In modern German, *allemal* means "certainly."

imagined that he had committed that sin. In fact, as a result he even planned to commit suicide. He remembered that the Holy Spirit had indeed knocked at the door of his heart many times while he was listening to a sermon, but in his youthful foolishness he had allowed these invitations to slip from his mind. Miraculously, however, God rescued him from his great anguish of conscience. Approaching his seat in the classroom one day, he found a page torn from a precious devotional written by Master Spangenberg. And of all things, it contained remarks about that very sin against the Holy Spirit. In particular it mentioned that one particular person, after committing that sin, was **unwilling to repent until his dying day**. That saved Hunnius. And it was because even in his youth he had to undergo such great tribulations that he became the great theologian that he was.

It is even more difficult to properly distinguish Law and Gospel when a pastor is ministering to individuals privately. In the pulpit he may say various things, hoping they will strike home. But when people seek his pastoral counsel, he has to deal with a far greater difficulty. He will soon observe: "This one is a Christian; and this one, not." This is not saying that the holy airs and manners of hypocrites may not deceive the pastor. However, if he can rightly distinguish Law and Gospel, even though those receiving his counsel may have deceived him, it is not his fault. The pastor only bears the responsibility if it is *his* fault that his people misunderstood him.

Pastoral fault

But if people act like Christians only to deceive you, they deceive themselves rather than you. A pastor must treat any person as a Christian if he appears to be one, and vice versa. However, not all unbelievers are alike. Some are coarse and despise religion and the Bible, while others are orthodox yet possess only the dead faith of the intellect. But the pastor notices to himself: "You are yet blind and still in the bonds of spiritual death." Of course, if you—though a preacher—are still steeped in sin yourself, you will not be able to judge even such a person.

Pastoral judgment

Now, if an unbeliever is truly alarmed and filled with an unnamed dread because he has committed various sins, yet is still unbroken, the pastor must say to himself: "This person must first be crushed." Some are addicted to a vice; others are self-righteous. Discovering to which class these various unconverted persons belong and applying the proper medicine to them—that is the real difficulty of which I am speaking. My goal is to convince all of you that a preacher can be truly equipped for his calling only by means of the Holy Spirit.

Finally, the greatest difficulty is dealing with true Christians according to their particular spiritual condition. Some have a weak faith; others, a strong faith. Some are cheerful; others are sorrowful. Some are sluggish; others are burning with passion. Some have only a little spiritual knowledge; others are deeply grounded in the truth.

One last word: In order for a pastor to correctly judge and counsel people, it is of the utmost importance for him to understand in his mind's eye the various human temperaments.[17] When observing the faults of a particular temperament, your mind must not become blind to that person's good traits. For instance, a person with a sanguine disposition will mainly be of good cheer and never troubled with gloomy thoughts. Yet he may still not be a Christian. That person is simply born with those "sunny" traits. On the other hand, if you determine that someone has a sanguine temperament and he becomes sad when you preach the Law to him, you will know that the Word has sunk in. Then when you preach the Gospel to him and he becomes happy again, you have to determine whether that is the Gospel at work or only his nature.

Conversely, if you meet a person with a melancholy disposition and observe that he always tends to be sad and is always wearing a frown, do not immediately conclude that he is sorrowing over his sins. But if he suddenly becomes lively while you proclaim the Gospel to him, and if you notice something in his demeanor that is contrary to his natural temperament, you may safely conclude that the Gospel has done its job.

Or you might meet a phlegmatic person who loves a life of ease and hates to be disturbed in his reflections. If you succeed in soothing such a person, do not think that you have done so by preaching the Gospel.

Or, finally, you may have to deal with someone with a choleric disposition. If he becomes despondent after you have ministered to him, you may be assured that it was because God's Word sank in.

---

17 Walther shows his classical education in this discussion of temperaments. In classical, medieval, and Renaissance medicine, the four *elements* were air, fire, water, and earth. The corresponding bodily *humors* were sanguine (blood; hot and moist; amorous/optimistic), choleric (yellow bile; hot and dry; ambitious/angry), phlegmatic (phlegm; cold and moist; cowardly/lazy), and melancholic (black bile; cold and dry; depressed/gluttonous). Temperaments were associated not only with proportions of the humors but also with the classical orbits of the planets and their astrological influence: lunatic, mercurial, venusian, solar, martial, jovian, and saturnine.

I f Holy Scripture were really such an unclear book that the meaning of all those passages that form the basic articles of the Christian Creed could not be definitely discovered, and if, as a result of this, we would have to acknowledge that without some other authority it would be impossible to decide which two or three interpretations of Scripture passages were the only correct ones—if all this were true, the Scriptures could not be the Word of God. After all, how could a book that left us groping in the dark and uncertain regarding its essential contents serve as a revelation?

In particular, the old Jewish Bible scholars of the Middle Ages declared that the literal meaning of the Scriptures was indeed plain but that there was a secret meaning of Scripture that is of the highest importance. This secret meaning could not be explored without the aid of the *Cabala*,[18] they claimed. For instance, they pointed out that in the first and last verse of the Hebrew text the letter *alef* occurs six times. Now, an ordinary person, they say, cannot know why that is so, but the *Cabala* gives the explanation, that is, that the world will last six thousand years.

This claim is, of course, quite absurd. However, even within the Christian Church—in the papacy—it is taught that the Scriptures are so unclear that one can scarcely understand a single passage in them. At any rate, very many important teachings of the Christian religion, it is declared, cannot be confirmed from Scripture. To this end, the traditions of the Church are said to be absolutely necessary. This claim of the Papists is evidence of their blindness. What St. Paul says in 2 Corinthians 4:3 applies to them: "And even if our gospel is veiled, it is veiled only to those who are perishing."

2 Cor. 4:3

Luther is right when he says in his exposition of Psalm 37 (St. Louis Ed. 5:335):

> There is not a plainer book on earth than Holy Scripture. It is, in comparison with all other books, what the sun is compared to all other lights. The Papists are giving us their twaddle about Scripture for the sole purpose of leading us away from Scripture and raising themselves up as masters over us in order to force us to believe their preaching of dreams. It is an abomination, a disgraceful defamation of Holy Scripture and the entire Christian Church, to say that Holy Scripture is obscure, that it is not clear enough for everybody to understand how to teach and prove what he believes.

W² 5:335

In his *Appeal to the Counselors of All Cities of Germany in Behalf of the Establishment and Maintenance of Christian Schools,* **Luther** says (St. Louis Ed. 10:473):

---

18 The *Cabala* is a collection of Jewish writings that have a strong Gnostic or "New Age" influence.

W² 10:473
(cf. AE 45:363)

The Sophists[19] have claimed that Scripture is unclear, meaning that it is the very nature of the Word of God to be unclear and to speak in a strange fashion. But they do not see that all this trouble is caused by the **languages**. If we understood the languages, there would not be anything that has ever been spoken that would be easier to understand than the Word of God. Of course, a Turk[20] will talk obscure things to me because I do not know Turkish; but a Turkish child seven years old can understand him readily.

Luther is absolutely right. Not only is Holy Scripture as crystal clear as the plainest human writing, but even much clearer because it has been set down by the Holy Spirit, the Creator of the languages. It is, therefore, absolutely impossible to prove an error or even a contradiction in Scripture if you stick to its words. Thus we express it in our beautiful Communion hymn "Lord Jesus Christ, You Have Prepared":

> Your Word stands as a rampart firm
> That none may ever overturn;
> Be they howe'er so cunning.[21]

1 Cor. 2:14

However, while the historical-grammatical meaning of Scripture can readily be opened up by anyone who understands its language, without the Holy Spirit it is impossible for anyone to understand Holy Scripture for his salvation, no matter how great a linguist, how famous a philologist, how keen a logician he may be. The apostle Paul declares in 1 Corinthians 2:14: "The natural person does not accept the things of the Spirit of God, for they are folly to him, and he is not able to understand them because they are spiritually discerned."

1 Cor. 1:23

Again, he says in 1 Corinthians 1:23: "But we preach Christ crucified, a stumbling block to Jews and folly to Gentiles." Now, the primary condition for a salutary[22] knowledge of Holy Scripture is the correct understanding of how to distinguish Law and Gospel. The Bible is full of light to everyone who has this knowledge. But wherever this knowledge is lacking, all Scripture remains a book sealed with seven seals.[23]

W² 9:806–7

Before we move on to the fourth thesis, let us hear a few quotes from Luther. When you listen to the sermons of inexperienced preachers, you

---

19   Luther uses the term "Sophists" to identify his Papist opponents.

20   Luther uses the term "Turk" to identify Muslims.

21   The Dau edition gives the hymn title from the *Evangelical Lutheran Hymn-Book*: "Lord Jesus, Thou Art Truly Good." That hymnal was the precursor to *The Lutheran Hymnal* (St. Louis: Concordia, 1941) in the Missouri Synod. The text here, part of stanza 3, is a close translation of the German. See also *LSB* 622:3.

22   Walther uses *heilsam* in the sense of the Communion liturgy: "meet, right, and *salutary*."

23   See Revelation 5:1.

might not be able to claim that they have perverted either Law or Gospel, but you *will* frequently notice that Law and Gospel have been merged with each other. **Luther** testifies in his *Sermon on the Distinction between Law and Gospel* (St. Louis Ed. 9:806f.) that the proper distinction of Law and Gospel is the greatest skill of theologians: "To express in words that the Law is a different kind of teaching than the Gospel—that everybody can do. But to reduce this distinction to the real world and to make it operative, that is a huge task. St. Jerome, among others, wrote a great deal on this matter, yet he talks like a blind man about seeing colors."

Luther treated learned men with great respect. As such, he called Erasmus a valuable man because he had caused the study of the [biblical] languages to flourish; but Luther did not call him a doctor of Holy Scripture. Why not? Because this was one skill Erasmus did not possess. A person may be most highly gifted and may have trained fifty years for the sacred Office of the Ministry, yet he will still not be able to properly distinguish Law and Gospel if he has not received the Holy Spirit. This is where the theologian meets his personal Scylla and Charybdis.[24] In either direction he can lead souls to their destruction and become guilty of a serious offense to poor Christians.

In his commentary on Galatians 2:14, Luther says (St. Louis Ed. 9:159): "Let anyone who knows well how to distinguish Law and Gospel thank our Lord God, for he can easily pass for a theologian. In my tribulations I did not, alas, understand this as well as I should have." An ordinary preacher may be an excellent theologian, yet another preacher—even though he has studied all the languages and God knows what else—may not be worthy even of the name of theologian. It is not man but *God* who makes theologians. If you think this statement is exaggerated, you are still blind. But if you have had any experience, you will admit that this is a very difficult skill.

W² 9:159
(cf. AE 26:115)

---

24 In Greek mythology, Scylla and Charybdis were sea monsters located on opposite sides of the Strait of Messina between Sicily and Italy. Avoiding one meant passing too close to the other. Homer described Scylla as having six heads on long necks, and it ate sailors, while Charybdis sucked in water, creating a whirlpool that captured any ships that sailed too close. Only Jason and the Argonauts successfully navigated between these obstacles.

This drawing shows the faculty of Concordia College, circa 1880. From left to right: Martin Günther, J. M. Gottlieb Schaller, C. F. W. Walther, and C. H. Rudolph Lange. While serving as professors, these men also served St. Louis congregations as pastors in an assistant or supervisory capacity. All four men were published authors of books and articles (even entire periodicals in the case of Walther and Lange). Schaller and Walther also held important leadership positions in the LCMS. Image courtesy of Concordia Historical Institute.

THESIS IV

Understanding how to distinguish Law and Gospel provides **wonderful insight** *for understanding all of Holy Scripture correctly. In fact, without this knowledge Scripture is and remains a sealed book.*

EDITOR'S NOTE: Walther stresses that the proper distinction between Law and Gospel is not simply the best way to understand Scripture, it is also the only true way to read and apply the Bible, as proven by Scripture itself.

If you were to glance at Holy Scripture while still ignorant of the distinction between Law and Gospel, you would probably get the impression that there are a great number of contradictions in the Scriptures. In fact, all of Scripture seems to be full of contradictions, worse than the Qur'an of the Turks. Here Scripture pronounces you blessed; there it condemns you. When the rich young ruler asked the Lord, "What good deed must I do to have eternal life?" the Lord replied, "If you want to enter into life, keep the commandments."[1] When the jailer at Philippi addressed the same question to Paul and Silas, he received this answer: "Believe in the Lord Jesus, and you and your household will be saved."

Solve contradictions;
Matt. 19:16–17;
Acts 16:31 Luther

On the one hand, we read in Habakkuk 2:4: "The righteous shall live by his faith." On the other hand, we note that John in his First Epistle, chapter 3, verse 7, says: "Whoever practices righteousness is righteous, as He is righteous." Over and against this, the apostle Paul declares: "For all have sinned and fall short of the glory of God, and are justified by His grace as a gift, through the redemption that is in Christ Jesus."

Hab. 2:4;
1 John 3:7;
Rom. 3:23–24

On the one hand, we note that Scripture declares that God does not want sinners;[2] on the other hand, we find that it states: "Everyone who calls on the name of the Lord shall be saved."

Rom. 10:13

In one place Paul cries: "For the wrath of God is revealed from heaven against all ungodliness and unrighteousness of men"; and in Psalm 5:4 we read: "For You are not a God who delights in wickedness; evil may not dwell with You." Yet in another [place], Peter says, "Set your hope fully on . . . grace."

Rom. 1:18;
Ps. 5:4;
1 Pet. 1:13

---

1   Walther cites only the Matthew text here.

2   See, for example, Romans 6:23.

John 3:16   On the one hand, we are told that all the world is under the wrath of God;[3] on the other hand, we read: "For God so loved the world, that He gave His only Son, that whoever believes in Him should not perish but have eternal life."

1 Cor. 6:9–11   Another remarkable passage is 1 Corinthians 6:9–11, where the apostle first makes this statement: "Do you not know that the unrighteous **will not inherit the kingdom of God**? Do not be deceived: neither the sexually immoral, nor idolaters, nor adulterers, nor men who practice homosexuality, nor thieves, nor the greedy, nor drunkards, nor revilers, nor swindlers will inherit the kingdom of God," and then he adds: "**And such were some of you.** But you were washed, you were sanctified, you were justified in the name of the Lord Jesus Christ and by the Spirit of our God."

Would not a person who knows nothing of the distinction between Law and Gospel be swallowed up in complete darkness when reading all this? Would he not indignantly cry out: "What? This is God's Word? A book full of such contradictions?"

The key to Scripture   Do not think that the Old Testament reveals a wrathful and the New Testament a gracious God, or that the Old Testament teaches salvation by a person's own works and the New Testament salvation by faith. No. We find both teachings in the Old as well as in the New Testament. But the moment we understand how to distinguish between Law and Gospel, it is as if the sun were rising upon the Scriptures, and we behold all the contents of the Scriptures in the most beautiful harmony. We see that the Law was not revealed to us to put a notion into our heads that we could become righteous by it, but to teach us that we are completely unable to fulfill the Law. Then we will know what a sweet message—what a glorious doctrine—the Gospel is and will receive it with exuberant joy.

The history of the Church, too, illustrates the importance of understanding this distinction. Corruption entered the Church when Law and Gospel began to be mingled. A review of the writings of the Church Fathers soon reveals the cause of the Church's misery in those early days: people did not know how to distinguish properly between Law and Gospel. Until the sixth century we still find glorious testimonies regarding this distinction, but from that time forward we notice that this light starts to grow dim and that the distinction is gradually forgotten.

One instance that illustrates this fact is that monastic life had begun to achieve ever greater importance. They[4] understood the reply of the Lord to

---

3   See, for example, Romans 1:18.

4   Walther refers to St. Anthony and other monks who interpreted both literally and personally the words of Jesus in Matthew 19:21: "If you would be perfect, go, sell what you possess and give to the poor, and you will have treasure in heaven; and come, follow Me."

the rich young man as necessary for a person's salvation. They brought the Law to the very same people to whom they should have brought the Gospel.

Following the course of history to the time when the papacy had become dominant, we find that the knowledge of this distinction [between Law and Gospel] became completely extinct; a truly hellish darkness settled in, and sheer paganism and idolatry worked their way into the Church.

Remember the agonies of our dear Luther! Considering the darkness that reigned in his day, we must say that, compared with others, he had acquired a great deal of knowledge at the beginning of his career, but even *he* did not know how to distinguish Law and Gospel. Oh, the toil and torments he had to suffer! His self-punishment and fasting brought him to the brink of death. The most crushing, the most fear-inducing statement in his estimation at that time was this: that righteousness which is valid in the sight of God is revealed in the Gospel. "Alas!" he mused. "What a woeful state of affairs! First, we are approached by the Law, which demands that we fulfill it; and now, on top of that, we must be made righteous by obeying the Gospel!" Indeed, Luther says that sometimes he had blasphemous thoughts.

Suddenly a new light shone upon [Luther], showing him the kind of righteousness of which the Gospel is speaking. He relates that from that moment on, he began to run through all of Scripture to get a clear understanding as to which portions of Scripture are Law and which are Gospel. He says that he pried into every book in the Bible, and now all of it became clear to him. Once he understood this distinction, he became the reformer. This is also the reason he was so incredibly successful when he went public with these ideas. With his new insight, Luther freed the poor people from the misery into which the Law-preaching of their priests had driven them.

You are preparing to become pastors and counselors, my friends. I urge you to grasp the immense importance of this matter for your future vocation. **Fundamental for pastors** Imagine that someone is in anguish and distress and comes to you. Whenever a parishioner is anguished in his soul like this, you know that the Law has grabbed hold of him, and it would never occur to him to be saved by the Gospel. He would never think of the Gospel while wailing, "Alas! I am a poor sinner; I am worthy of damnation," etc. To such a person you must say: "You are indeed a lost and condemned creature. But the passage of Scripture that told you that is the Law. There is, however, another teaching in Scripture. The Law has done its work in you. The Law needs to give you the understanding

---

Walther's point is that Jesus says these words to hammer the rich young man with the hopelessness that the condemnation of the Law brings. Jesus did not say these words in the manner of Gospel, as if this were a possible path to salvation. What we see is a fundamental confusion of Law and Gospel in Anthony's model of the monastic life. Compare Athanasius's *Life of St. Anthony* (NPNF[2] 4:196).

that you have sinned. Now quit Sinai and go to Golgotha. Look at your Savior, bleeding and dying for you!"

Not until you enter the ministry will you realize the great importance of distinguishing between Law and Gospel. Only when you understand this distinction will you be capable of discharging the office whose job it is to save the world. The matter of primary importance, of course, will always be that you have experienced this distinction yourself. I am not referring to those among you who have never been in anguish over their sins, who consider themselves orthodox because they have been reared in Christian homes. I am referring to those who are concerned about their salvation. There will be moments when you will imagine that you are God's children. Again, there will be times when you think your sins have not been forgiven. If on such occasions you desire genuine peace, it can come to you only if you can distinguish between Law and Gospel.

Ap V (III) 65   In the *Apology* of the Augsburg Confession (Müller, 119) we read: "For to rightly understand the benefit of Christ and the great treasure of the Gospel (which Paul extols so greatly), we must separate as far as the heavens are from the earth the promise of God and the grace that is offered from the Law."[5] Although the Word of God may preach the Gospel to us with the greatest comfort, unless we know that Holy Scripture also contains the Law (from which we have escaped), and unless we know that we are lost and doomed sinners and have embraced the Gospel, we shall nevertheless not obtain the peace that the Gospel offers. If we come across a comforting passage, we say to ourselves, "I have the forgiveness of sins." But then we may read another passage that makes us believe that we are lost—all because we do not know the distinction between Law and Gospel.

FC Ep V 2   The Epitome of the **Formula of Concord** states: "We believe, teach, and confess that the distinction between the Law and the Gospel is to be kept in the Church with great diligence as a particularly brilliant light. By this distinction, according to the admonition of St. Paul, God's Word is rightly divided."[6] This is repeated in the Declaration, Article V as follows (Müller, 633):

FC SD V 1   The distinction between the Law and the Gospel is an especially brilliant light, which serves so that God's Word may be rightly distinguished and the Scriptures of the holy prophets and apostles may be properly explained and understood. We must guard it with special

---

5   This text is near Ap V (III) 65. See also *Triglot Concordia*, 173; *Concordia*, 110. For more information on the Müller text of the Apology, see "Walther's Book of Concord," pages 467–68.

6   *Concordia*, 484. This English text follows essentially the Müller text used by Walther. See also Müller, 533–34; *Triglot Concordia*, 801.

care, so that these two doctrines may not be mingled with each other, or Law be made out of the Gospel. This mingling **hides the merit of Christ** and **robs** troubled consciences **of their comfort**, which they otherwise have in the Holy Gospel when it is preached genuinely and in its purity. The Gospel supports them in their most severe trials against the terrors of the Law.[7]

If these two doctrines are not kept separate, the merit of Christ is hidden. For if I am afraid of the threats of the Law, I have forgotten Christ, who says to me: "Though your sins are like scarlet, they shall be as white as snow. Come to Me, all who labor and are heavy laden, and I will give you rest."

Isa. 1:18;
Matt. 11:28

The preacher will not rightly proclaim these facts unless the distinction between Law and Gospel is burned into his brain. Only then can the listener lie down and die in peace on his deathbed. Even if the devil whispers every kind of insinuation at him, he can say to Satan: "So what if your charges against me are quite correct? I have another doctrine that tells me something altogether different. I am glad that the Law has put me in such a woeful situation, for now I can appreciate the Gospel all the more."

At the conclusion of Article V, we read in the **Formula of Concord** (Müller, 639):

> Let us take care that both doctrines—Law and Gospel—are not mingled and confused with each other and are not attributed to each other. This easily hides the merit and benefits of Christ and, once again, turns the Gospel into a doctrine of the Law, as happened in the papacy. This deprives Christians of the true comfort they have in the Gospel against the terrors of the Law and, once again, opens the door of the Church of God to the papacy. For this reason, the true and proper distinction between Law and Gospel must be observed and preserved with all diligence, and whatever might cause confusion between Law and Gospel,[8] that is, whatever might confuse and mingle the two doctrines, Law and Gospel, into one doctrine—that should be diligently prevented.[9]

FC SD V 27

We, too, are in the same great danger. Read the writings of those who claim to be the best preachers. They terrify, to be sure, but their incisiveness is caused by the fact that they mingle Law and Gospel. As a result, many people who read these writings are often plagued with doubts when they die. Many of them die with this thought in their heart: "I wonder whether God

---

7   Müller's German text is followed here in order to illuminate best the points that Walther makes. See also *Triglot Concordia*, 951; *Concordia*, 552.

8   Latin: *inter legem et evangelium.*

9   The translation is of Müller's German in order to see the connection with Walther's points. See also *Triglot Concordia*, 961; *Concordia*, 557.

will receive me." Anyone dying in such uncertainty does not depart in saving faith. Now, whose fault is it—at least in many instances? It is the preacher's fault.

Rom. 4:5

However, the preacher also must be careful not to say that the Law has been done away with, for that is not true either. The Law remains in force. It has not been ended. But we have another message besides that of the Law. God does not say, "The Law brings righteousness," but rather, "The Law brings knowledge of sin." Yes, we read in the Epistle to the Romans: "And to the one who does not work but believes in Him who justifies the **ungodly**, his faith is counted as righteousness." Therefore, we are on the right track to salvation the moment we are convinced that we are ungodly.

Commenting on Galatians 3:19, **Luther** says (St. Louis Ed. 9:415):

W² 9:415
(cf. AE 26:313)

If the Gospel is not fundamentally and plainly set apart from the Law, it is impossible to keep the Christian doctrine **pure**. On the other hand, when this distinction has been rightly and firmly established, we can have a fine and correct knowledge of how we are to become righteous in the sight of God. Where this illuminating knowledge prevails, it is easy to distinguish faith from works, Christ from Moses, the Gospel from the Law of Moses and from all other secular laws, statutes, and ordinances.

In conclusion, **Chemnitz** writes in his *Loci Theologici*, in the topic of justification (*Loc.* XIII, Cap. II): "Because Paul clearly states that the righteousness that is valid before God is[10] revealed in the Gospel without the Law, therefore the key point in this inquiry (regarding justification) is that the true and proper distinction between Law and Gospel be established and carefully maintained."[11] Is there any other light, besides the one supplied by the proper distinction between Law and Gospel, that has so forcibly broken up the dense darkness of the pope's dominion?[12] The darkness of the papacy has not been dispelled by any other light than the teaching that a distinction must be made between Law and Gospel. Great councils of the Church wanted to make an attempt to reform the Church. Mighty emperors had undertaken this task. What did they accomplish? Nothing. Matters went from bad to worse. Why did a poor, miserable monk succeed in this work? No doubt because he put the

---

10 The original Latin text by Martin Chemnitz reads: "of God has been." Walther states: "that is valid before God is." Walther also adds to this quotation the parenthetical remark "regarding justification."

11 Walther's references correspond with Chemnitz, *Loci Theologici* (Sterling Heights, MI: Lutheran Heritage Foundation, 2000). See also the English text on page 449 in volume 2 of the paperback English translation by J. A. O. Preus (St. Louis: Concordia, 1989) and page 825 in volume 8 of Chemnitz's Works (St. Louis: Concordia, 2008).

12 All previous editions of *Law and Gospel* include this sentence as part of the Chemnitz quotation. It is actually Walther's commentary, as this edition shows.

candlestick of this doctrine back in the Holy Place. Even if he had preached in an extremely evangelical fashion, Christians would not have been comforted. For the moment they had come across the Law, they would have exclaimed: "Ah, I was wrong after all! I have to keep the Commandments of God if I want to enter into eternal life."

Here is where most of the reformers before the Reformation were at fault. Hus preached the Gospel exceedingly well, but he did not show his hearers the proper distinction between Law and Gospel. For that reason his work, his attempt at reformation, did not endure.

May God, then, who has kindled this light for us, preserve it for us! I am thinking of you men in particular when I say this. We who are old will soon be in our graves. The light has begun to shine once more in our time. See to it that it is not put out again. You are on the wrong track if you think that you have understood this whole teaching in these few hours. If this light is not carefully guarded, it will soon go out. For instance, we find that this light was still burning in the days when the earliest writings of the Church Fathers were composed. But in the writings of the church teachers who followed them, no definite statement can be found regarding the distinction between Law and Gospel. That is the reason the papacy, in a later age, was able to burrow its way in so quickly. That same danger threatens us now.

The principal passage of Scripture establishing our thesis is Romans 10:2–4: "I bear them witness that they have a zeal for God, but not according to knowledge. For, being ignorant of the righteousness of God, and seeking to establish their own, they did not submit to God's righteousness. For Christ is the end of the law for righteousness to everyone who believes." Rom. 10:2–4

When he says in this passage "not according to knowledge," to what ignorance is the apostle referring? It is this: "They do not recognize the righteousness that is valid in the sight of God." *That* is the ignorance to which he is referring. [The believers in Rome] imagined they had to be zealots on behalf of the Law. Because that was most certainly God's Law, they thought, how could anyone dare depart from it? But if they had paid attention to Paul's preaching, they would soon have noticed that he actually had allowed the Law to remain in force. If they had understood that, they would not have become enemies of the Gospel, and the dreadful darkness that settled upon them like the pall of night would have been dispelled.

According to the latest statistics of ethnologists, the present population of the earth is estimated to be 1.4 billion. Not quite 400 million of these people—that is, not even one third of the human race—profess faith in Christ as the only Savior. To be sure, that is a terrifying state of affairs, pitiful enough to push us to the point of tears. However, still more terrifying and lamentable is the fact that, of these 400 million nominal Christians, nearly one half are still followers of the pope, the Antichrist. The mystery surrounding these shocking and depressing conditions is such that even sincere Christians dread to look with open eyes into this abyss of indescribable misery and wretchedness.

Pope as Antichrist

A fair amount—in fact, the majority—of those who claim to be Lutherans refuse to believe that the pope is the Antichrist and that the papacy is the power of the Antichrist. In line with the entire Church of the Reformation and in agreement with the Confessions of that Church, the orthodox American Lutheran Church of our time still and in full earnestness maintains the position that the pope is the Antichrist. But that is, at best, regarded as an odd fancy of narrow-minded men who refuse to keep up with the times.

Were you to ask why this is so, I would reply that it is chiefly because people no longer know what constitutes the Antichrist and the dominion of the Antichrist. People say, "We admit that, especially in the Middle Ages, there were many popes who were truly abominations and, even in the view of Romish writers, were swallowed up by hell." They admit that the papacy still practices many shocking abominations, but this is offset by the reminder that not one church is free of errors and even of Judases. They also admit that the papacy continues to allow the most horrible heresies to remain in fashion, but over against this they stress the fact that even the papacy holds strictly to the three Ecumenical Creeds.[13] For at the opening session and solemn organization of the Council of Trent in 1545, those three creeds were recited. They point out that even the popes believe the Bible of the Old and the New Testament to be the revealed Word of God, that God is triune, and that Christ is God and man in one person and the Savior of the world. They note: "The Papists confess, just as we do, their faith in a future resurrection of the dead; a last judgment, before which all men will be cited; and heaven and hell." These people[14] claim: "Far, then, from being the dominion of the Antichrist,

---

13 That is, the Apostles' Creed, the Nicene Creed, and the Athanasian Creed. For more information on these creeds, see *Concordia*, 15–18.

14 Walther means Philip Schaff. Concordia Seminary professor Martin S. Sommer delivered an important essay that details the attempts of both the papacy and of Schaff's movement to foist a man-made, false unity on the Church. See "The Unity of the Christian Church," in *Proceedings of the Twelfth Convention of the Evangelical Lutheran Synod of Missouri and Other States* (St. Louis: Concordia, 1911), 6–44.

the papacy is rather a powerful dam shutting out the fearful flood of unbelief that has come down on the Christian Church."

People do recognize the rule of the Antichrist in pantheism, materialism, atheism, socialism, nihilism, anarchism, and all the other horrible "-isms" that the modern age has inherited. But, I ask you, why is it that—based on the premises just mentioned—people draw the conclusion that the papacy is *not* the rule of the Antichrist and the pope *not* the true Antichrist? The chief reason is that people fail to consider that the pope claims to be the vicege-rent[15] of Christ on earth and the visible head of the entire Christian Church. In order to be this, he must, of course, profess many Christian doctrines. But he has to wear a mask; otherwise, the Antichrist could not possibly exist amid the Christian Church. Moreover, [the pope] has to appear to declare war on the enemies of all religions and on the enemies of the Christian religion, because he knows that, if Christ were to fall, the Antichrist would fall too. For if Christ were to fall—whose vicegerent the pope claims to be—that would be the end of the pope's vicegerency. Even though the pope seems to be fighting for Christ and the Christian Church, in reality he is fighting for himself and his dominion.

But here is a point of supreme importance: Since we can ignore all those groups that deny the triune God and that are thus outside the pale of the Christian Church, in the entire Christian Church only the pope is the outspo-ken enemy of the free grace of God in Christ. He is an enemy of the Gospel under the guise of the Christian religion because he is aping its institutions. The thesis that leads us to this fact [follows.]

---

15 That is, a deputy tasked with administration.

From 1839 to 1849, Trinity congregation in Altenburg, Missouri, operated a parish school in a log cabin. It also served as a school for pastors, producing five pastoral candidates. The school, but not the log cabin, was moved to St. Louis in 1849 after the formation of the Missouri Synod.

Thesis V

The most common way people mingle Law and Gospel—and one that is also the easiest to detect because it is so crude—is prevalent among Papists, Socinians, and Rationalists. These people turn Christ into a kind of new Moses or Lawgiver. This transforms the Gospel into a doctrine of meritorious works. Furthermore, some people—like the Papists—condemn and anathematize those who teach that the Gospel is the message of the free grace of God in Christ.[1]

Editor's Note: In this thesis, Walther begins to present twenty-one ways of confusing Law and Gospel. He presents as the heart of Scripture the Gospel, the Good News that Christ fulfilled the Law for all people and opened the way to eternal life. He shows that turning the Gospel into a set of morals totally skews the manner in which one reads and applies the Bible.

Romish legalism

I would like to submit two testimonies to demonstrate that the Papists actually do what the thesis charges. Two months before Luther's death, as you know, the Council of Trent was opened. Its task was to heal the mortal wounds that had been dealt the papacy by the Reformation of Luther and to rebuild the papacy.

Session IV says: "The most holy, ecumenical, and universal Council of Trent, lawfully convened in the Holy Spirit . . . always bearing in mind to remove errors and to preserve in the Church the purity of the Gospel, i.e., that which was first promised by the holy prophets in their writings, then preached with His own mouth by the Lord Jesus Christ, the Son of God, and then commanded to be preached to all creatures by His apostles, both as the source of all saving truth and **a moral norm**," etc.[2]

Mark 16:15

This does not sound too awful to begin with. In fact, the whole mob[3] of the Antichrist's wickedness even says that the Gospel contains doctrines of

---

1   For more on the groups that Walther mentions, see the Index of Persons and Groups.

2   In Thesis X, Walther provides a clue that he cites the canons and decrees of the Council of Trent contained in the edition of Wilhelm Smets, ed., *Des hochheiligen, okumenischen und allgemeinen Conciliums von Trient Canones und Beschlusse* (Bielefeld: Velhagen & Klasing, 1851). A number of English editions exist, several of which are in the public domain and available via the Internet.

3   Walther uses *Geschmeiß*, usually meaning a swarm of gnats, midges, or some other biting insect. By derivation, it means a mob of the lowest rabble in society. In the nineteenth

salvation. However, they immediately add that the Gospel also prescribes morals. That is how they interpret what Christ intended when He said, "Go into all the world and proclaim the gospel to the whole creation." They claim that He really wanted to say, "Tell them the Gospel, tell them what morals they need to keep and what good works they should do."

Here you can see that [the Papists] do not want the Gospel in the true sense of the word, that they do not accept it. The way they understand it, it is—at best—a law such as Moses proclaimed. Nor do they urge upon people only the Commandments of God, but rather the commandments of their church. They do not trouble a person who has broken the Commandments of God. But if anyone breaks the commandments of their church—say, if he has eaten meat on Friday—he is tortured until he acknowledges that he has committed a mortal sin.

In session VI, canon 21, this synagogue of the devil[4] decrees: "If anyone says that Christ Jesus has been given by God to men that He should be their Redeemer, in whom they are to trust, and not also their **Lawgiver**, whom they are to obey, let him be anathema." This decree overthrows the Christian religion completely. If Christ came into the world to bring us new laws, then we could practically say that He might as well have stayed in heaven. Moses had already given us such a perfect Law that we were not able to keep *that*. Now, if Christ had given us additional laws, that would have to drive us to despair.

Mark 16:15–16

The very term *gospel* contradicts this view of the Papists. We know that Christ Himself called His Word *gospel*, for He says in Mark 16:15: "Go into all the world and proclaim the **gospel** to the whole creation." And so we would know what He meant by the word *gospel*, He adds this content: "Whoever believes and is baptized will be saved," etc. If the teaching of Christ were a law, it would not be a *gospel*[5] (a glad tiding), but a *sad* tiding.

---

century, social, political, and even religious groups did not avoid name-calling. Walther stated elsewhere: "God fill you with hatred of the pope!" (William Dallmann, *My Life* [St. Louis: Concordia, 1945], 23).

4   Walther uses a saying of Luther's: *synagoga diaboli*. The phrase can be traced to Revelation 2:9 in the Vulgate: *et blasphemaris ab his qui se dicunt Iudaeos esse et non sunt sed sunt synagoga Satanae*. Luther's increasingly positive attitude toward the Book of Revelation helped form his position that the Bible points to the papacy as the Antichrist. This position was based on the papacy's opposition to Scripture and evangelical preaching. Lutherans maintained that position for at least two centuries after Luther's death—and the Missouri Synod does so to this day: "As to the Antichrist we teach that the prophecies of the Holy Scriptures concerning the Antichrist, 2 Thess. 2:3–12; 1 John 2:18, have been fulfilled in the Pope of Rome and his dominion" (*Brief Statement of the Doctrinal Position of the Missouri Synod* [St. Louis: Concordia, 1932], 20). This statement refers to Melanchthon's Treatise on the Power and Primacy of the Pope, paragraphs 10, 39–41, and 45 (*Concordia*, 295, 300–301).

5   Walther emphasizes that the Greek word *euangélion* means *good* news.

If we turn to the Old Testament, we see even there what the character of the teaching of Christ is. We read in Genesis 3:15: "He shall bruise your head." What do these words mean? It is this: The Messiah, the Redeemer, the Savior will not come to tell us what to do, what works we are to perform in order to escape from the terrible dominion of darkness, sin, and death. These things the Messiah is not going to leave for us to accomplish, but He will do all that Himself. "**He will bruise the serpent's head**" means nothing less than that He will destroy the kingdom of the devil. All that man has to do is to know that he has been redeemed, that he has been set free from his prison, that he has nothing more to do than to believe, accept this message, and rejoice over it with all his heart. If the text were to read "He shall save you," that would not be so comforting; or if it read "You *must* believe in Him," we would be at a loss to know what this faith means. This First Gospel[6] in the Old Testament was the fountain from which the believers in the Old Testament drew their comfort. It was important for them to know: "There is One coming who will not only tell us what we must do to get to heaven. No, the Messiah will do everything Himself to get us there." Now that the rule of the devil has been destroyed, it would not make any sense if *I* had to do something. If the devil's dominion is demolished, I am free. There is nothing for me to do but to *appropriate* this. That is what Scripture means when it says, "Believe!" That means: "Claim as your own what Christ has acquired."

We could cite many additional prophecies to prove the correctness of this interpretation. But let me call your attention to only one, which shows clearly what the doctrine of the Gospel really is. In Jeremiah 31:31–34 we read:

> Behold, the days are coming, declares the LORD, when I will make a new covenant with the house of Israel and the house of Judah, not like the covenant that I made with their fathers on the day when I took them by the hand to bring them out of the land of Egypt, My covenant that they broke, though I was their husband, declares the LORD. But this is the covenant that I will make with the house of Israel after those days, declares the LORD: I will put My law within them, and I will write it on their hearts. And I will be their God, and they shall be My people. And no longer shall each one teach his neighbor and each his brother, saying, "Know the LORD," for they shall all know Me, from the least of them to the greatest, declares the LORD. For I will forgive their iniquity, and I will remember their sin no more.

A **new** covenant, then, is what God is going to make. Note this well. This covenant is not to be a legal covenant like the one that He established with Israel on Mount Sinai. The Messiah will not say, "You must be people of such

Side notes:
Gospel— the heart of Scripture; Gen. 3:15

Jer. 31:31–34

---

6   Latin: *Protevangelium.*

and such character; your manner of living must be like this or that; you must do such and such works." The Messiah will introduce no such doctrine. He writes His Law directly into the heart, so that a person living under Him is a law unto himself. He is not coerced by a force from *without* but is urged from *within*. "For I will forgive their iniquity, and I will remember their sin no more." These words state the reason for the preceding statement. They are a summary of the Gospel of Christ: forgiveness of sin by the free grace of God, for the sake of Jesus Christ.

Matt. 22:4;
Luke 5:31–32

Therefore, anyone who imagines that Christ is a new Lawgiver and has brought us new laws cancels the entire Christian religion. For that would get rid of what makes the Christian religion different from every other religion in the world. All other religions say, "You must become just so and so, and do such and such works, if you wish to go to heaven." But the Christian religion says: "You are a lost and condemned sinner. You cannot be your own savior. But do not despair on that account. There is One who has acquired salvation for you. Christ has opened the gates of heaven to you and says to you, 'Come, everything is ready. Come to the wedding feast.'" That is also why Christ says, "Those who are well have no need of a physician, but those who are sick. I have not come to call the righteous, but sinners to repentance."

Mark 2:16;
Luke 15:1, 9

Whenever He converses with people, we see [Jesus] surrounded by sinners, while behind Him the Pharisees are lurking. Hungering and thirsting, the sinners huddle around Him. He has won their hearts. Although the divine majesty shines forth from Him, they are not afraid to approach Him. Their trust in Him grows. Bitterly, the Pharisees reproach Him: "This man receives sinners and eats with them."[7] The Lord overhears their remarks. But even if He had not heard them, nevertheless He would have known what they were saying. What does He do? He makes no apologies. He does not say, "I do not wish to have sinners but only righteous people about Me!" No, He confirms their statements by saying, "Yes, I want sinners about Me," and then goes on to prove His point by telling the parable of the lost sheep.[8] The shepherd picks up the lost sheep, even though it is **bloody** and **bruised**. He places it on his shoulder and, rejoicing, carries it to the sheepfold. The Lord also explains His conduct by telling the parable of the lost coin.[9] The woman seeks her lost coin throughout the house, searching for it even in the dirt. When she has found it, she calls her friends, saying, "Rejoice with me, for I have found the coin that I had lost." Finally, the Lord adds the incomparably beautiful parable of

---

7   Walther joins the parallel in Mark 2:16 with the Luke 15 text.

8   See Luke 15:1–7.

9   See Luke 15:8–10.

the prodigal son.[10] What the Lord is saying in these parables is this: "There you have My doctrine. I have come to seek and to save that which was lost."

If you were to take a survey of the entire life of Jesus, you would see that He does not walk around like some proud philosopher or a moralist, surrounded by champions of virtuous behavior, whom He would teach how to reach the highest degree of philosophical perfection. No, rather He goes about seeking lost sinners and does not hesitate to tell the proud Pharisees that harlots and tax collectors will enter the kingdom of heaven rather than they. In this way He shows us quite plainly what His Gospel really is. All of His apostles confirm His teaching.

John 1:17: "For the law was given through Moses; grace and truth came through Jesus Christ." Here John places the Law over against grace and truth, so John apparently regards grace and truth as doctrine too. What he is saying is that Christ's doctrine is the doctrine of grace and truth. Of course, I do not need to explain to you what grace is, and by "truth" Christ means this: "I teach the essence of the things that were only foreshadowed in the Old Testament. The Old Testament was only a shadow of things to come; but I bring the essence." The entire temple service of the Levites was figurative. But Christ brought the reality of what was only figurative in the Old Testament. *[John 1:17]*

John 3:17: "For God did not send His Son into the world to condemn the world, but in order that the world might be saved through Him." This verse clearly demonstrates that Christ most certainly did not come into the world to proclaim a new law. Because if that had been His aim, He would have come to judge the world, for the Law passes judgment on sinners. However, God did not send His Son to pass judgment on the world, but to save the world through Him. By the term *world* the Lord refers to mankind in its apostate and lost condition—made up of the lost, accursed, and condemned sinners. To these the Savior brings this blessed doctrine: "Even though you have broken every commandment of God, do not despair; I am bringing you forgiveness and salvation now and forevermore." *[John 3:17]*

Romans 1:16–17: "For I am not ashamed of the gospel, for it is the power of God for salvation to everyone who believes, to the Jew first and also to the Greek. For in it the righteousness of God is revealed from faith for faith, as it is written, 'The righteous shall live by faith.'" In 1 Timothy 1:15 we read: "The saying is trustworthy and deserving of full acceptance, that Christ Jesus came into the world to save sinners, of whom I am the foremost." In light of these plain passages, is it not horrible that the Papists teach that what is called Gospel in the Scriptures is, according to them, nothing else than a new Law? *[Rom. 1:16–17; 1 Tim. 1:15]*

Elsewhere they explain what they mean more fully, namely, that Christ stated many laws of which Moses knew nothing. For instance, the law to *[Deut. 6:5; Lev. 19:18]*

10 See Luke 15:11–32.

love our enemies, the law not to seek private revenge, the law not to demand the return of what has been taken from us, etc. All these matters the Papists declare to be "new laws." This is wrong. For even Moses said, "You shall love the LORD your God with all your heart and with all your soul and with all your might" and "You shall love your neighbor as yourself."

Christ fulfilled the Law; Matt. 5:17

Now, Christ did not set aside this Law of Moses, but neither did He publish any new laws. He only opened up the spiritual meaning of the Law. Accordingly, He says in Matthew 5:17: "Do not think that I have come to abolish the Law or the Prophets; I have not come to abolish them but to fulfill them." This means that He did not come to issue new laws, but to fulfill the Law for us, so that we may share in His fulfillment.

Let us hear now how the Council of Trent wants nothing to do with the Gospel. In fact, it even damns and curses those who teach the Gospel as a message of the free grace of God in Christ. Session VI reads:

> If anyone says that men are made righteous solely through the impu-tation of the righteousness of Christ or solely through the forgive-ness of sin, to the exclusion of the grace and love that is poured out in their hearts by the Holy Spirit and is inherent in them; or that the grace by which we are made righteous is nothing else than the favor of God—let him be accursed. If anyone says that the faith which makes men righteous is nothing else than trust in the divine mercy, which pays for sins for Christ's sake, or that it is only this trust that makes us righteous—let him be accursed. . . . If anyone says that a justified person does not, by reason of the good **works** that are done by him through the grace of God and the merit of Jesus Christ, whose living member he is, truly **merit** an increase of grace, eternal life, and the actual obtainment of eternal life, provided he dies in grace—let him be accursed.

Grace alone

Unless you are completely blind and know nothing of the Christian reli-gion, I believe there can be no plainer proof that the pope is the Antichrist. Everywhere the Papists set up the cross and make the sign of the cross, but that is sheer hypocrisy. While they may have the cross, they do not have Christ. Again and again we read that they call on Mary to keep the little ship of Peter from dying. They struggle with saying, "*Jesus* is our fortress, our rock," etc. Without a doubt, the worst sects within the Christian Church do less damage than the pope. For without exception, every sect admits: "If a person wants to be saved, that only happens by believing in the grace of God in Christ Jesus." And while all sects, by their teaching, hide the Gospel, they do not anathema-tize and curse it—as the pope does.

Inasmuch as all sects allow this thesis to stand—namely, that salvation is by the grace of God through faith in Christ Jesus—they are incomparably superior to the papacy. These sects are corrupted churches,[11] but the papacy is a *false* church. Just as counterfeit money is no money at all, so the Papist "church"—as a false church—is no Church at all. Compared with the corrupted sectarian churches, the papacy is a nonchurch, a denial of Christ's Church. Let me make it clear that I am not speaking of the *Roman Catholic* but of the Papist "church," the "church" that submits to the pope, accepts his decrees, and repeats his anathemas. This "church" is the one that history knows as the malignant church, the synagogue of Satan.[12]

However, you might raise the objection: Christ says in Matthew 11:28–30: "Come to Me, all who labor and are heavy laden, and I will give you rest. Take My **yoke** upon you, and learn from Me, for I am gentle and lowly in heart, and you will find rest for your souls. **For My yoke is easy, and My burden is light**." So they say that Christ, too, lays a burden on His followers. As it is, the Romanists claim this yoke and burden of Christ—which they interpret to mean self-denial and bearing one's cross—is much more severe than the Law of Moses. Moses, they say, prohibited only coarse outward sin. They think that the remark of Christ, "You have heard that it was said to those of old," refers to Moses. But what Christ really means to say is this: "Your *elders* have taught you by their traditions that you are keeping the Law when you refrain from the coarse acts prohibited by the Law." And then He proceeds to expound the true meaning of the Law.

Matt. 11:28–30; 5:21

Regarding this matter, Luther writes in his *Glosses on the Gospel of Matthew* (St. Louis Ed. 7:143): "Those are greatly in error who interpret 'the yoke of Christ' in this passage [Matthew 11:28–30] to mean the so-called 'evangelical law,' that is, commands issued by Christ." In the opinion of Romanists, the Gospel and the "evangelical law" are synonymous. They even call it "the new law."[13]

W² 7:143

Luther proceeds: "In expounding this text, the Sophists[14] have been at great pains to show that the yoke of Christ is easier than the yoke of Moses, despite their belief that Moses prohibits only the external act, while Christ even prohibits every useless word and any evil thought in one's whole heart." By their contention that the yoke of Moses was easier for the reason stated, the Sophists to whom Luther refers meant to prove that people in the Old Testament were saved by the Law because it was not so hard to keep. The Law in the Gospel, they say, is easy only insofar as it has done away with

W² 7:143

---

11   Latin: *ecclesiae corruptae.*

12   Latin: *ecclesia maligna; synagoga Satanae.*

13   Latin: *nova lex.*

14   Luther uses the term "Sophists" to identify his Papist opponents.

circumcision and the ceremonial laws. But the yoke and the burden of which Christ speaks is nothing less than the cross that His followers bear.

Luther continues:

W² 7:143

Finally, these blind people arrived at the conclusion that Law and Gospel are related to each other like that which exceeds something compared to that which is exceeded,[15] namely, in this way: that the Law is easier than the Gospel because it lays its commands not on the heart but on the hand, or on the coarse external act. By the same token, the Gospel is easier than the Law in the sense that it has done away with circumcision and the Mosaic ceremonies. That is indeed blindness befitting people who despise the Gospel and refuse to read it.

Rom. 5:3

This is what they *should* have taught: The power of Christ is marvelous in His saints. For by faith in the heart of these people, Christ changes death into laughter, punishment into joy, and hell into heaven. For those who believe in Him laugh at all those ills from which worldly and carnal minds flee in terror and which they detest. **That** is what Christ calls a pleasant yoke and a light burden, namely, to bear the cross joyfully, even as Paul did, who says, "We rejoice in our sufferings" (Romans 5:3).

The moment a person attains a living faith through genuine repentance, he is saved and has arrived at the very gates of heaven. When death comes, the doors are opened, and that person enters. But since it is dangerous for Christians to pass their days at ease in this present life, the Savior has taken the precaution of putting the cross upon them. Whenever a Christian professes his faith by word and deed, people become hostile to him. Even where this hostility is not demonstrated publicly, it is still noticeable and irritates the Christian quite a bit. How many have had to lay down their lives for Christ! But how light is the burden of Christ compared with that of the Law! Feeling the burden of the Law, a person will groan: "Oh, I am a most miserable wretch!" It makes people despondent and fills them with despair.

Neutrality impossible; Matt. 11:30

Some people spend their lives subject neither to the Law nor to the Gospel. These people live no differently than animals. But woe to them when their eyes are opened after death! But Christians are able to rejoice in the hope that God will deliver them from the misery and suffering of this life. They can sing hallelujah! The examples of the martyrs make this clear. They did not go to their execution weeping and wailing, but met their martyr's fate with joy and exultation. In them the words of Christ were fulfilled: "My yoke is easy, and My burden is light."

---

15   Luther's text uses the Latin: like the *excedentia* to the *excessa*.

Do not ignore these words, but apply them to yourselves. The primary goal of these evening lectures is to move you forward in your Christianity. I pray to God that these talks may not be in vain.

While it is a happy and important resolution for a person to decide that he wants to become a true Christian, this resolution cannot make him truly happy and save his soul if he does not take it seriously. Many thousands have resolved to quit the world with body and soul and—after having drained to the dregs the cup of the world's joys—to choose the narrow path of the children of God. After having come to know the truth of the Bible passage "Sin is a reproach to any people" by some sad experience, these people decided to quit their sins—even their pet sins.

Tenth Evening Lecture: Nov. 28, 1884

Prov. 14:34

Many thousands have been tormented with uncertainty day and night as to whether they were in a state of grace, whether they had been accepted by God as His dear children, and whether their sins had been forgiven. They have been filled with anguish when they asked themselves, "If I were to die today, will I be saved?" In this state of mind, they resolved to seek the grace of God and the forgiveness of their sins.

What was the outcome? Most who had made up their minds did not follow through. They put off their resolution for days, weeks, months—even years. But their resolution was as far as they got. Finally, death overtook them, and they were lost forever.

Faith needs action

What happened? They were not serious about following through on their resolution. True, God is so patient, kind, and gracious that He forgives Christians their sins of weakness and frailty every single day—and richly too. But He does this only for those who are really serious about being Christians. If this earnestness is lacking, a person is not a true Christian.[16] This is why wise Sirach wrote (18:23): "If you want to serve God, be serious about it."[17]

This is similar to when a person resolves to become a servant of Christ, a servant of Christ's Church and His Word. This, too, is a momentous resolution, but a blessed one only if backed by earnest effort. If a person wants to become a preacher, he must be so disposed toward his Lord Jesus Christ that he can say to Him: "My dear Lord Jesus, You are mine; therefore, I wish to be Yours. All that I possess—my body and my soul, my strength and my gifts,

---

16 Compare Theses IX and following. Walther is speaking against backsliding or mere historical faith. He is trying to steer between the errors of dead historical faith, on the one hand, and experience-based enthusiastic doctrine, on the other. Among true Christians, Word and Sacrament do have a real effect, which recalls Walther's Thesis I on the Church (see *Church and Ministry* [St. Louis: Concordia, 1987]).

17 The Dau text does not include Walther's reference to Sirach 18:23.

and all that I do, my entire life—I will consecrate to You, to You alone. Lay on me any burden You please; I will gladly bear it. Lead me anywhere—through sorrow or joy, through good fortune or misfortune, through shame or honor, through favor or disfavor of men. Grant me a long life or an early death. I will be satisfied with everything. Lead the way, and I will follow." That is the sentiment that our dear Paul Gerhardt has expressed in one of his hymns:

> I cleave now and forever
> To Christ, a member true;
> My Head will leave me never,
> Whate'er He lead me through.
> He rends asunder death,
> Suff'ring, and all the earth;
> He tears dread hell in twain;
> His comrade I'll remain.[18]

Gal. 1:16   This was how devoted the apostle was from the moment the Lord appeared to him and spoke to him. Paul relates that, when he received the divine call to go and preach the Gospel of Christ among the Gentiles, he did not consult with flesh and blood but obeyed promptly.[19] Blessed be Paul! His activities were favored with success beyond telling. And now he has been face-to-face with His God and Savior for more than eighteen hundred years and is praising and magnifying Him forever and ever.

O my dear friends, I know you are all resolved to enter the Holy Ministry, in which you intend to serve Christ and His Church by preaching His saving Word. Oh, please take this matter seriously. If not, your resolution will be in vain. If God leads you to this resolve at an early stage, but you refuse to follow Him and stifle the voice of the Holy Spirit in your heart, all those blessed moments of prompting from God will bear testimony against you at His throne.

On the other hand, you are blessed men if you carry out your resolution. You will never complain about the heartache and anguish and distress through which you had to pass. Rather, you will be full of joy on the day that the Lord with His nail-scarred hand places the crown of glory on your head.

Now, then, what will your chief task be when you enter the sacred ministry? You are to proclaim to a world of sinners both Law and Gospel. You are to do this clearly, perfectly, and with a passionate spirit. This reflection leads us to the consideration of Thesis VI.

---

18   "Awake, My Heart, with Gladness," stanza 6. Compare with *LSB* 467:6.

19   See Galatians 1:16–17.

THESIS VI

You are not rightly distinguishing Law and Gospel in the Word of God if you do not preach the Law in its full sternness and the Gospel in its full sweetness. Similarly, do not mingle Gospel elements with the Law or Law elements with the Gospel.

EDITOR'S NOTE: Walther stresses that the proper way of reading and applying Scripture passages is to understand that Law and Gospel always are proclaimed in full purity and at full strength. The Law does not "half condemn," even as the Gospel does not "half save."

Our task is to meditate upon the distinction between Law and Gospel and on the ever-present danger and harm of mingling one with the other. In our last lecture, we began to discuss the second part of this thesis. However, the two doctrines are also confused when Gospel elements are mingled with the Law, and vice versa. Let us investigate what Scripture says regarding this matter. To begin with, what does it say concerning the Law? How does it show us that we must definitely not mingle any Gospel ingredient with the Law?

Galatians 3:11–12: "Now it is evident that no one is justified before God by the law, for 'The righteous shall live by faith.' But the law is not of faith, rather 'The one who does them shall live by them.'" A precious text! A person becomes righteous in the sight of God by faith alone. What conclusion can we draw from this? The Law cannot make any person righteous because it has nothing to say about justifying and saving faith. That information is found only in the Gospel. In other words, the Law has nothing to say about grace.

Romans 4:16: "That is why [righteousness] depends on faith, in order that the promise may rest on grace and be guaranteed to all his [Abraham's] offspring—not only to the adherent of the law but also to the one who shares the faith of Abraham, who is the father of us all." Faith is demanded of us, not so there might be at least some little work that we were to do (because otherwise there would be no difference between those who go to hell and those who go to heaven). No, righteousness is of faith, so that it may be of grace. Both statements are identical. When I say, "A person becomes righteous in the sight of God by faith," I mean to say, "He becomes righteous for free—by grace—by God making righteousness a gift to him." Nothing is demanded of the person. He is told only: "Stretch out your hand, and you will have it." That

Gal. 3:11–12

Rom. 4:16

is what faith is—stretching out your hand. Even if a person has never heard a single word about faith, once he hears the Gospel, he will rejoice, accept it, put his confidence in it, and draw comfort from the fact that he has the true, genuine faith—even though he may never have heard a word about faith.

Keep Law and Gospel separate

No Gospel element, then, must be mingled with the Law. Anyone explaining the Law shamefully corrupts it if he adds grace to it—the grace, loving-kindness, and patience of God who forgives sin. That person would be like a nurse who fetches sugar to sweeten bitter medicine, which the patient dislikes. What is the result? Why, the medicine would not work, and the patient would remain feverish. In order to retain its strength, the medicine should not have been sweetened. A preacher must proclaim the Law in such a way that nothing in it is pleasant for us lost and condemned sinners. Any sweet ingredient injected into the Law is poison. It renders this heavenly medicine inactive. It neutralizes its effectiveness.

The Lord says in Matthew 5:17–19:

Matt. 5:17–19

Do not think that I have come to abolish the Law or the Prophets; I have not come to abolish them but to fulfill them. For truly, I say to you, until heaven and earth pass away, not an iota, not a dot, will pass from the Law until all is accomplished. Therefore whoever relaxes one of the least of these commandments and teaches others to do the same will be called least in the kingdom of heaven, but whoever does them and teaches them will be called great in the kingdom of heaven.

Whenever you preach the Law, you must always bear in mind that it makes no concessions. That would be completely contrary to the character of the Law, because it makes only demands. The Law says, "You must do this. If you fail to do it, there will be no patience, loving-kindness, and long-suffering of God for you. You will have to go to hell." To make this point quite plain to us, the Lord says, "Whoever relaxes one of the least of these commandments and teaches others to do the same will be called least in the kingdom of heaven." That does not mean he will have assigned to him the lowest place in heaven, but that he will not go to the kingdom of heaven at all.

Gal. 3:10

Galatians 3:10: "For all who rely on works of the law are under a curse; for it is written, 'Cursed be everyone who does not abide by all things written in the Book of the Law, and do them.'" If you direct people to do good works and—just for their comfort—add a remark such as: "You should indeed be perfect. Yet God does not demand the impossible from us. Do what you can in your weakness; just be sincere in your intention!" I say, if you were to speak like this, you would be preaching a damnable doctrine, for that is a shameful corruption of the Law. God never spoke like that from Mount Sinai.

Romans 7:14: "For we know that the law is spiritual, but I am of the flesh,   Rom. 7:14
sold under sin." When a minister preaches the Law, he must by all means bear
in mind that the Law is spiritual. It works on the *spirit*, not on some part of the
body. It is directed to the *spirit* in humans, to their will, heart, and affections.
That is always the case. When the Law says, "You shall not murder," it sounds
as if it applies only to the hand. But it applies to the heart, as we can see from
the Ninth and the Tenth Commandments, which prohibit evil desires of the
heart.[1]

A sermon on the Law that you deliver from the pulpit must measure up
to these standards if it is to be a proper preaching of the Law. Do not rant
about horrible vices that may be running wild in the congregation. Continual
ranting will prove useless. While people may quit the practices that have
been rebuked, in two weeks' time they will return to their old ways. You must
indeed testify against such outbreaks with great earnestness, but you must
also tell the people: "Even if you were to quit your habitual cursing, swearing,
and so on, that would not make you Christians. You might go to hell for all
that. God is concerned about the attitude of your heart." Explain this matter
with the utmost composure, but state it quite plainly.

Let me give you an example. You may say: "Look, when God says, 'You
shall not kill,' that does not mean that you are not murderers if your hand
has not killed anyone, if you have not assaulted anyone like a highway robber
or put another's life in jeopardy. Do not think that you have kept the Fifth
Commandment just because you have refrained from such outward acts. By
no means! The Law aims at the heart, at the spirit in man." If you say merely
in passing, "The Law is spiritual," the people will not catch the drift of your
speech. You must explain this matter to them quite thoroughly. If you do this,
you will be handling a sharp knife that cuts into the life of people, and your
hearers will go home in a daze. The Word works; they fall on their knees at
home and confess: "I am not as God would have me to be. I have to become a
different person."

Romans 3:20: "Through the law comes knowledge of sin." God does not   Rom. 3:20
tell you to preach the Law in order to make people godly. The Law makes no
one godly. Rather, when the Law begins to take effect, the person begins to
fume and rage against God. He hates the preacher who has shouted the Law
into his heart, feeling that he cannot slip off its coils. When this happens, you
sometimes hear people say: "I will never go to that church again. Why, that
preacher strikes terror into my soul. I prefer to attend the services of the Rev.
So-and-so. He makes you feel good. When you listen to him, you realize what
a good person you really are." Alas! Down in hell these same people will want

---

1   See *Concordia*, 321, 325–26. Cf. *Concordia*, 378–81, 392–95.

to take revenge on the preacher when they see how that false prophet got them thrown into the pit.

There was nothing pleasant, nothing comforting, at Sinai. Even on the day before, Moses had announced to the people that God was going to come to them. And He did come—with thunder and lightning!

At early dawn, a terrible tempest sweeps up from the horizon![2]

Finally, the mountain begins to quake, and the people are thrown into a still greater fright when the mountain starts to tremble!

The mountain turns into a majestic furnace!

Flames shoot skyward; smoke, steam, and vapors rise up!

Suddenly a loud trumpet begins to blare, hurling its thunderclaps across the mountains and valleys, sounding like thunder![3]

Exod. 20:5 Luther But the climax comes when the people hear the voice of Jehovah, blaring the Ten Commandments at them, with that rhythmic refrain: "You shall! You shall! You shall!" This concludes with: "I am a strong, jealous God, visiting the iniquity of the fathers on the children," etc.[4]

Everyone in the camp of Israel went to pieces from dread and fright.

Was it really a coincidence that terrible weather blew in precisely on that day? Just one day earlier, Moses had built a wall around the mountain to prevent anyone from approaching Mount Sinai. He had told the people they would drop dead if they crossed the barrier because everyone was in a state of confusion. No one would have survived. Only Moses, under the protective hand of God, was permitted to approach the mountain.

With this spectacle God indicated how we are to preach the Law. Of course, we cannot reproduce the thunder and lightning of that day, except in a spiritual way. But sermons are just as beneficial when the people sit in their pews and the preacher begins to preach the Law in its fullness, explaining its spiritual meaning. There may be many in the audience who will say to themselves, "If that man is right, I am lost."

---

2   Walther switches from the "narrative past" tense to the "historical present" as he speaks excitedly and dramatically of past events as if they were happening now. Cf. Exodus 19:9–20:21.

3   The original German notes suggest that Walther was thundering forth each sentence like a volley of cannon fire. He was a lively speaker who riveted people with his booming voice, his emotional delivery, and his razor-sharp wit. He could rise up to the height of stately prose, then plunge down to innuendo and the occasional swearword. The Dau edition edits out many of these swings in tone in order to present a consistent literary composition. The purpose of this edition is to present Walther as he spoke.

4   Walther has in mind Exodus 20:5 from Luther's translation, which he paraphrases here. Walther also uses the word order from Luther's Small Catechism, which makes the conclusion of the prohibition against idolatry and false gods a conclusion to all the Commandments.

Indeed, some may say, "That is not the way for a Lutheran[5] minister to preach." But, in reality, it is. In fact, he could not be a Lutheran preacher if he did *not* preach the Law in this way. The Law must precede the preaching of the Gospel. First you need Moses, then Christ. Or: first John the Baptist, then Christ. At first the people will exclaim, "How terrible this all is!" But then the preacher—with a glow in his eyes—arrives at the Gospel. This cheers the hearts of the people. Now they understand why the pastor had preached the preceding remarks: he wanted to make them see how terribly contaminated with sin they are and how desperately they need the Gospel.

When you are teaching, you must adopt the same method. When you are explaining the Law, never, ever, add Gospel elements—except in conclusion. Even little children need to experience anguish and terror. The reason so many people assume that they are really good Christians is because their parents reared them to be miserable Pharisees. Their parents never made them aware of the fact that they are poor, miserable sinners. A person may have fallen into the most dreadful sins, but if he has been brought up properly, when he hears the Law preached, he will say to himself, "Sure enough, I am an awful sinner!" Yet that Pharisee has sunk even lower. It is much tougher to convert such Pharisees.

Converting Pharisees is a far more difficult task than [converting] persons who acknowledge their sin. That was the chief sin of the Jews in Christ's day, and it is the chief sin of the Papists in our time. The Jews had mingled Gospel elements with the Law by telling the people: "If you do not actually kill somebody, you are not a murderer. If you do not actually commit fornication, you are not guilty of adultery." They declared that even concupiscence[6] was something quite natural. The Papists say the same thing, though they do admit that **Christ** explains the Law by mentioning a few things that cannot really be categorized as breaking the Law in a coarse way. They claim that Christ merely recommends we do these things and that only those who strive for an exceptionally exalted place in heaven need to do them. They claim these good works are extras.

Commenting on the words of Christ "You have heard that it was said to those of old, 'You shall not kill,'" etc., Luther says (St. Louis Ed. 7:429f.): **Matt. 5:21** Luther

---

5   Walther makes wordplay between the German *evangelisch*, "Protestant/Lutheran," and the German *Evangelium*, "Gospel." One cannot rightly be *evangelisch* without the proper distinction between "Law" (German: *Gesetz*) and *Evangelium*. Yet such a distinction is also the heart and soul of Lutheran preaching, as is translated here.

6   *Concupiscence* is defined by AC II as being in the state of original sin, worthy of condemnation (*Concordia*, 31–32). The Augsburg Confession follows the teaching of Augustine of Hippo and Hugh of St. Victor. The Papists, on the other hand, declared concupiscence to be a fairly benign natural state, like tinder that has the potential to flare into a roaring fire.

W² 7:429
(cf. AE 21:74);
Acts 5:28

Christ takes up some of the Ten Commandments for the purpose of explaining them properly. He shows that the Pharisees and scribes, when teaching the Law, did not push their explanation and interpretation beyond the literal meaning of the Commandments and thus made them applicable only to coarse, external acts. For instance, in the Fifth Commandment (which He introduces first) they considered no more than the word *kill*, which they interpreted to mean actual slaying, and they allowed the people to stick to the notion that nothing beyond this is forbidden in this commandment. Moreover, in order to escape the charge of manslaughter for delivering a person to the magistrates to be condemned to death—the way they delivered Christ to the pagan Pontius Pilate—they came up with a flimsy pretense for keeping their own hands from being stained with blood. They stressed their ceremonial purity and sanctity to the point of refusing to enter the governor's palace and forcing Pilate against his will to kill Jesus (John 18:28f.). Later, still pretending to be perfectly pure and innocent, they even rebuked the apostles for preaching Christ, charging them with the intention of bringing "this man's blood" upon them. What they were insinuating was: "The *Gentiles* killed Christ—*we* did not."

A similar trick is recorded regarding King Saul (1 Samuel 18:25f.). Saul was nursing a grudge against David and wanted to kill him. But because he wanted to be holy, Saul did not plan to kill David himself, but [he planned] to send him to the Philistines, so they would kill him. That way Saul's hands would remain pure.

The Jews were sticking to a literal reading of the Fifth Commandment. The teachers told the people: "If you avoid such and such acts, then you will keep the Fifth Commandment well." These great champions of the Law had emptied the Law of its contents and retained the mere shell. Our present-day rationalists do the same. Their aim is merely to uphold the reputation of decency in their lives, that is, not to rush into unspeakable vices of which any moral citizen would have to be ashamed. Upright conduct, too, is the sole object of their preaching. Even so-called Christian preachers are known to do this.

The Papists have taken up this practice of the Pharisees too. Papists and Pharisees are as alike as two peas in a pod. The Papists declare: "The Church does not thirst for blood.[7] True, many of our heretical enemies have been

---

7   Latin: *Ecclesia not sitit sanguinem.* This is the age-old false claim of the Inquisition that the church never put heretics to death; instead, the church left it for the state. Yet the nobility, if they were placed under the greater ban by the pope or an archbishop, would be excommunicated, and their lands, titles, and possessions would also be forfeit. Thus the civil authorities were forced into doing the Roman Church's will in the matter.

killed. However, *we* did not do that; it was the authorities." Yet when the authorities refused to do it, they were placed under the greater ban. In this way the Papists want to wash their hands of the blood of the martyrs. But they will not succeed. One day they will have to appear before God and will be stained with the damning witness of this blood.

With the Jews it was no different. Had they known the spiritual meaning of the Law, they, too, would have acknowledged: "Yes, we are the ones who killed Christ, for we were the ones who cried, 'Crucify, crucify Him!'"

Luther proceeds:

> Look at this fine Pharisaic[8] holiness, which whitewashes and retains the reputation of godliness, provided it does not use its own hand for killing. In reality, their hearts are filled with wrath, hatred, and envy, hiding evil and murderous plots, while their mouths spew curses and blasphemies.

W² 7:429–30
(cf. AE 21:74)

> This is just like the sanctity of our Papists, who have become experts at these tricks. To guard their sanctity against censure and to avoid being bound by the Word of Christ, they have figured a convenient way out in the **twelve** evangelical **counsels** that they have extracted from the teachings of Christ. They claim that not all that Christ taught has the nature of a command and is a necessary requirement for discipleship, but that some of His teachings were meant only as **good counsel**, which was left to everybody's discretion whether they wanted to follow it or not. Those wishing to achieve some special merit over against others could adopt these counsels.

> For the average person, however, they claim that these counsels were an extra teaching that one could well do without. If you ask how they base these counsels on the teaching of Christ and how they would prove their case, they would say: Well, you see, it would be an excessive burdening of the Christian law[9] and would make Christianity too burdensome an affair if all the teachings of Christ were understood as actual commands. That is what the theologians of Paris unblushingly published in the treatise directed against me.[10]

> Yes, yes, here we have some clever reasoning: "Be kind to your neighbor, and do not forsake him in distress, just as you would wish that people should treat you." And because they deem it too onerous, they decree that it will not be regarded as a command but should be optional for those who would like to do it. Those, however, who are

---

8 The reference to "Pharisee" can also intend the generic hypocrite.

9 Latin: *nimis onerativum legis Christianae.*

10 The theological faculty of the University of Paris condemned Luther in 1521.

unwilling to do it should not be burdened with it. That is how they twist Christ's speech, lord it over His Word, and remake its meaning according to our pleasure.

Matt. 5:22 Luther

But He will not let Himself be cheated like this, nor will He revoke the verdict that He laid down when He said, "Unless you can show a better kind of godliness, heaven will be closed for you, and you will be damned," or as He expresses it in a later statement: "If you say to your brother, 'You fool,' you shall be guilty of hellfire." From this we can readily gather whether He offered counsels or issued commands.

Matt. 5:40–42

Christ says: "And if anyone would sue you and take your tunic, let him have your cloak as well. And if anyone forces you to go one mile, go with him two miles. Give to the one who begs from you, and do not refuse the one who would borrow from you." The Papists say: "True, Christ did say that, but His words are merely counsels with some Gospel elements. If you want to make it to heaven, you need to keep the Law. But if you want to climb to a really high place in heaven, you must carry out these counsels."

Matt. 19:21; 19:12; 23:3; 7:5

In his *Loci Theologici*, **Chemnitz** enumerates these counsels.[11] By the way, the surplus of works that results from following these counsels is the treasure from which the pope distributes his indulgences. All told, there are twelve counsels: **(1) Voluntary poverty.** The words of Christ "Sell what you possess and give to the poor, and you will have treasure in heaven; and come, follow Me" are understood by the Papists to be merely good counsel. In their view, those who enter a monastery follow this counsel. **(2) Celibacy.** The Papists extract this from Matthew 19:12: "For there are eunuchs who have been so from birth, and there are eunuchs who have been made eunuchs by men, and there are eunuchs who have made themselves eunuchs for the sake of the kingdom of heaven. Let the one who is able to receive this receive it." "Behold," they say, "our monks and nuns have adopted this good counsel." Or they put it this way: "They lead a life of chastity." **(3) Unconditional obedience** to your superior in a religious order. This good counsel, too, is followed by monks and nuns. **(4) Taking revenge.** It seems almost beyond belief that anyone would arise in the Church and declare the divine command not to take revenge to be merely good counsel. That would be the same as saying, "You might be allowed to get revenge, but if you decline to do so, that is a splendid good work." **(5) Patiently suffering insult. (6) Giving alms. (7) Refraining from swearing. (8) Avoiding opportunities to commit sin.** This is awful! Accordingly, it is not really necessary to avoid all opportunities

---

11   Part II, page 104, of the Latin facsimile edition (Sterling Heights, MI: Lutheran Heritage Foundation, 2000). Locus IX is not translated by J. A. O. Preus in the English translation (St. Louis: Concordia, 1989).

for sinning; but if you do so, you will climb to the top of perfection! **(9) Having a good intention in whatever you do.** This would mean that, no matter what prompts you to do a good work, it is in every case a good work in the sight of God. But if you are guided by a right motive, you are an exceptionally saintly person. **(10) Doing what Christ says in Matthew 23:3: "For they preach, but do not practice," and in Matthew 7:5: "First take the log out of your own eye." (11) Not being concerned about earthly affairs.** In the view of Papists, this, too, is merely good counsel. **(12) Admonishing a brother.** Imagine—this should not be regarded as a real duty because it is not a part of the Law!

You can see how horribly the Papists have corrupted the Law. In fact, they have gutted the innermost spirit of the Law. They imagine that it would be asking too much if everybody were required to obey all these teachings of Christ. Of course, we cannot all enter a monastery. If we did, who would provide bread and meat? No, indeed—that would be asking too much! Oh, what an abomination!

Then the Jesuits came forward, proclaiming: "Until now, the poor Chris- **Matt. 5:22** Luther
tians have been excessively oppressed with moral regulations. Therefore, we, the Jesuits, have formed a society to relieve Christians of the most severe moral regulations." And they actually put their plan into operation, with the happy result that—according to their ethical standards—the most infamous scoundrel can still be a good Christian. Their moral code is the reverse of the Decalogue:[12] a person may commit the most horrible abominations, as long as he does so with good intent. He may poison his father if he has the good intention of becoming his heir. However, this entire ethical system of the Papists and Jesuits has been overthrown by the words of Christ: "Whoever says, 'You fool' shall be guilty of hellfire." This means that anyone who fails to fulfill the Law in its spiritual meaning deserves to burn in hell. Thus Christ overthrows all the morals of the Papists and Jesuits.

You can find many solemn warnings against false teachers in Holy **Eleventh**
Scripture. One of the most solemn of them, though not even the *most* **Evening Lecture:**
solemn, is in Jeremiah 23:22, where the Lord says regarding false teachers: Dec. 5, 1884
"But if they had stood in My council, then they would have proclaimed My
words to My people, and they would have turned them from their evil way, **Jer. 23:22**
and from the evil of their deeds."

This shows that, by teaching false doctrine, a preacher may himself be the reason that the souls entrusted to his care are not converted, which—as awful as it is to contemplate—will cause them to be eternally lost! True, it is their

---

12   That is, the Ten Commandments.

own fault that people who permit themselves to be led astray by false teachings are lost, for in innumerable passages of His Word, God with great earnestness warns people about false teachers and prophets—describing them in great detail. So anyone who despises these warnings finally cries a curse upon himself.[13]

Heb. 13:17   Still, this does not excuse the false prophets and teachers who proclaim false teachings. On the contrary, their guilt is increased because not only did they choose the false way for themselves, but they also pointed out that way to the souls entrusted to them. For it is written, Hebrews 13:17: "Obey your leaders and submit to them, for they are keeping watch over your souls, as those who will have to give an account."

Alas, what terror will seize all those false teachers on the great day of account when all the souls led astray by them will stand before the judgment seat of God and raise accusations against them! What terror will seize Arius, who questioned the deity of Christ and wanted to snatch the crown of divine majesty from Christ's head! What terror will seize Pelagius, who denied that a person is made righteous and is saved solely by the grace of God! What terror—even greater than these—will seize the popes, who have combined all anti-Christian doctrines into one system! How they will quake with terror when innumerable souls whom they have led astray and whose hearts they have poisoned will stand in the presence of God! On that day every false teacher will wish that he had never been born and will curse the day when he was inducted into the sacred Office of the Ministry. On that day we will see that false teaching is not the trifling and harmless matter that people in our day think it is.

Isa. 66:2   My dear friends, heed well what God inspired His prophet Isaiah to write in chapter 66, verse 2: "But this is the one to whom I will look: he who is humble and contrite in spirit and **trembles at My word**." Of the men serving in the sacred Office of the Ministry and of those who are training for the same—that is, of us all—God requires not only that we love His Word but also that we tremble at it, that is, that we sincerely dread to deviate from a single letter of the divine Word. This is so we do not dare add anything to it or take anything from it. We need to be ready to shed our blood rather than yield a jot and a tittle of God's Word.

W² 20:788   Choose our beloved **Luther** as a role model, who says, "I feel like one
(cf. AE 37:40);   passage of Scripture could push me off the face of the earth."[14] He means
Ps. 119:120

---

13   The Dau text assumes this act of self-cursing occurs after death. The German text includes this self-cursing even in this life.

14   For example, the confession and practice of the Lord's Supper affects how one generally interprets Scripture. Luther makes some of his most profound observations regarding Scripture in relation to the doctrine of the Lord's Supper. Luther's writing *That These Words, "This Is My Body, &c.," Still Stand Fast*, in addition to *Bondage of the Will* (*De servo*

to say: "If I ever noticed that the doctrine that I proclaim to the people were contradicted by one passage of Scripture, I would have no rest, day or night. I would not know where I could flee. The situation would be too terrible for me." Strive to have the mind of David, the royal prophet, who says in Psalm 119:120: "My flesh trembles for fear of You, and I am afraid of Your judgments."

Indeed, such a mind is impossible to have—at least you cannot grasp a mind such as David's—if you are still without a clear and thorough knowledge of all doctrines of Holy Scripture. For how can you keep what you do not possess? Make the most of your time here at the seminary, during which you can make yourself familiar with all of Holy Scripture and can get to know each article of faith by itself, as well as in connection with and in its relation to all the other doctrines.

The seminarian's task

That is also the object of our Friday evening lectures, in which we are discussing how to distinguish between Law and Gospel. For that is the primary issue: that you would learn to rightly distinguish Law and Gospel.

I am simply assuming you men will not become apostates, and I am also not afraid that you might set up new articles of faith. But I *do* fear that you will not rightly distinguish Law and Gospel. For this requires that you deviate neither to the right nor to the left, becoming neither despondent nor lax.

arbitrio), are cited in theses 15 and 16 from the 1867 Northern District *Proceedings*. See pages 24–29 of the *Lehrverhandlungen*.

These engravings were created from small portraits of C. F. W. Walther's parents, Johanna and Gottlob. Little is known of Johanna, but Walther remembered his father as a strict disciplinarian who did not spare the rod: "A young man must endure much pain, ere he becomes a gentleman" ("*Ein junger Mann viel leiden muss, eh' aus ihm wird ein Dominus*"). Nevertheless, this strict father deprived himself in order to pay for his children's education. Of his twelve children, six predeceased Gottlob, and three sailed to North America, never to be seen by him again. Walther visited his father's grave when he traveled to Germany in 1851. His mother lived with his sister at the time. See also August Suelflow, *Selected Letters of C. F. W. Walther* (St. Louis: Concordia, 1981), 19; and Suelflow, *Servant of the Word* (St. Louis: Concordia, 2000), 210. Images from Martin Günther, *Doctor C. F. W. Walther: Lebensbild* (St. Louis: Concordia, 1890), 2–3.

Thesis VII

You are not rightly distinguishing Law and Gospel in the Word of God if you first preach the Gospel and then the Law; or first sanctification and then justification; or first faith and then repentance; or first good works and then grace.

Editor's Note: In this thesis, Walther begins to warn against the teaching and practice common among Moravians. Walther emphasizes at several points the Moravian settlement of Herrnhut in Saxony.[1] The Moravian bishop, Count Nikolaus Ludwig von Zinzendorf, tried to unite Protestants in Europe and North America. He funded many missionaries. Yet he was opposed to those who took a strong stand on doctrinal confessions. Both Lutherans and Reformed viewed his followers as a serious problem.[2] Even Henry Melchior Muhlenberg, who helped to organize the Pennsylvania Ministerium, did not consider the Herrnhuters to be Lutheran.

Walther characterized his erstwhile leader Martin Stephan as "never really Lutheran."[3] Stephan came from Moravian roots and had some connections with Herrnhut. Walther was familiar with many of the same Pietists who he says influenced Stephan. Walther even found some of their books to be helpful in certain cases. Yet Walther disagreed with these authors on several points, and we see identified in the Law and Gospel lectures some of his strongest differences.

Proper sequence

We now need to discuss another way people sometimes incorrectly distinguish the Word of God. This happens when they do not present the various doctrines in their proper sequence: when something that should

---

1   See also the entries for the Moravians, page 497, and Count Nikolaus Ludwig von Zinzendorf, page 501, in the Index of Persons and Groups. See also the map of Saxony in the front of the book.

2   See also Augustus Graebner, *Geschichte der lutherischen Kirche in America* (St. Louis: Concordia, 1892), 257; G. Friedrich Bente, *American Lutheranism* (St. Louis: Concordia, 1919), 1:61.

3   Walther was the ghostwriter of the first chapter of J. F. Köstering, *Auswanderung der sächsischen Lutheraner im Jahre 1838* (St. Louis: August Wiebusch & Sohn, 1866). This book is an important eyewitness account of the Saxon emigration and the early Missouri Synod. Walther mentions Pietism as the basis for Stephan's doctrine, coupled with Stephan's belief that his ordination was a means of grace, an apostolic—indeed a divine—mandate (see Köstering, *Auswanderung der sächsischen Lutheraner*, 8–9).

come last is placed first. This practice can inflict tremendous damage in the heart and the understanding of those listening to you. There are four different ways to get this sequence wrong.

In the first place, you may distort the sequence if you preach the Gospel prior to the Law. You might be thinking: "How could anyone get it so wrong? Why, every catechumen at school knows quite well that the Law comes first and then the Gospel." However, this still can happen quite easily.

There are instances in history that show how even entire religious communities have succumbed to this error, for instance, the Antinomians in Luther's time (with Agricola of Eisleben as their leader) and the Moravians at Herrnhut in the eighteenth century.[4] The latter preferred not to have the Law preached at all. Their chief belief was "The Gospel must be preached first; start your preaching with the suffering and bleeding of Christ." This was fundamentally wrong. We should readily admit that the Herrnhuters did make an impression on many, but it was merely superficial. Their hearers were never made aware of their deep sinful depravity; they were never made to realize that they were enemies of God, worthy to be thrown into hell rather than to be saved. By the way, when we use the term "Gospel" in this context, we are, of course, referring to the Gospel in the strict sense of the term, namely, as the opposite of the Law.

Mark 1:15; Acts 20:21; Luke 24:47

In Mark 1:15 we read: "Repent and believe in the gospel." "Repent" is plainly a statement of the Law. When we preach of our Lord, this comes first, and it is followed by the Gospel summons: "Believe in the Gospel." Regarding this practice, the holy apostles followed Christ. Acts 20:21: "Testifying both to Jews and to Greeks of repentance toward God and of faith in our Lord Jesus Christ." The apostle preached repentance first and then faith, the Law first and then the Gospel. Luke 24:47: "And that repentance and forgiveness of sins should be proclaimed in His name to all nations, beginning from Jerusalem." The Lord does not reverse the divine order, saying, "Forgiveness of sins and repentance." No—that would be a wrong way and would absolutely not lead to salvation.

A second corruption of the correct sequence would occur if you were to preach the sanctification of life before justification, the forgiveness of sins. For justification by grace is the same as the forgiveness of sins. I become righteous by appropriating the righteousness of Christ as my own.

Ps. 130:4; 119:32

Psalm 130:4: "But with You there is forgiveness, that You may be feared." So the psalmist is saying to God: "First, You must grant us remission of sins; after that we will begin to fear You by walking in a new, sanctified life." The term "fear" in this text does not signify merely awe in God's presence but the whole work of sanctification. Psalm 119:32: "I will run in the way of Your

---

4   See the Luther to Walther timeline, pages xxxiv and xl.

commandments when You enlarge my heart!" First come the consolations, justification, the granting of pardon to the sinner, and the remission of sins. After that the psalmist expects to "run in the way of God's Commandments." What he is saying is this: "Because You, O God, receive me into Your grace, therefore—*because* of this gracious act of Yours—I start to love Your Commandments. As long as my sins are still unforgiven, I cannot love You and Your Commandments. No, I hate You. But as soon as I have been pardoned, I obtain a new heart and gladly quit the world, for I find with You something better than what the world can give me."

First Corinthians 1:30: "He is the source of your life in Christ Jesus, whom God made our wisdom and our righteousness and sanctification and redemption." Here we have the true sequence. The first requirement is to obtain wisdom, [that is,] knowledge of the way of salvation. This is the primary step. Next comes righteousness, which we obtain by faith. Not until this has been attained does sanctification come. I must first know that God has forgiven my sins, that He has cast them into the depth of the sea, before it gives me real joy to lead a sanctified life. Before that it was a serious burden to me. At first I was angry with God; I hated Him for demanding so many things of me. I would have liked to cast Him from His throne. I thought in my heart: "It would be better if there were no God." But once I was pardoned and justified, I delighted—not only in the Gospel but also in the Law. *1 Cor. 1:30* Luther

John 15:5: "I am the vine; you are the branches. Whoever abides in Me and I in him, he it is that bears much fruit, for apart from Me you can do nothing." The Savior desires us to be grafted in Him like branches on a vine. Of course, that does not mean that we should be physically incorporated in Him, but that we should believe in Him with our whole heart, put our confidence and trust in Him, and embrace Him completely with the arms of faith, so that we live only in Him, our Jesus, who has rescued us and saves us. When this takes place, we will bear fruit. What the Savior shows us is that we must first be justified before we can lead a sanctified life. But if we are disconnected, severed branches, we wither and can bear no fruit. *John 15:5*

Acts 15:9: "He made no distinction between us [Jewish Christians] and them [Gentiles], having cleansed their hearts by faith." Only after being justified by faith am I thus purified, renewed, and sanctified by that same faith. To confuse justification and sanctification is one of the most horrid errors. The most beautiful preaching is rendered useless by this error. Only when you strictly separate justification and sanctification can you make a sinner understand clearly and give him certainty that God has received him into grace; and this knowledge equips him with strength to walk in a new life. *Acts 15.9*

People make the third mistake when they confuse the correct sequence—which should be first Law, then Gospel. When they make this mistake, they preach faith first and *then* repentance, as the Antinomians did and as is still done by the Herrnhuters in our day. They teach: "Faith is key; after that you must become contrite and repent." How foolish is that! How can faith enter a heart that has not yet been crushed? How can a person feel hungry and thirsty if he detests the food set before him? No, indeed; if you wish to believe in Christ, you must first become sick, for Christ is a doctor only for those who are sick. You must first be a lost and condemned sinner, for He came to seek and to save that which is lost. First you must be a lost sheep, for He is the Good Shepherd who goes in search of the lost sheep.

Acts 2:37–38   Acts 2:38: "And Peter said to them, 'Repent and be baptized every one of you in the name of Jesus Christ for the forgiveness of your sins, and you will receive the gift of the Holy Spirit.'" That is what Peter said in reply to the question of the Jews: "Brothers, what shall we do?" This is what he replies: first, repentance; next, the remission of sins. As such, faith *follows* repentance.

Acts 20:21   All the passages cited above belong under this heading, especially Acts 20:21: "testifying both to Jews and to Greeks of repentance toward God and of faith in our Lord Jesus Christ." Anyone who reverses this order will have his teaching disproved by this verse. For a preacher, these passages are the true guiding lights to prevent him from straying from the right path.

In the fourth place, it is also wrong when good works are preached first and then grace. All these errors are similar; one is as bad as any of the others.

Eph. 2:8–10   Ephesians 2:8–10: "For by grace you have been saved through faith. And this is not your own doing; it is the gift of God, not a result of works, so that no one may boast. For we are His workmanship, created in Christ Jesus for good works, which God prepared beforehand, that we should walk in them." Note that the apostle does not say, "We must do good works so that God will be gracious," but rather the very opposite: "*By grace you have been saved, but by grace you are created for good works.*" First you have to receive grace, then God creates you anew. In this new state you *have* to do good works; you can no longer remain under the dominion of sin.

Titus 2:11–12   Titus 2:11–12: "For the grace of God has appeared, bringing salvation for all people, training us to renounce ungodliness and worldly passions, and to live self-controlled, upright, and godly lives in the present age." Here we are told that grace must be preached to us first, and then this grace does not begin a work of chastisement, but it begins a work of chastity upon us.[5] We are placed under the divine teaching of grace. The moment a person receives the grace that brought God down from heaven, that grace begins to train him.

---

5   One could also use *castigation* and *education* to illustrate Walther's wordplay. He draws from the Latin *castigare—castitas*, using the German *züchtigen* ("to chastize") in order to become *züchtig*, "chaste or modest."

The object of this training is to teach him how to do good works and lead an upright life.

The character of the Old Testament is chiefly legalistic, though the Gospel is proclaimed in that part of the Bible as well. Conversely, the character of the New Testament is chiefly Gospel oriented, though the Law is not absent. The Law was solemnly revealed in the Old Testament, while the Gospel was solemnly revealed in the New Testament. The Gospel was indeed present as far back as the days of Paradise, but its solemn inauguration had not yet taken place.

The full revelation of the Law occurred at Mount Sinai amid thunder and lightning, accompanied by an earthquake. It seemed as if the world were coming to an end. In the New Testament era, at the outpouring of the Holy Spirit on Pentecost, fire appeared as well, but it did not consume anything. Tongues of fire were visible on the heads of the apostles, but their hair was not singed. A mighty wind came roaring out of the sky, yet it destroyed nothing; not a thing was moved out of its place.[6] The purpose of this phenomenon was to indicate that at that moment an entirely different—a comforting—revelation was about to take place.

Let us move on to the apostolic Epistles, especially to the one addressed to the Romans, which contains the Christian doctrine in its entirety. What do we find in the first three chapters? The toughest preaching of the Law. Then toward the end of the third chapter and in chapters 4 and 5, the doctrine of justification is addressed. Beginning at chapter 6, the apostle deals solely with sanctification. Here we have a true pattern of the correct sequence: First the Law, threatening men with the wrath of God; next the Gospel, announcing the comforting promises of God. This is followed by instruction regarding the things we are to do after becoming new people.

When they wished to convert people, the prophets, too, began by preaching the Law to them. Then, after the chastising of the Law had done its work, they comforted the poor sinners. No sooner had their hearers shown that they were alarmed, then the apostles comforted them and pronounced Absolution on them. Only when that was done would they say to their people: "Now you must show your gratitude toward God." They did not issue orders. They did not threaten if their orders were disregarded, but they begged and pleaded with their hearers by the mercy of God. Genuine sanctification *follows* justification, and genuine justification comes *after* repentance.

Using a few sermon outlines, let me show you how sermons can reveal whether the preacher is distinguishing Law and Gospel or not. I am choosing very coarse examples, as Luther was inclined to do, for such examples readily

---

6   See Acts 2:1–3.

help us understand the matter under discussion. I want to do as Luther did; for if I have achieved anything worthwhile, I have learned it from him.

INCORRECT SERMON OUTLINES

First Topic: The way of salvation consists of (1) faith and (2) true repentance. An error such as this would make you genuine Antinomians and Herrnhuters.

Second Topic: Good works. A discussion of (1) what they consist of, (2) that they must be performed in faith. In such an outline you would state what good works are, without having spoken of faith. A description of good works needs a statement that they must be performed by believers. Otherwise, you would have to judge good works according to the Law. But, of course, that is wrong. For viewed in the light of the Law, any good work—even that of a Christian—no matter how good it may appear, is damnable in the sight of God.

Third Topic: Concerning prayer. (1) True prayer is based on the certainty of our being heard. (2) True prayer is based on faith. According to this outline, the first part of your sermon would be entirely wrong.

Fourth Topic: Prophecies and threats contained in the Word of God. (1) Prophecies. (2) Threats. When I hear these parts of a sermon, I say to myself: First, the preacher is going to comfort me, then he will throw rocks at me, causing me to forget everything that he said at the start. No. First, you must come down on your hearers with the Law, and then bind up their wounds with the divine promises. When a preacher concludes his sermons with threats, he has done a fine job of making that sermon unproductive.

Fifth Topic: True Christianity consists of (1) Christian living, (2) true faith, (3) a blessed death. This outline is simply horrible.

Sixth Topic: What must people do to become certain of salvation? (1) They must amend their life and become different people. (2) They must repent of their sins. (3) They must also reach out for Christ by faith. How can you lead a better life when you have not yet reached the stage at which you hate sin and a wicked life? The worst section is part 3, for there is nothing that gives me greater assurance of being saved than my own subjective faith.

Accordingly, the Pietists were certainly wrong when they claimed that the Sermon on the Mount[7] describes the various stages of the order of salvation. They were tempted to adopt this view because—at the opening of that great sermon—Christ says, "Blessed are the poor in spirit, for theirs is the kingdom of heaven."

Problems with Pietism; Matt. 5:3

But that view is defenseless. For, in reality, the phrase "poor in spirit" means "to have nothing to which the heart becomes attached." Even a millionaire may be poor in spirit. If his heart is not attached to his money and possessions, he does not really possess them. On the other hand, a beggar may be at the very opposite end of the scale if he puts his trust in the little bit of money he still has. The former is a "blessed" man, while the latter is not.

In the view of the Pietists, the second beatitude that Christ pronounced— "Blessed are those who mourn, for they shall be comforted"—refers to mourning over sin. They called this the second stage in the order of salvation. But, in reality, Christ is referring to the sorrow and cross-bearing that His followers have to suffer in this life for His name's sake.

Matt. 5:4

Furthermore, Christ says, "Blessed are the meek, for they shall inherit the earth." Here the Pietists have worked mightily to find a suitable meaning. They were troubled by the fact that until this point no mention had yet been made of justification by faith. That messes up their whole "order of salvation" scheme. They do marvelous mental somersaults in an attempt to evolve their "stages" from the Beatitudes, but their efforts are unsuccessful.

Matt. 5:5

Next, Christ says, "Blessed are those who hunger and thirst for righteousness, for they shall be satisfied." This is supposed to be the fourth "stage." But does meekness actually precede the other stages? If you ever preach on the Beatitudes, be careful not to follow those pietistic preachers!

Matt. 5:6

The Antinomians were opposed to Luther, so he was forced to declare his position over against them. They contended that *grace* must be preached first and *then* repentance. Indeed, they insisted that the Law must not be preached in churches at all. They claimed that the Law belongs in the town hall and on the gallows; it is to be preached to thieves and murderers, not to honest people—least of all to Christians.

Antinomian errors

In his treatise *Against the Antinomians*, written in 1539, **Luther** writes (St. Louis Ed. 20:1618):

The Antinomians have invented a new method by which grace is to be preached first and after that the wrath of God. The word *Law* should not to be mentioned at all within earshot of Christians, they claim. In reality, this is just a clever teeter-totter,[8] which pleases them

W² 20:1618
(cf. AE 47:114)

---

7   See Matthew 5:1–7:29.

8   German: *Katzenstühlchen* (literally, "kitty's little stool"). This word comes from the concept of toy furniture or small, decorative furniture, e.g., *Katzentisch*. The English word

wonderfully, because by this trick they can turn the Scriptures up or down and think they have become the marvel of the world.[9] They force their notion upon the statement of St. Paul in Romans 1.

Rom. 1:16, 18; 3:23

The Antinomians use verse 16 [of Romans 1]: "For I am not ashamed of the gospel, for it is the power of God for salvation to everyone who believes, to the Jew first and also to the Greek." They claim that it really says something else. "Look," they exclaim, "the apostle begins with the Gospel!" But the introduction comes first before this. Verse 16 states the subject of the entire Epistle. In verse 18, [Paul] begins with part 1 and concludes it by saying, "What I have demonstrated so far is that 'all have sinned and fall short of the glory of God.'" Not until he launches into part 2 does he start preaching the Gospel.[10]

Luther proceeds:[11]

W² 20:1618 (cf. AE 47:114)

They do not see that St. Paul teaches the very opposite: he begins by exhibiting—first—the wrath of God from heaven. He denounces all men as sinners and as guilty in the sight of God. After that he teaches those who have been made aware of their sin how to obtain grace and how to become righteous in the sight of God. That is his powerful and plain argument in the first three chapters. It is extraordinarily blind and stupid of the Antinomians to imagine that the wrath of God is something distinct from the Law. That cannot be, for the revelation of God's wrath is the Law in its operation upon the intellect and will of man. St. Paul expresses this fact when he says, "The Law brings wrath."[12] Now, then, have they not scored a fine point by doing away with the Law, in consideration of the fact that, after all, they have to teach it when they teach the wrath of God? But they put the shoe on the wrong foot, trying to teach us Law *after* Gospel and wrath *after* grace. I am well aware of the devil's aim. I see what horrible errors he is bent on introducing by using this exegetical teeter-totter. But I cannot address them at this time.

When he calls the way the Antinomians interpret Scripture a "teeter-totter," Luther means this: the Antiniomians have "rigged" matters in such a way that they can set up Law or Gospel as they please.

---

toadstool follows the same general idea. The involvement of cat or toad is a playful literary image that is appropriate for playground equipment.

9   Latin: *lux mundi.*

10   Walther divides Romans thus: Introduction (1:1–1:15), Theme (1:16–17), Law (1:18–3:23), Gospel (3:24ff.).

11   Walther provides no transitions but jumps back and forth from the Luther text to his commentary on it. The identification of the "speaker" in the Dau edition has been used to help the reader. As Walther becomes more excited, he becomes choppier in his delivery. It seems that his words can barely keep pace with his thoughts.

12   Latin: *lex iram operatur.*

In his *Commentary on Genesis* (21:12, 16), *Luther* writes (St. Louis Ed. 1:1427f.):

> It is indeed correct to say that people must be raised up and comforted. But an additional statement must be made, showing *who* needs to be comforted. Namely, those people who, like Ishmael and his mother,[13] have been thrust out of their home and fatherland, who are nearly famished with hunger and thirst in the desert, who groan and cry to the Lord, and who are on the brink of despair. Such people are proper hearers of the Gospel.

W² 1:1427
(cf. AE 4:49)

> Hagar and Ishmael had to be sent into misery before they could be freed from their pride. Humans are by nature conceited. They say, "What wrong have I done? I have committed neither manslaughter nor adultery nor fornication nor larceny." Wrapped in these miserable rags of civil righteousness, we try to make our stand before God. That spirit of pride in ourselves must be cast out. You need the hammer of the Law to crush stony hearts. Luther continues: "Therefore, the Antinomians deserve to be hated by everybody, despite the fact that they cite us as an example in order to defend their teaching."

W² 1:1428
(cf. AE 4:50)

The Antinomians had pointed to the fact that Luther himself at first had preached nothing but comfort. They claimed that he had then departed from his former teaching and had become a legalist. That, they said, explained his opposition to them. But they misjudged Luther. When he began his public activity, he did not have to instruct the people at great length in the Law. The people were so crushed that barely any of them dared to believe that they were in a state of grace with God. For in their best efforts at preaching, the Roman priests preached the Law, placing alongside the divine Law the laws of the church and the statutes of former councils, theologians, and popes. By the time Luther was on the scene, he had passed through the same agony that had harassed the people. He knew that the best help he could provide the people in their misery was to preach the Gospel. That was the reason the entire Christian Church in those days felt as if dew from heaven or life-giving spring showers were being poured out upon them.

Accordingly, **Luther** proceeds:

> They [the Antinomians] cite us as an example to defend their teaching, while the reason we had to start our teaching with the doctrine of divine grace is as plain as daylight. The accursed pope had completely crushed the poor consciences of people with his human regulations. He had taken away all proper means for bringing aid and comfort to hearts in misery and despondency and rescuing them from despair. What else could we have done back then?

W² 1:1428–29
(cf. AE 4:50)

---

13   See Genesis 21:8–21.

W² 1:1429
(cf. AE 4:51)

If Luther had struck these miserable people still more, he would have been the meanest kind of torturer. But times have changed. In those days people dreaded the Law of God and were in anguish of hell. Now their slogan is: "Let us eat and drink, for tomorrow we die, and death ends all." Even those who are not *that* extreme imagine that things are not *so* bad. To such people you must preach the Law, or you will not accomplish anything. Luther continues: "Of course, we know, too, that people who are stuffed, delicate, and overfed must be addressed differently. But back then we were all like castaways—severely tormented. The water in our jugs was gone, that is, there was nothing left with which to comfort people. Like Ishmael, we all lay dying under a shrub."[14]

The people of Luther's day were all like Ishmael, who wanted only to lay down and die. The little bit of water that Hagar and Ishmael had taken into the desert had soon evaporated from the heat of the sun. It was all gone.

W² 1:1429–30
(cf. AE 4:51)

We needed teachers to let us behold the grace of God and to teach us how to find refreshment.

Matt. 11:28 Luther

The Antinomians insist that the preaching of repentance must begin with the doctrine of grace. I have not followed that method. For I knew that Ishmael had first been cast out and made despondent before he could hear the comforting words of the angel. Accordingly, I followed that advice and did not offer comfort to any person who had not become contrite and was not sorrowing because of his sin. These were people who had despaired of self-help. The Law had terrified them like a Leviathan that had pounced upon and almost crushed them. For these are the people for whose sake Christ came into the world, and He does not want a burning wick to be quenched (Isaiah 42:3). That is why He calls in Matthew 11:28: "Come to Me, all who labor and are heavy laden."

Ishmael had not been reduced to this state until he was expelled from home. Rather, he was proud and secure and an antinomistic epicurean.[15] Because he had been born before Isaac, he had said, "I am lord and heir in this house; Isaac and Sarah will have to yield to me." Now, should this pride of his have been praised and tolerated, or should he have been rebuked for it? If the latter, in what other way could he have been rebuked than by being driven from the house, along with his mother, and not being permitted to take anything with him out of Abraham's house except the wages of the Law: bread and water?

For that is the way the Law usually acts: it leads the thief, handcuffed, to the gallows. Before he is strangled, the Law refreshes him with a sip

---

14   See Genesis 21:15–16.

15   See "Antinomianism" and "Epicureanism" in the Glossary, pages 474, 479.

of water. But at last there is no more water, and there is nothing left to do but to die. This is all the Law ever does.

Let us learn the lesson, then, that God is an enemy of every proud person. But those who have been humbled and who have felt the power of the Law He comforts, either by men or by an angel from heaven. For He does not want such people to perish. On the other hand, He will not let the secure and proud abide in Abraham's house.

Now, a teacher and preacher must be trained in these two things. He must possess skill and experience in them. That is, he must both rebuke and crush the obstinate, and, again, he must be able to comfort those whom he has rebuked and crushed, lest they despair completely and are swallowed up by the Law.

The biggest problem with modern preaching, my dear friends, is this: these sermons lack point and purpose. And this fault is particularly noticeable in the sermons of our contemporary preachers who are believers. While unbelieving and fanatical preachers have a definite goal—too bad that it is not the right one!—believing preachers, as a rule, imagine that they have fully discharged their office as long as they have preached the Word of God.

That is about as correct a view as when a hunter imagines he has discharged his office simply by sallying forth with his loaded gun and blasting aimlessly into the forest, or as when an artilleryman thinks he has done his duty by taking up his position in the line of battle and merely firing his cannon into the blue. Just as the latter are poor hunters and soldiers, the former are poor and useless preachers because they have no plan in mind and do not take aim when preaching. While their sermons may contain beautiful thoughts, they do not have any impact. They may occasionally make the thunder of the Law roll in their sermons, yet there is no lightning that strikes. Again, they may water the garden assigned to them with the fruitful waters of the Gospel, but they pour water on the flower beds and the paths of the garden indiscriminately—and their effort is lost.

Neither Christ nor the holy apostles preached in that fashion. When they had finished preaching, every hearer knew: he meant *me*, even though the sermon had contained no personal hints or insinuations. For instance, when our Lord Christ delivered the powerful, awful parable of the murderous tenants in the vineyard,[16] the high priests and scribes confessed to themselves: "He means us."

Twelfth Evening Lecture: Dec. 12, 1884

Sermons must be targeted

---

16   See Matthew 21:33–44.

Acts 24:25   When the holy apostle Paul, on a certain occasion, preached before the immoral and unjust Governor Felix concerning righteousness and self-control and the coming judgment, Felix perceived immediately that Paul was aiming his remarks at him. He trembled, but being unwilling to be converted, he said to Paul, "Go away for the present. When I get an opportunity I will summon you." But Felix never did call Paul. He had heard the sermon tailored to his spiritual condition, and Paul's well-aimed remarks had struck home.

My dear friends, the reason unbelieving preachers are nearly always in control in the "Lutheran" congregations of our former home country Germany is unquestionably this: the sermons of the "Christian" preachers are only hot air. Unbelievers are increasing in the congregations about as fast as the "Christian" preachers are increasing—of whom there are considerably more now than when I was young. Why do those preachers not accomplish anything? Oh, would to God that these dear men had the humility to sit at Luther's feet and study his postils! They would learn how to preach with great effectiveness. For—when preached as it should be—the Word of God never returns empty.

May God help you in your future ministry not to become aimless prattlers. That way you would not have to complain that you accomplished so little. And were you to become aimless prattlers, you would have only yourselves to blame because you did not have a definite goal when preparing your sermons and because you did not reflect that "*these* are the particular people to whom I want to drive home a lesson—not this or that person whom I am going to name specifically, but persons whose condition I know to be such and such."

Have the proper target   However, while it is important that sermons need a specific goal, it is equally important that your aim be the **right one.** If you do not aim properly, your preaching will be useless—regardless of whether you preach Law or Gospel.

Thesis VIII

You are not rightly distinguishing Law and Gospel in the Word of God if you preach the Law to those who are already in terror on account of their sins or the Gospel to those who are living securely in their sins.

Editor's Note: The first seven theses in this book appear in Walther's first and second lecture series on Law and Gospel.[1] Walther added to the content and kept the central arguments unchanged.

Thesis VIII is new material that establishes the context of the remaining theses. Walther expands Theses IX–XII.[2] Thesis IX alone grows from fourteen to eighty pages of German text. Theses XIII–XXI are new. Theses XXII and XXIII are expanded from the first series.[3] The remaining theses (XXIV–XXV) are new.

The new theses are Walther's response to the Election Controversy,[4] and in some cases they represent a reworking of his thought. This is especially true for Theses XIV and XVI, which deal with conversion, repentance, and eternal predestination.[5]

Especially from this point forward, Walther becomes more critical of authors in the Lutheran tradition. There are extended discussions of theological errors, even by Lutherans, because churchmen in the Iowa and Ohio Synods had accused the Missouri Synod of taking its doctrine from theological writings, not from Scripture. Walther shows that Scripture, not the Church Fathers, really is the source of doctrine in the Missouri Synod.

In this thesis, Walther reads a letter by Luther and offers a running commentary on preaching Law and Gospel.

---

1   Walther delivered his first lecture series on Law and Gospel in 1878. He gave his second, expanded, lecture series in 1884–85. See also the preface, page xii.

2   These were Theses VIII–XI in the 1878 lectures.

3   Theses XII and XIII.

4   See the earlier section on this topic, pages lxxiii–lxxvii.

5   See Walther's extensive list of citations in Johann Wilhelm Baier, *Compendium Theologiae Positivae*, ed. C. F. W. Walther, 3 vols. (St. Louis: Concordia, 1879). The Baier *Compendium* was the scholarly dogmatics used in the Missouri Synod. Heinrich Schmid's *Doctrinal Theology of the Evangelical Lutheran Church*, translated by Henry E. Jacobs and Charles Hay, serves as a good alternative. The dogmatics text used by the laity in the early Missouri Synod was Christian Löber, *Evangelisch-lutherische Dogmatik* (St. Louis: Fr. Dette, 1872). The Baier *Compendium* formed the basis for Franz Pieper's *Christian Dogmatics*.

Recap In the opening lecture on our series of theses, we made ourselves aware of the six points of difference between Law and Gospel. [These doctrines] differ (1) regarding the way they were revealed to human beings, (2) regarding their contents, (3) regarding the promises held out by either doctrine, (4) regarding their threats, (5) regarding the function and effect of either doctrine, (6) **and regarding the persons to whom either one or the other doctrine should be preached**. As a rule, point six is named last. The reason for this is not that it is less important, for in this last point Law and Gospel are quite distinct from each other. Rather, the reason is this: the Gospel must be preached only to crushed, contrite, and miserable sinners, while the Law must be preached only to secure sinners.

Pastor, know your people Inverting this order would result in mingling both doctrines with each other, which is most dangerous. We convinced ourselves of this truth in our first lecture, namely, from the statement in 1 Timothy 1:8–10:

1 Tim. 1:8–10 Now we know that the law is good, if one uses it lawfully, understanding this, that the law is not laid down for the just but for the lawless and disobedient, for the ungodly and sinners, for the unholy and profane, for those who strike their fathers and mothers, for murderers, the sexually immoral, men who practice homosexuality, enslavers, liars, perjurers, and whatever else is contrary to sound doctrine.

The Law is not given to persons made righteous by Christ, but only to the unrighteous and disobedient. *These* are the persons to whom you must preach the Law. To preach the Law to a miserable, contrite sinner is to commit a serious sin against him, for you ought to preach the Gospel to him.

Isaiah says in chapter 61, verses 1–3:

Isa. 61:1–3 The Spirit of the Lord God is upon me, because the Lord has anointed me to bring good news to the poor; He has sent me to bind up the brokenhearted, to proclaim liberty to the captives, and the opening of the prison to those who are bound; to proclaim the year of the Lord's favor, and the day of vengeance of our God; to comfort all who mourn; to grant to those who mourn in Zion—to give them a beautiful headdress instead of ashes, the oil of gladness instead of mourning, the garment of praise instead of a faint spirit.

The phrase "day of vengeance" does not mean a day of judgment on people, for to proclaim such a day would not be proclaiming a year of mercy. Rather, the meaning is this: the Son of God means to take vengeance on *Satan*, who hurled the human race into misery. For this reason the proclamation of "the day of vengeance" is a cheering, comforting message to us. If God had *not* punished Satan because of our fall, we would be lost. If Christ had *not* redeemed us from the devil, we could not rejoice but would have to remain in sadness. The illustrations that follow in this text are to be understood figuratively, as they point to spiritual gifts of grace.

These texts show us that, according to God's Word, we should not give a single drop of evangelical consolation to those who are still living securely in their sins. On the other hand, we should not address the slightest threat or rebuke to the brokenhearted—but only promises delivering consolation and grace, forgiveness of sin and righteousness, life and salvation.

That was the practice of our Lord and Savior. One day a woman "who was a sinner" approached Him (Luke 7:37). In the presence of the self-righteous Pharisees, she kneels down, washes His feet with her hot tears, and dries them with her hair, which at an earlier point in time she—no doubt—had frequently displayed in a show of vanity. She is crushed when she comes to Jesus. There is no one to comfort her. But she turns to Him, for she realizes that where *He* is, *there* is the throne of grace.[6] What does the Lord do on that occasion? He does not speak a single word of rebuke because of the sins she had committed secretly, for she had—no doubt—lived in the worst sins of fornication. No, not a word! He simply says to her, "Your sins are forgiven." He dismisses another[7] guilty woman with the assurance: "Neither do I condemn you," adding only the brief warning: "From now on sin no more." *(Luke 7:37; John 8:11)*

This is the same way the Lord treats Zacchaeus, the dishonest tax collector, who had defrauded people throughout the land. This man probably had heard some things from Christ directly and many more things about Him third hand. Zacchaeus had come to realize that he could not continue in his sinful ways and had to change his behavior. When the Lord is about to come through town, Zacchaeus climbs into a sycamore tree because he wants to see this holy man. What does the Lord do? Catching sight of him in the tree, He calls to him, "Zacchaeus, hurry and come down, for I must stay at your house today," and He cheerfully went into the tax collector's house. *(Luke 19:5)*

Most certainly, Zacchaeus expected the Lord to go over a long list of sins with him and show him all the evil things he had done. But Jesus does nothing of the kind. On the contrary, in the house of Zacchaeus Jesus says, "Today salvation has come to this house, since he also is a son of Abraham." Then Zacchaeus says, "Behold, Lord, the half of my goods I give to the poor. And if I have defrauded anyone of anything, I will restore it fourfold."[8] *(Luke 19:9; 19:8)*

---

6   The present tense is used instead of Walther's past tense to clarify the "present" situation of the woman and Jesus over against her "past" life of sin.

7   Walther treats the passages from Luke and John as if they engaged the same event. Following the Dau edition, the two passages have been separated here.

8   Walther presents the verses out of order as he speaks about them. He stresses the basis for Luke 19:8 in verses 9–10, that "the Son of Man came to seek and to save the lost."

The Lord does not demand this of [Zacchaeus]. Rather, the man's own conscience—first alarmed and then at peace—demands that he do this joyful act of generosity to the poor. No doubt, Zacchaeus kept his promise.

Luke 15:23–24
Luther The parable of the prodigal son is another illustration. The Lord tells us that, after wasting all his possessions on harlots, the young man returns to his father with a contrite heart. The father receives his son without a single word of rebuke and even hugs and kisses him, exclaiming: "Let us be merry, for this one, my son, was dead and is alive again; he was lost and is found." A joyful feast is prepared, but not a word of rebuke is spoken.

Luke 23:41–42 This is the same attitude the Lord maintains—even while hanging on the cross. Next to Him hangs a man who has led an infamous life. The patient suffering of Christ has given him a new understanding, which he voices to the other criminal in these words: "We are receiving the due reward of our deeds; but this man has done nothing wrong." Finally, turning to the Lord, he says, "Jesus, remember me when You come into Your kingdom."

He recognizes that Jesus is the Messiah.

Luke 23:43 Note carefully that the Lord does not reply: "What! *I* am supposed to remember *you*? You, who have done so many wicked things?" No, He does not confront the man with his sins but simply says, "Truly, I say to you, today you will be with Me in Paradise."

With these examples the Lord shows us—even today—how to deal with poor sinners who may have led a shameful life yet who have become crushed and contrite, full of terror because of their sins. In these cases we should not waste any time censuring and rebuking them. Rather, we should absolve and comfort them. This is how we distinguish Gospel from the Law.

Acts 16:28, 30–31 The holy apostles distinguished Law and Gospel the same way our Lord did. I only need to recall the jailer at Philippi who was about to commit a shocking deed—the mortal sin of suicide—when Paul called to him: "Do not harm yourself, for we are all here." All night long the man had heard Paul and Silas singing praises to God. No doubt something inside the jailer was beginning to click. When he heard Paul's warning, the jailer called for a light and came in trembling. He fell down before Paul and Silas, saying, "Sirs, what must I do to be saved?" They do not give him a long list of things he has to do first, such as feeling contrite. They simply say to him, "Believe in the Lord Jesus, and you will be saved, you and your household." They simply invite him to accept the mercy of God. For that is what faith is—accepting divine grace.

Let me now cite an example from Luther's writings. This is not one of those passages in which he insists that one must proclaim the Gospel in a pure and untainted way. Rather, hear now about this particular incident that shows how Luther brought consolation to a person who had fallen into a great and serious sin.

The party in question was that splendid man Spalatin (born in 1482), who greatly contributed to the work of the Reformation. Spalatin lived at Altenburg and was ecclesiastical counselor[9] to the elector of Saxony,[10] as well as a close friend of Luther's. Now, along with some people, Spalatin had advised a certain pastor to marry the stepmother of his deceased wife. This marriage was absolutely contrary to God's Word, and Spalatin's advice was all the more horrifying because the apostle Paul, in dealing with a similar offense in 1 Corinthians 5, had declared that such fornication was shocking even to the Gentiles. When the truth finally dawned on our good friend Spalatin, he refused to be comforted. Luther learned that he had fallen into a deep depression. Nothing would comfort him. Spalatin imagined that no consolation in Scripture could apply to a man such as he—even though he knew the Word of God so well and had taken so much consolation from it.

How did **Luther** proceed to comfort this man? He wrote him a letter, which began as follows (St. Louis Ed. 10:1728–33):

> Grace and peace from God in Christ and the consolations of the Holy Spirit to my worthy master in Christ, George Spalatin, superintendent of the churches in Meissen, most faithful pastor of Altenburg, the beloved in the Lord. Amen.

W² 10:1728

> My dearest Spalatin, I heartily sympathize with you and earnestly pray that our Lord Jesus Christ would strengthen you and give you a cheerful heart. I would like to know and am making diligent inquiries to find out what your trouble may be or what has caused your breakdown. Some people are telling me that this is nothing more than depression and heaviness of heart, caused by the affair of a pastor who was publicly united in marriage to the stepmother of his deceased wife. If this is true, I beg you most urgently not to become self-centered and listen to the thoughts and sensations of your own heart, but to listen to me, your brother, who is speaking to you in the name of Christ. Otherwise, your desperation will grow beyond endurance and will kill you. For St. Paul says, 2 Corinthians 7:10, "Worldly grief produces death." I have often passed through the same experience and

2 Cor. 7:10 Luther

---

9   German: *Kirchenrat*, a church overseer who advises a prince.

10   The 1356 Golden Bull, a decree of the Diet of Nuremberg under Holy Roman Emperor Charles IV, established the imperial Electoral College. The "secular" prince-electors included the king of Bohemia, the Count-Palatine of the Rhine, the prince of Saxony, and the margrave of Brandenburg. The "churchly" electors included the prince-bishops of Cologne, Mainz, and Trier.

witnessed the same in 1540—in the case of Master Philip[11]—who was nearly consumed by heaviness of heart and desperation on account of the landgrave's affair.[12] However, Christ used my mouth to raise him up again.

I say this on the assumption that you have sinned and are partly to blame for the previously mentioned marriage, because you approved it.

Luther says thus: I have to admit, you have committed a serious sin in this matter. Spalatin approved the marriage and advised that the marriage should be contracted.

W² 10:1728–29

Yes, I would go even further and say: Even if you had committed more numerous and greater sins in this particular instance (or in other instances) than did Manasseh,[13] the king of Judah—whose offenses and crimes could not be purified throughout the entire time of his posterity, down to the time when Jerusalem was destroyed—your offense is very light, because it concerns a worldly interest and can be easily cured. Nevertheless I repeat, granted you are to blame, are you going to worry yourself to death over it and—by killing yourself— commit an even more horrible sin against God?

What Luther means to say is this: This marriage can be dissolved, for it is not legitimate. It would be a greater sin to doubt the mercy of God than to have advised this marriage. For to doubt God's mercy is always the most horrible sin, because it means that we make God out to be a liar.

W² 10:1729

Luther writes: "It is bad enough that you made a mistake in this matter. But do not let that sin stick in your mind—get rid of it. Quit your despair, which is a far greater sin." Namely, that he will not let go of this grief. Again, Luther:

W² 10:1729–30;
Ezek. 33:11 Luther

Listen to the blessed consolation that the Lord offers you through the prophets, which He speaks in Ezekiel 33, verse 11: "As truly as I live, I have no pleasure in the death of the sinner, but that the sinner repent

---

11 Luther habitually refers to Philip Melanchthon as "Master Philip" because the latter held only a master's degree. Nor was Melanchthon ever ordained into the Office of the Holy Ministry.

12 Philip, landgrave of Hessen (1504–67), had ruled Hessen since 1519. Married in 1523 at the age of nineteen to Christine of Saxony, Philip started committing adultery within the first year of marriage. In 1526, Luther rejected Philip's proposal to commit bigamy. Philip saw a new solution, however, when Melanchthon proposed a morganatic marriage (see the Glossary, page 482) as a means to solve the situation of Henry VIII, Catherine of Aragon, and Anne Boleyn. In 1539, Luther and Melanchthon approved in principle such a marriage for Philip, not knowing that Philip had already picked Margarethe von der Saale. Philip of Hessen married Margarethe on March 4, 1540. This affair weakened the Protestant cause and strengthened the power of Emperor Charles V.

13 See, for example, 2 Kings 21.

and live." Do you think that the Lord's hand is too short (Isaiah 59:1)? Or that He has forgotten to be gracious and has withdrawn His compassion from you alone (Psalm 77:10)?[14] Or are you the first man to sin so awfully that there is no longer a High Priest who would be able to sympathize with your weaknesses (Hebrews 4:15)? Or are you surprised that a person living this life in the flesh—with innumerable arrows of so many devils flying about him—is occasionally wounded and knocked down?

It seems to me, my dear Spalatin, that you are not very experienced in battling sin, an evil conscience, the Law, and the terrors of death. Or that Satan has removed from your vision and memory every consolation that you have ever read in the Scriptures. . . . Back when you were not afflicted, you were well comforted and knew very well what the office and benefits of Christ are. It seems to me that the devil has now plucked from your heart all the beautiful Christian sermons concerning the grace and mercy of God in Christ with which you used to teach, warn, and comfort others with a cheerful spirit and great, uplifting courage.

Or could it be that until now you have been only a trifling sinner, conscious only of unimportant and insignificant faults and weaknesses?

Luther offers only two reasons to explain why Spalatin refuses to be comforted. Either Spalatin has until now failed to understand adequately his misery and wretchedness under sin—and thus is [for the first time] aware of the fact that he is a great sinner by nature. As such, his great fall *had* to occur before the moment when his eyes were opened to these facts. Or, second, perhaps Satan hid every consolation from Spalatin's sight. In effect, Luther is saying to Spalatin: Had you fully realized the awful corruption of your heart in its relation to God, you would not be so inconsolable, for you would say to yourself: Alas! The fountain is so polluted that filth *has* to flow from it.

But let us get back to Luther, who writes: "Therefore, my faithful request and warning would be that you would join and associate with us—all of us coarse and hardened sinners." Luther wanted Spalatin to associate with people who were truly coarse sinners, truly condemned, and apparently Luther thought that he, too, belonged to that group. W² 10:1730

Luther continues: "By no means must you make Christ seem unimportant and trifling to us, as though He could only be our helper if we wanted to rid ourselves of imaginary, nominal, and childish sins." If we make our sins look

---

14 According to Luther's 1545 German translation, this is Psalm 77:10, which corresponds to Psalm 77:9 in English Bibles.

small, we make *Christ* look small. That would be the same thing as saying: He is capable of forgiving small sins but not big ones.

Again, Luther: "No, no! That would not be good for us. Rather, He must be a Savior and Redeemer of real, great, serious, and damnable transgressions and iniquities, yes, of the very greatest and most shocking sins—in short, of the grand total of all our sins." Christ can no longer help a person who has committed such a great sin yet is unconcerned about it. But if that person actually worries about his sin, his help has already come.

Thus Luther: "Dr. Staupitz comforted me on a certain occasion when I was a patient in the same hospital, suffering from the same affliction that you are." Luther went to Dr. Staupitz[15] to grieve over his distress. Luther had never committed any coarse or public sins. It was all about the sinful condition of his heart. God granted Luther an extraordinary degree of understanding about human corruption. "'Aha!' Staupitz said. 'You are trying to be a pretend sinner and, accordingly, expect Christ to be a pretend Savior.'" I do not want a pretend Savior; that is why I should not be surprised that I am a real true sinner.

W² 10:1730 Get used to believing that Christ is a *real* Savior and that you are a *real* sinner. For God is neither joking nor is He dealing in imaginary affairs, but He was deadly serious when He sent His own Son into the world and sacrificed Him for our sake, etc. (Romans 8:32; John 3:16). Satan—who is alive and well—has snatched these and similar reflections, which come from soothing Bible passages, from your memory. Therefore, you are not able to recall them in your present great anguish and depression. For God's sake, then, turn your ears my way, brother, and hear me cheerfully sing. I am your brother. At this time I am not afflicted with the desperation and depression that is oppressing you. Therefore, I am strong in my faith. The reason I am strong in the faith—while you are weak and harried and harassed by the devil—is that you may lean on me for support until you regain your old strength.

Ps. 118:3; Then you can look the devil in the eye and cheerfully sing: "I was
Acts 3:6 Luther pushed hard, to the point of falling, but the LORD helped me" (Psalm 118:13). Imagine now that I am St. Peter, extending my hand to you and saying to you, "In the name of Jesus, rise up and walk!" (Acts 3:6). My dear Spalatin, listen and believe the words of Christ that He is speaking to you through me.

---

15 Johann von Staupitz, head of the Augustinian monks in Germany, mentored Luther, pointing him to the consolation of the Means of Grace.

Christ is speaking through me because I am proclaiming His word to you. Luther writes: "For I know I am not mistaken." In this, Luther is not referring to himself, but he says this because he is proclaiming God's Word to Spalatin.

> Nor is the devil talking through me, but it is Christ who speaks to you through me (because I am proclaiming the Word of Christ to you). He bids you to obey and trust your brother who is of the same household of faith. It is Christ who absolves you from this and all your sins, and we[16] share your sin by helping you bear it.

W² 10:1730–31

When a preacher absolves a person who has confessed his sin to him, he takes that sin of the other person upon his own conscience. He can cheerfully do this, however, because the party who came to him to confess perhaps the most horrible sins came with a crushed heart. That preacher may cheerfully pronounce Absolution to such a person and say: "I will assume the responsibility for what I am doing, for I know that, on the great Day of Judgment, Christ will say to me: 'You did the right thing. For that person came to you with a broken conscience, and the only correct thing to do was to administer the Gospel to him.'"

> Therefore see to it that you accept and claim for yourself the comfort we are offering you. For this comfort is true, certain, and reliable, since the Lord has commanded us to communicate it to you and has invited you to accept it from us. For even though we are cut to the quick to see you in such awful distress because of your deep depression, it displeases God much more to behold it, "for He is gracious, merciful, patient, and abounding in steadfast kindheartedness; and He relents over disaster" (Joel 2:13).

W² 10:1731;
Joel 2:13 Luther

You should share our sins, but you should also share our consolation. God does not like it when someone is crushed[, nor does He like it] when someone tries hard to remain stuck in that desperation and repentance. No, when the hammer of the Law strikes a blow, then we should flee from Moses and run to Christ. That is the right way to go about it.

> Therefore, please do not turn away from the one who is coming to comfort you, to announce the will of God to you, and who hates and condemns your desperation and depression as a trial of Satan. Do not by any means allow the devil to portray Christ to you differently than what He really is. Believe Scripture, which testifies that "the reason the Son of God appeared was to destroy the works of the devil" (1 John 3:8).

W² 10:1731;
1 John 3:8 Luther

---

16   In Luther's German original, he switches from using the singular "I" to the royal "we" because Christ Himself is speaking the Absolution through Luther. See also SC V (*Concordia*, 341). Luther remains careful to refer to Spalatin using the polite forms of his day: "you" and "yours" (German: *Ihr, Euch, Euer*).

Your depression is a work of the devil, which Christ wants to destroy, if you will only let Him. You have had your fill of anguish. You have sorrowed enough. You have exceeded your penance. (Therefore, do not refuse my consolation; let me help you, etc.)

Luther's exegesis of 1 John 3:8 is beautiful. The phrase "works of the devil" is usually interpreted to mean horrible and coarse sins, but in this phrase Luther interprets doubt and depression as being the most serious sin. Christ did not come to fill us with sadness but with peace and joy in the Holy Spirit.

W² 10:1731

Luther writes: "Behold my faithful heart, dear Spalatin, in the way I am dealing with you and speaking to you. I would consider it the greatest favor I have ever received from you if you would allow the comfort that I am offering you—or, rather, the Absolution, pardon, and restoration of our Lord Christ—to remain in you." This is the gratitude that Luther would like to have for his efforts. Luther sat down and most certainly was crying to the Lord as he composed this letter. In fact, he was even on the road when he wrote it because it was dated in Zeitz.[17]

W² 10:1731–33;
Ps. 147:11; 34:19;
51:17 Luther

If you do this, you will—once you recover—be forced to confess that you offered the most pleasing and acceptable sacrifice to the Lord by your obedience. For Psalm 147:11 states: "The LORD takes pleasure in those who fear Him, in those who hope in His love." (And again, in Psalm 34:19: "The LORD is near to the brokenhearted and saves the crushed in spirit."[18] And again in Psalm 51:17: "The sacrifices that please God are a broken spirit; a broken and contrite heart, O God, You will not despise.")

Therefore, let the accursed devil and his desperation scamper away like a whipped dog. He wanted to make me sad on your account; he wanted to dash my joy in the Lord. Yes, if he could, he would swallow us all up in one gulp. But may Christ, our Lord, rebuke and punish him, and may He strengthen, comfort, and preserve you by His Spirit! Amen. Comfort your wife with these and your own even more effective words. I do not have the time to write her a letter as well. Zeitz, August 21, A.D. 1544. Yours, Martin Luther.

---

17   From 1542 until 1548, a power struggle between Emperor Charles V and Prince-Elector John Frederick resulted in conflict over the bishopric of Naumburg. Zeitz, a town south of Leipzig, was located in that bishopric. Charles supported the tolerant, moderate Roman Catholic nominee for bishop, Julius von Pflug (1499–1564). John Frederick supported Nikolaus von Amsdorf. Luther went to Zeitz in 1544 to settle a clergy dispute on behalf of Amsdorf.

18   According to Luther's 1545 German translation, this is Psalm 34:19, which corresponds to Psalm 34:18 in English Bibles.

I wanted to share this letter with you in its entirety, hoping that it might please you so much that you would frequently reread it. Think of it especially whenever a sorrowing, miserable sinner approaches you in your pastoral capacity. Read this letter as a preparation for the Gospel that you need to administer to such a sinner. Luther admits that Spalatin has sinned, but [he] realizes that at that particular moment he must not, for God's sake, say anything to Spalatin that might pierce his friend's heart like an arrow.

Let me read you another letter that Luther wrote as early as 1516. He wrote it to an Augustinian friar named Spenlein,[19] who was in great agony concerning his state of grace. Spenlein had been a fellow monk of Luther's in the Augustinian monastery at Wittenberg. Everyone familiar with Luther's writings agrees that this letter is most excellent. We can only marvel that Luther could write such a letter even at such an early a date. It is pure gold, pure honey. **Luther** writes (St. Louis Ed. 21a:20–21):

> I wish to know the condition of your soul, namely, whether you have at last come to hate your *own* righteousness and, instead, desire to rejoice in the righteousness of Christ and to be of good cheer because of it. For these days, people are desperately tempted to be arrogant, particularly people who work mightily to be righteous and godly and who do not know of the immaculate righteousness of God that is freely given us in Christ. For this reason they keep searching for something good in themselves, until they become confident that they can pass muster before God as people who are properly dressed with virtuous and meritorious deeds—all of which is impossible. While you were with us, you held this opinion or, rather, this error—just as I did. For my part, I am still wrestling with this error and am not quite rid of it yet.
>
> Therefore, my dear brother, learn Christ—Christ crucified. Learn to sing praises to Him and to despair completely of your own works.

W² 21a:20–21
(cf. AE 48:12)

What Luther is saying is this: Do not be surprised that you can find nothing worthy in yourself and only sin. You should learn to sing praises to Christ and to completely despair in yourself—a person in whom one can find nothing good, unless God once did something good in you. You should not try to acquire such righteousness that you would no longer appear to be a sinner. It would be disgraceful to act like that, even if you knew the Word of God. That would be to deny the Savior.

---

19   George Spenlein, an Augustinian monk, had been a friar in Wittenberg since 1512. Spenlein was transferred to Memmingen, and he asked Luther to sell the belongings that he could not take with him and send the money later. Luther gives an account of what he received for the belongings as well as addressing Spenlein's worries. Spenlein would later quit the Augustinians and become a Lutheran pastor.

W² 21a:21
(cf. AE 48:12–13)

Say to Him: You, my Lord Jesus, are my righteousness. I am Your sin. You have taken from me what is mine and have given me what is Yours. You became what You were not and made me to be what I was not.

Beware of your ceaseless working for righteousness, which is so great that you no longer appear as a sinner in your own eyes and do not want to be a sinner. **For Christ lives only in sinners.**

Walch[20] comments that it is obvious what this means: Bold sinners do not acknowledge that they are sinners. What others call "sin" they call "human weakness" or a "natural, inborn tendency." Their occasional display of godliness is complete hypocrisy. They may say, "We are such poor sinners," but they do not mean that statement in the scriptural sense. They say, "Well, we cannot help it that we are weak mortals," but at the same time one is a drunkard, another a fornicator, the third a thief, etc. All these vices are supposed to be mere *weaknesses*? Truly, Christ lives only in sinners who regard themselves to be sinners. Christ first lived among the angels, then He wanted to live with sinners as well. That is why He came down to this earth.

W² 21a:21
(cf. AE 48:13)

Luther continues: "For He came down from heaven—where He had lived among the righteous—to now live among sinners. Think about His love and you will realize His sweetest consolation. For if our consciences could find peace when we struggle and suffer on our own, **then why did He die?**"

What a wonderful statement! Anyone who is troubled on account of his sins is a fool for not immediately taking refuge with Christ and for imagining that his evil conscience proves that he may not come to God. No. **This** is what an evil conscience indicates: You *should* come to Jesus. Then you will receive a cheerful conscience, causing you to praise God with a joyful heart when you rise in the morning and lie down to rest at night.

For why did Christ die for you?

In the same way, when you have committed this, that, or the other sin and are confused about how to find a way out of your sin, do not try to find that way yourself. Go to the One who alone knows the way. Go to Jesus.

W² 21a:21
(cf. AE 48:13)

So Luther: "Therefore you should find peace in Him only when you completely despair in yourself and your works." This is a remarkable statement of Luther's: "only when you completely despair in yourself"! Yet it is true! If a poor sinner looks to himself, he will despair. But if He looks at Jesus, he will be made confident.

---

20 Johann Georg Walch (1693–1775) was a professor of rhetoric, poetry, and theology at the University of Jena. He supervised the Halle edition of Luther's works (1740–53). In his research and writing, Walther primarily used the Halle edition (W¹).

Luther writes: "Learn from Him, too, that He received you and took your sins upon Himself and made His righteousness your own. In the same way, have strong faith in Him, as you should. Because whoever does not believe this is accursed!" W² 21a:21 (cf. AE 48:13)

This is the most beautiful Gospel that I am able to preach, because it says: Christ came for everyone. He took upon Himself everyone's sin. He calls everyone to Himself. Everyone should believe in Him. Everyone should be happy and be certain that all their sins are forgiven. And everyone should be certain that when they die, they will die in a blessed state.

To achieve worthy results, my friends, a preacher needs to preach the Word of God in its truth and purity—without any changes whatsoever. This is the first and foremost requirement for success. Some preachers in our day stifle certain teachings that are offensive to worldly people. They do this with the good intention of not shocking their hearers. But this is a great mistake. You cannot make a person a true Christian by speech-making—be it ever so lofty or passionate—but only by the Word of God. Only the Word of God produces repentance, faith, and godliness and preserves people therein to the end. **Thirteenth Evening Lecture:** Jan. 9, 1885

The second requirement for effective preaching is not only that the preacher himself would believe the things he preaches to others but also that his heart would be full of the truths that he proclaims, so that he would enter his pulpit with the passionate desire to pour out his heart to his hearers. In the best sense of the word, he must be "high-spirited" regarding his topic. Then his hearers will have the impression that the words shooting from his lips are flames from a soul on fire. However, that does not mean that the Word of God must receive its power and life from the living faith of the preacher, for the Lord clearly says, "The words that I have spoken to you are spirit and life" (John 6:63). John 6:63

Moreover, the writer of the Epistle to the Hebrews says, "For the word of God is living and active, sharper than any two-edged sword, piercing to the division of soul and of spirit, of joints and of marrow, and discerning the thoughts and intentions of the heart" (Hebrews 4:12). But when a preacher proclaims what he has often experienced in his own heart, he will easily find the right words to speak convincingly to his hearers. When his words come from the heart, they, in turn, penetrate the heart of his hearers, according to that old saying: "It is the **heart** that makes eloquent."[21] This is not the fake Heb. 4:12

---

21 Latin: *Pectus disertum facit.*

eloquence gained in speech class, but the healthy *spiritual* skill of reaching the heart of hearers.

For when your hearers feel that a preacher is deadly serious, they feel drawn by an irresistible force to pay the closest attention to what the preacher is teaching in his sermon. That is the reason sometimes many simple, less-gifted, and less-learned preachers accomplish more than the most highly gifted and deeply learned men.

My dear friends, first and foremost, I would wish that you all were real Christians, filled with burning passion for the truth. That is the main tool you need, over time, to become powerful preachers—preachers whose spirit grabs hearers by an irresistible force, as the example of the apostles demonstrates. The people could not tell why, but the preaching of these simple men made a most powerful impression on them.

Far from suggesting that great gifts and thorough theological learning are not of tremendous value, I would rather claim the opposite to be true. For if you add great gifts and thorough learning to the living faith of a preacher, he will eventually become a mighty, efficient tool in the hands of God.

God does not relegate all our natural skills and whatever we might have gained by our personal enthusiasm to some corner when we enter the ministry. Rather, these skills are purified and pressed into His service. That is why great things have taken place and great results have been achieved in the kingdom of God whenever great gifts and thorough learning have been coupled with living faith. First and foremost, I would point to the apostle Paul, who was the only scholar among the apostles. According to his own testimony, he worked more but also accomplished more than the rest. Another example is Luther, the great reformer. If he had merely had a heroic faith and had not at the same time been a great, highly gifted, and learned man, he would never have become the reformer who gloriously accomplished the greatest work of his age.

So, during this period of your studies, I would urge you to work day and night to get the best grades in every area of theological knowledge, not only in dogmatic theology but also in practical theology.[22] I wish you the best, and I pray to the Lord that your wishes may be granted. If they are, you will be living proof of the importance of joining these two factors—living faith and natural skills—with faithful and diligent study. That will be enough for now on this subject.

Let us move on to another point, but do not regard my remarks until now as only an introduction. No, it was merely a preamble. I wish my words—even though they were spoken in weakness—would find a permanent place in your heart. May God the Holy Spirit grant it! For much, my friends, *very* much

---

22 See the definition of "theology" in the Glossary, page 487.

depends not only on your lifting high the light when you enter upon your public activity but also on being lights yourselves. This is your task—not by immediate but rather by mediate illumination.[23] Let us now move on to our topic.

We finished considering the first part of Thesis VIII, which declares that the Word of God is not rightly distinguished when the Law is preached to those in *terror* of sin. Let us now continue on to the second part of the thesis, which states that the Word of God is not rightly distinguished if the Gospel is preached to those *secure* in their sins.

The latter error is as dangerous as the former. Incalculable damage is done if the consolations of the Gospel are offered to secure sinners or if you preach to a crowd in such a way that secure sinners in the audience would imagine that the comfort of the Gospel is meant for them. That would be the preacher's fault.

By doing this, a preacher could conceivably preach whole crowds of people into hell instead of into heaven. No, the Gospel is not intended for secure sinners. We cannot, of course, prevent secure sinners from coming into our churches and hearing the Gospel. However, it is up to the preacher's skill to offer the entire comfort of the Gospel in all its sweetness in such a way that secure sinners would realize that this comfort is not intended for them. The whole manner of the preacher's presentation must make them realize that fact. Let me offer you a few proof texts from Scripture for my claims.

In Matthew 7:6 our Lord says to His disciples: "Do not give dogs what is holy, and do not throw your pearls before pigs, lest they trample them underfoot and turn to attack you." A remarkable saying! What does "holy" mean? Nothing other than the Word of Christ. What does "pearls" mean? The consolation of the Gospel, with the grace, righteousness, and salvation that it proclaims. We should not speak these things to dogs (that is, to enemies of the Gospel) nor to pigs (that is, to those who want to remain in their sins and are seeking their heaven and their bliss in the filth of their sins). | Matt. 7:6

Isaiah 26:10 reads: "If favor is shown to the wicked, he does not learn righteousness; in the land of uprightness he deals corruptly and does not see the majesty of the LORD." It is quite useless to offer mercy to the godless. Either they imagine that they do not need grace or that they already have obtained it. They claim that the unimportant sins of which they are guilty were forgiven long ago, and that grass has grown over it.[24] We must not preach the Gospel to | Isa. 26:10

---

23 In this context, "immediate" means when God directly appears in a vision, while "mediate" refers to the action of the Holy Spirit through Scripture, the Word of God.

24 This is a European expression that refers to ruins and burial mounds that are so ancient they have become part of the landscape because grass has grown over the ruins. A pithy equivalent would be "water (or whiskey) under the bridge."

such people. In other words, we should not offer them grace—for that is what preaching the Gospel means—because they will not benefit from it.

The devil is capable of binding people not only with the ropes of filthy and coarse sins but also with the delicate threads of sins such as pride, envy, and lovelessness. A wicked person who wants to remain in his sins—whether they be those coarse or refined sins—such a wicked person, Isaiah says, does "not see the majesty of the LORD." They do not discern what a great treasure is being offered them. They do not understand the doctrine of salvation by grace. Either they reject it, or they shamefully misapply it. They think: "If mere faith is all that I need for salvation, then my sins, too, are forgiven. I can remain as I am, and I will still go to heaven. I, too, believe in my Lord Jesus Christ." Preachers who cause secure sinners to misapply the Gospel load upon themselves great guilt and responsibility before God.

Prov. 27:7   Proverbs 27:7 reads: "One who is full loathes honey, but to one who is hungry everything bitter is sweet." If you place honey before a person who has eaten his fill, even this delicious food will make him sick, whereas a hungry person will enjoy it. The Gospel—which is sweeter than honey and the honeycomb—should be preached only to hungry souls. The "bitter" thing—that is, the Law—is for those who are not hungry.

In the first place, we can model our preaching on our dear Lord Jesus Christ. If we study His behavior in the Gospel records, we will find that whenever He meets secure sinners—such as the self-righteous Pharisees of His day—He does not have a drop of comfort to offer them. Rather, He calls them serpents and a vipers' brood, denounces a tenfold woe against them, reveals their nasty hypocrisy, sends them to hell, and tells them that they will not escape eternal damnation.[25] Although He knows that these very same people will nail Him to the cross, He fearlessly tells them the truth.

That is a very important point for us preachers to note. Even though we know in advance that we will share the same fate of our Lord Jesus, we must preach the Law in all its severity to secure, reckless sinners, to hypocrites, and to people who are our enemies.

Now, I do not mean to say that we would be able to endure what our Lord endured. We cannot drink the cup that He drank. But we *will* feel the hatred of people. They will either oppose us openly or continually plot against us in secret. There is no way out of this difficult sitation. Whenever a preacher faces these kinds of people, he dares not preach anything other than the Law to them. Moreover, when he preaches before a crowd, his hearers need to get the impression that what he says does not apply to all of them indiscriminately, but only to the would-be righteous—those who claim the Gospel for themselves.

---

25 See Matthew 23.

True, our Lord says, "Come to Me, **all**," but He immediately adds: "who   Matt. 11:28
labor and are heavy laden." Thus He serves notice upon secure sinners that
He is not inviting *them*. They would only mock Him if He were to lay His
spiritual, heavenly treasures before them.

On a certain occasion a rich young man[26] approached Jesus and said to   Mark 10:17
Him: "Good Teacher, what must I do to inherit eternal life?" Jesus rejected the
title "Good Teacher" because it would have put Him in the same class with the
self-righteous young man, who considered *himself* to be a "good teacher." The
rich young man was not sincere when he addressed the Lord in this manner.
If he had regarded Christ as the Son of God and the Savior of the world, if he
had believed in Christ and **for that reason** had called Him "Good Teacher," it
would have been quite proper. But because he merely meant to offer the Lord
a bit of flattery, Christ declined the title.

And what does the Lord do next? He asks the young man a counterques-   Luke 10:25–27
tion: "What is written in the Law? How do you read it?" Then the young man
replies with great passion, quoting the main passages of the Law, and says,
"You shall love the Lord your God with all your heart and with all your soul
and with all your strength and with all your mind, and your neighbor as
yourself."

And the Lord says, "You have answered correctly; do this, and you will   Luke 10:28;
live." Oh, the young man replies, "All these I have kept." What the young man   Matt. 19:20
means to say is this: "If You have no other teachings to propose, You are not
as wise as some consider You to be. What You just told me I have known for
a long time. I thought I would get all kinds of new teachings from You. What
else do I need?"

How does Christ answer the young man's last question? Does He say,
"What you lack is faith"? By no means. Since He is dealing with a miserable,
secure, and self-righteous person, He does not preach one word of Gospel to
him. Even though He knows in advance—by reason of His omniscience—
that all His efforts will have no success, He feels that He must first bring the
young man to a realization of his spiritual misery.

God, in His love, does many things that to us may seem useless so that   Matt. 19:21–22
on Judgment Day no one would have an excuse for not coming to faith in
Christ. God will say to many, "This and that I did for you, but you rejected
Me." Accordingly, Jesus says to the rich young man, "If you would be perfect,
go, sell what you possess and give to the poor, and you will have treasure in
heaven; and come, follow Me." Now the record states: "When the young man
heard this he went away sorrowful, for he had great possessions."

---

26   Walther cites Luke 10:28–29, adding elements from Mark 10:17–22 and Matthew 19:16–22.
      Walther is not trying to misquote Scripture. Rather, he clearly is speaking from memory.
      He remembers a particular Bible story and constructs a kind of Gospel harmony.

He departed with a guilty conscience, which, no doubt, told him: "That is, in fact, a different doctrine from the one I used to hear. What He is telling me I cannot do. I have become too greatly attached to my possessions. I would rather give up my fellowship with Him than to do what He says. I am not going to roam around the country with Him like a beggar." Probably his conscience also testified to him that, according to the teaching of Christ, he was damned, that he was on his way to hell. That was the effect that the Lord had intended to produce when He dealt with the young man.

Whether he was converted later, we do not know, nor is that relevant at this time. The point is that here we have an example that guides us when we are dealing with people who are still secure in their sins and self-righteous. True, we cannot give orders as did Christ, the Lord of lords. But there are enough questions that we can ask to make this kind of person realize that he is still deeply steeped in sins and a lost creature.

We find that the apostles did the same. First they preached the Law—and with such force that their hearers were cut to the heart.

Acts 2:37–38 Let us examine Acts 2. In his first Pentecost sermon, Peter begins by accusing his hearers of murdering Christ. And that charge hits home. They are frightened and ask, "Brothers, what shall we do?" And then the apostle Peter says to them, "Repent and be baptized every one of you in the name of Jesus Christ for the forgiveness of your sins, and you will receive the gift of the Holy Spirit." Preaching the Gospel to them, he tells them that all their sins can be forgiven—even the very worst ones.

Thus we see the same among the apostles everywhere—not only in Jerusalem but also in Athens, Corinth, Ephesus, and elsewhere. Wherever they were, they preached repentance first, and then faith. For they knew that wherever they were—as a rule—they were facing secure sinners who had not yet realized their most miserable, sinful condition. However, they applied the Law sternly, both to those who had not yet heard anything about the Christian religion and also to those who pretended to be Christians but were still living securely in their sins.

2 Cor. 12:20–21 There is also a remarkable example in the two concluding chapters of 2 Corinthians. The holy apostle writes: "For I fear that perhaps when I come I may find you not as I wish, and that you may find me not as you wish—that perhaps there may be quarreling, jealousy, anger, hostility, slander, gossip, conceit, and disorder" (2 Corinthians 12:20). What he means to say is this: "You probably think that I am going to preach the Gospel to you. But will you be surprised when I come and you hear me preach!" In his preaching, Paul does not even mention swindling, fornication, theft, blasphemy, and murder. Rather, he addresses the habits of all sinners, including those of hypocrites, whom you can find in every Christian congregation. Just look at verse 21: "I

fear that when I come again my God may humble me before you, and I may
have to mourn over many of those who sinned earlier and have not repented
of the impurity, sexual immorality, and sensuality that they have practiced."

To be fair, at that time those people were not living in fornication and
uncleanness, but they had at an earlier point in time. Because they had
become Christians only by a process of reasoning, they had not truly repented
of their sins. They professed the Christian religion with their lips, but their
faith was not faith of the heart. They had not been regenerated and renewed
by the Holy Spirit. Moving on, the apostle says: "This is the third time I am
coming to you. Every charge must be established by the evidence of two or
three witnesses. I warned those who sinned before and all the others, and I
warn them now while absent, as I did when present on my second visit, that if
I come again **I will not spare them**" (2 Corinthians 13:1–2).

2 Cor. 13:1–2

Here we have an excellent example for a preacher to follow. If people begin
to engage in all manner of sinful practices without fear of punishment and
imagine that everybody will regard them as good Christians as long as they
attend church and go to Communion, the pastor must say to himself: "It is
time for me to lay down the Law to my people. After all, I do not want to live
in careless ease while my flock goes to hell. . . . I certainly do not want them
to accuse me on the Last Day, saying: It is your fault that we have to suffer
eternal torment."

Presumably, the apostle concluded that, when he resumed his ministry in
the Corinthian congregation, he would still find secure members whom he
would once again have to cut to the heart. He did not care whether the people
would turn against him and become his enemies in that godless environment—much like Sodom.[27] He sent advance notice to Corinth that he was not
going to spare them. He would tell them to their faces that their fate would
be eternal damnation unless they repented. He would rebuke them as people
who had been unmasked as habitual sinners against their consciences, while
claiming to be Christians.

Accordingly, we must not preach the Gospel but rather the *Law* to secure
sinners. We must preach them into hell before we can preach them into
heaven. By our preaching our hearers must be brought to the point of death
before they can be restored to life by the Gospel. They must be made to realize
that they are terminally ill before they can be restored to health through the
Gospel. First, expose their so-called righteousness, so they may see of what
filthy rags it consists. Second, by preaching the Gospel, cloak them in the
righteousness of Christ. Make them admit from the heart: "I am a lost and
condemned person," as the Creed puts it,[28] so that—in the next step—you can

**Against
historical faith**

---

27 See Genesis 18:20–19:29.
28 See *Concordia*, 329.

make them joyfully exclaim: "Oh, blessed person that I am!" We must first reduce them to nothing by means of the Law. Then we have to make them into people to the glory of God's grace by means of the Gospel.

Of course, we cannot prescribe to sinners the **degree** of their repentance,[29] for an examination of the Holy Scriptures on this point will reveal that every person whose conversion is recorded there has a different degree of repentance. But every one of them must experience something of the bitterness of repentance, or he would never begin to enjoy the sweetness of the Gospel. **When God leads such people to faith and salvation—without letting them experience a lot of fear and terror—He always compensates for that later.** So even though God in His mercy sometimes "fast-tracks" people to faith and joy in their Savior, He sometimes by that same mercy, at a later point, drowns them in genuine sorrow over their sins, so they do not fall away from the faith. The Lord describes these "fast-track believers" as follows: the seed of the divine Word immediately takes root in them, causing faith to spring up in them rapidly. They receive the Word with joy but do not profit from it. Unless the Law has pulverized the rocky places in their hearts, the sweet Gospel is of no benefit to them.[30]

It is indeed a common observation that all those who have passed through great and deep sorrow at the beginning of their faith life become the best and strongest Christians. In the same way, those who in their youth were deeply submerged in floods of anguish and sorrow on account of their salvation turn out to be the best pastors and theologians.

Just look at our beloved Luther. The Reformation of the Church—the greatest task that anyone could have accomplished in that age—had been entrusted to him. Without giving Luther any forewarning, God had prepared him for that task—not only by making him very smart, or by filling him with a keen knowledge of men, or by immediately giving him a very clear understanding of the Word of God, for at first Luther did not understand the Bible all that well, nor did he really grasp it, until the Holy Spirit kindled the true light in his soul. Rather, God forced Luther to his knees in anguish and terror—in fact, so much so that he was constantly in danger of yielding to blasphemous thoughts. That, however, was the proper school from which the future reformer needed to graduate.

---

29   Walther uses the term *penitence* or *penance* (German: *Buße*; Latin: *poenitentia*), which means more than just "repentance" in the sense of "feeling sorry." The term arises from ancient legal codes and includes both sorrow for sin as well as an earnest desire to make amends. Here Walther stresses that, apart from Christ, no one can fulfill the Law and be righteous before God. No one can make amends apart from Christ.

30   With his reference to "rocky places," Walther suggests the parable of the soils found in Mark 4:3–20; Luke 8:5–15. He sees the application of Law and Gospel as the way to move from the poor kind of soil to the good kind.

Another example is that of Flacius,[31] who, beyond question, was the greatest theologian of his time—second only to Luther. Too bad [Flacius] fell into error at a later point in time and would not accept correction. For a long time, he, too, was at the edge of despair. Luther ministered to him until he was in a condition to at last receive the consolation of the Gospel.

Furthermore, we read that when Johann Gerhard—one of the very greatest dogmaticians[32]—was a young man in preparatory school,[33] he was in deepest anguish and sorrow for more than a year. Nobody was able to console him until Johann Arndt,[34] his spiritual doctor, was able to heal him with the comfort of the Gospel. Once he came out from this hellish anguish and realized that he was a miserable sinner, Gerhard became a great man.

As a rule, most of the biographies of the great theologians have not been published and will not be known except in eternity. If we could know their stories now, we would probably observe that all those great men became great only after previously being made small and worthless. They became great men in the kingdom of God—acknowledged as His great instruments—only after being freed from their anguish and distress, *after* they started to believe the Gospel, and *after* becoming new men.

A young man who has arrived at "faith" in God's Word only by a sterile conviction of his intellect is a pitiful sight. If he has a sharp mind, he can easily fall into all sorts of errors and become a heretic, because he has never passed through any real anguish of the soul.[35] But anyone who has experienced the power of the Word and passed through the ordeal of genuine and serious repentance will not easily slip into those hidden spiritual sinkholes, for he has been made cautious by experience. Then, when his reason starts to get the upper hand, he can cling to the Word and command his reason to be silent. God grant that you have not only been politely listening to my remarks and have resolved to put them into practice in your ministry but that you may also experience these struggles in your own hearts.

Let me submit a few testimonies from **Luther** on this matter. First, from his *Commentary on Chapters in Exodus* (St. Louis Ed. 3:858–59):

---

31 Matthias Flacius (1520–75) met Luther in the 1540s and became active in the Reformation, especially as a professor at the Universities of Wittenberg and Jena. However, Flacius taught an incorrect understanding of original sin, an error that is specifically addressed in the Formula of Concord.

32 A dogmatician studies how to express biblical doctrine using an organized set of categories.

33 German: *Gymnasium.*

34 Johann Arndt (1555–1621) is remembered chiefly for his devotional works, such as *True Christianity.*

35 German: *Herzensangst.*

W² 3:858;
Luke 1:53

The Gospel should not be preached to coarse, vulgar, reckless sinners, who spend their lives without a thought of eternity. Rather, it is a consolation intended for afflicted souls (Matthew 11:28). For it is a delicate food, which requires a hungry soul. Accordingly, the blessed Virgin Mary sings in her Magnificat in Luke 1:53: "He has filled the hungry with good things."

Otherwise, the rude masses will fall upon it—all claiming to be evangelical and Christian brethren—and will then start schisms and all sorts of distress. They go wherever the devil leads them.

When you rebuke a person and he becomes angry with you, that shows he is not a true Christian. For a Christian receives rebukes meekly, even if the rebuke is uncalled for. He is not greatly surprised that people should charge him with wrong-doing, knowing that no person still in his natural state can be expected to do good. If he knows he is innocent of the charge, he says, "Praise God! I am not guilty."

W² 3:858

Luther continues: "Christians are not reckless, wild, and vulgar. Rather, their conscience is timid—humble and timid. They feel the gnawing of their sin and tremble at the wrath of God, the power of the devil, and the thought of death."

This is an important remark of Luther's: stating that people certainly are *not* Christians who do not feel the gnawing of their sin, are not wrestling with it, and are even likely to ask, "Why, what wrong am I doing?" People who speak like this are in a sorry state. Were these people true Christians, they would say: "Indeed, I am drowning in sin. That was my problem—not only back then, before my conversion, but even today. I do not believe this merely because I read about it in my Bible but because I experience every day what a wicked thing my heart is and how weak my old Adam is."

W² 3:858–59

A heart bruised and crushed like this yearns for the Lord Christ. In the same way, redemption from sin, death, devil, and hell are much appreciated by those who are being swallowed up by death, who feel their distress and yearn for rest. They obtain this rest if they have believing hearts. But, at the same time, they feel what a weak thing their old Adam is.

W² 16:2241
(cf. AE 41:113)

Furthermore, in his treatise *Concerning the Councils and the Church*, **Luther** writes (St. Louis Ed. 16:2241–42): "My friends the Antinomians preach exceedingly well—and I cannot but believe that they do so with great earnestness—concerning the grace of Christ, forgiveness of sin, and other contents of the article of redemption."

As you know, the Antinomians were followers of Johann **Agricola** of Eisleben,[36] who taught that the Law must not be preached in Christian churches because it belongs in the town hall,[37] on the gallows, etc.

But they flee from this conclusion[38] as from the devil, namely, that they need to tell people about the Third Article of the Creed, sanctification, that is, about the new life in Christ. For they hold that we must not terrify people and make them sorrowful but must always preach to them the comfort of grace in Christ and the forgiveness of sin. They tell us for God's sake to avoid statements such as these: "Listen, you want to be a Christian yet at the same time keep on hanging on to your sins of adultery, fornication, obesity—full of pride, greed, envy, revenge, evil, practicing usury, etc." Rather, they tell us that *this* is the proper way to speak: "Listen, so you *are* an adulterer, fornicator, you are miserly, or are addicted to some other sin. Now, if only you will believe, you will be saved and need not dread the Law, for Christ has fulfilled all." My dear friend, does this not amount to conceding the premise and denying the conclusion? **To be sure, it does amount to this: that Christ is taken away and made worthless in the same breath as in which He is most highly preached.**[39]

W² 16:2241
(cf. AE 41:113–14)

None of you would readily use such a crude method, but it is easy to fall for something similar. Rather, if you truly want to comfort people who are in anguish and distress because they imagine that their sins are too great or that they have sinned for too long, etc., then rise to the occasion by glorifying grace and saying, "Even if you had committed every sin that has ever been committed on this earth, even if you were a Judas or a Cain and had personally persecuted Jesus, you need not despair of the mercy of God." However, you must deliver this correct statement in such a way that reckless sinners understand that this applies only to sinners who are alarmed and in distress over their sins—and not to people such as themselves, who think that things are not really as bad as the preachers say. So, for God's sake, be careful when you preach the Gospel. Do not make sinners secure and thus become preachers of sin and defenders of sin.

Luther continues: "This is like saying 'Yes' and 'No' on the same issue. A Christ who would die for sinners who do not quit sinning after they have been forgiven of their sins and who do not lead a new life—that kind of Christ would be worthless." Luther's remark about the class of sinners for whom

W² 16:2241
(cf. AE 41:114)

---

36   For the location of Eisleben, see the map of Saxony in the front of the book.

37   German: *Rathaus.*

38   Latin: *Consequens.*

39   The Dau text adds: "Luther has given an extreme description of Antinomian preaching."

Christ died must not be interpreted to mean that Christ did not die for all sinners. All Luther means to say is that Christ did not die to make sinners secure. Thus Luther: "According to the logic[40] of Nestorius and Eutyches,[41] these people preach a Christ who is—and at the same time is *not*—the Redeemer. **These people are excellent preachers of the Easter truth but miserable preachers of the truth of Pentecost.**"

Take note of this! It is well and good if you emphasize with great force the victory of Christ over sin, death, devil, and hell—at Easter. But you must also be good Pentecost preachers and say to your hearers, "Repent! For then the Holy Spirit will come with His grace and comfort, enlighten, and sanctify you." We will never achieve perfect sanctification in this life, but we must make a beginning and progress in this effort. For if you do not increase, you will decrease. And if you decrease, you will ultimately completely stop using what God has given you. Finally, you will die off.

W² 16:2241–42
(cf. AE 41:114)

For in their preaching they ignore sanctification through the Holy Spirit and being awakened into a new life.[42] They preach only about the redemption of Christ. Without a doubt, they praise Christ highly in their preaching (as is fitting). But Christ is the Christ because He achieved our redemption from sin and death for the very purpose that the Holy Spirit should change our old Adam into a new man, so we can die to sin and live to righteousness. St. Paul teaches in Romans 6:2ff. that we are to begin this change and increase in this new life here on earth and bring it to completion there.

For Christ has gained for us not only *grace*[43] but also the *gift*[44] of the Holy Spirit. He gives us not only **forgiveness** of sin but also helps us **cease** from sinning (John 1:16–17). Therefore, anyone who does not cease from sinning but continues in his former evil way must have obtained a different Christ—presumably from the Antinomians. **The genuine Christ is not with them, even if they cry with the voice of all angels, "Christ! Christ!" They will have to go to hell with their new Christ.**

Luther's remarks are certainly stern—known, as he was, throughout the Christian Church as the greatest witness for the greatness and riches of the

---

40 Latin: *Dialectica*.

41 Nestorius (d. 451) denied the union of the divine and human natures in Christ. Eutyches (ca. 378–ca. 454) opposed Nestorius, yet taught that Christ's human nature was swallowed up in the divine. Both taught contrary to the witness of Scripture regarding the divine and human natures in Christ.

42 Latin: *de sanctificatione et vivificatione Spiritus Sancti*.

43 Latin: *gratia*.

44 Latin: *donum*.

grace of God in Christ. Few men in the Christian Church had the gift of speaking words of comfort to people as did Luther. But he was not one-sided. You see, when it is necessary for him to preach the Law, he is stern and sharp; he spares no one; he brings down the rod of "woe" on everyone who is secure in his sins.[45]

In his *Instruction for Visitors*, written in 1528, **Luther** writes (St. Louis Ed. 10:1636–37):

> As far as doctrine is concerned, among other things, we find *this* to be the chief fault: that while some preach the faith that makes us righteous, they do not explain adequately how we are to **attain** faith. Thus nearly all of them leave out a key part of Christian doctrine, without which no one can understand what faith is or what deserves the name of faith.

W² 10:1636
(cf. AE 40:274)

Shouting at masses of people: "Believe, just believe in Christ, and you will be saved," leaves them uninformed as to the preacher's meaning. The ax of the Law must first come down on them. When they hear the thundering of the Law and look up at the preacher, startled, they begin to reflect: "If the preacher is right, what will become of us? Woe upon us!" Then they are ready for the consolation of the Gospel.

> For Christ says in Luke 24:47 "that repentance and forgiveness of sins should be preached in His name." However, these days many speak only of forgiveness of sin and say little or nothing about repentance, **regardless of the fact that without repentance there is no forgiveness of sins, nor can forgiveness of sins be understood without repentance**. If forgiveness of sins without repentance is preached, the people will imagine that they have already been forgiven of their sins, which makes them secure and unconcerned. **This is a greater error and sin than all errors of former times**, and we can rightfully fear we are in danger of what Christ points out when He says in Matthew 12:45: "The last state of that person is worse than the first."

W² 10:1636
(cf. AE 40:274);
Luke 24:47;
Matt. 12:45 Luther

What a noteworthy saying! Before Luther began his work, the Law alone held sway. Those miserable people were in anguish and terror. But when Luther came to understand the Gospel, he preached it in all its sweetness to these poor, stricken sinners. Many misunderstood him. They concluded that, to preach like Luther, pastors would have to preach faith, justification, and righteousness without works of the Law every Sunday.

Luther denounced this practice of theirs as an error greater than the error of the Papists. By preaching faith alone and saying nothing about repentance,

---

45   See Zechariah 11:7. See also the note on pages 39–40 n. 11.

these preachers led their hearers to that awful condition in which people imagine they are not in need of repentance. Finally, they become so bad that they are beyond being helped.

W² 10:1636–37
(cf. AE 40:275);
Matt. 23:24 Luther

Accordingly, we have instructed and warned pastors to do their duty and preach the Gospel[46] in its entirety, not only one part (the Gospel) without the other (the Law). For God says in Deuteronomy 4:2 that we are not to add to His Word, nor are we to take from it. Our preachers these days scold the pope for having made many additions to Scripture, which, alas, is all too true. But these men who do not preach repentance tear a great portion out of the Scriptures and, instead, talk about eating meat and such other irrelevant matters. Of course, when appropriate, we should not pass over these matters in silence—for Christian liberty must be defended against tyranny. But what else are these preachers doing than "straining out gnats and swallowing camels," as Christ says in Matthew 23:24? We have therefore warned them to urge the people diligently and frequently to repent, be contrite, and be sorrowful over their sin and to fear the judgment of God. We have warned them not to quit teaching the important and necessary element of repentance, for both John the Baptist and Christ rebuke the Pharisees more sharply for their saintly hypocrisy than they do ordinary sinners. In the same way, pastors are to rebuke the common people for their coarse sins, but they should urge them to repentance much more sternly if they discover hypocritical sanctity.

Of course, this does not mean that you should preach the Law vigorously only when you are preaching against **coarse** sins. This kind of preaching produces only Pharisees. Nevertheless, pastors should preach against those **coarse** sins.[47]

---

46 Luther refers here to the "Gospel in the loose (or wide) sense" (Latin: *evangelium late dicta*; German: *Evangelium im weiteren Sinne*), which refers to the whole counsel of God, namely, all of Scripture. He immediately follows with a reference to the "Gospel in the strict (or narrow) sense" (Latin: *evangelium stricte dicta*; German: *Evangelium in engeren Sinne*), meaning the preaching of forgiveness through Christ's person and work over against the Law.

47 The Dau text adds: "Luther's statement about the greatness of the Antinomian error as surpassing the errors of former times deserves to be noted."

Fourteenth
Evening Lecture:
Jan. 16, 1885

Dear friends, regarding the differences between the Lutheran and the Reformed Church, your average Lutheran—at least way back when—imagined that there are only two important differences: When they recite the Lord's Prayer [in German], Lutherans put the word *Father* first, whereas the Reformed place the word *Our* first.[48] Similarly, the average Lutheran held that, during the Lord's Supper, Lutherans use a wafer, which they do not break, whereas in Reformed churches they use ordinary bread, which they *do* break during or before the distribution. This horrible ignorance on the part of the people is completely the fault of the unfaithful ministers of our own church. They have shamefully neglected their flock.

In view of this ignorance, it is, of course, not surprising that those poor Lutherans finally gave in to overtures for a union with the Reformed. Recently, however, a change has taken place: the violently enforced establishment of the Union Church in the place where it was attempted first—in Prussia—has given the opportunity to our beloved Lutheran people to reconsider the points of difference between the Reformed and the Lutheran Church.[49]

The Lutheran awakening

In 1817, when the union was instituted, **Claus Harms**, a pastor and professor at the University of Kiel,[50] published a new series of Ninety-five Theses for use at the celebration of the three-hundredth anniversary of the Reformation. In Thesis 95 he says, "A union is now being contemplated, which is to enrich that poor handmaiden, the Lutheran Church." However, he adds this warning: "Do not dare try it—over Luther's dead body. His bones will take on new life, and then the Lord have mercy on you!"

[Harms's] prophecy has been fulfilled. These days any Lutheran child who has received at least a passable instruction in Christian doctrine knows that there is indeed a great difference, involving the principal articles of Christian doctrine, between the Lutheran and the Reformed Church. Today the Lutheran people are well-informed on this point: Lutherans cling firmly to the words of Christ, forever true: "This *is* My body. This *is* My blood."

---

48 Lutherans follow the Latin word ordering of the Our Father (*Paternoster*): *Vater unser, der du bist im Himmel.* The Reformed follow the Heidelberg Catechism: *Unser Vater, der du bist im Himmel.*

49 In 1817 King Frederick William III of Prussia established the Evangelical Christian Church, a forced union between Lutherans and Reformed. Those Lutherans who resisted the union were deprived of their rights and property. Many emigrated to Australia and the United States. Prussia grew out of the Mark Brandenburg. It added some of the lands formerly held by the Order of the Teutonic Knights, the rest of which became Estonia, Latvia, and Lithuania. Prussia gained more territory toward the end of the eighteenth century when, along with Russia, and Austria-Hungary, it partitioned Poland among the three countries. Finally, Prussia swallowed up smaller German states on its road to becoming the dominant member of the German Empire, stretching from the Baltic to the Rhine.

50 Kiel is a German city in the state of Schleswig-Holstein on the Baltic Sea, south of Denmark.

Fundamental differences

Accordingly, every Lutheran knows that the body and blood of Christ are substantially and truly present in the Holy Supper. The elements are distributed and received by the communicants, whereas the Reformed interpret those clear words—plain as broad daylight—to mean: "This *symbolizes* the body of Christ. This *symbolizes* His blood." Accordingly, the Reformed contend that the body and blood of Christ are removed from the Holy Supper as far as the heavens are from the earth, because Christ is locked up in heaven—and His return to earth is not to be expected until the Last Day.

These days, every Lutheran knows that according to Scripture—the book of eternal truth—Holy Baptism is the washing of regeneration, a means by which regeneration is effected from on high through the Holy Spirit. On the other hand, the Reformed contend that Baptism is merely a sign, symbol, or representation of something that previously took place in a person.

These days every Lutheran knows that the human nature of Christ, through its union with the divine nature, also received divine attributes, namely, that omniscience, omnipotence, omnipresence, and the honor of adoration have been communicated to it.[51] On the other hand, the Reformed contend that there is only a difference of degree between the man Christ and other men, namely, that Christ has received greater gifts. However, even the highest gifts that His human nature has are claimed to be creature gifts, the same as in other creatures.

These days every Lutheran knows that, according to the Holy Scriptures, the saving grace of the Father is universal; so is the redemption of the Son and, likewise, the effective calling of the Holy Spirit through the Word. On the other hand, the teaching of the Reformed Church on these three points is "particular." This means that the Reformed most emphatically contend that God created the majority of the human race to eternal damnation and has accordingly assigned them to everlasting death—even for eternity. In the clear light of the precious, saving Gospel this is a terrifying and horrible doctrine.

In a nutshell, every Lutheran these days knows that there is a major difference between the Lutheran and the Reformed Church—not just regarding tangential [matters] but in key doctrinal issues.

Many remain uninformed; Eph. 4:5

Why, then, have so many who claim to be Lutheran allowed themselves to become entangled in the spiderweb of the union? How can they claim to be Lutheran yet calmly remain in this forced union? The church established by the Prussian Union was not established by Christ—but by an earthly king. It is a church in which everyone does not speak the same things or hold the same views, as the apostle requires in 1 Corinthians 1. This is a church in

---

51 Jesus' divine nature has divine attributes. These include knowing everything (omniscience), having power to accomplish anything (omnipotence), being present everywhere (omnipresence), and having the sole right to be worshiped (adoration).

which there is *not* "one faith, one Baptism," and one hope, which the apostle requires of the Church of Christ Jesus in Ephesians 4.

Why is this? There is only one reason: Because people feel that—despite the many and grave errors of the Reformed Church—the Reformed and the Lutheran Church agree in the key points. They claim that the relationship between these two churches is entirely different from the one between the Lutheran and the Papist Church. There is probably truth to this claim. But if God wanted the Reformed Church to agree with us in the key points,[52] it would quickly reach an agreement with us in the few points of minor importance as well!

But what the Reformed Church lacks is this: it cannot correctly answer the question "What must I do to be saved?" Ironically, it is in the doctrine of justification—the cardinal doctrine of the Lutheran Church—that the Reformed Church does not agree with us. It does not point the correct way to grace and salvation. There are very few in our day and age that understand this point. It is true that all the Reformed, and the sects that have come from the Reformed Church, do affirm that a person is saved by grace alone. But the moment you examine their *practice*, you will immediately discover that—even though they hold this truth in theory—they do not put it into practice. Rather, they point people in the opposite direction.

Justification rejected

This evening's thesis addresses this very issue.

---

52   The Dau edition adds: "a consummation devoutly to be wished."

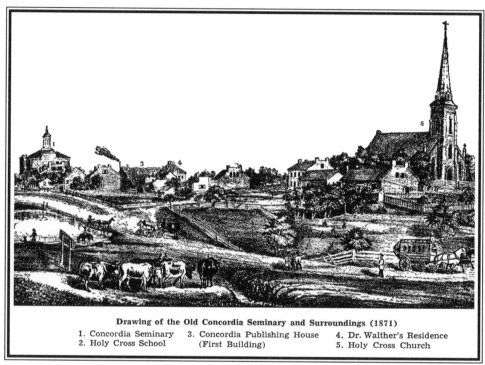

Drawing of the Old Concordia Seminary and Surroundings (1871)

1. Concordia Seminary
2. Holy Cross School
3. Concordia Publishing House (First Building)
4. Dr. Walther's Residence
5. Holy Cross Church

This engraving was made from an original color drawing, at least one copy of which is in the holdings at Holy Cross Church, St. Louis. Its perspective makes the distance between the seminary (left) and Holy Cross (right) much larger in order to frame the picture. The area was also less rural than depicted. Compare the aerial image in the front of the book. Image from Ludwig Fürbringer, *Persons and Events* (St. Louis: Concordia, 1947), 213.

THESIS IX

You are not rightly distinguishing Law and Gospel in the Word of God if you point sinners who have been struck down and terrified by the Law toward their own prayers and struggles with God and tell them that they have to work their way into a state of grace. That is, do not tell them to keep on praying and struggling until they would feel that God has received them into grace. Rather, point them toward the Word and the Sacraments.

EDITOR'S NOTE: This one thesis takes up almost one-quarter of the book. In this thesis, Walther remains completely committed to salvation by grace alone through faith in Christ Jesus because discarding the Gospel in favor of the Law results in the loss of salvation. Some critics had labeled Walther as a Calvinist. He responds to that criticism throughout the rest of the book. Walther shows his critics that they have fallen prey to American theology of either the Calvinist or of the Methodist variety.

Walther's theology stood much closer to the Lutheran confessional awakening in Europe than to the American religious landscape. In Europe, the nineteenth century saw confessional Lutherans rediscovering historic Lutheran doctrine from the sixteenth and seventeenth centuries, spurred on in 1817 by the lone voice of Pastor Claus Harms in Kiel, Germany. The doctrinally lax, rationalist Lutheran establishment called the confessionals "Neo-Lutherans" in order to lower their status. The confessionals called themselves "Old Lutherans" because they held to Scripture and the Lutheran Confessions, which the Rationalists had abandoned in favor of false, human doctrine. Every confessional Lutheran church body today comes from this awakening, which sent a wave of immigrants from Germany to North and South America, South Africa, and Australia.

From the earliest days of *Der Lutheraner* in 1844,[1] Walther considered the distinction of Law and Gospel to be a central part of his task. Walther left this emphasis as a legacy to future Missouri Synod Lutherans. Thesis IX, in particular, takes aim at the revivalism that was a feature of the U.S. religious landscape

---

1   See also the biography of Walther, beginning at page xxvi.

of Walther's day. Yet it also speaks against Pietism and its major role in nineteenth-century Lutheranism. Walther lifts up the Gospel message of Christ as the central content of Scripture. He shows how this central doctrine needs to be applied in order not to lose it.

The doctrine denounced in this thesis is common to all the Reformed and to the sects of Reformed origin, including Baptists, Methodists, the so-called "Evangelical Church,"[2] Episcopalians, and Presbyterians. All of these are offshoots of the great tree of the Reformed Church, and they all teach what we condemn in this thesis. These people do not proclaim the pure Gospel doctrine of how poor, alarmed sinners can arrive at the assurance that God is gracious to them. None of these sects shows this way.

The gravity of error

In order to obtain divine assurance about the proper way of rightly distinguishing the Word, let us examine a few examples recorded in Scripture. We observe that the holy apostles were filled with the Holy Spirit and—prompted by God—no doubt rightly distinguished His Word. They showed alarmed sinners the correct way to rest and peace and to assurance regarding their state of grace before God. In order to remove every possible doubt, let us examine how the apostles dealt with the most serious and obvious sinners.

In Acts 2 we have a record of how the apostle Peter treats people who only a few weeks earlier had cried, "Crucify, crucify Him!" Curiosity had led the same pitiful creatures—who at the tribunal of Pilate had shouted, "Away with Him! To the gallows with this cursed wretch! We would rather have Barabbas!"—to the place where the outpouring of the Holy Spirit occurred. They had heard the roaring of the mighty wind and had come to investigate the phenomenon. Notice that—at the very outset—Peter rebukes those who had mockingly said that the apostles were filled with new wine. He shows them that the outpouring of the Holy Spirit is precisely the fulfillment of Joel's prophecy.[3]

Acts 2:36

Next, Peter reviews the story of the suffering, death, resurrection, and final ascension of Jesus and concludes with these words: "Let all the house of Israel therefore know for certain that God has made Him both Lord and Christ, this Jesus whom you crucified" (Acts 2:36). Although only a few words long, that was a horrific Law sermon.

---

2   This is a group of originally German-speaking Methodists (*Albrechtsbrüder*), part of which joined the United Methodist Church in 1968 and part of which remains independent. It is not the similarly named Evangelical Synod of North America, which was an offshoot of the Prussian Union in North America and is now a part of the United Church of Christ.

3   See Acts 2:1–36.

Accordingly, we are told in verse 37: "Now when they heard this they were cut to the heart." When these words of the apostle struck their heart, they had the sensation of having been stabbed by a dagger. They trembled. They were horrified, and the Holy Spirit drove the apostle's thrust home and made them realize what a terrible sin they had committed by crucifying their own Messiah. And they "said to Peter and the rest of the apostles, 'Brothers, what shall we do?'" Acts 2:37

How does the apostle react at this point? Does he say: "You need to make a personal effort to change your behavior. You need to recognize more deeply how sinful you are. Get down on your knees and cry for mercy. Perhaps God will help you and receive you into grace"?

No, nothing of the kind. He says to them: "Repent and be baptized every one of you in the name of Jesus Christ for the forgiveness of your sins." [The Greek word] literally means "turn your minds around."[4] This is obviously the second part of repentance, that is, faith. Here the term is used for the whole of Law and Gospel,[5] because the Law had already done its work upon these hearers. Accordingly, the last thing the apostle Peter would want to do is bring about their salvation by hurling these people into still greater distress, anguish, and terror. Now that they are cut to the heart, it is time to move on. They are now prepared to hear the most blessed Gospel and receive it into their heart. Acts 2:39

For this reason the apostle now addresses them as follows: "Turn your minds around and believe the Gospel of the Crucified One. Dismiss all your errors, and be baptized in the name of Jesus Christ—right now—for the remission of your sins." And they, for their part, are baptized.[6]

The apostle witnesses to them by saying, "Your sins are forgiven. Your terrible sins will be remembered no more." The apostle adds these words:

> And you will receive the gift of the Holy Spirit. For the promise is for you and for your children and for all who are far off, everyone whom the Lord our God will call to Himself. And with many other words he bore witness and urged them, saying, "Save yourselves from this crooked generation." So those who gladly received his word for their part were baptized, and there were added that day about three thousand souls. Acts 2:38–41
Luther

---

4   Greek: *metanoeite*.

5   The original reads "in synecdoche," a figure of speech in which a part substitutes for the whole or the whole for the parts. For example, one may refer to a sports car as "hot wheels."

6   English does not have an easy way to translate the German *sich etwas lassen*. It recalls the "middle voice" in Greek: for their own benefit, they were baptized. That brings the Spirit's revelation, faith, and the act of Baptism together as a unit (see Mark 16:16).

That is the whole story. That is all the apostle expects them to do. All his hearers have to do is listen to him talk and take comfort in these soothing words of consolation, this promise of the forgiveness of their sins, of life and salvation. We do not hear the slightest thing about any additional requirements such as the ones that the sects use these days. But more about all that later.

Acts 2:42 Luther   That was the first sermon Peter delivered, coming fresh from the forge of the Holy Spirit, as it were. He went to work with the most intense faith and with that one sermon gained three thousand souls, to whom he brought rest and peace and the assurance of salvation. In verse 42 we are told: "And they remained steadfast in the apostles' teaching and fellowship, in the breaking of bread and in prayer."

This was not a "flash in the pan," such as is frequently sparked in our day by traveling enthusiasts at their revivals.[7] No—the hearts of these people had been deeply stirred and completely changed. They rejoiced and cheerfully took upon themselves all the shame and persecution, all the sufferings, that Christians of that era had to endure.

Acts 16:19–20   After this first example that reveals the apostles' practice, let me add a second one: the conversion of the jailer at Philippi, which is recorded in Acts 16. While we dealt with Jews in the first example, in this one we are told about a heathen—and a very godless heathen at that. In verses 19–20 we read: "But when her owners"—the owners of the slave girl from whom Paul had cast out the soothsaying spirit of divination—"saw that their hope of gain was gone, they seized Paul and Silas and dragged them into the marketplace before the rulers. And when they had brought them to the magistrates, they said, 'These men are **Jews**, and they are disturbing our city.'"

Acts 16:21   That was the custom back then—Jews were universally hated and despised. Furthermore, the owners raised this charge in verse 21: "They advocate customs that are not lawful for us as Romans to accept or practice." The nobility claimed to be several notches better than any other nation.

Acts 16:22–24   The record continues: "The crowd joined in attacking them, and the magistrates tore the garments off them and gave orders to beat them with rods." Mind you, without being given a required hearing! Verses 23–24: "And when they had inflicted many blows upon them, they threw them into prison, ordering the jailer to keep them safely. Having received this order, he put them into the inner prison and fastened their feet in the stocks."

---

7   In the original lectures, Walther used the English word "revivals" in order to point specifically to this American phenomenon. He spoke similarly in the 1884 Synodical Conference *Proceedings* when he criticized the idea of "common sense," using the English term as a way to punctuate the false idea that people, left on their own, are basically good.

The jailer had not been ordered to throw them into the **inner** prison and put their feet in the stocks. He simply took pleasure in doing this. He did not know whether the apostles had been lawfully committed to jail—and neither did he care. This was an inhuman brute.

The story continues in verse 25: "About midnight Paul and Silas were praying and singing hymns to God, and the prisoners were listening to them." Acts 16:25
Undoubtedly the jailer, too, heard them—and it must have made a most powerful impression on him. Without a doubt he had expected them to be sitting in their cell, gnashing their teeth and cursing him. But instead he heard them chanting praises to God. He must have thought: "These men are weird. I have never had prisoners like this in my jail."

And now we read in verses 26–27: "And suddenly there was a great earthquake, so that the foundations of the prison were shaken. And immediately Acts 16:26–27 all the doors were opened, and everyone's bonds were unfastened. When the jailer woke and saw that the prison doors were open, he drew his sword and was about to kill himself, supposing that the prisoners had escaped."

Dereliction of duty was no laughing matter in the Roman Empire. If prisoners escaped from jail, the jailer was held responsible. In the case of especially dangerous criminals, the jailer could pay with his life if the prisoners escaped. Now, this jailer did not believe in a God who would judge him. Accordingly, he figured: "Since I am going to be sentenced to death anyway, why keep on living? I would rather be my own executioner and strangle myself."

Verse 28: "But Paul cried with a loud voice, 'Do not harm yourself, for we Acts 16:28 are all here.'" Imagine the impression this cry must have made on the jailer! Here he had tossed the apostles into the inner prison, but instead of seething with anger against him and plotting revenge, they stopped the jailer from committing suicide by shouting out to him as they did.

From what the apostles had been singing, the jailer had very likely under- Acts 16:30 stood that these were men who wished to tell people how to find happiness beyond Hades. In his great distress he now begs the apostles in verse 30: "Sirs, what must I do to be saved?"

If the apostles had been enthusiasts, they would have said to him: "My dear friend, this is no easy matter. Before a godless, reckless man such as you can be saved, an elaborate and extensive cure is necessary, which we will prescribe to you." No, they do not say a single word to this effect. Rather, they see that the jailer is ready to receive the Gospel. True, he is still just as godless as before. He does not yet hate sin. He says nothing about any of that. All he wants is to escape the punishment of sin and obtain a happy, blessed fate beyond the grave.

Nevertheless we read in verses 31–33: "And they said, 'Believe in the Lord Acts 16:31–33 Jesus, and you will be saved, you and your household.' And they spoke the word of the Lord to him and to all who were in his house. And he took them the same hour of the night and washed their wounds; and he was baptized at once, he and all his family."

That same night the jailer is converted. He receives the gift of faith and the assurance that he is accepted before God—and reconciled. He is now a beloved child of God.

What requirements do the apostles demand of him? They do nothing except proclaim the Gospel in a simple manner.[8] Without any requirements they say, "Believe in the Lord Jesus." That makes the apostles' practice clear. Whenever their word produces faith, they immediately administer Baptism. They do not say, "We need to walk you through an extensive course of instruction and explain accurately and thoroughly all the articles of the Christian Creed. After that, we will have to put you on probation to see whether you can become an approved Christian." Nothing of the sort. The jailer asks to be baptized because he knows this is how he will be received into the kingdom of Christ, and the apostles immediately baptize him.

Compare this practice of the apostles with that of the Reformed Church in our day and age. (I am referring to all the sects that have sprung from the Reformed Church.) If they were to see a Lutheran pastor adopting the practice of the apostles, they would cry out: "How can that godless and lax preacher act that way? Why, he first ought to impress on the sinner that he must *feel* the grace of God in his heart. Instead of doing that, this worthless pastor is comforting and even baptizing so-and-so."

But whether the Reformed like it or not, that is the biblical method, and since it is biblical, it is also the Lutheran method. For the Lutheran Church is nothing else than the Church of the Bible. It does not deviate from the Bible; it does not take away or add to it, but stands squarely on the Word of God. In all its teachings and in its practice, the Lutheran Church lives by this key principle.

Acts 16:34   In conclusion we read: "Then he brought them up into his house and set food before them. And he rejoiced along with his entire household that he had believed in God."

The jailer had good reason for rejoicing. He meant to declare that, while he did not formerly have a God and was without any hope in this world, he had now found a God and Savior who had saved him and redeemed him with His precious divine blood. And this God had given him the promise that He would come again and receive him into the kingdom of glory.

That is the second example that I wanted to give you. It shows the apostles' way of doing things. It demonstrates how they went about leading people to the assurance of the grace of God.

---

8   German: *unverklausuliert*. It means "straightforward, without all the legal language."

Now let us discuss the example of the apostle Paul himself. How is this   Acts 22:1–2
disgraceful man, who had persecuted the Christians so horribly, converted?
He describes it best in the most beautiful chapter, Acts 22. It says in verses
1–2: "'Brothers and fathers, hear the defense that I now make before you.'
And when they heard that he was addressing them in the Hebrew language,
they became even more quiet."

Nearly every time he appears in public, especially before an audience of   Acts 22:3
Jews, Paul tells the story of his conversion. On this occasion he addresses
them in Hebrew in order to attract their attention. Few people at that time
understood Hebrew well, but Paul, being a learned man, understood it well.
In the deathly silence that follows, his audience hangs on Paul's every word.
He tells them in verse 3: "I am a Jew, born in Tarsus in Cilicia, but brought up
in this city, educated at the feet of Gamaliel according to the strict manner of
the law of our fathers, being zealous for God as all of you are this day." What
he means to say is that he used to be the same kind of person they are.

He continues in verses 4–5: "I persecuted this Way to the death, binding   Acts 22:4–5
and delivering to prison both men and women, as the high priest and the
whole council of elders can bear me witness. From them I received letters to
the brothers, and I journeyed toward Damascus to take those also who were
there and bring them in bonds to Jerusalem to be punished." By "the Way" he
means the Christian religion.[9] He, too, had persecuted the new religion and,
by painfully torturing them, had forced Christians to renounce and curse
Christ.

He continues in verses 6–9:

> As I was on my way and drew near to Damascus, about noon a great   Acts 22:6–9
> light from heaven suddenly shone around me. And I fell to the ground
> and heard a voice saying to me, "Saul, Saul, why are you persecuting
> Me?" And I answered, "Who are You, Lord?" And He said to me, "I am
> Jesus of Nazareth, whom you are persecuting." Now those who were
> with me saw the light but did not understand the voice of the one who
> was speaking to me.

God wanted Paul to know that **he** alone was the intended one; that is why
only Paul heard the voice. For that reason, too, Jesus addressed him by name.

> And I said, "What shall I do, Lord?" And the Lord said to me, "Rise,   Acts 22:10
> and go into Damascus, and there you will be told all that is appointed
> for you to do."

---

9   The Dau text adds: "Paul classifies the Jews in their present state with himself in his
unconverted state."

Paul is to be converted by nothing else than the Word. At this point, the Savior does not preach conversion to him. Paul has to learn by means of human beings what he has to do to be saved.

Acts 22:11–13

And since I could not see because of the brightness of that light, I was led by the hand by those who were with me, and came into Damascus. And one Ananias, a devout man according to the law, well spoken of by all the Jews who lived there, came to me, and standing by me said to me, "Brother Saul, receive your sight." And at that very hour I received my sight and saw him.

Ananias had had a vision from the Lord in which he had been told what to say when he saw Saul. Because of the instruction he had received, when he entered, he addressed Saul as "brother." Continuing his account, Paul relates:

Acts 22:14–16

And he said, "The God of our fathers appointed you to know His will, to see the Righteous One and to hear a voice from His mouth; for you will be a witness for Him to everyone of what you have seen and heard. And now why do you wait? Rise and be baptized and wash away your sins, calling on His name."

At this point Ananias does not say: "First, you have to keep praying until you have a sensation of grace deep down inside." No, he tells him: "After you have come to a knowledge of the Lord Jesus, your first step must be to receive Baptism so your sins would be washed away. *Then* you call upon the Lord Jesus."

That is the true order of saving grace: Again—we do not start by praying to obtain the grace of God. Rather, we *first* receive the grace of God, *then* we pray. Only in that sequence are we able to pray acceptably.

This is how the Lord Himself did it. Needless to say, *He* knows how to deal with poor sinners. As soon as Saul becomes alarmed about his sins, Jesus approaches him with His consolation. He does not require him to experience all sorts of feelings, but immediately proclaims to [Paul] the Word of grace. These examples show us how a true minister of Christ is to proceed when his goal is to lead sinners—*after* they have been crushed by the Law—to the assurance of the grace of God in Christ Jesus.

Improper preaching of Law

In contrast, how do the sects go about it? They do the exact opposite. To be fair, they also preach the Law first with great sternness, which is quite proper. After all, we do the same, following the method of the apostles and of Christ. The only wrong feature in this part of their preaching is their depiction of the torments in hell, which is usually done in such a drastic manner as to trigger the imagination rather than to make their words sink deep into the heart.

True, using its awful threats, they frequently preach excellent sermons on the Law. Only they do not bring out its spiritual meaning. Here is the problem with the way most sects go about this: instead of crushing their hearers to the point where they profess to be poor, lost, and condemned sinners, deserving everlasting wrath, the sects put them in a state of mind that makes them say, "Is it not terrible to hear God speak such awful threats on account of sin?"

If you do not use the Law to get a person to the point where he strips off his *own* robe of righteousness and declares himself a miserable, wicked person—whose heart sins day and night with his evil lusts, thoughts, desires, tendencies, and wishes of all kinds—if you do not get the person to that point, you have not preached the Law correctly. A preacher of the Law must make a person distrust himself—even in the smallest things—until his dying hour and keep him confessing that he is a miserable creature, with no record of good deeds except those that God has accomplished through him. This person must say, "What I really do is ruin, poison, and mess up the good things that God wants to do through me." If their hearts are not put in such condition, people are not properly prepared to receive the Gospel.

But the incorrect preaching of the Law is not even the worst feature of the sects. To make matters even worse, the sects do not preach the Gospel to people who are alarmed and in anguish. These pastors imagine they would commit the worst sin by immediately offering consolation to such poor souls. They give them a long list of works they have to do, so that they will be received into grace—if at all. They tell them how long they have to pray, how forcefully they have to struggle and wrestle and cry, until they supposedly feel the Holy Spirit and divine grace and can rise from their knees shouting, "Hallelujah!"[10]

Failure to preach Gospel

In order to speed up this process in larger gatherings, Methodist preachers have fellow brothers and sisters kneel around the person who is to be converted and urge that person to start calling out to God. They plead with God to forgive that particular person. Sometimes their effort is without success; sometimes the desired result is not achieved for weeks or months. If a sincere candidate confesses that he still does not feel that he has been forgiven but only feels his inability to do good and tendency to do evil, he is told that he is still in a very sorry state and must continue to wrestle in prayer until he finally experiences that feeling of divine grace. At that point he is told to praise God because he is finally rid of sin. All is well, his penitential agony is over, and he has become a child of God's grace.

But this is a false foundation.[11] Indeed, that feeling can have another basis. It might not be the testimony of the Holy Spirit in that person's heart after all, but only a physical impact, worked up by the lively presentation of the

---

10   See the entries for "anxious bench" and "revival" in the Glossary, pages 474, 485.

11   Walther does not oppose the place of sincere emotional response in religion. Rather, he means this: Any feeling that can be ambiguous is a false foundation. Since this is a feeling

preacher. That would explain why—frequently—sincere persons who have become believers feel one minute that they have found the Lord Jesus and the next minute that they have lost Him again. At times they imagine that they are in a state of grace. Other times they imagine that they have *fallen* from grace.

Imagine the distress this causes for such souls in their dying hour—when they have no sensation of grace and think: "Woe is me! I am damned and lost eternally!"[12] I have no doubt, however, that the Holy Spirit comes to the aid of the poor souls who have been at the mercy of such bad apples for pastors. He enables them to cast overboard all their reliance on their own works and struggles and to throw themselves into the arms of the free grace of God—and die peacefully. However, wherever this occurs, that blessed result is not the result of Methodist preaching, but it is the result of the work of the Holy Spirit—**despite** Methodist preaching.

Three errors in review

In review, this faulty practice results from three horrific errors:

In the first place, the sects neither believe nor teach real and complete reconciliation of man with God because they regard our heavenly Father as a God who is very hard to deal with, whose heart must first be softened by passionate cries and bitter tears. That amounts to a denial of Jesus Christ, who long ago turned the heart of God to men by reconciling the entire world with Him.[13] God does nothing halfheartedly. In Christ, He loves all sinners without exception.[14] The sins of every sinner have been canceled. Every debt has been canceled. There is no longer anything that a poor sinner has to fear when he approaches his heavenly Father, with whom he has been reconciled by Christ.

2 Cor. 5:20; 5:14

However, these sects imagine that, now that Christ has done His share, man must still do *his*—and man is not reconciled to God until both efforts meet. These sects picture reconciliation to mean that the Savior made God *willing* to save people—provided they, on their part, are *willing* to be reconciled. But that is the complete reverse of the Gospel. *God* is reconciled—not man. Accordingly, the apostle Paul calls to us: "Be reconciled to God" (2 Corinthians 5:20). This means that since God has been reconciled to *you* by Jesus Christ, grasp the hand that our Father in heaven extends to you. Moreover, the apostle declares in 2 Corinthians 5:14: "One has died for all, therefore all have died." This means that since Christ died for the sins of all

---

of divine grace that is based on emotion, it can be ambiguous. The feeling creates a false foundation.

12 Walther says "you" instead of "me" in the original German because he envisions someone having a dialogue with his soul. Since this literary motif may be foreign to current readers, "me" has been substituted to avoid confusion.

13 See, for example, Romans 5:10; 2 Corinthians 5:18–19; Colossians 1:21–22.

14 See 1 Timothy 2:3–4.

people, everyone has died and made satisfaction for their sins. Therefore, nothing at all is required on the part of mankind to reconcile God. He *already is* reconciled. Righteousness is ready and waiting. Humans must not first achieve it. If we were to attempt to do so, that would be an awful crime, a battle against grace and against the reconciliation and perfect redemption accomplished by the Son of God.

Second, these sects teach false doctrine concerning the Gospel. They regard it as nothing but a set of instructions for man, teaching what man must do to secure the grace of God. In reality, the Gospel is God's *proclamation* to people: "You are redeemed from your sins. You are reconciled to God. Your sins are forgiven." No sectarian preacher would dare make such a bold statement. If one of them—say, Spurgeon[15]—*were* to state that in one of his sermons, that would be a decidedly Lutheran element in his sectarian teaching, and thus an exception to the rule. Moreover, his sectarian brothers will immediately jump on him for going too far.

Third, the sects teach false doctrine concerning faith. They regard faith as a quality in people that "improves" them, that increases their sanctification. This is why they consider faith to be such an extraordinarily important and beneficial matter.

It is true indeed that genuine faith does change a person completely. It brings love into a person's heart. Faith can be without love just as little as fire can be without heat. But the fact that faith contains love is not why faith justifies us and gives us what *Christ* has acquired for us and what is thus *already* ours and only needs to be received by us. These people do not teach what Scripture teaches in response to the question "What must I do to be saved?" Rather, the correct response to that question is: "You must believe, that is, you do not need to do anything yourself." Because when the apostle answers the jailer's question by saying, "You must believe in the Lord Jesus Christ." That is the same as saying, "You do not need to do anything. Just receive what God has already done for you. That is all. Now you are saved." **Acts 16:30**

Since we have this doctrine, what exceedingly happy and blessed people we Lutherans are! This teaching takes us directly to Christ—without any detours. It opens heaven to us when we feel hell in our heart. It enables us to obtain grace at any moment—without losing time by following a wrong way as we work for grace by our own effort, as we sometimes do, even with the best intentions. We can approach Christ directly and say: "Lord Jesus, I am a poor sinner. I know it. I have known this in the past, and when I reflect on what is going on in my heart now, I must say, that is still my experience. But You have called me by Your Gospel. I come to You just as I am. For I can **Why be Lutheran?**

---

15   Charles Haddon Spurgeon (1834–92). For more information, see the Index of Persons and Groups, page 500.

come no other way." That is the saving doctrine that the Evangelical Lutheran Church has learned from Christ and the apostles.

Use this doctrine to your own personal advantage, my friends. It would be horrible if one of you were to go to bed tonight with this thought in his heart: "I am not sure whether God is gracious to me, whether He has accepted me as His child, or whether my sins are forgiven. If God were to call me home tonight, I would not be sure whether I would die saved."

God grant that none of you would go to bed tonight in that frame of mind. For whoever among you that did so would lie down to rest with the wrath of God smothering *him*. The way you imagine God to be—that is the way He is for you. If you believe that God is gracious to you, you will certainly imagine Him to be a gracious God. If you dress up our heavenly Father as a scarecrow—as a God who is angry with you—you *have* an angry God, and His wrath will smother you. However, our Savior has removed the God who used to be angry with us. We now have a God who *takes pity* on us.

I have another wish concerning you: that you may be filled with good cheer, to some day joyfully proclaim this most blessed doctrine to your respective congregations. If you had to preach nothing but sterile ethics, you might consider that a boring task, yielding meager results. But if you have experienced in your own heart what it means to communicate to poor, lost, and condemned sinners the consolation of the Gospel and to say to them: "You are indeed lost and condemned sinners, yet come, just believe: you are redeemed"—if you believe this and think about the full meaning of this, you cannot but look forward with joy to the day when you will stand before your congregation for the first time and deliver this most blessed message. In fact, you will not help but reach the conclusion that you certainly have chosen the most beautiful and glorious calling on earth. For a messenger of good news is always welcome. May this happen to you as well, with the help of God!

Fifteenth Evening Lecture:

Jan. 23, 1885

False doctrine of purgatory

My Dear Friends, Beloved in the Lord:—

You know that the Papists teach that even godly persons do not enter heaven immediately after death. Rather, before they are allowed to see God, they supposedly must first pass through what the Papists call "purgatory." That is where they claim the dead are purified from sins for which they had not made full atonement by being tormented in fire. Even worse, the Papists teach that no one—not even a sincere Christian—can be assured in this present life that he is in a state of grace with God, that he has received forgiveness of sins and will go to heaven. Only a few, they say, are excused from this rule, namely, the holy apostles and extraordinarily great saints, to whom

God has given advance information by revealing to them in an extraordinary manner that they will reach the heavenly goal.

This is the doctrine of the Antichrist—absolutely without comfort. As you know, our Lutheran Church teaches the very opposite. It is a pity that the vast majority of nominal Lutherans, even though they cherish some kind of human hope that God accepts them and that they have obtained forgiveness of sin and will be saved, nevertheless have no assurance in these matters. This sad fact proves that such Lutherans—far from having received the Lutheran doctrine into their hearts—have no knowledge of it at all.

How can the Christian doctrine be called the Gospel, that is, "Good News," if those who accept it must be in constant doubt as to whether their sins are paid for, whether God looks upon them as righteous people, and whether they will go to heaven? If even a Christian cannot know what his relationship to God is and what his fate will be in eternity—whether damnation or salvation—what difference is there between a Christian and a heathen, with the latter living without God and without hope in this world?

Does Holy Scripture not say, "Faith is having a **sure** confidence regarding things hoped for and not doubting things unseen" (Hebrews 11:1)?[16] Does our blessed Lord Jesus Christ not say, "Come to Me, all who labor and are heavy laden, and I will give you rest" (Matthew 11:28)? Does He not say, "Whoever drinks of the water that I will give him will never be thirsty again" (John 4:14)? Does He not say, "My sheep hear My voice, and I know them, and they follow Me. I give them eternal life, and they will never perish, and no one will snatch them out of My hand" (John 10:27–28)? If the Papists' doctrine of doubt mentioned above were true, would all these sayings not be empty delusions and—I shudder to say it—full of lies and deception?

Heb. 11:1 Luther; Matt. 11:28; John 4:14; 10:27–28

Our dear Lord Jesus Christ requires of His followers that they wrestle with their own flesh and blood, the world, and the devil, and that they be faithful to death.[17] He requires of them to renounce all they have, to come to Him, to take His cross upon themselves, to deny themselves, and to follow Him. He tells them in advance that, if they live in Him, the world will hate, revile, and persecute them to death.[18]

If the Papists' doctrine of doubt were true, who would desire to come to Christ, cling to Him, and fight all the great and dreadful battles of this life, following His crimson banner? Who could gather the strength to follow after holiness if there was any doubt whether the heavenly goal would ever be reached? Indeed, anyone who would receive this doctrine of doubt into his heart is an unhappy person. He remains forever as a sorry slave of the Law.

16   Walther makes a specific point of using Luther's German translation here.
17   See, for example, Revelation 2:10.
18   See, for example, Matthew 19:21; 16:24; 5:11; 1 John 3:13.

His conscience tells him constantly: "It is *not* well with you. Who knows what God's thoughts are concerning you? Who knows what punishment is awaiting you?"

Unquestionably, this doctrine of doubt is the most horrible error into which a Christian can fall. For it puts Christ, His redemption, and the entire Gospel to shame. It is no laughing matter.

What is the root cause of this error? It is nothing else than the mingling of Law and Gospel. Let us learn, then, to rightly distinguish the Word of God—Law and Gospel—which the apostle Paul requires of every servant of God.[19]

Points in review　A week ago we gained the belief that preaching the Word of God—that is, the Gospel—to people who are sincerely alarmed over their sins is the only correct way to give them assurance of the forgiveness of sins and assurance of salvation. You simply call upon them to believe and to apply this belief to themselves—and never to question the truth of this heavenly message of grace.

Next, you urge them—if they are still unbaptized—to receive Baptism for the remission of their sin. As evidence that this is the only right way, we have three examples from Holy Scripture, all of which recount instances of conversion. First, the conversion of the three thousand at the first festival of Pentecost by the preaching of the apostle Peter. Then, the conversion of the jailer at Philippi. Finally, the marvelous conversion of the apostle Paul, which he told himself in Acts.

We also learned that it is incorrect to force alarmed sinners to observe all kinds of rules for their behavior, to tell them all the things they have to do (how earnestly and how long they must pray, wrestle, and struggle, etc.), until they hear a mysterious voice whispering in their heart: "Your sins are forgiven. You are a child of God. You are converted." Or until they *feel* that the grace of God has been poured out in their heart . . . . This is the approach for conversion that all the Reformed sects and their followers use.

Pietist errors　If only this method of conversion were not in use in the Lutheran Church! But, alas, this is the case. At first the **Pietists** tried to convert people by this method. In some points they were quite right. Back then the Lutheran Church had fallen asleep, as it were. It lay wrapped in spiritual death. The Pietists wanted to come to the rescue. However, instead of going back to the purity of teaching that the Church of the Reformation had used, and instead of learning from that age how to make the spiritually dead come alive, some Lutheran churches adopted the approach of the Reformed. Let me illustrate this by using the example of **Dr. Johann Philipp Fresenius** (1705–61).

19　See 2 Timothy 2:15.

From 1748 on, Fresenius was *senior* of the ministerium at Frankfurt am Main.[20] This was a most excellent man, unquestionably a sincere Christian, a godly, pious author of many beautiful devotional writings in which there is little to criticize. With great earnestness he wrote against the Papists, Jesuits, and Herrnhuters.[21] But his attacks on the Herrnhuters placed him under a cloud of controversy among the believers of that time.

Even in his boyhood, Fresenius had been a passionate Christian. Whenever the boys in his town came together, he tried to evangelize them and convert them. He kept this passionate spirit until he entered the University of Strassburg, where he studied with great enthusiasm and became a profound scholar. However, his father, who was struggling financially, did not approve of his son going to university. But Johann Philipp went to Strassburg anyway, relying on the help of God. He had to struggle to pay his way, living for quite a while on only bread and water in a miserable lodging until his professors heard of the young man's difficult situation and secured free room and board for him.

One of Fresenius's most popular works is his *Book on Confession and Communion*, published in 1745. All eight editions sold out in no time. In fact, there was not a single believer in those days who did not own a copy. In 1845 it was published in a new edition by Meyer,[22] who not only failed to remove its errors but even added some more of his own.

The reason I am quoting this book is to show how even Lutherans mingle Law and Gospel. I had a very sad personal experience with this book. After graduating from secondary school,[23] I entered university. While I was not an outspoken unbeliever—after all, my parents were believers—I had left home at the age of eight and all my peers were unbelievers. So were all my professors, with the exception of one, who seemed to have a faint trace of faith.[24]

Walther's pietistic past

---

20 A *ministerium* is an association of pastors. In this case, the association extended to a territory of the Holy Roman Empire. Until 1866, Frankfurt am Main was chartered as a free city, and its ministerium chose a leader, the *senior*. See also the entry for Fresenius in the Index of Persons and Groups, page 494.

21 Herrnhuters were the Moravians who had taken residence on the Berthelsdorf estate of Count Nikolaus von Zinzendorf. See the entries for the Moravians and Zinzendorf in the Index of Persons and Groups, pages 497, 501.

22 Heinrich A. W. Meyer (1800–73) is best known for his work as general editor of the *Kritisch exegetischer Kommentar über das Neue Testament*. This was a leading historical-critical commentary series.

23 German: *Gymnasium*.

24 Walther's uncle, Franz F. W. Walther, was responsible for his elementary education at the parish school in Hohenstein. Walther's brother-in-law, H. W. F. Schubert, was the director of the *Gymnasium* at Schneeberg. Walther's father was a third-generation pastor in the Saxon Territorial Church. The split between Rationalists and the confessional awakening divided Walther's family, as well as other families connected with the Saxon immigrants. For the sake of faith, many severed ties with loved ones.

When I entered university, I did not know even the Ten Commandments by heart and could not recite the books in the Bible. My knowledge of the Bible was pitiful, and by then I did not have the smallest idea of the true faith.

However, I had an older brother who had entered the university ahead of me. Just before I got to university, he joined a society of converted students. When I arrived, he introduced me to this circle of Christians. I had no clue as to what was awaiting me, but I had great respect for my brother, who had invited me to join him. At first I was attracted merely by the friendly and kind way these students treated me. I was not used to such treatment, for in our secondary school the students had treated one another quite roughly.[25]

It was the way these university students treated one another—and people in general—that attracted me at first, not even the Word of God. I soon began to appreciate the company of these Christian students so much that I gladly attended even the prayer meetings they held.

And then—lo and behold! It was there and then that God began to work on my soul by His Word. In no time I had really become a child of God, a believer, who trusted in His grace. Of course, at that point I was not yet deeply grounded in Christian knowledge.

This went on for nearly half a year. Then a theology student who was a good deal older—a genuine Pietist—joined our group. He figured he would never receive a call to a state church[26] because at that time Rationalism was in control everywhere. The other students thought we were crazy and avoided us as if we were afflicted with some contagious disease. That was the sad state of affairs in Germany at the beginning of the nineteenth century.

Then this theology student came to us and said, "You think you are all converted Christians, do you? But you are not. You have not yet passed through any real penitential agony." I fought this view day and night, thinking at first that he meant to take us away from the Gospel and put us back under the Law. But he kept repeating his claim until I finally began to ask myself whether I really was a Christian. At first I had felt so happy, believing in my Lord Jesus Christ. Now a period of severest spiritual affliction began for me.

I went to the student and asked him, "What must I do to be saved?" He prescribed a number of things I had to do and gave me several books to read, among them Fresenius's *Book on Confession and Communion*. The more I

---

25 German student life, similar to the English boarding school, can have its dark side. Dueling fraternities (*Burschenschaften*) exist to the present day. In Walther's student days, it was not uncommon for fraternities holding different political beliefs to have running, deadly feuds. For example, students occupied the Wartburg in 1817, voicing nationalist sentiments. Police stormed the castle and restored order with a notably heavy hand.

26 Since 1555, the Holy Roman Empire permitted each primary ruler to establish the church in his territory, thus a state church or territorial church. In many cases, church workers were civil servants.

read in that book, the more uncertain I became as to whether I really was a Christian. An inner voice kept telling me: "There is not enough proof that you truly meet the requirements of a Christian." To make matters worse, the student was more pietistic than Fresenius himself. At that time, whenever I opened any religious book dealing with grace and salvation, I would read only the chapter on repentance. When I got to the chapters on the Gospel and faith, I would close the book, saying, "That is not for me." An increasing darkness settled on my soul as I tasted less and less of the sweetness of the Gospel. God knows I did not mean to deceive myself—I *wanted* to be saved. In those days I thought the best books were those that spoke a stern language to sinners and left nothing of the grace of God.

Then one day I heard about a man who was said to be a real spiritual doctor.[27] I wrote to him, but in reality I planned to throw his letter into the stove if he said anything about the grace of God and the Gospel. However, his letter was so full of comfort that I could not resist its arguments. That is how I was freed from the miserable state into which I had been led chiefly by Fresenius.

How happy students of Jesus are when they are immediately given the blessed and comforting doctrine of the Gospel! However, we know from experience that the more someone receives the pure doctrine of the divine Word, the more they despise it. This is disgraceful indeed.

In his book, Fresenius separates all communicants into nine different classes. I did not fit into any one of them. By the way, the sainted Pastor Keyl,[28] who certainly was a sincere Christian, assured me that he had no better luck either. That is what happens when you dissect a person's spiritual condition the way Fresenius did, listing the types of communicants as follows: (1) Unworthy communicants. (2) People who sincerely seek grace but who have obtained no assurance. (3) People who are assured of their state of grace, especially spiritual infants or "weak" beginners in Christianity. (4) "New" or "young" Christians or people who have attained some strength of faith. (5) Experienced Christians or spiritual "parents" of other believers. (6) Christians who suffer from great spiritual afflictions. (Even though I was afflicted, I still did not seem to fit in this class.) (7) People who rejoice in God. (8) People who have fallen from God's grace. (9) People who are in a state of distress.

Speaking of the first type, Fresenius writes (in ch. 3, paragraph 11):

Errors in Fresenius's book

---

27   An allusion to Martin Stephan. Walther does not use Stephan's name in order to insulate the positive aspects of Stephan from the tragic events that Stephan's name would otherwise bring to mind.

28   Ernst G. W. Keyl, one of the Saxon immigrants. For more information, see the Index of Persons and Groups, page 496.

> If sinners of this type are to obtain the forgiveness of sins and to receive the body and blood of Christ worthily, everything depends on their conversion. Accordingly, I will here offer faithful instruction regarding the points that need to be observed on their part for them to be thoroughly converted in a short period of time.

The remark "in a short period of time" sounded like Gospel to me, and I wished that it might be so in my case.

> I have tested the good quality of this instruction on many sinners and have found that it resulted in the certain salvation of everyone who faithfully followed it. With great, heartfelt joy, I observed that even sinners who had been bound by Satan with exceptionally strong chains were—by this method—in a short period of time brought into a state where they could be regarded as new creatures in Christ. It is a simple and straightforward method and requires no effort on the part of the "patient." All they have to do is to let God work in them. For it is He, after all, who must give us everything that we need.

> Everything depends on three rules that the sinner must observe. They are taken from the innermost nature of the divine order of salvation and, if faithfully applied, will help even the worst slave of Satan. If anyone is not helped, he must blame his own unfaithfulness for it, and not the rules.

I resolved to gladly obey all the rules.

> The first rule is: Pray for grace. The second: Be watchful lest you lose grace. The third: Meditate upon the Word of God in a proper manner.

> Since sinners cannot convert themselves, they must pray for the grace of conversion. Since the grace that they have obtained in answer to prayer can easily be lost, they must be watchful. Since the Word of God is the Means of Grace by which we are enlightened and regenerated—that is, our hearts are changed—sinners must cherish the Word of God. This shows that these three rules have been taken from the inmost nature of the divine order of salvation.

> A brief explanation of these rules—one by one—will help us learn how to observe them. Regarding the first rule, the person desiring the grace of conversion must pray for it.

As if an unconverted person could seriously pray for conversion! Fresenius should have said, "This person must hear the Word of God." But he addressed that in his third rule. Fresenius's whole plan makes conversion depend on man's own effort to obtain grace.

He continues: "This prayer must be of a different quality than when that person was still under the rule of sin. It must not be a frigid, unfamiliar, lifeless operation of the lips, but it must be offered up with great, heartfelt earnestness." So Fresenius actually speaks of a person in whom sin is still dominant—with his primary error being the false distinction between being *converted* and *awakened*. In reality, anyone who has been awakened, that is, raised from spiritual death, is already converted. After conversion, that person must indeed pray and wrestle. At that point his faith is like an infant that can easily die if not given nourishment. You are not able to do this until you are converted, until you believe.

How do you do this? Well, you enter your room, as the Savior advises in Matthew 6:6 (or wherever you can speak to God in private), kneel, and with all your might cry out for grace—not only for the grace that God may forgive your sins but also for the grace that your heart may be changed and the love of sin destroyed in you. Fresenius speaks as if forgiveness of sins and renewal of the heart were two different things, occurring at different times. The fact is: when your sins are forgiven, your heart is changed and the love of sin is destroyed.

Now about all that crying toward God until He gives grace: Where in the world did Fresenius hear that God is so hard-hearted that He must first be softened by a person's prayers and by that person wrestling with Him?

Fresenius writes: "Since Christ has acquired for us the first kind—converting grace—we base even our first prayer on *His* merit." He speaks of converted people as if they still had to be converted, for to base one's prayer on the merits of Christ means to believe in Christ. And Fresenius claims we should cry to God so He would grant us that converting grace because our Lord Jesus paid such a precious ransom for us. No matter how good the intention of Fresenius might have been, what he writes is awful. Even though he speaks about the merits of Christ, he directs man to his own works, by which nothing will ever be achieved.

"You should offer this prayer," Fresenius claims, "not once or twice, but daily, with sighs and weeping, until you obtain grace." What is that supposed to mean? His advice to cry to God "until you obtain grace" means, as the words that follow show, "until you have a *feeling* of grace." The sweet sensation that satisfies the heart—that is what these people call grace. But grace is not something for which you must look in your heart. It is in the heart of God. Grace cannot be found *in* me. It is *outside* of me. He says, "From your own experience this assures you that your heart has been truly changed."

If our good friend Fresenius had said all these things about believing Christians, [the statements] would be correct. Christians must do all those things. But before they are Christians, they are spiritually dead; they cannot see spiritually, hear spiritually, or feel spiritually.

Fresenius continues: "Some may say: Granted that grace is obtained by praying, yet how can a sinner pray in such a way? Is not prayer itself the result of divine grace, something we do not produce in ourselves while we are still dead in sins?" Dead in sins! Yet he goes on:

> Answer: This kind of prayer is indeed an operation of grace that the sinner—being dead—cannot perform by his own power. But we know that prevenient or awakening grace quite often and earnestly knocks on our hearts in order to awaken us from our sleep in sin. Whenever this happens, grace offers to sinners something they do not have, namely, the strength to offer sighs and cry for help from the depths of sin as they should.

As if people who are dead in their sins were able to do anything by their own power!

He goes on: "Sinners themselves can observe this if they are attentive. Often the Word of God, sickness, the death of other people, terrible dreams, the thought of their own death, of future judgment, of hell and heaven, and similar things make them uneasy about their condition." This is extremely dangerous! If they have not experienced everything that—according to hearsay—they feel they *should* be experiencing, some righteous souls might start to think: "Yes, I presume I am awakened, but I am not yet converted!" Thousands and millions of people have tortured themselves by thinking: "I am not converted."

He states: "In that moment a feeling wells up in them that makes them yearn for salvation. They secretly sigh for grace." What else is this secret sighing for grace than a first spark of faith? It is not something that is given to people so they can *work* their way into grace.

> Now, this desire and sighing is not an action of one's own nature. Rather, it comes from an energy that awakening grace has already produced in them. If they accept this energy, it is no longer impossible for them to call upon God, pray, and cry as their condition requires. By doing this, their strength for praying is continually increased by grace.

This desire for grace is never a power that is given to a person for the purpose of achieving grace by using it. Where do we find any of this in Scripture? Nowhere! **After** we become believers, Fresenius tells us we will have to wrestle with the devil because he will want to rob us of the grace we have received. It is indeed as I have stated: When a person is still unconverted, he is spiritually dead and thus without any strength. Even if strength were breathed into him, he could not use it as long as he is dead. Try breathing strength into a statue and see whether it will move. No, that statue will remain dead and not move.

Modern theology is completely in the grip of this error because it claims that man is able to convert himself by some spiritual powers that are conferred upon him. Fresenius continues:

> Other readers may object and say that even Scripture declares: "God does not listen to sinners" (John 9:31). Therefore, it is useless for them to want to pray, for God testifies distinctly to the Israelites: "When you spread out your hands, I will hide My eyes from you; even though you make many prayers, I will not listen" (Isaiah 1:15). I would answer: "These and similar passages of Scripture refer only to sinners who pray that God would turn aside His vindictive judgments, for forgiveness of sin, or for nothing better than help in their worldly affairs. They do not refer to having a change of heart."

Fresenius is right in what he says. But only a person in whom such change has begun will offer a prayer for a change of heart. Only believers are such people. While they are still unbelievers, people are dead in their sins. They take serious matters lightly; they are unconcerned about whether they will go to heaven or hell or whether they might die tonight. They trust in God's goodness in a merely physical fashion.

> While these people "offer their prayers," they remain entrenched in their particular sins and say their prayers by their natural powers, not by the power of the Holy Spirit. It is obvious that they cannot be heard while they are still in their wicked condition and are still cherishing these false purposes. David says (Psalm 66:18): "If I had cherished iniquity in my heart, the Lord would not have listened." However, the sinners to whom we are referring seek not only forgiveness but also a genuine change of heart, and they earnestly desire to be converted.

If people are serious about wanting to be converted, they *are* already converted. Everyone else is not even interested in it. Only true Christians are worried about the state of their salvation.

Fresenius says, "Now, God cannot despise His own work. It follows, then, that the prayers of such people are truly heard, and the experience of many people confirms this fact." Well, of course, when one makes a false distinction between being awakened and being converted and even says people still in spiritual blindness are enlightened.

"The second rule," Fresenius continues, "is this: A person earnestly desiring to be converted must be on his guard to keep the grace that God has conferred on him." In other words, Fresenius claims that even *before* their conversion people are able to be spiritually watchful.

He writes: "When God gives the power to pray, at the same time He gives the power to be watchful, and this power must be exercised with great care and earnestness." What Fresenius says is well enough when said in reference to a beginner in the Christian faith.

> Such a person guards his own heart, lest it be ruled by sinful thoughts, which prevent the operation of divine grace. He guards his eyes and ears, lest new filth be carried into the heart and the inner work of the Holy Spirit be disturbed. He guards his tongue, lest by insincere and sinful words it grieve the Spirit of God (Ephesians 4:29–30) and the heart be deceived (James 1:26). He is careful about the people with whom he associates, so as to keep away from anything evil, to quit once and forever the sinful friendship of the world, which is hatred against God (James 4:4). Whenever his professional duties lead him into the company of evil people, he needs to make his heart firm against their evil doings, lest he become a partaker of other people's sins.[29]

[Fresenius] describes the complete work of sanctification and expects all these things of an unconverted person! It is almost inconceivable that such a learned and experienced pastor should have failed to see this point.

> He should guard the operations of divine grace, so as to give them more room. He should cherish the seasons of gracious visitation, when God once again awakens him to prayer, alerts him to meditate on His Word, to wrestle with sin, and to exercise neighborly love.

Even love toward one's fellow human being is assumed prior to conversion! That is the dangerous feature of this "instruction." Any honest person will ask himself: "All these things are supposed to take place in me first—while I am still an unconverted person?"

Again Fresenius: "He should take advantage of such times to enter more thoroughly into grace by his sighing and supplications." It is horrible to hear Fresenius speak of trying to penetrate more deeply into grace, since grace is something in the heart of God. Grace is obtained either completely or not at all. It is never given piecemeal, as Luther puts it. A person is either a child of the devil or a child of God; either in the kingdom of darkness or in the kingdom of light; either in a state of grace with God or under His wrath.[30] There is no middle ground.

> This watchfulness is greatly needed in conversion, and the person who fails in it and gives room to sin in his inner life or outward behavior cannot possibly be brought around to the right way. Many people

---

29   The Dau text adds: "He guards his entire conversation, lest he be contaminated again with intentional sins."

30   See, for example, AE 51:70–71.

take the beginning of their conversion seriously. They beg and cry for grace, and God gives them as much grace as they are willing to accept.

What Fresenius says about the necessity of watchfulness for conversion involves an ambiguous[31] use of the term "grace," which is the cause of his error when he cites: "For a while they run well (see Galatians 5:7)." He overlooks that Paul's charge against the Galatians was directed against people who were already converted.

> But they are not serious about being watchful, they are not faithful, and thus they lose the grace that they had obtained—and the enemy again takes possession of their heart.

> In this context it is to be noted that watchfulness offers some difficulties at the beginning of a person's conversion. However, if you are but faithful, it becomes increasingly easy, until—after much practice—you become so skilled in this that being watchful becomes second nature.

> But in view of the previously mentioned difficulties, it occasionally happens at the beginning of conversion that a person—as the result of carelessness—suffers damage from the enemy either in his inner life or in his outward behavior.

This would all be true if it were not being claimed about someone who has yet to be converted.

Fresenius writes: "Whenever this happens, we should not despair but take fresh courage, flee to Jesus, and heartily pray for forgiveness for the careless act and for the grace of greater caution." Eventually, that, too, will happen! He states: "And you need to pray from the bottom of your heart and ask that this carelessness may be forgiven and that you would receive the grace to be more careful. Accordingly, praying and watching take turns in Christians and cooperate harmoniously."[32]

Now comes the third rule: The Word of God must be meditated on in the proper manner. We will see that Fresenius is speaking exclusively of the power of the divine Word to change the heart of man. He is not speaking of—and he seems to be entirely uninformed about—the collative[33] power of the Word of God, which not only describes gifts such as justification but also

Mark 16:16

---

31 Walther uses the hybrid German/Latin word *Aequivocation*, which is related to the English *equivocation*. "Equivocation" happens when someone uses two or more different meanings of a word at the same time, creating an imprecise definition that can mean different things to different people.

32 The Dau text adds: "The dangers attending a person's carelessness which he depicts are true, but it is wrong to say that by the opposite conduct a person is converted. It seems a mere afterthought in the plan of Fresenius to remind his readers of the refuge that is open to them in Christ."

33 See the entry "Word of God" in the Glossary, page 488.

at the same time confers and communicates them. The statement "Whoever believes and is baptized will be saved" produces faith in itself and also communicates the blessing described. When we listen to a preacher, we need to imagine that God is standing behind him. When he speaks words of comfort to us, we must say to ourselves that it is *God* who is speaking to us. When he pronounces forgiveness of sin to us, we must not merely think that because these words are in the Bible we are to receive some benefit from them, but we also must say to ourselves, "By these words God Himself imparts forgiveness of sin to me." But this doctrine, alas! This all vanished from the Lutheran Church a long time ago.

Fresenius writes: "A person desiring to be converted must meditate upon the Word of God in a proper manner. This is done by *reading* as well as by hearing the Word. The Word is read properly when a person reads it for the purpose of being enlightened and transformed into a new person by virtue of its power." He does not mention at all that this Word not only speaks, but it also offers and gives, and that the person who believes it has it. The Word distributes and gives. But, according to Fresenius, everything depends on the behavior of the person.

He says: "You have to pray for this grace before, while, and after reading. You must not read too much at one time, but only a little—and you have to pause at every powerful message, lift your heart to God, and present the contents of your prayer to God with a short sigh, and then ask Him to make the Spirit inside of you grow."

Fresenius's advice to read only a little bit raises some concerns. Of course, you sometimes need to pause at various verses, but true Christians must read the whole Bible **quickly**, so they will generally remember what it says. At the same time, you should study the Word quietly.

Beginners, in particular, should read the Bible this way: first, the four Gospels, because they set before us the Lord Jesus with His grace and example. After that the same method may be followed for the reading of the rest of the New Testament, the Psalms of David, and the other books of Holy Scripture. Anything readers fail to understand they should reverently skip—not stopping for doubtful musings, but holding on to what is clear and plain—in the certain hope that God will gradually reveal the troublesome spots to them, inasmuch as they need them. The Word of God is heard properly when it is heard from preachers who present it in its purity; when it is heard with the same purpose as when it is read; when God is invoked for His gracious power and work before, during, and after hearing the Word; when it is gladly received and those passages, in particular, are noted that apply to that person's condition; and, finally, when it is kept and meditated on and permitted to enter ever more deeply into the heart.

All of this is fine. The problem is that Fresenius says all of this should be done by people who have yet to be converted.

Fresenius concludes his explanation of the three rules for "people who are not yet converted but who would like to be" with these remarks: "Anyone who puts these three rules into practice with the utmost sincerity will, in a short period of time, become a different person, and the grace of God will work in him so powerfully that he will discover in himself more and more clearly the marks of a new creature in Christ."

Let me ask you now: Where do we find advice like this in the Bible? Whenever the apostles preached and their hearers asked them, "What must we do to be saved?" all they answered was: "Believe in the Lord Jesus Christ." That is the only correct method for a preacher who wants to lead people to faith and to an assurance of the forgiveness of their sins and of eternal life. When he follows this method, the preacher must not forget to recommend constant prayer, personal struggles in wrestling with sin, and the proper use of the Word of God. This correct way assures people that their sins are forgiven and that they are in a state of grace. Just because orthodox Lutherans oppose Fresenius's wrong method, we must not draw the conclusion that they oppose genuine, earnest Christianity, earnest and unceasing prayer, earnest wrestling with sin, and constant watchfulness. On the contrary, sincere Lutherans are just as passionate in these matters as they are in refusing to lead people to Christ in a roundabout way.

No doctrine of the Evangelical Lutheran Church is more offensive to the Reformed than the doctrine of the grace of God, the forgiveness of sin, righteousness in the sight of God, and the fact that eternal salvation is obtained only by believers who put their confidence in the written Word, in Baptism, in the Lord's Supper, and in Absolution. The Reformed—especially their theologians—declare that this approach of getting into heaven is too mechanical. When they hear the Lutheran teaching, they denounce it as "dead-letter worship," quoting the apostle Paul: "For the letter kills, but the Spirit gives life" (2 Corinthians 3:6).

Again, they say, "What are the benefits of baptizing with earthly water? True baptism is baptizing with the Spirit and with fire." And again: "What are the benefits of eating and drinking the natural body and blood of Christ?" No, they say, "The food and drink that still the hunger and thirst of the soul is the truth that came down from heaven." Finally, they say, "How can a mortal,

Sixteenth Evening Lecture: Jan. 30, 1885

2 Cor. 3:6

sinful man, who cannot look into my heart, help me by saying, 'Your sins are forgiven'?" No, they say, "My sins are forgiven only when God Himself speaks these words into my heart and makes me feel their force." That is the Reformed view.

Now, does this view agree with Scripture? Not at all!

Letter and Spirit; 2 Cor. 3:6

In the scriptural meaning of the term, the "letter" is not something dead. The context in 2 Corinthians 3:6 shows, in the first place, that the apostle refers not to the Word of God as such, but to the Law. *That* is what kills. On the other hand, the "Spirit" signifies the Gospel. *That* is what gives life. Consider, furthermore, that when the apostle says, "The letter kills," he cannot mean that the letter itself is dead. For something that is dead cannot kill.

Baptism; Acts 22:16; John 3:5; Gal. 3:27; Titus 3:5–7

According to the Holy Scriptures, Baptism is not a mere washing with earthly water. Rather, the Spirit of God—or, more precisely, Jesus, with His blood—connects with it in order to cleanse people of their sins. Therefore, Ananias says to Saul, "Rise and be baptized and wash away your sins" (Acts 22:16), and Jesus says to Nicodemus, "Truly, truly, I say to you, unless one is born of water and the Spirit, he cannot enter the kingdom of God" (John 3:5). He mentions the water first, and then the Spirit, for it is by this very baptizing with water that the Spirit is to given to us. In Galatians 3:27 the apostle says clearly and distinctly: "For as many of you as were baptized into Christ have put on Christ"; and in Titus 3:5–7: "He saved us, not because of works done by us in righteousness, but according to His own mercy, by the washing of regeneration and renewal of the Holy Spirit, whom He poured out on us richly through Jesus Christ our Savior, so that being justified by His grace we might become heirs according to the hope of eternal life."

The Lord's Supper

According to the Holy Scriptures, the Lord's Supper is not an earthly feast but a heavenly feast on earth, in which bread and wine, the body and blood of Christ, and also forgiveness of sins, life, and salvation are given to us and sealed for us. For when He distributed the bread that He had blessed, Christ said, "This is My body, which is given **for you** . . . This do in remembrance of Me." By the words "for you," He invited the disciples to think about the fact that they were now receiving and eating His body and that by His bitter death on the cross the entire world would be redeemed. He was reminding them that they ought to explode with joy and gladness because the ransom that would be paid for the sins of the whole world was, so to speak, being put in their mouths. Offering the disciples the cup that He had blessed, Christ said, "This cup is the new testament in My blood, which is shed for you." Why did He add the words "shed for you"? His point was: "When you receive the blood of redemption in this Holy Supper, at the same time you also receive what has been acquired on the cross by this sacrifice."

Finally, according to the Holy Scriptures, the Absolution pronounced by a poor, sinful preacher is not *his* Absolution but the Absolution of Jesus Christ Himself. For the preacher absolves a person by the *command* of Christ, in the *place* of Christ, and in the *name* of Christ. Christ said to His disciples: "Peace be with you. As the Father has sent Me, even so I am sending you" (John 20:21). Why are these words important? Because of this very point: "I am sent by My Father. When I speak to you, My words are the words of My Father. Ignore the humble form in which you see Me. I come in the name of the Father, in the place of the Father, and the word of promise that proceeds from My mouth is the word of My Father. Now, in the same manner as My Father has sent Me, I am sending you. You, too, are to speak in My name and in My place." Therefore, He continues: "Receive the Holy Spirit. If you forgive the sins of any, they are forgiven them; if you withhold forgiveness from any, it is withheld."

Absolution;
John 20:21;
20:22–23

Observe, then, the lack of appreciation, the contempt, and the scornful ring in the words of the Reformed when they speak of the sacred Means of Grace, the Word and the Sacraments. This contrasts with the grand, majestic ring in the words of the Lord and the apostles when they speak of these matters. Who is right: Christ or the Reformed? the holy apostles or the ministers of the Reformed Church? I would be ashamed to answer these questions. You all know the answers.

The true reason for the Reformed view is this: They do not grasp how a person can come into possession of divine grace, the forgiveness of sin, righteousness in the sight of God, and eternal salvation. They point to another way. They want to know nothing of the means that God has provided. They have invented new approaches. We discovered this in our previous evening lecture. May the Lord grant us His Holy Spirit so that tonight we may be strengthened and confirmed in this belief and be blessed with a cheerful faith.

The ninth thesis that we are studying is one of the most important. For when the Reformed mingle Law and Gospel—a common practice among the sects—this is what it boils down to: instead of pointing people to the Word and the Sacraments, the Reformed instruct alarmed sinners to struggle their way into a state of grace by prayer and inward wrestling until they *feel* grace living within themselves. This *looks* like a very godly and Christian procedure, and an inexperienced person can easily be deceived by it.

But God be praised! We have God's Word, which does not deceive us, a Word on which we can rely and by which we can remain in the present darkness, which it lights up for us. When death summons us and says, "Come along," even though we feel nothing, we can follow it confidently and say, "I will gladly go with you. I praise God for my escape from this terrible prison. I am absolutely certain that I will stand before the throne of a gracious God.

Why? Not because I have a certain *feeling*, not because I have performed any good works, not because I have become a better person. All these things of mine would be sinking sand." For it is quite possible that in my hour of death I will not have any feelings of gladness. But if you are accustomed to relying on the Word, you have a trusty staff, which you will need as you walk through the dark valley of death.

May our heavenly Father equip you with His Word when you enter the ministry so your efforts do not turn out merely to be a beating of the air! May you always know that "this is the Word of the eternal, living God. And let not the devils in hell try to convince me to deny this fact." Just tell those devils: "When the Lord speaks, let all keep silence; for He is Lord over all, and all must be subject to Him."

Until now I have been explaining this doctrine to you—as it is stated in the Holy Scriptures—to the best of my ability. But so you may see that I am not presenting my personal opinion but the doctrine of our dear Lutheran Church, let us hear what the Confessions of our Church say about this matter.

Zwingli's errors   First, listen to a testimony of Zwingli, the grandfather of all Reformed churches, on behalf of Reformed teaching. Apparently the influence Zwingli wielded was not as great as that of *Calvin*. Nevertheless Zwingli did lay the foundation for the Reformed Church before God snatched him out of the world of the living by sudden death. Calvin polished the clumsy work of Zwingli. By the finesse of Calvin's workmanship, he gained the English and the French to his side, though he accomplished little among the German people. Be that as it may, the doctrine of Zwingli is the source from which all false teachings of the Reformed churches have sprung. What does he say about the relationship of the Means of Grace to faith?

Most of you know that in 1530 the Zwinglians wanted to participate in the Augsburg Confession, but the Lutherans denied them fellowship. Accordingly, Zwingli wrote a so-called "Augsburg Confession" of his own and sent it to the emperor.[34] The most dismaying feature of this confession was this: Six months prior to this event, Zwingli had endorsed the very opposite doctrine, for in the late fall of 1529—at the Marburg Colloquy—he had, among other things, signed the following statement:

> In the eighth place, the theologians have agreed that the Holy Spirit . . . gives faith to no one except through previous preaching and by and with the Word creates and works faith how, where, and in whom He pleases. In the ninth place, that Holy Baptism is a Sacrament, by which man is regenerated.

---

34   Compare Philip Schaff, *Creeds of Christendom*, 6th ed. (New York: Harper & Brothers, 1919), 1:366–68.

Luther had presented the pure, plain Lutheran doctrine before the Zwinglians and even before Zwingli himself. They accepted it because they desired a union with the Wittenberg theologians. With tears in his eyes, Zwingli stood before Luther, offering his hand and asking for brotherly fellowship. Going as far as he thought he could, Zwingli declared: "By the spoken Word of God, faith is produced in people; by Baptism a person is regenerated." Half a year later he denied all of this, for in his confession he writes: "In the seventh place, I believe and know that all Sacraments, far from conferring grace, do not even offer or present it." Remember, at Marburg, Zwingli had subscribed to the opposite teaching and pledged that it was his too.

Zwingli continues:

> Most Powerful Emperor, it may appear to you that I am speaking too freely. Nevertheless this matter is settled. For grace is worked and given by the Holy Spirit, and therefore this gift must be attributed to the Holy Spirit. (I am using the term *grace* in its Latin meaning. I understand it to mean forgiveness, kindness, and blessing—without any merit and not as a payment for the same.)

What Zwingli means to say is this: "This is why preaching, Baptism, and the Lord's Supper are useless (they are mere empty symbols): Because the Spirit requires no conveyance or vehicle, for He is Himself the conveying force by which everything is transferred. He does not need to *be* transferred."[35]

Look at the crude terms in which Zwingli speaks of these sacred matters! When the Holy Spirit wants to approach man, He does not need the Word of God, the Gospel, Baptism, or the Lord's Supper. He does not need these things; He can come without them!

Zwingli says: "Nowhere in Holy Scripture do we find a teaching"—what a strange Bible Zwingli must have had!—"that external objects, among which one includes the Sacraments, bring the Spirit with them to people in a sure manner. On the contrary, whenever external objects have accompanied the Spirit, it is in every instance the Spirit—not the external objects—that did the conveying."

---

35 Zwingli developed his position concerning the sacraments and preaching from the Renaissance era revival of Cicero's writings. Surprisingly, Cicero's writings on moral obligations and on divination had a twofold effect. The papacy used them and other writings to support its claim that the pope controls the Means of Grace and determines the meaning of Scripture because Scripture is said to be basically unclear. Zwingli and the radical reformers claimed from these documents and from Greek philosophy that all possible ways that God comes to us through means (preaching and the Sacraments) are vague. They said that working through means cannot result in the clarity that the Holy Spirit supposedly gives in the heart of the elect as a result of divine providence. Luther alone bases the Means of Grace on the clarity of Scripture. Luther alone has the true, biblical doctrine.

Acts 10:44

Zwingli inserts the word "sure." That is ambiguous. The Means of Grace **really** convey grace, but not by forcing a person to receive them. To the person receiving Baptism, God says, "I will be your God, and you will be in grace and favor with Me." If the person refuses to receive this offer, he does not obtain grace; the reason for that is not because there is no grace for him to receive, but because he despises it. The whole Bible is full of testimonies to the fact that the Word and the Sacraments actually convey the Holy Spirit. For instance, in Acts 10:44: "While Peter was still saying these things, the Holy Spirit fell on all who heard the word." Here the coming of the Holy Spirit is attributed to the Word.

Concerning Baptism, you have already heard that streams of the Holy Spirit are poured out with Baptism. Zwingli continues:

> For instance, when a mighty wind began to blow, the languages came at the same time, by the power of the wind. But the wind was not supported by the power of the languages. Likewise, one wind brought quail, another carried away locusts; but never have quails and locusts been so light and nimble that they would have brought wind. Likewise, when a wind so strong that it could have blown away mountains blew by Elijah, the Lord was not in the wind.

> In sum, "the Spirit (wind) blows where it wishes," that is, it blows in a way agreeable to its nature. "You hear its sound, but you do not know where it comes from or where it subsides.[36] So it is with everyone born of the Spirit," that is, who is enlightened and drawn in an invisible and intangible manner. Truth speaks these words. Therefore, the grace of the Spirit is not conveyed by this "immersing," "drinking," or by "unction."[37]

He also mentions extreme unction because he is addressing the Roman emperor. What Lutheran ever regarded unction to be a sacrament? That was only a temporary ceremony, which was used in the time of the apostles.[38]

Thus Zwingli:

> For if this were so, we *would* know how, where, in which direction, and by what vehicle the Spirit comes. For if the presence and efficacy of grace is attached to the Sacraments, they will operate wherever

---

36   German: *wo er stille wird.*

37   In the first paragraph, Zwingli recalls (rather loosely) Acts 2:1–2; Numbers 11:31–32; Exodus 10:18–19; and 1 Kings 19:11. In the second paragraph he does likewise with John 3:8. Extreme unction is the Roman Catholic sacrament of last rites for the dying; here Zwingli refers to the anointing with oil that is part of the rite.

38   Walther refers to the anointing with oil mentioned in James 5:14.

they are applied; and wherever they are not applied, all will be broken down and miserable.

At this point, theologians should not babble about the substance or the person receiving grace, namely, that the grace of Baptism or the Lord's Supper should be given only to those people who are fit to receive it, as they say. For if anyone receives grace by means of the Sacraments, as they claim, they either make themselves suitable on their own or the Spirit prepares them to receive the Sacrament.

If they do it on their own, they must have some natural ability, and **prevenient grace** would not apply. But if a person is prepared for the reception of grace by the Spirit, I would ask, "Does this occur in connection with the Sacrament or without it?"

If it occurs by means of the Sacrament, then a person is prepared for the Sacrament *by* the Sacrament. This process would have to continue *ad infinitum*, since a Sacrament would always be required as a preparation for the Sacrament.

But if a person is prepared without a Sacrament for the reception of sacramental grace, surely the Spirit with His grace is present **prior** to the Sacrament. Thus **grace is conveyed and present before the Sacrament comes**. This leads to the conclusion (which I gladly admit and concede in the negotiations on the Sacrament) that the Sacraments are offered as **public evidence of that grace** which exists **previously** in every individual.

Remember—according to Zwingli's teaching—Baptism is worthless because the Holy Spirit does not require a vehicle for His conveyance.

Zwingli continues:

The Church, then, receives by Baptism those who have previously obtained grace. **Accordingly, Baptism does not confer grace.** Rather, it testifies to the Church that the person receiving it has already obtained grace. . . . In the tenth place, I believe that the office of prophesying, or preaching, is sacred because it is highly necessary above all other offices. For, to speak with canonical correctness, we observe that, in every nation, external preaching by the apostles and evangelists or bishops has come before faith.

Zwingli mentions this because it is an undeniable fact, and he calculates that his opponents will now be unable to charge him with hiding this fact: "and yet we attribute man's faith to the Spirit alone. For, alas! We behold a great number of people **who hear the external preaching of the Gospel** and yet do not believe **because the Spirit is lacking**."

There is the fanatic for you. From such teaching, fanaticism is bound to crop up. It certainly has cropped up. We have the best evidence of it here in America, where the appeal to the Spirit is heard everywhere.

Zwingli concludes: "If, notwithstanding this, the prophets or preachers of the Word are sent to any place, that is an indication of the grace of God, who wants to reveal the knowledge of Himself to the elect." He means to say: "When the Word is preached and there are still so many people who are unconverted, the reason is not that the Word has not been efficacious but because there is no efficacy in the Word.[39] The Spirit must produce the impact. God permits preaching only because He wants to convert the elect. Accordingly, He applies His Spirit to some and takes Him away from others."

This plainly shows what the Reformed Church teaches regarding the relation of the Means of Grace to grace, righteousness, and the salvation of sinners. Now, listen to a few testimonies from our own Confessions.

SA III VIII 10 Smalcald Articles III VIII 10: "Therefore, we must constantly maintain this point: **God does not want to deal with us in any other way than through the spoken Word and the Sacraments. Whatever is praised as from the Spirit—without the Word and Sacraments—is the devil himself.**"[40]

The Spirit comes to people only by means of the Word. A person may imagine that he is about to burst because he is so full of the "Spirit," but this is his own spirit of fanaticism. The true Spirit is obtained only through the Word of God. In every passage of Holy Scripture that recounts the conversion of people, we see that God wants to deal with people only through Word and Sacrament.

Apology IV 68 (Müller, 99) states:

Ap IV (II) 68; But God cannot be dealt with. **God cannot be apprehended except**
Rom. 1:16 Luther **through the Word. Accordingly, justification occurs through the Word, just as St. Paul says in Romans 1:16: "The Gospel is a power of God for everyone who believes."**

Rom. 10:17 Luther Likewise, in Rom 10:17: "**Faith comes by hearing.**"

From all of this it should be crystal clear that **only faith in God saves**. For if justification occurs only through the Word and the Word is apprehended only by faith, it follows that *faith justifies*.[41]

---

39 The terms *efficacious* and *efficacy* are from Latin and refer to the power or ability of the Word of God to do what it says and to actualize its purpose. These terms are technical, theological terms that also refer to the serious commitment of God to bring about our salvation. See also the entry "Word of God" in the Glossary, pages 488.

40 *Concordia*, 281. See also Müller, 322; *Triglot Concordia*, 497.

41 This text is near Ap IV 67. See also *Triglot Concordia*, 139; *Concordia*, 91. For more information, see the appendix, "Walther's Book of Concord," pages 467–68.

This important statement demonstrates that everyone who rejects the Means of Grace does not believe from the heart that people are saved solely by grace. For what does their objection to the Means of Grace amount to? They like to argue: "How can a person really obtain forgiveness of sins by the mere application of the letter, Baptism, the Lord's Supper, and Absolution? That would be too easy."

But if we are saved by pure grace, why should our salvation be such a difficult task—provided it is really grace that saves us? It is precisely *because* we are saved by grace that God must have arranged matters so that we need nothing but the means by which God offers us forgiveness of sins, grace, and salvation. When God says to the sinner, "Only believe," He is saying, "Accept what I give you; have confidence in Me. What I am telling you is the truth. Just come, lay hold of My gift, and take it." When I hear the Gospel preached to me, I am supposed to believe that it is God who is bringing me these glad tidings by means of the preacher's proclamation. At the same time, God is saying to me: "Why do you keep on working to accumulate good works? Christ has acquired all that you need. Just believe, and all is yours. I am not lying." That is what God says.

Now, whatever is true for the Word of God is, of course, also true for the Sacraments, for they also are Means of Grace. They are the visible Word. The Word of God—the Gospel—is only audible, but the Sacraments are also visible, for they are acts attached to objects of the five senses. Therefore, it is a horrible error—promoted in our time particularly by so-called "modern believers"—to claim that the Word has its own efficacy. They claim that Baptism is a special medicine for other ills and that the Lord's Supper a cure for still others. But these are useless human theories, of which not a word is found in the Scriptures. Let us hear our Confessions on this matter.

In **Apology** XIII 5 (Müller, 196) we read:

> But just as the Word enters the ear to strike our heart, so the rite itself strikes the eye in order to move the heart. **The impact of the Word and of the rite is the same**, as Augustine said so well, namely, that a **Sacrament** is a **visible Word**, because the rite is received by the eyes. It is a picture of the Word, as it were, meaning the same things as the Word. **Therefore the impact of both is the same.**[42]

Ap XIII (VII) 5

This is an important point. We can preach the Gospel to a hearing person by using words. But in the case of a person with a hearing impediment, whom we cannot teach by that method, we could use a picture representing the crucifixion or the birth of Christ with the angels coming down from heaven. Using

---

42   See also *Triglot Concordia*, 309; *Concordia*, 184–85.

pantomime, we could explain those pictures and instruct that person without speaking a word.

It is the same with the Sacraments. They show us in a picture, so to speak, what God proclaims audibly in the Word. "The Sacraments are the visible Word" is an excellent statement of truth by Augustine. Some people speak disparagingly and disdainfully of the Sacraments and say the same kinds of things against the Word. They do not consider the terrible guilt they are heaping upon themselves. They mock God, turning Him into a wretched master of ceremonies who has prescribed all sorts of pantomime for us, merely for the purpose of exercising our obedience. No, God does not occupy Himself with such unimportant things now that the era of shadows and "types" is past. The body itself and the essence of God's gifts have arrived now that the time of the Old Testament is past.[43]

Luther writes on Isaiah 20:2 (St. Louis Ed. 6:285):

W² 6:285
(cf. AE 16:168)

> Just as the Holy Spirit operates by means of the Word, He operates also through signs, which are, so to speak, nothing else than the acted Word, inasmuch as the same things are expressed by an act as by the words sounding in people's ears. And since the Word never returns empty, the signs cannot be without result either. Thus Baptism and the Lord's Supper are signs, which raise up and strengthen our faith.

This quote shows that our church does not teach that mere hearing of the Word or immersing a person in water and drawing him out again leads to faith and the obtaining of grace. If that were so, we would be saved by works, would we not? No, the crucial point, as we are engaged in pious meditation of the Word, is that we say to ourselves: "That is the voice of my God speaking to me." Baptism without faith is useless, even if the act were repeated ten times a day. Communing without faith would not benefit us, even if we received the Sacrament daily. No, these acts—if performed in this way—would rather increase the blindness and darkness that cover us; they would intensify our hardness of heart and spiritual stubbornness and, in the end, our damnation. The doctrine of our church, then, is this: The Word and the Sacraments

---

43 Walther makes an indirect reference to Johann Gerhard's *Loci Theologici*. Taken from Walther's article "Theologische Axiome," *Lehre und Wehre* 7 (1861): 9–13, the text reads: "As in the Old Testament one discerns the darkness[, that is, types or prefigures of Christ,] so in the New one searches for what [the words plainly] mean, not another type" ["*Ut in Veteri T. umbra cernitur, ita in Novo res significata quaerenda est, non alius typus*"]. The Old Testament always points to the New as its fulfillment. The proverbs from Gerhard, Luther, and others included in Walther's article appear frequently as sayings in this book. The full citation of the article is Walther, "Theologische Axiome," *Lehre und Wehre* 7 (1861): 4–14, 33–39, 65–67, 87–90, 129–32, 161–64, 193–95, 225–27, 257–64, 289–93, 353–57; *Lehre und Wehre* 8 (1862): 6–12, 129–35, 257–65; *Lehre und Wehre* 9 (1863): 46–47, 161–65, 193–98, 225–31, 268–70, 303–5; *Lehre und Wehre* 10 (1864): 15–19, 97–100, 129–34, 192–95.

operate in such a manner as to raise us up in faith and prompt us to lay hold of the blessings that are offered us.

In a general way **Luther** treats this topic by commenting on Deuteronomy 4:28. This quote is taken from a sermon that Luther preached at the Marburg Colloquy. He speaks out against the fanatics, the Zwinglians, the Anabaptists. Zwingli was such an enthusiast. For though Zwingli admitted the correctness of Luther's teaching, we can see that half a year later he revoked his admission in a solemn address to the emperor.[44] Zwingli was hoping that the emperor would read his confession at an open session of the Diet. But this was not done, and not until after Zwingli's death was that confession published by his son-in-law, who thought he needed to use this document to raise a monument to his late father-in-law. It is, truly, a sorry monument.

So, this sermon of Luther's was preached in 1529. Note the timeline carefully! Did Zwingli in 1529 not agree with Luther on a common confession? Did Luther, then, do Zwingli a serious wrong by preaching as he did? Not at all! At the time the sermon was preached, Zwingli had not yet made this confession. This explains Luther's language.

[Luther] writes (St. Louis Ed. 3:1691–94):[45] "Notice that our new fanatics and enthusiasts are leading the people to trust in their own works!" True enough, the fanatics do not issue orders such as "You must give this certain amount to the poor, or you must forgive your enemy. These things will get you to heaven." But simply by declaring that people need to *do* things in addition to believing the Good News of the Gospel, we have enough evidence to define these new sects as non-Christian. For only people who believe that they are saved by *grace* are Christians. Once a person becomes a Christian, it is all right to tell him that he must now work and struggle because he already *has* faith. In fact, we *must* tell him this—so he does not mistakenly believe that he will get to heaven because of the work and worry he went through **first**.

"Just take the Anabaptists. What are they doing, and what do they teach? They declare that Baptism is worthless." These *Schwärmer* caused a rift [in the Church] on account of Baptism, even though they claimed that Baptism is useless. They said it was a mere act of outward obedience that—how disrespectful!—a person must perform in order to fulfill all righteousness. That is how Anabaptists equate themselves to Christ. When they receive Baptism, they view it as an act of goodwill on *their* part. They claim they are doing God a service by it. And that is still their teaching, as I know from my personal experience and through my reading.

W² 3:1691

W² 3:1691

---

44 See Walther's comments concerning Zwingli above, page 170ff.

45 Walther does not always cite Luther continuously here. He picks up sections of the Luther text that he wishes to highlight as they pertain to his remarks.

W² 3:1691   "They remove the element of grace from Baptism, so that there are no longer grace and the mercy of God, no longer forgiveness of sin in it. As such, Baptism becomes a sign of one's own godliness **prior** to Baptism, etc., a **mark** that one now **possesses** godliness." In other words, they claim that one needs to acquire grace *first*. Thus you receive Baptism as a sign that you have *already* attained grace. This is horrible!

W² 3:1691   "The Anabaptists separate grace from Baptism and leave us with a merely external sign, in which there is **not a single ounce of mercy**. Every scrap of grace has been removed. Now, if the grace of Christ has been removed from Baptism, nothing is left except a pure work." In that case, Baptism is nothing more than a work we must do.

W² 3:1692   Likewise, concerning the Sacrament of the **Lord's Supper**, the enthusiasts remove the promise offered us in this Sacrament. They tell us that what we eat and drink is nothing but bread and wine. Here, too, the offered grace is removed and renounced. These people teach that the only good work that we do by communing is to profess Christ alone. But when we merely eat bread and drink wine in the Lord's Supper, there is no grace in it for us.

So they claim you are doing a good work by professing Christ at the Lord's Supper. But you need to bring your own grace.

W² 3:1692   That is what happens when you fall away from the First Commandment: you immediately set up an idol in the form of some meritorious work in which you trust. Therefore, Moses says: My dear children, be careful to remain in God and follow Him. Otherwise, you cannot avoid idolatry. You will fall into that sin. For at all times the devil assaults the grace of God. **No heresy can stand against the teaching of divine grace.**

Luther's remark about the hatred of all heretics toward the grace of God is an important axiomatic[46] statement. Every heresy that has sprung up was caused by the inability of the heretics to believe that man becomes righteous in the sight of God and is saved by grace alone. That is the real bone of contention against which all heretics, all false teachers, dash their heads. But there is no escape from this difficult situation: either you believe this truth or you are left to your own devices. For since the great God came down from heaven, I may not treat this matter lightly.

But do I not need to add something to make God's work complete? No. What you need is to fall prostrate before God as a poor sinner—like that leper[47]—and praise and magnify God for His plentiful grace. When you do

---

46   An "axiom" is a rule or proverb; Walther cites many "theological axioms" in this book.
47   See Luke 17:15–16.

this, you will understand how senseless is the fanatics' insistence on having the Spirit. You will then receive the Spirit of God and become passionate in your love for God. You will realize that this is not a mechanical way of getting into heaven, but the most spiritual way that can be pointed out. This Spirit is no delusion. Spirit and life spring from the Word of God.

> The fanatics of today all urge the First Commandment, saying: We, too, proclaim grace and mercy through Christ. We do not reject the doctrine of the First Commandment. They charge that I, Luther, am telling lies about them. However, put them to the test: **True, they confess Christ crucified who died for us and saved us, but they renounce the means by which we obtain Him. They demolish the way, the bridge and path, leading to Christ.**

W² 3:1692

That is the main point![48] What good is it if someone tells me: "There is a great treasure. Go get it! All you have to do is haul it off," yet he does not tell me where the treasure is, how to get there, what methods to use to get it. Then I would say, "Enough of your foolish talk about your great treasure!" But that is exactly how the fanatics talk about the great treasure that lies hidden in the Christian religion. When you ask them how to gain it, they cannot tell you. It is true in that hymn:

> Your Baptism, Supper, and Your Word
> Console me in grief's vale, O Lord;
> There lies my dearest treasure.[49]

Whoever does not go to these places to get the treasure will not fetch any gold. What you get may *look* like gold, but it is mere tinsel. If only I could squeeze this truth deeply into your hearts, so that the sound of my words would not simply rush past your ears but would bring energy and life to you! Oh, what witnesses you would become by refusing to deny the grace of God in Christ, as the fanatics do!

> The Jews, too, believe that there is a God, but they despise the way that leads to God, namely, through Christ—the man, Christ Jesus. On the other hand, the Turks [Muslims] confess God, yet they renounce the means, or bridge, by which we come to God, namely, by the grace of God. They refuse Christ and any Sacraments by which a person obtains grace.[50] They act just like people to whom a preacher might say, "Here, I have a treasure," yet he does not put the treasure plainly

W² 3:1692–93

---

48   The Dau edition adds: "Luther touches the main point of the controversy when he speaks of the bridge to Christ that has been demolished by the Anabaptists and Sacramentarians."

49   Again Walther recalls the hymn "Lord Jesus Christ, You Have Prepared." This is from stanza 6. See *LSB* 622.

50   In Luther's time Islam was considered to be a Christian heresy.

before them or give them the key to unlock it. Then what good would this treasure be to them? **They lock up the treasure in front of us** that they ought to lay plainly before us—and thereby they lead me out on a limb to step on the monkey's tail.[51]

If someone wanted to be secure regarding this issue and were still misled, then he would realize on what shifting sand he is standing, when he looks around and sees that he was played for a fool!

W² 3:1693

These people are refusing to give me my treasure and are preventing me from accessing, using, and possessing it.

Granted, the fanatics talk a great deal about God, forgiveness of sins, the grace of God, and the death of Christ. Yet when the question is raised as to how to come to Christ and how to obtain grace, they tell us that the Spirit alone must do this. They mislead us by saying that the external and oral proclamation of the Word, Baptism, and the Sacrament are worthless. And yet they preach grace. That amounts to proclaiming the existence of a treasure in fine terms, and then taking away the key and bridge that would put me in possession of the treasure.

Now, God has ordained that this treasure should be offered and conveyed to people by means of Baptism, the sacrament of the Lord's Supper, and the external Word. These are the means and instruments by which to obtain the grace of God. They deny this truth.

I must confess: For a long time that caused me considerable worry. When I first read that, I was but a student. I thought that way too easy and therefore wrong, until one day I was thrown into great anguish and distress and found out that it is the right way after all. Since then I have, by the grace of God, stuck to this way. I say "by the grace of God," for no one arrives at this knowledge or clings to it by his own strength.

We are all by nature much more inclined to choose the wrong way than the right way. In the end—even in sectarian circles—if people are children of God, they turn to the right way, at least in their hour of death. They may not decide to become Lutherans, but that is not of such key importance. For a person may bear the name of Lutheran and still go to the devil. Without fully realizing what they are doing, these people cast aside everything in which they had placed their confidence, and when they are at death's door, they fling themselves upon the mercy of God. The reason why—even in the papacy—

---

51 Luther uses the slang phrase *"und führen mich auf den Affenschwanz,"* which means to mislead someone. The picture is of a person led onto a false branch that is really a monkey's tail, thus he falls.

many are saved is because in the end they cast everything else overboard and cling only to the mercy of God.

The goodness and grace of God are marvelous. A person may have despised the grace of God for fifty years, and may have been burdened with millions of dreadful sins, but finally collapses and cries, "God have mercy on me, a sinner!" and God receives him. But this truth must not be abused in an arrogant manner. A person may not conclude that he can continue sinning at his ease, yet in his last hour simply repeat the cry of the penitent tax collector.[52] Plotting of this kind hardens the heart. The outcome may be that this person is snatched from life before he can formulate a single godly thought. And then suddenly he will find himself in eternity, standing before the judgment seat of God.

> I state these matters because the devil is so cunning that he **professes the words** of this truth but renounces the **means** by which we obtain what the words declare. These fanatics do not renounce the treasure, just the **use** and **benefit** of it. They deprive us of the method—of the ways and means—of getting at the treasure so that we can enjoy it. They shut us out from the grace that we would very much like to have. They tell us that we must have the **Spirit**, but they do not concede to us the means by which we may **have** the Spirit. How can we receive the Spirit and believe when the Word of God is not preached and the Sacraments are not administered to us? We must have the means, for "faith comes from hearing, and hearing through the spoken word" (Romans 10:17). In sum, all sects must collide with the First Commandment and stumble over Christ Jesus. All heretics end up being piled at the foot of the First Commandment.

W² 3:1693–94;
Rom. 10:17 Luther

The only way you can obtain the Holy Spirit is simply by believing the Word of God. Even if you feel nothing but still say, "God said it; I believe it!" then you will notice that the Holy Spirit has moved into your heart and that you will be filled with peace and joy in the Holy Spirit!

> Let us then live by this article: "You shall have no other gods," and let us diligently hold in esteem its object and scope. For if we lose sight of this commandment, we are opening the doors wide to all schismatic spirits. **God never meant to set up His worship in this world without external means.**

W² 3:1694

This must be enough for tonight. But the discussion of this matter is so important that I will take it up once more next week. I owe you a thorough discussion, for I am aware of my great responsibility toward you. I will soon

Walther's Legacy

---

52   See Luke 18:10–14.

stand before the throne of God to give an account of the great number of dear souls to whose care thousands will someday be entrusted. God will demand of me a statement whether I have fully discharged my office. Therefore, I must speak to you about this subject, whether you like it or not.

However, I have no doubt that you *will* like it, especially those of you who have known the precious Word of God since early childhood. I hope you have had spiritual experiences that have taught you that the only source of comfort when you are afflicted is the Word of God. Only *it* assures you of your salvation.

Seventeenth Evening Lecture:
Feb. 6, 1885

MY DEAR FRIENDS:—

In 1529, Philip, landgrave of Hesse, organized a colloquy at Marburg. Luther, with his followers, his fellow soldiers of the Reformation, gathered on the one side, while Zwingli and some of his followers gathered on the other. At first it seemed that the desired objective of reaching a brotherly and ecclesiastical union could really be achieved, for the Swiss made one concession after the other. But this progress was brought to a halt when the two groups started to discuss the doctrine of the Lord's Supper. For the sake of peace, the Swiss offered to adopt Luther's terminology concerning the substantial presence of the true body and the true blood of Christ in the Lord's Supper—except that the Zwinglians understood that to mean a **spiritual** presence. Despite all this, with great earnestness, the Swiss hoped that brotherly and ecclesiastical fellowship would not be refused them on account of this single difference. In fact, Zwingli even had tears in his eyes.

And what did Luther do on this occasion? He soon noticed that the Swiss were not acting quite honestly. As you know, his suspicion was well-founded because six months later Zwingli overthrew the entire agreement and denied every concession he had made at Marburg.[53] Accordingly, Luther said to Zwingli, "Your spirit is different from ours." This figure of speech—this memorable, world-renowned phrase of Luther's—struck the heart of Zwingli and his followers like a bolt of lightning. In a letter to his friend Dr. Propst,[54] a pastor at Bremen, Zwingli refers to the impact of Luther's statement. Zwingli relates that whenever he repeated those words of Luther to himself—and he did that often—he felt their consuming force. Why? He and his friends knew they were beaten. They knew they had been found out and had to reveal their insincere goal of trying to create a mere *external* union.

---

53   This refers to Zwingli's confession that he sent to the emperor. See above, page 171ff.

54   Jakob Propst remained not only a friend of Zwingli but also of Luther. For more information, see the Index of Persons and Groups, page 498.

What did Luther mean when he spoke those words: "Your spirit is different from ours"? Undeniably this: "If you poor people were merely caught in an error because of your human weakness, we could—in fact, we would *have* to—regard you as weak, erring brothers, but still as our brothers, because you would surely soon be rid of this single error of yours. But that is not the case. The difference between you and us is this: your spirit is alien to ours."

What spirit did Luther find lacking in the Swiss? Undeniably, the spirit to which the Lord refers when He says in Matthew 18:3: "Truly, I say to you, unless you turn and become like children, you will never enter the kingdom of heaven." Indeed, my friends, that is the spirit which Zwingli and his followers lacked and which those who follow in his footsteps in our day are still lacking. They lack the spirit of childlike simplicity, which takes the Father in heaven at His words. The spirit of the Zwinglian, Calvinist, and unionist churches is nothing else than the rationalist spirit, the spirit of doubt and uncertainty that one embraces when confronted by every mystery of the Holy Scriptures, like the unenlightened, unregenerate Nicodemus: "How can these things be? I do not understand it. That goes against reason."[55]

Matt. 18:3

When people of this character make concessions, they provide no assurance of reliability. This is obvious when they team up with people who teach doctrines contrary to their own. Moreover, as a rule, they betray that they are ashamed of their own religion. In their hearts they admit more than they do with their mouths.

On the other hand, the spirit of Luther and of the entire genuine Lutheran Church is the spirit of childlike simplicity, the spirit of faith, the spirit that submits to the Word of God and takes human reason captive under the wisdom from on high. It is the spirit that finds expression in one of our glorious hymns, namely, in the words:

> You have now spoken; it is true.
> You are almighty, and with You,
> Impossible is nothing.[56]

Only someone who is able to confess these words along with that pious poet[57] may call himself a Lutheran. If not, they belong to one of the fanatical sects.

The characteristic mark of our church is unquestioned submission to the divine Word. On the other hand, our sectarian teachers are continually tossed about like the waves of the sea, betraying the fact that they are not founded on the rock of the Word of God. Now, every church that lacks this spirit of childlike simplicity, even when professing the truth, is not to be trusted. Is

Lutheranism is biblical

---

55 See John 3:9.

56 Again, Walther cites from "Lord Jesus Christ, You Have Prepared," this time from stanza 4. See *LSB* 622.

57 Samuel Kinner (1603–68).

that not horrible? That is indeed a serious charge, but from what I have stated in my previous remarks, you know that it is not without foundation. Let me offer you a few additional proofs.

False charges of Papism

So-called "Protestant" churches, which are outside the pale of the Evangelical Lutheran Church, know nothing of the true way to forgiveness of sin by means of the Word and—in general—by the Means of Grace. In particular, this is evident from the way they reject Absolution as pronounced by the pastor from the pulpit or in general and private confession.

These so-called "Protestant" churches claim that, of *all* Protestant churches, the Lutheran has really been "reformed" the least, for they claim that it still retains much of the leaven of the Roman Church. For proof they cite clerical robes, the wafers we use at Communion instead of ordinary bread, the crucifix on the altar, candles in the church, the chanting of our ministers in front of the altar, making the sign of the cross, and bowing the head at the mention of the name of Jesus.[58] All these matters are innocent ceremonies. Our church does not bind a person's salvation to them, yet it also does not allow them to be pronounced as sin. For no creature has the right to declare something a sin that God has not declared to be a sin. Anything that God has neither commanded nor forbidden is a matter of freedom. But the churches mentioned previously are simply going too far when they claim that the worst Papist leaven and the most offensive remnant of the papacy in the Lutheran Church is Absolution.

First, their claim is based on ignorance concerning what we really teach about Absolution. They have made a total misrepresentation of our doctrine. They are not diligent enough to ask us what we really mean by Absolution. They are not that honest. Rather, behind our backs they slander us and call us "Papists" who would lead our poor people back to Rome. As a rule, these people imagine that we teach that, once ordained, a pastor is given a certain mysterious power that enables him to forgive sin. They assume that we teach that Absolution is his *privilege*, so that sins are forgiven whenever an ordained pastor pronounces the words "Your sins are forgiven." They assume that we regard these words to be without impact when pronounced by a layman.[59]

Who has the Keys? SC V

Now, everybody knows that this is not our doctrine. Rather, it is the doctrine of the Papists. They could even find out from our Small Catechism that our doctrine is entirely different. The Small Catechism states in the Fifth Chief Part—the Office of the Keys—that the authority to forgive sins has

---

58   During Walther's time, there were many Protestants and some Lutherans who considered these practices to be either of little worth or even extinct. The Missouri Synod maintained these historic Lutheran practices that so many mocked, yet the Synod still experienced significant growth.

59   Walther specifically means a male member of the laity.

been given to the **Church** on earth. For it says: "The Office of the Keys is that **special [churchly] authority** which Christ has given to His **church** on earth to forgive the sins of repentant sinners, but to withhold forgiveness from the unrepentant as long as they do not repent."[60]

Note the phrase "special [churchly] authority." It means that this authority has been given not to pastors, but to the Church. Pastors are not the Church but only *servants* of the Church. If these men are Christians, they are part of the Church; but if they are not Christians, they do not belong to it. In that case they are mere cutters of wood and drawers of water for the sanctuary, like the Gibeonites in the Old Testament.[61] If they are Christians, they are joint owners of the Office of the Keys. However, the Keys do not belong exclusively to the pastors, but to the Church, to every individual member of the Church.

The most humble day laborer has the Keys just as much as the most high- Tr 67
ly honored general superintendent.[62] Our church stated this fact plainly, among other things, in a remarkable story told by Augustine. We read in the **Treatise**: "In a case of necessity even a layman absolves and becomes the minister and pastor of another. Augustine tells the story of two Christians in a ship, one of whom baptized the catechumen, who after Baptism then absolved the baptizer."[63] Here is the story:

Once upon a time two men were sailing on a ship. One of them was a converted Christian; the other, a pagan. They became friends. The Christian proclaimed the Gospel to his new friend, and through the Holy Spirit the pagan became a believer. Suddenly a fearful storm arose. Death was staring the passengers in the face, and they doubted they would be saved. The former pagan's one wish was that he might receive Holy Baptism before drowning, while the Christian craved Absolution. Amid this difficult situation, the Christian suggested to the pagan a plan by which both of their wishes could be fulfilled: he would baptize the pagan, and the pagan, once a Christian, would then

---

60 *Luther's Small Catechism with Explanation*, 29.

61 See Joshua 9:21.

62 Walther's choice of terms is interesting. In 1854, the Missouri Synod established the office of district president (*Distriktpräses*), the leader of a district-synod (*Distriktsynode*), usually geographic, that serves as an administrative component of the general Missouri Synod (*allgemeine Synode*). See also the maps in the front of the book. Walther could have used that terminology, yet he chooses to use the German term *General-Superintendent*, the overseer of a Protestant denomination organized in a given European territory, usually the highest elective office in such a church body.

63 *Concordia*, 304. See also Müller, 341; *Triglot Concordia*, 523. Older editions and Walther's original German refer to the Treatise as part of the Smalcald Articles. The story itself comes from medieval canon law (Gratian, *Decretum* III, dist. 4, c. 36) regarding the validity of Baptism administered by a layman in an emergency situation. Such a situation is defined as facing imminent death. The writings of Gratian and other testimonies from the early and medieval Church Fathers that agree with Scripture are cited throughout the Book of Concord.

absolve the Christian. The plan was carried out, and when by the protecting providence of God they had safely weathered the storm and reached land, the bishop to whom these activities on board ship were reported did not pronounce them invalid. Rather, both the Baptism and the Absolution were acknowledged to be valid.

Basis of Absolution

On what doctrine is the Lutheran practice of Absolution based? It is based on the following facts that we teach:

John 1:29

1. Christ, the Son of God, took upon Himself every sin of every sinner, counting them as His own. Accordingly, John the Baptist points to Christ and says, "Behold, the Lamb of God, who takes away the sin of the world!" (John 1:29).

2 Cor. 5:21 ESV;
Isa. 53:5 ESV;
Ps. 69:5 Luther

2. By leading His life in abject poverty, by His suffering, crucifixion, and death, Christ wiped out the record of the world's sin and gained for us remission of all sins. No person living—from Adam to the last human yet to be born—is excused from this plan. For Paul writes in 2 Corinthians 5:21: "For our sake He made Him to be sin who knew no sin, so that in Him we might become the righteousness of God." Isaiah states in 53:5: "But He was wounded for our transgressions; He was crushed for our iniquities; upon Him was the chastisement that brought us peace, and with His stripes we are healed." And even in an Old Testament prophecy written earlier than Isaiah, we hear the Messiah wail: "I am forced to pay back what I did not steal" (Psalm 69:5).

3. By raising His Son, Jesus Christ, from the dead, God the Father confirmed and put His stamp of approval on the work of reconciliation and redemption that Christ had finished on the cross. For by the resurrection of Christ, the Father, in the presence of heaven and earth, angels and people, declared: "Just as My Son cried out on the cross, 'It is finished,' so I announce, 'It is finished indeed!' You sinners are redeemed. Forgiveness of sins is prepared for everybody. It is already here. It must not first be acquired by you."

4. In addition to Christ commanding that the Gospel be preached to every creature, He at the same time commanded that forgiveness of sins should be preached to all people.[64] This is what we call the Good News: "All that is necessary for your salvation has been accomplished. When you ask, 'What must we do to be saved?' please remember that all has been done. There is nothing more to do. All you have to do is believe that everything has been done for you—and you will be saved."

5. Christ issued a general command to His apostles and their successors in office to preach the Gospel, that is, the forgiveness of sin. Yet He also

---

64 See, for example, Matthew 28:19–20; Luke 24:46–47.

commanded us to minister to each individual who desires forgiveness by offering this comfort: "You are reconciled to God." For if forgiveness of sin has been acquired for **all**, it has also been acquired for **each individual**. If I can offer it to **all**, I can offer it to **each individual**. Not only *am I allowed* to do this, I am *ordered* to do it. If I fail to do it, I am a servant of Moses and not a servant of Christ.

6. Now that forgiveness of sin has been acquired as stated, not only does a pastor have a special commission to proclaim it, but also every Christian—male or female, adult or child—is commissioned to do this. Even a child's Absolution is just as certain as the Absolution of St. Peter—yes, even as the Absolution of Christ would be, were He again to stand visibly before people and say, "Your sins are forgiven." There is no difference, because, note well, it is not a question of what humans must do but what has been done by Christ.

Suppose there was a rebellious uprising and an entire city had formed a conspiracy against its sovereign lord, had killed the king's son, and all the citizens had to pay for that crime with their lives. To stretch this parable even further, suppose one of the king's other sons had come to intercede for the rebels and had persuaded his father to pardon them, to issue a document of amnesty. Then the son announces this to the rebels—either personally or by messengers—assuring his father that the rebels will then again become good and grateful citizens and loyal subjects. Suppose the king yields to his son and, while remaining quietly in his castle, sends out messengers to read the document of amnesty on every street corner, calling to the rebel citizens: "You have been pardoned!" And this to the very same citizens who a few days previously had fearfully viewed themselves as defeated, expecting soon to be executed! What would you think if these rebels were to say to the messengers: "We do not believe you. The king will have to come himself and make the announcement to make us believe it." That would be unparalleled disrespect. In this case no one would be so reckless. Everyone would be glad that the messengers had come with the royal document—signed and sealed—and would read the proclamation: "I hereby pardon all rebels. I want them to accept this pardon and become good citizens, the way they used to be."

Let us suppose, furthermore, that the messengers did not reach every place, but others who had heard of the pardon went into every nook and cranny and spread the news. Their announcement would be just as much a decree of pardon as what the messengers were proclaiming. For the pardon would be valid, not because of a special authority of the messengers who are offering it, but because the pardon had been decreed, embossed, and sealed. In a nutshell, this amnesty would be valid because it had been confirmed and circulated in the king's name and by his order.

Now, the case of all humanity is identical to that of those rebels. *We* are, of course, the rebels. And our heavenly Father is the King against whom we have rebelled, and the Son of God has done everything necessary to cause our heavenly King to pardon us. All of this has happened. When a Lutheran pastor announces the forgiveness of sins or absolves a sinner, he does nothing else than communicate to his congregation the news that Christ has interceded for them in their sorry situation and that God has restored them to favor. Moreover, the Lutheran pastor does this by the explicit order of Christ.

If someone commissions me to tell so-and-so that he has forgiven so-and-so, and I carry out this order, that forgiveness is just as valid and effective as if the party himself were to deliver it. Or suppose you had a friend in Germany who had severely offended you, and you find out that he is suffering great regret over his action and is full of unrest and worry over his sins, which are torturing him to death and causing him to fear that God will not receive him into His grace—in a case like this, would you have to go to Germany to see your friend? Why, you could either write him a letter or ask some acquaintance of yours who is going to Germany to tell your friend that you forgave him long ago and that he should no longer worry about the wrong he had done you, because you are fully reconciled to him. Your friend would certainly accept the information as reliable. That is what happens at the moment of Absolution.

False penance   I ask you now: Is there any Papist element in this? Surely not. Just for the sake of comparison, the doctrine of the Papists goes like this: When a priest absolves, this power of forgiving sins has been vested in him because of his priestly ordination and the anointing with chrism that he received.[65] Regarding the person receiving absolution, the power—or efficacy[66]—of this absolution lies in the person's contrition, confession, and satisfaction. The Papists declare that the conditions of a valid and salutary[67] absolution are (1) oral confession,[68] (2) heartfelt contrition,[69] [and] (3) compensation by means of good works.[70]

In the first place, there must be full—or plenary—confession. In the opinion of the Papists, any omission in the confession renders the entire

---

65 This anointing ceremony is designed to show the Roman Catholic teaching concerning the priesthood, namely, that the priest receives an indelible character that allows him to control access to the sacraments.

66 As with the Word of God, the *efficacy* of the Sacraments is a technical term that means their ability to do what they offer.

67 Here we see the original meaning of *salutary*, namely, something that has the capacity to grant salvation.

68 Latin: *confessio oris.*

69 Latin: *contritio cordis.*

70 Latin: *satisfactio operis.*

confession and absolution invalid and noneffective. In the second place, the person making confession must feel perfect contrition and heartfelt regret; otherwise, the Keys will fail to open heaven to him. In the third place, the person confessing must render the satisfaction prescribed by the priest.

Our Lutheran Confessions contain none of this. What we say is that the power—or efficacy—of Absolution is not taken from the ordination or consecration of the pastor. In fact, its efficacy is most certainly not taken from the pastor, but (1) from the perfect reconciliation and redemption of Christ; (2) and from the command of Christ to preach the Gospel to all people, which means nothing less than to absolve all people—to assure them of the forgiveness of their sins.

True Absolution

We have examples from the Confessions of our Church and from Luther's writings. Article XXV of the **Augsburg Confession** (Müller, 53–54): "The people are very carefully taught how comforting Absolution is and how they should highly prize Absolution. It is not the mere voice or word of the person standing there, but it is God's Word that forgives sin."[71]

AC XXV 3

This is usually understood to mean that the words of Absolution are taken from the Bible and in that sense are the Word of God. But the meaning is that a pastor announcing to a poor sinner, "Your sins are forgiven," is just like God pronouncing those words. For the pastor absolves not because he is an individual who might have extraordinary power, but because God has commanded that in His name and in His place people's sins are to be forgiven. It makes no difference whether God or the pastor makes the announcement. Accordingly, our Confessions tell us to believe firmly that what the pastor says at Absolution is what almighty God Himself—who determines this issue—is saying to us.

But some raise the objection: "How can a pastor forgive sins?" That is the same wicked and foolish objection that the Pharisees raised when they said about Christ: "This man is blaspheming" (Matthew 9:3). They imagined that Jesus was attempting something that was impossible. But how can I forgive sins on God's behalf?

Matt. 9:3

Of course, Absolution would be invalid if God had not commanded it. But God *did* command it, just as I can tell someone to communicate to an enemy of mine on my behalf that I am reconciled to him. At Absolution we say nothing but what has happened, that is, the precious truth that forgiveness of sins has been acquired. If we would only truly believe in Absolution, with what joy we would attend church whenever Absolution is pronounced!

---

71 See also *Concordia*, 50; *Triglot Concordia*, 69. See the section "Walther's Book of Concord," pages 467–68. The Dau edition adds: "The Augsburg Confession wants us to regard absolution, not as the word of a human being who happens to pronounce the same, but as the word of God forgiving men's sins."

AC XXV 3   But who believes it? There are few who do. There are very few people—even among Lutherans—who truly believe in Absolution. That is the curse of false doctrine. Incorrect *preaching* deprives people of their most precious treasures. The fanatics admit that Absolution is taught in the Bible, but these Bible statements must not be taken as they read.[72] Herod would be proud![73] Indeed, I must surely take the Bible at its word. Are we to get its meaning by reading between the lines? God will call everyone to account who treats His Word in such slanderous fashion. A true Lutheran relies on God's Word and would not worry about it even if the whole world mocked and despised him for it. He does not consider the world an authority in religious matters. He rests his faith on higher authority: "Because it is pronounced on behalf of God and by His command."[74]

AC XXV 4   Many Unionists[75] claim that they subscribe to the Augsburg Confession: "Yes, we subscribe to it as well." They do not really mean it. If they did, they would cry, "Away with that Papist book!" when reading the above statement concerning Absolution. They have never examined the Confessions of our Church, nor have they investigated our doctrine of Absolution. "Concerning this command and authority of the Keys, it is taught how comforting, how necessary it is for terrified consciences."[76]

Among the fanatical sects, many people spend their lives in a state of despair because they do not "feel" what they would like to feel. They eventually surrender to their despair and are lost. If they only knew our doctrine of firm faith in Absolution! They would approach God and say, "Heavenly Father, I have been absolved according to Your command by so-and-so. I know that You are always truthful and cannot lie to me." God would answer them, "That is right. I do not lie. I keep My promises." But the people must be diligently taught how to arrive at this assurance.

AC XXV 4   "God requires faith in Absolution—no less than as if it were His own voice speaking to the sinner from heaven."[77] Some of you might raise the objection: "Should a godless person, then, believe that he has been absolved?" Indeed, that is what God requires, and that person is required to believe this—or lose the salvation of his soul.

---

72 The Dau edition adds: "That is a teaching worthy of the devil's reward."

73 In the tradition of German literature, invoking the name of Herod is like invoking the name of Satan.

74 AC XXV (Müller, 54; see *Concordia*, 50). The Dau text adds the following: "Agreeably with the Augsburg Confession, [a true Lutheran] regards absolution as an announcement in God's stead and by God's command."

75 Walther specifically refers to members of the Prussian Union.

76 AC XXV 4 (Müller, 54; see *Concordia*, 50).

77 AC XXV 4 (Müller, 54; see *Concordia*, 50).

A different question would be whether [the godless] can believe it. For their conscience will denounce their attempt to believe it by suggesting that they do not intend to come to God because they are currently living—and intend to continue living—in sin, without any regard for God. Nevertheless, they ought to believe it. Should God not require that we believe what He says? God has commanded the Gospel to be preached to the whole world. We humans are to believe the Gospel. When Absolution is pronounced to a person, the Gospel is brought to that individual, for the Gospel is nothing else than Absolution.

> And thus we are cheerfully comforted that we attain forgiveness of sins by this faith. It used to be that preachers who taught so much about confession did not say a word about these important things. Rather, they tortured consciences by listing all the sins and by going on and on about satisfaction, indulgences, pilgrimages, and the like.[78]

AC XXV 4–5

The Papists regard absolution as a key point. When a Catholic layperson confesses and receives absolution, the idea that he is now reconciled with God would never enter his mind. He is only concerned that he made a clean sweep of everything. If he omitted something in his confession because he wished to avoid a great and difficult satisfaction that would be imposed on him, he departs from the confessional booth with the tormenting reflection that all has been to no benefit.

But we Lutherans tell the poor sinner to come and receive Absolution, to believe that he has been forgiven when the words are pronounced, even though he were coming to confession fresh from committing the most horrible crime. We tell him that God requires nothing of him except that he accept what Christ by His meritorious life, suffering, and death has gained for him.

Even this teaching used to be neglected to a great extent. Rather, those poor sinners were warned to feel genuine contrition, to be truly crushed, and to have truly good resolutions. But they were *not* told to come, even if they had to crawl, even if they had to confess themselves the worst sinners. They were *not* told that the door of grace is open to them and that they need only accept what is offered them.

If these latter facts had been emphasized, there would have been more Christians. For these facts do not make people secure in their sins, but they awaken them to faith and a renewal of their lives. People begin to feel the great love that God has shown them and to rejoice because of His own free grace. He has taken all their sins from them and dressed them with the cloak of Christ's righteousness.

---

78 Müller, 54; see *Concordia*, 50. The Dau edition adds: "The Augsburg Confession charges the papists with suppressing absolution by their doctrine of confession."

Ap XII 39   **Apology** XII 39 (Müller, 172) has: "The Power of the Keys administers and presents the Gospel through Absolution, which proclaims peace to us and is the true voice of the Gospel."[79] This was the assurance our forefathers had: Absolution proclaims the Gospel to us, for Absolution is basically shorthand for the Gospel, an extract drawn from it, addressing faith and Christian justification. This statement is the bottom line: "On Christ's behalf I forgive you all your sins in the name of the Father and of the Son and of the Holy Spirit." For the word of Absolution proclaims to us peace and the Gospel itself.

Luther says (St. Louis Ed. 12:1586):[80]

W² 12:1586   This, then, is the benefit of the suffering and resurrection of Christ: that these acts were performed not on *His* own but on *our* behalf, so that He might bruise under His heel the devil[81] and all my sins that He bore in His body on Good Friday. The devil flees at the mere mention of Christ's name. Now, then, if you want to make use of these great treasures, behold, He has given them to you. Only give Him this much honor: that you would accept them gratefully.

W² 11:1104   You need not kneel down and pray that He would give you these treasures. He has *already* given you all. In the *Church Postils*, **Luther** says (St. Louis Ed. 11:1104): "It is not of our doing, neither can it be merited by our works. Everything has already been given and is being offered to you. All you have to do is to open your mouth—or, rather, your heart—hold still, and let Him fill it (Psalm 81:11)."[82]

Large Catechism III 88 says:

LC III 88   There is here again great need for us to call upon God and to pray: "Dear Father, forgive us our trespasses." It is not as though He did not forgive sin without and even before our prayer. (He has given us the Gospel, in which is pure forgiveness, before we prayed or ever thought about it.) But the purpose of this prayer is that we may recognize and receive such forgiveness.[83]

---

79 See also *Triglot Concordia*, 261; *Concordia*, 172. See the section "Walther's Book of Concord," pages 467–68.

80 Luther preached this sermon on Mark 16:1–8 during the first service of Easter Sunday 1530 while staying at the Coburg fortress during the Diet of Augsburg. It belongs to a collection of miscellaneous Luther sermons. Walther mistakenly recalls it as one of Luther's *Church Postils* because it is in the same volume of the Halle edition that contains those postils.

81 See Genesis 3:15.

82 This is Psalm 81:10 in English Bibles. Walther correctly identifies this sermon as one of the *Church Postils*. Compare the translation in John Nicholas Lenker, ed., *Complete Sermons of Martin Luther*, trans. John Nicholas Lenker et al. (Grand Rapids: Baker, 1983, 2000), 2.1:360.

83 *Concordia*, 419. See also Müller, 485; *Triglot Concordia*, 723.

This is a remarkable passage. Let us not think that the Fifth Petition of the **SC III** Lord's Prayer proves that to obtain forgiveness we must first pray for it. The object of this petition is *not* to show that there is no forgiveness until we pray for it, but to remind us that it lies ready for us and that this fact should strengthen our faith. Similarly, Luther says regarding our prayer at meal-times: "God gives daily bread, even without our prayer, to all wicked people; but we pray in this petition that He would lead us to realize it and to receive our daily bread with thanksgiving."[84]

In his *House Postil*, **Luther** says (St. Louis Ed. 13a:917): "Now, after our **W² 13a:917** dear Lord Christ thus addressed the paralyzed man and forgave him his sins, the scribes start up and charge Him with blaspheming God by pretending to forgive sins."[85]

As you know, the Gospel reading for the Nineteenth Sunday after Trinity **Luke 5:21;** deals with the Absolution of the paralyzed man by Christ, which leads to the **Matt. 9:8** angry question of the Pharisees: "Who is this who speaks blasphemies? Who can forgive sins but God alone?" (Luke 5:21). Christ shows them that as the **Son of Man** He has absolved the paralyzed man. Moved by the Holy Spirit, "when the crowds saw it, they were afraid, and they glorified God, who had given such authority to men" (Matthew 9:8). Why did Matthew document this exclamation of the people in his Gospel? Because it was a statement that the Holy Spirit had stirred up the people to make. Christ does not say, "Oh, no! God did not give this power to **people** the way He gave it to Me," but He assures us that this power was indeed given to **people**.[86] The Lord Christ does not intend to walk about in the world in visible, human form, proclaiming to people the forgiveness of their sins, but He has commanded His Christians to do this. In fact, He ordained a particular office, the holders of which have nothing else to do than to keep saying to people what Christ said to the paralyzed man. We are to proclaim this truth to all our fellow human beings. Why? Because everything necessary for our salvation has been accomplished, and any person believing this believes not us but God, and—in their belief— has what Absolution declares.

Luther continues:

> Now, here is an essential point of great importance, which we are to **W² 13a:917** note diligently. For in all the fanatics and the whole rabble of sectarians we observe the error that they fail to understand how sins are

---

84 *Concordia*, 335. See also Müller, 371; *Triglot Concordia*, 547.

85 Compare the translation in Eugene F. A. Klug, ed., *Complete Sermons of Martin Luther*, trans. Eugene F. A. Klug et al. (Grand Rapids: Baker, 1986, 2000), 7:83.

86 When Walther speaks of *Menschen* here, he refers to Christians in general, to the royal priesthood (see 1 Peter 2:9). Walther later refers specifically to those who hold the Office of the Holy Ministry.

forgiven. Ask the pope and all his scholars and you will find that they cannot tell you what Absolution accomplishes. **The entire papacy is built on the teaching that grace is infused into people by some secret operation**, obtained by contrition, confession, and satisfaction.

Luther notes that the papacy is built on this teaching—and I would add that this includes the sects. Without exception, they teach that forgiveness of sins must be obtained by praying, struggling, and wrestling with God until you feel the soothing sensation that grace has been infused into you. However, that is a complete deception, for grace cannot be infused into people, since it is the disposition of God outside of ourselves, in heaven. It can only be *proclaimed* to us. True peace, therefore, can be given to us only through the Word, either when we hear it preached or when we read it. From every chapter of the Bible we can get Absolution, for there is not a chapter that does not tell us: "Your sins have been forgiven." Every little passage in which it says that God will be merciful is an Absolution. That is why Luther says that true Gospel-oriented pastors are not capable of opening their mouths without pronouncing Absolution. This is really true.

Note well, I am speaking of *genuinely* Gospel-oriented pastors. A Law-oriented preacher cannot do this. He preaches people into despair and hell, while a Gospel-oriented preacher lifts even the greatest sinner out of hell. Of course, when sinners talk like the rebels of whom I spoke—who, when they heard that their king had pardoned them, refused his grace and wanted to murder his son by hanging him—such people will obviously go to the gallows, not because grace has not been offered them but because they would not accept it. Thus this doctrine of infused grace is the whole secret of the papacy and all of our sects.

W² 13a:917   Luther continues: "If you ask them what Absolution and the Keys effect, they will tell you that it is an external regulation observed in the Church. Accordingly, they do not base the forgiveness of sins on God's Word and on faith, on which they must be based, but rather on *our* contrition, confession, and satisfaction."

When reading a letter of indulgence issued by the pope, some people say: "Of course, people must also repent of their sins. Moreover, you must go to confession and render the satisfaction imposed by the priest; otherwise, the letter of indulgence will be of no benefit." And these uninformed, deceived people claim that the pope is not really so bad because he demands three conditions for absolution: contrition, confession, and satisfaction. But this is horrible, hellish, devilish blindness! It[87] overthrows the entire Gospel. According to the pope's teaching, the sinner seeking absolution must do those

---

87   The Dau edition adds: "the pope's practise."

three things, and, what is even worse, faith is not one of the requirements, the pope—the Antichrist—says. The people are told merely to be contrite, crushed, and to confess. But the priests will let some of it go; if they cannot get contrition, they will be satisfied with attrition.[88] Indeed, they admit that, for a plenary absolution from all sins, it is better to have contrition. Moreover, as a rule, the priests are so accommodating as to impose on the people only a really insignificant satisfaction, such as reciting ten Our Fathers or dropping a contribution into the almsbox, etc. By dropping in a small contribution, the people imagine they have settled their account. Or they may be told to eat fish on a day on which they usually eat meat. All this is nothing but devilish nonsense, a despicable spirit that leads the people astray.

Luther continues: "But this is an altogether fictitious teaching, by which   W² 13a:917
people are misled and pointed the wrong way."

However, our time is up. I believe this subject is of enough importance to justify taking it up once more in order to examine a few beautiful testimonies. Then we will study in greater depth these words in our thesis: "until they would feel that God has received them into grace." This important part of our thesis has not been fully treated as yet. And yet it is necessary. You need this instruction more than the people in Germany, for you are living in the land of sects.[89] Our poor people observe the great show of sanctity that the sectarians display and are easily misled by it. For they imagine that to really save their souls they must join the strictest sect, which would guarantee their salvation. Alas! Can the sects save anyone? There is but one Savior—and a person who does not trust Him alone and completely to bring him into heaven truly will not enter heaven. For Jesus Christ alone is the door to heaven.[90]

My friends, imagine how a prisoner on death row for his misdeeds would   **Eighteenth**
feel if he were unable to verify a vague rumor that he had been par-   **Evening Lecture:**
doned. How dreadful that would be! He would jump every time the door of   Feb. 13, 1885
his cell block opened because he would not know whether the person coming

---

88   The Dau edition adds as an explanatory footnote SA III III 16: "Furthermore, since no one could know how great the contrition ought to be in order to be enough before God, they gave this consolation: He who could not have contrition at least ought to have 'attrition.' I call that half a contrition, or the beginning of contrition. The fact is, they themselves do not understand either of these terms, anymore than I do. But such attrition was counted as contrition when a person went to Confession" (*Concordia*, 273; see also Müller, 319; *Triglot Concordia*, 483).

89   Walther means the United States. England experienced centuries of continual, widespread sectarian division after Henry VIII declared himself head of the Church of England in 1534. Many Anglican theologians refer to this as the problem of "Home Reunion." England passed this sectarianism to its colonies in North America.

90   See John 10:9.

No true atheist to see him were bringing him his authentic and definite pardon or were about to take him to the executioner. At such a time only a completely crude, depraved, and reckless atheist would be capable of joking and frolicking.

From a spiritual point of view, every person is by nature in a similar condition. Since the ancestors of the human race fell away from God, every person has by nature been under a divine sentence of both earthly and eternal death. True, each person has heard a vague rumor that God has pardoned him, but he cannot arrive at any certainty about it. In any mortal illness, in any great difficulty, especially in moments when our heart and conscience are filled with unrest, dread, and terror, we have the sensation that the doors of eternity are swinging open to receive us, but we poor wretches do not know whether we are entering into eternal death or eternal life. In such a state of mind only the most abandoned would remain outwardly calm, while every other person would quake and tremble. Although they may have laughed at holy matters, those abandoned people would not feel like laughing at that point.

How could it be that our loving, kind, gracious, and merciful God has done nothing to make us certain that we have the forgiveness of our sins and that we will enter the mansions of eternal peace and rest "over yonder"? Has He really done nothing to rescue us from our dreadful condition? That would be unthinkable. You can be sure—God *has* done something. Yes, He has done something so great that we are unable to understand it.

Gospel certainty God has sent His only-begotten Son into this world, making Him a human being like us. He has laid the burden of our sins upon Him and given Him up to be crucified for the atonement of our sins. After doing all this, would [God] really leave us for our entire life in a dreadful state of ignorance concerning whether He is still our enemy and whether our dying day will also be our Judgment Day?

Luke 2:10–11;
Mark 16:15;
Matt. 28:20 No, as soon as the eternal Son of God became man and entered this world, the highest messenger was dispatched from the throne of grace to this earth to proclaim to the shepherds at Bethlehem—and in them, to us, to all of us, to the entire world—"Behold, I bring you good news of great joy that will be for all the people. For unto you is born this day in the city of David a Savior, who is Christ the Lord" (Luke 2:10–11). After Christ had finished His great work; after God the Father had raised Him from the dead and thereby pronounced Him (our Bondsman and Substitute) free from all guilt; after God the Father justified and absolved us all in Him, Christ commanded His disciples: "Go into all the world and proclaim the gospel," that is, the joyous message of the finished redemption, "to the whole creation" (Mark 16:15), adding these words: "And behold, I am with you always, to the end of the age" (Matthew 28:20). With these words, Christ testified that the joyous message that He

committed to His disciples is to echo throughout this earthly globe until the Last Day.

In view of this, are we not blessed, highly favored people? Yes, our bliss is beyond description. Heaven and earth are full of the goodness and grace of the Lord, our God. Anywhere and everywhere all things cry to us: "You are redeemed; your sins are forgiven; heaven is thrown open to you! Oh, believe it, do believe it, and you will have this bliss!"

But, alas! This unspeakable joy given to our highly favored race is polluted by false doctrine. This is what we have been pointing out in our lectures these past three evenings. Let us strengthen the belief that we have gained, first, so we would not make bitter for ourselves this cup of inexpressible joy that our Father in heaven has filled for us. Second, so that, when you enter into the office in which you proclaim reconciliation, you would not withhold from people what God gave them long ago—in fact, what He has designed for them from eternity.

This ninth thesis now before us is really the central thesis in this entire series. Anyone who understands this thesis will be able to rightly distinguish Law and Gospel. But anyone who does not understand it will never learn how to distinguish it—no matter what other theses they apply. This is the main point when we state this thesis:

Central thesis

> You are not rightly distinguishing Law and Gospel in the Word of God if you point sinners who have been struck down and terrified by the Law toward their own prayers and struggles with God and tell them that they have to work their way into a state of grace. That is, do not tell them to keep on praying and struggling **until they would feel that God has received them into grace**. Rather, point them toward the Word and the Sacraments.

We have seen that particularly the way sectarian preachers reject Absolution proves that they do not know how to distinguish Law and Gospel. Not only do they have an entirely incorrect concept of the character of Absolution and of *our* doctrine of Absolution, but by claiming that—outwardly—*we* seem to be doing the same things the Papists do, they think *our* doctrine of Absolution is Papist. But no, even though the Papists use ever so sweet terms in pronouncing Absolution, nevertheless they are offering the people only husks—with the kernel removed. We keep the precious words of Absolution, but we also seek to offer the kernel to those who seek Absolution and invite them to enjoy it.

Absolution important

Let us hear more about the Gospel reading for the Nineteenth Sunday after Trinity, which Luther discusses in his *House Postil*. Here we have the story of the paralyzed man whose sins the Lord forgave. This action of the

Mark 2:7; Matt. 9:5

Lord Jesus causes the hypocritical Pharisees to murmur, saying, "This man is blaspheming. Who can forgive sins but God alone?" They imagine that they are displaying great wisdom by criticizing the Lord. But the Lord immediately hushes them. He asks them, "Which is easier, to say, 'Your sins are forgiven,' or to say, 'Rise and walk'?" (Matthew 9:5). [The Pharisees] refuse to reply because they know the Lord will catch them in their own words. If they say, "It is easier to say to a person, 'Your sins are forgiven,' than to say to a paralyzed man, 'Rise and walk,'" they are afraid that He might say the latter, for the Lord had by that time performed many amazing miracles. And, sure enough! The Lord proves His ability to cure the man's paralysis miraculously. For upon His Word, this man suffering from paralysis takes up his bed and goes to his house, rejoicing. The people who witness all this know that Christ is a man—which He is indeed. His miracle does not offend them because He had already given powerful evidence that He is also the Son of God. And now they begin to glorify God for having given the power to **men**.

If this had been a superstitious notion of the people, the Holy Spirit surely would have added something like: "The poor people *thought* that such power had been given to men. But no, it had *not* been given to men." But we do not see a word of this in the evangelists' account, for the Holy Spirit inspired the people to make that statement, and they may have reflected on their happy condition under such a Messiah. For when sheep have been locked up in a spiritually poor pasture and the consolations of the Gospel are withheld, they become starved. Then they usually devour the luscious grass of the pure Gospel with great joy when it is presented to them.

We have examples of this in Germany. The churches of the rationalists are empty, but every church is packed whose pulpit is occupied by a man who is preaching with the manifestation of the Spirit and of power. The people still have their Bibles, their catechisms, and their old hymnbooks. They cling to the old Bible passages that they have learned. They enjoy their old devotional books, and when they get a lively minister who preaches the Gospel to them, they are overjoyed.

Keep it simple, pastor! But, alas! There are also other preachers who—even though they are believers—preach in such lofty language that the people do not grasp the message. What is obvious in these situations is that, while the preacher may well be a believer, the people are dead—dead in their faith. Not only must we pastors proclaim the truth, we also must speak so plainly that a peasant listening outside of the sanctuary can understand it and feel drawn into the church. We should preach so clearly that everyone would understand without a doubt that "this is the way to be saved. There is no other." I would not be surprised if God would hurl a lightning bolt at every preacher who fills his manuscript with fancy terms, intending to shine by his speech-making. The common people do not understand such language. At best, it may penetrate their minds, but it does not enter their hearts, where it ought to lodge. Let us hear **Luther**:

> The Anabaptists likewise say: How can we receive forgiveness of sins through Baptism? There is nothing but a handful of water there. If we are really to be purified from sin, the Holy Spirit must do it; water cannot do it. In this way they strip forgiveness of sins away from the Word and refuse to leave the matter where the good people here put it, who glorified God for giving such power to men.[91]

W² 13a:917

The Anabaptists look upon the baptismal water with cow eyes and think that we teach that the water "does the trick." Ah! They are missing the point. The water does not have any particular special force. Baptismal water is water—just like other water—but it is connected with this Word of God: "Whoever believes and is baptized will be saved." When these words are added to the water in Baptism, baptismal water becomes as precious as—in fact, even *more* precious—than heaven and earth and all the treasures of the world. Since God wants to save us only by grace and exclusively through faith, He tells us: "You wish to be saved. Very well, be baptized and believe My promise, and as truly as I am God, you will be saved."

Mark 16:16

You should not look at yourself and ask, "What should **I** do to gain salvation?" You remain a condemned sinner and obtain salvation from the free grace and mercy of God. The Anabaptists have constructed an entirely new way, about which the Bible does not say a word, namely, that people are to struggle until they can say, "Now I feel that I have obtained grace." That is an awful doctrine—much more harmful than most people imagine.

> In the same way, the Sacramentarian fanatics say that the Sacrament consists of mere bread and wine. As such, forgiveness of sin cannot be found there. The Spirit must provide that; the flesh benefits nothing.

W² 13a:917–18

> In sum, no sectarian spirit, no priest or monk, has ever been able to understand that the forgiveness of sins is a power conferred on men, as this Gospel lesson states. Learn, then, how to speak of this matter. I know well enough, and also confess, that God alone forgives sin. But we must know, too, how to recognize that our sins are forgiven and by what means this is done.

> Regarding this point, the Holy Scriptures teach us and every Christian that when we desire our sins to be forgiven, we should not sit down

---

91   Walther continues citing Luther's sermon on the Gospel reading for the Nineteenth Sunday after Trinity. Luther's "good people," literally, "good little people," refers to the crowd in the Gospel narrative. Compare Klug, *Complete Sermons of Martin Luther*, 7:83–87.

in some nook and pray, "My God, forgive me for my sins," and then wait for an angel to come from heaven and announce, "Your sins are forgiven."

Just reflect on a case like this: You have cruelly insulted someone, and every time you recall that event, it torments you. You desire pardon and the restoration of your friendship with the person you have insulted. How can you be assured that he has forgiven you? Will you wait until your heart feels some kind of relief, which would make you think that your former friend has forgiven you? If you take that approach, everybody will tell you: "You are an idiot.[92] The important point is not how **you** feel, but how the **person** whom you insulted feels."

Forgiveness via the Means of Grace

Or will you obtain assurance that you have been forgiven when you receive a gift from your former friend? No, that would make you feel even more uncertain, for the insulted party may want to make you feel that he is not a wretch like you. He may want to make you thoroughly ashamed of yourself by pouring burning coals upon your head.

Now, what other way is there to arrive at the assurance that you have been forgiven? There is no other way than this: the insulted party must tell you that he has forgiven you. When he comes to tell you not to worry about his anger because of the way you insulted him, when he says, "Your action was indeed disgraceful, but all has been forgiven. Cheer up, let us be friends again," then you know that he has forgiven you—do you not?

It is the same way with God. You cannot conclude from your feelings or from the divine blessings showered upon you that God has forgiven you. For He makes His sun rise on the evil and on the good alike, and He sends rain upon the just and the unjust.[93] You can only know anything about the matter because He **says** that you have been forgiven. A person seeking this assurance in any other way will not find it but will only deceive himself by imagining that he has found it some other way.

But where does God tell us that He has forgiven us? Why, in His Word, in the Gospel, in Baptism, in the Lord's Supper, at Absolution. In the Holy Supper, the real gift of grace that we receive is not that we partake of the body and blood of Christ. The real gift of grace is the promise of the forgiveness of sins. Christ attached that forgiveness to the promise of His body and blood to be received by us. It is "the body that is given for you and the blood that is shed for the remission of sins."[94] The body and blood of Christ are only the royal seal that the Savior affixes to His words. In short, the Word occupies first place in everything that God does to assure us of His grace.

---

92 German: *Du bist ein Narr.*

93 See Matthew 5:45.

94 See, for example, Matthew 26:26–28.

This also applies to Absolution. Here, too, the Word is of primary importance. That is the reason we should not waste much precious time waiting for an angel to come from heaven, announcing our forgiveness. God has given us no promise to that effect. If He had, we could indeed confidently ask for such a messenger. For though we are poor sinners, God is willing to give us the greatest gifts. What He has promised He will perform. He says, "Open your mouth wide, and I will fill it" (Psalm 81:10). He has promised to forgive our sins. If we believe that, we have it. But people will not believe this.

Luther says: "For God promises that He will descend in His Word and will personally assure me of the forgiveness of my sins." But the people do not want to believe this. Calvin was unhappy with Zwingli's interpretation of the Lord's Supper, but his own interpretation was wrong as well. Calvin claimed that a person desiring to receive the body and blood of Christ could not get it under the bread and wine but had to climb up to heaven by faith, where the Holy Spirit would negotiate a way to feed him with the body and blood of Christ. This is mere speculation, originating in Calvin's imagination. But this example shows that people will not believe that God has such great love for us poor sinners that He is willing to come to us. The fanatics think they must ascend to Him, but He has already descended to us. This is not surprising, for the Gospel is a doctrine that was a stumbling block to the Jews and foolishness to the Greeks.[95] It is that still, not only to the circumcised Hebrews and to the uncircumcised heathen but even to thousands upon thousands in Christendom.

Now, faith is given first in Holy Baptism, which is connected with God's command to baptize people in the name of the Father and of the Son and of the Holy Spirit.[96] Furthermore, faith is given with the promise: "Whoever believes and has been baptized will be saved."

Someone might object: "Is Baptism not mere water?" True, but this water is not by itself. God's Word goes with it. It is the same when you go to your pastor, who has been given a special commission—or, for that matter, to any other Christian.

Luther makes no difference here, as we will hear at a later point.

And when you desire to be comforted and absolved from your sins. He will say to you, "By Christ's authority I forgive you all your sins." When this happens, you can be certain that by such an external word your sins are truly and surely forgiven. For Baptism and God's Word will not lie to you.

Ps. 81:10

W² 13a:918

W² 13a:918;
Mark 16:15

W² 13a:918–21

---

95   See 1 Corinthians 1:23.
96   See Matthew 28:19.

Such things were not preached in the Roman Church, and to this day no Papist preacher understands them. Therefore, thank God for this mercy and learn that God wants to forgive sins. But how? In no way other than is written here, that is, by giving such power to forgive people.

Matt. 18:18;
John 20:23 Luther

Christ teaches this and later commands that from that point on—to the end of the world—the Church should observe that repentance and forgiveness of sins are to be preached. Let everyone, then, learn that he must seek forgiveness of sins from fellow human beings and from nowhere else. For thus reads the command of our Lord Christ: "Truly, I say to you . . . whatever you loose on earth shall be loosed in heaven" (Matthew 18:18). Likewise, "If you forgive the sins of anyone, they are forgiven" (John 20:23). For God will not tolerate the building of special ladders and stairways to heaven to suit every individual. He alone wants to be the sole Architect.

Accordingly, if you desire your sins to be forgiven, go and be baptized, if you are still unbaptized. Or if you *have* been baptized, remember the promise that God made at your Baptism and *do not be unbelieving.* Likewise, go and be reconciled to your neighbor, and then ask for Absolution. And when you hear the announcement of the forgiveness of your sins in the name of Jesus, believe it, and truly you will have it. After that go to the most venerable Sacrament and receive the body and blood of Christ in the assurance that this precious treasure is meant for you and that you may enjoy it as your own, etc.

Baptism, Absolution, preaching, and the Sacrament are not to be despised, but in *them* forgiveness of sin is to be sought and obtained. To this end, God has called and commissioned your pastor, your father and mother, and your closest fellow Christians and has put His Word in their mouth, that you are to seek consolation and forgiveness of sin from them. For though human beings are talking to you, still what they say is not their own [word] but God's Word. Therefore, you should believe it firmly and not despise it.

. . . This is why Anabaptists and other sects have lost in one stroke the forgiveness of sins, Baptism, the Sacrament, the Christian Church, and all Christian works: because they reject the Word when they hear it from their fellow man, regarding it as nothing better than the bleating of a calf. Well, suppose God were to speak to you through some cow or other animal, as He once spoke through a donkey?[97] . . . Still,

---

97 See Numbers 22:28–30.

you are not to despise His Word, but regard it as valid. Why, then, would you despise it when men speak it by the command and order of God? For though you indeed hear a man's voice, you do not hear a man's [word] but *God's* Word, and you surely will receive the forgiveness of sins attached to it, if you will only accept it by faith.

Furthermore, commenting on the words "As the Father has sent Me, even so I am sending you. . . . Receive the Holy Spirit. If you forgive the sins of any . . ." etc. (John 20:21ff.), Luther writes in his *Gospel Postil* (St. Louis Ed. 11:731–33):[98]

John 20:21–23

> What Christ is saying is this: Whenever you pronounce a word of Absolution upon a sinner, it is spoken in heaven and is as valid as if God Himself had spoken it. For He is in your mouth. Therefore, your speaking amounts to His speaking. Now, it is certainly true that when Christ—Lord over sin and hell—speaks these words over you: "Your sins will be removed," they must be removed, and nothing will prevent it. Again, when He says, "Your sins will not be forgiven," they remain unforgiven; and even if you were to exhaust yourself to death in the effort, neither you nor an angel nor a saint nor any creature could forgive your sin. The power to do this, however, is given to every Christian. . . . It is a power that we have taken from the resurrection and ascension of Christ.

W² 11:731–32

If Christ had not arisen, we could not administer Absolution, for on what would we base it? Only when God the Father acknowledged the work of Christ's reconciliation and redemption—only when He had absolved Christ (and, in Him, all men) by raising Christ from the dead—did we mortals become justified and become able to say to a fellow human being: "Be of good cheer! All your sins are forgiven, and their record is wiped out. Just believe!" This declaration is based on the fact that God the Father glorified Christ—our Substitute—and thereby proclaimed in the presence of heaven and earth that all people are redeemed and reconciled and their sins forgiven.

> However, so we do not fall into the ways of the pope, we must treat this matter carefully. The Papists have forced upon the words of Christ a different meaning, namely, that **they** have the power of which Christ speaks; and whatever **they** speak and however they speak it must come to pass **because they have said so**. That is a power you [the pope] do not have. Only the Divine Majesty has it. They say that when the pope speaks one word conveying absolution, a person's sins are gone, even

W² 11:732–33

---

98 Walther refers to Luther's *Church Postils*, the Gospel portion. Compare John Nicholas Lenker, ed., *Complete Sermons of Martin Luther*, trans. John Nicholas Lenker et al. (Grand Rapids: Baker, 1983, 2000), 1.2:360–62.

if he is neither contrite nor believes. Accordingly, they imagine it is in their power to give or take away, open or close heaven, or cast people into hell. It will be a long time before that happens. For from this claim it would follow that our salvation is based on human works, power, and authority.

During my first visit back to Germany, to my regret, I heard with my own ears a highly honored and believing pastor[99] state: "A layman[100] may proclaim truths of great comfort to others, but he cannot administer Absolution because that is a privilege that God has reserved for pastors who are ordained and installed by the Church." I wonder what this man thought of Absolution? He must have thought nothing other than what the Papists think. Anyway, that is more than thirty years ago. I vigorously opposed the view he expressed, but he remained immovable. To echo the pope's statement that sins are forgiven when a minister absolves someone but not when a *layman* does is simply awful.[101]

No, the removal of sins is not based on a mysterious power of the pastor but on the fact that Christ took away the sins of the world a long time ago, and everybody should share this wonderful news with his fellow human beings. Of course, this is the duty of preachers in particular—not, however, because of a special power inherent in them, but because God has ordained their office for the administration of the Means of Grace, the Word and the Sacraments. In an emergency it becomes evident that a *layman* has the authority to do what a prelate or a superintendent does, and it will be just as effective.[102]

You can see from these facts that our doctrine of Absolution is the very opposite of the Papists' doctrine. It does not contain a trace of Papism. The pope curses and condemns our doctrine. Does he not make the sweeping statement that no person can be certain of his salvation or his justification? Bellarmine, called the greatest of the Papist theologians, writes in his chapter on "Justification" (ch. 3):

> The doctrine that in this life people cannot achieve an assurance
> of faith regarding their righteousness—with the exception of a few

---

99 From 1859 to 1860, Walther and Friedrich C. D. Wyneken, who was serving as the general president of the Missouri Synod, met with many Lutheran pastors and professors who were leading the confessional awakening in Germany. Walther's comments here could point to several pastors among the confessionals. Walther tends to avoid mentioning by name those with whom he disagrees yet with whom he still wishes to have some kind of fellowship.

100 Walther specifically refers to a man.

101 Walther may be referring indirectly to a running debate within the Missouri Synod at that time concerning private Absolution, the role of the laity, and the pastoral office.

102 *Prelates* are clergy of higher rank in an episcopal hierarchy. They have the power to exercise church law over those who are below them in rank. Superintendents have similar power in German Protestantism; they preside over a geographic area.

whom God decides are worthy to have this fact revealed to them by a special revelation—this doctrine is a current opinion among nearly all theologians.[103]

He means to say: "I will give you the Bible and ask you to find your name in it—particularly the assurance that your sins have been forgiven. You will not find it. But there are a few men, such as Peter or Paul, to whom God revealed this fact in a supernatural manner. But *you* cannot be certain of your justification and salvation."

Is this not a disgraceful doctrine of the devil? The Roman Church calls itself the mother of all churches, yet it robs Christians of all comfort. It tells them to their face: "You cannot be certain that you will be saved. You have to wait until after your death, until you enter eternity, to find this out from your actual experience." A terrible, satanic cruelty! Luther continues:

> Therefore, because that is against all Holy Scripture, it cannot be that when you [the pope] bind or loose, it is bound or loosed by **necessity**. Thus one must understand properly that when Christ says, "Whosoever sins you loose, they are loosed," etc., **He does not institute the authority of the one who is speaking, rather of those who believe**.

W² 11:733; Matt. 16:19 Luther

My Absolution is valid because faith saves, not because I say it. Were I a completely holy person; were there no wrong in me, so that no one could find any fault in me; were I completely sanctified; were I even an archangel—not even all of that would aid in the least in making Absolution valid. But when I speak the word of the Gospel, without which no one can be saved, that is effective and good.

Let me give you another quote from Luther's incomparable treatise *On the Keys*. As far as I am concerned, I have to confess that it was from this treatise that I first learned what the Gospel is, at a time when I thought I knew it but actually did not. I will praise and thank God for this forever. When I became a Christian, I dealt a lot with the Pietists, as you know. Then I happened across Luther's writings and read them as well.

Luther had written a treatise on the Keys prior to this. When rereading it, he did not like it and wanted to rewrite it. Veit Dietrich heard of his intention and begged him most earnestly to send him the treatise. Luther agreed to the request, on the condition that the treatise not be published and that Dietrich was not to show it to anybody, because it did not measure up to

---

103 Robert Bellarmine's great work is the 1581 *Disputations Concerning the Controversies of the Christian Faith against the Heretics of Today* (*Disputationes de Controversiis Christianae Fidei adversus hujus temporis Haereticos*). This citation is from the first volume, which deals with the Word of God, Christ, and the pope. Walther only cites Bellarmine indirectly via Lutheran theological writings that, in turn, cite Bellarmine. See also Bellarmine in the Index of Persons and Groups, page 490.

Luther's standard and Luther was planning to write another treatise. But in the eighteenth century it was published nevertheless. I own a copy of it. It is a very excellent treatise, but is, in fact, surpassed by the second treatise, from which I will quote.

W² 19:943
(cf. AE 40:364)

Luther says (St. Louis Ed. 19:943–48): "Consider, furthermore, that the Keys, or the forgiveness of sins, are not based on our contrition or worthiness, as they[104] teach and corrupt. Their teaching is completely Pelagian, Muslim,[105] pagan, Jewish, Anabaptist, fanatical, and anti-Christian."

Now there is a fine list of predicates that come out of Luther! But he is right. As soon as my interests are staked on *my own* contrition, I do not need Christ. Contrition is necessary, but not as a means for acquiring forgiveness of sins. If you are a proud Pharisee, what do you care for the forgiveness of sins? You would be like the overfed glutton who turns up his nose at the finest food and drink that is set before him. Most who are Christians in name only are so completely overfed that they will decline this precious food for their soul with a disgusted, "*N.O.!*"[106]

Contrition, then, is necessary. Let us not misunderstand our good Luther. He did not proclaim the consolation of the Gospel to sinners living in carnal security.[107] He gave them no comfort. But if a person were contrite and longed for forgiveness of sins, he would say to him, "Here it is; take it, and it is yours."

W² 19:943
(cf. AE 40:364)

On the contrary, our contrition, our works, our believing heart, and all that we are must build on the Keys. With complete boldness we must confidently trust in the Keys as God's Word, never doubting in the least, as dearly as we love our body and soul, that what the Keys state and confer is as certain as if it were stated and conferred by God Himself. For it is certainly He who is speaking in this matter, since it is His command and Word—not the word or command of man.

Luther is saying, "You must not ask yourself about the state of your contrition." For any person who builds his hope on that would be building on sand. On the contrary, a person needs to praise God for the Absolution he has received; that makes his *contrition* salutary.[108] The right procedure is not to base the validity of Absolution on our own *contrition*, but to make our *contrition* rest on our Absolution.

---

104 Luther's "they" refers to the papacy, yet it certainly can include all who teach a false doctrine of the Office of the Keys.

105 Luther: *türkisch.*

106 Here Walther said, "*N.O.*," in English, as he had earlier used the English word "revivals."

107 Carnal security occurs when people are comforted instead of terrified by the Law. They think that the thoughts, words, and deeds of their sinful flesh are good enough to satisfy God's Law. It is the opposite of *Anfechtung.* See the entry "security, carnal" in the Glossary, page 486.

108 "Salutary" means something that is capable of saving you.

If you doubt this, you make God out to be a liar, pervert[109] His mandate, and base His Keys on your contrition and worthiness. True, you must be contrite, but to think that the forgiveness of sins is made certain and the work of the Keys is confirmed by **your contrition** means to forsake the faith and deny Christ. He does not propose to forgive and remit sins for your sake, but for His own sake, from pure grace, by means of the Keys.

W² 19:943–44
(cf. AE 40:364)

Christ Himself said, "Your sins are forgiven." If He said it, then believe it. If you do not believe it, then you yourself call Christ a liar. Even if we pastors were to pronounce the Absolution to such a person ten times, it would not benefit him. We cannot look into people's hearts. But that is not necessary anyway. We should look only at the Word of our heavenly Father, which informs us that God has absolved the entire world. That assures us that all sins of all humans have been forgiven.

You might ask: "Does this also apply to an ungodly scoundrel who might be plotting a burglary tonight—intent on stealing and robbing?" Indeed it does. The reason this person does not benefit from Absolution is because he does not accept the forgiveness offered him, for he does not believe in his Absolution. If he believed the Holy Spirit, he would stop stealing.

You might also ask: "Is it right to absolve such a scoundrel?" Answer: If you know he is a scoundrel, it would be wrong to absolve him because you know that he will not accept forgiveness. If you know this, you would commit a great and serious sin by performing the sacred act of Absolution for him and thus casting your pearls before swine. But Absolution itself is always valid. If Judas had received Absolution, God would have forgiven his sins; but Judas would have had to accept forgiveness. To obtain this treasure, there must be someone to give it—and someone else to receive it. An unbeliever may imagine and even say that he accepts forgiveness, but in his heart he is resolved to continue his sinful life and to prefer serving the devil. Therefore, the true doctrine of Absolution does not make people secure but thoroughly and radically plucks them out of the devil's kingdom. That is something altogether different from what moralists do when they paint a white veneer on a black personality.

Christ says, "Whatever you bind on earth," etc. Note that He promises most certainly that what **we** bind or loose **on earth** will be bound or loosed. **These Keys work without fail.** He does not say, "What I bind or loose **in heaven** you will also bind or loose on earth," as the teachers

W² 19:944
(cf. AE 40:364);
Matt. 16:19

---

109 German: *verkehren*. In this context it means to transform something into its opposite. One who does such transformation is understood to be perverse or evil.

of faulty keys would deceive us into believing.[110] When will we learn what God binds or looses in heaven? Never. Well, then, the keys would be useless, and using them would be ineffective.

Thus the Papists speak with their shameful, false doctrine. When you ask them whether they absolve scoundrels as well, and what the benefit of absolution is in such a case, they reply that in such cases the key is faulty because it will not fit into that particular keyhole, and the right key has not been provided to them. Our Key is never faulty, because we only repeat what God has spoken. It is man who is at fault. If he is impenitent, he does not benefit from the "releasing Key." Rather, he only doubles his damnation.

W² 19:944–45
(cf. AE 40:364–65)

Nor does He say, "You must know what I bind or loose in heaven." Who could know that? But this is what He says: "Bind and loose on earth, and I will help you bind and loose in heaven. Do the work of the Keys, and I will do it also. Yes, when you have done it, it will be counted as done, and there will be no need for Me to do it after you. I am telling you that what you bind or loose does not need to be bound or loosed by Me, but it will be bound or loosed without My binding and loosing. Your work and Mine will be one identical operation, not two operations. Do **your** work, and *Mine* will already be accomplished. Bind and loose, and I will have bound and loosed."

He promised to enter into our work. Yes, He commands us to do His own work. Why, then, should we make everything uncertain by inverting the process and claiming that He must first bind and loose in heaven? As if His binding and loosing in heaven were different from our binding and loosing on earth, or as if He had Keys in heaven that were different from those on earth—even though He plainly and clearly states that these Keys are the Keys of heaven, not of earth.

We have heaven's Keys here on earth.

W² 19:945–46
(cf. AE 40:365–66)

These ideas of two kinds of Keys pop up when people do not regard God's Word as God's Word, but as man's word because it is spoken by man. People imagine God to be up in heaven—far, far, far away from His Word here on earth. They stand, gaping toward heaven for His Word, and make up other keys, different from those that we already have.

. . . Do not be deceived by such pharisaical prattle, by which they deceive themselves, saying, "How can a man forgive sins when he can give neither grace nor the Holy Spirit?" Cling to the words of Christ, and **be assured that God has no other way of forgiving sin than by**

---

110 German: *narren*. It means to fool someone with a hoax.

the Word that He has commanded us to speak. If you do not seek forgiveness in His Word, it is pointless for you to stand, gaping toward heaven for grace or for what they call "inner forgiveness."

The enthusiasts[111] say that this depends on the so-called "inner forgiveness." Of course, they never know whether theirs is really the inner forgiveness of the Holy Spirit or whether it arises from their own fanatical spirit.

I hear you raising the same objection that sectarians and sophists[112] raise, namely: "Nonsense, many hear of the binding and loosing by means of the Keys, but they ignore it and stay unbound and unloosed. Therefore, something else is necessary besides the Word and the Keys: **the Spirit, Spirit, Spirit needs to be involved.**"[113] Do you really believe that when a person refuses to believe in the binding Key that he does not remain bound? Let me tell you that in due time he will find out that his being bound on account of unbelief was not a pointless act, and the intended effect was, in fact, present. **In the same way, a person who refuses to believe that he has been released and that his sins have been forgiven will discover in due time that, in fact, his sins had been forgiven him, even though he did not want to believe it.** Like St. Paul says in Romans 3:3, for the sake of our faithlessness, God will not fail.[114] This discussion is not about believing or *not* believing in the Keys. We are well aware that few believe in them. But we are speaking of what the Keys bring about and provide.

W² 19:946
(cf. AE 40:366–67)

Many will be surprised on the Last Day when God recounts to them all the Sundays on which He stood ready to absolve them, while they would not believe Him and thus made Him out to be a liar. They will see that they had often been standing at the gate of heaven and refused to enter.

Of course, if a person does not accept what the Keys give, he has nothing; but that is not the fault of the Keys. Many do not believe the Gospel, but that does not make the Gospel a failure or a lying message. Suppose a king gives you a castle; if you do not accept it, that does not make the king a liar nor his gift deceptive. You have cheated yourself. It is entirely your own fault; the king most certainly did give you the castle.

W² 19:946–47
(cf. AE 40:367)

This must be applied to Absolution. In doing that, God really offers forgiveness to all, even to unbelievers and scorners of a gift that they think cannot

---

111 German: *Schwärmer.*

112 Luther uses "sophist" to refer to Roman Catholic theologians who support the pope using philosophical arguments in place of Scripture.

113 Luther repeats "Spirit" (*Geist*) three times.

114 In Luther's discussion of the Keys, he paraphrases Paul's words. Paul says in Romans 3:3: "What if some were unfaithful? Does their faithlessness nullify the faithfulness of God?"

be real because it is given to them by a man like themselves. These deluded people do not consider that it is God Himself—not man—who does the forgiving. The pastor may personally be a son of hell, yet he forgives people's sins when he pronounces Absolution to them. Why? Because what he does is in the name and by the command of God. Sometimes kings have sent out wicked servants with orders to their subjects, and these commands are just as valid as if the king had published them in person.

W² 19:947–48
(cf. AE 40:368)

Thus Luther: "It is God's command and word that the confessor speaks and the penitent hears. They are **both** duty bound—and this is as true as their salvation—to firmly and stoutly believe this doctrine, just as any other article of faith."

Indeed, the pastor as well is duty bound to believe that all the sins of his parishioners are forgiven. If he does not do this, he is a miserable sinner who dares to open his yap[115] to pronounce Absolution, while in his heart he regards the whole action as some kind of comedy designed to fool the uninformed masses.

Nineteenth Evening Lecture:
Feb. 20, 1885

During the first half of the eighteenth century, the so-called Pietists disagreed with orthodox Lutherans on a number of doctrinal issues. The most important was this: The Pietists, you know, the disciples of Spener, August Hermann Francke, and Johann Jakob Rambach—and, in any case, they were not true disciples—the Pietists held that anyone unable to state the exact day and hour when he was converted and entered into grace was certainly not a true Christian. The Pietists claimed that neither should such people consider themselves to be Christians nor should they be viewed as such. On the other hand, orthodox Lutherans rejected this.

Now, it is indeed true that conversion does not require a day or an hour, but only a split second. For, according to Holy Scripture, conversion is nothing other than an awakening from spiritual death into spiritual life. Put differently, conversion is leaving the broad way leading downward and turning onto the narrow way leading upward. It is the transfer from the realm of the devil to the kingdom of Jesus Christ, the Son of God.

Just as there is no "middle way" between death and life, just as there is no "middle way" between the narrow way leading upward and the wide way leading downward nor an intermediate realm[116] between the realm of Satan

---

115 The German *Maul* here means a coarse, bestial mouth, as in "Shut your trap" (*"Halt's Maul"*).

116 In this paragraph, Walther uses the German word *Reich*, which may be translated as "realm" or "kingdom." In this paragraph, "kingdom" and "realm" are used alternately to avoid the idea of Christ and the devil as coequal counterparts of good and evil.

and the kingdom of Christ, we are all either spiritually dead or spiritually alive. We are traveling either on the narrow or on the wide way. We are either in the kingdom of Jesus Christ or in the realm of the devil. In other words, a person is either converted or not. There is nothing in between.

True, Holy Scripture cites some examples of people who could actually name the time when they were converted to God and obtained grace—down to the actual day and hour. Let me cite a few of these.

The first human beings, who fell from grace on the first day of their existence,[117] were also converted again on that same day. By hearing the promise of the woman's Seed, which was to bruise the serpent's head, they rose at once from their fall and obtained grace, righteousness, life, and salvation.[118]

Or just think of David, who, after his fall from grace, spent an entire year in carnal security. We know likewise that, when the prophet Nathan came to rebuke David for his awful sin, he became terrified and confessed his sin. Immediately the prophet told him: "The LORD also has put away your sin; you shall not die" (2 Samuel 12:13). At that moment David was converted, and he praised and magnified God in the words of Psalm 32 for the forgiveness of his sins.

2 Sam. 12:13

Take Saul, for instance. That persecutor of Christians was promised great mercy when the Lord appeared to him in person. Upon hearing that terrible address: "Saul, Saul, why are you persecuting Me?" he collapsed and cried: "Who are You, Lord?" The Lord told him: "I am Jesus, whom you are persecuting. It will go ill with you if you kick against the goads."[119] At that moment Saul lay crushed before the Lord, and he became a child of God, a "chosen vessel unto Him," because two or three days later he arose and, filled with the Spirit and with power, began to preach Christ crucified.

Acts 26:14–15
Luther

Remember the three thousand who listened to the first Christian sermon at Pentecost? We read that they were cut to the heart (Acts 2:37) when the apostle charged them with murdering Christ. But the moment they were told to believe in the Lord Jesus, they received power from the Holy Spirit and believed.

Lastly, we read of the conversion of the jailer at Philippi on the night that he tortured two disciples of the Lord, Paul and Silas, by putting their feet in

Acts 16:30–31

---

117 Scripture is silent on the exact timing of the fall into sin. We do know that Adam and Eve were created on the sixth day (Genesis 1:31) and that no sin had yet occurred on the seventh day, for it was holy (Genesis 2:2–3) amid a very good creation. After that, no specific length of time is given until the first sin is recorded in Genesis 3.

118 See Genesis 3:15.

119 Middle Eastern farmers used goads, the precursors of modern cattle prods, to keep the oxen plowing forward in a straight line. If the oxen did their job, they were left alone. If they rebelled, they felt the sting of the goad: a nail or sharp point at the end of a pole. The intent in this passage in Acts is that Saul would continue to be disciplined if he did not stop persecuting the Church.

the stocks in the inner prison. That same night—during the earthquake—he was about to run his sword into his own heart. His question "Sirs, what must I do to be saved?" was answered by the apostle: "Believe in the Lord Jesus, and you will be saved, you and your household," and the jailer became a believer.

Every one of these people could say, "On that particular day and at that hour I was converted and brought out of death into life, out of darkness into light, from my desperate condition under the wrath of God into a state of grace." But of the many others we have no such record in the Scriptures. The history of the Church during the first nineteen centuries of its existence shows that millions upon millions who were raised within the pale of the Church were unable to name the day and hour of their conversion. Nevertheless, they were well aware of the fact and could prove, too, that they had become different people by being brought by the Holy Spirit to a living faith in Christ, thus attaining grace, righteousness, and the hope of everlasting life.

What could be the reason that the Pietists—who really meant well—came up with a doctrine that no one could be a Christian unless he knew the exact day and hour of his conversion? The reason is that they imagined that people must suddenly experience heavenly joy and hear an inner voice telling them that they have been received into grace and have become a child of God. Once they had invented this notion of how conversion takes place, they were forced to declare that people have to be able to name the day and hour when they were converted, became a new creature, received forgiveness of sins, and were robed in the righteousness of Christ.

However, we have already learned to some extent what a huge and fatal error this is. Tonight we will take up the last part of Thesis IX, which tells us in particular that the Word of God is not rightly distinguished when one directs sinners who have been struck down and terrified by the Law to win over into a state of grace through prayer and struggling—in other words, to keep on praying and struggling **until they would feel** that God has pardoned them.

Faith not based on feelings

The Methodists have also adopted this approach. But before we discuss their view, we first have to warn against a misunderstanding of the doctrine that a person must certainly not base his salvation and state of grace on his feelings. For this doctrine is horribly abused by many.

There are people who regard themselves as good Christians, even though they are spiritually dead. They have never felt real anguish and have never been filled with terror on account of their sins. They have never been horrified by the thought of hell, even though they are worthy of hell. They have never been on their knees before God, wailing with bitter tears about their awful and damnable condition under sin. Much less have they wept sweet tears of joy and glorified God for His mercy.

They read and hear the Word of God without being particularly impressed by it. They go to church and receive Absolution without feeling refreshed. They attend Holy Communion without any inward sensation and remain as cold as ice. Occasionally, they become inwardly stirred up because of their indifference in matters of salvation and because of their lack of appreciation of God's Word. Then they try to calm their hearts with the reflection that the Lutheran Church teaches that a lack of spiritual feeling is irrelevant. They reason that this lack of spiritual feeling cannot harm them and that they can be good Christians anyway because they *consider* themselves to be believers.

However, these people are suffering from a great, horrible self-delusion. People in that condition have nothing but the dead faith of the intellect, a fake faith, or—to put it yet more drastically—they pay lip service to their faith.[120] They may say with their mouth, "I believe," but their heart knows nothing of it. No, God's Word calls to us: "**Taste** and see that the LORD is good." Whoever has never tasted how compassionate the Lord is should not regard himself as being in a state of true faith. Moreover, the apostle Paul says in Romans 8:16: "The Spirit Himself bears witness with our spirit that we are children of God." How can the Holy Spirit bear this witness in us without our feeling it? A witness in court must speak loudly enough for the judge to hear. The same is true in this case. According to God's Word, those who have never felt the testimony of the Spirit that they are a child of God are spiritually dead. They can offer no testimony in still considering themselves to be Christians and do wrong by doing so. **[Dead faith defined; Ps. 34:8; Rom. 8:16]**

Again, the apostle says in Romans 5:1 that being "justified by faith, we have peace with God through our Lord Jesus Christ." Objective peace, established through the shedding of Christ's blood, exists before our justification. Accordingly, the apostle must be speaking of a peace that is sensed, felt, and experienced. **[Rom. 5:1]**

Furthermore, the apostle Paul writes in Romans 14:17: "For the kingdom of God is not a matter of eating and drinking but of righteousness and peace and joy in the Holy Spirit." The joy of which the apostle speaks is not worldly or carnal joy, but spiritual joy. A person who has tasted all the other joys except the last is spiritually dead. **[Rom. 14:17]**

The examples of the saints recorded in the Bible confirm this point. The saints are continually praising God because of what He has done for them. That presupposes that their hearts were aware of the mercy that the Lord had shown them. Without an inward experience, how could David have exclaimed: "Bless the LORD, O my soul, and all that is within me, bless His holy name! Bless the LORD, O my soul, and forget not all His benefits, who **[Ps. 103:1–3]**

---

120 German: *Maulglauben*. Think of a horse's mouth or a donkey's mouth trying to confess the faith.

forgives all your iniquity, who heals all your diseases." David certainly had a very passionate feeling of these matters when he spoke those words.

Lastly, ask any person who meets all the requirements of a true, living Christian whether he has experienced all the things of which they speak, and he will answer, "Yes, indeed, I have! I experienced the terror that God sends to a sinner whom He wants to rescue. But then I experienced the sweetness of God's grace in Christ. Oh, every time I think about my Savior's love, my heart melts within me! Although I know that I have found grace, I am ambushed frequently by fright and anguish at the sight of the Law."

When we say that no one must base one's salvation and state of grace on feelings, this does not mean that a person can be a good Christian without having experienced anything regarding religious matters. That is not what we teach. Let me offer a pertinent testimony of Luther, who differed, for instance, from Melanchthon in the sense that the reformer was most certainly not a sentimentalist, which Melanchthon was in the highest degree. Melanchthon based his joy on his feelings; but no matter what Luther's feelings were, he clung to the Word.

Confirm feelings with Scripture; Gal. 4:6

In his *Church Postil* (St. Louis Ed. 12:239–41), Luther comments on the words "And because you are sons, God has sent the Spirit of His Son into our hearts, crying, 'Abba! Father!' (Galatians 4:6)."[121] Although he endeavored never to rely on changeable and deceptive feelings, Luther writes as follows:

W² 12:239; Rom. 8:15 Luther

> At this point everyone is to investigate and to prove whether he **feels** the Holy Spirit in his heart and **experiences** Him speaking. Note well: the text says that the Spirit **cries**, "Abba, Father." For in this passage St. Paul says that in every heart in which the Spirit lives, the Spirit cries, "Abba, Father." Likewise, in Romans 8:15 he says, "You have received the Spirit of gracious adoption as God's children, by whom we cry, 'Abba! Dear Father!'" You feel this crying when your conscience knows for sure—without wavering or questioning—that your sins have been forgiven and that you are a child of God. You are assured of your salvation, and with a cheerful and assured heart and with all confidence you may call God your dear Father and cry to Him.

That is the great sorrow in our time: such faith is rare. Either people are spiritually dead and therefore are unconcerned about their soul's welfare because they imagine that they will get to heaven anyway. Or they are filled with anguish and uncertainty. Many who have spent their lives in their horrible "faith"—which *looks* like faith but is not—die with the thought in their hearts: "What will become of me now? Am I going to heaven or not?" You

---

121 See also John Nicholas Lenker, ed., *The Complete Sermons of Martin Luther*, trans. John Nicholas Lenker et al. (Grand Rapids: Baker, 1983, 2000), 1.1:292–96.

must be more certain of these things than of your very life. You must be ready to suffer every kind of death—and hell too—rather than allow this assurance to be taken from you by yielding to doubt.

As you know, the Roman Church rejects this. They declare not only that people **cannot** but even that they **should not** obtain assurance of salvation. The Roman Church regards striving for such assurance as a crime and a cheeky undertaking. It declares that only when you receive a special, extraordinary revelation from heaven are you able to say, "I know and am certain that I have been received into grace by God and will be saved." That is an "inverted gospel," and the entire teaching of the papacy is nothing but the most miserable corruption of the Gospel into new law, that is, into Roman church laws.

> It would be an offense to the rich life of Christ and to His suffering if we were not to believe that He obtained everything for us to the point of overflowing, if we did not allow His great living and dying to urge us to—and to confirm us in—this confidence with the same force as sin and affliction[122] prevent us from this confidence and make us hopeless.

W² 12:239–40

Some people would say, "Oh, I know well enough that Christ has redeemed the whole world, but here is the question: What about me?" People who speak like this have no knowledge of either Law or Gospel. For a person who has learned the Gospel will say, "Since the Son of God has redeemed the whole world, He has redeemed me too. Since He has redeemed me, He wants me to believe that. He does not prevent me from believing it by the pietistic warning: 'Do not believe too soon!'"

We can never believe too soon. The moment the Gospel is preached to us, we need to believe it for the salvation of our souls, lest we fall under the displeasure and wrath of God. But unless people cling to the Word, they cannot feel assured. They will waver and dither[123] every day and hour. One moment they imagine themselves to be Christians; the next hour they will think that they have deceived themselves.

Luther continues: "Some might argue that a person could worry that he is not a child of God." Luther is not claiming here that the witness of the Holy Spirit is only in the heart of a child of God. There is still disagreement about this.[124] Thus Luther: "And he might imagine and feel that God is an

W² 12:240

---

122 German: *Anfechtung.*

123 The English expression "to waver and dither" reflects the German "*wanken und schwanken.*"

124 A clue regarding this remark appears in resources such as the article "Holy Spirit," in Richard Watson, *A Biblical and Theological Dictionary*, 2d ed. (London: John Mason, 1832), 496. Watson cites John Wesley's occasional sermons almost word for word. The

angry, stern judge, as happened to Job and many others. But in a conflict of this kind, childlike confidence—even though it might be trembling and quaking—must conquer in the end, or everything is lost."

Hope must be there—yet even though there is hope, we sometimes fear and tremble. But we can fear and tremble yet still be sure of our salvation. I can cross a terrible gulf that falls into darkness, thinking, "Oh, what if I toppled into the depths!" But I have a barrier on both sides of my path, so I gather confidence and cross over, certain of safety. That is the strange paradox in the heart of a Christian: we fear and tremble and are still assured.

W² 12:240   If Cain were to hear this, he would make the sign of the cross with his hands and even his feet and say with great humility: "God keep me from this awful heresy and disrespect! Am I—a poor sinner—so conceited as to call myself a child of God? No, no. I will humble myself, acknowledge that I am a poor sinner, etc."

These are the kind of people you should avoid. Beware of them as the greatest enemies of the Christian faith and your salvation. Of course, we know indeed that we are poor sinners. But in this business we are not to consider what we are and what we do, but what *Christ* is, has done, and is *still* doing for us. We should not talk about our human nature but about the grace of God that is so much greater than we, of which Psalm 103:11 says [it is] as high as the heavens are above the earth, as far as the dawn is from the sunset.

Do you consider it to be a great thing to be a child of God? Then do not consider it unimportant that the Son of God has come, born of a woman and placed under the Law,[125] for the purpose of making you such a child of God. Everything that God does is great. That is why it produces **great joy and courage** and fearless spirits that are not afraid of anything and able to do all things.

Cain's attitude is narrow and produces nothing but miserable hearts. Such people are full of anguish and are neither fit to suffer for Christ nor to live for Him. They shiver at the sound of a leaf blowing, as Moses says in Leviticus 26:36. Cling, then, firmly to this text, and know that **you must feel the crying of the Spirit in your heart**. For how can you

---

argument is that the witness of the Spirit arises from the Word of God and from inner experience. The requirement of experience also arises among German theologians in the nineteenth century; see the section "Scripture, Theology, and Philosophy," page lxxiv. Here Walther corrects John Wesley's belief that only children of God have a direct testimony of the Spirit. Walther, following Luther, speaks of "our spirit" hearing the Holy Spirit in a special, spiritual way, but he qualifies this by directing such hearing to the confirmation of the Word. Walther rejects inner feelings as the final judge.

125 See Galatians 4:4.

fail to feel it when it is the crying of your own heart? Moreover, St. Paul uses the word "crying" when he might have said the Spirit lisps or speaks or sings. Paul wanted to use a far stronger term than these.

This does not mean "The Spirit gives a general witness," but He does it "with our spirit." Accordingly, our spirit must hear the witness of the Spirit in a spiritual way, and that is the "feeling" of which we speak.

> The Spirit cries and calls with all His might—from a full heart—so that everything seems full of life and energy through the confidence that He produces. Regarding this effect, the apostle says in Romans 8:26: "The Spirit in us pleads for us with sighing so deep that none may express it in words," and again in Romans 8:16: "The Spirit Himself bears witness to our spirit that we are children of God." How could our hearts not feel this crying, groaning, and witness-bearing?

W² 12:240–41; Rom. 8:26 Luther; Rom. 8:16

It is strange that a Christian who is beginning to doubt will hear a voice telling him: "Christ has died for you despite your sins. You do not need to fear or yield to despair. You belong to the redeemed of the Lord, and your destination is heaven. Be of good cheer!" Coming spontaneously, this voice, which we cannot produce at random, is the witness of the Holy Spirit. It comes to us especially at a time of spiritual trial. You do not need such a witness every day, but when you are being accused, you go in search of one. The same happens in our spiritual life: when a poor Christian is in very great distress, the Holy Spirit calls to him: "Do not despair."

> And oh! Affliction[126] and suffering provide a precious service for Christians, urging them to cry and awakening the spirit.[127] However, we are afraid of the cross and flee from it; therefore, we never feel the Spirit and remain with Cain. If you do not feel the crying of the Spirit, resolve never to quit praying until God hears you. For you are a Cain, and your spiritual condition is not what it should be.

W² 12:241

Cain roamed about and did not know his true relationship with God.[128]

Luther writes: "**Indeed, you should not covet the idea that such calling might be purely in you alone.** By necessity a murderous cry will arise along with it that will drive and work you into its own calling, as has happened with everyone else." While a Christian may be sure of his state of grace, nevertheless there will come a voice whispering in his ear: "Oh ho! You are not yet rid of your sins! What evil thoughts have you had again this very day?

W² 12:241

---

126 German: *Anfechtung.*

127 German: *die treiben zu solchem Rufen und wecken den Geist auf.* This refers to the sleeping human spirit. Luther then speaks about feeling the Holy Spirit in connection with this awakening.

128 See Genesis 4:11–12.

What sinful lusts have arisen in you? What useless words have come from your mouth? Whatever good you have done has become a mere sham." Those are the murderous arrows from Satan's bow. In such moments the Holy Spirit steps forward to bear testimony for us if we are Christians.

W² 12:241

Also your sin will cry, causing your conscience to despair horribly. But the Spirit of Christ must drown out these cries, that is, produce in you a confidence stronger than your despair. For St. John says in 1 John 3:19–22: However much our heart might punish us, God remains greater. Therefore, dear brothers, as much as our heart might punish us, we have the confidence that we will receive everything from Him that we ask. We thereby know that we are born of truth, that we may comfort our heart in His presence.[129]

This calling and crying of the Spirit within us, then, is nothing else than a strong, unwavering, trustful crying with our whole heart to God—as to our dear Father. It is the way we react as His dear children.

Faith precedes feeling

We will now move on to the particular point in our thesis that is our topic tonight, namely, that Law and Gospel are horribly mingled by those who claim: "If you want to be certain that your sins are forgiven, you must pray, struggle, and grapple until you finally feel joyful in your heart." This would indicate in a mysterious way that grace is now in your heart and that you can be of good cheer because your sins have been forgiven.

Now, properly speaking, grace is never in a person's heart, but in *God's* heart. **First** a person must **believe**. **After that he may feel.** Feeling proceeds from faith—not faith from feeling. If a person's faith proceeds from feeling, it is not genuine faith. For faith requires a divine promise to which it can hold. Accordingly, we can be sure that the faith of those who can say, "The only thing I hang on to in the world is the precious Gospel. That is what I build on," is of the right sort. The devil may terrify and harass such people until they have no pleasant feeling of grace, but they will nevertheless sing:

> Though "No!" should be my heart's refrain,
> E'en surer does Your Word remain.

> or:

> I will believe, though void of feeling,
> Till before You I am kneeling.

1 John 3:19–20

The key passage for this point of doctrine is 1 John 3:19–20: "By this we shall know that we are of the truth and reassure our heart before Him; for whenever our heart condemns us, God is greater than our heart, and He knows everything."

---

129 Here Luther paraphrases the Bible text.

Christians may feel the accusation of their own heart, that is, their conscience, and when they try to calm their heart, they may hear a voice telling them that they are condemned, that they have no forgiveness of their sins and no grace, that they are not children of God and cannot hope for eternal life. To such people the beloved John says, "If our heart condemns us, God is greater than our heart." That is to say, our heart is indeed a judge, yet only a local judge. There is a higher Judge, namely God, presiding above our heart. I can say to my troubled heart: "Be still, my heart! Be still, my conscience! I have appealed to another Judge to determine if I am free of my sins. That Judge is the great God, who is greater than you. That is a higher court." A higher court can always reverse the verdict of a lower court. When we hold fast to the Word, then the higher Judge speaks to us: "Your sins are forgiven."

Whoever by the grace of God is capable of believing this—oh, what a blessed person! Hell is closed, and heaven is opened wide for him. Even if all the devils in hell were to roar at him, "You are lost!" he can answer them: "Wrong! I am not lost, but forever redeemed. Look at the written evidence in God's Word!" In due time that feeling of grace will return. That is true, even though a Christian might be only at the point of thinking: "Oh, I cannot feel anything. I am a miserable and lost person! I am so cold and so dead! The Word of God to me is like eating rotten wood! Absolution will not quicken me to life! The witness of the Spirit is not in me!" When he finally thinks, "I am done for," then great joy would suddenly enter his heart. God will not leave him stuck like that.

To be sure, we cannot lay down rules for God. There are all kinds of Christians. Some have been highly favored because God has led them down an easy path. They have always been privileged to enjoy beautiful, pleasant feelings, and they never have had to struggle. For one thing is certain: when people recognize that what they are experiencing is in harmony with the Word of God, they do not need to struggle to achieve that harmony.

However, God almost always leads others through darkness, great anguish, serious doubts, and diverse afflictions. In the case of these people, we must be careful to distinguish between someone who is spiritually dead and someone who is afflicted.[130]

This distinction is not difficult: If you are worried about not feeling grace—for which you earnestly long—that is proof that you are a true Christian. For people who desire to believe are already believers. For how could a person possibly desire to believe something that he regards as untrue? No one wants to be deceived. As soon as you want to believe something, you already secretly believe it.

---

130 German: *Anfechtung.*

This is a good point for pastors to note when they deal with individuals. Good congregation members may come to the pastor, complaining of great spiritual misery, claiming that they cannot believe at all. If you ask them whether they would like to believe and they eagerly answer in the affirmative, then comfort them with the assurance that they may confidently consider themselves to be believers. Tell them to wait until God permits the hour of their affliction to pass—when they will suddenly observe their faith break forth in great strength and joy.

John 20:29 In John 20:29 we read: "Jesus said to him, 'Have you believed because you have seen Me? Blessed are those who have not seen and yet have believed.'" Thomas refused to believe that Christ had risen from the dead, unless he could place his finger into the nail marks on Christ's body. Out of great compassion, Christ granted him that privilege. Thomas fell down before Him, exclaiming, "My Lord and my God!" Then the Lord spoke the words we just quoted.

Now, seeing is basically the same as feeling. For whether you sense something through your nervous system or see something with your sense of vision or hear something with your auditory nerves—it is all the same. The Lord's remarks to Thomas mean that we must **first** believe and **then** see. He does not mean to say, "I should first see, then believe." It is certain, therefore, that we must not desire first to **feel**. Rather, we must first believe and **then** wait for God to grant us the sweet sensation that our sins have been taken from us.

Heb. 11:1 Hebrews 11:1 states: "Now faith is the assurance of things hoped for, the conviction of things not seen." Here we have a definition of faith. If faith is what is stated here—a firm confidence, not doubting, not wavering—it is self-evident that faith dare not be based on sight, feeling, and sense. If it is built on such sand, the entire structure will soon collapse. Pity the person who is accustomed to regarding himself as pardoned only when he is enjoying pleasant feelings. As a rule, these pleasant feelings vanish in the hour of death, when the final agony drives them away. Blessed is a person who in that hour can say:

> I cling to what my Savior taught
> And trust it whether felt or not.

That person can depart in peace. On the other hand, pity the poor, unhappy wretch who in his hour of death discovers that he completely lacks any feeling of grace and must die without Jesus living in his heart. Many who have joined the fanatical sects may have died eternally because they let go of Jesus in their dying hour, thinking that they were not permitted to grab hold of Him. For all the fanatics claim that only a feeling of divine grace conveys the privilege of coming to Jesus and taking comfort in Him.

When they ask one of their brothers, "What do you feel?" and that man tells them that he is not aware of any particular feeling, they cry, "You poor wretch!" They say, "Come, let us pray, fight, and struggle together until you attain that feeling." The feeling that this man does obtain, however, is merely physical—not the feeling of the Holy Spirit.

When put under an extraordinary strain, human nature will probably turn a person's mind. Suddenly every nerve seems as though it snapped, and you feel like a drowning person who has been rescued from a watery grave. Such a person, too, has a sensation of delight, but it is not the delightful sensation of the Holy Spirit.

In his *Church Postil* (St. Louis Ed. 11:1577–78),[131] **Luther** writes:

W² 11:1577

> The second quality of faith is that believers do not demand knowledge or assurance of whether they are worthy of God's grace or whether He has heard their prayers. This is something that doubters do—people who are reaching for God and who are testing Him.

> Doubters grope around, looking for God like a blind person groping along a wall. The first thing they want to do is feel and be sure that He cannot escape them. Hebrews 11:1 reads: "Now faith is the certain assurance of things hoped for; it points toward things not seen." That means that faith clings to things that it does not see, feel, or sense—whether in body or soul. On the other hand, faith is trust in God, for whom you are willing to risk and stake anything, never doubting that you will come out a winner. If believers feel good about God, they submit to that feeling, they trust it, they do not doubt that those things that they assume will happen. And these things certainly do happen to them. **These feelings and perceptions come to believers in a manner that is both unsought and undesired—indeed, by means of their assumption or belief.**

Heb. 11:1 Luther

That is exactly the true manner of faith: it declines to know and be assured by such knowledge before it believes. Rather, it simply believes the moment God's Word is spoken. This is indeed followed by assurance—sooner for some people, later for others.

The common experience is that a person who becomes a Christian immediately has a pleasant sensation. God treats His young children just as an earthly father treats his. He feeds them light snacks, gives them sweets, etc. In the same way, God gives new Christians the sugar bread of pleasant feelings. But when they have passed through a number of spiritual experiences that exercise their faith, the sugar bread stops, and they are given black rye

---

131 See also John Nicholas Lenker, ed., *The Complete Sermons of Martin Luther*, trans. John Nicholas Lenker et al. (Grand Rapids: Baker, 1983, 2000), 3.1:66–67.

bread, which sometimes is quite hard and has a strong taste.[132] God's thinking is that, since these Christians have gained enough experience in Christianity simply by living the Christian life and having matured in the faith, this new food will not be too rough on them. For new believers, on the other hand, this spiritual food would be indigestible.

When tribulations come, many Christians fondly remember, "Oh, what a happy person I was once! How I just wallowed about in the sweet experience and the joyful assurance that I have a gracious God in heaven, something of which I had no clue before I was converted! Back in those days, I went to bed every night, knowing that I would rest in the arms of Jesus. I rose cheerfully in the morning, knowing that Jesus and His angels would accompany me in all my ways. How sure I was that no misfortune would happen to me." And even if any *should* happen to them, they thought it would be a blessing in disguise, as Paul Gerhardt phrases it when he sings:

> My heart from care is free,
> No troubles trouble me.
> Misfortune now is play,
> And night is bright as day.[133]

Mature Christians are able to digest this hard rye bread quite well. On the other hand, if God were to withdraw His comfort from a new believer, that person would say, "Thanks for making me so miserable. In their sermons, pastors always paint the Christian life as being glorious. But in reality I can see that Christians are the unhappiest people. Their whole life is filled with anguish, misery, and terror."

What a kind Father, then, is God to His Christians! He does not lay heavy burdens on them from the very beginning. He gradually accustoms them to how He deals with them. Then He gradually withdraws His *comfort* from them so they would learn to lay hold of Him in the dark as well. Accordingly, we must not think that we have fallen from grace or have forsaken our first love when we no longer have the blessed experiences of former days—or at least not in the same degree. The love that a more mature, experienced Christian bears toward his Savior may not have the sweet flavor of his earlier

---

132 A reference that may be familiar to those of European heritage. One makes sugar bread (*Zuckerbrot*) by buttering white bread and sprinkling it with sugar. On the opposite extreme are the dark breads—rye, pumpernickel, and *Vollkornbrot* with whole kernels of grain in it—which are coarser in texture, more difficult to digest, and often are an acquired taste.

133 Walther again cites "Awake, My Heart, with Gladness." This is the published translation of stanza 5 (see *LSB* 467). A more literal rendering, though not metrical, is: "Affliction does not depress me, Neither my heart nor my appearance. Misfortune is my fortune, And night is my sunny day."

Christian life, but it is purer, because many dregs that it contained at the beginning have been strained out of it.

Luther continues:

> Tell me, had anyone promised those lepers[134] in writing that Christk   W² 11:1577–78
> would hear their prayer? In what way do they sense or feel His mercy?
> Do they have any information, knowledge, or certainty of His good-
> ness? We can see none of these things in them. Well, what *do* we see
> in them? They are bold risk takers and cheerfully assume He will treat
> them with kindness, which they have not felt, tested, or discovered.
> They do not see any marks that would indicate what He intends to do
> for them. They look solely to His goodness, and this sparks in them
> the daring thought that He will not leave them in the lurch. Where do
> they get their knowledge of His goodness? For though they had never
> experienced it, they had to have some previous knowledge of it. No
> doubt, they had gathered it from public rumors about all the good that
> He had done, though personally they had never experienced it. For the
> goodness of God must be proclaimed through His Word, and people
> must rely on it before they can test it or experience it.

After reciting the Lord's Prayer with proper devotion—something that, by the way, happens very rarely among most people—I can cheerfully conclude by saying, "Amen," even though during my prayer I may not have felt that it is really the Holy Spirit who is urging me to pray. Even though I struggle with my prayers, nevertheless my prayer is heard.

In another place **Luther** writes (St. Louis Ed. 11:453–55):[135]

> What I have said is this: God will not permit us **to rely on anything**   W² 11:453–55
> **or to cling with our hearts to anything that is not Christ as revealed**
> **in His Word, no matter how holy and full of the Spirit it may seem.**
> **Faith has no other ground on which to stand.** Accordingly, Joseph
> and the mother of Christ experience that their own wisdom, thoughts,
> and hopes fail them and turn out to be useless while they are hurrying
> from place to place, seeking Him.[136] For they do not seek Him where
> they should, but consult their own flesh and blood, which is always
> staring about for some comfort other than that offered by God's
> Word. Flesh and blood always desire something that can be seen and
> touched—something that can be grasped by the senses and human
> reason. For that reason, God lets them fail and forces this lesson upon

---

134 These are the ten lepers whom Jesus healed in Luke 17:11–19.

135 This is Luther's second sermon for the First Sunday after Epiphany. Its text is Luke 2:41–
     52. Compare with Klug, *Complete Sermons of Martin Luther*, 1.2:42–44.

136 See Luke 2:41–51.

them: no amount of comfort, aid, and advice that people seek from flesh and blood—or from other human beings or from any other creature—is worth anything unless God's Word is grasped. The mother of Christ and Joseph[137] had to abandon everything—their friends, acquaintances, the entire city of Jerusalem, every clever idea, every stroke of intelligence, all that they themselves and other people could do. All these things did not provide them with the proper assurance until they sought Him in the temple, where He was about His Father's business. There Christ is surely found, and there the heart recovers its cheer, while it would otherwise remain cheerless, since neither we ourselves nor any other creature comfort can provide us comfort.

Therefore, when God sends us such great afflictions,[138] we, too, must learn not to follow our own thoughts or the advice of such people who send us here and there and direct us to our own or to other people's resources. Rather, we should remember that we must seek Christ in His Father's house and about His Father's business. We must simply cling solely to the Word of the Gospel, which shows us Christ correctly and teaches us how to know Him. Learn, then, from this and from any other spiritual affliction that whenever you wish to communicate genuine comfort to others or to yourself, you must say with Christ: Why are you are running here and there, tormenting yourselves with anxious and sad thoughts, imagining that God will not keep you in His grace and that there is no longer any Christ for you? Why do you insist on finding Him within yourselves, insist on feeling holy and without sin? You will never succeed. All your effort will be worthless.

Do you not know that Christ will be nowhere, nor permit Himself to be found anywhere, except about His Father's business—not in anything that is man-made? This is not the fault of Christ or His mercy. He can never be "lost." He can always be found. Rather, it is your fault because you are not seeking Him where you ought—namely, in the place where He should be sought. You are being guided by your feelings and think you can grasp Him with your thoughts. Come to the place that is driven neither by your own nor by any human being's business, but by God's business and rule. So come to His Word. There you will find Him and hear and see that there is no wrath and disfavor against you in Him, as you fear in your despair. Christ has nothing but grace and warm love in store for you. He acts as your kind and

---

137 Luther always reserved high honor for Mary. Here Luther places Mary, according to her office as the mother of Christ, ahead of Joseph in honor.

138 German: *Anfechtung.*

loving Mediator with the Father, speaking the kindest and best words possible on your behalf. Nor does He send you trials with the intention of casting you off, but so that you may learn to know Him better and cling more firmly to His Word and in order to rebuke your unreasonableness. This forces you to learn by experience how cordially and faithfully He cherishes you.

This is Luther's verdict that condemns all fanatical sects. No matter what other false doctrines they may teach, they all have this great error in common: They do not rely solely on Christ and His Word, but chiefly on something that takes place in themselves. As a rule, they imagine that all is well with them because they have turned from their former ways. As if that were a guarantee of reaching heaven! No—we should not look back to our conversion for assurance. Rather, we must go to our Savior again and again—every day—as though we never had been converted. My former conversion would be of no benefit to me if I became secure in my sins. I must return to the mercy seat every day, otherwise I would make my former *conversion* my savior, and not Christ, because I would be relying on it. That would be horrible, for at the end of the day that would mean that I would make myself my own savior.

My Friends:—

Twentieth Evening Lecture: Feb. 27, 1885
Practical advice

When a Lutheran candidate of theology is assigned to a parish where he is to discharge the office of a Lutheran preacher, for him that place ought to be the dearest, most beautiful, and most precious spot on earth. He should be unwilling to exchange it for a kingdom. Whether it is in a metropolis or in a small town, on a bleak prairie or in a clearing in the forest, in a flourishing settlement or in a desert—for him that place should be a miniature paradise. Do not the blessed angels descend from heaven with great joy whenever the Father in heaven sends them to minister to those who are to inherit salvation?[139] Why, then, should **we** poor sinners be unwilling to hurry after them with great joy to a place where we can lead other people   fellow sinners—to salvation?

However, no matter how joyful a young, newly called pastor is when he enters his parish, he should be completely serious and determined to do all he can to save every soul entrusted to him. It may often seem to him that the majority of—if not all—the members of his congregation are still spiritually blind and unconverted people. That observation must not make him gloomy or discourage him, but rather [it should] fire him up with the burning desire

139 Walther does not base this remark on a specific Bible passage, but he draws from the sense of several passages, including Matthew 18:10 and Luke 15:10.

to wake them out of spiritual death through the divine Means of Grace, to make them living Christians. He should not let the devil stop him; he should take up his work in the power of faith!

Even if he observes that some members of his new parish are living in open shame and vice, he must not despair. Rather, he should keep in mind that he has a powerful Word by which he can make an effort to free these slaves of sin. If he observes that his congregation has little knowledge regarding how salvation works, that his people are still sadly uninformed of what the Gospel really is, then he must cheerfully resolve: "I will take up the task of teaching these poor, uninformed people with patience and enthusiasm until they see the light."

Or he may notice that there are people in his congregation who are sincere but, because of their pietistic training, tend to be legalistic. For that reason they would regard some things as sinful that are not. In that case he must not exercise his Christian freedom, lest he offend souls that regard as sinful something that *he* feels free to do.

1 Cor. 9:22   On the other hand, he may discover that there are people with an Antinomian tendency in his congregation, people who are inclined to go too far in their Christian freedom because they are not accustomed to having the Law preached to them in its severity. In these cases, he must *not* decide on the spot to oppose them forcefully and to preach nothing but the sternest Law to them for a whole year. Rather, he must go after them gently and *gradually* make them see the stern demands of the Law. For the apostle Paul says about himself: "I have become all things to all people, that by all means I might save some" (1 Corinthians 9:22). Paul wants every servant of Christ to take this statement to heart. What he means is that a pastor must not be content with merely proclaiming the truth. He must proclaim the truth in such a way as to meet the needs of his people. He may have to delay saying many things until his people have gained confidence in him and his teaching, until he knows that he may frankly tell them anything without fear of driving them off. In sum, he must resolve to turn his congregation from a dreary desert into a flourishing garden of God.

Or he may make the very heartening discovery that most members of his congregation are mature, believing, and active Christians and that there are only a few who appear to be unconverted. In that case he must resolve—before anything else—to bring the unconverted to Christ. Of course, in due time he must also resolve to give those people who are well-grounded in the truth the strong meat that they need.

Matt. 7:23   How pitiful is the young pastor who enters this office thinking: "Hooray, the time of hard work and drudgery is over. Now I have come to the haven of rest and peace! I will enjoy that! I am my own boss and need not take orders from any person in the world!" This is just as pitiful as the pastor who looks upon his office as his craft, or trade, and thinks: "Now all I have to do is to set up for myself a nice, comfortable parish! I will be really careful not to make enemies and do everything to make everyone my friend." Oh, what a pitiful man! These pastors plan to use their spiritual assets for worldly gain. They are not true ministers of Christ, and on the Last Day He will say to them, "I never knew you; depart from Me, you workers of lawlessness" (Matthew 7:23).

But blessed is the pastor who starts his official work on the very first day, determined to do everything that the grace of God will enable him to do, so that not one soul in his congregation would be lost on account of him. A pastor like this would resolve that by the grace of God he would do all he can, so that, when the day comes for him to lay down his shepherd's staff, he may be able to say what Christ said to His Father: "Here I am. Of those You gave me, not one is lost."[140] This pastor resolves that even the blood of those who will stand on the left side of the judgment seat would not be on his hands.

But this raises the question: What would be the main way for him to reach this glorious goal? He must approach the Lord with heartfelt prayer and earnest pleas on behalf of his congregation. He must preach the Word of God with great passion—publicly and privately—and rightly distinguish the Word of truth. For that is what Paul demands in 2 Timothy 2:15 when he says, "Do your best to present yourself to God as one approved, a worker who has no need to be ashamed, rightly handling the word of truth."

2 Tim. 2:15

During this academic year at the seminary, this very thing is the subject of our study, as you know, to properly distinguish the Word of God: Law and Gospel. These two are the key doctrines of all Holy Scripture. Holy Scripture is based on Law and Gospel. Any passage of Scripture—why, any historical fact recorded in Scripture—can be classified as belonging either to Law or to Gospel. No one should be permitted to graduate from a school of theology if he is unable to determine whether a given passage of Scripture is Law or Gospel, or whether in any compound clause of Scripture the main clause is Law and the subordinate clause Gospel or vice versa. It is your duty to become perfectly clear on this subject.

No mere "stuff"

Many things might still be said regarding the ninth thesis, but we must not spend any more time on it, or else we will never get done.

---

140 See John 17:12.

This portrait of C. F. W. Walther was drawn by Gustav Pfau between 1840 and 1843. Image courtesy of Concordia Historical Institute.

THESIS X

You are not rightly distinguishing Law and Gospel in the Word of God if you preach that "dead" faith can justify and save in the sight of God—while that believer is still living in mortal sins. In the same way, do not preach that faith justifies and saves those unrepentant people because of the love and renewal it produces in them.

EDITOR'S NOTE: In this thesis, Walther rejects both Roman Catholic and Reformed sources that claim godless people can have faith, albeit for different reasons. Walther's opponents in the Election Controversy had called him a Calvinist, while he responded by calling them Papists. Walther takes aim at the Canons of Dort[1] in order to distance himself and the Missouri Synod from the charge of Calvinism. He does the same with the Puritan Oliver Cromwell (1599–1658) for the same reasons.

Lutherans have always affirmed that sin, even minor sin, is very dangerous and that one cannot continue to embrace evil thoughts, words, and deeds and still retain a living faith. Walther takes the stricter position that even a minor willful sin causes one to lose salvation. He states that immediate repentance restores grace. This argument rests on a 1544 opinion of Luther, Johann Bugenhagen, and Philip Melanchthon against a commentary on 1 John by Thomas Naogeorg that claims a Christian can commit premeditated murder and other coarse sins yet not lose faith.[2] The reformers correctly see this as contrary to Scripture.

The Missouri Synod, however, did not affirm Walther's opinion about falling in and out of grace.[3] This opinion only appears in these lectures, which may suggest that it was not a central part of Walther's teaching. The main point of this thesis nevertheless

---

1   The Synod of Dordrecht (Dort) established a summary presentation of the basic points of Calvinism.

2   The best source of this opinion is *D. Martin Luthers Werke: Briefwechsel* (Weimar: H. Böhlau, 1947), 10:509–15. Perhaps in haste, the reformers paraphrase citations from Scripture and these paraphrases are presented in several editions of Luther's works as direct quotations. At one point, the reformers claim that one of these paraphrases is the clear word of Scripture. This shows how all Christians are human and can err. Everyone must look carefully to Scripture as the source, standard, guide, and measure of faith.

3   Neither Franz Pieper's *Christian Dogmatics* (St. Louis: Concordia, 1950–57) nor any doctrinal resolutions between 1880 and 1918 show that Walther's position on falling in and out of grace was accepted. This aspect of Walther's thought was quietly set aside.

remains based on Scripture. The Missouri Synod did affirm that Walther is correct when he states that mere intellectual or historical knowledge of Jesus cannot save, for it is not true faith. Missouri Synod doctrinal resolutions affirm from Scripture that true faith is both knowledge and action; faith cannot help but produce good works. Walther correctly shows that one cannot preach Gospel comfort to those who have only an intellectual or historical knowledge of Jesus and who continue in sinful lives.

No cheap grace   This evening we wish to consider the first part of this thesis, once again referring to how people mingle Law and Gospel. This problem occurs chiefly in the papacy and is the principal reason they reject Luther and his doctrine.

As you know, Luther taught that only *faith—apart* from good works—saves a person. Correspondingly, he taught that good works do *not* save. Based on Luther's rejection of good works, Papists draw the conclusion that he must have been a wicked man. They have claimed that Luther said that, in order to get into heaven, you need only believe and not do any good works. But this is not Luther's doctrine at all. In fact, Luther taught the exact opposite. He did not say, "You need faith—but also good works and love." Rather, what Luther said was that "you need faith that is so strong that it will produce love on its own, generating an abundance of good works."

This does not mean that faith saves *on account of* the love that springs from it. What it means is that the faith which the Holy Spirit creates *cannot help* but do good works. This faith justifies because it clings to the gracious promises of Christ. It justifies because it lays hold of Christ. This faith is active in good works *because* it is genuine faith.

There is no need to urge believers to do good works. Their faith generates good works automatically. Believers engage in good works—not from a sense of duty, in return for the forgiveness of their sins, but chiefly because they cannot *help* but do them.

It is completely impossible for genuine faith not to gush forth from the believer's heart in works of love. This is a point that the Papists simply do not grasp. They imagine that a person may have true faith and still live in mortal sin.[4] This is why they sneer at the teaching that "faith saves." They call this a "fine religion," meaning that it is the worst and most wicked religion that has ever been invented. This is what they teach about Luther.

However, it never entered Luther's mind to teach only a kind of faith that merely believes what the *Church* believes. The Papists claim that faith is the

4   See "sin, mortal and venial" in the Glossary, page 486.

firm belief that the teaching of the Church is correct. Therefore, in their view, as long as anyone has that belief, they also have the true faith. Nevertheless when believers in the Roman version of faith die, they do not immediately go to heaven, Rome claims. This is why, as far as Rome is concerned, people can be fornicators, adulterers, drunkards, thieves and at the same time be good believers.

In Galatians 5:6 we read: "For in Christ Jesus neither circumcision nor uncircumcision counts for anything, but only faith working through love." If faith is lacking love, the reason it is not effective is not because of its lack of love but because it is not genuine, righteous faith in the first place. It is not that love must be *added* to faith. Rather, love must *grow* out of faith.

Gal. 5:6

A fruitful tree does not produce fruit because someone ordered it to grow fruit but because, as long as there is still some life in it and it is not dried up, it *cannot help* but produce fruit spontaneously. Faith is like that tree. If it fails to bring forth fruit, it is obviously withered. In the same way, the sun does not need to be told to shine. It will continue shining until the Last Day—without anyone commanding it to do so. Faith is like the sun.

Acts 15:9 documents the effect of the mission work of the early Church: "And [God] made no distinction between us [Jews] and them [Gentiles], **having cleansed their hearts by faith**."

Acts 15:9

A person who claims to have a firm faith that he will never abandon—but who still has an impure heart—must be told that he is in great darkness. For, in reality, he has no faith at all. For instance, you may regard all the doctrines preached in the Lutheran Church as true, but if your heart is still in its old condition, filled with the love of sin—if you still act contrary to your conscience—then your whole faith is a mere sham. Then you do not have the faith of which the Holy Spirit speaks when He uses the word "faith" in the Scriptures. For *real* faith purifies the heart.

Christ says in John 5:44: "How can you believe, when you receive glory from one another and do not seek the glory that comes from the only God?" What a terrible verdict! What the Savior is saying is: "Anyone who would be a believer yet accepts honor from people really has no faith." From the moment faith begins to grow up in a person's heart, one of the first fruits of faith is that he gives all honor to God alone. But if a believer does happen to receive honor from his neighbor, then that person is inwardly convinced that he does not deserve it. Then he says to God:

John 5:44

> Whate'er of good this life of mine
> Has shown is altogether Thine.[5]

---

5 German: *Ist etwas Gut am Leben mein / So ist es wahrlich lauter dein.*

Thus a true believer returns to God any honor given to him. In the same way, if a person *without* faith finds himself looked down upon or despised, he at once becomes depressed and miserable because he is not getting what he seeks.

Preachers who are conquered by this faithless mind-set step into the pulpit full of ambitious passion: "Now the folks are going to see what a real preacher is!" They are flattered by the admiration of people who may be completely unqualified to evaluate them: "Oh, that was so beautiful! Oh, the young man presents it all so well! Someday he is going to be somebody!"[6] These preachers prefer such flattery to being slipped, say, ten dollars,[7] though they would probably take the money too.

But seriously, *all* of us are haughty, proud, and ambitious. And only the Holy Spirit can drive this harmful vice from our heart. But we can never get rid of it entirely. An evil root remains in our heart. When a believer notices this nasty tendency within himself, he detests it, rebukes himself, feels ashamed of himself, and asks God to deliver him from these disgraceful ideas of pride.

That this statement is true is beyond question. For the Savior is asking a rhetorical question, saying, "How can you possibly think that you could receive honor from one another?" There is no way that "looking for honor" and "faith" can be compatible with each other. Rather, when faith enters a person's heart, this should make the believer humble in the presence of God and other people.

We should despair when we occasionally eavesdrop on our own heart because we must remember that a poisonous root of vanity is still in our heart. And as soon as our heart begins to stir up those vain thoughts in us, we must fight it. This will keep us from despair. Yet a person who does not fight his vanity has no faith and thus is not a Christian. Or he has already lost his faith.

1 John 5:4   First John 5:4 says: "For everyone who has been born of God overcomes the world. And this is the victory that has overcome the world—our faith." Accordingly, a person who is still in his old nature and is not born of God, a person who still loves the world and seeks to satisfy his heart with foolishness and vanity, that person has no faith. For faith overcomes the world.

James 2:1   In James 2:1, the apostle says: "My brothers, **show no partiality** as you hold the faith in our Lord Jesus Christ, the Lord of glory." If you prefer the rich over the poor because of their wealth, this means you are focusing on the person and thus have no faith. That is an attitude that faith will not **tolerate**, as James says quite correctly.

---

6   Here Walther mimics what people might say to the preacher or about the preacher after the service.

7   Walther's ten dollars would buy perhaps as much as $200 worth of goods today.

This means that where there is faith, this kind of attitude must disappear, because faith does not focus on the person but on the relationship that person has with God. Faith thinks: "This poor beggar has been redeemed by the blood of the Son of God. As far as I am concerned, this makes this man worth as much as a king or an emperor." These are the kind of huge miracles that faith works in our hearts.

Now, if you say that faith is merely the lifeless mental act of regarding certain matters as being true—even if that person sins habitually—that means you are treating faith as a work that a person can produce in himself and preserve in himself even while sinning. That would be like claiming: "Well, I might have stumbled into this or that sin, but I want to believe, so I will get to heaven." True faith is a treasure that only the Holy Spirit can give us.

Faith without works is dead

Now listen to what the Papists taught in the Council of Trent.[8] As you know, it convened a few months before Luther's death, with the purpose of healing the wounds that the Reformation had dealt to the papacy. The council put its seal of approval on all the errors that had been adopted by the Roman Church over time, but it presented them in a subtler manner than most of the theologians of that age had done. This is what the council passed in its sixth session, as translated by the Roman theologian Smets: "We must claim that salvation can be lost by other means than simply by unbelief, through which faith itself is lost."[9] They admit that someone can lose faith by unbelief. This is an extremely important truth! They start with this in order to blind and mislead people. "Salvation can also be lost **by any other mortal sin, though faith itself is not lost by it**."

Roman Catholic errors

As such, they teach that salvation may be given up, while faith is retained. This is quite correct when applied to the religion of **Papists**. For the most depraved Catholic can be the best member of the Catholic Church. They teach that "the Gospel, grace, justification, and forgiveness of sins can all be lost in defense of the divine Law—which excommunicates not only unbelievers but also believers, namely, fornicators, adulterers, pederasts, drunkards, robbers, and all who commit mortal sin."

So, according to the religion of Rome, there are such things as believing thieves, believing fornicators, believing adulterers and child molesters, believing misers, drunkards, blasphemers, and robbers. Note that these unfortunate people[10] have no concept of what faith is. If they had but an inkling of it, they would see that wicked people cannot have genuine faith. On the other hand, they would see that the Lutheran Church does not believe

---

8   Walther uses the Latin: *Concilium Tridentinum.*

9   Wilhelm Smets, ed., *Des hochheiligen, okumenischen und allgemeinen Conciliums von Trient Canones und Beschlusse* (Bielefeld: Velhagen & Klasing, 1851).

10   Walther means the Papists.

what they think we believe. Far from placing good works on the back burner, the doctrine of Luther points to the true source from which good works must spring. For a person who by the Holy Spirit and the grace of God has obtained a living confidence in Christ cannot live in sin. His faith changes and purifies his heart.

Calvinist error One can barely believe it, but the Calvinists have fallen into the same error—from a different angle. We read in the **Decrees of the Synod of Dort,**[11] chapter V, articles 3–8:

> Because of the remnants of sin living in them—moreover, because of the temptations of the world and Satan—the converted cannot persevere in grace[12] when left to their own natural resources. But God is faithful and mercifully confirms them in the grace given to them and keeps them powerfully in the same until the end.[13] Although the power of God that confirms and keeps true believers in grace is too great to be overcome by their flesh, nevertheless the converted are not always urged and moved by God in such a manner that in certain, particular actions they do not depart from the guidance of grace, are not seduced by the lusts of the flesh and obey them. For this reason they must continually watch and pray that they not be led into temptation. If they fail to do this, they **may not only be dragged into serious and awful sins by the flesh, the world, and Satan**, but also occasionally they **are dragged** into such sins by a just, permissive providence of God. Instances of this kind are the **sorry fall of David, Peter, and other saints**, which are recorded in Scripture. By such dreadful sins, however, they greatly offend God, bring mortal guilt upon themselves, grieve the Holy Spirit, interrupt **the exercise of their faith,**[14] grossly violate their conscience, and sometimes lose the *consciousness* of their faith for a season—until they return to the right way by earnest repentance, and God again makes His fatherly face to shine upon them. For because of His unalterable decree of predestination, God, who is rich in mercy, **does not entirely take His Holy Spirit away from His own in such sorry instances in cases of sin, nor does He permit them to**

---

11 In this confession, a number of subpoints are organized under five chapters or "heads" that define the five main doctrines of Calvinism, which can be identified by the acronym TULIP: **t**otal depravity of man, **u**nconditional election, **l**imited atonement, **i**rresistible grace, and **p**erseverance of the saints.

12 Taken from chapter V, this material speaks about the Calvinist doctrine of the perseverance of the saints, the **P** in TULIP. Lutherans regard this teaching on perseverance, which goes together with the Calvinist doctrine of predestination, to be contrary to Scripture.

13 This is another way of saying, "Once predestined, always saved."

14 Walther comments here: "They only interrupt the exercise of their faith! So they keep it!" Walther is speaking with sarcasm. He means, of course, that they do not keep their faith.

lapse to a point where they would fall from the grace of the adoption to sonship and from the state of being justified. . . . For, in the first place, He preserves in them that imperishable seed of His out of which they were born again, so that it cannot be lost or driven out from them.

The first proof[15] cited for this view is taken from 1 John 3:9: "No one born of God makes a practice of sinning, for God's seed lives in him, and he cannot keep on sinning because he has been born of God." This is not to say that converted people cannot lose the seed. It means that, while the seed is in them, the effect it has on them keeps them from living in mortal sin.

1 John 3:9

Second, He renews them certainly and powerfully to repentance by the Word and His Spirit, in order that in conformity with God they may heartily grieve over the sins they committed (by His permission); may with contrite heart pray for, and obtain by their faith, forgiveness in the blood of the Mediator; recover the feeling of the grace of God reconciled with them; worship His mercy by faith; and thereafter show forth greater enthusiasm in working out their salvation with fear and trembling. So it is not by their own merit and strength, but through the gracious compassion of God, that they do **not entirely fall from faith and grace nor remain in their fall until the end and be lost**.

Thus Calvinists claim that, when David committed adultery and even murder, he lost neither his faith nor the grace of God. Rather, his faith merely withdrew somewhat, so that he could not exercise it. That was all. He did not fall from grace or lose his faith, they claim, and so would *not* have gone to hell if he had died in that state.

This is a horrible doctrine because people who believe this will not worry about repenting if they commit crimes such as adultery and murder. When Cromwell, the miserable person who had sentenced his king to death and launched murderous and bloody trials throughout England, was on the verge of death, he became alarmed. Summoning his chaplain, Cromwell asked him whether a person who had once been a believer could lose his faith. That miserable chaplain replied, "No." Cromwell thus concluded that all was well with himself because he knew that once upon a time he had been a believer. Remembering the deep impressions that the Word of God had made upon him at certain times in his life, Cromwell relied on the comfort of this shameful chaplain, namely, that since he had had faith at one point in time, he *still* had it. This example shows the awful effect of this doctrine.

Let me now present a testimony from our own Confessions, namely, from the Smalcald Articles, Part III, Article III, paragraphs 42–44:

Lutheran response

---

15 Walther disagrees with these proofs. He is relating the Calvinist position.

SA III III 42   On the other hand, certain sects may arise; some may already exist. During the peasant rebellion, I encountered some who held that those who had once received the Spirit or the forgiveness of sins or had become believers—even if they later sin—would still remain in the faith. Such sin, they think, would not harm them. They say, "Do whatever you please. If you believe, it all amounts to nothing. Faith blots out all sins," and such. They also say that if anyone sins after he has received faith and the Spirit, he never truly had the Spirit and faith. I have seen and heard many such madmen. I fear that such a devil is still in some of them.[16]

So this is what Luther calls the devil!

SA III III 43   The Smalcald Articles continue: "So it is necessary to know and to teach this: When holy people—still having and feeling original sin and daily repenting and striving against it—happen to fall into manifest sins"—manifest sins are those that are not only in your heart—"(as David did into adultery, murder, and blasphemy), then faith and the Holy Spirit have left them."[17]

When he fell into sin, David had ceased to be a prophet enlightened by the Holy Spirit and a child of God. Had David died during that period in his life, he would have gone to hell. Yes, that could have happened to him that entire year before Nathan came to preach repentance to him. David condemned the man who had committed the crime narrated by Nathan. When Nathan told him, "You are the man," that showed David that he had declared his own sentence: if he did not repent, he would go to hell and be damned.

SA III III 44   The Holy Spirit does not permit sin to have dominion, to gain the upper hand so it can be carried out, but represses and restrains it from doing what it wants. **If sin does what it wants**, the Holy Spirit and faith are not present.[18]

Not only coarse sins but also any willful, intentional sin can snuff out the light of faith.[19] Accordingly, people fall from the faith far more often than we

---

16   *Concordia*, 276.
17   *Concordia*, 276, 278.
18   *Concordia*, 278. See also Müller, 324; *Triglot Concordia*, 491.
19   See also Pieper, *Christian Dogmatics*, 1:367, which draws on the *Loci Theologici* of Martin Chemnitz. The understanding of willful sin does not necessarily include what one does when the rational will recedes in favor of emotion, such as fear, passion, partisan fervor, and ignorance. Christians may also have sins of weakness, meaning the wicked thoughts that may arise suddenly from the sinful flesh but are not acted upon. In contrast to this we have the conscious, premeditated sins of Judas (Matthew 26:14–16) and Absalom (2 Samuel 15). One can group together murder, rebellion, adultery, robbery, and any sin that requires planning. A true believer cannot plan and do evil acts. Those evildoers stand condemned, each by his own conscience. That puts one very near to committing the sin against the Holy Spirit and thus falling into a state of living death. See additional points

imagine. Faith dies in those who lead a life of shame, but it also dies when people permit themselves to be led astray against their better knowledge and the warning of their conscience. They plan to do a certain sinful thing and carry it out, even though they know that it is contrary to God's Word. In such instances faith simply evaporates.

However, people caught in this snare can quickly recover their faith, if they immediately quit their wrongdoing, as the example of Peter shows.[20] Peter did not harden his heart. When Jesus looked him in the eyes, Peter went out and wept bitterly. That look of the Savior made Peter repent of his sin, causing him to realize the enormity of his offense and the unspeakable greatness of his Lord's mercy. Jesus' look seemed to say, "Poor Peter, repent! I have forgiven you all your sins." That was like a sword run through the heart. Blessed is the man who—after falling—immediately gets up and repents, so he does not reach a stage when his heart is hardened.

St. John says in 1 John 3:9: "No one born of God makes a practice of sinning . . . and he cannot keep on sinning." This is also the truth that St. John speaks in 1 John 1:8: "If we say we have no sin, we deceive ourselves, and the truth is not in us." *1 John 3:9; 1:8*

In conclusion, I will submit a testimony of **Luther** from his private writings. In 1536 a certain preacher sent a commentary that he had written on the First Epistle of John to the faculty at Wittenberg, requesting that it be reviewed for publication.[21] The commentary contained the error that the elect supposedly do not lose the Holy Spirit even when they lapse into conscious sinning and coarse vices. Luther opposed the publication of the commentary and wrote a theological opinion on that point, signed by the other members of the faculty. It can be found in his works, St. Louis Ed. 10:1706ff. *W² 10:1706*

> When a person sins against his conscience, that is, when he knowingly and intentionally acts contrary to God, such as an adulterer or any other criminal does who knowingly does wrong, he is without repentance and faith and does not please God—as long as he consciously persists in this intent.

> Or, for example, when a man keeps the wife of another man, it is obvious that he lacks repentance, faith, and sanctification. For the faith by which we are made righteous must be associated with a good conscience.

---

regarding willful sin in John W. Kleinig, *Leviticus*, Concordia Commentary (St. Louis: Concordia, 2003), 123, 136.

20 See Luke 22:54–62.

21 The actual date of the document is Jan. 25, 1544. All editions of Luther's works available to Walther date the document uncertainly to 1536.

How dare I come before God with an evil conscience and say, "Oh, dear God, You have forgiven me my sins. Praise be to You eternally!" No, God will reject you if you say that. If you care nothing for God, you will remain in sin. How, then, can you come to God in an intimate way? It is impossible! Suppose someone who has treated you shamefully came to you and said, "I treated you in a disgraceful manner. I beg you, forgive me. But I intend to keep on doing it." Would you forgive him? No! Only a madman would say, "Pardon me, but I am just going to keep on doing it. Furthermore, every time I see you, I will insult you.[22] Yet I still want you to forgive me." People who want to be comforted by His mercy yet keep on sinning treat God in just this manner.

W² 10:1706   Luther continues: "It is absolutely impossible for these two things to coexist in a person, that is, to have faith in God while at the same time having a wicked intent or, as it is also called, an evil conscience." Conscience is a damaging witness, preventing us from keeping our mouths shut—no matter how hard we try. Of course, we are all poor sinners. But if we attempt to sin, our conscience tells us: "Do not try it. You are God's enemy and want to remain His enemy. You do not really want to go to God!"

W² 10:1706–7   Thus Luther: "Faith and calling out to God are very tender things." They can be easily wounded. Furthermore: "If your conscience is damaged even a little bit, it will push away faith and calling out to God." It is not the external outrageousness of their sin that casts such people out of their state of grace and snuffs out the heavenly light of their faith, but rather the attitude of their heart toward that sin.

Yet if you are suddenly overtaken by sin, God forgives you. He is not angry with you and does not charge that sin against you. These acts do not snuff out faith. Or you might be tossed into sin by your temperament. You do not want to sin but have been angered to such an extent that, before you know it, you sin. That would not be a mortal sin, which would remove you from the state of grace. But when a person *persists* in a sin against his conscience—even though he knows it to be a sin, even though he deliberately continues to sin for a long time—he no longer has faith and cannot truly pray to God.

W² 10:1707   In this situation, the Holy Spirit leaves one's heart because another spirit, an evil one, rules in it, [a spirit] whom the sinner has admitted into his heart. The Holy Spirit yields His place to this evil spirit and departs, as Luther says, "something every tried-and-true Christian frequently encounters." Christians notice that, when they yield to sin in the smallest detail, their trust in God is immediately diminished. They also feel that, if they do not turn away from that sin on the spot, sin will rule over them, and they will be unfit to believe.

John 21:17   In moments such as these, Christians fall to their knees and call upon God with tears—though that is not an essential part of repentance—crying,

---

22   German *beleidigen* means "to offend, slight, bad-mouth, talk trash," and so on.

"You know, O God, that I do not want to sin." Likewise, Peter declared to Christ: "Lord, You know everything; You know that I love You." Peter was able to call upon the Lord as his witness. With a good conscience, he could say to Christ: "You can look into my heart, is that not so? Why, then, do You ask me?" That is the language every Christian must be able to use when speaking to God: "My God, You know that I do not want to sin, and yet I am sinning. You know that I have become an enemy to sin."

Thus Luther: "Accordingly, Paul joins the following two pieces: 1 Timothy 1:5, 'This is the summary of doctrine: Love from a pure heart, a good conscience, and a sincere faith'; and 1 Timothy 1:19, 'Hold faith and a good conscience.'" The only true love is the love that is made up of sincere faith. Sincere faith means faith that does not just look like faith but which is living, active, and really faith of the heart. Luther continues: "And again in 1 Timothy 3:9, 'They must hold the mystery of the faith with a clear conscience,' etc. These and similar passages, to be cited further below, indicate that where good consciences are lacking, there is neither faith nor sanctification." *W² 10:1707; 1 Tim. 1:5, 19; 3:9 Luther*

Faith and good conscience must go hand in hand. Where there is faith, there a good conscience is too. But a person who does not have a good conscience certainly is without faith, because the two belong together. The apostle in 1 Timothy 1:19 says that such people have suffered a shipwreck of their faith. Whoever does not have a pure conscience also has not maintained the precious treasure of faith.[23]

Therefore, only faith in our Savior, Jesus Christ, obtains the grace of justification, that is, only a believer has forgiveness of his sins and is accepted by God. Nevertheless, this person must drop his former evil intentions so that a good conscience will start to grow in him. Now, where there is faith and a good conscience, there the Holy Spirit certainly is as well. Yet those who are justified do not build their confidence on their own worthiness or good conscience, but on Christ. Therefore, we conclude from Christ's promise that we have been received into grace for His sake and may offer our prayers to God acceptably, as John says in 1 John 3:20: "For whenever our heart condemns us, yet we may confidently address God, and what we ask, we will receive from Him." *W² 10:1707; 1 John 3:20 Luther*

Luther continues: "Sin remains in the saints: hereditary misery and evil tendencies, that the heart does not seriously fear God, trust God, etc." Because even after we are converted, we are not truly able to fear God, nor are we able to fully trust Him. [Luther says:] "All of these are not unimportant problems, but rather huge sins." All sins are huge sins. Even the so-called sins *W² 10:1707*

---

23   The Dau text adds: "They have cast the precious treasure of faith overboard."

of weakness, which justified people cannot avoid, are not to be regarded as unimportant. Even though these sins of weakness do not snuff out one's faith, they should not be treated lightly.

W² 10:1707–8   Thus Luther: "Nevertheless, this weakness should be distinguished greatly from conscious assent and evil intent, which pollute one's conscience." That is the big difference! [Luther continues:] "These latter sins do not coexist with sanctification. In this context we must not discuss predestination, but the wrath of God that is revealed in His Word, and then seek grace."

What Luther is saying is we should not assume that, just because we are predestined, we are guaranteed to go to heaven. To be sure, anyone who is predestined will certainly go to heaven. But the key issue is: Are you *really* predestined? Any person living in sin and continuing that kind of lifestyle makes it clear that he is not predestined. God does not insist on keeping that person out of heaven. Rather, He had foreseen that this wicked person would abuse His grace. No, if you are such a person, you are not in His grace. And if you stay like that, you are condemned!

W² 10:1708   The sins into which the elect fall strip away their sanctification and drive the Holy Spirit from them. This is quite evident, first, in Adam and Eve, who were elect but who nevertheless lost their holiness and the Holy Spirit in a miserable way, so that by the wounding of these first people all their descendants have become feeble and sinful by nature.[24]

Nobody can deny that Adam and Eve were elected, and yet they fell, lost the image of God, the Holy Spirit, their holiness—in short, everything. But they repented and were thus restored to a state of grace.

W² 10:1708   Had they not been raised up again, they would have remained condemned forever. In the meantime, they were truly under the wrath of God. These are not fake events. For in clear terms Paul says in Romans 5:12 that through one man sin came to all men to damnation. Everybody knows what damnation is. Likewise, when David slept with the wife of Uriah and had caused her godly husband to be killed, etc., he was under the wrath of God and had lost his sanctification and the Holy Spirit until he was converted again. We could list many similar examples.

Once faith is lost through some mortal sin, the grace of God is also lost, and that person becomes a child of death and condemnation. He may return to faith and ultimately be saved, but in the meantime he is not blessed, but rather a completely miserable, lost creature.

---

24 See Genesis 3:1–19.

The truth of what I have stated is clearly established from the following passages: 1 John 3:7, "Do not be deceived! Whoever does righteousness is righteous. Whoever does sin is of the devil." For instance, when David permitted his heart to be set on fire with the flames of wrong desire and lost his footing, he was whipped up by the devil. After conquering David with that first sin, the devil drove him to still greater sins, namely murder, etc. That the Holy Spirit had been driven out of David's heart is evident from the words of Paul in Galatians 5:19: no adulterer is an heir of the kingdom of Christ.[25]

W² 10:1708;
1 John 3:7–8 Luther

Paul is clearly speaking of the adultery that is still taking place. When adulterers persist in their sin, they are not heirs of the kingdom of Christ.

Consequently, he is not righteous and holy and does not have the Holy Spirit. Furthermore, because of these things, the wrath of God comes upon the disobedient.[26] In Romans 8:13 Paul introduces a distinction that we must make among sins. He says, "If you live according to the flesh you will die, but if by the Spirit you put to death the deeds of the body, you will live."

W² 10:1708–9;
Rom. 8:13 Luther

Now, it is clear that in this passage Paul is preaching to saints, teaching them how they may remain holy, namely, by resisting their evil tendencies. On the other hand, he says, "If you live according to the flesh you will die," that is, if you yield to your evil desires, you will again be under the wrath of God. For that is what he calls dying. Ezekiel 33:12: On the day a righteous person does evil, I will forget all his righteousness, etc., and on the day the godless one repents and does good, I will forget his sins.[27] This is a clear text: it proves that if righteous people knowingly and intentionally fall into sin, they are no longer justified.

In Revelation 2:14 the Holy Spirit rebukes the church at Pergamum for tolerating false doctrine and fornication, and He says with clear words, "What I hate."[28] When God is angry with someone, that person is not holy and accepted by Him, etc. And among those there were, without a doubt, elect and nonelect.

When God is angry with someone—for when He hates someone, His wrath burns against them—that person is not acceptable. There may have been elect persons in the congregation at Pergamum, but God also hated

---

25   This is a paraphrase that combines Galatians 5:19 and 5:21.

26   The Dau text has a reference to Galatians 5:6.

27   This is a paraphrase of Ezekiel 33:12. Luther's text attributes it to Ezekiel 33:13.

28   Luther's text attributes the content of Revelation 2:6 to 2:14, referring to the Nicolaitans, a Gnostic sect also tolerated at Pergamum, as indicated in Revelation 2:15.

those elect persons and was angry with them because, for the time being, they had driven out of their hearts His grace, faith, and the Holy Spirit.[29]

W² 10:1709;
Matt. 10:22 Luther

Based on these and many other testimonies, the Church has always taught unanimously that when saints knowingly and deliberately act contrary to God's command, they are no longer saints. Rather, they have lost the true faith and cast away the Holy Spirit. But if they turn again, He will keep the gracious oath that He has sworn, saying: As surely as I live, I have no desire for the sinner to die, but to repent and remain alive.[30] Accordingly, for Christ's sake God once again takes back into His grace those people who turn to Him and rekindles in their hearts the true faith through the Gospel and His Holy Spirit. He has not commanded us to ask first whether we are predestined. Rather, it is enough for us to know that whoever perseveres to the end in repentance and faith is certainly elect and will be saved, as Christ says, "Blessed are those who persevere to the end."

**Twenty-first
Evening Lecture:**
March 6, 1885

**Christianity
is unique**

My Friends:—

The world of unbelievers regards the doctrine of the Christian religion—that salvation is brought about solely through a person's faith—to be impossible. The world discredits this concept. To them this teaching seems to be complete nonsense. In fact, they regard it as proof that even the Christian religion—like all the other religions that claim to have been revealed supernaturally—is intent on deceiving people.

They claim that Christianity is not superior to Hinduism, which requires faith in the Vedas, the sacred books of the Hindus.[31] Or they would cite Muhammad—that prophet of lies, as everyone knows—who demands faith in the Qur'an, the holy book of Muslims, claiming that only *it* contains the true religion of salvation.[32] The world equates these two religions with Christianity because, according to the world, Christianity states that it, too, is a religion that has been supernaturally revealed and that it, too, demands faith in its doctrines as the only way to salvation.

---

29   Scripture states that God "has something against" the congregation in Revelation 2:14, not that His hatred is directed against them as a whole. Only some in the congregation accept the ways of the Nicolaitans (Revelation 2:6, 15). Yet it is clear that the congregation in Pergamum displeases God because it tries to serve both God and pagan ways (the sin of Balaam). If the members of the congregation do not repent, God will act on His wrath against them. See Louis A. Brighton, *Revelation*, Concordia Commentary (St. Louis: Concordia, 1999), 78.

30   See Ezekiel 33:11.

31   This was popularized by Friedrich Max Müller, a professor of Sanskrit at Oxford.

32   Walther speaks of the Qur'an in a sharply negative light in his writings.

The world's argument is that the Father in heaven does not care what a person believes or disbelieves, since true religion consists only of leading an upright life, exercising virtue, and doing good works. Why should it be a sin, they say, if a person fails to believe something that is completely contrary to his God-given reason? The world claims that if there is such a thing as God and final judgment, on the Last Day people will not be asked what they have believed, but what kind of lives they have led.

Faith is not a work

Others wish to dig deeper into these matters. They claim that if the Father in heaven is especially pleased with a person's faith, it is because that faith is such a glorious work and such a beautiful virtue. Thus they can see no reason whatsoever why He should not be equally well pleased, say, with a person's love, patience, bravery, justice, impartiality, truthfulness, and similar qualities.

What causes these objections to the role of faith in Christian doctrine? Without question, coarse ignorance is the primary source. People simply do not know what faith is according to the Holy Scriptures. Far from regarding saving and justifying faith as nothing else than stubbornly sticking to certain religious teachings (as the Hindus and Muslims do), Christian doctrine declares that simply sticking to the teachings revealed in Holy Scripture is useless. In fact, this approach leads straight to hell.

Christianity says that anyone who builds on those teachings is building on sand. While these other religions claim that we Christians lift up faith and say it is a glorious work and a precious virtue, on the contrary, we teach that faith does not justify and save a person because it is such a good work. Rather, what saves is the redemption accomplished by Jesus Christ, which faith grasps. This reflection takes us back to our tenth thesis.

A week ago we discussed that faith is not dead and lifeless, but something that transforms and renews the heart. It regenerates a person and brings the Holy Spirit into his soul. Tonight we will focus on the second part of the tenth thesis, which states that the Word of God—Law and Gospel—is not rightly distinguished, but mingled, **when one preaches that faith justifies and saves because of the love and renewal it produces**.

The Holy Scriptures emphatically testify that there can be no genuine faith without love, without a renewal of heart, without sanctification, or without an abundance of good works. But at the same time Scripture testifies that the renewal of heart, love, and the good works that faith produces is not the justifying and saving element in a person's faith. Innumerable passages of Scripture could be cited to prove this statement. We will focus only on the principal passages.

Romans 4:16 states: "That is why it depends on faith, in order that the promise may rest on grace and be guaranteed to all his offspring." Here Paul

Rom. 4:16

declares that the very reason we teach righteousness by faith is because we teach that a person is saved by grace, which justifies him before God. Now, if faith were to make us righteous because of some good quality inherent in us, it would be wrong to conclude that the reason we teach that people are justified by faith is because they are justified and saved by grace.

Justification takes place by grace *through* faith—not because of any good qualities inherent *in* faith. In justification, it is not the person's faith that is taken into consideration, but the fact that Jesus Christ has redeemed the entire world. Justification is based on the fact that Jesus has already done what was necessary and has suffered all that mankind ought to have done and suffered, and that people merely have to accept this.

Therefore, the way to salvation is this: We contribute nothing—absolutely nothing—toward our salvation. Rather, Christ has already done everything for us, and we must merely cling to what He has done, drawing consolation from His finished work of redemption and trusting in it for our salvation. This passage in Romans is a precious text, a text that deserves to be remembered. If something that we ourselves must do belonged to the justifying quality of faith, the apostle would be drawing a false conclusion here. In that case Paul should have said, "By faith, insofar as it enables us to accomplish something good." But that is not the reason faith justifies. It justifies because it accepts the merit of Christ. Faith is only the hand with which we grasp what God offers. Philippians 3:8–9:

Phil. 3:8–9   Indeed, I count everything as loss because of the surpassing worth of knowing Christ Jesus my Lord. For His sake I have suffered the loss of all things and count them as rubbish, in order that I may gain Christ and be found in Him, not having a righteousness of my own that comes from the law, but that which comes through faith in Christ, the righteousness from God that depends on faith.

This is another precious passage! As bright as the sun, it sheds bright light on the real essence of faith. The apostle declares that he is indeed righteous. However, the righteousness that he has obtained by faith is not at all his own righteousness, but the righteousness of Christ. Accordingly, when we become righteous by faith, we are made righteous by an "alien righteousness." God sees in us absolutely nothing that He could credit to us as righteousness. The righteousness that we have by faith is foreign to us; it is from another. We have not purchased it or contributed anything toward it. Had we contributed love toward it, and were God to justify us on *that* account, our righteousness would not be an alien righteousness, or at least it would be only half alien, to supplement our own imperfect righteousness. For the apostle declares: "I have no righteousness of my own, but only the righteousness that God credits to faith."

Romans 4:5: "And to the one who does not work but believes in Him who justifies the ungodly, his faith is counted as righteousness." When a person is justified, though he was previously a godless—not a godly—person, he is now made godly by faith. Anyone having genuine faith acknowledges that he has been godless, deserving hell and damnation, lost, contaminated with sin from head to toe, and that a divine miracle of grace was performed on him when God said to him the moment he believed in his Savior: "You are counted as righteous. I see in you no righteousness of your own, yet I am covering you with the righteousness of My Son. From now on, I will see in you nothing but righteousness." Whoever does not come to Christ as an ungodly person does not come to Him at all. *Rom. 4:5*

Ephesians 2:8–9: "For by grace you have been saved through faith. And this is not your own doing; it is the gift of God, not a result of works, so that no one may boast." This almost sounds as if the apostle felt he was not saying enough to keep the reader from falling into self-righteousness, because he first says, "By grace you have been saved." Next, he adds "through faith." Lest people think they had achieved this feat by their faith, the apostle continues: "and this is not your own doing." Well, from where does it come, if not from us? "It is the gift of God." And completely to ward off any thought of a person's own merit, he adds "not a result of works," such as a person's love, or charity, would be. He concludes with the statement "so that no one may boast." *Eph. 2:8–9*

Now, a person who claims that faith justifies on account of the love that follows it could say, "I have been justified by faith, but that was because I also loved, because I had also performed good works, because I had also become a different person. *That* is why God regards me as righteous." The apostle tosses out this thought in his concluding remarks. Anyone who imagines that there is a little "halo," a little glory, that he might claim as his own is *still* without the faith that justifies. These people are *still* blind and are not walking in the way of salvation. Rather, they are headed straight for hell.

Romans 11:6: "But if it is by grace, it is no longer on the basis of works; otherwise grace would no longer be grace." The apostle cannot emphasize strongly enough that this is all by grace. He invites his readers to reflect that, when they admit that their salvation is "by grace," it cannot be by merit, for that would destroy the idea of grace. As soon as one adds merit to grace, that cancels out grace. That makes all talk of grace complete nonsense. "If salvation is by the merit of works, grace does not count either—or merit would not be merit."[33] There is no alternative, then, for a person other than to believe *Rom. 11:6*

---

33 Walther demonstrates his classical education by taking the essence of Romans 11:6 ("if *grace*, then not *works*") and, following Paul's meaning, declaring the contrapositive: "if

firmly that he has been made righteous solely by God's pure, everlasting mercy—by the gift of faith.

Even when one's faith bears good fruit, these follow later—*after* that person has received all that is necessary for salvation. First a person is saved, then he becomes godly. *First* he must be made an heir of heaven, *then* he becomes a different person.

Here we have the wonderful quality of the Christian religion in particular. If a person wants to do everything on his own to get to heaven, he is lost. No, first you must be made an heir of heaven and be saved; *after* that you begin to thank God.

That is why Luther says that the Christian religion is—in a nutshell—a religion of gratitude. All the good that we Christians do is not done to merit something. We would not even know how to acquire merit. Everything has been given to us: our righteousness, our everlasting heritage, and our salvation. All that is left for us to do is to thank God.

In fact, God is so gracious that, for the person who is especially faithful in this life, He even adds to his salvation an additional, eternal glory. That is not an unimportant matter for eternity. For when God gives extraordinary gifts, He is outrageously generous. That is why there will be such a great difference among Christians in the life to come. In heaven, even a trifling "more" becomes infinitely great throughout eternity.

Good works defined   For this reason we must be truly grateful to God—not only for receiving eternal life but also for all that we are and have. Only works that proceed from gratitude are genuinely good works. Even in our secular relationships, when a person is very willing to render services to another and hope for a reward, we accuse that person of being a miserable cheat. They pretend to love us while speculating on financial gain. We find out later: "That guy just did it because he wanted to be paid." That is when we say, "What a rotten guy! I thought he was doing it out of kindness—and now I see that he was just eyeing my wallet! I thought he was being helpful and selfless, but he just wants to be paid! That lousy creep can take a hike!"[34] Such people nauseate us; they do us some service not because we are especially dear to them, but they figure they will *get* more from us than they *do* for us. And they become nasty and hostile to us when their hopes are dashed.

---

works, then not *grace*." Doing so makes *grace* and *works* mutually exclusive in classical logic.

34 Walther emphasizes his point through role-playing. He does that more often in this thesis than elsewhere. Perhaps after moving so carefully through Thesis IX, Walther had to "loosen up." When he resorts to role-playing—such as the church ladies complementing the pastor, the Jesuit insulting the Lutherans, the angry person telling his false friends to get lost, and so on—Walther tends toward dramatic excess. He takes advantage of being "among the boys" to make his point.

Truly "good" works, therefore, are works that we do out of thankfulness toward God. True believers would never think of earning or obtaining good for themselves. They cannot help but express their gratitude by love and good works. Their hearts have been changed, softened by the richness of God's love that they have experienced. On top of it all, God is so gracious that He rewards even the good works that *He* accomplishes in us. For the good works done by Christians are God's works.

Some people object that in the matter of sanctification a person must add at least something of his own to it. Yet a person can never really begin any good work of his own ability. God must prompt him and work in him even to *want* to do the good work that he is to perform. Accordingly, whenever Christians seem to be doing something good, it is only by the power and operation of God in them that they are doing it.

The Papists occasionally say that a person is justified and saved by faith, but they add: "provided love is added to faith." They do not mean to say merely that a person who has no love has no faith. That is what we teach too—just as Scripture does. What they mean is this: A person may have true faith created in him by the Holy Spirit. But if love is not added to it, they claim that faith is absolutely worthless. That is why they call love the *forma* of faith. In theological terms, as you know, *forma* makes matter what it is—its essential quality.[35] The Papists declare that if love is not added to faith, such faith may be genuine, but it is not justifying faith. Love is the *forma* of faith, which they say makes justifying faith what its name indicates. Such faith they call *fides formata*, faith that has received the proper form. However, if love has not been added, they call that faith *fides informis*, that is, faith without its proper form.[36]

"Justification" by works

The Decrees of the Council of Trent, ch. VII, canon 28: "When love is not added to it, faith neither forms a vital union with Christ, nor does it make a person a living member of the Body of Christ." The Papists do not speak of "faith from which love does not proceed." That would be correct. If faith does not produce love, it is a mere fake. Rather, what they mean is this: You might have good faith, but that does not justify you if you do not add love to it. Love should not *flow* from one's faith; that is something altogether impossible according to their teaching. They understand faith to be mere lifeless agreement with the doctrines of the Church. Love, they say, must be added to faith. *Then* faith will justify you.

---

35 In Aristotelian philosophy, matter (the material cause) changes form as the result of thought (the formal cause) acting on it.

36 One finds this language already in Bonaventure's commentary on the *Sententiae* of Peter Lombard and the *Summa Theologiae* of Thomas Aquinas.

Well, if that is the case, then what *does* justify? Only love, only a person's good works. They do not say this in plain terms, but any person who reflects even a little on what they are saying cannot help but draw out of their remarks this meaning: If faith does not justify in the first place, then something must be added that on its own achieves justification.

"Catechumens receive the faith that obtains eternal life, which faith without love cannot obtain." By "catechumens" the Papists mean those who want to join their church. See, without love this so-called "faith" cannot attain eternal life! "Therefore, they hear the word of Christ: If you want to enter into eternal life, then keep the Commandments." Here we have the Papists' real faith! Faith, though admittedly necessary, does not obtain everlasting life. They say: If a person does not keep the Commandments, faith is of no help to him. After he has satisfied the one command of Christ to believe, another is added, namely, to keep the Commandments.

Matt. 19:16–17   In Matthew 19, a rich young man asked the Lord, "What good deed must I do to have eternal life?" His question was not "What must I do?" but "What good deed must I do?" Accordingly, Christ had to tell him: "Keep the commandments." That did not mean that the rich young man would really be able to keep them. The Lord was simply answering the question of this man who was drowning in self-righteousness. When the Lord failed to cure him of his awful blindness—even after telling him that he had to love God above all things and his neighbor as himself—He gave him an additional lesson. He told him to sell all that he had and to give the money to the poor. That lesson sent the young man away sorrowful. Without a doubt, he was cut to the heart because he now realized that he did not love God above all things. He had to acknowledge that Jesus had judged him correctly.

Yet [the young man] was not seriously concerned about his salvation. If he were, he would have admitted that he was unable to do what the Lord commanded and that he would be lost if that was the only way to obtain everlasting life. Had he admitted that, the Lord would have told him: "There is One who can save you. Believe in Me—and even though you are a despicable man and break the Commandments, you will be saved." But the young man went away. Without a doubt, if he had become a believer, Scripture would have recorded that fact.

Someone might think that—at the end of the day—the Papists just mean that dead, superficial faith does not justify a person, which is exactly what we ourselves teach. But no, what they mean to say is: "No matter how good a person's faith is, it will not save him unless love is added to it." That is about as wise a saying as "No matter how good the apple tree, unless you add the fruit to it, it is not an apple tree." Why, the opposite is true. Apples do not make an apple tree. Rather, the apple tree produces apples.

However, the Papists have been quite clear on this matter. In the chapter and canon of the Council of Trent mentioned earlier,[37] it says: "If anyone claims that when grace is lost because of sin, faith is lost in the process as well; or that the faith that remains in a sinner is not genuine faith, even though it may not be a living faith; or that the person who has faith without love is not a Christian—let him be accursed."

They claim, then, that a person who falls into mortal sin does not lose faith. *We* would say that a person living in mortal sin may have a perfect historical faith but that such faith is not genuine—just a mere sham. The Papists, however, declare that it is genuine faith. They speak of faith as something apart from love. In their view, love must join faith in order to make that faith valid. They regard faith as a fine container that has no worth beyond storage. Love is the treasure to be added. When that happens, the treasure chest becomes far more precious than it had been. Thus the Papists maintain that faith is made precious when Christians add love. They say, "Faith justifies," but only if it has love.

In the days of Johann Gerhard, the theologians of Cologne—at that time Rome's best theologians—published the *Censura Coloniensis*. In this treatise they state: "People who are justified live by faith. But this is not solely because of Christ or His work. In fact, the *forma* or power of faith does not stem from Christ, whom it apprehends and possesses, but from our love." Not only does this statement declare that a person must add love to faith, but it also declares that love is the only reason justification does what it does.

Let us now hear a few testimonies from **Luther** on this so-called faith. Its Roman Catholic champions claim that it is the true essence of faith, thus true faith, but not justifying faith.[38] On Galatians 3:11 (St. Louis Ed. 9:357f.):

Justification by grace

W² 9:357
(cf. AE 26:268–69)

> The Sophists,[39] as they are always prepared to distort Scripture, make these hairsplitting remarks on this passage: "The righteous one lives by faith,"[40] certainly, but by faith that operates,[41] does works, or has obtained its proper form through love.[42] If faith lacks this form,[43] it does not justify. This gloss[44] is pure invention. With this statement they are doing violence to the prophet's words.

---

37 *Decrees of the Council of Trent*, ch. VII, canon 28.

38 Latin: *fides formata* as opposed to *fides informis*.

39 Walther notes: "By which he [Luther] means the Papist theologians."

40 Luther speaks of this as one passage, but he refers simultaneously to Habakkuk 2:4; Romans 1:17; and Galatians 3:11.

41 Latin: *efficax*.

42 Latin: *formata caritate*.

43 Latin: *informis*.

44 Ancient and medieval Bibles were written in Greek and Latin. Monks and other learned churchmen would write study notes between the lines of text and in the margins. These

They have twisted and distorted this precious, comforting passage. Indeed, they do admit that both the apostle Paul as well as the prophet Habakkuk stated: "The righteous one lives by faith." But what faith does he mean? An active faith that does good works, that has love, and that has renewed the person. This alone is the faith that he means—and only for this reason does man live by faith.

W² 9:357
(cf. AE 26:269)

Luther continues: "I would not mind their gloss if by 'faith properly formed' they understood genuine, theological faith or what Paul calls sincere faith." Please note that Luther permits the phrase "properly formed faith,"[45] only if it means genuine faith of the heart. He knows that faith that does not purify the heart does not justify, but keeps that person in sin. But the Papists always present it in this manner: "Oh yes, the Lutherans say that a person is justified by faith without good works. That is an entirely shameful doctrine. It is calculated simply to repel and discourage people from doing good works. They would like no one to do good works anymore. They always say, 'Believe, believe, believe, believe!'[46] Then, from that moment onward, one will go to heaven."

Of course, the better-informed Papists say this, knowing that this is not so. However, there are so many Papists, even among the priesthood, who actually believe that the Lutheran Church is a disgraceful mob that says, "The mere act of admitting something to be true makes a person righteous and saves him," so that he goes to heaven—no matter what kind of life he leads.

Luther says that if they understand *fides formata* to be faith created by the Holy Spirit and now the source of all good works, if they claim that this faith justifies, then Luther is in full agreement with the Papists. But they should not add a statement such as: "Faith saves because it has a wonderful quality." No, faith first justifies and saves a person. Then it also produces fruit. Luther continues:

W² 9:357–58
(cf. AE 26:269)

For in this case, faith would not be set up over against love, but it would be in opposition to a useless opinion that people may have of faith. We, too, distinguish between fake and genuine faith. "Fake faith" exists in people who have heard about God, Christ, and all the mysteries of the incarnation and redemption and who have understood these matters intellectually—knowing how to talk about them beautifully. Yet it all remains useless imagination. What these people have heard

---

notes were often in the language of the people, not of the Bible text. Thus the notes were called *glosses* because they translated and explained the text for more common use. Later, glosses were compiled in books to guide the interpretation of Scripture. The word *gloss* comes from the Greek word that means "language."

45   Latin: *fides formata.*

46   German: *Glaube! Glaube! Glaube! Glaube!*

has merely left an echo of the Gospel in their hearts—and they babble about it. But it is not really faith, for it does not renew and transform their heart or produce a new person. Rather, it leaves them stuck in their former opinions and behavior. Such faith is actually extremely harmful. It would be better for this person not to have it at all. A moral philosopher of this world is better than a hypocrite who has this kind of faith.

It would be better if such a person had never found out about the Gospel, were he only to grasp it with mere intellectual understanding. Yes, he can chatter about it, he can preach on it—he can even preach on it in a meaningful way. Yet he is only a noisy gong or a clanging cymbal.[47] It would be better for him if he had not had that faith.

Accordingly, if they were to distinguish "properly formed faith"[48] from false or fake faith, this distinction would not be so offensive to me. But they speak of faith that receives its proper form through *love*. Thus they establish two kinds of faith: "unformed faith" and "properly formed faith."[49] I must reject this harmful and devilish gloss in the strongest terms. For they say: Even where there is infused faith— which is a gift of the Holy Spirit—and, in addition, acquired faith,[50] which we produce ourselves by many acts of believing, yet both kinds are unformed[51] and only receive their proper form when love is added.

W² 9:358
(cf. AE 26:269)

Oh, take care to remember that! The Jesuits[52] have snared countless people, and when Lutherans rebuke them for not teaching justification by faith, they reply: "Your Lutheran preacher is just making false claims. We do not teach that doctrine at all. We are teaching a better doctrine than yours. You Lutherans say, 'All you have to do is believe, and you will go to heaven.' We Catholics say, 'A person is justified by faith, namely, by faith that works through love. That is what the apostle Paul teaches.'"

Now, if a person did not realize that the Jesuits are just talking nonsense, he could think that he had been misinformed about the doctrine of the Catholic Church. However, let no one be deceived. The Jesuits do not speak of faith as a *source* of love, but of faith that has love existing *alongside of it*. Thus they are lying when they seem to agree with us and say that a person is justified by faith. When they add the term *formata* ["properly formed"] to *fides*

---

47 See 1 Corinthians 13:1.

48 Latin: *fides formata*.

49 Latin: *informis et formata*.

50 Latin: *fides acquisita*

51 Latin: *informis*.

52 The Jesuits, or Society of Jesus, is a religious order founded by Ignatius of Loyola. For more information, see the Index of Persons and Groups, page 496.

["faith"], what they really mean is works. For they say that a person is justified by faith only if he has works in addition to faith.

That is just as if I had some play money and thought: "If I had dollars in addition to that, I could really buy something." If I went to the store, the merchant might take the play money along with the real money, but he would give me nothing for the play money. He would only exchange the real money for his products. I really could buy nothing at all with the play money. The Papists turn faith into play money while giving true worth to love. They say, "Faith has to be there; it is necessary for the doctrine to be true. But if it is to save, then love, then good works, must be added, and they are the real things that buy my way into heaven."

Thus the Roman doctrine of justification is nothing less than a complete denial, total destruction, and condemnation of the Gospel. Any sect is incomparably better than the papacy, the Roman Church, because even though sects worry a lot about their works of piety, their wrestling for grace, and their prayers, they still hold fast to the teaching that faith in the Lord Jesus alone justifies and saves a person. When poor Methodists or Baptists are in their final agony, they realize that faith alone saves, and they die saved—taking refuge in the Lord Christ.

But when Papists die, they are forced to think of purgatory and how long they might be stuck there because they lack love and good works. They would have to consider themselves lost. That was the devil's aim when he founded the papacy; he wanted to destroy the redemption of Christ by this damnable doctrine[53] that faith does not justify and save—except when you add another element that acquires salvation.

Luther writes:

W² 9:358
(cf. AE 26:269)

Thus [the Sophists] dream up the idea that faith without love is just like a painting or something beautiful to behold that is placed in the dark and cannot be seen until light, that is, love, is added to it. And in this way they claim love is the form [or essence][54] of faith, while faith itself is only the material[55] on which love works. That means one puts love ahead of faith and credits a person's righteousness to love instead

---

53 German: *diese verdammte Lehre*. Walther cursed in order to make a strong point. Yet he would not advise church workers to follow his example of cursing and of casual reference to the devil. Nor do the doctrinal theses and their discussions in the Missouri Synod during Walther's time follow this example. The literature on the Antichrist clearly points to papal abuses, papal wealth, the political power of the papacy, and the end-time biblical prophecies regarding a universal Christian leader who has been co-opted by Satan in order to persecute true Christians. Of all the Christian bishops, the papacy ultimately stands out because of the amount of blood that it has spilled in Jesus' name.

54 Latin: *forma*.

55 Latin: *materia*.

of to faith. For whatever gives a certain quality to something has that quality in a higher degree. Therefore, they really give no credit at all to faith because they attribute righteousness to faith only on account of love.

The Papists do not say that if you could create your own faith, it would not save you—because they claim that even if you had true faith created by the Holy Spirit in your heart, that faith would not save you if you did not add love. They hold to the Council of Trent, which states you can have true faith but still be drowning in mortal sins.[56]

> Moreover, these people who distort the Gospel of Christ say that infused faith, which has not been obtained by preaching or some other activity[57] but is worked in a person by the Holy Spirit, can exist in a person guilty of a mortal sin and can be found in the worst scoundrels. For this reason they declare it to be a lifeless and useless thing when it is alone, even if it works miracles. Thus they rob faith entirely of its function and attribute it to love, declaring faith to be completely worthless unless we add to it love, which is what gives faith its proper form.[58]

W² 9:358–59
(cf. AE 26:270)

On Galatians 2:19, **Luther** writes (St. Louis Ed. 9:218):

> When I have thus grasped Christ by faith, I become dead to the Law, justified from sin, and freed from death, the devil, and hell by Christ. Then I begin to do good works, to love God, to show Him gratitude, and to practice love toward my neighbor. But this love, or the works that follow from faith, neither give the proper form to faith nor do they adorn it. Rather, faith gives love its proper form and adorns it.

W² 9:218
(cf. AE 26:161)

Love is not the form of faith; rather, faith is the form of love.[59] Why? It is not that love creates faith, but that faith creates love. It is not love that gives faith its true essence. Rather, faith gives love its true essence.

---

56 Here Walther makes an important point, but he communicates only part of his thought process. He knows that the Church rejected Pelagius and salvation by works at the Council of Ephesus in 431. Therefore, if the Papists were true to the ecumenical councils, they would affirm that one cannot be saved by trying to work or create one's own faith. Roman Catholic sources tend to limit Pelagian issues to the Greek Church. Pelagius argued a "faith alone" doctrine (*sola fides*) in which faith alone grasps justification, but this merely opens the external path to God that works and sanctification must complete internally. Luther argued for "by faith alone" (*sola fide*), in which Christ justifies, faith receives, and works flow from justification. Before Vatican II, Roman Catholic sources such as the *Catholic Encyclopedia* slandered Luther by calling his doctrine Pelagian. It is the papacy that has remained truly faithful to the Pelagian heresy.

57 Latin: *operatione*.

58 Latin: *forma*.

59 Walther uses the Latin: *Caritas non est forma fidei, sed fides est forma caritatis.*

Gal. 5:6

Galatians 5:6 states: "In Christ Jesus neither circumcision nor uncircumcision counts for anything, but only faith working through love." The Papists argue that this verse supports their thesis, yet these words say something completely different. This is why **Luther** comments on this text (St. Louis Ed. 9:632ff.):

W² 9:632–33

The Sophists force this text to support their view that we must be justified by our love and good works. For they declare that even faith infused into a person by God does not justify unless it is given its proper form by love, because they call love "grace that makes a person acceptable in the sight of God"[60]—what we with our words, yet more so with those of Paul, would call justifying grace.[61] At this point I do not wish to say anything about the faith that a person obtains by his own effort.[62]

Gal. 5:6 Luther

Moreover, [they say that] love is obtained by our own merit, which God rewards according to His good pleasure,[63] etc. In fact, they even maintain that infused faith can exist in a person living in mortal sin. Thus they completely remove justification from faith and attribute it (in this manner) to love alone. They would establish this doctrine of theirs by St. Paul: "faith that works through love," as if Paul meant to say: See, faith does not justify; it amounts to nothing unless works-producing[64] love is added to it, which gives faith its proper form.

This is the error of the Antichrist.

W² 9:633–34

However, unspiritual men have made up all these strange, horrible ideas. Could anyone tolerate the doctrine that faith—the gift of God that is poured into people's hearts by the Holy Spirit—can exist alongside mortal sin? We could tolerate such teaching if they were referring to faith acquired[65] by one's own effort or to historical faith or to the natural opinion that comes from historical matters. Indeed, they would be speaking correctly about historical faith.

Gal. 5:6

But since they speak of infused faith, they plainly reveal that they have no true understanding whatsoever of faith. Besides, (as one is careful to say) they read this passage in a mirror dimly.[66] They corrupt the text and twist it according to their fancy. Paul does not say "faith that

---

60   Latin: *gratia gratum facientem.*

61   Latin: *iustificatione.*

62   Latin: *de acquisita.*

63   Latin: *nostro merito congrui.*

64   Latin: *operatrix.*

65   Latin: *acquisita.*

66   An allusion to 1 Corinthians 13:12.

justifies by love" or "faith that makes a person acceptable by love." They falsify such a text and forcibly declare for it that meaning. Even less does Paul say, "Love makes a person acceptable." No, *this* is what the apostle says: "Faith working through love." He states that works are performed by faith through love—not that people are justified by love.

They get it backward. The text does not state what faith makes happen in God's eyes, but what faith does within itself. For it is active through love, *after* it has obtained righteousness before God and everlasting salvation for the believer.

The Papists invariably teach this error. Among so-called Protestant churches, many teach this point incorrectly as well. Even though they declare that everything is received by grace through faith, many Protestants add: "Of course, faith must also produce good works," because they are afraid that the above statement might offend people. As soon as they add this, however, they falsify and undermine their whole preaching. For with that one qualification all their preaching about grace and faith is useless and a wasted effort. That makes it sound as if faith were not enough for justification and needed love to be added to it.

This is how you must preach on this issue: "Of course, if a person does not have love, then let him understand that he does not have faith either. Therefore, he cannot be righteous in God's sight." Not because love justifies a person in God's sight, but because faith is only genuine when it is worked by God through the Holy Spirit, which flows forth in love of God and one's neighbor.

My friends, it is an undeniable fact that there are more believing theologians today than when I was young—some fifty years ago. In those days, basically only vulgar Rationalists occupied the ecclesiastical offices and pulpits created by the government. Back then, the small number of believing theologians were tolerated—provided they behaved and kept quiet, made no serious attempt to confess their faith, and, above all, did not passionately oppose the forces of unbelief.

What a change has taken place since then within the so-called Protestant Church! Those vulgar Rationalists turn the Bible into a code of ethics and specifically declare Christian doctrines to be "magic carpet" myths and fantasies—valuable only as far as moral lessons may be drawn from them. These men appear to have left the scene and fizzled away.

Twenty-second Evening Lecture: March 13, 1885

These days the so-called "intelligentsia" refuses to be classified as vulgar Rationalists. True, the so-called Society of Protestants[67] *has* made an attempt to reintroduce and rehabilitate vulgar Rationalism, but without success. Even the spokesmen of that society declare that vulgar Rationalism is outdated. These days, if you want to be regarded as a person of intelligence, it is absolutely necessary to acknowledge that the Christian religion is supernaturally revealed. Yet they still have watered down the authority of the Bible, maintaining that it only *contains* God's Word.

By what process did these new "believers" attain their "faith"? Was it by personally recognizing the misery of their sinful condition? Or was it by clearly recognizing their damnable condition and their need of redemption? Alas! There is pitifully little evidence of that. A careful observer can barely help but get the impression that they arrived at their faith by rationalist speculation. That is why nearly all of them reject the verbal inspiration of the Bible. They subject all books of the Bible to criticism, such as would be engaged in only by enemies of the Bible. Of course, they are not aware that they are enemies of the Bible. They have turned the Christian religion into a religious philosophy.

Regarding its essential qualities, modern theology is something entirely different from what theology used to be. It does not pretend to be a system of faith. Rather, it wishes to be a system of science. Starting with the principles of human knowledge, modern theologians propose that they are able to *prove* as absolute truth what the common people merely *believe.*

Ps. 119:120   Accordingly, modern theologians do not have that fear that drove David when he said, "My flesh trembles for fear of You." These days, such reverence for Holy Scripture is hard to find. They treat nearly everything in the Bible as they would the fables of Aesop. I am telling you the truth when I say this. And later on, when you compare the old and the modern theologians, you will see that I am not exaggerating. Science has been placed on the throne, and theology is made to sit at her feet and await the orders of philosophy. Accordingly, as soon as someone becomes prominent in a new field of science, he is also immediately awarded a doctorate of *theology,* as if science and learning were identical with theology.

My dear friends, if you do not keep the light of the pure Gospel shining in this **land** of the West, which was recently devastated by God,[68] it will not be possible to delay the Day of Judgment. In our day we are down to the dregs of the cup. The end is at hand. May God help us to remain faithful in this part of the world that has been the last region to be penetrated by the Gospel.

---

67 German: *Protestantenverein.* See "Protestants, Society of" in the Index of Persons and Groups, page 498.

68 This is likely a reference to the U.S. Civil War.

Do not forget, my dear friends, that there is only one way to arrive at true faith. God did not provide several ways to salvation—one for the learned and the other for common folk. God is not a respecter of persons. If the learned scholar wants to become a believer and be saved, he must come down from his lofty perch and sit with poor sinners, regardless of whether they are cowboys or other regular folk. There is no other way to faith than through a person's knowledge of sin and his damnable condition and through the inward crushing of the heart in contrition and sorrow. A person who has not come to faith in this way is not a believing Christian—much less a theologian.

I hope you will not misunderstand me when I say that this is the only way to faith. If this statement is not understood correctly, it may lead to a horrible mingling of Law and Gospel. In these "Luther Lessons" of ours, this reflection leads us to consider the next thesis.

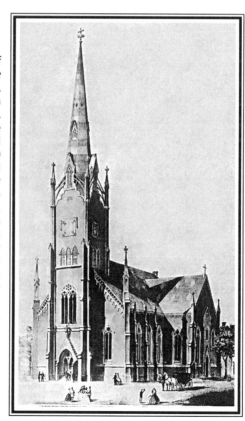

The church building of the *Dreieinigkeitskirche* (Trinity Church) in St. Louis was dedicated on December 3–4, 1865. On May 27, 1896, the tornado that damaged or destroyed 8,000 buildings in St. Louis and East St. Louis severely damaged this structure as well as Holy Cross. Both church buildings were rebuilt. Trinity's steeple is lower today and less ornate and does not have a clock in the belfry. Image courtesy of Concordia Historical Institute.

This photograph of the pastor and teachers of Holy Cross congregation was taken circa 1880. Top left is the Rev. Dr. [Licentiate] K. Georg Stöckhardt (served 1878–87). To his right stands Teacher A. Troeller (served 1879–83). Seated left to right are Teachers Reinhold Koerner (served 1868–94) and Heinrich Erck (served 1850–91). Image courtesy of Holy Cross Church.

THESIS XI

You are not rightly distinguishing Law and Gospel in the Word of God if you only want to comfort those with the Gospel who are contrite because they love God. You also need to comfort people with the Gospel who are only contrite because they fear His wrath and punishment.

EDITOR'S NOTE: In this thesis, Walther emphasizes that we can only love God in a state of spiritual life and activity, not spiritual death. Before we first have faith, either through Baptism or through the Word of God, we cannot love God. God has to give us that spiritual life through faith. If He has not done that, we cannot "love" God merely through our sorrow over our sins. That sorrow in the hearts of unbelievers is really a selfish, sinful act. Yet contrite sorrow is God-pleasing when it comes from the hearts of believers.

In a more general sense, even though God works through "every-day" means such as human language, water, bread, and wine, those means do not themselves set limits for God. It is God in His grace who stoops to the level of humans. We cannot capture or manipulate God. We cannot take hold of the Gospel on our own before God comes to us in grace.

Contrition through Law

The entire Roman Church violates this thesis. Yet within the so-called Protestant Church, one sees [this violation] among all the fanatics[1] and Pietists as well.

If a Protestant is alarmed over his sins and is in a state of contrition and sorrow because of them, people ask him to state the source of his contrition. They ask: "My dear fellow, why are you contrite? Are you contrite only because you realize you will be going to hell because of your sins? Or are you contrite because you realize you are condemned because you see God's wrath above you and the pit of hell below you?" The Papists and even the fanatics say, "No, real contrition must come from love for God. Only then is your contrition worth anything. Only then can I preach the Gospel to you."

This is a fear-inducing error—and I hope I do not have to prove to you that this is obviously a terrible confusion of Law and Gospel. As you know, since

---

1   German: *Schwärmer.*

the fall, the Law has only one single function: to lead people to the knowledge of their sins. It has no power to renew [people]. *That* power is vested solely in the Gospel. Only faith is active through love. We, however, do not become spiritually active through "love" [when that means] through sorrow over our sins.[2]

On the contrary, as long as we are still uninformed concerning the fact that God has become our reconciled God and Father through Christ, we hate Him. An unconverted person who claims to love God is stating falsehood and is guilty of miserable hypocrisy—even though he may not be aware of it. That person is making a false claim because only faith in the Gospel regenerates a person. Accordingly, a person cannot love God as long as he is still without faith. To demand of a poor sinner that he must be alarmed because of his sins and that he must feel sorry for them—out of a love of God—that is a terrible way of turning Law and Gospel completely backward.

Love from Gospel No, this is what the Bible's teaching *really* states: Sinners should come to Jesus just as they are, even if they have to acknowledge: "I have only hatred for God in my heart. O God, what should I do? What can I do to be saved?"

A genuine preacher of the Gospel will ask: "Do you know that you are lost and condemned sinners and that you cannot find the help you are seeking? Then come to Jesus with your evil hearts and your hatred of God and of God's Law, and Jesus will receive you just as you are. He is full of glory. Everybody knows that 'Jesus receives sinners!'[3] There is no need for you to change your behavior, there is no need for you to cleanse yourself first, and there is no need for you to improve yourself **before** you come to Jesus. No, the only one who can improve *you* is Jesus! And He will, if only you would believe in Him."

Rom. 3:20 The proof for this doctrine from God's Word is in that most general statement in Romans 3:20: "Through the law comes knowledge of sin." Here the apostle states the function of the Law: it does not produce love, but the knowledge of sin. In fact, a person really can have that knowledge even without the love of God.

Rom. 5:20 Romans 5:20: "Now the law came in to increase the trespass, but where sin increased, grace abounded all the more." The Greek text reads: "that sin might be **increased**."[4] Many sins are sleeping in a person who is still uninformed

---

2   This statement is difficult to understand, whether in the original German notes or otherwise. Here Walther makes the all-important distinction between spiritual life and death that governs the rest of this thesis. Spiritual life and death does not come from human feelings. Spiritual death comes from original and actual sin. The German forms of these theological terms are perhaps clearer in translation: inherited sin and sin of deeds. Many people who are spiritually dead lead happy lives. Many Christians are sad. Spiritual truth ultimately transcends the small scope of human thought and experience. Recalling Luther, we are beggars, not lords; this is true.

3   See Luke 15:2.

4   Walther said this in Greek.

concerning the Law. Forcefully preach the Law to such a person, let the Law strike his conscience with lightning force, and the person will become worse. He will begin to rear up against God and say, "What! I am going to hell? True, I know that I am an enemy of God. But that is not my fault; I cannot help it."

That is what preaching the Law does. It drives people to despair. Blessed are the people who have been brought to this point: They have taken a great step forward on the way to their salvation. Such people will receive the Gospel with joy, while other people who have never experienced such things will only yawn when they hear the Gospel preached. They will say, "That is an easy way to get to heaven!" Only a poor sinner, on the edge of despair, will realize what a message of joy the Gospel is and will joyfully receive it.

Romans 4:15: "The law brings wrath." It stirs up people to burn with wrath against God, not to love God.   **Rom. 4:15**

Romans 7:7–8:

> What then shall we say? That the law is sin? By no means! Yet if it had not been for the law, I would not have known sin. For I would not have known what it is to covet if the law had not said, "You shall not covet." But sin, seizing an opportunity through the commandment, produced in me all kinds of covetousness. Apart from the law, sin lies dead.   **Rom. 7:7–8**

We always reach out for what is clearly forbidden. Human beings are always tempted to act contrary to an injunction or a prohibition. Even Ovid, that dirty old man, knew that when he wrote: "We strive after the forbidden thing and always lust after those things that are denied us."[5] To be sure, even a heathen could figure that out. He was always turning his thoughts toward himself. Ovid was a genius, but still a dirty old man.

Galatians 3:21: "Is the law then contrary to the promises of God? Certainly not! For if a law had been given that could give life, then righteousness would indeed be by the law." Why does the apostle ask this question? Why the hypothetical if/then clause? No doubt, the apostle wants to negate the question even more strongly. Often when a question is raised about something that everybody knows to be false, the intention is to bring about a very strong negation. That is the case in this text. The apostle means to say: the Law most certainly cannot save people.   **Gal. 3:21**

---

5   Latin: *Nitimur in vetitum, semper cupimusque negata.* Walther also referred to this quotation from Ovid in Thesis I.

2 Cor. 3:6 Luther Second Corinthians 3:6: "The letter kills, but the spirit gives life."[6] The members of the Union Church[7] have horribly corrupted this precious text. They claim that it is wrong to insist on the letter of Scripture, that it is the spirit—general ideas drawn from Scripture—to which we must hold.

Remember when Luther wrote the words "This is My body"[8] at Marburg and pointed to those words again and again? The Union Church feels that Luther was not acting in a Christian way when he did that. In actual fact, what Luther did was not unionist. It *was* genuinely Christian. These words certainly mean: "The letter kills, but the spirit gives life." We do not have enough time to explain this in greater detail, but, if you study the matter further, you will see that *letter* means the Law and *spirit* means the Gospel.

These Bible passages are illustrated by beautiful examples recorded in Scripture. They relate the behavior of certain persons *before* and *after* their conversion. While few instances are recorded, all of them show that contrition does not flow from a *love* for God; rather, [it flows] from the Law.

Acts 2:37–38 At the first Christian feast of Pentecost, a crowd of people had gathered and heard the apostle Peter preach. His main point[9] was that they had murdered the Messiah, Jesus of Nazareth, and thus needed to tremble when considering the judgment. They listened to the whole sermon, but when he reached the point at which he raised this charge against them, they became alarmed by the Holy Spirit. The record says, "They were cut to the heart." They felt as if Peter had run a dagger into their heart. They reasoned: "If we have done that, we are all doomed. What will God say to us when we appear before His judgment seat? He will charge us with the killing of the Messiah."

We are not told that they said, "Oh, we are so sorry that we grieved our faithful God." It was not love for God but fright and terror that made them cry, "What shall we do?" Nor does the apostle Peter say to them: "My dear people, we now need to investigate the quality of your contrition, whether it is flowing from a love for God or from fear of the punishment you deserve for your sins, that is, from the fear of hell." There is not one word of this.

Acts 2:37–38 When the listeners pose their frightened and terrified question, "Brothers, what shall we do?" the apostle says, "Repent and be baptized every one of you in the name of Jesus Christ for the forgiveness of your sins." Since these

---

6   Lutheran tradition, such as that in the great Ernestine Bible (*Das weimarische Bibelwerk*), connects this verse with Romans 10:4 and interprets "letter" as Law and "spirit" as Gospel, as Walther does here.

7   In North America, the counterpart to the Prussian Union, into which Lutherans and Reformed were forcibly merged, was the German-speaking "Evangelical Church," now part of the United Church of Christ, which also includes the New England Congregationalist tradition.

8   Walther said the Lord's Words in Greek, following Luther's example from the 1529 Marburg Colloquy.

9   Latin: *summa summarum*.

people were already in terror over their sins, the word *repentance* here refers not to what is called the first part of repentance, which is contrition, but to the second part, namely faith. We are told that they immediately let themselves be baptized.[10] They desired change of mind—in the sense that they no longer desired to be murderers of Jesus, but rather wished to believe in Him. Accordingly, the apostles received them, and these converts were numbered with those who were saved.

The example of the jailer at Philippi—to which I have referred a number of times—also illustrates this point. I need to refer to it over and over because it is the most glorious passage that we have in Scripture. The jailer was a scoundrel and enjoyed the task of beating the servants of the Lord, casting them into the inner prison or deepest dungeon, and putting their feet in the stocks, which he had not at all been ordered to do. But once he thought that all his prisoners had escaped during the earthquake, this same man was seized with despair and wanted to commit suicide. Paul cried out to him: "Do not harm yourself, for we are all here." Writhing and trembling, the jailer fell at the apostles' feet and asked, "Sirs, what must I do to be saved?" It was complete fright and terror that moved him to do that. Now, Paul does not say to him: "But first you must show contrition as proof that you love God." Rather, he said, "Believe in the Lord Jesus, and you will be saved, you and your household." *Acts 16:28, 30–31*

Saul had the same experience. He had persecuted the Church of God, snorting wrathfully that he would murder all Christians. He had been on his way to a place where he wanted to shed the blood of Christians when the Lord Himself met him in a vision. Saul fell to the ground and was "astonished." That is all! Then Jesus said to him, "It will go ill with you, if you kick against the goads."[11] *Acts 26:14* Luther

Once the Gospel with its sweet heavenly power had entered into [Saul's] heart, this wretched man was free from his distress and misery. And now the Lord prescribed for this sinner, who was first terrified and crushed and then comforted, no other lesson than this: instead of persecuting Him, Saul was to confess the Lord. Saul was to be baptized, receiving the seal that his sins had been forgiven.

When you preach, do not be stingy with the Gospel. Bring its consolations to all, even to the greatest sinners. But only when they are terrified by the wrath of God and hell are they fully prepared to receive the Gospel. True, this goes against our reason; we think it strange that such scoundrels should be comforted immediately. We would think that they should be forced to suffer much greater agony in their conscience. Fanatics adopt that method when **Only God works contrition**

---

10 See Acts 2:41.

11 See the note on "goads" in Thesis IX, page 211.

they deal with alarmed sinners. But a genuine Bible theologian resolves to preach the Gospel and faith in Jesus Christ to a person whom God, by His Law, has prepared for such preaching.

2 Cor. 7:10   Second Corinthians 7:10: "For godly grief produces a repentance that leads to salvation without regret, whereas worldly grief produces death." Some people think "godly grief" means contrition out of *love* for God. This is incorrect. Rather, the apostle is referring to sorrow that a person has not produced *himself* but that *God* has caused in him by His Word. The Greek text reads: "sorrow in accordance with God or produced by God."

It is a horrible corruption of Christian doctrine to tell an alarmed sinner that he must first experience contrition and, when he asks how he must go about that, to tell him that he must sit down and meditate and try to draw, or elicit, repentance from his heart, of his own ability. That is what the Papists teach. But their teaching is complete hypocrisy. In the whole, wide world there is not one person who can produce contrition in himself. They may work to bring it forth until they become "unglued" in tears, but that is all a hypocritical sham. **Godly** sorrow is required because faith is required. By terrifying us, God wants to produce this sorrow. We must not imagine that contrition is a good work that we do. Rather, it is something that God works in us. God comes with the hammer of the Law and crushes our soul.

A person who wants to make *himself* sorrowful wants to drag himself down more and more. On the other hand, a person suffering from the *right* kind of sorrow strongly desires to be rid of it. These people are tormented day and night. They may frequent bars and make an unsuccessful attempt to drive away their sorrow by drinking. With their buddies they tend to be braggarts, but when they get home, their conscience tells them: You are damned. If you die tonight, you will go to hell. That is godly sorrow, produced not by man but by God Himself. God has no regard for any miserable product of man.

The **Apology** (Müller, 168–69) reads:

Ap XII (V) 8   Moreover, [our opponents] teach and write many things that are still more awkward and confusing. They teach that grace may be merited by contrition. When they are asked to explain why Saul and Judas, in whom there was quite an awful contrition, did not merit grace, they ought to answer that Judas and Saul lacked the Gospel and faith, that Judas did not comfort himself with the Gospel and did not believe. For faith is the deciding factor between the contrition of Peter and Judas. But our opponents give no thought to the Gospel and faith, but to the Law. They say that Judas did not love God but was afraid of the punishment.[12]

In the Papists' view, the reason Judas was condemned was because his contrition did not flow from love of God. If it had, he would have gained merit. Papists are always looking for some merit, either of the congruent or of the condign kind.[13] The Apology continues:

> Is this not an uncertain and awkward way of teaching repentance? In the real and great distress described in the Psalms and prophets, when will an alarmed conscience know whether it fears God as its God out of love—or whether it flees from Him, hating His wrath and eternal damnation?[14]

Ap XII (V) 9

How can one know this? It would be simply horrible to ask a poor, terrified sinner, "Well, what is the story? What is driving your contrition?" He responds: "I am afraid of going to hell. If I die tonight, I will go to hell. That is why I am contrite." But no matter what is driving him, we can see that he is terrified and we console him. Then love will come!

The Apology continues: "It would seem that those who claim these things have never really experienced such a situation—those who play around with words and distinguish matters according to their dreams." The Papists talk about contrition like a blind man talks about color. They have never experienced beneficial terror on account of their sin. When a poor sinner comes to one of their learned theologians, they ask him, "What kind of contrition is causing you anxiety?" The poor person may be unable to explain this point adequately, and he says that he knows nothing about it, except that he feels terribly distressed. Then the learned doctor may send him to a barber-surgeon for some bloodletting. He will feel better when he is rid of his sluggish blood. Good heavens, what pitiful theologians these people are! Lord, have mercy!

Ap XII (V) 9

Back to the Apology: "But deep down inside, when the test is applied, the matter turns out quite differently. One's conscience cannot be put at ease with shoddy syllables and words, as these nice, leisurely, and idle Sophists dream up."[15] Those good, kind, and lazy Sophists! How can they speak properly

Ap XII (V) 10

---

12 See also *Concordia*, 159; *Triglot Concordia*, 254–55. See also the section "Walther's Book of Concord," pages 467–68.

13 The Dau text adds this footnote taken from Ap V (III) 255: "[The adversaries] . . . infer that works merit grace, sometimes *de congruo* and at other times *de condigno*, namely, when love is added" (*Triglot Concordia*, 223). Cf. *Concordia*, 140. Scholastic theologians, both medieval and some modern ones, claim that *congruent* merit is what God awards when someone tries to do good but fails. God supposedly awards merit to make the imperfect attempt satisfactory. *Condign* merit is fully deserved merit. Scholastics believe salvation is awarded on merit.

14 See also *Concordia*, 159.

15 See also *Concordia*, 159.

of matters that they have never experienced and about which they merely speculate?

Again, the *Apology* says (Müller, 171–72):

Ap XII (V) 29   When we speak regarding genuine contrition,[16] we cut out those innumerable questions that they advance, such as whether a person's contrition flows from love of God or from fear of punishment. For these are nothing but mere words and a useless babbling of persons who have never experienced the state of mind of a terrified conscience. But we say that true repentance[17] happens when the conscience is terrified, begins to feel its sin and the great wrath of God raised against sin, and is sorry for having sinned. And this contrition takes place in this manner when our sins are punished by the Word of God.[18]

Now that truly is sweet comfort! When God has given me the grace to be alarmed on account of my sins, I am in the right state to approach the throne of grace, where I receive forgiveness—the true cure. Of course, I need to have contrition—however, not for the purpose of acquiring some merit by it, but in order that I might gladly accept what Jesus offers me.[19]

Ap XII (V) 32   Amid these terrors, the conscience feels the anger of God against sin, which is a matter entirely unknown to such idle and carnal men as the Sophists and their kind. It is at that point that one's conscience first becomes aware what a great disobedience to God sin is. And it is at that point that the terrible anger of God weighs down on the conscience—and human nature cannot possibly bear up under it, unless it is raised up by the Word of God.[20]

Even when there is love of God in a person's heart, the devil will spoil it. Wherever false teaching has free reign, a dying person may be led into despair. [People] may feel contrite, but that feeling does not flow from a love of God, but rather from their fear of the anger of God and of hell, into which they fear they are about to be hurled. But when they have been taught the true doctrine, people know that they believe in the Lord Jesus and cling to Him. Therefore, the love of God will also enter their heart. You see, this teaching is not a matter to be treated lightly.

---

16   Latin: *de contritione.*

17   Latin: *contritio.*

18   See also *Concordia*, 161; *Triglot Concordia*, 259.

19   Walther is not afraid to put himself at the point of being the miserable sinner, fully under the hammer of God's judgment. When Walther criticizes someone, he is willing to stand under that same criticism and be judged fairly by it.

20   See also *Concordia*, 162.

Thus St. Paul says, "By the Law I am dead to the Law." For the Law does nothing but accuse the conscience. It commands people what to do and terrifies them.[21] Our opponents do not say one word about faith. Therefore, they do not teach one word regarding the Gospel or Christ, but their teaching is entirely from the Law. They tell people that with their pain, contrition, sorrow, and anguish they are meriting grace, provided their contrition is from a love of God and provided they love God. Good heavens, what kind of preaching is that for consciences that are in need of comfort![22]

Ap XII (V) 33–34;
Gal. 2:19 Luther

Thus reads our Confession. Our theologians did not just sit themselves down and weave together a system of doctrine. They sat down to write our Lutheran Confessions as true Christians. They knew how a poor sinner is given rest and the comfort of salvation. In the Apology, dear Melanchthon speaks like a straightforward Christian. What makes this Confession all the more precious is that he speaks from the fullness of Scripture and from experience.

How can we love God when we are stuck in great distress and immense agony, when we feel the great and terrible earnestness and anger of God, which is stronger than any person could express in words? Why, this is nothing less than complete despair that these preachers and scholars are teaching, when they preach to poor consciences in distress. They proclaim neither the Gospel nor any comfort, but only the Law.[23]

Ap XII (V) 34

In the preface to the first part of the 1545 Latin edition of [his] works, Luther tells us how things looked in his heart before he had received the light of the Gospel. He makes a personal confession, saying that, while in bondage to the Law, he had read the words of the apostle Paul, namely, that the righteousness of God is revealed in the Gospel.[24] This statement terrified him. The Law already had terrified him greatly, and now he reads that God's justice is also revealed in the Gospel? That was simply too terrible. The Law damned him, and now God apparently was sending him the Gospel to do the same! So, even there, God seemed to demand righteousness of sinners!

We cannot thank and praise God enough for giving Luther, shortly before his death, the leisure to relate some of the inner experiences of his life that had prepared and equipped him for the work of the Reformation. He writes (St. Louis Ed. 14:446ff.):

---

21   Walther comments: "That is all the Law does."

22   See also *Concordia*, 162.

23   See also *Concordia*, 162.

24   See Romans 1:16–17.

W² 14:446–47;
Rom. 1:17 Luther

[In 1519] I truly had a hearty desire; indeed, I was yearning to understand the Epistle of St. Paul to the Romans. Until that point, nothing had stopped me except the single phrase "the righteousness of God" in 1:17, where Paul says, "The righteousness of God is revealed [in the Gospel]."

Now, I hated the term "righteousness of God" because I had been taught in agreement with the usage and practice of all teachers of that period. I had been taught to understand that term according to the philosophers who claim that God is righteous in Himself. As such, He does and works good, and He punishes all sinners and the unrighteous. This righteousness is called essential[25] or active righteousness.[26]

Now, my condition was this: Although I was leading the life of a holy and blameless monk, I discovered that, in the sight of God, I was a great sinner. Moreover, my conscience was troubled and distressed.

W² 14:447

Luther's life as a monk had been without reproach. He had almost tormented himself to death trying to keep his monastic vows, but despite all his efforts, he was brokenhearted. This was the case because, by means of the Law, the Holy Spirit had revealed to him that his heart was corrupt. He did not regard this condition of his heart to be an unimportant matter. Rather, it filled Luther with anxiety: "I also did not trust my ability to ease the anger of God with my satisfaction and merit."[27]

W² 14:447

Luther was always insecure. He truly desired to make full satisfaction for his sins and to keep not only the Ten Commandments but also the commandments of the Church, which were not in the slightest ordered by God. Thus he lived on in papistic blindness.

W² 14:447

But then he would ask himself: "What does God care whether I am lying on a sack of straw or on a couch of velvet and satin?" Luther confesses: "For this reason **I did not at all love this righteous and angry God** who punishes sinners. **Rather, I hated Him** and was full of secret anger toward Him."

W² 14:447

Now, just ask any modern theologian whether he had loved God prior to his conversion, and he will say, "Why, of course. Who would not love God? We have always been taught to do that." But that shows his blindness. Luther confesses that he used to hate God.

If we were observant, we would become aware that our condition—before faith was kindled in our heart—was identical to that of Luther's: "And so I

---

25   Latin: *iustitia formalis.*

26   Latin: *iustitia activa.*

27   The Latin *satisfactio* means "to make good." The German word is *genugtun*, to "do enough." The Roman Catholic model of penance includes feeling sorry for sin (contrition of the heart), listing the sins to a priest who is approved to hear confession (oral confession), and making up for the sin (satisfaction of works).

secretly and intensely hated God (though not through secret idolatry)."²⁸ Before he came to know the Gospel, Luther had been angry with God. Anyone who has ever been hit between the eyes by the Law will not be surprised about Luther's confession.

> Frequently I would say: Is God not satisfied that He has ravished us poor, miserable sinners with all kinds of misery and affliction, with the terrors and threats of the Law? Even though we are already condemned to everlasting death on account of original sin! Must He pile heartache on heartache even more by the **Gospel**? On top of it all, by preaching its message, must He proclaim His righteousness and serious anger—and thus only add to our terror? In my confused conscience, I was full of hostility.

W² 14:447

Already terrified and distressed by the Law, Luther read in Paul's Epistle to the Romans that the Gospel also reveals the righteousness of God. At that time, Luther did not yet have a clue concerning the sweet consolation contained in that statement. These days every child knows that the text does not refer to the righteousness that God requires of *us* in the Law. It refers to the righteousness of Christ that God wants to give us and that Luther expressed so well by translating the Greek with "the righteousness before God." By this translation even the most simple person can understand that this passage does not refer to the righteous life that we have lived and according to which we will be judged, but to the gracious righteousness that Christ acquired for us on the cross.

> Nevertheless, I continued my meditation on blessed Paul, working—with a great yearning for knowledge and a hearty desire—to understand what he meant in this passage. I spent night and day thinking about these things until—by the grace of God—I finally understood **how these words are connected: The righteousness of God** is revealed in the Gospel, as is written: "The righteous shall live by **faith**."

W² 14:447; Rom. 1:17

> From this context I learned to understand the righteousness of God by which the righteous live by the gracious gift of God, through faith alone, and I realized that this is what the apostle means: The Gospel reveals the righteousness that is valid in the sight of God and through which God—out of grace and pure mercy—makes us righteous by faith. In Latin this righteousness is called passive,²⁹ and this is the

---

28 The St. Louis edition (W²), which is translated here, offers a much clearer text than the older Halle edition (W¹). The text of the Halle edition could make one think that Luther did commit idolatry. Indeed, that is how Walther understood the passage from that older edition.

29 Latin: *iustitia passiva*.

righteousness to which the passage "The righteous shall live by faith" refers.

Luther would not remain stuck in that difficult situation. With his natural heart raving against God, he was but a short step from the edge of despair. He picked up his Bible again and again, and [he] kept staring at Romans 1:17. He began to think that possibly the text had a different meaning after all.

W² 14:447

During his persistent musing, reading, and meditating, God helped him to see the light, and he has shared with us what happened to him when he had finally seen: "*That* is what those words mean!" [He writes:] "At that point I immediately felt that I had been born again and had found a door wide open, leading straight to paradise." The same man who previously had hated God and had been grumbling against Him was now filled with unspeakable joy. He began to love God with all his heart after hearing the most blessed news of joy: *Christ,* the Son of God, acquired righteousness for the whole world. All you need is to believe in this righteousness.

May God grant to all of you, as He did to Luther, that you would see the gates of paradise open wide to receive you! Then your congregations will get a taste of your own happiness, and you [will] keep from falling into dead orthodoxy.

In his *Sacred Scripture Vindicated*,[30] paragraph 79, p. 125, Hülsemann comments on 2 Corinthians 7:10:

Paul does not say, "You have awakened sorrow in yourselves out of your love for God, but you were given a godly sorrow by me, that is, a sorrow that is in accordance with the will or commandment of God." . . . Accordingly, St. Paul interprets "godly sorrow" to mean a sorrow that had been awakened in the Corinthians by the power and the command of God. On the other hand, the "sorrow of the world" means a sorrow that arises from worldly causes, such as the fear of earthly punishment, the loss of personal honor, an evil conscience, and other causes that produce sorrow over some crime even in heathens and unregenerate persons.

This kind of sorrow, then, refers to a person who is alarmed because of his sins and who is sorrowful in the presence of God. When you are terrified by the thought of your sins, hell, death, and damnation and realize that God is angry with you—that is godly sorrow. Since you are under His wrath, you are damned on account of your sins. This is the case, even though you may be in the same situation Luther was in before he truly came to understand the Gospel. Such sorrow comes from God!

---

30 Johann Hülsemann, *Vindiciae sacrae scripturae* (Leipzig, 1679). Here and elsewhere, longer Latin titles are abbreviated for clarity.

On the other hand, when a fornicator, lecher, or drunkard begins to sorrow because he has wasted the glory days of his youth, when he has ruined his body and has become prematurely senile—that is a sorrow of this world. When a vain person is plunged into sorrow over his sins because he has lost some of his prestige, when a thief sorrows over his thieving because he has landed in jail—all of that is worldly sorrow.

However, when a person grieves over his sins because he sees hell before him, where he will be punished for having insulted the most holy God— that is godly sorrow, provided that it has not been produced by imagination through a person's own effort. God alone can produce genuine godly sorrow. May God grant us all such sorrow!

Among the various functions and official acts of a minister of the Church, the most important of all, my friends, is preaching. And since there is no substitute for preaching, a minister who accomplishes little or nothing by preaching will accomplish little or nothing by anything else he may do.

Twenty-third Evening Lecture: March 20, 1885

Of course, here is where the Papists differ from us. They call their ministers "priests" and declare that the most important of all the functions of a priest is to baptize, hear confession, pronounce absolution, administer Communion, and, above all, to offer to God the sacrifice of the Mass. Apart from the fact that the sacrifice of the Mass is the greatest horror that has ever been practiced in the Christian Church, we are forced to say that all their baptizing, pronouncing of Absolution, and administering of Communion is useless if these topics had not been previously dealt with in sermons. For these are not the works of men, but of God Himself, who has connected with the Sacraments a promise that faith must grasp.

Accordingly, without faith, none of these Sacraments benefit anyone. On the contrary, without faith they are even harmful. If these works of God are to be of any use, it is absolutely necessary that [the people should] first be thoroughly taught [about these works] from the Word of God in sermons.

When Christ was about to return to the glory that He had with the Father before the foundation of the world,[31] He gave His disciples this instruction: "Go into all the world and **preach** the Gospel to all creatures," or as Matthew puts it: "Go, therefore, and **teach** all peoples." Only then does [Jesus] add: "And baptize them in the name of the Father and of the Son and of the Holy Spirit." Not satisfied with this, He concludes His instruction with the words: "teaching them to observe all that I have commended to you." Behold, the

Mark 16:15; Matt. 28:19–20 Luther

---

31 See John 17:24.

first and the last, the alpha and omega of the apostolic office (or the ministry of the Church): preaching and teaching.

This function, however, is not only the most important but also the most difficult task assigned to a minister of the Church. There are preachers who imagine that preaching is easy for them—and the longer they are in the ministry, the easier preaching becomes. They believe that if only they are careful to preach nothing but the pure Word of God—without adding any heresy—that must be enough. Such preachers have given in to a horrible and very dangerous error. Mere pious talk without any purpose or logical order is not genuine preaching.

Rather, only the Holy Spirit through His Word inspires genuine preaching. Accordingly, a genuine sermon comes about only after all the spiritual and intellectual energy of a truly believing preacher has been applied to the utmost, after passionate prayer, after all earthly cares have been chased from his mind, and after the preacher has been freed from all vain desires. This is a difficult task.

Administering Baptism properly is easy. Anybody can do it. Likewise, pronouncing Absolution correctly is also quite easy. Even a boy can do it. Administering Holy Communion correctly is very easy as well. Any intelligent Christian can do it. But to preach properly is difficult. For this reason a student of theology ought to make proper preaching his highest aim. For if he is unable to preach, he does not belong in the ministry.

In our orthodox Church, a minister of God is a servant of Jesus Christ, and his value does not lie in a certain undefined quality that is imparted to him at his ordination or consecration. This value is not something that other people do not have, which would make him "holier than thou" and invaluable. By no means. The value of a true minister of the Church lies exclusively in his ability to preach properly. If he does not have this ability, the pulpit is not the place for him. That is because the pulpit is for preaching. Preaching is the central element of every Divine Service.

What is he supposed to bring about by his preaching? Remember that the preacher is supposed to shock secure souls who are asleep in sin. Next, his job is to lead those who have been shocked to faith. Next, he gives believers assurance of their state of grace and salvation. Next, he leads those who have become sure of their salvation to a life of sanctification. And last, he is to confirm those who are sanctified and to keep them in their holy and blessed state to the end. What a task!

Here is a most important point that we must not forget: To achieve this task, it is so important to rightly distinguish the truth, as the apostle says, or to rightly distinguish Law and Gospel. If a preacher does not understand how to do this and always mingles one doctrine with the other, his preaching is completely ineffective. It is useless. More than this, a preacher of this kind does harm and leads astray the souls of people. He leads them to a false faith, false hope, and false contrition. He makes them mere hypocrites and frequently hurls them into despair.

To distinguish Law and Gospel properly is a very, very difficult task. As Luther says, all preachers cannot help but remain mere apprentices in this skill until death.[32] Nevertheless, a young theologian must be able to recite at least the first lesson in this curriculum. He must know the goal he is to reach, and he must have made a start toward reaching that goal. $\quad$ W² 11:1255

In our previous evening lectures, we learned something about the difficulty of distinguishing Law and Gospel. Let us increase that belief we have already arrived at by considering another example of how these two doctrines are sometimes mingled.

Martin Stephan Sr. had a pleasant appearance, perhaps more so than Walther, yet his deeds had distinctly unpleasant results. From Bishop Athanasius of Alexandria, who preserved biblical Christianity in the fourth century, to more recent figures, God has been pleased to bless the Church greatly through people whom the world has not esteemed greatly with regard to their appearance. This image of Stephan is from Ludwig Fürbringer, *Persons and Events* (St. Louis: Concordia, 1947), 88.

---

32 This is Walther's application of Luther's statement in the second sermon for the Third Sunday after Trinity, contained in Luther's *Church Postils*. Luther states that he and those who share his profession practice "the sort of skill that no one can have except for Christians, and we must remain students [or apprentices] and continue to learn [this skill] our whole life." Compare with the translation in John Nicholas Lenker, ed., *The Complete Sermons of Martin Luther*, trans. John Nicholas Lenker et al. (Grand Rapids: Baker, 1983, 2000), 2.2:80.

This photograph from June 11, 1875, shows Concordia College on its twenty-fifth anniversary on Jefferson Avenue. Martin Stephan Jr. designed the building, which was built in 1850. He studied under Walther after the elder Stephan died. The long exposure times of early photography caused flags and some leaves to be hand-drawn. Image courtesy of Holy Cross Church.

Thesis XII

You are not rightly distinguishing Law and Gospel in the Word of God if you teach that the reason our sins are forgiven is because we both believe and are contrite.

Editor's Note: In this thesis and elsewhere, Walther carefully revised and reworked his message for the second lecture series. For example, Walther used a technical theological term[1] in the 1878 lectures that could be misunderstood to mean that contrition (sorrow for one's sins) contributes to forgiveness. Walther intended to say that being contrite does *not* contribute to forgiveness; only faith is the root cause for being forgiven. To correct the original language in this thesis, which was confusing, Walther simply used "cause"[2] or "reason" to clearly state his point in the second lecture series. This shows Walther's humility and willingness to look for ways to improve his own study and grasp of the subjects that he taught.

There is no question that contrition is necessary if a person wishes to obtain forgiveness of sins.

Contrition is necessary;

At His first public exercise of the preaching function, our Lord cried, "Repent and believe in the gospel." He cites repentance first. Whenever this term is placed in opposition to faith, it means nothing else than contrition. When Christ gathered the holy apostles about Him for the last time—as He was about to ascend to heaven and withdraw His visible presence from the Church—He said to them, "Thus it is written, that the Christ should suffer and on the third day rise from the dead, and that repentance and forgiveness of sins should be proclaimed in His name."

Mark 1:15; Luke 24:46–47

Why is repentance required in addition to faith? What do you think? Our Lord gives the reason in these words: "Those who are well have no need of a physician, but those who are sick. . . . For I came not to call the righteous, but sinners." With these words the Lord testifies that the reason contrition is absolutely necessary is that without it no one can be made a believer. People's stomachs are full, as it were. They reject the invitation to the heavenly marriage feast.[3] Even Solomon said, "One who is full loathes honey" (Proverbs

Matt. 9:12–13; Prov. 27:7

---

1 German: *Mitursache.*

2 German: *Ursache.*

3 Perhaps an allusion to the parable of the great banquet (Luke 14:12–24), which follows immediately the parable of the wedding feast (Luke 14:7–11).

27:7). Where there is no spiritual hunger and thirst, the Lord Jesus is not received. As long as a person has not been reduced to the state of a poor, lost, and condemned sinner, he has no serious interest in the One who saves sinners.

Contrition defined

However, as you keep this in mind, do not think that contrition is the cause for sins being forgiven. Contrition is in no way the cause for a person to receive forgiveness of sins.[4] Rather, it is faith that grasps forgiveness of sins. Why do you think I have been stressing that people who claim *contrition* to be the cause of the forgiveness of sins are mingling Law and Gospel?

1. Contrition is solely a result of the Law. People who regard contrition as the *reason* sins are forgiven are basically turning the Law into a message of grace, and the Gospel into Law. This corrupts the entire Christian religion.

2. Contrition is not even a good work. For contrition that comes before faith is nothing but suffering on the part of human beings. It consists of anguish, pain, torment, and a feeling of being crushed—all of which God has caused in human beings with the hammer of the Law.

Contrition is not an anguish that a person has produced in himself, for he would gladly be rid of it, yet cannot, because God has come down on him with the Law, and that person sees no way to escape from this ordeal.

If someone were to sit down, meditate, and try to generate contrition in himself, he would never be able to reach the goal. You cannot generate contrition. Those who think they can are miserable hypocrites. They want to persuade themselves that they are contrite, but that is not so. God produces genuine repentance only when the Law is preached in all sternness and when human beings do not willfully resist its influence.

False teaching

It is not likely that someone who calls himself a Lutheran preacher will ever openly admit that contrition leads to forgiveness of sins. Only Papists will say that, but never a Protestant preacher who has some concept of pure doctrine. Still, it sometimes does happen that preachers who claim to be true Lutherans mingle Law and Gospel in the way they describe contrition. There are two ways they could speak of contrition as if it caused the forgiveness of sins: either by saying too little or by saying too much about contrition.

Many apprentice preachers are afraid they might lead people to despair. They *do* preach that contrition must come before faith—which is quite correct—but they fear that unless they add some saving clause to that

---

4   A more literal, though more awkward, translation from the German reads: "Contrition is not, to some extent, necessary for the forgiveness of sin; indeed, contrition is not necessary at all for such forgiveness." Walther himself struggles at times with the language. Contrition has to happen because the Law must condemn before the Gospel can offer forgiveness. Yet contrition never merits forgiveness. That is hard to express in only a few words.

statement, someone in their congregation may despair. For that reason they qualify their statement by saying, "Even though you do not feel much pain, as long as you just *wish* you were contrite, God will receive you."

Softening contrition in this way actually makes the claim that contrition is the true cause for the forgiveness of sins. This is false comfort. What makes God happy is not that I might wish to be contrite. Rather, what makes Him happy is when the Gospel is being preached to me and my contrition would prepare me to believe that I am a poor, lost sinner.

The preacher ought to say this: "Look! When you have come to the point that you are hungering and thirsting for the grace of God, you have all the contrition you need. God does not require contrition as the way to atone for your sins, but only for the sake that you may be awakened from your security and ask, 'What must I do to be saved?' "

Accordingly, Luther says that, when he had grasped for the first time the meaning of the word *repentance*,[5] no word seemed sweeter to him. It did not mean that he had to do penance for his sins, but simply that he had to be alarmed on account of his sins, desiring the mercy of God. The word *repentance* was the true Gospel to him. From that moment on, he finally understood that God had brought him to the point of acknowledging that he was a poor and lost sinner, that he needed Jesus. Now Luther could go to God with the assurance that He would receive him as Luther was—with all his sins and anguish and misery.

A person should not ask whether his contrition is enough to be received by Jesus. Just the fact that he is worried whether he will be admitted shows that he may come to Jesus. At the same time, if someone has the desire to come to Jesus, he has true contrition even if he does not feel it. It is just as when a person begins to believe. I know from personal experience that a person can have contrition without being aware of it:

For years I had been genuinely contrite and on the edge of despair because I did not have the sweet feeling of a broken heart over the fact that I had seriously offended my Father in heaven. Yet I had an intense feeling that I was a lost sinner. At that point I turned to a person who was more experienced in these matters than I was, and in a few minutes he opened my eyes.[6]

The statement that God is satisfied when a person merely desires contrition is evidence of mingling Law and Gospel, for a statement such as that describes contrition as a merit on account of which God is gracious to sinners

---

5   Latin: *poenitentia*.

6   Walther refers to Martin Stephan, again separating the positive aspects of his career from the negative. When Walther wants to agree or disagree only in part with someone, he tends not to mention the individual's name in order to stress and isolate the point of agreement or disagreement.

and forgives them their sins. That is the same mistake as when a pastor is completely satisfied with only a slight sign of contrition in his parishioners. For example, the conscience of wicked people who have lived in sin and shame for a long time can suddenly awaken and say, "You have perjured yourself. Woe to you!" Fear and terror grasp them. Or their conscience may rebuke them: "You have blood on your hands! You are a murderer!" However, these people do not become alarmed by thinking: "I am a poor sinner." No, only that particular deed frightens them. With the exception of that one sin, they imagine that they are good at heart.

I once witnessed a thing like this in Germany. A wicked man had committed perjury.[7] He would not admit it, but he started to become agitated every time someone brought it up. Once I visited him, and he actually had to grab hold of the table to stop from shaking. Yet he could not be brought to confess his sin. The result was that I could not preach the Gospel to him.

There are many wicked people like this—people who have already heard their death sentence. "I admit that I did this, Pastor. I know it was wrong. But believe me, Pastor, I am a good person at heart. True, I did mess up in this area. It just happened—I could not help it." If a pastor is satisfied with a partial contrition of this sort, he is actually treating contrition as a merit. In reality, this is nothing else than an ulcer bursting open. If you see that there is still pus in the wound, you cannot preach the Gospel. When a healing salve is applied to an open wound that still contains pus, the infection will eat deeper into the person, and the wound will not heal.[8]

On the other hand, there are also pastors who demand too much when they tell their poor listeners: "You need to repent, as Scripture testifies on every page. Your own common sense will tell you that God cannot forgive sins that *you* do not really care about yourself. You simply must repent. So let me tell you what this repentance must look like."

Ps. 38:6–8; 6:6–8

Then they start reading passages such as Psalm 38:6–8: "I am utterly bowed down and prostrate; all the day I go about mourning. For my sides are filled with burning, and there is no soundness in my flesh. I am feeble and crushed; I groan because of the tumult of my heart." Or Psalm 6:6–8: "I am weary with my moaning; every night I flood my bed with tears; I drench my couch with my weeping. My eye wastes away because of grief; it grows weak because of all my foes. Depart from me, all you workers of evil, for the LORD has heard the sound of my weeping."[9]

---

7   Similar to a doctor discussing a medical case outside the caregiver-patient relationship, Walther preserves the anonymity of his parishioners, both present and past. Otherwise, he would bear false witness.

8   The Dau text adds: "The healing balm in spiritual therapy is the Gospel."

9   In Luther's German Bible cited by Walther, the references are to Psalm 38:7–9 and 6:7–8. Luther's enumerations followed the Vulgate.

Legalistic pastors will ask: "Have you said such things about yourself too? Have you ever walked around, bowed down and prostrate, mourning for a whole day? Has there ever been a time when your sides were filled with burning? Can you, too, say, During that time there was no soundness in my flesh? Did you groan because of the tumult of your heart? Did you flood your couch with weeping? Did you look like you had aged fourteen years in fourteen days? Well, if you have never experienced such things, then you have not really experienced repentance. That is the only true repentance."

Needless to say, this approach is completely wrong. True, these texts do describe David's repentance. But show me a text that prescribes the same **degree** of contrition for everyone. Such a Bible passage does not exist. Shortly after they were cut to the heart on the first Pentecost, the people were moved to cry, "What shall we do?" Peter immediately preached the mercy of God to them. | Acts 2:37

David's own case serves as an illustration. He had been living in a state of impenitence for an entire year when Nathan pointed out his awful sin to him. With a contrite heart David then cried, "I have sinned against the LORD." That was all. Immediately the prophet Nathan noticed that David was crushed. Accordingly, he said to him, "The LORD also has put away your sin." | 2 Sam. 12:13

This is the same thing that we read about the jailer at Philippi. Only a few minutes earlier, he had been so terribly upset that he was about to take his own life. When he fell down before the apostles and cried, "Sirs, what must I do to be saved?" they did not tell him that he needed to generate serious repentance in himself. They did not remind him of the penitential acts of David. Rather, they told him, "Believe in the Lord Jesus, and you will be saved, you and your household." The apostles saw plainly that the man was crushed and was craving mercy—and they considered that to be enough. When a person has been made to hunger and thirst for mercy, repentance has done its full work on him. | Acts 16:30–31

The Pietists claim that faith must be preceded by a long period of penitence. In fact, they warn people not to believe too soon, telling them that they must allow the Holy Spirit to work them over thoroughly. They say a person cannot be converted in two weeks' time. Sometimes it might even take many months and years—during which [time] God prepares them for conversion.

That is simply awful doctrine. These preachers do not consider what a tremendous responsibility they assume when they warn a person against believing too soon. What will become of such people if they die before they are ready to believe?

I know the awful effect of this teaching from personal experience. A pietistic theology student had once instructed me the way I just described to you. I did everything to become truly penitent—and finally fell into despair. When I came to him to tell him about my condition, he said, "*Now* is the time for you to believe." But I did not take his advice. I thought he was deceiving me because his last instruction was out of line with what he had described to me previously. Accordingly, I said to him, "If you knew the state I am in, you would not comfort me. What I want is rules for my further conduct." He gave me those rules too. But it was no use.

If we assume, in all fairness, that a person has been pried loose from his self-righteousness and wants to be saved by grace alone, we should for God's sake confidently preach the Gospel to him. It is never too soon. A person cannot possibly come to Jesus too soon. The trouble is that people frequently do not really go to Jesus. They call themselves poor sinners but do not mean it. They want to present to God some merit of their own. It is complete hypocrisy when they say that they are going to Jesus, for as a matter of fact they do not come to Him as poor beggars with all their sins.

If you have received the grace to be "beaten and bloodied" by God; if you can no longer find consolation in yourself; if everything has become dark and depressing—that is when you cry out: "Where can I find consolation?" This would be a true state of contrition. It would be wrong to warn you against going to Jesus. In this case you would need to have the Gospel preached to you. It would be horrible doctrine to say those things to you.[10] This is when they should tell you that you need to boldly come to Jesus and not think that you are coming too soon. If such a person were to die after I had told him that he cannot yet come to Jesus, God would demand from me the soul of that sinner.

Kinds of repentance   A basic reason many in these situations mingle Law and Gospel is that they fail to distinguish the *daily* repentance of Christians from the repentance that *comes before faith*. Daily repentance is described in Psalm 51. David calls it a sacrifice that he brings before God and that pleases Him. This is not the kind of repentance that comes before faith but that *follows* it.

The vast majority of sincere Christians whose faith is based on pure doctrine repent *after* becoming Christians—not before. That is because they had good preachers who led them to Christ directly—and not in a roundabout way. And they still go to those same churches. And, even though they are now Christians, their former self-righteousness can still crop up, even though they have been crushed many times. God must strike these poor Christians again and again to keep them humble. David's example may serve to illustrate this point. He had come to faith in a moment, but what misery did he have to pass through later! A prophet had spoken the word of the Lord to him, but to his dying day his heart was burdened with anguish, distress, and misery. God

---

10   Here Walther means the preaching of the Law.

had ceased to prosper his undertakings. David met with one misfortune after another until God released him through death.

But all that time David had repentance alongside faith. That is indeed a sacrifice with which God is pleased. Contrition of this kind is not merely the result of the Law, produced by the Law alone. Rather, it is at the same time an operation of the Gospel. Love for God enters a person's heart through the Gospel. When repentance follows from love for God, it is indeed a truly sweet sorrow, acceptable to God. It pleases God, for we cannot offer Him greater honor than by throwing ourselves in the dust before Him, confessing: "You are righteous, O Lord, but I am a poor sinner. Have mercy on me for the sake of Jesus Christ."

Let me submit a testimony from the **Smalcald Articles**, Part III, Article III.[11] It is a precious passage, one of the gems in our Confessions. For the true doctrine of contrition is not found in any of the sects, but only in our Lutheran Church, and it is laid down in this passage. As you know, Luther wrote the Smalcald Articles himself. We should bless him even in his grave for having handed down to us this heritage. He says:

> The New Testament keeps and urges this office ‹of the Law›, as St. Paul does when he says, "The wrath of God is revealed from heaven against all ungodliness and unrighteousness of men" (Romans 1:18). Also, "The whole world may be accountable to God. . . . No human being will be justified in His sight" (Romans 3:19–20). And, Christ says, the Holy Spirit will convict the world of sin (John 16:8).
>
> SA III III 1–2
>
> This is God's thunderbolt. By the Law He strikes down both obvious sinners and false saints. He declares no one to be in the right, but drives them all together to terror and despair. This is the hammer. As Jeremiah says, "Is not My word like . . . a hammer that breaks the rock in pieces?" (23:29). This is not active contrition[12] or manufactured repentance. It is passive contrition,[13] true sorrow of heart, suffering and sensation of death.

Manufactured contrition is nothing more than a mere sham.

> This is what true repentance means. Here, a person needs to hear something like this, "You are all of no account, whether you are obvious sinners or saints ‹in your own opinions›. You have to become different from what you are now. You have to act differently than you
>
> SA III III 3–15

---

11 The following lengthy quotation is taken from *Concordia*, 272–74. See also Müller, 312–14; *Triglot Concordia*, 479–88.

12 Latin: *activa contritio.*

13 Latin: *passiva contritio.*

are now acting, however great, wise, powerful, and holy you try to be. Here no one is godly."

But to this office ‹of the Law›, the New Testament immediately adds the consoling promise of grace through the Gospel. This must be believed. As Christ declares, "Repent and believe in the gospel" (Mark 1:15). That is, become different, act differently, and believe My promise. John the Baptist (preceding Christ) is called a preacher of repentance, but this is for the forgiveness of sins. That is, John was to accuse all and convict them of being sinners. This is so they can know what they are before God and acknowledge that they are lost. So they can be prepared for the Lord[14] to receive grace and to expect and accept from Him the forgiveness of sins. This is what Christ Himself says, "Repentance and forgiveness of sins should be proclaimed in [My] name to all nations" (Luke 24:47).

Whenever the Law alone exercises its office, without the Gospel being added, there is nothing but death and hell, and one must despair, as Saul and Judas did.[15] St. Paul says, through sin the Law kills.[16] On the other hand, the Gospel brings consolation and forgiveness. It does so not just in one way, but through the Word and the Sacraments and the like, as we will discuss later. As Psalm 130:7 says against the dreadful captivity of sin, "with the LORD is . . . plentiful redemption."

However, we now have to contrast the false repentance of the sophists with true repentance, in order that both may be understood better.

It was impossible for them to teach correctly about repentance, since they did not know what sin really is. As has been shown above, they do not believe correctly about original sin. Rather, they say that the natural powers of human beings have remained unimpaired and uncorrupted. They believe that reason can teach correctly, so that the will can do what is right, and God certainly bestows His grace when a person does as much as he can, according to his free will.

According to that dogma, they need to do penance only for actual sins. Those would include only the evil thoughts that a person yields to. Or evil words and deeds that free will could easily have prevented. (According to these people, wicked emotions, lust, and improper attitudes[17] are not sins.)

---

14   See Mark 1:3.

15   See 1 Samuel 31; Matthew 27:5.

16   See Romans 7:10.

17   A more literal translation of *Reizungen* is "arousing temptations."

They divide repentance into three parts: contrition, confession, and satisfaction. They add this consolation and promise: If a person truly repents, confesses, and renders satisfaction, he merits forgiveness. He has paid for his sins before God. So even in repentance, they taught people to put confidence in their own works. This is where the expression comes from that was used in the pulpit when Public Absolution was announced to the people: "Prolong, O God, my life, until I can make satisfaction for my sins and amend my life."

There was here no mention of Christ and faith. People hoped to overcome and blot out sins before God by their own works. With this intention, we became priests and monks, so we could protect ourselves against sin.

As for contrition, this is how it was done. No one could remember all his sins (especially those committed over an entire year), so they inserted this provision: If an unknown sin is remembered later, it too must be repented of and confessed, and so on.

Some went to Communion only once a year. They found out that they could not say, "I still know every sin that I did on every day of the year." They had to do it, but they could not do it. The priest would tell them, "Okay, whenever the leftover sins come to mind, you will have to confess them in order for Absolution to be of help to you."

Luther continues: "Until then, the person was commended to God's grace."[18] This meant (for [the Papists]) that Absolution was not yet in effect. It still had to be added. For instance, "commended to the grace of God" meant: "If the person were to die the next day, I could not say whether that person would go to hell or into purgatory." However, it was presumed that he was not going to hell. **SA III III 15**

Furthermore, since no one could know how great the contrition ought to be in order to be enough before God, they gave this consolation: He who could not have contrition at least ought to have "attrition." I call that half a contrition, or the beginning of contrition. The fact is, they themselves do not understand either of these terms, anymore than I do. But such attrition was counted as contrition when a person went to Confession.[19] **SA III III 16**

What Luther means to say is this: What they meant by attrition I do not know; but for the Papists it was a sufficient contrition.

---

18   *Concordia*, 273.
19   *Concordia*, 273.

SA III III 17   Luther writes: "If anyone said that he could not have contrition or lament his sins (as might be the case with making love with prostitutes[20] or the desire for revenge, etc.), they asked whether he wished or desired to have contrition."[21] Ask a Roman Catholic priest! If he is sincere, he will admit that this practice still prevails: "We proclaim absolution, even when there is only attrition." The true Catholics tell it the way it is. One says, "I would really like to have contrition, but I cannot. Whenever my whoring about comes to mind, I just want to keep on doing it.[22] Whenever I think about my enemy, I still want to hurt him."

SA III III 17   Again Luther: "When one would reply 'yes'—for who, save the devil himself, would say 'no'?—they accepted this as contrition. They forgave him his sins on account of this good work of his. Here they cited the example of St. Bernard and others."[23] Without a doubt, under the papacy there exists a most horrible religion!

SA III III 18   Luther comments: "Here we see how blind reason gropes around in matters belonging to God.[24] According to its own imagination, reason seeks consolation in its own works and cannot remember Christ and faith."[25] They talk about these excellent things like a blind man talking about colors. Just read their confession in the decrees of the Council of Trent! They discuss all kinds of things that are so obvious from Scripture. They make it clear that they do not have a clue about what they are discussing.

SA III III 18   Viewed in the light, this contrition is a manufactured and fictitious thought. It comes from our own powers, without faith and without the knowledge of Christ. When he reflected on his own lust and desire for revenge, the poor sinner might have laughed rather than wept— unless he had either been truly struck by the lightning of the Law[26] or had been tormented by the devil with a sorrowful spirit.[27] Otherwise, this kind of contrition was certainly mere hypocrisy and did not put to death the lust for sins. They had to be contrite, but if they were free, they would rather have kept on sinning.[28]

When he wrote these words, Luther undoubtedly remembered his own life among the Papists. When engaged in his penitential exercises, he certainly

---

20   German: *Hurenliebe*.
21   *Concordia*, 273.
22   German: *Wenn ich an meiner Hurerei denke, so möchte ich die gerne noch länger betreiben*.
23   *Concordia*, 273–74.
24   See 1 Corinthians 2:14.
25   *Concordia*, 274.
26   See Psalm 77:18.
27   See 1 Samuel 16:14.
28   *Concordia*, 274.

did not feel like laughing. He took these words so seriously and was filled with dread to such an extent that he sometimes fainted in complete terror during these penances. As you know, one time he locked himself in his cell for several days in order to do penance. When his fellow monks forced the door open, they found him unconscious, so great was the anguish of his soul. The devil's melancholy soul had gripped [Luther], and nothing was able to console him. So they awakened him with music. This is one reason Luther regarded music so highly: he had felt the powerful impact that music has on the human mind.

About 120 years ago, my friends, Rationalism became dominant in the so-called Protestant Church of Germany. This was a time of the deepest disgrace and humiliation through which the nation had ever passed. It was also a period of complete abandonment of the Gospel. The shallowest minds, the most brainless men, without any considerable learning, were regarded as great lights and far ahead of their time.

Twenty-fourth Evening Lecture: April 10, 1885

For theologians to achieve some fame in that period, all they needed was enough boldness—or, rather, the audacity—to declare the mysterious doctrines of Christianity to be errors of the former Dark Ages, a period without "enlightenment." They claimed that the main point of the Christian religion is the teachings of God, virtue, and immortality.

What a horrible era that was! Things became so bad that, in order to counteract the claim that they had now become unnecessary in the real world, Rationalist preachers meant to prove their usefulness by preaching from their pulpits on topics such as "Intelligent Agriculture," "How to Make Potato Growing Profitable," "Why It Is Necessary to Plant Trees," "The Importance of Good Health," etc. The various Rationalist books with sermons on such topics were celebrated with great fanfare. These books are enough evidence that my claims are true and that I am not slandering the Rationalists of that era.

Some Rationalists were ashamed of these typical products of the school of Rationalism. As such, a book was published in 1772 that bore the title *Of the Usefulness of the Ministry, Written for the Consolation of My Colleagues*. The author was Joachim Spalding, a writer of some fame in his day. In his book he states that topics such as the ones I just mentioned are indeed not proper topics for sermons. He submits his own opinion, namely, that if sermons are to be useful, the preacher must never speak of the doctrines of faith *first*, because these issues only confuse people's minds. Rather, he must exclusively present "real world" ethical lessons.

So it is not surprising, then, that in those days many souls had hearts that were upset by the question: "What must I do to be saved?" They left our devastated Church or sought refuge with the sect of the Moravians or even turned to the demonic Church of Rome.[29]

Praise and thanks be to God that those awful times are past—let us hope forever! After the successful ending of the so-called Wars of Liberation[30] from that monster Napoleon I, something like the breath of a new spiritual spring blew through Germany.[31] Countless people have experienced a truly marvelous awakening from their deadly sleep in Rationalist unbelief. Among these there are a fair number of ministers.

Since then, many preachers have begun to discard the dry, comfortless, powerless pagan Rationalist morality; rather, they preach Christ and faith in Him as the only way to salvation and to true peace of heart in the present life. Oh, may it be that this has come to pass for good and for all, not just as a temporary fad!

However, it is undeniable that even well-intentioned preachers are still mingling Law and Gospel and thus causing horrible injury to their listeners. May God, by His grace, preserve you from this danger when you go to your future congregations, with which you will one day appear before the throne of God. You will have to give an account of whether you were a faithful watchman over the souls entrusted to you and [whether you] shared with them the true Bread of Life—or whether you gave them unwholesome, harmful food, which caused their souls to fall ill or even to die. May the study of our thirteenth thesis help in preparing you for your future work!

---

29   Walther consistently refers to Moravians as *Herrnhuter* because of their association with Zinzendorf. See the map of Saxony, xlix. In addition, two handpicked former colleagues on the faculty of Concordia College, Carl A. Baumstark and F. R. Eduard Preuss, converted to Roman Catholicism. As William Dallmann recalls in *My Life* (St. Louis: Concordia, 1945), Walther reacted on a very personal level to what he saw as betrayal. That may be showing here in the reference to the "demonic Church of Rome."

30   This is the War of the Sixth Coalition (1813–14) that followed the disastrous Russian campaign of Napoleon in 1812. Napoleon I controlled France as first consul (1799–1804) and as emperor (1804–14). The era between the Congress of Vienna in 1815 and the start of the Great War (1914) marked the rise of Prussia, the resurgence of German nationalism, and the establishment of modern German identity.

31   This refers to the confessional awakening that began in 1817 with Claus Harms.

THESIS XIII

You are not rightly distinguishing Law and Gospel in the Word of God if you explain faith by demanding that people are able to make themselves believe or at least can collaborate toward that end. Rather, preach faith into people's hearts by laying the Gospel promises before them.

EDITOR'S NOTE: In Theses XIII and XIV, Walther takes aim at his opponents in the Election Controversy, also called the Predestinarian Controversy. In these two theses, Walther offers some of his strongest criticism of Melanchthon. In other theses, Walther refers positively to Melanchthon and values the Apology of the Augsburg Confession that Melanchthon wrote. Here, however, in order to highlight the problems among those who followed various points of Melanchthon's thought, Walther looks to the Formula of Concord as the "heart and soul"[1] of the Lutheran Confessions in order to help read and apply the Bible.

In this thesis, we are not claiming that it is wrong for a pastor to demand—even passionately—that his listeners have faith. That was what all the prophets demanded, all the apostles, and, yes, even the Lord Jesus Christ Himself.

Faith as gift

When we demand faith, we do not lay down a demand of the Law. Rather, we extend the sweetest invitation, saying to our listeners, "Come, for everything is now ready." If I invite a half-starved person to sit down to a well-set table and to help himself to anything he likes, I do not expect him to tell me that he will take no orders from me. In the same way, the demand to believe is to be understood not as an order of the Law, but as an invitation of the Gospel.

Luke 14:17

No, the error we are addressing is that man can produce faith in himself. Such a demand would be an order of the Law and would turn faith into a human work. Clearly, that would be mingling Law and Gospel. A preacher must be able to preach a sermon on faith without ever using the word *faith*. It is not important to use the literal word *faith*. Rather, the preacher needs to frame his address in a way that he would awaken in every poor sinner the

---

1   Walther wrote a book for the 1877 300th anniversary of the Formula of Concord that refers to it as the "heart and soul" of the Book of Concord: *Concordienformel: Kern und Stern* (St. Louis: M. C. Barthel, 1877). Franz Pieper followed that with a book on the Augsburg Confession in 1880 for its 350th anniversary. The Missouri Synod also printed a 300th anniversary edition of the 1580 German Book of Concord.

desire to lay the burden of his sins at the feet of the Lord Jesus Christ and say to Him, "You are mine, and I am Yours."

Here is where Luther reveals his true greatness. He rarely appeals to his listeners: "Believe, really believe!" Rather, he preaches the work of Christ, salvation by grace, and the riches of God's mercy in Jesus Christ. Everyone gets the idea: "All I have to do is to receive; all I need to do is rest in the lap of divine grace." That is the great art that you must seek to learn, so each listener will think: "If that is true, then I am a blessed person. All my anguish and unrest has been unnecessary. I am completely redeemed. I am reconciled with God. I am among the saved, among those on whom God has made His gracious face to shine." The moment a person thinks these thoughts, he attains faith.

Suppose you were describing the Lord Jesus to a group of American Indians, telling them that He is the Son of God who came down from heaven to redeem humankind from its sins by taking the wrath of God upon Himself. He overcame death, devil, and hell in their place and has opened heaven to all people, and that every person can now be saved by merely accepting what our Lord Jesus Christ has brought to us. And suppose that the deadly bullet of a hostile Indian lying in ambush suddenly struck you down. It is possible that—even though you lie there dying—you might leave behind a small congregation of Indians, though you may not even once have pronounced the word *faith* to them. For everyone in that audience who did not spitefully and willfully resist divine grace would have to think: "I, too, am redeemed."[2]

On the other hand, you could spend a lot of time telling people: "Indeed, one must truly believe in order to be saved." Your listeners might get the impression that they are required to do something. They will begin to worry whether they are able to do it and, if they have tried to do it, whether they have done exactly what is required of them. Thus you may have preached a great deal about faith without really delivering a true sermon on faith. Anyone who understands "Here I need merely to receive" has faith. Indeed, to be saved by faith means: "Please, just take it, then you will be saved."

I do not mean to say that you must not preach about faith. In this era, in particular, we lack a proper understanding of this matter. The best preachers imagine they have accomplished a great deal when they have beat their listeners over the head with the saying "Faith alone saves." But by their preaching they merely make their listeners sigh: "Oh, if only I had faith! Faith must be something very difficult to get, for I have not yet obtained it."

These unfortunate listeners would go home from church with a heavy heart. The word *faith* would still be ringing in their ears, but it would give them no comfort. Even Luther complained that many in his day were preaching about faith without showing their listeners what faith really is and how to

---

2   Walther lived in the era of the "Wild West," with its social classes and expectations.

attain it. Such a preacher may struggle for years, yet his congregation remains spiritually dead. No wonder so many people talk as if they are uncertain about their salvation. You can tell that they stagger and totter back and forth with doubt. In fact, they actually become terrified and distressed when they are told that they are at death's door. Whose fault is it? The preacher's—because he preached about faith in the wrong way.

To say that faith is required for salvation is not to say that a person can produce faith himself. Scripture requires everything of a person. Every commandment is a demand, crying: "Do this and you will live." Scripture demands that we "purify [our] hearts." We are told: "Awake, O sleeper, and arise from the dead, and Christ will shine on you." But just because these demands are given does not prove that a person can meet them. There is an old trustworthy saying: "Based on an obligation, one cannot be certain of its fulfillment."[3]

Gen. 42:18; James 4:8; Eph. 5:14

When a creditor demands payment, this does not prove that the debtor can pay. In everyday life, a creditor who knows that his debtor is insolvent may demand payment of a debt merely because he has observed that the debtor is a shiftless person and, moreover, is full of vanity and conceit. The creditor's point in making the demand might be simply to get the debtor to quit his proud behavior and to humble himself.

God deals with people the same way. By serving notice on me that I have to obey all His Commandments, God leads me to realize that I cannot meet my obligations—no matter how hard I try. Once He has humbled me, He approaches me with His Gospel. Modern preaching lacks the concept that the natural heart must be humbled. When a person says to a preacher, "I simply cannot believe," and the preacher tells him, "Oh yes, you can. All you need is the earnest desire to believe. You can get rid of your sins. All you have to do is to struggle against them," that is a horrible way to preach.

Alas, the synergists have poisoned the Gospel, denied the Lord Christ, and made His grace worthless. As you know, Melanchthon is the father of

---

3   Latin: *A debito ad posse non valet consequentia*. This emerged from Luther's rebuttal of Erasmus in *Bondage of the Will* (AE 33). It also appears in Walther's article, "Theologische Axiome," *Lehre und Wehre* 7 (1861): 98. Erasmus argued in the so-called *Diatribe* (on the freedom of the will) that if God issues a command, the obligation of that command assumes that people have the ability to fulfill it. Erasmus maintained that if people cannot fulfill God's commands, then God would not command them. This argument looks correct from the standpoint of a book on classical logic, yet this argument falls apart in light of Romans 3:23: "All have sinned." Therefore, Lutherans developed the saying "Based on an obligation [or a command], one may not conclude its fulfillment." Walther knew, however, that Melanchthon and Johann Pfeffinger from the sixteenth century, Johann Latermann from the seventeenth century, and Christoph Luthardt from the nineteenth century all used forms of the argument made by Erasmus. Walther and the Missouri Synod opposed these arguments as a part of the Election Controversy. Walther's rebuttal also speaks against modern arguments for decision theology.

synergism.[4] Let me submit a few statements in which Melanchthon reveals his synergism. It is all the more important for today's theologians that these statements of Melanchthon have betrayed his synergism. Some who are familiar with them declare that these very statements are what is good about Melanchthon's teaching. Orthodox Lutherans, however, would not agree.

Leonhard Hutter, the well-known orthodox theologian, wrote a book entitled *Concordia Concors*.[5] It is a history of the Formula of Concord, showing what prompted the writing of each article of this confessional document. From it we see, among other things, that Melanchthon's teaching was the reason Article II was inserted into the Formula of Concord. As evidence, Hutter cites incorrect statements in Melanchthon's writings. I am presenting these statements in order to demonstrate that Missourians are not the only ones who rigorously detect synergism wherever it may lurk. This is what **Melanchthon** taught:

1. "There is and must be a cause in human beings why some people are predestined to salvation while others are cast away and damned."[6]

Hutter declares this statement to be synergistic. Compare this to the publications of our opponents in the Election Controversy, and you will find that they are saying the same thing as Melanchthon, thereby proving that they are coarse synergists—as Melanchthon was.

The problem with Melanchthon's statement is not his declaration of a human cause of blame and damnation, but [his declaration] that a cause in people must also exist that predestines them to *salvation*. No such cause exists in any person. All the saints, full of the deepest heartfelt thanks, will proclaim eternally: "I have done nothing to be here in heaven! In me there was no cause of salvation. In me there was enough reason to be in hell right now, but nothing, not the slightest cause, for me to be in heaven."

Again, Melanchthon says:

2. "Since the promises of grace are universal and there cannot be contradictory wills in God, there must necessarily be some different cause in us that accounts for the salvation of some and the damnation of others. That is, there must be in each person a different kind of action."

The different kind of action is not the reason anyone would find himself in heaven. True, grace *is* universal. But the reason some are condemned is

---

4   That is, synergism within the Lutheran Church.

5   In English, *Harmonious Concord: About the Origin and Progress of the Formula of Concord of the Churches of the Augsburg Confession.* Original: *Concordia Concors* (Witebergae: C. Berger, 1614).

6   Hutter's summaries of Melanchthon's teaching correspond with the later editions of Melanchthon's *Loci Communes*. The Latin text is in *Corpus Reformatorum* XXI. Several English translations are available. See also the entries on Melanchthon's *Loci* in the section Law and Gospel timeline, pages lx–lxi.

because they willfully resist grace. Here reason steps onto the stage with the claim that, accordingly, there must be a deciding factor in the other group because of which they are saved—and this must be because they did not resist grace.

But at this point we are confronted with an impenetrable mystery, and anyone who is unwilling to acknowledge this mystery is abandoning the Christian religion. Christianity's central teaching is that God has revealed to humankind a way of salvation that human reason could not have discovered or is not able to understand: "Oh, the depth of the riches and wisdom and knowledge of God! How unsearchable are His judgments and how inscrutable His ways! 'For who has known the mind of the Lord, or who has been His counselor?' 'Or who has given a gift to Him that He might be repaid?' For from Him and through Him and to Him are all things. To Him be glory forever. Amen." Rom. 11:33–36

Again, Melanchthon says:

3. "The cause lies in us, as to why some give their assent to the promises of grace, while others do not."

This is coarse synergism, for Melanchthon refers to a real primary cause.[7] How can his declaration stand over against the truth that we are all by nature dead in sins and that we become new creatures when we are regenerated?[8]

Finally, Melanchthon states:

4. "There are three reasons for a person's conversion: the Word of God; the Holy Spirit, whom the Father and the Son send to awaken our heart; and the human will, which gives assent to the Word of God and does not resist."

A person's faith comes under the same ruling as his contrition. I might sit in a corner and indulge in sad thoughts in order to coax contrition out of myself, but I will fail. If I were sincere, I would have to admit my inability. While I imagine that my heart has been softened and I am repenting of my sin, suddenly—deep down inside—I crave the very sin of which I have just "repented." If genuine contrition is to be produced in me, the thunder of the Law must roll over my head and the lightning bolts of Sinai must strike my heart. The same is true regarding faith—I cannot produce it myself.

Let me submit one more citation, which Hutter has not quoted but which is related to our topic. It is taken from **Melanchthon's** *Loci* from 1552.[9] On

---

7   The Dau edition inserts: "to what is termed a causating or impelling cause (*causa causans*)." Walther's phrase, *bewirkende Ursache*, is usually translated as "primary cause" for a cause that is directly responsible for an act, as opposed to a "secondary cause" or "attendant cause" that is not directly responsible.

8   See, for example, Ephesians 2:1–7.

9   See also the Law and Gospel timeline, page lxii.

page 101, Melanchthon writes: "You say you are unable to obey the voice of the Gospel, to listen to the Son of God, and to accept Him as your Mediator?" Melanchthon responds: "Of course you can!"[10] What a horrible answer this is!

When parishioners come to you complaining that they cannot believe, tell them you are not surprised by their statement, for *no one* can. It would be a miracle if they could. Teach them to do nothing but listen to the Word of God, and God will give them faith. Furthermore, warn them not to resist divine grace and not to snuff out the sparks beginning to glow in their heart. To say these things is fine, but it does not give them the strength they need. When the Gospel enters their heart like the blessed water of life from heaven—*that* is what kindles their faith.

At first this faith is weak—like a newborn babe, who sees, hears, tastes, moves, has a certain amount of strength, and can eat and drink. Not until this has taken place should you urge the person to cooperate with divine grace. By no means do we reject cooperation on the part of a person *after* his regeneration. Rather, we urge it upon them, lest they die again and become subject to the danger of being lost forever.

Melanchthon continues: "Just raise yourself up by means of the Gospel, ask God to help you and to let the Holy Spirit bring about this comfort in you. You must understand that the grace of God proposes to convert us in this manner, namely, when we, through the awakened promise, wrestle with ourselves, call on Him, and fight against our unbelief and other evil tendencies." Again, he says, "Free will in man is the ability to prepare oneself for grace."[11] This is the notorious statement that is usually cited to prove that Melanchthon was a genuine synergist. The previous horrible statements prove indeed that he was.

Finally, Melanchthon says, "What I mean is this: man hears the promise, makes an attempt to give his assent to it, and puts aside sins against his conscience." No way. First I must be converted, and then, only then, can I put aside sins against my conscience.

---

10 Walther starts reading on page 101 of his edition of Melanchthon's *Loci Communes*, but he gives no further indication. It is likely that the subsequent quotes from Melanchthon are on page 101 and following.

11 Latin: *facultas se applicandi ad gratiam.*

The tasks of a pastor of Jesus Christ are many, difficult, and demanding. The most difficult and demanding task of all—beyond question—is the task of proclaiming the pure doctrine of the Gospel of Christ and at the same time exposing, refuting, and rejecting teachings that are contrary to the Gospel. A pastor who does this will discover by experience the truth of the old saying: "Telling the truth makes enemies."[12]

If in his day faithful Athanasius had been content to proclaim his doctrine that Jesus Christ is true God, begotten of the Father in eternity, and also true man, born of the Virgin Mary, but if he had at the same time *not* vigorously attacked Arius and the Arians, who denied this doctrine, he would undoubtedly have finished his life in honor and pleasant peace, for he was a highly gifted man.

Or, had Luther followed the example of Staupitz, quietly teaching the pure Gospel to his fellow monks, but without at the same time attacking the horrors of the papacy with great earnestness, not a finger would have been raised against him. For even before Luther's day there were monks who had come to understand the Gospel and who made no secret of their knowledge. But they did not go public in their fight against the errors of the papacy. Accordingly, they were allowed to live in peace and quiet, as long as they held to the core of the Roman Catholic Church—the pope.

Worldly people and all false Christians cannot help but attack those who teach a faith and doctrine different from theirs. These fake Christians regard those with sound doctrine as "disturbers of the peace"—peace-hating, quarrelsome, and nasty people. These unfortunate people have no idea of the blindness that surrounds them. They do not know how gladly the boldest champions of Christ wish to keep peace with all people, how much they would prefer to keep silent. These fake Christians do not know how hard it is for the bold champions to go public and become targets for the hatred, enmity, slander, scorn, and persecution of people. However, they cannot help but confess the truth and at the same time oppose error. Their conscience forces them to do this because such behavior is required of them by the Word of God.

They remember that Jesus Christ said to His dear disciples not only "You are the light of the world" but also "You are the salt of the earth," that is, not only are you to proclaim the truth, but you also need to salt the world [that is] full of sins and errors. You need to sprinkle stinging salt on the world to prevent its corruption.

Matt. 5:14; 5:13

They remember that Christ distinctly said, "Do not think that I have come to bring peace to the earth. I have not come to bring peace, but a sword." It is not as if the Lord takes pleasure in wars that remove peace. . . . It is not as if

Matt. 10:34

12   Latin: *veritas odium parit.*

He had come into the world to spawn dissensions and discord among men. What He means to say is this: "My doctrine is such that, if it is properly proclaimed—in its thesis and antithesis—peace among people cannot possibly be preserved. For as soon as My Word is proclaimed, people will split into two camps. Some will receive it with joy; others will be offended by it and will begin to hate and persecute those who receive it."

Besides, righteous preachers remember that the Church is not a kingdom that can be built up in peace. It is located within the domain of the devil, the prince of this world. Accordingly, the Church has no choice but to be at war. It is the Church Militant[13] and will remain such until the blessed end. Whenever a church appears to be not a militant church but a church at ease,[14] that is a false church. You can rely on it!

Moreover, an honest preacher knows that he is also a pastor, that is, a shepherd. Of what use, however, is a shepherd who leads the sheep to good pastures yet flees when he sees the wolf approaching? He is obligated to fight the wolf that wants to eat the sheep. That means he has to "fight" for the kingdom of God.

Finally, an honest preacher knows that he has to be a regular sower of seed. Of what use is it for him to sow good seed and then to look on while another sows the weeds of false doctrine among his wheat? Soon the weeds will outstrip the wheat and choke it.

Keep these facts stored up in your memory, my dear friends. If you wish to be a faithful servant of Christ, you cannot possibly do so without striving and fighting against false doctrines, a false gospel, and false belief. In the view of worldly people, your lot will not be particularly enviable. Even wise Sirach says, "If you come to serve the Lord, prepare your soul for temptation" (Sirach 2:1). What he means is this: It is impossible for you to escape affliction if you wish to be a faithful servant of God. Anyone who is without affliction may be ever so passionate about fulfilling the duties of his office, yet his passion is nevertheless not of the right sort. Where there is genuine passion, not only does one plant and build, but the workers will also have the sword strapped to their waist, going out to wage the wars of the Lord. Let this be your slogan:

> Here, through taunt and scorn, yonder glory's crown.
> Here I'm hoping and believing;
> There I'm having, touching, seeing—
> For the glorious crown follows taunt and scorn.[15]

---

13   Latin: *ecclesia militans*.

14   Latin: *ecclesia quiescens*.

15   This is a fairly literal translation of stanza 13 of the 1697 hymn *"Seelenbräutigam"* ("Bridegroom of My Soul") by Adam Drese. Included in the German hymnal of the Missouri Synod, this hymn text binds the Christian life explicitly to the two natures in

At the same time, let this slogan be your comfort, for, as I have said, your cause will be rejected as evil. So ignore any view that people would express in opposition to your teaching. Doing this will let your cause shine with even greater luster in heaven. On the Last Day, God will say to you, "Well done, good and faithful servant. You have been faithful over a little; I will set you over much. Enter into the joy of your master." We will be refreshed when we quit this wicked world and the association of false Christians who shamefully slander our best efforts, calling them the worst horrors. Then our Lord Jesus will say, "Well done! Good job. You did not look for ease and comfort. Rather, you focused on keeping what was entrusted to you."

Matt. 25:21

But remember that, when errors are hidden, they are all the more harmful. It is, therefore, necessary that they be exposed to the light and fought against. We are reminded of this duty by the fourteenth thesis.

Christ and makes our suffering Christ's suffering, our joy Christ's joy, and it grounds our perseverance in our Savior. Although the Drese hymn text has not appeared in English hymnals of the LCMS, Johann Sebastian Bach used the hymn's melody in several of his works. English speakers will recognize the tune because it was used for the hymn "Jesus, Lead Thou On" (see *LSB* 718). This latter hymn was composed by Christian Gregor in 1778 out of two hymns written by Count Nikolaus Ludwig von Zinzendorf, a Moravian. This hymn came into the Missouri Synod via the English Synod, later the English District, as "Jesus Still Lead On" in the *Evangelical Lutheran Hymn-Book*. The Zinzendorf/Gregor hymn had become popular among English-speaking Protestants in the nineteenth century. It also appeared in *The Lutheran Hymnal* (St. Louis: Concordia, 1941) and in subsequent LCMS hymnals.

In this print, an older Walther listens to a young seminarian read his sermon. Walther owned a number of large, long-stemmed pipes—all well used. Indeed, he often filled his office with smoke. Although he did not have a cat, as depicted here, he did have a canary. See William Dallmann, *My Life* (St. Louis: Concordia, 1945), 29. Image courtesy of Concordia Historical Institute.

Thesis XIV

You are not rightly distinguishing Law and Gospel in the Word of God if you demand that faith is a condition for justification and salvation. It would be wrong to preach that people are righteous in the sight of God and are saved not only by *their faith, but also* on account of *their faith,* for the sake of *their faith, or* in view of *their faith.*

Editor's Note: In this thesis Walther takes direct aim at the words and arguments of his opponents about the role of faith in salvation. He will show that their position remains fundamentally destructive to faith by confusing Law and Gospel. The *intuitu fidei* language, salvation "in view of faith," is the central element of disagreement.

There are quite a few people who think that as long as a pastor consistently preaches that a person is saved and made righteous in the sight of God *by faith*, this is obviously a genuine "evangelical" preacher. "What more could you ask for?" They claim everybody knows that salvation by faith is the marrow and essence of the Gospel and the entire Word of God.

Clearly define faith

If this is really the case, it is indeed right. A minister who preaches that kind of doctrine is certainly a genuine evangelical preacher. But a genuine evangelical preacher is not defined merely by saying, "A person is saved and made righteous in the sight of God by faith alone." Rather, the key point is in which context he says and uses the word *faith.*

By *faith* the preacher must mean the same thing that Scripture means when it uses that word. But here is where many preachers are wrong. When many of them say "by faith," they mean something different from what the prophets, the apostles, and our Lord and Savior understood. Not to mention the Rationalists, who used to preach that a person is indeed saved by faith. By "faith" in Jesus Christ, *they* understood only accepting the excellent moral teachings that Christ proclaimed. They held that a person becomes a true disciple of the Lord and is made righteous and saved by accepting this doctrine of virtue. Look at any Rationalist book of the radical type from that era and you will see that this was the preaching of vulgar Rationalism.

False definitions

Nor are the Papists unwilling to say that faith makes a person righteous in the sight of God and saves him. When push comes to shove, the Papists will even say that faith alone makes a person righteous and saves him. But when they say "by faith," they actually mean that it is joined with love.[1] Accordingly, they manage to say many excellent things about faith. But by "faith" they mean the exact opposite of what Scripture teaches regarding faith.

Moreover, in the postils and devotional writings of all modern theologians, you can find the doctrine that a person is made righteous in the sight of God and saved by faith. But, again, by "faith" they understand what a person gives himself, what he himself achieves and produces. Their "faith" is a product of human energy and resolution. Such teaching, however, subverts the entire Gospel.

God's Word really means nothing else than this when it says that a person is justified and saved by faith alone: A person is **not saved by his own acts**, but **solely** by the doing and dying of his Lord and Savior, Jesus Christ, the Redeemer of the whole world. Over against this teaching, these modern theologians declare: "Indeed, there exists two kinds of activity. First, there is something that God must do. His part is the most difficult, for He must accomplish the task of redeeming people. But, second, something is required of *man*. For a person cannot go to heaven just like that, without doing anything. No, a person must contribute something—something really great: he has to believe."[2]

This teaching overthrows the Gospel completely. It is a pity that many beautiful sermons of modern theologians ultimately reveal the fact that they mean something entirely different from the plain and clear teaching of Scripture that a person is saved not by what he **himself** does or achieves, but by what God does and achieves.

For instance, hear a statement from **Luthardt** in his *Compendium of Dogmatics*, [page] 202:[3]

> On the other hand, repentance and faith are **required of man as his [rendered] duty**: *metanoeîte kaì pisteúete*—**at every stage of the history of salvation**. The requirement of repentance can be met immediately by the person who is called by grace, Psalm 95:7; Hebrews 4:7ff., with **faith being a free act of obedience that man renders**.

---

1   Latin: *fides formata*.

2   This is a summary statement in which Walther appears to characterize theologians at the University of Erlangen and elsewhere who follow in the wake of Johann C. K. von Hofmann, whose heretical Christology also affected how one understands sin and repentance. See also Claude Welch, *Protestant Thought in the Nineteenth Century* (New Haven, CT: Yale University Press, 1972), 1:192–93, 218–27.

3   Christoph E. Luthardt, *Kompendium der Dogmatik*, 2d ed. (Leipzig: Dörffling & Francke, 1866), 188. Luthardt's dogmatics was revised often for more than fifty years, yet this statement was not changed in any of those revisions. The quotation used here is from the edition and pagination used by Walther and Timotheus Stiemke, a district president in the early Missouri Synod who also wrote negatively about Luthardt's position.

Note the term "[rendered] duty."[4] It refers to the fulfillment of a duty for which a person expects a reward. But faith is not such a duty. If it were, it would be a requirement that God set before me—as if God had said, "I have done My share; now you do yours. I am not asking much of you, but I do require that you repent and believe."

Now, can you consider anything to be a gift if you are required to do something for it? No. It stops being a gift when the donor specifies one condition or another that the recipient must meet. Here in America many kinds of donations are illegal. Accordingly, to make a legal donation of something quite valuable, sometimes the donor will state that he has received one dollar for it. This is done in a bill of sale by which a property worth millions of dollars is transferred. This gets around the law, but it plainly shows the essential difference between giving and selling.

In truth, believing the Gospel would be an immeasurably great and difficult task for us if God were not to accomplish it within us. But suppose it were not so exceedingly great and difficult. Even if it were an easy condition that God had proposed to us for our salvation, our salvation would not be a gift; God would not have **given us His Son**, but would merely have offered Him to us with a certain restricting condition. But that is not God's way. The apostle Paul says, "[They] are justified by His grace as a gift, through the redemption that is in Christ Jesus." We are justified gratuitously, without any contribution on our part—without even the least thing being required of us.

Accordingly, we poor sinners praise God for the place of refuge He has prepared for us, to which we can flee even when we have to come to Him as completely lost, dead broke beggars, who have not the slightest ability to offer to God something that we have achieved.

Blessed are we! We have a Gospel that proclaims: "Here is indeed a refuge for sinners!" Jesus Christ is the faithful Savior, to whom we all can flee. And we should offer Him nothing more than to say, "Here are my sins!"

Then Christ will ask me, so to speak, "Do you not have anything more?"

And I will answer, "No, all I have is my sins!"

Then He will say, "Fine, then you are the right one for Me."

As soon as someone comes up and wants to offer Him something, then that person is denying the Lord Jesus. "And there is salvation in no one else, for there is no other name under heaven given among men by which we must be saved." And that name is the dear name of Jesus. So remember: We should regard it as a horrible corruption of the Gospel to treat the command *to believe* as a condition of a person's justification and salvation.

Margin notes: Rom. 3:24 · Getting to the truth · Acts 4:12

---

4   Luthardt uses the German noun *Leistung*, which here means something one is expected to do. Walther refers to the verb *leisten*, "to render" such duty.

Suppose a beggar approaches you, asking for alms, and you say that you will give him something on one condition. He asks you what that condition is, and you tell him the condition is that he accept your gift. Would he not consider your condition a joke? He would laugh, saying, "Why, I will meet your condition most gladly—and the more you give, the happier I will be to take it!" The Gospel is horribly corrupted when you make faith a requirement.

2 Thess. 3:10   True, if a person refuses to believe, nobody can help him. But he must not say that grace was offered with a condition attached to it that he could not meet. God does not attach a condition to His grace when He offers it to a sinner and asks him to accept it. It would not be a gift if He were to attach a condition to it. In the same way, it would not be a gift if someone came up to me, wanting something, and I told him, "Sure, I will you give you something if you work in my garden." He would say, "What kind of present is that? Do you want me to work the whole day?" No, I would treat a person like that in accordance with 2 Thessalonians 3:10: "If anyone is not willing to work, let him not eat." So: "Just get to work and stop loafing."

Election Controversy   Our recent Election Controversy shows how easy it is to err in this matter. Our opponents struggle with our doctrine that God does not foresee anything in the elect that would prompt Him to elect them, but that His election is one of free grace. They are shocked because, in accordance with the Formula of Concord, we teach that there are only two causes of salvation, namely, the mercy of God and the merit of Christ. Why do they think this is so horrible?

They claim that God is partial, that He elects some and neglects others, consigning them to hell. We should reply with the old saying: "May they receive Herod's thanks for making such a conclusion."[5] They should consider that a person is justified and saved **by** faith, not **on account of** faith. But they think: "There must indeed be a difference among people, or there would be a partiality with God." Certainly, the old Lutheran theologians said that people who accuse God of being partial deserve to feel the cane.[6]

German theologians come out more boldly with their opinions, while our opponents here in America are more wary. The latter follow the old dogmaticians' formula *intuitu fidei* and say that God elected people "in view of their faith." They are trying to hide behind the old dogmaticians. But this strategy is unsuccessful because they use the formula differently than how the old dogmaticians used it.

---

5   The German idiom "To receive Herod's thanks" means to be punished or to go to hell for one's efforts. In effect, Herod is a stand-in for the devil. The Dau edition reads: "This is an inference which they draw, and it is one for which they deserve no commendation."

6   The German *stäupen* means to receive a prescribed sentence of strokes with a switch, cane, or club. Even in Walther's time, the cane was used on school-age boys who became lazy in their studies.

Our opponents plainly state that God decreed to elect certain people in view of their "conduct"[7]—or something similar. But let them turn and twist as much as they will, they are declaring that something that a person does is the cause of his salvation. If Johann Gerhard and Aegidius Hunnius rose from the dead and could see that our opponents in the current Election Controversy are quoting *them* as their authorities, they would grasp their heads in anger and explode.[8] For we can plainly show that they would have rejected and condemned the doctrine of our opponents.

Faith accurately defined

In his ***Loci Theologici***, **Johann Gerhard** writes (*Locus de evangelio*, paragraph [40]): "The promises of the Law are conditional, for they require perfect obedience and demand the complete fulfillment of this condition."[9] Leviticus 18:5: "You shall therefore keep My statutes and My judgments. If a person does them, he shall live by them." But the promises of the Gospel are gratuitous and are offered as gifts.[10] Accordingly, the Gospel is called the word of God's grace, as Romans 4:16 states: "That is why righteousness comes through faith, in order that it may be of grace."

Lev. 18:5;
Rom. 4:16 Luther

There, you see it. That is why this thesis belongs here. A person teaching [that] "faith is a condition that the Gospel stipulates" makes the promises of the Gospel conditional—like the Law—and removes the distinction between Law and Gospel. The Law promises nothing good, unless that person meets its demands perfectly, while the Gospel promises everything unconditionally as a free gift.

In short, the promises of grace demand nothing of humankind. When the Lord says, "Believe," He does not speak a demand. Rather, He extends an urgent invitation for people to apprehend and to appropriate what He is giving, without asking anything in return for it. This gift must, of course, be accepted. Needless to say, the person who does not accept it loses the gift, but not because there was a condition attached to it.

Again, **Gerhard** says (*Locus de evangelio*, paragraph 26): "Faith is not placed in opposition to grace, just as the beggar's act of accepting a gift is not placed in opposition to the free benevolence of the giver." A beggar would be insane if he said to the donor, "What? Now you want me to accept it too?" I would tell that person to hit the road. Gerhard continues:

---

7   Here Walther uses the English word "conduct" in his German lectures. He does that, as with his use of "revivals," to emphasize the position of his opponents as being American in character.

8   German: *Die Hände über den Kopf zusammenschlagen.* It is a gesture that shows either great fear or great anger and frustration. Here it means to become so angry that one grabs the top of his head with both hands in anger and then goes on a rampage. One might suggest a biblical motif: "They rip out their beards in anger."

9   All prior editions of Walther's lectures refer only to paragraph 26. According to the Latin editions of the *Loci Theologici*, Walther is citing paragraphs 40 and 26.

10 Latin: *donative.*

The word "if" is either etiological or syllogistic. That is, it means either a cause or a consequence. In the preaching of the Law, in the statement "If you do this, you will live," the word is etiological; it means the cause or reason. For obedience is the reason eternal life is given to those who keep the Law. But in evangelical promises, the word "if" is syllogistic. It means a consequence, for it relates to the mode of application[11] that God has appointed for these promises—and that is faith alone.

If faith is called a human achievement, the demand for it makes faith a condition that a human being must meet by his own effort. This is the reason Luthardt's error, as mentioned above, is so great. It poisons his entire theology.

In his *Collegium Theologicum*, book V, 140, **Adam Osiander** writes: "Faith does not justify, insofar as it is obedience in compliance with a command, for, thus viewed, it is an action, a work, and something required by Law. Rather, it justifies only **insofar as it receives** and is attached to justification like a passive instrument."[12] This quote once again shows that our thesis belongs in this series regarding the distinction between Law and Gospel. If faith is obedience, it is a work of the Law. That would make the apostle Paul altogether wrong when he declared that a person is justified without the deeds of the Law, by faith alone.[13]

However, it is not Paul who is wrong, but the modern theologians. Faith is merely a passive instrument, like a hand into which someone places a dollar. The hand is a *passive instrument*.[14] The person who receives the dollar does not withdraw his hand; beyond that he does not have to do anything. It is the *donor* who is doing the essential part by placing the gift into the recipient's hand—not the other party, who holds out his hand. Just let a beggar approach a miser and see what good holding out his hand will do. The miser might even turn his dogs loose on the beggar if he becomes too annoying.

To quote **Gerhard** once more, who writes (*Locus de justificatione*, paragraph 179): "It is one thing to be justified *on account of* faith and another to be justified *by* faith. In the former case, faith is the meritorious cause; in the latter, it is the instrumental cause." There must be a tool by which you come into the possession and enjoyment of what the other person is offering you. "We are not justified *on account of* faith as a merit, but *by* faith, which lays hold of the merit of Christ." It is not *my own* merit that saves me, but the merit of Christ.

---

11 Latin: *modus applicationis.*

12 Johann Adam Osiander, *Collegium theologicum* (Tubingae, 1683).

13 See Romans 3:20–22.

14 In this sentence and the previous sentence, Walther repeats the Latin phrase *instrumentum passivum*, thus stressing this concept for his hearers.

However, regarding this simile, let us not forget the old saying: "In every simile there is some element of dissimilarity."[15] Otherwise, it would not be a simile but an identity.[16] When I hold out my hand, I am making a motion. One should not press this point in the case of a person's faith. For it is God who prompts sinners to hold out their hands after He has prepared them for the Gospel by means of the Law. Of course, God cannot prompt a person who continues, and is determined to continue, in his sinful life and thus makes a mockery of God's Word.

John Olearius, who completed that splendid treatise of Carpzov, *Isagoge in Libros Symbolicos*[17] (*Introduction to the Symbolical Books*), says (page 1361), "In relation to salvation, faith is **not our work**."[18]

In a certain sense we could say that "faith is a person's work" because it is not God who believes, but man. However, this could be misunderstood, which is why we should not speak like this. Faith is not an achievement of ours. God alone works in me. I contributed nothing to my faith. Olearius writes:

Rather, faith belongs to the order ordained by God, which is why it is **by no means an actual, so-called condition** depending on a person, but rather a blessing from our Father in heaven, or a requirement that is provided to a person who merely allows it to be provided to him, or an instrument that lays hold of salvation. It is in no way the active cause that comes from a person, nor does it have any so-called influence in bringing about a person's salvation.

Remember this well: Faith is not the requirement but the tool. Of course, the old dogmaticians called faith an instrumental cause.[19] There you see how dangerous it can be to dissect everything into a series of causes. When they came to the element of faith, they thought: "Now, what kind of cause is that?" So they called it an instrumental cause.[20]

---

15 Latin: *Omne simile est dissimile.* See also "Theologische Axiome," *Lehre und Wehre* 7 (1861): 11, where Walther cites a similar proverb in Greek: "Everything similar is dissimilar." Walther tirelessly stressed the importance of being careful with definitions when interpreting Scripture.

16 *Identity* is a technical term. A *simile* is proven by showing that all objects in a set share in common a number of attributes. Proving *identity* shows both that all attributes are the same and that none are unlike. For example, every object in a box of wooden blocks is similar because every object is made of wood. Yet objects in that set are only *identical* if they are alike in all respects—color, size, shape, etc.—and not unlike in any way.

17 *Isagoge in libros ecclesiarum Lutheranarum symbolicos* (Lipsiae: D. Fleischeri, 1699).

18 The Dau text adds: "but it belongs to the order of salvation which God has laid down."

19 Latin: *causa instrumentalis.* This is a cause for change that does not achieve change by itself; rather, it acts as a tool, catalyst, or conduit for the root cause of change.

20 This is another instance in which Walther repeated a Latin phrase—this time *causa instrumentalis*—for emphasis.

Read through the entire Bible and show me one single passage that states that a person is justified **on account of** his faith. Oh, you might as well let it go! The Bible never states: "You are justified and saved because of your faith, that is, because you believe." As soon as the Bible mentions the correlation between faith and justification, it uses terms that declare faith to be a *means*, not a *cause*. I think that is enough proof of what the biblical doctrine is. There is no getting around it: either you put the Bible aside and choose a different vocation or—if you must enter the ministry because God has captured you—then teach only in strict accordance with God's Word!

Heerbrand writes in his *Compendium*,[21] page 379—this *Compendium*, a summary of theology of the excellent Württemberg theologian Heerbrand, was even translated into Greek and sent to the patriarch[22] of Constantinople. Okay, Heerbrand says:

> Faith is not a condition, nor is it, properly speaking, required as a condition, because justification is not promised and offered on account of the worth or merit of faith or insofar as faith is a work. For faith, too, is imperfect; however, it is a mode[23] of receiving the blessing offered to people through and on account of Christ.

Now, it would be absurd to call faith a condition. Says Heerbrand: "The hand is not called the condition, but rather the instrument for receiving alms."

Finally, **Calov**, in his *Biblia Illustrata*,[24] commenting on Romans 5:10, says:

> We have not been redeemed and reconciled—nor have our sins been atoned for—conditionally. Rather, we have been absolutely redeemed in the most perfect and complete manner, as far as merit and effectiveness of the act are concerned. Although, regarding the actual enjoyment and appropriation of salvation, faith is necessary, which is nothing else than the appropriation of the atonement, satisfaction, and reconciliation of Christ. For, in the judgment of God, if One has died for all, it is the same as if all had died (2 Corinthians 5:14).

This is a golden text, which shines with the radiance of the sun—even in the luminous Scriptures. Since the death that Christ died for all is a death for the purpose of reconciliation, it is the same as if all had suffered death for this purpose. It follows, then, that, without the slightest doubt, I can say

---

21   Jakob Heerbrand, *Compendium theologiae* (Tubingae: Georgius Gruppenbachius, 1579). Other printers published subsequent editions into the seventeenth century. The publisher Louis Volkening in St. Louis printed an edition in 1879.

22   The leading bishop in the Eastern Orthodox Church.

23   Latin: *modus.*

24   *Biblia: Illustrata* (Francofurti ad Moenum: Typis & Sumptibus B. C. Wustii, 1672–76).

with perfect assurance: "**I am** redeemed; **I am** reconciled; salvation **has been acquired for me**."

I n order to be a true Christian, genuine faith is essential. However, in order to be a true preacher, genuine faith is not enough. In addition to faith, you must have the ability to express in proper terms the things that need to be believed. Accordingly, the holy apostle Paul urges his assistant Timothy with great earnestness regarding this duty: "Follow the pattern of the **sound words** that you have heard from me, in the faith and love that are in Christ Jesus" (2 Timothy 1:13).[25]

Twenty-sixth Evening Lecture:
May 1, 1885
2 Tim. 1:13

It is indeed essential for a preacher to have genuine faith in his heart—and to guard in his heart this mystery of faith. However, it is equally essential that he presents the true faith in "sound words," as the apostle expresses it, that is, in clear, plain, unmistakable, and adequate terms.

It is important that this is heard by young theologians who, according to the apostle Paul, were not reared in the sound words of faith, as Timothy was. These would be people who have not heard the true doctrine from childhood on, but rather grew up on the teaching of Rationalist preachers or of believing preachers of the modern type. As such, some completely wrong thought may well have stuck in their minds, and they will probably make use of it in their sermons, which will cause damage to their listeners.

Guard against your bias

As you know, Rationalist preachers referred to repentance and conversion as amending or reforming one's life. They called sanctification "walking in the path of virtue." They called the wrath of God "the serious purpose of God." They called the predestination of God "a person's fate." They called the Gospel "the teaching of Jesus." Anyone who has heard such phrases from childhood could easily adopt this dangerous Rationalist terminology in his sermons, even if he does not necessarily do so because his faith is misguided.

However, even believing theologians of the modern type are frequently too timid to use those specific theological terms that are fully warranted by biblical and church usage, because they are afraid that these terms might prove offensive to their listeners. In their sermons, they avoid speaking of original sin or of proclaiming the wrath of God against sinners, of referring to the blindness of natural man or to spiritual death, to which all people are subject by human nature. They do not like to speak of the devil prowling around like a roaring lion, seeking someone to devour,[26] because that would make them unpopular with their listeners. They are unwilling to speak of the everlasting

Modern errors

---

25 In this section Walther draws heavily from the proverbs of Johann Gerhard and others collected in Walther's *Lehre und Wehre* article "Theologische Axiome."

26 See 1 Peter 5:8.

fire of hell, of eternal torment and damnation. They prefer to mention these matters to their listeners in terms that do not seem so strange, faulty, and offensive to them, preferring to use phrases that are more in harmony with "the religious sentiment of an enlightened people."

Now, there is no doubt that these men wish to convert people, but they want to do so using these false terms. They believe that they can convert people by hiding things from them or by presenting matters in a way that is pleasing to people in their natural state. They are like sorry doctors who do not like to prescribe a bitter medicine to weak patients, or if they do prescribe it, they add so much sugar to it that the patient does not taste the bitter medicine, with the result that its effect is spoiled. Accordingly, preachers who do not clearly and plainly proclaim the Gospel, which is offensive to the world, are not faithful in carrying out their ministry. Rather, they cause great injury to people's souls. Instead of advancing Christians in the knowledge of pure doctrine, they allow them to search about in the dark, nurse hallucinations, and hurtle down their false and dangerous path.

The history of the Church shows how dangerous it is when theologians—who are otherwise regarded as orthodox—use wrong terms, which can be misunderstood easily. As a result and in order to cover up their errors with a deceptive appearance of sanctity, the most horrible heretics have established their claims using phrases that genuine orthodox teachers had once used, but [the heretics] give them new and twisted meanings. They wonder why people want to condemn them because the teachers to whom they refer were genuine orthodox teachers.

True, these heretics use incorrect expressions—which the orthodox teachers had used correctly—to hide their error. Nevertheless, the men who first used those expressions and believed that they were using them in the right sense are not completely without blame. As previously stated, Arius, Nestorius, all the scholastics, etc., appealed to men whose orthodoxy was acknowledged, thus creating the impression that they were still teaching the doctrine of the old Church and that it was their *opponents* who were the false teachers.

Bear this in mind, my dear friends, and consider that as ministers of the Gospel it is your duty not only to **believe** as the Church believes but also to **speak** in harmony with the Christian Church. Accordingly, before you memorize your sermons and deliver them to your congregations, you must subject your manuscripts to a severe critique. You need to determine whether your sermons are according to the analogy of faith and whether you have chosen proper terms throughout, lest you unintentionally destroy where you want to build up. This is of primary importance. That is the reason our Church from the very beginning has declared that it requires its preachers "not to depart an inch" from its Confessions, not to turn aside from the doctrines laid down in them, regarding not only *what* is taught but also *how* it is taught.[27]

This is indeed a great task, which requires diligent study. However, in three years you can accomplish a great deal.[28] At the end of your theological triennium, those of you who have faithfully applied yourselves will know—some more, some less—not only what the true doctrine is but also how it must be presented.

This task will be somewhat more difficult for those of you who have had to listen to wayward teachers most of your lives. Those seminarians will reveal in their sermons that they have not been brought up in the **sound words** of faith. Proper terms must be used, for the apostle Paul urges the entire congregation at Corinth to "agree" (1 Corinthians 1:10). They should not use divergent terms when explaining the same doctrine. The apostle adds another important remark: "that you be **united in the same mind and the same judgment**."

1 Cor. 1:10

But teaching a unified doctrine is worthless if it is not done with a unified meaning and focus. The Union Church[29] is a good example of this. While its teachers may speak as we do, they do not apply our meaning and focus. These two things, then, are required of you: unified doctrine and speech, and unified meaning and focus. In our fifteenth thesis we will study an example that shows how destructive it is to express oneself incorrectly.

---

27 Latin: *non tantum in rebus, sed etiam in phrasibus.*

28 In Walther's time, the program of theological education consisted of six years in *Gymnasium* (which would correspond to modern seventh through twelfth grades) and three at seminary. Most men were pastors by age twenty-two. A typical day began at 5:30 a.m. and continued until 8 p.m. Textbooks were copied class notes and whatever students could buy from German antiquary shops. There was no vicarage or internship year. Graduates received a theological diploma of vocation, not an academic degree.

29 German: *die unierte Kirche.*

This picture, taken in the early 1870s, shows an integrated school class at the "second" school building of Holy Cross at Ohio and Potomac, slightly northwest of Concordia Publishing House. Here is a concrete example of how German Lutherans were offering African Americans freedom in the Gospel—seventy years before some St. Louis schools. Teacher Erck stands in the midst of the girls, who also came from different social strata. Image courtesy of Holy Cross Church.

Thesis XV

You are not rightly distinguishing Law and Gospel in the Word of God if you turn the Gospel into a preaching of repentance.

EDITOR'S NOTE: In this thesis Walther focuses on how Scripture uses the word *Gospel* in both a general sense to mean the whole counsel of God and a specific sense that means the Good News of forgiveness through faith on account of Christ. By making this distinction clear, Walther helps Christians read and apply the Bible in the manner that Scripture itself intends.

To understand these words correctly you have to keep in mind that the word *Gospel* is used similarly to the word *repentance*. In the Holy Scriptures the word *repentance* is used in a wide and in a narrow sense. In the wide sense it means conversion viewed in its entirety, embracing knowledge of sin, contrition, and faith. This meaning is found in Acts 2:38, where we read: "Repent and be baptized every one of you," etc. The apostle does not say, "Repent and believe." Accordingly, he refers to conversion in its entirety, including faith. Nor could he have said, "Be contrite and then be baptized." He must have understood contrition as being joined with faith. What he means to say is this: "If you acknowledge your sins and believe in the Gospel that I have just preached to you, then let yourself be baptized for the forgiveness of sins." — **Meanings of repentance; Acts 2:38**

The word *repentance* is used in a narrow sense to mean the knowledge of sin and heartfelt sorrow and contrition. In Mark 1:15 we read: "Repent and believe in the Gospel." In this statement, when John the Baptist uses *repentance*, he obviously does not mean *faith*, otherwise his statement would be unnecessary repetition. — **Mark 1:15**

In Acts 20.21 Paul relates that he had been "testifying both to Jews and to Greeks of repentance toward God and of faith in our Lord Jesus Christ." Since faith is listed *separately* in this text, the word *repentance* cannot mean knowledge of sin, contrition, and faith either, because right afterward it says, "**and** of faith." — **Acts 20:21**

Likewise, concerning the Jews, the Lord says that, despite the preaching of John the Baptist, they did not afterward repent and believe him, and He adds: "that you would also have otherwise believed him" (Matthew 21:32). By *repentance* [Jesus] refers to the effects of the Law and means to say that, since they had not become alarmed over their sins, it had not been possible — **Matt. 21:32 Luther** for them to believe. For there can be no faith in a heart that has not first been terrified.

Meanings of Gospel

It is similar with the word *Gospel*. Sometimes this word is used in a wide [sense], then again in a narrow sense. The narrow sense is its proper meaning. In its wide sense it is used merely by way of synecdoche,[1] meaning anything that Jesus preached, including even His very poignant preaching of the Law, for instance, as in the Sermon on the Mount[2] and His rebuking of wicked people.[3] Furthermore, the term *Gospel* is also used in contrast to the Old Testament, which often means only the teaching of the Law.

Rom. 2:16; John 3:18; 5:24

For instance, in Romans 2:16 we read: "On that day when, according to my **gospel**, God judges the secrets of men by Christ Jesus." Here the apostle cannot be referring to the Gospel in the narrow sense, for that has nothing to do with the judgment, since Scripture declares: "Whoever believes in Him is not condemned"—"He does not come into judgment." In this text, when Paul uses the word *Gospel*, he means the doctrine that he had proclaimed and that was made up of both Law and Gospel.

Rom. 1:16

The word *Gospel* is unquestionably used in the narrow sense in Romans 1:16: "For I am not ashamed of the gospel, for it is the power of God for salvation to everyone who believes." First, it is called a Gospel of Jesus Christ. Next, a Gospel that saves **all who believe it**. This is not what is said of the Law, which requires that we **keep** it. Accordingly, here the apostle is speaking of God's gift to the world—and we are called to believe it. Therefore, here we are speaking of the Gospel in the narrow sense, to the exclusion of the Law.

Eph. 6:15

Another pertinent text is Ephesians 6:15, which speaks of "the Gospel of peace." Since the Law does not bring peace, but only unrest, the apostle in this text is speaking of the Gospel in the narrow sense, that is, of the glad tidings that Jesus Christ has come into the world to save sinners.

Our Lutheran Confessions follow the lead of the Bible, sometimes using the word *Gospel* in the wide [sense], sometimes in the narrow sense. This is how we can explain a statement such as "the Gospel preaches repentance." You should note this fact in order to understand our thesis correctly: You would be mingling Law and Gospel horribly if you were to turn the **Gospel of Christ**, that is, the Gospel in the narrow sense, into a preaching of repentance.

---

1   That is, a figure of speech in which a part substitutes for the whole or the whole for the parts. For example, one may refer to a sports car as "hot wheels."

2   See Matthew 5:1–7:29.

3   Although Jesus begins the Sermon on the Mount with the Beatitudes, the repeated blessings, He then qualifies that with stark preaching of the Law, beginning with Matthew 5:17. Elements of Law and Gospel, with the latter including the Lord's Prayer (Matthew 6:9–13), occur throughout the rest of the sermon. Yet the balance of the sermon reveals that people cannot keep the Law and are driven to seek refuge in the Gospel.

In the **Apology**, Article XII, paragraph 29 (Müller, 171), we read: "For in these two parts there stands the summary of the **Gospel**: First, it tells us: 'Improve yourselves,' thus denouncing everyone as a sinner. Second, it offers forgiveness of sin, everlasting life, salvation, every blessing, and the Holy Spirit through Christ, by whom we are born again."[4]   Ap XII 29

It is quite clear that in this passage Melanchthon uses the word *Gospel* in the wide sense. Luther does the same in so many places throughout his writings, whenever he speaks of the Gospel punishing people. But when he teaches what the Gospel really is, he talks only about consolation, mercy, forgiveness of sins—in other words, what the Gospel truly teaches in the narrow sense.

So you do not think that Melanchthon, who cannot always be trusted, misspoke even in our Confessions, let me submit another quotation from the **Apology**, Article XII, paragraphs 53–54 (Müller, 175):

> Accordingly, all Scripture urges these two doctrines. One is the Law, which reveals our misery and punishes sin. The other doctrine is the Gospel, for the promise of God [is] where He offers grace through Christ. And the promise of grace is repeated again and again throughout the Scriptures—ever since the days of Adam. For at first the promise of grace, or the first Gospel, was given to Adam in these words: "I will put enmity," etc.[5] Later, promises concerning the same Christ were made to Abraham and the patriarchs. Later, the prophets preached it, and finally Christ Himself preached the same promise among the Jews when He had come. Ultimately, the apostles spread it among the Gentiles throughout the world. For by faith in the Gospel, that is, the promise of Christ, all the patriarchs and all the saints since the beginning of the world have been made righteous before God, not on account of their contrition or their sorrow or any given work.[6]

Ap XII 53–54

From this statement you can see that when Melanchthon says a few pages earlier: "First, [the Gospel] tells us: 'Improve yourselves,'" he uses the term *Gospel* in the wider sense, referring to the tidings of grace together with the preaching of the Law, and vice versa. But in this last passage he speaks of "both parts" as contrasting each other, naming the two doctrines that distinguish all of Scripture.

When a pastor in his sermons essentially regards the Gospel as a preaching of the Law—that is, as repentance in light of the wrath of God against sinners—this is extremely dangerous and actually harmful to people's souls.

---

4   See also *Concordia*, 161; *Triglot Concordia*, 258. For more on Walther's use of the German Book of Concord, see pages 467–68.

5   See Genesis 3:15.

6   See also *Concordia*, 164; *Triglot Concordia*, 264.

If that pastor is not cautious about the terms he uses, it is a great and serious error—even if the preacher's personal faith may be orthodox. Accordingly, the Lutheran Church has from its very beginning kept a close watch on men who are likely to say, "The Gospel is a preaching of repentance." What the Lutheran Church wants to see is whether he is speaking of the Gospel in the wide [sense] or in the narrow sense.

False teachings   When Melanchthon published the Altered Augsburg Confession, the *Variata*, he was regarded with suspicion because of the new explanation he gave on this matter. He was immediately taken to task by Matthias Flacius, who never took false teaching lightly. Melanchthon backed off from his position and admitted that he had indeed used inadequate—in fact, even wrong—expressions. This was satisfactory to Flacius, who did not wish to argue about terms, since heresy is not so much a question of the words one uses as the way one teaches, though the terms should not be regarded as irrelevant either. When using words that do not correctly express a certain thought, we are not heretics, but careless speakers. Accordingly, Flacius did not rush at Melanchthon, shouting, "For God's sake, man, what have you done!"

The first one to teach entirely false doctrine on this point was Johann Agricola, the antinomian fanatic. He was an untrustworthy, completely careless person who abused the Gospel. He was highly conceited, though a learned man. During an illness that everyone thought would prove fatal, he remarked humorously: "You cannot kill a weed." He started to make a name for himself when Luther began preaching stern Law sermons to secure sinners. He presumed that Luther had fallen away from his own teaching of the blessed Gospel, which he had proclaimed at a time when he had an entirely different audience, namely, people who had been totally crushed by the Law. Agricola thought the time had come for him to show that *he* was the real reformer, so he anonymously published eighteen "Theses Spread among the Brethren,"[7] which can be found in the St. Louis edition of Luther's Works, 20:1624ff.[8]

W² 20:1626   Thesis 18 reads: "For the Gospel of Christ teaches the wrath of God from heaven and at the same time the righteousness that is valid in the sight of God (Romans 1:17). For a preaching of repentance is attached to God's promise, which reason does not grasp by nature but only by divine revelation."

Rom. 1:18 Luther   In Romans 1:17 the apostle begins a new section of his treatise. After announcing the topic of his Epistle, he takes up the Law. He keeps his focus on the Law from the second half of the first chapter through the first half of the third chapter. He begins this part of his teaching with the quote: "The wrath

---

7   Latin: *Propositiones inter Fratres Sparsae.*

8   This quotation is one of the few in the original German text of *Law and Gospel* that Walther draws from the St. Louis edition, because volume 20 was one of the earliest published in that edition. Otherwise, Walther used the Halle edition.

of God from heaven," etc. Paul declares that everybody carries in their heart the judge that condemns them because they feel and observe the judgments of the holy and righteous God everywhere. Only after preaching the Law does the apostle take up the Gospel.

Now, Agricola interprets the apostle's words to mean that the wrath of God is revealed in the Gospel—using Gospel in the narrow sense of the term. He indulges in foolish talk when he calls the Gospel "a preaching of repentance . . . attached to God's promise, which reason does not grasp by nature but only by divine revelation." He declares that it cannot be understood, yet he attempts to preach it to people who have not yet been crushed. He is contradicting himself—but that is what heretics always do.

Next, the Philippists—the followers of Melanchthon—took up Agricola's teaching. But our dear friend Melanchthon could not prevent his fanatical followers from declaring Agricola's teaching to be completely orthodox, instead of admitting, as Melanchthon had done, that he had used inadequate terms that did not express his real meaning.

The worst of these fanatics was Caspar Cruciger the Younger. His father had been an excellent theologian, and at one time Luther had even wanted him to become his own successor. But Cruciger Junior did not turn out well. In 1570 he wrote a treatise on justification in which he said: "In this office (of the Gospel) God wants to terrify people by the preaching of repentance, which reveals both all the sins that are set forth in the Law and also the saddest of all sins is exposed in the Gospel, namely, the failure to know the Son of God—that is, to despise Him."[9]

Cruciger contrasts the Gospel with the Law, claiming that it is not the Law that shows us our worst sins but the Gospel. Some thought that Agricola was not completely wrong because the Law has nothing to say about faith that justifies a sinner. Therefore, the sin of unbelief is obviously revealed in the Gospel. This, however, is only *apparently* the case. The Gospel is the preaching of consolation. Although we must conclude that contempt of the Gospel is the most horrible sin, still it is not the Gospel that teaches that. Rather, it is a conclusion drawn *from* the Gospel. But certainly, by inverting it, you can strip the comfort from even the most comforting doctrine—and make it bleak and hopeless.

No, it is the Law that rebukes unbelief. Where does it say this? In the First Commandment, which states: "We should fear, love, and **trust** in God above

---

9   *Disputatio de Justificatione Hominibus* (1570), Thesis 10. See Leonhard Hutter, *Libri Christianae Concordiae . . . Explicatio plana et perspicua* (Wittebergae: Zachariae Schüreri, 1608), 472. Subsequent citations use Walther's nomenclature: *Libri Concordiae Christianae Explicatio.*

all things."[10] Of course, the Law does not know when this occurs. This you can find only in the Gospel. But when God calls to me in His grace, saying, "Believe in My grace; trust My promises!" it is the Law that commands me to believe God and to trust Him. The Gospel does not command me in any way.

Unbelief, no matter in what context, is forbidden in the First Commandment. When we commit the sin of unbelief, we *sin* because we break the Law, which demands that we trust in God and believe His Word. The Gospel did not come into the world to reveal the sin of unbelief because sin had previously been revealed by the Law.

You must bear this in mind if you want to succeed in any way against the Antinomians.

Making the same mistake as Agricola, Christoph Pezel wrote a treatise against Johann Wigand, saying, "The Gospel in the narrow sense contains the sternest threats and rebukes sin, namely, the sin of unbelief, that is, when a person refuses to know[11] the Son, despises the anger of God, and, finally, despairs."[12] It is complete nonsense when Pezel says in this context that the Law does not mention at all that despair is sin. Are we not to love and trust in God? That rules out despair. Therefore, despair is obviously the most unspeakable and horrible sin because the Gospel says, "Believe, and you will be saved."[13] From this one can infer: If I do not believe, I will not be saved, but that is because the Law requires me to believe in God.[14]

You must burn this fact in your mind, so you do not fall for the claim of the Antinomians and their horrible confusing of Law and Gospel. Do not fall for their claims! When preaching the Gospel, do not present it with a black cloud hanging over it. Rather, proclaim free grace and unconditional consolation. When we are in the agony of death, we must have a sound rope that we can grasp. We must know that what we are grasping is not the Law.

The Antinomians who opposed Luther may have meant well, but they were Pharisees. In their pitiful blindness they imagined that they were helping the world by their teaching. In reality, they were depriving the world of its only means of rescue. In this context, let us note Paul Crell's treatise against Wigand in 1571. He says, "Since the greatest and chief sin is revealed,

---

10   See *Concordia*, 317, Walther's emphasis. Cf. *Concordia*, 359–63.

11   Latin: *ignoratio.*

12   *Disputatio Adversus Johannem Wigandum.* See Hutter, *Libri Concordiae Christianae Explicatio*, 472.

13   See, for example, Mark 16:16.

14   Walther means that the Gospel's imperative to believe actually has no threats to it, only a kind invitation and creation of belief. On the other hand, the Law's command to believe only threatens unbelief; it never fosters belief. Rejecting the Gospel imperative causes God's wrath only on the basis of the Law's command. If someone refuses the imperative to grab the life preserver, it is not the life preserver that kills but the raging sea.

rebuked, and condemned only by the Gospel, it is, strictly speaking, the Gospel **alone** that is really and truly the preaching that calls for repentance or conversion in the true and proper sense."[15]

Let us hear now what our Confessions say about this issue that has caused so much confusion. That was why the Formula of Concord was designed to restore harmony regarding this point of doctrine. As it says in the **Epitome**, [Article] V, points 6 and 7, and paragraph 11:

Correct teaching

> 6. The Law and Gospel are also contrasted with each other. Likewise also, Moses himself as a teacher of the Law and Christ as a preacher of the Gospel are contrasted with each other.[16] In these cases we believe, teach, and confess that the Gospel is not a preaching of repentance or rebuke. But it is properly nothing other than a preaching of consolation and a joyful message that does not rebuke or terrify. The Gospel comforts consciences against the terrors of the Law, points only to Christ's merit, and raises them up again by the lovely preaching of God's grace and favor, gained through Christ's merit.[17]

FC Ep V 7

Because Scripture does not always use the word *Gospel* in the same sense, the Antinomians had credited something to the Gospel in the narrow sense that one can say only about the Gospel in the wide sense. We must keep in mind that there is also a Gospel that does not rebuke sin but provides only comfort to sinners. When reading the Scriptures, we must be able to tell whether the word *Gospel* in a certain passage is intended in the wide [sense] or in the narrow sense—and we must be particularly careful to find the passages in which it is used in the latter sense.

> 7. Concerning the revelation of sin, Moses' veil hangs[18] before the eyes of all people as long as they hear the bare preaching of the Law, and nothing about Christ. Therefore, they do not learn from the Law to see their sins correctly. They either become bold hypocrites ‹who swell with the opinion of their own righteousness› like the Pharisees,[19] or despair like Judas.[20] Therefore, Christ takes the Law into His hands and explains it spiritually (Matthew 5:21–48; Romans 7:14). In this way God's wrath is revealed from heaven

FC Ep V 8, 11

---

15 *Disputatio Adversus Johannem Wigandum.* See Hutter, *Libri Concordiae Christianae Explicatio,* 471.

16 See John 1:17.

17 *Concordia,* 485. See also Müller, 534–35; *Triglot Concordia,* 802–5.

18 See 2 Corinthians 3:12–16.

19 See Matthew 23.

20 See Matthew 27:3–5.

against all sinners,[21] so that they see how great it is. In this way they are directed back to the Law, and then they first learn from it to know their sins correctly—a knowledge that Moses never could have forced out of them.

. . . We reject and regard as incorrect and harmful the teaching that the Gospel, strictly speaking, is a preaching of repentance or rebuke and not just a preaching of grace. For by this misuse the Gospel is converted into a teaching of the Law. Christ's merit and Holy Scripture are hidden, Christians are robbed of true consolation, and the door is opened again to ‹the errors and superstitions of› the papacy.[22]

The same teaching that is rejected here existed already in the Interim[23] and in the *Decrees of the Council of Trent*.

Next Friday we will try to determine in which passages of Scripture the word *Gospel* is clearly used in the narrow sense. This matter is quite important, especially for young preachers, if they are to learn how to express their thoughts correctly.

Twenty-seventh Evening Lecture:
May 8, 1885

Ps. 111:3

All humanity, as you know, consists of three estates[24] appointed and ordained by God Himself: the churchly or preaching estate, the estate of family and economic life, and the political estate.[25]

None of these three estates should be thought of as being lesser than the others. Thus we have David's statement in Psalm 111:3: "Full of splendor and majesty is His work." In each one of these areas of vocation, a person can walk along the path to heaven, please God and God's children, and serve God and his neighbor. What more do we need? In the churchly estate, we find teachers

---

21 See Romans 1:18.

22 *Concordia*, 485. See also Müller, 534–35; *Triglot Concordia*, 802–5.

23 The Augsburg Interim and the Leipzig Interim established a state of compromise after the Smalcaldic War between Lutherans and Roman Catholics. For more information, see the Luther to Walther timeline, page xxxvii.

24 German: *Stände*.

25 The German *Lehrstand, Nährstand*, and *Wehrstand* roughly translate the Latin *status ecclesiasticus, status oeconomicus*, and *status politicus*. The German *Lehrstand* is the estate or class of teachers of public doctrine, that is, preachers, bishops, and others called to church office (AC V, XIV, XXVIII). Those involved in business, nurture, and daily provision occupy the *Nährstand*. Those appointed to defend the order and peace of society are in the *Wehrstand*. The German terms rhyme, which explains their use. One of the clearest expressions of these terms in the Missouri Synod occurs in the 1870 doctrinal proceedings (*Lehrverhandlungen*) of the Western District.

in both church and school.[26] In the economic estate, we have farmers, trade professionals, artists, and the learned. In the political estate, we find rulers,[27] public officials, lawyers, and soldiers.

True, the world has reserved the greatest scorn and hate for the churchly office; nevertheless, it is and remains the most glorious estate of them all, for the following seven plain reasons:

Church vocation

1. The work of this estate has the most glorious object of its activity: humankind. The theologian deals with people only insofar as man has an immortal soul and is meant for eternal life.

2. The churchly estate uses the most beneficial medium and instrument in its work, namely, the Word of the living God.

3. It has the most beneficial and glorious goal, namely, to make people truly happy in this present life and to lead them to a life of eternal bliss.

4. It has the most wholesome occupation, one that entirely satisfies the souls of its members and advances them in the way of salvation.

5. Its work yields the most precious result, namely, the salvation of man.

6. It has the most glorious promise of the cooperation of the Lord, so that the work of a teacher of the Church will never be entirely unsuccessful and in vain.

7. It has the promise of a most gracious reward, which consists of glory in the world to come that is unspeakably great and so overflowing in abundance that it goes beyond anything they could ever have asked for and prayed for in this life.

If people would only stop and consider these points, they would come crowding into the holy office of preaching and teaching[28] in the same way that they crowd in droves to the great governmental offices, which yield them honor and rich rewards. Parents would consider it a high honor and a special grace of God if they could have their sons trained for this sacred office. Every day young theologians would feel compelled to drop to their knees and praise

---

26 German: *die Lehrer in Kirche und Schule*. At this time, all called teachers in the Missouri Synod were male. Many pastors and teachers had similar educations, and, in fact, it was possible for a pastor to receive a call to be a teacher or a teacher to receive a call to be a pastor. As women began to teach, usually in the lower grades, male teachers and pastors began to become distinct in identity and education. In 1911, one still expected a man to teach from the level of confirmation instruction upward in the school, specifically because the office of catechist was viewed as an adjunct to the pastoral office.

27 Walther uses the German *Regent*.

28 German: *das heilige Predigt- und Lehramt*. It is one office (*Amt*) with two activities: preaching (*predigen*) and teaching (*lehren*). One sees this from the use of *das* (the singular article) and the hyphen after *Predigt*, which means the words form a compound singular noun.

and magnify God's holy name for having done such great things for them, [appointing them] from eternity to this exalted and sacred office.[29]

Yes, I must say that if the holy angels—confirmed in eternal bliss—were capable of envy, they would, even in their state of heavenly glory, unquestionably envy every teacher of the Gospel. For all that is recorded concerning angels in Holy Scripture does not equal the greatness of the office of teachers and preachers,[30] in which they become helpers in the task of bringing fallen creatures back to their Creator. Without a doubt, these rescued people will eternally thank those by whose ministry they were saved from damnation and brought into life everlasting.

Yet if the estate is more glorious, the need is even greater for preachers and teachers to be extra faithful as they continue with their teaching. They must use extra caution to ensure that their doctrine is pure and untainted, presenting it in such a way that their listeners will learn to know, on the one hand, their own misery and, on the other, the goodness of God. Thus the listeners would come to faith, be kept in the faith, and would finally come to the place where they see God, praising and magnifying Him eternally.

We have already seen that the principal task of a preacher is rightly to distinguish the Word of truth.[31] He must not be like a carpenter trimming a block of wood, careless as to where the chips fall, which he then tosses into the fire. Rather, he must be like a goldsmith working with precious metal, careful to pick up even the smallest speck that drops from his workbench.

Rev. 14:13   May God grant you His Holy Spirit abundantly and make you faithful guardians of the immense treasures that will be entrusted to you when you enter the ministry! May you truly provide for the precious souls that God puts in your care, so that it may be said of you once you have finished your work: "Their deeds follow them!" Then you will never regret—neither during these years of study nor later in the ministry—that you had to submit to tough conditions. You will praise God when you see that by pure grace He makes you shine as brightly as the heavens and as the stars—eternally.[32]

Gospel no Law   We have already examined the principal proofs for the fifteenth thesis and have rejected some of the objections raised against it. Now I wish to call attention to two additional objections.

---

29 Walther states that the teaching office of the Church consists of male pastors and male teachers. He clearly indicates that the sons (*Söhne*) are its incumbents. The conclusion of the sentence alludes to Ephesians 2:10 in describing this office.

30 German: *das Amt der Lehrer und Prediger.* By reversing the order, Walther effectively stresses the coequality of male teachers and pastors. He does not include *Lehrerinnen*, female teachers, in this group

31 See 2 Timothy 2:15.

32 See Daniel 12:3.

In the first place, we reject the claim that Scripture itself calls the Gospel *law* and that, therefore, it would be permissible to define the Gospel as *preaching of repentance*, because the Law serves the purpose of leading people to repentance. These people quote Romans 3:27, which reads: "Then what becomes of our boasting? It is excluded. By what kind of law? By a law of works? No, but by the **law of faith**." Rom. 3:27

"Aha!" someone says. "See, according to the apostle's own expression, the Gospel is also a law." Such a person draws a false conclusion from the apostle's words. In this passage the apostle is using the so-called figure of *antanaclasis*. That is when someone uses the same word that his opponent has used, albeit in a different meaning, in order to show that his opponent is wrong. One can also do that by using the same word with different meanings, one after the other.

To illustrate: The Jews self-righteously asked Christ: "What must we do, to be doing the **works** of God?" Jesus answered, "This is the **work** of God, that you believe in Him whom He has sent." They had misunderstood the term "works of God" that the Lord had used, imagining that He was referring to works that people must do to please God. Christ keeps the term, but uses it in an entirely different meaning. He means to say: "Works do not save a person. But there is no need to do works in order to achieve some merit. All you need to do is rely solely on Christ the Redeemer and His grace—*that* is what saves." Therefore, a person is made righteous in the sight of God by what he receives from God. John 6:28–29

One uses this figure of speech also in daily life. When a son who has been sloppy in his work comes to his father and disrespectfully asks for his **wages**, the father will say, "Indeed, I will give you your **wages**—with the cane." This, too, is an anticlastic use. Even the most dull-witted people make great use of this figure of speech.

In a similar way, death is called the **wages** of sin.[33] Now, death is not really a reward that God has put on sin. Likewise, in Matthew 24:51 the Lord says [the master] will appoint to the evil servant his **wages** "with the hypocrites. In that place there will be weeping and gnashing of teeth." Therefore, one cannot establish from Romans 3:27 that the Gospel is a preaching of repentance. Only a person not familiar with rhetoric would cite this passage for proof. If you wish to understand Holy Scripture properly, you need to know the rules of rhetoric. For Scripture is quite rhetorical and full of such figures of speech and rhetorical devices. Matt. 24:51

---

33 Walther typically uses *Lohn*, the normal German word, to refer to "wages." At this point, however, he follows Luther's text of Romans 6:23, using the German word *Sold*, the pay of a mercenary soldier (*Soldner*). The latter German words come from the Latin *solidus*, a gold coin regularly minted from the time of Constantine I (ca. AD 312) to the tenth century. It was the standard unit of military pay. A "soldier of sin" earns the devil's wages.

Quenstedt says:

Properly speaking—and in contrast with the Law—the Gospel is not a doctrine that commands people to be righteous. Such a doctrine would demand faith as a good work—either as a subset of good works or as a personal tendency.

Rather, the Gospel proclaims the gracious forgiveness of sin and the righteousness that is valid in the sight of God as something to be accepted by faith as the receiving tool. **For this reason** the Gospel is called "the ministration of righteousness," 2 Corinthians 3:9.[34]

Rom. 10:16   Another objection is raised on the basis of Romans 10:16: "But they have not all **obeyed** the Gospel." Some argue that, since it is really the Law that demands obedience, the Gospel is not merely a message of joy but an improved Law.

However, it is a complete corruption of this text to try to prove from it that the Gospel in the narrow sense is a preaching of repentance. Of course, we are to obey the will of God not only as expressed in the Law but also in His gracious will. But the latter is not a will of the Law. By His gracious will, God offers and gives us all things. If we accept what He gives, this is known as obedience. It is an act of kindness on God's part to call it obedience. And, indeed, when we do obey Him this way, we are also fulfilling the First Commandment, for faith is commanded in the Law—not in the Gospel. The Gospel is called "glad tidings." But glad tidings cannot be anything that impose a task on a person, things that one has to do. The only glad tidings are the ones that tell a person to put away all fear because God is gracious, taking a step toward us to meet us.

Gerhard writes: "The accusation of unbelief belongs to the Law, as illuminated by the light of the Gospel. Luther recognizes this fact when he says that the work of believing in Christ and the contrary sin of unbelief are related to the First Commandment."[35] We noted earlier that Luther speaks of faith as a return to the First Commandment. To accept the grace of God as soon as it is offered to you, to take comfort in it, to thank God for it, and not to be so arrogant as to try to achieve by your own effort what our Father in heaven is offering by grace—that is the glorious way of fulfilling the First Commandment.

Hear the testimony from **Luther's** *Preface to the New Testament* (St. Louis Ed. 14:85–90), explaining what is the Gospel in the narrow sense:

---

34 Johann Andreas Quenstedt, *Theologia didactico-polemica* (Wittebergae: Johannes Ludolphus Quenstedt et Elerdi Schumacheri Haeredes [Matthaeus Henckelius], 1685), citing from the locus or chapter on the Gospel (*cap. de evangelii*), s. 2, q. 4, f. 1029.

35 *Locus de evangelii*, paragraph 111.

The Old Testament is a book in which the Law and Commandments of God have been recorded—together with the history of those who kept them and of those who did not keep them. Similarly, the New Testament is a book in which the Gospel and the promises of God have been recorded—together with the history of those who believed them and those who did not believe them.

W² 14:85–86
(cf. AE 35:358)

For the term *Gospel* is a Greek term. In German it means "a good message," "glad tidings," "good news," a "good report" of which men speak and sing cheerfully.

In other places, Luther says that the Gospel punishes humankind. What he means is that, when the word *Gospel* is used in synecdoche, in certain passages it may mean *Law*. But it is noteworthy that, while you find the word *Law* frequently used to include the Gospel, you never see *Gospel* (narrow sense) used for Law. Go look it up! See if Law ever means Gospel. Never!

For instance, when David conquered the great Goliath, a good report—the good news—circulated among the Jewish people that their worst enemy had been killed and that they had been delivered and restored to happiness and peace.

W² 14:86
(cf. AE 35:358)

In the same way, the Gospel of God and the New Testament are glad tidings and a glad report—spread throughout the world by the apostles—concerning the One who was a true David, fighting against sin, death, and the devil and conquering them. By His victory He redeemed, justified, awakened, saved, and restored to peace with God all those who were in bondage under sin, tormented by death, and overcome by the devil. As a result, they sing, thank, and praise God and rejoice forever, provided they firmly believe in this deliverance and remain steadfast in this faith.

What Luther says when he defines the Gospel in the narrow sense should make you extremely careful not to mingle any elements of the Law with statements regarding the Gospel. Proclaim the Law forcefully. Your pulpit must reverberate with its thunder and lightning. But the moment you begin to speak of the Gospel, the Law must be hushed. Moses set up a barrier around Mount Sinai, but Christ and the apostles did not place a barrier around Golgotha. Here everybody is allowed free access. People approaching the God of the Law must be righteous, while people approaching the reconciling God on Golgotha may come just as they are. Yes, they are welcome precisely because they are sinners. All they need to do is come.

This good report and comforting message, these divine evangelical glad tidings, are also called a **new testament**, because, as in a last will

W² 14:86
(cf. AE 35:358–59)

and testament through which a dying person disposes of his goods and orders them to be distributed among his appointed heirs after his death, Christ, prior to His death, gave a command and directions to His followers to proclaim this Gospel throughout the world after His death. This gave to believers—as their own possession—all His goods, that is, His life through which He swallowed up death. It gave them His righteousness through which He wiped out sin and His salvation through which He defeated eternal damnation.

According to Luther's description of the Gospel as the last will and testament of Christ, the Gospel is not a doctrine that teaches us how to make ourselves worthy in the sight of God. Rather, the Gospel teaches what we are to receive from God.

Luther occasionally uses this expression that—objectively—every person is already righteous in the sight of God because of the living and dying of Christ in their place. But when God justifies an individual by offering him the Gospel and he refuses to accept it, he is, indeed, not justified, but is and remains a condemned sinner. To such a person the chief torment of hell will be the fact that he knows: "I *was* redeemed; I *was* reconciled to God; I *was* righteous. But because I would not believe it, I am now in this place of torment."

The joyful message that you are to bring to your people is this: "You are redeemed. You are reconciled to God. You have been made righteous. You are blessed people. Salvation has been acquired for you too. Just believe it! What good would it be if someone were to offer you hundreds of millions of dollars and you would not think it worthwhile to extend your hand and take the money? You would still remain a beggar until your dying day." Untold numbers of people remain in their state of condemnation despite the perfect redemption of Christ proclaimed to them and offered to them in the Gospel.

W² 14:86–87 (cf. AE 35:359) Luther writes: "You cannot tell a poor human being—dead in sins and consigned to hell—anything more precious than this blessed, lovely message concerning Christ. If that person believes it is true, he must rejoice in his heart of hearts and be glad." Merely believing that the Gospel is true is not faith that justifies a person. That is a correct statement. But Luther goes one step further. He says that what distinguishes **Christians is that they believe this statement is true for themselves personally**. For whoever does not consider **himself** redeemed does not believe that the Gospel is true. The Gospel is God's message to every individual throughout the world, telling each person: "You have been received into grace by God. God is no longer angry with you. His Son has wiped out all your sins. All you need to do is to accept this message."

Adopt this as a principle for your work in your congregation, always proclaiming this glad message in your pulpit, so that your congregation will rejoice that they have a pastor who is a true evangelist. Do not follow your reason, which will tell you that by preaching the Gospel to them you will make your listeners secure in their sins. That is not so.

When the grace and glory of the Gospel are truly proclaimed to people, this wakes them up, makes them joyful and, therefore, willing to do good works. This kindles a heavenly fire in their heart, as it were. This effect is certain. Anyone coming into contact with this fire starts to glow. Any person coming into contact with the fire of divine love starts to glow with love toward God and neighbor. But it also goes without saying that the Law must be preached continually. Because when people become too "stuffed" on the Gospel, it will cease to help them.

> The Gospel, then, is nothing else than preaching about Christ, the Son of God and David's Son, true God and man, who by His death and resurrection overcame sin, death, and hell for all those who believe in Him. Accordingly, the Gospel can be defined in a brief or in a long statement, depending on whether the writer gave a brief or a long description. The four evangelists, who recount many works and words of Christ, give an extensive account. For instance, St. Peter and [St.] Paul, who do not describe the activities of Christ, give a brief account. Yet they do indicate briefly how by His death and resurrection Christ conquered death and hell for those who believe in Him.

W² 14:88
(cf. AE 35:360)

You may be assured that the Lutheran Church is distinct from all others by the fact that it preaches perfect redemption and, therefore, does not portray faith as a work, but merely as the receiving hand by which the sinner accepts the gifts of God. Furthermore, the Lutheran Church invites all sinners who are alarmed over their sins, no matter how horrible their behavior may have been, saying, "Come, for everything is now ready." This is also why our Church has the true doctrine of the Sacraments, because it teaches the true doctrine of salvation by grace alone.

Luke 14:17

Luther says, "See, then, that you do not turn Christ into a new Moses or Christ's Gospel into a book of law or instruction." The Gospel is not a book of the Law—or even a book of instruction—but a message of joy. People cannot rejoice over it too soon, and whenever it enters their heart, their joy is a heavenly, divine joy. If people constantly complain that they cannot see how they would benefit from the Gospel, and if the preaching of the Gospel leaves their heart empty, they have no one to blame but themselves and their refusal to believe.

W² 14:88
(cf. AE 35:360)

W² 14:88
(cf. AE 35:360)

Again Luther: "This has been done in some prefaces that have been written on the New Testament—for instance, by St. Jerome." Next to Origen, Jerome was the greatest expert in languages of the first few centuries of the Christian Church, but Luther hated to read Jerome's writings because there was precious little of the Gospel in them.

W² 14:88–89
(cf. AE 35:360)

For, actually, the Gospel does not require our works to save us and make us pious. In fact, it condemns our works. Rather, it demands that we believe in Christ, namely, that He has conquered sin, death, and hell for us and makes us godly, awakens us, and saves us—not by *our* works, but by *His* works and *His* suffering and dying. In this way we may appropriate His death and victory—just as if we had achieved it ourselves.

When David had killed Goliath, all the children of Israel had to do was to make use of their freedom.[36] After the defeat of their leader, the enemies fled. In the same way, Christ conquered *our* enemies and did everything to set us entirely free. We have no more to do than the Israelites did when David returned victoriously from his battle. They no longer had to be afraid of a defeated army. In the same way, we no longer need to be afraid of the Law, sin, death, the devil, and eternal damnation. All these were our enemies—and they have been put to flight. To continue fearing them is a reproach to Christ, which stirs God to anger. If you believe that God is angry with you, you certainly have an angry God. But if you believe He is kind to you, then you have a kind God, and you should not think: "Well, maybe He is, but probably not."

W² 14:89
(cf. AE 35:360–61)

However, we should understand the many commandments, teachings, and explanations of the Law that Christ has given in the Gospel—and which St. Peter and [St.] Paul have given as well—just as we understand the other works and blessings of Christ. If you are familiar with the works and history of Christ, that does not necessarily mean that you know the true Gospel and embrace the knowledge that He has conquered sin, death, and the devil.

In the same way, if you are familiar with the doctrine and commandments recorded in the New Testament, you do not necessarily know the Gospel yet. Rather, the Gospel is this: It is when you hear the voice that tells you that Christ is your own—complete with His life, teaching, works, His dying, His rising from the dead, and everything that He is, has, does and is able to do.

Whenever Luther spoke of the Gospel as being about preaching of repentance and the wrath of God, he most certainly was not referring to the Gospel

---

36 See 1 Samuel 17:1–54.

in the narrow sense. The above quotation shows you how Luther speaks whenever he refers to the Gospel in the strict and proper sense. He wrote that preface in the time of his first love, in 1522.[37] He repeated and expanded it in 1527. His whole discussion is glowing with such burning and personal love that a poor sinner—upon hearing this testimony—feels like leaping for joy. Of course, if someone is still a slave of sin, wallowing in manure, then they do not enjoy this food for the soul. They are like the animal that loves acorns more than anything else.

> Accordingly, we see that [Christ] is not compelling people, but inviting them with kind words, saying, "Blessed are the poor," etc. Similarly, the apostles use terms such as "I urge," "I beg," "I plead." All of this shows that the Gospel is not a book of the Law, but, properly speaking, a sermon concerning the blessings of Christ, given to us to have as our own if only we would believe. Moses, on the other hand, in his writings drives, compels, threatens, beats, and punishes people in a horrible fashion, for he is a writer and enforcer of the Law.

W² 14:89 (cf. AE 35:361); Matt. 5:3

In our Lutheran congregations we must preach the Gospel—the truly precious Good News—and the Gospel spirit must fill the entire congregation. If that is the case, our people are not continually terrorized by the Law but are made glad by the Gospel. When we preach the Law, it is not to make people saints, but sinners. Thus Luther: "That is the reason the Law is not laid down for the just, to make them righteous in the sight of God, as St. Paul says in 1 Timothy 1:9, for believers are made righteous, are awakened and saved, by Christ. And when they are no longer anxious, they must demonstrate their faith with works."

W² 14:89 (cf. AE 35:361)

Works are not necessary of themselves. In God's accounting they are not necessary at all for our salvation. But they are necessary for the sake of people, so that others would see Christians exercising their faith by works and so may praise the Father in heaven and accept Him as their God.[38] Luther writes: "Indeed, when there is faith, believers cannot help but do good works. Christians prove themselves, they break forth, in their good works. They confess their faith, teach people the Gospel, and risk their lives in the process."

W² 14:89 (cf. AE 35:361)

We should test our own faith by these remarks of Luther. Faith cannot be shut in. It is like a body of water that can be tapped. It rushes through any opening that is made for it. Believers are ready to serve anybody, wherever they can. They cannot help but profess the Gospel before other people; in fact, they bet their life on the Gospel.

---

37 Walther refers to the first edition of Luther's New Testament translation, which was completed in 1522 and is known as the "September Testament."

38 This acceptance happens after the work of the Holy Spirit, as Walther has already noted.

Matt. 10:32

Believers know that if they refuse to do these things, they will have to forsake Christ. At this point the light of faith will be snuffed out in them. Accordingly, they confess Christ not merely because Christ said, "So everyone who acknowledges Me before men, I also will acknowledge before My Father who is in heaven," but because they cannot help but do it.

W² 14:89–90
(cf. AE 35:361)

During their life, everything believers do helps their fellow human beings—not only so they would also obtain the grace of the Gospel but so that they also would follow the example of Christ and sacrifice their lives, possessions, and honor for others, as Christ did for them.

That is what Christ means when, at the end of His life, He gives His disciples only one commandment: that they should love one another. He tells them that so people would see who are His disciples and sincere believers. For unless it breaks forth in works of love, faith is not genuine. In such persons the Gospel has not yet taken root, nor have they come to know Christ properly.

That is Luther's *Preface to the New Testament.* It is quite brief, but of much greater value than the modern scholars who have made it their life's goal to tear down the foundation of faith by making the Bible unreliable.

Let us now study the Bible passages that refer to the Gospel in the narrow sense and learn by what attributes we may know them. There are five indicators.

1. Whenever the Gospel is contrasted with the Law, it is quite certain that the word *Gospel* does not refer to the Gospel in the wide [sense], but in the narrow sense. In Ephesians 2:14–17 we read:

Eph. 2:14–17 Luther

For He is our peace, who has made one of both and has broken down the wall between by abolishing through His flesh the enmity, namely, the Law set up as commandments, that He might create in Himself one new man out of two, thus making peace, and might reconcile both to God in one body through the cross, thereby through Himself killing the hostility. And He came and preached peace in the Gospel to you who were far off and peace to those who were near.

The Law, which does not bring peace, comes first. But then the Gospel, which brings peace, follows it.

John 1:17

2. Whenever the Gospel is presented as the particular teaching of Christ or as the doctrine that proclaims Christ, it cannot refer to the Law at the same time. For in John 1:17 Christ Himself says, "For the law was given

through Moses; grace and truth came through Jesus Christ."[39] He did not first give the Law simply for the sake of giving it. He did so in order to clear the Law of the false interpretations of the Pharisees, because the proper knowledge of the Law is necessary before a person is able to accept the Gospel.

Luke 4:18–19: "The Spirit of the Lord is upon Me, because He has anointed Me to proclaim **good news** to the poor. He has sent Me to proclaim liberty to the captives and recovering of sight to the blind, to set at liberty those who are oppressed, to proclaim the year of the Lord's favor." In this text, our Lord Jesus declares why He has come into the world and what He is to preach as the Christ, the Savior of the world. He concluded the foregoing statement by saying in verse 21: "Today this Scripture has been fulfilled in your hearing." Previously, He had not spoken one word about the Law but had referred only to the doctrine that is offered to the poor, the sick, those with broken hearts, and those in the bondage of sin and the devil.

Acts 17:18: "Some of the Epicurean and Stoic philosophers debated with [Paul]. And some said, 'What does this idle chatterer want to say?' Others said, 'It seems that he wants to preach about new gods.' That was because he was preaching Jesus and the resurrection to them." The doctrine that here has Jesus Christ as its object is the Gospel in the narrow sense.

The following passages belong under this heading as well:

First Corinthians 15:1–4: "Now I would remind you, brothers, of the gospel I preached to you, which you received, in which you stand, and by which you are being saved, if you hold fast to the word I preached to you—unless you believed in vain. For I delivered to you as of first importance what I also received: that Christ died for our sins in accordance with the Scriptures, that He was buried, that He was raised on the third day in accordance with the Scriptures."

Romans 16:25–26: "Now to Him who is able to strengthen you according to my **gospel** and the preaching of Jesus Christ, according to the revelation of the mystery that was kept secret for long ages but has now been disclosed and through the prophetic writings has been made known to all nations, according to the command of the eternal God, to bring about the obedience of faith."

Galatians 1:6–7: "I am astonished that you are so quickly deserting him who called you in the grace of Christ and are turning to a different

Margin notes:
Luke 4:18–19, 21

Acts 17:18 Luther

1 Cor. 15:1–4

Rom. 16:25–26

Gal. 1:6–7

---

39 Walther believes that the prologue of John's Gospel is spoken by Christ in the same way that Christ speaks in the first chapter of Revelation. This has considerable merit. In both books the introduction connects with the final sections regarding those who are faithful and the return of Christ.

gospel—not that there is another one, but there are some who trouble you and want to distort the **gospel of Christ**."

Matt. 11:5;
Luke 4:18 3. Whenever poor sinners are the ones to whom the Gospel is addressed, you may be certain that the reference is to the Gospel in the narrow sense. Matthew 11:5: "The poor have **good news** preached to them." Luke 4:18: "The Spirit of the Lord is upon Me, because He has anointed Me to proclaim **good news** to the poor."

Furthermore, we are dealing with the Gospel in the narrow sense in the following points:

Rom. 1:16;
Eph. 1:13 4. Whenever forgiveness of sins, righteousness, and salvation by grace are named as the effects of the Gospel. Romans 1:16: "For I am not ashamed of the **gospel**, for it is the power of God for salvation to everyone who believes, to the Jew first and also to the Greek." Ephesians 1:13: "In Him you also, when you heard the word of truth, the **gospel** of your salvation, and believed in Him, were sealed with the promised Holy Spirit."

Mark 1:15;
16:15–16 5. When faith is correlated to the Gospel, the reference is to the Gospel in the narrow sense. Mark 1:15: "Repent and **believe the gospel**." Mark 16:15–16: "Go into all the world and proclaim the gospel to the whole creation. Whoever believes and is baptized will be saved, but whoever does not believe will be condemned." Also, the passage cited last certainly refers to the Gospel in the narrow sense. The remarks of the Lord about unbelievers who will be condemned are indeed not a part of the Gospel, but Law. The Lord adds these remarks in order that those who reject the Gospel would know that by their unbelief they are causing themselves to be thrown into hell.

Twenty-eighth Evening Lecture:
May 15, 1885

Sermon preparation

Every time a pastor is preparing to write a sermon that he will deliver from his pulpit, he should approach this task with fear and trembling, that is, with the reverent concern that he would preach nothing contrary to the Word of God. He must examine everything he has written down most carefully to see whether it is in harmony with the Word of God and the experience of Christians. Every time he should weigh everything that he is to speak in public, using the holy scales of the temple to weigh the true gold content, as it were. He should see whether it agrees with the writings of the apostles and prophets.

But after writing a few paragraphs, a pastor could become impressed: "Now, that is beautiful. Oh, you really got it that time! Now that will make an impression!" Do not be fooled. One more time he ought to go over carefully the very passages that seem so beautiful to him to see whether they might contain anything that is false or that has been expressed in such a manner as to be misunderstood, and which could awaken false impressions in his listeners.

As soon as he sees a problem, he must be stern—even cruel—toward himself and draw a thick black line through those sentences, even if he has invested much time and work on them. Even though those sentences are lost effort, they were merely the product of his genius—not of a clear knowledge drawn from the Word of God.

Indeed, a preacher may discover to his horror that an entire section of his sermon—or even the entire sermon—has turned out completely wrong. For God's sake, he should not think: "Should I let all this effort go to waste? Should I let all this worthless drudgery come to nothing? Will I let this whole sermon that took so much time and effort just go up in smoke? Ah, but the whole thing is just a sloppy mess that has gone wrong, all wrong!" Listen, the whole thing must be cashiered, deposited in the round file! It would be better for him to speak off the cuff than to deliver that original sermon—even though it had cost him so much time and effort.[40]

Fixing mistakes

What if an otherwise careful minister has had the misfortune of putting something into his manuscript that was wrong and has even said those incorrect things from the pulpit? If he notices his mistake while preaching, he must then immediately correct himself: "My dear listeners, I said such-and-such, but here is what I really meant."

If he notices his mistake later, and if the matter is very important, he must make the correction later, so that his listeners might not be led completely astray. In fact, he may not only have to correct his wrong statement but also solemnly revoke it. That will not lower him in the esteem of his listeners. On the contrary, the people will say all the more: "Now there is a reliable preacher; he is really accurate."

But the pastor must not think: "Oh, my hearers will already get the right idea and muddle through whatever it is that I messed up." Rather, he must speak in such a way that the people will not misunderstand his words.

1 Cor. 5:6

For this reason the apostle warns all preachers: "Do you not know that a little leaven leavens the whole lump?"[41] False teaching is a leaven. Yes, one might even call it a toxin that, even in the smallest dose, will course through every artery, poison, and kill a person. Daily experience teaches this. Yes, everyday life tells us that even a tiny bit of poison can have the most horrible effects. If someone were to eat a whole piece of arsenic and it became entirely

---

40 Walther did not approve of novice pastors speaking off the cuff. He reserves that for the experienced pastor. Here he is talking about choosing the lesser of two evils.

41 See also Galatians 5:9.

coated in mucus, that might not kill him;[42] however, a little poison can kill the entire person.

You can cause unspeakably great damage in only one incorrect sentence in a sermon. For instance, a preacher might be rebuking people incorrectly. Godly, diligent Christians, full of concern for their souls, trying to work out their salvation with fear and trembling, could hear that rebuke. It can easily happen that these dear souls become uncertain of their state of grace and dare not believe that they will be saved. For what they apply to themselves to make their faith uncertain would be what the preacher had rebuked incorrectly.

If the preacher notices this, he must not think: "Oh, on another Sunday I will talk about the same topic in a completely different way, so as to make everything good again." For the more confident his listeners are that their preacher is an orthodox man and a faithful, experienced Christian, the more difficult it will be for them to pull out the arrow that he had shot into their heart in the first place with his baseless rebuke.

In a similar way, on another occasion, when he *should* have administered a rebuke, he may have offered false comfort, to the delight of all false Christians, who would then disregard the remainder of his sermon and say to themselves, "Ah, now you just hang on to that part right there! You really are a good Christian!" Oh, the horror! This is an awful situation when a carnally secure person thinks that he is a good Christian but indeed he behaves himself quite differently—to remain in spiritual blindness until he passes away and is damned forever.

Mistakes such as these can happen even to a sincere pastor. In a moment of carelessness, when he is not on his guard and not praying while writing his sermon, God may let it happen and say to him, "You do not need Me, that is obvious. You do not call on Me. You are relying on your own strength. Fine, go figure it out yourself!" Imagine the anguish of a minister who has himself to blame when he sees a parishioner of his walking down a wrong path! Just think: "It is *your* fault that so-and-so is straying. That is why!"

Every one of your sermons must be the product of heartfelt prayer. When you sit down to the task of writing your sermon and feel that you are distracted, cold, and dead, you must not think: "I cannot help it. I must fill this page." No, lay your pen aside. Call earnestly upon your Father in heaven to lift you out of your miserable state of mind, to give you a passionate heart, to overcome everything in you that is not godly, to let the breath of His Holy Spirit enter your heart. And you will be able to do more than merely **write**

---

42 Arsenic was a common poison in the nineteenth century and even an ingredient in certain medicines and cosmetics during Walther's time. Walther refers quite loosely to the fact that elemental arsenic is far less poisonous than certain chemical compounds that include arsenic. Walther likely saw a tabloid headline and it emerged here off the top of his head. If nothing else, the reference jarred his students into paying attention.

down words of comfort, which you do not feel yourself and which leave your own heart cheerless. Then you will not think: "All I have to do is simply talk about everything that I see there in the Bible. It is all good." No, you cannot say that it is all good. When you prepare your sermon, your entire effort must be to answer: "Now, how do I begin, in order that I get the best possible catch using the net of the Gospel?"

Pastors sin in this area more often than you might imagine. Some of them waste a lot time during the week—occupied not with godless affairs, to be sure, yet not with the one thing needful. Then Sunday rolls around, and there they are, standing in their pulpits, unprepared to give their people the best that is in them. Their listeners get the impression that the pastor is merely reciting something because he has to, regardless of whether the sermon actually helps anyone. That is a horrible situation!

The forty-five minutes that you spend in the pulpit is most valuable time.[43] It may help determine the present and eternal salvation of many thousands of people. Woe to the preacher who does not redeem that time by offering his listeners the very best he is able to give. And if he is not in tribulation, he thinks: "This is what I want to preach! I know for a fact that—unless someone is rejecting the Holy Spirit—they will hear the testimony of the Holy Spirit and certainly get something out of that. And that is the truth!" But if he does not have confidence in his own sermon, how can he accomplish this with his preaching?

I said, "If he is not in tribulation." When he is in tribulation himself, a faithful preacher will be tempted to rip up the sermon manuscript he has written. In these tough exceptions God intends to humble him by using painful experiences such as these. But normally—after struggling and wrestling with God during the preparation of his sermon—a preacher is confident. He is certain that he has a sermon to offer that will bring souls to Christ as surely as the proper fishhook of a skilled fisherman will catch fish.[44]

But if a preacher talks without a plan and purpose, he need not wonder that he is not achieving his goal. Shame on pastors and students preparing for the ministry who go to work in a sloppy and careless manner, jotting down and reciting anything that comes to mind, anything that flows into their pen, and anything that leaps from their lips! As a rule, that is what happens when a pastor preaches off the cuff. What I mean here is not only pastors who have plagiarized their entire sermon but also those who have not adequately

---

43 Walther specifically mentions forty-five minutes as a standard sermon length in the German class notes.

44 Walther speaks about the fishhook, not a fishing pole. He is probably alluding to fly-fishing, which became a popular pastime in the nineteenth century and was marked by innovation in terms of equipment. Missouri offers numerous opportunities for fly-fishing in its many streams and rivers.

meditated upon the subject they intend to present to their listeners.[45] But after thoroughly meditating on it, their flow of words is much better.

There is also a difference between good judgment and genius.[46] I am even inclined to say that a preacher must gradually wean himself of his manuscript and thus give the Holy Spirit a chance to lay hold of him and suggest thoughts and words to him that had not come to him previously.

2 Tim. 2:15   This is why the apostle Paul writes in 2 Timothy 2:15: "Do your best to present yourself to God as one approved, a worker who has no need to be ashamed, rightly handling the word of truth." Thus the main point in a sermon is to rightly distinguish Law and Gospel.

This photograph shows C. F. W. Walther in his later years.
Image courtesy of Holy Cross Church.

---

45   The Dau text adds: "Some preachers cannot speak with any degree of self-assurance if they have not meditated their sermon."

46   Walther: *Judicium und ingenium sind verschieden.*

THESIS XVI

You are not rightly distinguishing Law and Gospel in the Word of God if you claim that people are truly converted when they get rid of certain vices and, instead, engage in certain works of piety and virtuous practices.

EDITOR'S NOTE: In this thesis, Walther argues against coarse works-righteousness. "Doing good" does not save people, yet saved people do perform good works. Walther cautions that if a person puts the cart before the horse by describing salvation as the decision to do good instead of evil, that makes it impossible for such a person to read and apply the Bible in a Christian manner.

This is a very important thesis because it addresses the worst possible way of mingling Law and Gospel. Woe to the pastor who, in his preaching, leads his listeners to imagine that they are good Christians just because they might have stopped robbing and stealing, and that over time they will most likely eliminate any weaknesses still remaining in themselves.[1] Such pastors twist the Gospel into Law because they claim conversion is a work of man. In reality, genuine conversion, which produces a living faith in a person, is brought about only by the Gospel.

Works-righteousness

This most serious way of confusing Law and Gospel is something of which Rationalists are especially guilty. The essence of their religion is to teach that people must quit their vices and then practice virtue—and thus become brand-new people. Yet the Word of God teaches us that we must become different brand-new people first. Only *then* will we put away our particular sins and begin to practice good works.

The doctrine proposing to make people godly by their own works is the doctrine of pagans, Reformed Jews, and Turks.[2] This is like trying to empty a

---

1   Walther knew that he could never hope to gain salvation through his own works. Walther would say that he probably could give up all bad habits, then he would smile and say, "Except smoking." Like all sinful humans, including us, Walther relied on salvation by grace alone in Christ Jesus. He never compromised on this important teaching of Scripture. The real Walther was very different from the "founding father" image that he was given in a number of essays in 1911. See William Dallmann, *My Life* (St. Louis: Concordia, 1945), 25, 29–31.

2   By pagans or heathen (*Heiden*), Walther means those who engage in magic, nature worship, and polytheistic traditions. He also included Asian Indian and Chinese religions in that category. Walther is aware that Orthodox Judaism retains traditional beliefs that are closer to Old Testament Scripture than Reform Judaism. Walther follows Luther in

great river of sin by dipping one bucket after another into it, and then expecting to reach the bottom at some point. If you want to dry up a river of sin, you must first stop up its foul source. Only *then* will the water become pure.

Rationalists love to cite the well-known saying "Genuine repentance is to stop sinning." Since it is possible to apply this saying correctly, our forefathers used it in *this* sense: "You people who are boasting of having the right faith while leading wicked lives: quit babbling about faith. Genuine repentance is to stop sinning." But Rationalists interpret it [the wrong way,] like this: "Do not beat yourselves up—genuine repentance is to stop sinning. What God wants is for you to stop sinning. That is how to become a true Christian."

That is the shameful teaching of moralists. The Christian religion gives us the correct teaching in one Greek word: *metanoeîte*,[3] which means: "All of you, turn your minds around" or, as Luther translates correctly, "Repent." (If he had rendered this word etymologically, in accordance with its derivation, he would have amazed his readers.)

With this word the Lord confronts the sinner, telling him, first, that a change of his innermost self must take place. What He requires is a new mind, a new heart, and a new spirit—not to quit one's vices and do good works. By making *this* the primary condition for being a Christian, He puts the ax to the root of the evil tree. Rationalism and the papacy prune the harmful tree, but for every branch they cut off, new branches sprout forth—all of them still harmful. A tree of this kind must be grafted; healthy branches must be inserted into it if it is to bear different fruit. Let us hear a few Bible passages.

John 3:3   John 3:3: "Truly, truly, I say to you, unless one is born again he cannot see the kingdom of God."

John 3:2   Nicodemus had approached the Lord with the statement: "Rabbi, we know that You are a teacher come from God, for no one can do these signs that You do unless God is with him." Of course, Nicodemus expects that the Lord will be pleased with such a statement coming from a Pharisee and that He will say to him, "That is excellent. Just keep on doing what you are doing." But there is not one word of this. In fact, Jesus slams the door of heaven in Nicodemus's face, practically saying to him, "I can see you are trying to butter Me up with flattery. But with that old mind-set of yours, you will not be able to enter heaven. You have to become an entirely new person. You have to be born again."

John 3:4–6   Now Nicodemus reveals his puzzlement by crying out: "How can a man be born when he is old? Can he enter a second time into his mother's womb

---

using the word "Turks" to mean all those who practice Islam, regardless of nationality. For more on Islam and Judaism, see the Glossary, pages 480–81.

3   This Greek word, a plural imperative, sounds similar to the English words *paranoia* and *noëtic*.

and be born?" But the Lord repeats His previous statement and even goes a step further: "Truly, truly, I say to you, unless one is born of water and the Spirit, he cannot enter the kingdom of God. That which is born of the flesh is flesh, and that which is born of the Spirit is spirit." What the Lord means is this: "Everything you do while still in your carnal nature is sinful. You must become spiritual before genuine spiritual fruits will begin to reveal themselves in your life."

Matthew 12:33: "Either make the tree good and its fruit good, or make the tree bad and its fruit bad, for the tree is known by its fruit." Plant a good tree, and it will bear good fruit. Plant a bad tree, and it will bear bad fruit. This means that unless a person is completely changed—unless he has become a new creature, has been born anew, with a new mind—all his doings will be bad fruit. For by nature everyone is a bad tree.

Matthew 15:13: "Every plant that My heavenly Father has not planted will be rooted up." Only works that God has produced are good. Any work that a person has produced by the power of his reason and natural will is a plant that will have to be rooted up. God will not recognize it. On the contrary, He will say, "Get out of My sight with this sin! What you have done, that is just plain sin, simply a disgrace. For this work has sprung from an evil heart, a heart that cares nothing for Me. It is polluted water, flowing from a stinking source."[4]

True Christians know full well that this is true and do not need to be told that this is so. No matter what they do, no matter how beautiful a job they do, they are aware that it is not right. You did not do it out of love for God and neighbor, but only in a mechanical fashion or because you acted in such a way that others would say, "Look, now there is a Christian."

A Christian can see right away whether a work has been planted by God— or by Adam. Any person still unable to discern this should know that he has not yet experienced a change of heart, a turning around of the mind.[5] The Holy Spirit is not yet in him. From the moment a person receives the Holy Spirit and he wishes to do what the Law demands, the Spirit immediately informs him that the deed is worthless.

That person may give someone a thousand dollars,[6] and the Spirit will immediately urge him to examine himself as to whether or not he was motivated toward the generous act by love for God or of neighbor. If not, he will be

Matt. 12:33

Matt. 15:13

---

4   In this thesis, Walther draws on the statements of Johann Gerhard regarding actual sin, statements that Walther collected in his *Lehre und Wehre* article "Theologische Axiome."

5   Walther used the Greek: *metánoia*.

6   In Walther's time, a Missouri Synod missionary's annual salary was usually $400 a year. Some pastors earned as little as $100 in a year. In today's money, Walther's $1,000 would be worth about $30,000.

told that his deed is worthless in the sight of God—nothing but a fraud—and that God does not bless this deed.

Jer. 4:3   Jeremiah 4:3: "For thus says the LORD to the men of Judah and Jerusalem: 'Break up your fallow ground, and sow not among thorns.'" What a remarkable statement! We know its meaning well enough. Sowing wheat into untilled land—soil that is still covered with brush—will not yield a worthwhile harvest. We must first clear the ground, remove all scrub growth, cut down the trees, or at least thin the forest enough to give the sprouting seed the necessary air. That is a picturesque description of conversion. A person must first be given a new heart in conversion, and only into this new heart may the seed of every good work then be sown.

1 Cor. 13:3   First Corinthians 13:3: "If I give away all I have, and if I deliver up my body to be burned, but have not love, I gain nothing." This remarkable passage has a special meaning for our thesis. What is all-important are not the works themselves, but the love from which they proceed. Even if you are so desperately poor that you are not able to do anything, in God's opinion you may be rich in works, if love awakens in you the desire to do good to all people and you think: "Oh, if only I could do good for all people! But, according to God's will, I must let *others* show *me* their love." God sees your goodwill for your good works. But the main point is your love, not your outward works.

Before his conversion, Paul kept the Law perfectly. Nobody could make any claims against him. While he said that he regarded it all as excrement, he regarded his works that were *truly* good not as excrement, but said that he would receive a great reward of mercy for them.

Romans 14:23: "For whatever does not proceed from faith is sin." This is a huge statement! Even surrendering one's body to the flames is worthless if the act does not spring from love, that is, from faith. For love only enters a person's heart through faith. How blind, then, must a preacher be who proposes to make people godly by urging them to do good works! A person must first become godly before he can perform good works.

Church discipline and . . .   Even pastors who are true believers may mingle Law and Gospel horribly—perhaps without being aware of it—not so much in their sermons but in their counseling and in the exercise of church discipline. Many pastors and congregations make mistakes when applying church discipline.

Addiction   They may be dealing with a true alcoholic and so bring him before them for discipline. There, in front of them, he says, "Oh, but I am so very sorry." Such people usually are quick to admit sorrow over their sins. An inexperienced pastor is easily deceived by such a confession. The drunkard may be suspended from church membership and monitored for three months. Then a fellow congregant brings the good news: "He has kept sober all that time and not lived in sin." The pastor decides that the drunkard is now converted, while in reality he is still quite a godless person. For God's sake, take this seriously, and avoid being deceived like this!

The same thing may happen with someone who curses all the time. He is called before the congregation and stops cursing for a while.

Cursing

Or take the lazy member who never comes to church and, therefore, certainly is not a Christian. After he has been brought before the congregation, he may come to church several Sundays in a row. But does this outward act alone make him a Christian? By no means. Any godless person can do what this person is doing.

Lapsed members

These people must be made to realize that Christians simply do not act like they do. If people do act like that, they cannot possibly be in a state of grace. But it requires hard work on the part of the pastor until these persons are born again by the Word of God. If a pastor is unwilling to perform this work, he is neglecting the souls of these persons.

Or take the case of tardy communicants who return to the Sacrament once the pastor has rebuked them. If the pastor is satisfied with that, he is guilty of mingling Law and Gospel.

Neglect of the Lord's Supper

Or take the sin of stinginess. A congregation may be so stingy as to refuse to take up a collection. [The congregation] may fail to pay the pastor his salary. In that case the pastor must not resolve to preach his people a stinging sermon in order to open their wallets and purses. Opening wallets by means of the Law is no achievement at all. He must preach in a manner that will awaken them out of their spiritual sleep and death. If he does not do that, he falls under the criticism of our sixteenth thesis.

Stinginess

Luther comments on John 3:3, which I just cited, as follows (St. Louis Ed. 7:1854): "Our doctrine, then, denounces all works as worthless and ineffective if the person doing them has not been born again." Some misguided orthodox preachers would say, "Nonsense, that is complete Pietism." No, that is what the Christian faith teaches!

W² 7:1854
(cf. AE 22:279)

For this reason we consider this to be the key part of the instruction that people need regarding how they must be born anew: One must first tell them that they are all spiritually dead and that whatever they may do in their lives—whether it be their monastic order, fasting, or anything else—will not help them to obtain forgiveness of sins until they are first born again and made into new people.

W² 7:1854
(cf. AE 22:279)

Remember, you have an excellent weapon when you tell them: "You must first be born again if you want to do good works. If not, all your good works are only a fraud." If you do not tell your people this truth, if you do not wield this trusty weapon in your ministry, the best-case outcome will be that you gather about yourself a congregation of completely legalistic Pharisees.

W² 7:1854–55
(cf. AE 22:279–80)

Let us now hear what this new birth must be like. Our teaching stands on the fact that Christ twice swears an oath, saying, "Truly, truly, I say to you, unless one is born again," etc. What He intends to say is this: "Nicodemus, do not think that you will be saved just because you are an honest, pious man. True, we should lead honest, decent, and peace-loving lives in this world. But if you ever fail to live in this way, then Master Hans the Hangman[7] will come along with his sword and noose and will enforce the Commandments that you have broken by putting you where you can no longer break them. This will teach you that, if you will not obey, you will have to suffer. But your good works are worthless if you assume that you can use them to work your way to heaven. For these works, this kind of pious living, only lay the groundwork for this earthly life. They keep you from being murdered, they keep your wife and family from kicking you out, they keep you from the executioner's gallows. The fact that you are an honorable citizen of Jerusalem secures your life, honor, and distinction in that city. But if you want to get to heaven and into the Church and kingdom of Christ, you need to understand that you have to become a new person. Think of yourself as a child, unable to do a single good work, one who has neither his [adult] sphere of activity nor his [adult role in] life yet.[8] That is what Christians preach.

Christian doctrine teaches us that we must first become different people, that is, that we must be born again. How is this done? By the Holy Spirit and by [the] water [of Baptism]. After I have been born again and have been made godly and God-fearing, I begin a new life. What I do in the reborn state is good.

---

7   In the Middle Ages, people invented nicknames such as "the Evil Man," *Meister Hans*, and *Meister Fix* for the executioner (*Scharfrichter*) because his identity was anonymous and they feared being cursed by evil spirits. "Master Hans" also maintained order among skinners, sewer-cleaners, prostitutes, and others kept out of upper-class society yet whose skills or services were used regularly by upper-class citizens. Luther's theology of Christian vocation helped condemn the sin of upper-class citizens (nobles, merchants, craftsmen, artisans, and members of holy orders) who considered themselves to be upright and clean while seeing those in the lower classes, including serfs, to be sinful and unclean. For example, our words "lewd" and "villain" were originally descriptions of lower-class people who may have been neither lewd nor villainous in today's sense, but they were thus stereotyped. Luther did condemn vocations that were sinful in themselves, such as prostitution. Yet his doctrine of vocation identified formerly "outcast" vocations, such as the necessary work of "Master Hans," as acceptable before God.

8   Here, Luther's use of *Wesen* refers to a sphere of activity; cf. WA 38:130.16. Luther sets up the contrast between a respectable, established citizen (*Bürger*) and a little child (*Kind*). Both the AE and the Dau edition do not provide the best interpretation at this point. They lead one to believe that Luther is speaking of an infant or unborn child.

If Adam had remained in the state of innocence in which he had been created, he could have spent his life doing anything he pleased: fishing for gobies,[9] catching robins, or planting trees. Everything he did would have been good and holy works, and there would have been no sin in them. Eve would have nursed and tended her babies—and her works, too, would have been altogether precious and good. For the person[10] had been created good, upright, pure, and holy, and, therefore, all his works—his eating and drinking and everything—would have been right and good.

In the new birth everything is God's work. Even when I treat myself to a hearty meal, eat, or sleep, I am doing a good work—not just when I engage in hard labor. If I should suffer as a servant of the Law, that is simply a martyrdom for hell. A Christian has the right mind in it all. Therefore, all his actions are God-pleasing. From a pure fountain nothing but good, fresh water can flow.

But since the man[11] strayed into sin, he has done nothing good after the fall. Rather, he sins in all his works, even when he prays. He does everything as a sinner. Whatever he does is wrong, even when he fasts and prays, leads the strict life of a Carthusian, puts on a monk's garb, and goes barefoot.[12] All these things are sin because the person[13] is evil and not born again. Nothing that he does gives him any help [before God].

W² 7:1855
(cf. AE 22:280)

When [a monk] in a cloister became a believer, all his activities, even wearing a friar's cloak, became good, because he was then acting from a right motive, convinced that God wished him to serve in his calling. That monk

---

9   The German *Schmirle* in W² (Latin *smerillus* or *mirlus*) means "goby," a small bottom-feeding fish that lives usually in salt water or brackish water.

10 German: *die Person*.

11 Luther includes all sinful people in his use of the German word *Mensch*, which is translated here as "man." A synonym would be "the old Adam." In this sentence, "man" refers back to the "person" (*die Person*) in the final sentence of the previous quotation. When the words *Mensch* and *Person* refer to sinful people, they refer to people of both genders. When Luther uses *Mensch* in reference to Adam and Christ, he means those two as *men* in the sense of Romans 5:12–21. This understands the "old Adam" and "new man" (Christ) as singular collective nouns of male gender in which, respectively, all unregenerate and regenerate humans of both genders are created (Genesis 1:27; 2:22), reborn (Romans 5:12–21), have their existence (1 Corinthians 6:14–20), and according to which they will be judged (1 Corinthians 6:9–13). The entry for *Mensch* in W² 23:1157–62 has much to offer regarding the German usage. Unfortunately, an English discussion of Luther's terminology for a general readership is not readily available. Luther's usage is theological, not political.

12 The Carthusians are a very strict order of monks. See the Index of Persons and Groups, page 491.

13 German: *die Person*.

thought: "God wants it to be like this. This is my vocation—this is why I am doing it."

W² 7:1855
(cf. AE 22:280)

Accordingly, Christ tells Nicodemus: "I have come to preach a different doctrine about how to become good: you must be born again. Even though Holy Scripture refers to this, you people do not read it. And even if you do read it, you do not understand it. The point is that, in order to do good works, a person must be born again, because sinners—being corrupt—cannot help but produce more sinners."

W² 7:1855
(cf. AE 22:280);
Matt. 7:16–17
Luther

The Old Testament is also full of this teaching that people need a new heart and a new spirit, that their hearts must be circumcised before they can be acceptable to God. Luther writes: "In Matthew 7, the Lord says, 'Whenever a tree is bad, it bears no good fruit. Thistles do not produce figs; neither do thorns yield grapes." Christ wants to make us godly from the ground up.

Let me give you another testimony of Luther from his *Sermon on the Liberty of a Christian*, from the year 1520.[14] This is the treatise that Luther dedicated to the pope. He attempted to enlighten the pope and tell him the truth in an amazing way. As you know, Luther was not afraid of his fellow human beings—not even of the devil. During his exile at the Wartburg, one day he was startled by a terrible racket, as if a hundred thousand barrels were being hurled down the stairs. He exclaimed, "What is going on?" but checked himself immediately, saying, "Ah, it is you, devil! If I had known that, I would not even have bothered to step out of my study." Any other person would have been seized with a deadly fright at the thought that he was being harassed by the devil, but Luther treated the devil with contempt, knowing that he is a haughty spirit, to whom nothing is more unbearable than contempt. That is why Luther despised the devil. Anyone else would have been scared to death and would have thought: "That is the devil!"

So **Luther** writes (St. Louis Ed. 19:1003f.):

W² 19:1003
(cf. AE 31:361);
Matt. 7:18 Luther

Good and pious works never produce a good and pious person. But a good and pious person produces good and pious works. In every instance, the person must first be good and pious before he can do any good work. Good works follow, and come from, a pious and good person, as Christ says in Matthew 7:18: "A healthy tree cannot bear bad fruit, nor can a diseased tree bear good fruit."

Now, it is evident that fruit does not bear the tree and that the tree does not grow on the fruit. Rather, the reverse is true: trees bear fruit and fruit grows on trees. There must be trees before there can be fruit,[15] and, likewise,

---

14 See AE 31:327–78.

15 No "tree and fruit" and "chicken and egg" problems exist here. God originally created His creatures in forms suitable for bearing young (Genesis 1:11–12, 20–22, 24–25, 28).

the fruit does not make the tree either good or bad—the tree produces the fruit. Likewise, man must first be either good or bad before he does good or bad works. His works do not make him either good or bad, but he does either good or bad works.

> We observe this in all trades. A good or a bad house does not make a good or a bad carpenter. Rather, a good or bad carpenter builds a good or bad house. No work produces a master corresponding to it, but as is the master, so is his work. Man's works come under the same rule. Accordingly, as man is either a believer or an unbeliever, his works are either good or evil, not vice versa, making him godly and a believer according to his works. Since works do not turn people into believers, they do not make them godly either. But faith, which makes people godly, likewise produces good works.

W² 19:1003–4
(cf. AE 31:361)

These are matters that are readily understood by us now, but before Luther was able to write beautiful passages such as this, he had to pass through many severe conflicts. It is surprising that, as early as 1520, he was able to picture the relation of works to faith as he does in the passage that I have cited.[16]

Without question, the words in Revelation 3:15–16 that Christ addressed to the bishop of the church at Laodicea are most strange and terrible. He said, "I know your works: you are neither cold nor hot. Would that you were either cold or hot! So, because you are lukewarm, and neither hot nor cold, I will spit you out of My mouth."

Twenty-ninth Evening Lecture:
May 29, 1885

Rev. 3:15–16

We see from these words that, in the perfect judgment of God, it is worse to be a lukewarm than a cold pastor. It is worse to be a sluggish and indifferent pastor, who serves in his office because it is the profession in which he is making his living, than to be obviously ungodly. For when a pastor—even though he is not teaching or living in a plainly unchristian manner—is so lethargic, so empty of all earnestness and passion for the kingdom of God and the salvation of souls, the unavoidable result is that the poor souls in his congregation become infected by him, and finally the entire congregation is lulled into spiritual sleep.

On the other hand, when a pastor leads a clearly ungodly life and teaches ungodly doctrine, the good souls in his congregation do not follow. Rather, they turn away from him with disgust. Now, though greater damage is inflicted on the church when a pastor is a lukewarm servant of God than

Matt. 7:23

---

16 In his early years as a pastor, Walther read and cited from Luther's early works as well as his later works. As he responded to different issues, Walther began to prefer Luther's later works to the reformer's earlier writings.

when he is obviously ungodly, at the Last Day both kinds of pastors will receive the same sentence. Both the lukewarm and the cold pastor will be addressed with those awful words: "I never knew you; depart from Me, you workers of lawlessness."

Matt. 25:21   In contrast, the truly faithful servants of Jesus Christ will one day hear these happiest of words addressed to them: "Well done, good and faithful servant. You have been faithful over a little; I will set you over much. Enter into the joy of your master."

2 Cor. 5:13   Faithful pastors must not only avoid being lukewarm or cold. They also must be warm. Their hearts must burn with love for their Savior, Jesus, and for the congregation that their Savior has entrusted to their care, so that they may be able to say with St. Paul and all the apostles: "For if we are beside ourselves, it is for God; if we are in our right mind, it is for you."

Rom. 10:2   This is a strange passage. St. Paul is saying that a pastor must demonstrate greater earnestness and enthusiasm than the majority of the members of his congregation may like or approve. The apostle does not mean to say that in his own ministry at Corinth he displayed "zeal, but not according to knowledge," but that he was more passionate than the Corinthians desired.

Every sincere preacher and minister of Jesus Christ should demonstrate much enthusiasm and earnest determination, even if the congregation responds with disdain, hatred, and enmity. A sincere pastor will suffer such experiences rather than gain anyone for himself by downplaying the truth, hiding it, or dulling its sharp points.

It is an undeniable fact, then, my friends, that a pastor—especially a really passionate pastor—**has to** take the **Office of the Ministry** seriously, or he will commit a serious sin. But he can also be committing a serious sin when he goes beyond **what the Word of God declares** in presenting Christianity and its demands. This brings us to our seventeenth thesis.

THESIS XVII

You are not rightly distinguishing Law and Gospel in the Word of God if you describe believers in a way that is not always realistic—both with regard to the strength of their faith and to the feeling and fruitfulness of their faith.

EDITOR'S NOTE: In this thesis, Walther expands on a statement he often made to his students: "We have no power but the power of the Word, but we *have* the power of the Word!"[1] As Franz Pieper said in the 1882 doctrinal proceedings of the Minnesota-Dakota District, the ultimate goal of Scripture is the salvation and eternal bliss of people. In service of the Gospel, the Law always curbs, condemns, and punishes outright sin; reveals our sin; and serves us as a guide. Going beyond what Scripture says and allowing the Law to dominate creates a truly harmful way of reading and interpreting the Bible.

Only Scripture defines sin

Young pastors who still have only a little experience frequently make this mistake. They want to make an impression on their people. They want to awaken them from their natural security. They imagine that they must keep on placing demands on those who are sincere Christians in order to prevent any hypocrites from regarding themselves as Christians. However, here is a point where the pastor must be careful not to go beyond the Word of God—or, by being too passionate, he will cause terrible harm to the souls of his listeners.

Alas! In many respects Christians are quite different from the descriptions truly given in good faith in sermons. Pastors want to awaken their people and warn them against self-deception. However, that cannot be their **ultimate aim.** Their ultimate aim must be to lead their listeners to the assurance that they have forgiveness of sins with God, the hope of the future blessed life, and confidence to meet death cheerfully.

Anyone who does not make these things his ultimate aim is not an evangelical, [that is, a Gospel-oriented,] pastor. For this reason, unless he is quite sure of his footing, he must be careful, for God's sake, not to say, "Anyone who does this or that is not a Christian." It is not uncommon for Christians to act in very unchristian ways.

---

1   William Dallmann, *My Life* (St. Louis: Concordia, 1945), 30.

Rom. 7:18   Romans 7:18: "For I know that nothing good dwells in me, that is, in my flesh. For I have the desire to do what is right, but not the ability to carry it out." It is plain that, in this passage, the apostle is describing Christians. In the previous chapter, he describes how a person becomes a Christian. Next, he goes on to show how a Christian ought to walk.[2]

In the above section of the Epistle, Paul begins to discuss the doctrine concerning spiritual tribulation.[3] Christians frequently have to endure such tribulation, so Paul discusses the topic in order to comfort them. He describes Christians as consisting of two parts. True Christians, he says, always desire what is good, but frequently they do not accomplish it. Now, then, if a preacher claims that Christians do not have a true, godly[4] will if they do not do good in everything—that is unbiblical.

To want what is good is the main characteristic of Christians. Frequently, they do not progress beyond the godly will to do something. Before they are aware of it, they have gone astray, sin within them has erupted, and they are ashamed of themselves. But by no means does that mean they have thus fallen from grace.

Rom. 7:14   Romans 7:14: "For we know that the law is spiritual, but I am of the flesh, sold under sin." What Paul is saying is this: "Who would not gladly be rid of sin? As for me, I am like a slave sold to a master. I cannot get away from him. I must always live under sin's tyranny." That is the situation Christians are in: they feel like slaves. But the difference is that they do **not** obey their master **gladly**, as **Christian** slaves are supposed to obey the Lord. They obey sin with the greatest reluctance.

Rom. 7:24   Accordingly, the apostle cries out in verse 24: "Wretched man that I am! Who will deliver me from this body of death?" Remember this, partly for your own comfort, partly for the task of comforting the members of your future congregation. The prevailing spiritual illness of our day is that Christians are not sure of their salvation. This is because they are not given any trustworthy teaching. Now, when a real Christian is shown what a miserable sinner he is, he clings to Christ all the more firmly and rejects the whispering of the devil, who keeps on telling him that he is fallen from grace and has lost God.

Phil. 3:12   Philippians 3:12: "Not that I have already obtained this or am already perfect, but I press on to make it my own, because Christ Jesus has made me His own." In this life we chase after many things, but we do not grab hold of them. Sometimes a Christian may think that there were times when he was

---

2   The Dau edition adds: "and to please God."

3   German: *Anfechtung*.

4   German: *der wahre, gute Wille*. Walther speaks of a godly will as both doing good and wishing to do that which is good. The discussion here concerns the ability of a Christian to make the desired good a reality.

more sanctified and was able to overcome sin better. That may actually have been the case, and his present condition may be the result of spiritual back-sliding. But this may also be the result of the fact that now he sees much more plainly what a weak person he is.

Brand-new Christians may imagine that at their conversion they are altogether pure, that they have forsaken the world, that they have heaven in their heart. But they are not aware of the starving beasts that lie in wait for them. When they stop receiving the sugar bread of their spiritual child-hood[5] and tribulations[6] arise for them, they imagine that they can no longer fight against sin the way they used to fight. In reality, the truth is that they are being attacked much more violently than before and that they are more acutely aware of their sinful cravings.

In Galatians 5:17, the apostle writes: "For the desires of the flesh are against the Spirit, and the desires of the Spirit are against the flesh, for these are opposed to each other, to keep you from doing the things you want to do." According to this text, a pastor has no right to denounce a person as an unbe-liever if he is not doing all that he should, as long as that person maintains that he does not want to do these things. But if he commits sin from weakness or in rashness, he can still be a Christian.[7]

Gal. 5:17

James 3:2: "For we all stumble in many ways. And if anyone does not stumble in what he says, he is a perfect man, able also to bridle his whole body." He means to say that there is no such thing as a perfect human, and by the use of the pronoun "**we**," he includes himself, all the apostles, and all the saints in this understanding. Christians sin not only in thoughts, desires, gestures, and words but also in their actions, which makes it evident to the whole world that they are still poor, weak humans.

James 3:2

Hebrews 12:1: "Therefore, since we are surrounded by so great a cloud of witnesses, let us also lay aside every weight, and sin which clings so closely, and let us run with endurance the race that is set before us." According to this text, Christians are always putting away sin—yet it is continually clinging to them. They cannot get it out of their hearts, and this makes them so sluggish. If only they did not have to carry their evil flesh around with them, their behavior would be quite different, and, like heroes, they would walk cheer-fully with their God.

Heb. 12:1

Isaiah 64:6: "We have all become like one who is unclean, and all our righteous deeds are like a polluted garment. We all fade like a leaf, and our iniquities, like the wind, take us away." The prophet does not say, "All the righ-teous deeds of natural man are like a polluted garment," but "all our righteous

Isa. 64:6

---

5 Regarding sugar bread, see page 222 n. 132.

6 German: *Anfechtungen*.

7 For more on the Lutheran understanding of premeditated sin, see pages 229–42.

deeds" are [that way]. Therefore, in God's eyes the life of a true Christian cannot look very beautiful. If God had not spread the cloak of Christ's righteousness over us, we would be eternally damned and lost—even though we have become true "Christians."[8]

Job 14:4

Job 14:4: "Who can bring a clean thing out of an unclean? There is not one."

Ps. 32:6

Psalm 32:6: "Therefore let everyone **who is godly** offer prayer to You at a time when You may be found." Immediately before this text, the psalmist speaks of the forgiveness of sin. He says that it is especially the genuinely godly people who need to pray every day for the forgiveness of their sins.

False descriptions of Christians; Matt. 6:12 Luther

But why spend so much time searching the Scriptures for proof texts? Our Savior taught all Christians to offer up this daily petition in the Lord's Prayer: "Forgive us our debts."[9] Every day, then, apparently adds a new burden of guilt on our heart and conscience. Some people claim that Christians are perfect. You do not need to be a Methodist[10] to make that claim—you can make those claims as an individual too. Well, people who make these claims, saying that Christians are something they are not (or at least that most Christians are not like that), these people are describing Christians incorrectly and do tremendous harm.

For from such incorrect descriptions Christians with a very tender conscience will think: "Oh, I am not a Christian! I was often suspicious of that, but today the preacher said it: I am not a Christian!" This impression may become so firmly lodged in their heart that they are unable to remove it. Then they torment themselves until their dying day with efforts to keep from falling into this or that sin, and still they commit that same sin over and over. Therefore, pastors must provide Christians with the proper cure when these people sin, namely, to immediately get up after having slipped—provided their sin was not intentional.

For an intentional sin would indeed drive the Holy Spirit from them.[11] But Christians learn by experience to sense danger. And when they have sinned, they feel urged to seek immediately their Father in heaven, to confess their sin, and to ask to be forgiven for Jesus' sake. They also feel inwardly assured that they have been forgiven, and even if they have no such feeling, they will say with the poet:

---

8   Here Walther makes the distinction between the apparent Christian according to outward behavior and the Christian whose heart is clothed in the righteousness of Christ.

9   The German text, similar to the King James Version, reads: "And forgive us our debt[s], as we forgive our debtors." This follows both the Greek and Latin texts of the New Testament.

10 Methodism started as a group of church leaders and laypeople in England who adopted a "method" to reach a state of holiness. For more on Methodism, see the Glossary, page 482.

11 For more on the Lutheran understanding of premeditated sin, see pages 229–42. Walther explains his position on pages 236–42.

Oh, indeed shall I e'er trust Him,
Till I come there to behold Him,
Till He holds our wedding feast.[12]

Some preachers claim that Christians have nothing but pleasant feelings. I have frequently observed this claim in some of your sermons. You [seminarians] say things like: "To be sure, unbelievers are miserable beings. As long as they serve the world and sin, they will be chased by demons." That is simply not true. Many unbelievers live without any worries of conscience. "In contrast," some of you say, "how happy Christians are! They are free from all anxiety, free from doubt," etc. That is not true either. On the contrary, thousands upon thousands of Christians are filled with anguish and despair and are continually struggling and crying out: "Oh, what a wretched person I am!"

In your sermons, you students sometimes like to preach on topics such as "The Blessed State of a Christian" and the like. Well, do not forget that **the blessedness of Christians is not based on pleasant feelings** but on the assurance that, despite the bitterest feelings imaginable, Christians are accepted by God. In their dying hour they will be received into heaven. **That** is indeed a great blessedness.

You can easily make a mistake here without being aware of it. Never say anything that is contradictory to the experience of Christians. Simply search your minds and imagine: "What would it be like if I were sitting among my own parishioners and another pastor preached this. How would I grow fearful? How would I react if asked, 'Are you a Christian?' I would have to answer, 'No!' " Would it not be frightful for me to make a sermon in which I called judgment on myself? If I had to think: "If another man preached that to me, I would be frightened to death if I did not know the truth"?

Of course, in your sermons it is proper for you to depict the happy moments that Christians do occasionally enjoy when given a foretaste of their future happiness. But, at the same time, you must tell your listeners that these are merely passing moments in the lives of Christians—sunbeams that find their way into their hearts once in a while. If you describe these moments of bliss properly, this will cause your parishioners neither to be in anguish nor to grieve nor to doubt their faith. Rather, it will give them a heartfelt longing for the experience you are describing.

How to preach correctly

---

12 This appears to be a poem from a devotional book, similar to those written by Johann Starck. Walther does not provide enough information to identify the poet. The poem's scansion and meter match that of the melody for *"Alles ist an Gottes Segen,"* which has been translated as "All Depends on Our Possessing" (*LSB* 732). The poem itself does not match any of the common German hymns set to that melody, but it reflects a very common theme and contrast in German devotional literature.

It is especially Christians who have fought the good fight faithfully[13] who will feel that way. First, they are flat on their backs in spiritual distress, imagining that God has rejected them. And then—lo and behold—their heavenly Father is pleased to pour such heavenly joy into their hearts that in their ecstasy they believe they are no longer on earth but already in heaven.

Furthermore, you must keep in mind that Christians retain their natural temperament even after their conversion. A person with an irritable temper will keep that tendency, and it may frequently get the better of him. So do not say that, when a person becomes a Christian, he turns from a bear into a lamb, in the sense that he is willing to take rebukes and scorn from everybody and will always be ready to forgive others. No, [some] Christians often have great trouble keeping their temper. Frequently they cannot control it, and nobody can calm them down. Their nasty temperament will always get the upper hand. Yet we must not think that if that person were to die tonight, he would go to hell.

Judgmental Christians might tend to think such thoughts, whereas that fellow Christian [with the nasty temper] might be on his knees in his closet, pleading with God for forgiveness and for strength to control his temper. Is it not disgraceful to judge someone else so uncharitably? The next day you may meet the Christian with the nasty temper and he might say to you: "Please forgive me for losing my temper yesterday. I am truly sorry."

Job 1:21 Frequently, Christians are described as being as patient as Job. Some preachers say, "Take everything away from a Christian, and he will cheerfully say, 'The LORD gave, and the LORD has taken away; blessed be the name of the LORD.'" And the preacher may think that his remarks have been quite biblical. Job did indeed say those words, but not *all* Christians say them. It is inconsistent with the truth to make such a claim in a sermon. Many Christians grow impatient when trouble strikes. Their impatience may become violent—even over unimportant matters. Later, when they get a grip on themselves, they are ashamed of themselves.

No one can say that Christians never commit a coarse sin. These things do happen occasionally. But whenever this is the case, Christians surrender unconditionally to the Word of God, even though they may not do so immediately. At first, they may be so blinded by the devil that they think they did no wrong. In the end, however, God's Word convinces them that they were wrong, and then they humbly ask for forgiveness, whereas hypocrites claim as long as they can that they did the right thing.

Many preachers describe Christians as people who do not fear death. That is a serious misrepresentation, because most Christians are afraid of dying. If a Christian does not fear death and declares that he is ready to die at any

13 See 2 Timothy 4:7.

time, God has given him a special grace. Some have expressed this sentiment before their doctor told them that they would not survive the night, but after that they are seized with a terrible fear. It is indeed a special gift from God if someone is not afraid of dying.

For God's sake, do not paint a false picture of Christians. But whenever you describe Christians, see whether you can personally identify with that picture. Even pride can pop up in a Christian in a very obvious way. This is one of the worst vices because it is a sin against the First Commandment. By nature we are all proud—except that some of us are even more strongly inclined toward that sin than others.

As a rule, choleric[14] people with a so-called "strong will" and an abundance of energy have a great deal of self-confidence. They expect others to be respectful toward them—a result of the most shameful pride.[15] This sin sometimes breaks forth even in true Christians. Just recall the disciples of the Lord, arguing with one another about who among them was the greatest.[16] If this were not in the Bible, we could barely believe that the apostles went around like little children, saying, "I am the greatest!"—"No! I am the greatest!" Indeed, the mother of Zebedee's sons foolishly requested that one of them be placed at the right and the other at the left hand of the Lord.[17] From the account in Luke, we gather that the disciples were uneasy during this argument.[18] They knew that they had sinned greatly. When the Lord rebuked them, they felt so deeply ashamed that they wanted only to sink through the floor.[19]

Again, it is completely incorrect and false to describe Christians as always being enthusiastic in prayer and as if praying were their most cherished occupation. This is simply not the case. It requires much struggle on the part of the Christian to make himself fit for prayer, passionate in it, and confident that he will really receive from God that for which he is praying. How often are we Christians distracted—speaking to God yet thinking about this person or that!

That is why the Lord's Prayer, which is recited so often, has been called the greatest martyr on earth. This happens to true Christians as well. True, if a person regularly babbles the Lord's Prayer without knowing what he is

The Lord's Prayer is best

---

14 Hot-tempered. For more on Walther's understanding of temperaments, see page 64 n. 17.

15 Walther occasionally had to deal with his own energy and temper. Yet he usually had the ability to master himself and channel his energy in more fruitful ways. See, for example, Dallmann, *My Life*, 25.

16 See Mark 9:33–37.

17 See Matthew 20:20–28.

18 See Luke 22:24–30.

19 Walther treats the Synoptic Gospels as different aspects of one story. This was a common approach in his time.

saying, he is certainly not a Christian. A Christian who becomes aware of his lack of attention during prayer feels deeply humiliated and immediately starts the Lord's Prayer over again. However, there *are* times when the Christians' flesh and blood are forced into the background and they are full of bliss, as if they were in heaven, speaking with God—even though they retain their natural flesh and blood.

Christians are even tempted by the desire to grow rich. Business people, in particular, are in great danger of turning into misers. If they were not warned and admonished, they would be dragged into hell as if caught in a snare and would be lost forever.

It is so important to know whether someone loves the Word of God and his Savior, or whether his heart is hardened and he is leading a shameful life. There are people who want to make a show of being holier-than-thou. They avoid conversation, piously raise their eyes to heaven, constantly quote Scripture, and read their Bible in their spare time—preferably by themselves—in order to impress people with their exemplary Christianity.

Outward piety can mislead By putting on such a show, the "heavenly prophets"[20] succeeded in deceiving good Melanchthon. We must not think that **only** people who make a display of their godliness are true Christians. I am not claiming that every one of these people is an unbeliever, but I am sure that whoever fits perfectly the description above is a miserable hypocrite. Read the Gospels! Notice how the disciples spoke with the Lord and how they acted in His presence. They spoke their minds plainly—even John, the beloved disciple. Christ did not denounce them as being unconverted because of this. Rather, He treated them as converted people who, nevertheless, still carried a sizable portion of the old Adam with them.

In your sermons, you may refer to actions of **strong** or exceptionally **faithful** Christians. It will not harm your listeners to think that they have not yet reached such a degree of faithfulness. On the contrary, it will be a motivation to them to make more progress.

When new members are received into the congregation and you have to talk to them, do not regard them as godless, unconverted people if they do not immediately engage in a religious conversation with you. Some people cling to their Savior yet are unable to talk much about their faith, though on other

---

20 In 1521, while Luther was translating the New Testament at the Wartburg, Melanchthon and Carlstadt were in Wittenberg welcoming the "heavenly prophets," Nicholas Storch and Markus Stubner, from Zwickau. Storch and Stubner, along with Thomas Münzer, were members of the early Anabaptist movement that wanted to overthrow the existing government and create a theocracy. Their activity peaked with the Peasants' War in 1525. Carlstadt joined the radical reformers, while Luther had the "prophets" and their movement expelled from Wittenberg and brought Melanchthon back in line. See the map of Saxony in the front of the book, as well as the related entries in the Glossary and the Index of Persons and Groups.

topics they may be ready talkers. Others, again, may not have much experience in spiritual matters and for that reason may not be able to say much.

In conclusion, let me submit a citation from Luther's *Church Postil*. He says (St. Louis Ed. 12:911ff.):[21]

> That explains why St. Paul warns his Christians to such an extent as to make it appear that he were overdoing it. In all his Epistles, he insists on beating these matters into the people, implying that they are stupid, uninformed, inattentive and forgetful. He is implying that they do not know these things and would not do them on their own, unless told and urged to do them. He knows that—even when Christians are taking their first steps in the faith and are at the point where the fruits of their faith should start to show—these things are not happening yet, nor are they completed. Accordingly, it is not enough to say that it is sufficient to preach the doctrine to them—and once the Spirit and faith are at work, the fruits of faith and good works will follow all by themselves. For even though the Spirit is present and, as Christ says, it operates in believers and makes them willing, nevertheless the flesh is also present, and the flesh is always weak and tardy. Moreover, the devil never rests. Using tribulations and temptations, he attempts to trip up Christians and make them fall because of the weakness of their flesh, etc.

W² 12:911–13

> For this reason we must not treat our listeners as if they did not need to be warned and urged by God's Word to lead a godly life. Beware of negligence and laziness in carrying out this duty! For the flesh is too slothful to obey the Spirit. In fact, the flesh is so strong that it will resist the Spirit, as St. Paul says in Galatians 5:17: "For the flesh lusts against the Spirit, etc., to keep you from doing the things you want to do." Therefore, God must act like a good and diligent manager of an estate or a magistrate who has a lazy servant or slothful officials under him, though in other respects these people are not unfaithful or wicked. Do not think that, just when the manager has issued one or two orders, the job that he wants done will be completed. He must continually be after his workers and urge them to do their work.

Gal. 5:17 Luther

> Likewise, we have not yet reached the point where our flesh and blood are active and leap forward with complete joy and delight to do good works and obey God—as our spirit desires and our faith demands. On the contrary, despite all our constant urging and prodding, we can scarcely get our flesh to move. What would happen if we were to stop

---

21 See John Nicholas Lenker, ed., *Complete Sermons of Martin Luther*, trans. John Nicholas Lenker et al. (Grand Rapids: Baker, 1983, 2000), 4.2:305–6.

prodding and urging and assume—as many secure spirits do—that everybody knows well enough what they have to do, just because they have heard their duties recited to them for so many years and have even taught them to others, etc.? I am convinced that, if we were to stop preaching and warning for one year, we would become worse than the worst heathen.

Thirtieth Evening Lecture:
June 5, 1885

Many young men whom God has blessed with splendid gifts that are especially suited for the Office of the Ministry—and who even have a certain tendency toward that office—nevertheless do not want to become pastors. They think that in the Office of the Ministry they would have to sacrifice their life's happiness and their freedom.

Pastors lead lives of faith and sacrifice

However, this is a great self-delusion. Anyone who wishes to be saved must be ready, if Christ so desires, to sacrifice his life's happiness and surrender his freedom for the Lord's sake. Not only a pastor but also every Christian must choose[22] the narrow path[23] that leads to heaven—assuming that he wants to get to heaven. He must forsake the world, fight against his flesh and crucify it, and work out his salvation with fear and trembling[24] if he does not wish to die eternally. Therefore, by refusing to become a pastor, a young man does not gain any advantage at all for his lustful flesh.

If a Christian does not wish to thrust the grace of God from himself, a Christian must be a part of the spiritual priesthood—even if he does not become a preacher. It is indeed true that men who wish to become pastors must, first, be sincere Christians. That is the necessary condition.[25]

1 Tim. 3:9

In 1 Timothy 3, the apostle Paul concludes his list of the qualities required for a bishop—or, what amounts to the same, a pastor—with these words: "They must hold the mystery of the faith with a clear conscience." This shows that a pastor must have a purified conscience—cleansed not only by the blood of Christ for the forgiveness of sins but also by the sanctification of the Spirit. A pastor must come to the important decision that he will not live for himself but for Him who died and rose again for his sake. By the time he is ordained—when he is separated from the world for service in the sanctuary—a pastor must have said good-bye to the world and become irrevocably divorced from

---

22   German: *erwählen*.
23   See Matthew 7:13.
24   See Philippians 2:12.
25   Latin: *conditio sine qua non*.

it. He must have reached the belief that the pious poet[26] has expressed in this way:

> Oh my heart, now be clear:
> In good faith, dare the venture!
> Or you will find no rest.
> Renounce the world henceforth;
> Your fleshly lusts throw off.
> With Christ now take your stand,
> And thus the matter end.

Blessed are you, my dear friends, if you make your heartfelt cry the poet's words: "With Christ now take your stand, And thus the matter end." **Not until you do this** will you "end the matter."

Accordingly, when a congregation has an orthodox yet unconverted pastor who does not believe what he preaches—even though he has grasped pure doctrine quite well with his intellect and memory—this is a real tragedy. Thanks to his pure doctrine, a pastor like this will generally lead his congregation to good pastures in his pulpit work. Yet he will be a sorry "watchman" and "caretaker of souls" and an even sorrier example for his flock. His congregation will not regard him as a Christian role model who has renounced himself and the world.

If it is to his advantage, he will indeed stick to pure doctrine and even fight bravely to maintain it. But if a situation arises that might cause him to be hated or that might produce unthankfulness as a reward for his enthusiasm, or if there is a risk of suffering dishonor and persecution for the sake of pure doctrine—he will drop it like a hot potato. In this case it would be obvious that his Christianity grew from a bad root and that his congregation has obtained a cheat.

For in times of tribulation, when wolves and foxes try to break into the flock, it is of primary importance that the shepherd take a firm stand and be ready to give his life, to shed his blood—for the truth and for his flock. An unconverted person would consider it ridiculous to sacrifice a pleasant life in a nice position with a comfortable income for what he would consider to be a subtle point of doctrine, because he has never truly understood how the doctrine of salvation works.

When the issue at hand is not about objective or speculative doctrine, but about teachings that from a purely practical point of view are based on true knowledge and experience of the heart—then a doctrinally sound pastor of this type will talk like a blind man about colors. At times, he will portray

---

26   Karl Friedrich August Westenholz (1736–89). He reached the position of director (*Kapellmeister*) at the court chapel in Schwerin.

Christianity in a better light than it is; at other times, in a worse light than it really is. At our last meeting, we saw how Law and Gospel can be confused by an exaggerated view of Christianity. Tonight, we will hear how a pastor portrays true Christianity in a worse light than it really is.

This photograph shows the faculty of Concordia College from 1887 to 1892. Standing, from left to right, are Licentiate K. Georg Stöckhardt, exegetical theology (Walther's former post); Franz A. O. Pieper, dogmatics and practical theology; and August L. Graebner, homiletics. Seated from left to right are C. H. Rudolph Lange, historical theology and philosophy; and Martin Günther, introductory courses, isagogics, and symbolics. Image taken from Ludwig Fürbringer, *Eighty Eventful Years* (St. Louis: Concordia, 1944), 102.

THESIS XVIII

You are not rightly distinguishing Law and Gospel in the Word of God if you describe the universal corruption of mankind so as to create the impression that even true believers are still under the spell of ruling sins and sin deliberately.

EDITOR'S NOTE: In this thesis, Walther points to the historic distinction between ruling sins and sins that are ruled.[1] For unbelievers, even their outward good works and prayers are sin before God because their hearts are sinful. That is what Luther means with his two kinds of righteousness.[2] Because something outwardly looks pious among people does not mean that God sees it that way. In the fall, man became totally sinful. Yet those in whom the Holy Spirit has kindled faith now struggle against their sin (Romans 7:14–24). The grace of Christ rules those sins; it hides them in the immeasurable sacrifice of Christ, and they are put away. God forgives the struggling believer. The sin that a believer has is completely evil and completely his; the righteousness that a believer has is completely righteous and completely of Christ, not of himself.

P lease note that I am speaking of the claim that the universal corruption of mankind includes the fact that true believers are *ruled* by deliberate sin. No one who is familiar with pure doctrine will make the unqualified statement that a Christian can be a fornicator and an adulterer. Such a thought would not enter the mind of a true teacher of the *Word of God*.

Ruling and ruled sin

But a preacher trying to give a very drastic description of the universal corruption of mankind might easily be tempted to stray from pure doctrine. I am speaking of mistakes that are frequently made by [overly] enthusiastic pastors and by theological students as well. In their first sermons submitted for review, they quite often say that all of mankind lives in this or that sin—even citing mortal sins, as though even Christians were wallowing in such sins.

Incredible damage is done when people are forced to hear that we human beings live in every horror, shame, and vice. What is missing here is a qualifying statement such as "as we are by nature" or "as long as a person is still

---

1 Latin: *peccata regnans* and *peccata regnata*.
2 Luther engages this in *The Bondage of the Will* (AE 33). See especially AE 33:54.

in the state of natural wickedness prior to his conversion." Once you add these qualifiers, of course, you cannot overemphasize the horrible qualities of man's natural condition.

Scriptural division of people

However, when addressing a Christian congregation, you have to be very careful not to speak as if all Christians live in shame and vice. It was a harmful and dangerous attempt on the part of the Pietists to separate humanity into so many different classes that nobody was able to tell to which class he belonged. But this must not keep us from pointing out in our sermons the two great groups into which humanity is truly separated, that is, believers and unbelievers, the godly and ungodly, the converted and unconverted, regenerate and unregenerate persons.

Mark 16:16; Matt. 9:13; 5:45; 13:38

This classification runs throughout Scripture. Christ always preaches: "Whoever believes and is baptized will be saved, but whoever does not believe will be condemned." "For I came not to call the righteous, but sinners." God "makes His sun rise on the evil and on the good, and sends rain on the just and on the unjust." In each one of these texts, Christ recognizes only two kinds of human beings. In Matthew 13:38, He speaks of "the sons of the kingdom" and "the sons of the evil one," of "good seed" and "weeds."

This thorough division, this either/or, must appear in every sermon of a sincere preacher. This is what your listeners must learn, that is, that they are either spiritually dead or spiritually alive, either converted or unconverted, either under the wrath of God or in a state of grace, either Christians or unbelievers, either asleep in sin or awakened to a new life in God, subjects in either the devil's [kingdom] or God's kingdom.

It is an accursed heresy to speak of Hades as modern [historical-critical] theologians do, [as a place or mode of existence] where man supposedly has another chance to be converted. Immeasurable harm is done by this doctrine. May God in His grace protect you from being tempted by Satan and embracing this teaching!

Matt. 7:13–14

Make plain to your listeners in all your sermons that there are only two places where we will end up at the end of this life: either heaven or hell. There will be only two sentences pronounced on people: either damnation or eternal life. Accordingly, there are only two kinds of people in the present life: the one kind is headed straight for hell; the other, straight for heaven. For Christ says as clearly as possible: "Enter by the narrow gate. For the gate is wide and the way is easy that leads to destruction, and those who enter by it are many. For the gate is narrow and the way is hard that leads to life, and those who find it are few."

There are only two gates, two roads, and two destinations at the end of life. To confuse these two kinds of people is to confuse Law and Gospel in the most horrible way. The Law produces condemned sinners; the Gospel, free and blessed people. So let us hear a few Bible passages on this matter—even though it seems so unnecessary to discuss this matter further because this whole thing is as clear as daylight. You can stumble into this error despite your best intentions if you claim that we are "**horrible sinners** who need a Savior."

When we speak of "horrible" sinners, we must not refer to Christians, in whom we find weaknesses, which are covered with the righteousness of Christ, yet also good deeds, which God does through them and which are pleasing to Him. All baptized Christians may apply to themselves the declaration of God: "This is My beloved Son, with whom I am well pleased." — Matt. 3:17

Romans 6:14: "For sin will have no dominion over you, since you are not under law but under grace." [Paul] is actually saying not only that sin **should** not dominate Christians but also that sin is not **able** to dominate Christians. In fact, it is absolutely impossible for a person who is in a state of grace to be ruled by sin. When a pilgrim traveling on a lonely road is attacked by a robber, the pilgrim will escape from the robber at the first opportunity because he does not want to be overcome and killed. Christians are pilgrims in this world and are on their way to heaven. Like a highway robber, the devil assaults them, and they collapse before him because of their weakness—not because they *want* to collapse. When true Christians collapse, they are forgiven because they turn to God in daily and tearful repentance—or at least with heartfelt sighs, begging for pardon. But if a person allows sin to rule him, that is a sure sign that he is not a Christian but a hypocrite—no matter how pious he pretends to be. — Rom. 6:14

In 1 Corinthians 6:9–11 we read:

> Do you not know that the unrighteous will not inherit the kingdom of God? Do not be deceived: neither the sexually immoral, nor idolaters, nor adulterers, nor men who practice homosexuality, nor thieves, nor the greedy, nor drunkards, nor revilers, nor swindlers will inherit the kingdom of God. And such were some of you. But you were washed, you were sanctified, you were justified in the name of the Lord Jesus Christ and by the Spirit of our God. — 1 Cor. 6:9–11

No one, then, who falls into these sins and fails to repent of them will inherit the kingdom of God. The Christian's repentance consists in this: that he no longer desires to commit these sins. Whoever commits these sins intentionally has proof that he is not a Christian but is condemned and moved not by the Spirit of God, but by the hellish spirit.

In 2 Peter 2:20–22, the apostle writes:

> For if, after they have escaped the defilements of the world through the knowledge of our Lord and Savior Jesus Christ, they are again — 2 Pet. 2:20–22

entangled in them and overcome, the last state has become worse for them than the first. For it would have been better for them never to have known the way of righteousness than after knowing it to turn back from the holy commandment delivered to them. What the true proverb says has happened to them: "The dog returns to its own vomit, and the sow, after washing herself, returns to wallow in the mire."

With this important passage, in particular, we confront the Calvinists who say that a person who has once obtained faith can never lose it. Here the apostle Peter is speaking of persons who had been children of God, who had a living knowledge of the Lord Jesus, and who had been in a state of divine grace. How, then, can anyone be so disrespectful as to declare that a person who had been truly converted stays converted, even when, like Peter and David,[3] they fall into some particular sin?

Rom. 8:13–14   Romans 8:13–14: "For if you live according to the flesh you will die, but if by the Spirit you put to death the deeds of the body, you will live. For all who are led by the Spirit of God are sons of God." The apostle does not say, "Do not worry about your sinning. God will keep you in His grace and bring you back." Rather, he says, "If you live according to the flesh, you will die. Those who are led by **the Spirit** of God—**they** are the sons of God." On the other hand, this means that those who are not led by the Spirit of God, but by their flesh, are not the children of God but servants of Satan.

In Galatians 5:19–21, Paul writes:

Gal. 5:19–21   Now the works of the flesh are evident: sexual immorality, impurity, sensuality, idolatry, sorcery, enmity, strife, jealousy, fits of anger, rivalries, dissensions, divisions, envy, drunkenness, orgies, and things like these. I warn you, as I warned you before, that those who do such things will not inherit the kingdom of God.

Stop and consider every word of this passage. In view of this text, is it not shocking when men who want to be Christian theologians say that people can be in a state of grace while living in shameful sins such as the ones mentioned in this text? This text shuts them out from the kingdom of God and announces the judgment of God to them.

In Ephesians 5:5–6, the same apostle writes:

Eph. 5:5–6   For you may be sure of this, that everyone who is sexually immoral or impure, or who is covetous (that is, an idolater), has no inheritance in the kingdom of Christ and God. Let no one deceive you with empty words, for because of these things the wrath of God comes upon the sons of disobedience.

---

3   Walther is referring to Peter's denial of Christ and David's adultery with Bathsheba and the subsequent murder of her husband, Uriah. See Matthew 26:31–35, 69–75; 2 Samuel 11.

The apostle's warning, "Let no one deceive you," means: Do not listen to those who tell you the opposite. Unbelievers will be condemned because they live in sins such as these. Consider, then, that if you were to live in the same sins, you would share their fate in hell. This is what Paul is asking the Ephesians to think about.

I wish to call your attention to the fact that passages such as the ones I have quoted are found in the Sunday lectionary readings.[4] They should prove valuable to you when you use them for a lively presentation of the doctrine we are discussing. I am always irritated when I attend church and find that these splendid texts are not used for the sermon. You ought to resolve that, when a lectionary reading that contains these texts comes up, you will explain them to your listeners and tell them that, as surely God lives, they will be condemned if they live in this or that sin. If you only tell them that Christians remain sinners until they die, they will often misunderstand you. Some will lull themselves to sleep with the idea that they are poor and weak human beings, yet they still have faith in the Lord Jesus Christ. This, however, is a false faith.

Using the lectionary

Let me urge you in general to take a survey of the lectionary readings on which you are going to preach and to note beforehand particular passages that suggest subjects on which you feel you ought to preach. If you fiddle around until Wednesday or Thursday, looking up the text for the coming Sunday and after a shallow reading decide on some topic that will yield eight pages of manuscript, enough for a talk of forty-five minutes,[5] you are acting like a shameful hireling.

Tips for writing sermons

Every Sunday evening the faithful pastor begins to consider the subject of his sermon for the coming Sunday and determines to redeem fully the precious minutes during which he will face his congregation. (The only thing that would keep him from following this practice would be a visit he might have to make or receive on that Sunday evening.) In so doing, he delights in storming this or that stronghold of the devil. True, he will not succeed in overthrowing every one of these strongholds, but it must be his earnest intention to do so. Otherwise, many worshipers will continue in spiritual misery—stuck in their sinful ways—and the pastor will have **himself** to blame for it. If you do what divine grace enables you to do, the Savior will not put you to shame on account of your deficiencies but will graciously reward you in the end with the crown of glory.[6]

---

4   The original text reads: "the pericopes."
5   Regarding sermon length, see also page 331.
6   See 1 Peter 5:4.

To strengthen the belief that I am trying to produce in you, let me cite a testimony from the Smalcald Articles, Part III, Article III, paragraphs 42–45:[7]

On the other hand, certain sects may arise; some may already exist. During the peasant rebellion, I encountered some who held that those who had once received the Spirit or the forgiveness of sins or had become believers—even if they later sin—would still remain in the faith. Such sin, they think, would not harm them. They say, "Do whatever you please. If you believe, it all amounts to nothing. Faith blots out all sins," and such. They also say that if anyone sins after he has received faith and the Spirit, he never truly had the Spirit and faith. I have seen and heard many such madmen. I fear that such a devil is still in some of them.

So it is necessary to know and to teach this: When holy people—still having and feeling original sin and daily repenting and striving against it—happen to fall into manifest sins (as David did into adultery, murder, and blasphemy),[8] then faith and the Holy Spirit have left them. The Holy Spirit does not permit sin to have dominion, to gain the upper hand so it can be carried out, but represses and restrains it from doing what it wants.[9] If sin does what it wants, the Holy Spirit and faith are not present. For St. John says, "No one born of God makes a practice of sinning . . . and he cannot keep on sinning."[10] And yet it is also true when St. John says, "If we say we have no sin, we deceive ourselves, and the truth is not in us."[11]

Now, so you do not think that we are ineffectively arguing about obvious matters, let me prove to you that the Calvinists have adopted as doctrine the very same error we reject in this thesis. [Listen to this statement] from the decrees of the **Synod of Dort**:[12] "God, who is rich in mercy, according to His immutable purpose of election, **does not completely remove the Holy Spirit from His own even when they sin outrageously**, nor does He permit them to fall entirely out of the grace of adoption as children of God and out of the state of justification."[13]

Anyone who falls into a mortal sin slips back entirely into the state of sin. But according to this confession of the Reformed, Peter, David, and others remained righteous people while they committed mortal sins. [The

---

7   *Concordia*, 276–78. See also Müller, 319; *Triglot Concordia*, 491.

8   See 2 Samuel 11.

9   See Psalm 51:11; Romans 6:14.

10   1 John 3:9.

11   1 John 1:8.

12   For information on the Synod of Dort, see page 229 n. 1 and the Glossary entry, page 478.

13   The Canons of the Synod of Dort, Part V, Article IV (Walther's emphasis).

Calvinists claim that] these people remained in a state of grace as children of God and retained the Holy Spirit. This we reject, while we indeed affirm that the elect **cannot** remain in a condemned state **until their death**—otherwise they could not be elect.

The fact that sin exists and the question of how it originated are two of the greatest problems with which we humans can wrestle. Even the more serious philosophers of pagan antiquity dealt with this highly important and grave subject. But they were uninformed of the fact that in the beginning God had created man perfectly good, according to His image. Yet soon afterward—after he was misled by the devil—man fell from this first estate. So, of course, those pagan philosophers were not able to discover the awful character of sin and its origin.

As a rule, they did not get any further in their reasoning than to state that sin is an inborn weakness and frailty of man. Others—such as Zoroaster, Manes, and many of the Gnostics—wished to push their investigation further and claimed a twofold primordial principle or primeval essence: one good, the other evil. They claimed that what is good in man comes from the good; what is evil in him, from the evil principle. But when all was said and done, they still did not understand what a terrible outrage sin is.

It is a tragedy that even in the midst of Christendom there are countless people—both baptized and unbaptized—who do not know what sin is. Some, such as the Rationalists, claim that man is naturally good and becomes evil and sinful only when influenced by evil examples, wrong teaching, and sensual enticements that he is not able to resist steadfastly.[14]

Others—such as the pantheists, atheists, and materialists—claim that sinning is no worse than eating when you are hungry or drinking when you are thirsty; it is merely satisfying a natural craving. Most of them go even further, claiming that sin is the indispensably necessary means by which man has developed his self-consciousness. The notorious philosopher Hegel[15] says flat out that if man had not fallen into sin, Paradise would have been nothing but a zoological garden. In fact, Hegel even considers sin necessary. He is unable to grasp that sin might be harmful. On the contrary, he treats sin as the transition from the state of barbarism to that of self-conscious thinking.[16]

Thirty-first Evening Lecture: June 12, 1885

---

14   This is the idea of the "noble savage" that was popular in the nineteenth century. Several English philosophers expressed similar ideas, which informed ideas about the natural rights of man in the American Declaration of Independence.

15   German philosopher Georg Wilhelm Friedrich Hegel (1770–1831). For more information, see the Index of Persons and Groups, page 495.

16   In the nineteenth and twentieth centuries, historical-critical scholars reinterpreted eating from the tree of the knowledge of good and evil (Genesis 3) to be an awakening event in

This blindness regarding sin is the chief cause of the almost universal rejection of the Gospel in our time. People who fail to recognize the horrible nature of sin decline to accept the sacrificial death of the Son of God for the reconciliation and redemption of this world of sinners. They consider His death completely unnecessary and, therefore, regard the story of the Gospel as a miserable fable.

It is, therefore, one of the most important requirements of a true, Gospel-oriented pastor that he would know how to explain to his listeners the true nature of sin in terms that are as loud and clear as they are terrible, drastic, and relevant. For without a real knowledge of what an awful thing sin is, a person cannot understand and accept the Gospel. As long as he is not alarmed that sin is his greatest enemy and the most awful horror living in him, he will not come to Christ. Law and Gospel can be distinguished even less if a person has no true and adequate knowledge of sin. This point leads us to our next thesis.

---

which Adam and Eve emerged from immaturity to maturity, as if doing good and evil were somehow greater or better than doing good alone.

THESIS XIX

You are not rightly distinguishing Law and Gospel in the Word of God if you preach about certain sins as if they were not damnable but only venial.[1]

EDITOR'S NOTE: In this thesis, Walther draws on a long-established element of doctrine that he researched in the Book of Concord, Luther, and Johann Gerhard's *Loci Theologici*.

Walther has already made the distinction between intentional, mortal sin and unintentional, pardonable, venial sin.[2] Sin is always a serious evil. It is not because of the sinner that venial sins do not bring spiritual death. Venial sins are pardoned because of the great suffering and death of the righteous Christ and, through Him, the struggle of faith against the devil, the world, and sinful flesh.

Much of the expanded material in these second lectures on Law and Gospel is Walther's collection and application of a lifetime of studying Lutheran sources. Walther wants to pass on what he received in order that his students and even generations yet unborn may properly read and apply the Bible.

Unless you reflect deeply on this hugely important matter, you will lack much of the clear vision that you need to properly carry out the pastoral office. We have already seen that we must distinguish mortal and venial sins. A person failing to make this distinction is not rightly distinguishing Law and Gospel. But the distinction between these two kinds of sin must be made with great care.

This distinction is necessary to prove that certain sins do, in fact, expel the Holy Spirit from the believer. Once the Holy Spirit has been driven out, faith, too, is ejected. For no one can come to faith or keep it without the Holy Spirit. Sins that expel the Holy Spirit and bring on spiritual death are called **mortal sins**.

Types of sin

---

1   *Venial* sins are otherwise mortal sins that, for the believer, are pardoned by Christ through faith and the Means of Grace. They are not pardoned because they are considered to be "no big deal."

2   All sin deserves death (Genesis 3:17–19). The cross does not remove punishment in this life, but it offers new life in Christ: forgiveness now and, at the hour of death, release from all punishment into blessedness. With this in mind, Gerhard and others distinguish between *mortal* sins that deserve death and *deadly* sins that actually cause death.

This can happen quite easily. If someone has been a Christian, as soon as he sins intentionally, he would know right away that the Holy Spirit has departed from him. He is no longer able to pray to God like a child.[3] He cannot resist temptation firmly and bravely—the way he used to do. He would notice: "I have become chained to sin; I am now a slave to sin." Good for him, if he should have at least this knowledge of his condition. He may yet be brought back to God. Yet as long as this condition continues, he is not in fellowship with God.[4]

Venial sins, on the other hand, are sins that Christians commit without losing the Holy Spirit. They are sins of weakness or rashness and are sometimes called the "daily sins" of Christians.

Venial sins not minor

While we need to impress this distinction on our listeners, for God's sake, we must be most careful not to create the impression that venial sins need not concern us and that we do not need to ask forgiveness for them. A preacher who does exactly that, insofar as it is possible for him to do, preaches his listeners straight into hell. He makes them carnally secure and drives the fear of God from their hearts. This would not be the truly evangelical way of preaching about these sins. At the same time, it would not be a truly evangelical, Gospel-oriented idea that only a pastor who does *not* preach the Law frequently is a real evangelical preacher.

Both Law and Gospel must be preached—the one in its sternness, the other in its sweetness. A preacher who does not preach both side by side does not deserve to be called an evangelical pastor. Rather, this man would be a false leader—sowing the Gospel as if casting wheat into the ocean, where no crop can be raised.

The heavenly seed of the Gospel can sprout only in a crushed heart. It happens all too often that, when distinguishing between venial and mortal sins, preachers create the impression that Christians need not worry about venial sins. "Since everybody is a sinner and no one ever gets rid of sin entirely, there is no reason you should feel disturbed because of these sins." Such talk is awful and ungodly.

In Matthew 5:18–19, the Lord says:

---

3   See Luke 18:15–17.

4   If a person commits an intentional sin, he is not forgiven because he feels sorry about it. In fact, if he does have faith, the Holy Spirit urges him to confess that sin either in private confession with the pastor or as a part of the general confession in the Divine Service in order to be restored by the Means of Grace. A Christian must be willing to accept punishment in this world so that he does not receive eternal punishment in the world to come (Matthew 5:29–30; 7:21–23). Sorrow can lead either to confession and forgiveness or to a hardening of the heart that, if unchanged, at the point of death is revealed to be the sin against the Holy Spirit.

For truly, I say to you, until heaven and earth pass away, not an iota, not a dot, will pass from the Law until all is accomplished. Therefore whoever relaxes one of the least of these commandments and teaches others to do the same will be called least in the kingdom of heaven, but whoever does them and teaches them will be called great in the kingdom of heaven.

Matt. 5:18–19

This is one of the toughest sayings in Scripture. The Lord does not say, "He will **be** the least," but, "He **will be called** least." "The least" means the most condemned, that is, people whom God does not acknowledge as His own. That will be the **sentence** passed on them in the kingdom of God and Christ. Therefore, for God's sake, be sure to approach the task of preaching both the Gospel and the Law with trembling! Make certain you say that every single iota of the Law—including the [falsely] so-called "minor" Commandments—is something about which Christians should be greatly concerned.

The context in which the Lord said these words is noteworthy. Immediately before this passage, He states that He has come to fulfill the Law. Now—especially given the fact that the Lord had to fulfill every law and every commandment in our place—it is shocking when people, poor, sinful worms that they are, would want to ignore a single law of God and to treat it as if it were a matter of no importance.

People who entertain such thoughts are not Christians. If anyone takes some kind of secret comfort from this idea, they have pitifully deceived and cheated themselves. On the contrary, in these matters true Christians are persons who are afraid to commit a single sin.

But the Lord adds: "and **teaches** others to do the same." It is bad enough when a pastor on his own disregards some law and leads a careless life. But it is even worse when he preaches his lax views and leads people to damnation by his preaching. Such pastors will have to give an account to God of their preaching, and on the Last Day they will not be able to excuse themselves by claiming that they were talking only about unimportant matters that are irrelevant.

Pastors, beware!
Matt. 5:19

A Christian grieves even over the smallest sins, but unbelievers imagine that they can "escape from their crimes."[5] That is the slogan of the godless. An unconverted person thinks: "Well, I will just make up for it, and the whole thing will blow over." If you do not ask God for forgiveness, that situation will never blow over.

In Matthew 12:36: "I tell you, on the day of judgment people will give account for every careless word they speak." Using a real-world[6] example, this

Matt. 12:36

---

5   See Psalm 56:7. The Dau text adds: "[Luther: 'What evil we do is already forgiven.']"
6   Latin: *in concreto.*

text shows us how horrible it is to claim that some sins are basically venial and are automatically paid for by God, as if He did not regard them to be a great evil.

1 Sam. 2:24   People who speak in this way picture God, the Holy and Righteous One, as a feeble, old man like Eli, who saw his sons sin and merely said, "No, my sons," thinking that he had already done his full duty. True enough: God is love. But He is also holiness and righteousness. For the people who rise up against Him, God becomes a terrible fire, and His fiery wrath follows these sinners into the depths of hell.

Let the people of the world mock and scorn this teaching. They will have to pay dearly for their laughter, like the people of Sodom.[7] Every evil word ever spoken will be dealt with. And when sinners are tried on Judgment Day, even one single evil word would be enough to damn them. Is there a single Christian who can say at the end of each day on which he has spoken much that he has not spoken a single idle word? Few Christians will be able to make that claim. Christians must ask God's pardon with a contrite heart—even for an idle word—and promise to guard their lips better in the future. If God did not forgive their idle words, these alone would condemn them. No sin is venial in itself. But there *are* sins that will not prevent a person from still believing in Jesus Christ with all his heart.

James 2:10   James 2:10 reads: "For whoever keeps the whole law but fails in one point has become accountable for all of it." Let us assume that Scripture contained a thousand commandments. (In reality there are more than a thousand, because the ones that have been recorded state only general principles for which we are to find specific applications.) Now, according to this text, if a person had kept 999 of the 1,000 commandments, he would be guilty of the whole Law. This applies to every one of the so-called "venial sins."

Unless Christians clearly understand this fact, they stop being Christians. What makes people Christians is this living knowledge:[8] "I am a miserable, accursed, damned sinner, who would have to be eternally condemned if Christ had not died for me. But I believe that Jesus Christ, true God, born of the Father in eternity, and also true man, born of the Virgin Mary, has redeemed me, a lost and condemned person, purchased and won me from all sins, from death, and from the power of the devil."[9] A Christian must regard himself as a lost and condemned sinner—or all his chatter about faith is useless and worthless.

Gal. 3:10   Galatians 3:10: "For all who rely on works of the law are under a curse; for it is written, 'Cursed be everyone who does not abide by all things written in

---

7   See Genesis 19:1–29.

8   Walther refers to this as living knowledge over against dead, historical, false faith.

9   Compare with *Concordia*, 329. The use of "born" follows Luther's German.

the Book of the Law, and do them.'" The curse recorded in this clear passage will descend on everyone who does not continue to do *everything* written in the Book of the Law. Therefore, there is no such thing as a sin that is venial by its nature. Sins are venial only for Christ's sake.

First John 1:7: "The blood of Jesus His Son cleanses us from all sin." **From all sin!** Indeed, the blood of Jesus Christ, the Son of God, must be required to cancel the so-called "venial" sins as well. Otherwise, it would say: "from all mortal sins, from all serious sins, from all coarse sins." But if the blood of Christ was necessary to cleanse us from venial sins as well, then those sins must **in themselves** be mortal sins.

1 John 1:7

Every sin is something awful because it is lawlessness.[10] It is rebellion against holy, omnipotent God—our supreme, heavenly Lawgiver. When a sinner adds willfulness to his act, he acts like a person who sees the law that the king ordered to be posted in public, tears down the proclamation notice from the wall, and tramples on it. What will happen to such a person? In an absolute monarchy the punishment for such a crime would be death.

We may not be tearing down the Law of God publicly, but we daily act contrary to it. For this we are to express our heartfelt **regret.** A true Christian is not a smart-mouth who goes around holding his head high—I think you know what I mean. A true Christian has a smashed heart. His heart is not hard. When one speaks God's Word to him, he accepts it immediately and humbles himself. Anybody may speak a warning or a rebuke to a Christian, and he will accept it. Occasionally, he may resist for a moment and, as Luther puts it, allow the devil to ride him.[11] But then [this act of resistance] begins to burn. He would have to be practically out of his mind if, in a short while, he did not see that he behaved himself in a very unchristian and godless manner. It will not take long before he begs God and other people for forgiveness.

Without a broken spirit, people can talk as much as they want about their Christian faith. All that talk is worthless because they are under the power of sin. Let us, then, be entirely certain that sin—no matter what it might be—is never venial in and of itself. Whenever someone does something contrary to the Law, the Law has to condemn the doer. Here is an example; take Matthew 5:21–22:

> You have heard that it was said to the ancient ones, "You shall not murder; and whoever murders will be answerable to judgment." But I say to you that whoever is angry with his brother will be answerable to judgment; whoever says to his brother, "Raca," will be answerable

Matt. 5:21–22
Luther

---

10   Walther uses the Greek: *anomía*.
11   See *Bondage of the Will*, AE 33:176.

to the council; and whoever says, "You fool!" will be guilty of the fire of hell.

Is there a Christian who has never been angry with a fellow Christian—if even only for a short time? Even though the lapse occurred in weakness, nevertheless that Christian committed a sin of which he needs to be ashamed. When Christ says, "He will be answerable to judgment," He treats anger and murder alike. [The Aramaic insult] "Raca," ["empty-head,"] means when anger in the heart breaks forth in angry words and gestures. It reaches its worst stage when the angry person cries: "You fool!" The Law immediately sends such an angry person to the fire of hell.

Rom. 8:1

All these texts prove that so-called "venial sins" are not venial in themselves according to their nature, but damnable, mortal sins. But Scripture speaks of believers only thusly: "There is therefore now no condemnation for those who are in Christ Jesus." But a believer is the very person who regards sin as **a very serious matter**.

Roman errors

So you do not think: "Oh, who could possibly preach that way," hear now what the Papists teach in their catechism. The **Roman Catechism** (*p.* II, *cap.* V, *q.* 46) says:

> All mortal sins must be told to the priest. For venial sins, which do not separate us from divine grace and into which we can fall rather often, though we may properly and usefully confess them, . . . may also be withheld from the priest without penalty and may be atoned for in many different ways. Mortal sins, however, . . . must be listed individually, . . . for it is their nature to cause a more serious wound on the soul than those sins that people are in the habit of committing freely and publicly.[12]

Matt. 5:19

Here it says that one does not need Absolution for venial sins. This is antichristian doctrine. They put it so naively, but it reveals a bottomless pit of evil. The Word of the Lord that applies here is: they "will be called least in the kingdom of heaven."

Over against this teaching, **Kromayer** writes (*Theologia positiva polemica* I, page 511): "There is no sin that in its nature is venial. We must steer a middle course between the Roman Scylla and the Calvinistic Charybdis."[13]

The Romanists and others count sinful desires that they do not actually do as venial sins. For example, there are many shameful rogues who do not

---

12 *Catechismus ex Decreto Concilii Tridentini ad Parochos*, ed. Pius V and Clement XIII (Rome: Press of the Congregation for the Propagation of the Faith, 1858), 177–78. Walther translated the Latin text into spoken German for his hearers. The German translation represented here is not literal, but it correctly captures the sense of the Latin text.

13 Hieronymus Kromayer, *Theologia Positivo-Polemica* (Lipsiae: Wittgau, 1668). Walther has already demonstrated that both Romanists and Calvinists err in the doctrine of sin.

actually carry out certain things, but they delight in all kinds of shameful pictures while lying on their beds. The only reason they refrain from doing the things [they think about] is because they are afraid of the scandal that would follow. Nevertheless, these people must be told that they are still living in mortal sin. Or a little thing, such as stealing a pin, is supposed to be a venial sin. In contrast, I still remember quite well that my parents deeply impressed on us children: "You must not steal even a stickpin!" Children must come to realize that father is an enemy of every sin and will get really angry, or at least very stern. They have to see that "Father is taking it very seriously"! It is really good when parents do that.

Let me cite a statement of **Socinus** in his *Commentary on the Gospel of St. John* (page 448): "It seems to be certain that, for a person who otherwise confesses the faith of Christ in his heart, **one** sinful act cannot have the effect of bringing him to death. When we are told about a sin that leads to death, the reference cannot be to a **single** sin, but to habitual sinning."[14] According to Socinian teaching, a person does not need to ask God's forgiveness for an occasional fall into sin. No, [this teaching says] that sin must first become a habit; it must become a vice before it excludes a person from the kingdom of God.

Let us hear a few testimonies from **Luther**. I will first cite a passage from his *Exposition of the Theses Discussed at Leipzig* (St. Louis Ed. 18:833ff.). The second thesis that Luther defends reads: "To deny that a person sins even in his good deeds, to deny that **venial sins are such not by their nature** but solely by the mercy of God, or to deny that sin remains in an infant also after Baptism, means to trample both St. Paul and Christ underfoot." Luther then comments on this thesis:

W² 18:833

> Therefore, it is another serious error of the theologians that they show barely any concern regarding venial sins and chatter away that a venial sin does not offend God, at least only to a pardonable degree. If venial sins are such unimportant sins, why is it that even the righteous are scarcely saved? Why can the righteous not endure the judgment of God and be declared righteous? Why are we urged with such intensity, and in no petty or figurative sense, to pray: "Forgive us our debts" and "Thy will be done; Thy kingdom come; Hallowed be Thy name"? Is it not obvious that these miserable "theologists"[15] first extinguish the fear of God in men, and then make soft pillows for people's arms and

W² 18:843

14 Faustus Socinus, *Commentarius in Epistolam Joannes Apostoli primam, Bibliotheca Fratrum Polonorum*, ed. Andreas Wiszowaty (Amsterdam, 1656–68) (Walther's emphasis).

15 Latin: *theologistas*. The English word "theologist" was commonly used before 1814. It meant either one who is learned in theology or one who makes theological speculations and comes up with strange doctrines or "theologisms." Here Luther intends the

heads, as Ezekiel says [13:18]?[16] They remove them from this prayer and quench the Spirit! Regardless of whatever they say, it is not an insignificant matter to depart from the Law and will of God even a hairbreadth, nor is the mercy of God that pardons venial sins an unimportant matter. These people, then, treat the Law and the will and the mercy of God as something that has no power. The result is that the prayer of the righteous is not fervent, nor is their gratitude kindled. Let us beware of this pharisaical leaven!

Again, *Luther* writes in 1518, in his explanation of the *Theses Concerning Indulgences, Against Tetzel*, in his comment on Thesis 76 (St. Louis Ed. 18:260):

W² 18:260;
Ps. 143:2

Here I should have explained carefully about venial sin, which is regarded lightly these days, as if it were not a sin at all—to the great harm of many people, I fear, who are securely snoring away. These people are not aware that they are committing coarse sins. I confess that during all my reading of the scholastic teachers I have never understood what a venial sin is, nor how great it is. I do not know whether they understand these things themselves. I want to state briefly: Any person who is **not in constant fear of being full of mortal sins, and does not act accordingly, has little hope**[17] **of being saved**. For Scripture says in Psalm 143:2: "Enter not into judgment with Your servant."

Not only venial sins, as they are called by everybody these days, but even good works cannot bear the careful examination of God's judgment. Rather, they are in need of His pardoning mercy. For the psalmist does not say: "Enter not into judgment with Your enemy," but, "with Your servant"—Your child who is serving You. This fear ought to teach us to yearn for the mercy of God and to trust in it. Where this fear is lacking, we trust not so much in the mercy of God as in our own conscience and in the fact that we are not aware of having committed any coarse sins. **Such people will meet with a fearful judgment.**

In evangelical, [Gospel-oriented] preaching, sin must be magnified. The pastor must pronounce a severe judgment on sin, for He is to proclaim the judgment of God. Even venial sins must not be regarded lightly. You must remember that all of us believers sin so much every day that God would have to cast us all into hell if we did not believe in Christ.

---

second meaning. The Latin ending *–ista* is often used as a slur, which is why people today associate negative ideas with groups identified as "–isms."

16 Luther follows the Vulgate text. For more information, see the note on this passage and the two rods "favor" and "woe" on pages 39–40 n. 11.

17 German *kaum* means "unlikely."

Always remind yourselves that, if God were to deal with us according to His justice, we would belong in hell—not in a comfortable bed. We need to have such fear and behave as if we were full of deadly sins. It is horrible to hear believers casually say, "Now my conscience is at ease." It is certainly pitiful for believers to have an unconcerned conscience while the Word of God pronounces condemnation upon them.

Dannhauer says (*Hodosophia*, p. 195): "Sin is as great as is the person who is offended by it." That is an important proverb! Since God is offended by sin, there are immeasurable wickedness and immeasurable guilt in sin.[18]

Finally, Christian experience also proves that by its very nature no sin is venial. Any true Christian will tell you: "Yes, I have experienced that myself. As soon as I had sinned, I felt uneasy. That continued until I asked God for forgiveness." The conscience of every true Christian immediately rings an alarm. A Christian merchant has no peace over five cents in his bookkeeping that do not belong to him.

Their consciences scold Christians for wrongdoing when they treat a brother impolitely or in a loveless fashion. [Christians] apologize for the slightest offense that they have given by any sinful behavior. They do not rest until they have done so. Is that not remarkable? It shows that venial sins, too, are something evil, a fire that can flare up and cast us into damnation. **Small sins become great when they are regarded as small.**

My Dear Friends:—

Thirty-second Evening Lecture: June 19, 1885

During the last quarter of the eighteenth century, Rationalism descended upon the so-called Protestant Church with the force of a hurricane. In the lecture halls of universities it was proclaimed as a new and great light to young theologians. They, in turn, preached it to the unfortunate common people as true Christianity, as Christianity purified. Thus Rationalism gradually became the dominant type of religion. The certain consequence was that the conscience totally lost the ability to say, "It is not all the same, whether a person is Lutheran or Reformed or [Roman] Catholic."

The small remnant of sincere Christians who still believed and confessed with their mouths[19] that the Holy Scriptures are the Word of God, that Jesus Christ is the Son of the living God, that man is justified before God by faith in Christ alone—these few Christians extended to one another the right hand

---

18 Johann Conrad Dannhauer, Ὁδοσοφία *Christiana seu Theologia* (Argentorati [Strassburg]: Sumptibus F. Spoor, 1649). Dannhauer ordained Philipp Jakob Spener. Walther cites this same proverb in his serial article "Theologische Axiome," *Lehre und Wehre* 7 (1861): 65.

19 See Romans 10:9.

of brotherly fellowship. They were like persons saved from a great shipwreck, who see most of their fellow passengers go down to a watery grave and now embrace each other with tears of joy—even though they previously had been total strangers.

In light of such conditions, as the general opinion began to grow in people's hearts, people everywhere decided that the hour had come to make an end of discord, as it was called, namely, doctrinal controversies among the denominations. People thought that the time had come to let fall the barriers that distinguished the denominations from one another. People thought it was especially the various confessions that had to be removed because, like tollgates along a highway, they were seen to prevent progress. In a nutshell, people felt that all denominations—well, at least the Protestant ones—had to be united.

But what happened? In the year 1817, when this plan was about to be carried out, **Claus Harms**, in whom at least a few drops of Lutheran blood still flowed, wrote ninety-five theses against Rationalism and the union of churches, which he intended as a counterpart to the Ninety-five Theses of Luther. In these theses he said to those who supported church union: "You are proposing to make the poor handmaiden, the Lutheran Church, rich by a marriage. Do not dare carry this out over Luther's dead body! He will come back to life, and then—woe to you!"[20]

His glorious prediction came true. When the Union [Church] was actually put into effect in Prussia, multitudes of Lutherans suddenly awoke from their spiritual sleep, remembering that they belonged to the Lutheran Church. They declared that they would never forsake the faith of their fathers. In fact, they even preferred to be deported, imprisoned, and driven out of the land rather than to consent to a union of truth with error, of the Word of God with man's word, of the true Church with a false church.

Rev. 3:11   Those were glorious days in the midnight-black period about the middle of the nineteenth century! It is a pity that from the glorious conflict of those trying times the old, pure, genuine Lutheran Church did not emerge. The reason was that the very men who wished to "hold fast what you have, so that no one may seize your crown" did not have a clear and pure knowledge of the truth. And so it happened that they went from one extreme to the other: from Rationalism, religious and ecclesiastical indifference to particularism and an anti-Lutheran hierarchism.[21] The same men who in those days had

---

20   This is Harms's Thesis 75. On Harms and his Ninety-five Theses, see the Index of Persons and Groups, page 494.

21   Here Walther had Johannes A. A. Grabau in mind, as well as those in Germany who had similar positions. When, for example, the Saxon immigrants adopted essentially a Presbyterian form of church government in their Parish Order (*Parochialordnung*) of 1839–40, Grabau blasted them for sinning, first, in following Martin Stephan, then

led others in firm opposition to the union of churches and forcefully insisted on being Lutherans went on to prove their point. They declared that only the true visible Lutheran Church is the Church mentioned in the Third Article of the Creed, namely: "I believe . . . in the holy Christian Church, the communion of saints."[22]

They held that the Lutheran Church is the Church *par excellence*, the Church in the most exalted and proper sense, the Church outside of which there is no salvation,[23] possibly with this limitation: "except that God in a miraculous and extraordinary manner may save a person also outside of this Church and lead him to eternal life."

It was a sad and serious error—and placed these men in direct contradiction to the Holy Scriptures and, moreover, overthrew the cardinal doctrine of Christianity. This is the doctrine that a poor sinner is made righteous in the sight of God for Christ's sake, by faith alone. This error plainly involved a most shameful confusion and mingling of Law and Gospel. This error is still popular in the separate Lutheran Church of Prussia.[24]

---

sinning again in limiting the Office of the Holy Ministry to a "teaching elder" in the Reformed tradition. Walther's victory in the 1841 Altenburg Debate defended both the laity and the clergy in their God-given roles and helped affirm a Lutheran form of church government among the Saxons. Walther rejected the one extreme in which the laity in the congregation constitute and run the church. He also rejected the other extreme in which the pastors constitute and run the church. Walther drew on Luther to confess a church in which pastors and laity are both biblically literate and mutually accountable. That remains the vision of the Missouri Synod to this day.

22 See *Concordia*, 330.

23 Latin: *ecclesia, extra quam nulla salus.*

24 Severe persecution in Prussia helped to shape the interpretation of doctrine in this church.

Emilie (pronounced like "Amelia") Walther died before her husband, Ferdinand, completed lecturing on this thesis. Her death would underscore for Ferdinand the eternal consequences of properly distinguishing Law and Gospel. This engraving comes from Martin Günther, *Dr. C. F. W. Walther: Lebensbild* (St. Louis: Concordia, 1890), 152.

THESIS XX

You are not rightly distinguishing Law and Gospel in the Word of God if a person's salvation is made to depend on his association with the visible orthodox Church and if you claim that salvation is denied to every person erring in any article of faith.

EDITOR'S NOTE: In this thesis, Walther steers a course between two great errors: unionism and sectarianism. Unionism errs by claiming that Protestants are all basically the same. In its worst form, unionism turns into universalism, that is, the belief that all paths to God are basically the same. This approach throws out basic truths proclaimed in Scripture concerning the particular origin of the Gospel in the one, true God. Humanity is the god of the false, universalist faith, and hell is its doom (Romans 1).

Sectarianism errs by claiming that only the people in a particular organization will be saved. This ignores the universal goal of the Gospel (Matthew 28) and the fact that God will call His people out of all groups by the action of the Spirit through the Means of Grace. The judgment on sectarianism is also hell (Matthew 23). By avoiding these errors, Christians properly read and apply the Bible.

The essential Church is invisible

It seems so bizarre that, after such a long time during which Rationalism and the greatest religious indifference were widespread, these men should have devised the doctrine that the visible Lutheran Church is the Church *par excellence*, outside of which there is no salvation. However beyond understanding it first seems to be, it is just as easily explained.[1]

They stumbled into this mistake by means of a different false belief. Every error bears much fruit.[2] The mother of that terrible false idea [that this thesis addresses] is the doctrine that the Church is a visible institution that Christ has established on earth—differing in no way from a kind of religious state. The authority and governing offices are, indeed, not in the hands of kings,

---

1   The Dau edition adds: "by the prolific nature of error."
2   This is yet another proverb that Walther picked up from orthodox Lutheranism.

emperors, generals, and mayors. Rather, they are in the hands of superinten-dents, bishops, church commissions,[3] pastors, deacons, synods, and the like.

Matt. 16:18   Everyone who is at least somewhat familiar with God's Word knows that **this view is in error**. Does the Savior not say, "And I tell you, you are Peter, and on this rock I will build My church, and the gates of hell shall not prevail against it"? This rock is Christ. No one is a member of the Church except the person who is built on Christ. Being built on Christ does not mean connect-ing yourself mechanically with the Church, but placing your confidence in Christ and hoping to receive righteousness and salvation from Him alone. Whoever fails to do this is not built on this rock. Therefore, this person is not a member of the Church of Jesus Christ.

Paul says in Ephesians 2:19–22:

Eph. 2:19–22   So then you are no longer strangers and aliens, but you are fellow citizens with the saints and members of the household of God, built on the foundation of the apostles and prophets, Christ Jesus Himself being the cornerstone, in whom the whole structure, being joined together, grows into a holy temple in the Lord. In Him you also are being built together into a dwelling place for God by the Spirit.

The only people built on the foundation of the apostles and prophets are those who believe and cling to the word of the apostles and prophets. Therefore, a person without a living faith cannot be a member of the Church.

Furthermore, the Savior calls Himself a bridegroom. Let no one who is *not* betrothed to Christ with the innermost affection of his heart claim to be a true Christian and a member of the Church. Regarding their relationship to Christ, these people are strangers. The Church, however, is the Bride of Christ.[4]

Again, Christ is called the Head of the congregation.[5] Therefore, you can be a member of the Church only when Christ—as the head, light, life, strength, and grace—flows into you. If someone does not have that spiritual connection with Christ, Christ is not his Head. Whoever is his own ruler and is not governed by Christ does not belong to the Church.

In another place the apostle calls the Church the Body of Christ.[6] This has motivated many of even the most faithful Lutherans to say that, since a body is visible, the Church, too, must be visible. But that is a shameful piece

---

3   German: *Kirchenkollegien*. This is a supervisory board similar to a consistory. August Hermann Francke envisioned a church commission working with the Prussian court to enforce Pietism in the Lutheran Church and duplicate the program at Halle in other cities. See also the introduction to Pietism, beginning on page lxvii.

4   See Revelation 19:7; 21:2, 9.

5   See, for example, Ephesians 1:22–23; 4:15; Colossians 1:18; 2:18–19.

6   See Colossians 1:18; 2:19.

of exegesis! The point of comparison[7] in this phrase is not the visibility of the Church. Instead of being made up of many dead members, the Church is a living organism of members through whom **one** faith and one life of faith is pulsating. This proves beyond contradiction that the Church is not visible, but invisible. Only a member of the Church can experience this constant radiation from Christ, the Head of the Church.

Again, Christ calls the Church His flock.[8] Therefore, no person who is not a member of the Church can belong to the flock of Christ, can be one of His sheep, can come to His pasture, and can obey His voice.

Some might raise the objection that Christ compares the Church to a field in which wheat and weeds are growing. But this objection is based on a wrong interpretation of that parable. Christ has given us the key that unlocks its meaning. He does not say, "The field is My kingdom." If that were true, the Church would be a society made up of good and evil members.[9] But He says, "The field is **the world**."

Matt. 13:38

The Apology of the Augsburg Confession emphasizes this fact.[10] The Savior compares His Church to a field in which weeds grow among the wheat, to a net in which good and bad fish are caught, to a marriage feast that foolish virgins join along with wise virgins and to which, according to another parable, people gain entrance even though they are not dressed in the proper wedding garment.[11] But with these parables Christ does not mean to describe the essence of the Church, but rather the outward form in which it appears in this world and how it appears among the people of this world.

Although it is composed only of good sheep, only of reborn persons, the Church never appears in the form of a congregation that is made up of only true Christians. In its visible form the Church can never purge itself of the hypocrites and ungodly persons who worm their way into it. Not until life eternal will the Church appear triumphant, entirely purified, and without blemish, separated from those who are not honestly and sincerely joined to it but only drawn to their own secular interests in an outward union with the Church.

The invisible Church always within the visible

While hypocrites and false Christians profess Christ with their lips, their heart is far from Him. They serve their carnal lusts and not the Lord alone. In Luke 14:26, the Lord says: "If anyone comes to Me and does not hate his own father and mother and wife and children and brothers and sisters, yes,

God sees the invisible Church; Luke 14:26

---

7   Latin: *tertium comparationis.*

8   See, for example, John 10:26–28; 21:15–16.

9   This was the position of Tychonius in the fifth century AD. See the Law and Gospel time-line, page lvii.

10   For example, Ap VII and VIII (IV) 1 (*Concordia*, 143).

11   See Matthew 13:24–30, 47–50; 25:1–13; 22:1–14.

and even his own life, he cannot be My disciple." In this passage, Christ passes judgment on all who do not want to renounce what they have. But not until all are gathered before the judgment seat of Christ will these people become known as hypocrites. **We may see people going to church, but we cannot see whether they belong to the Church.** It is impossible to declare whether individuals are true members of the Church. No person knows if he is or if he is not. Only God knows. The Church is visible to the eyes of God alone. To human eyes it is invisible.

The Church is one and imperishable

The error that we are now discussing is the primary falsehood of our time. It is indeed a horrible error! For those who surrender to this error pretend to be good Lutherans, opposed to the Papists—and yet the only difference is that they use different weapons than the Papists do. There was a time when it was the Papists who were the ones defending this false doctrine now under review. Now it is Lutherans—yes, Lutherans!—claiming that they are the Church outside of which there is no salvation. Such Lutherans become an object of mocking to the Papists. They play the part that the pope and his rabble used to play. The only conclusions that can be drawn from this sorry state of affairs are: either the pope's church is the true Church, or the true Church had stopped existing before Luther came.

But Scripture says that the true Church cannot stop existing. It will continue until the end of time. Yet until the sixteenth[12] century there was no "Lutheran" Church. Still, since the days of the apostles there has not been a single church with doctrine as pure as that of our [Lutheran] Fathers. This is the difficult problem that all those maintaining this false doctrine concerning the Church bring upon themselves: either Scripture must be full of lies, or the Roman Church was indeed the true Church and Luther's Reformation was rebellion.

The main thing, however, is undeniably this: when you make a person's salvation dependent on membership in the visible orthodox Church and communion with the visible orthodox Church, that means you are overthrowing the doctrine of justification by faith. This cannot be denied. People joining the Lutheran Church already have true faith before they come.

It would be a fatal mistake to think that Luther did not have the true faith *before* becoming a Lutheran.[13] Regardless of how highly we honor our church, may this shameful, fanatical idea be far from us: that our Lutheran Church is the only church that saves! The true Church extends around the globe

---

12 The German notes have: "fifteenth and sixteenth century." Walther probably said something similar to "fifteenth—uh—sixteenth century." English versions give the corrected text.

13 The Dau text adds a Latin phrase not in the original notes: *sit venia verbo*, "please pardon the expression." Walther did not ask for pardon.

and is found in all sects. For the Church is not an external organism with its own special arrangements, to which a person must adapt himself in order to become a member. Anyone who believes in Jesus Christ and who is a member of His spiritual body is a member of the Church. Moreover, this Church can never be torn apart. Although its members are separated from one another by space and time, the Church will always be one.

Now, in order to keep people from imagining that the pope is the Church, Luther renders the Greek *ekklesía* as "congregation,"[14] which is a correct rendering. People could draw a false conclusion from the fact that Scripture speaks of external church communities, such as those at Rome, Corinth, Philippi, Thessalonica, in Galatia, and those in Asia Minor, to whom the Lord issued letters through John. All these visible communities are called "churches." Therefore, they claim that the Church is visible. As a rule, to apply the word *ekklesía* to local churches would be to draw a wrong conclusion, because the Scriptures regularly use this word not when referring to a local congregation but to the Church in the absolute sense.

More than the local congregation

The Church is an invisible community. The term is applied to local organizations because the invisible Church is contained in them. In a similar manner, we speak of a stack of wheat, though it is not all wheat, but rather a good deal of hay and straw is in the pile as well. Or we speak of a glass of wine, though water has been mixed with it. In such instances the object is named according to its principal content.[15] Thus visible communities are called "churches" because the invisible Church is in them, because they contain a heavenly seed.

False Christians and hypocrites are called "members of the congregation," even though in reality they are not members. Since they claim to confess the name of Jesus, we give them this title charitably, assuming that they believe what they confess. We cannot look into their hearts. We leave that to God. We do not judge them, except when they are **obviously** ungodly persons. In that case we stop calling them members, but exclude them and call them heathen and tax collectors.

Now, as a visible community, in synecdoche[16] the Lutheran Church, too, is called a "church." Therefore, it is an awful mistake to claim that people can be saved only in the Lutheran Church. No one should be forced to join the Lutheran Church because it is believed to be the only way to get into God's Church. There are still Christians in the Reformed Church, among the Methodists—yes, even among the Papists.

False reason for being Lutheran

---

14 German: *Gemeine*, that in which all are (or have) in common.

15 Walther uses the Latin: *a potiore parte*.

16 Synecdoche is a figure of speech in which a part substitutes for the whole or the whole for the parts. For example, one may refer to a sports car as "hot wheels."

Isa. 55:11   We have this precious promise in Isaiah 55:11: "So shall My word be that goes out from My mouth; it shall not return to Me empty." Wherever the Word of God is proclaimed and confessed or even recited during the service, the Lord is gathering a people for Himself. The Roman Church, for instance, still confesses that Christ is the Son of God and that He died on the cross to redeem the world. That truth is enough to bring a person to the knowledge of salvation. Whoever would deny this fact would also be forced to deny that there are Christians in some Lutheran communities into which errors have crept. But there are always some children of God in these communities because they have the Word of God, which is always bearing fruit by converting a number of souls to God.

Correct reasons for being Lutheran; Matt. 10:32–33; 2 Tim. 1:8   This false doctrine regarding the Church mingles Law and Gospel in a most horrible way. While the Gospel requires faith in Jesus Christ, the Law makes all sorts of demands on people. Anyone who would demand additional requirements for salvation besides faith is mingling Law and Gospel. I belong to the Lutheran Church for the sole reason that I want to side with the truth. I would leave any denomination if I **discovered** that it harbors errors with which I do not wish to be contaminated. I do not wish to become a partaker of the sins of others. By leaving that heretical community, I would be confessing the pure and untainted truth. For Christ says, "So everyone who acknowledges Me before men, I also will acknowledge before My Father who is in heaven, but whoever denies Me before men, I also will deny before My Father who is in heaven." Furthermore, Paul writes distinctly to Timothy: "Therefore do not be ashamed of the testimony about our Lord, nor **of me** His prisoner, but share in suffering for the gospel by the power of God."

True believers seek the true Church   But just because people may be saved in all the sects and despite the fact that there are children of God in all sectarian churches, by no means does it follow that we can remain in communion with a sect. Many people cannot understand this. They imagine it is a completely unionist principle to hold that a person can be saved in any of the sects. But it is true, and the reason is that we are saved by faith, which some members of sectarian churches may have. However, if I recognize the error of my heretical community and do not forsake it, I would be lost because, even though I saw the error, I did not abandon that sect.

I can still remember the time when I became a believer. At that time, I also joined the Union Church.[17] Some people approached me with the intention of bringing me into the Lutheran Church. But I told them that I was a believer and did not want to belong to a church that claimed to be the **only** church that saves. Later, I found some good writings that showed me that this is not true after all. The Lutheran Church claims to be the **only church that has pure**

---

17   That is, the forced union of Lutheran and Reformed Churches.

doctrine, yet it does not claim to be the only church that saves. At the same time, those documents admitted that people can be saved even in sects, if they are not aware of that sect's error.

As soon as I understood this, I left the unionist community and joined the Lutherans. I had long known that the Lutheran Church has the truth, but I refused to endorse the above Papist principle. Then I understood that it is not necessary to condemn anyone who is in error regarding some article of the Creed, but only those who have seen their error and still want to stick to it.

Let me show you that this is indeed the doctrine of our church. In the **Preface to the Book of Concord**[18] we read:

> Now, about the condemnations, censures, and rejections of godless doctrines, and especially about what has arisen concerning the Lord's Supper. These had to be clearly set forth in this, our declaration, thorough explanation, and decision about controversial articles. This was done not only so that all may guard against these condemned doctrines, but also for certain other reasons that could in no way be ignored. So it is not at all our plan and purpose to condemn **people who err because of a certain simplicity of mind, but are not blasphemers against the truth of the heavenly doctrine. Much less, indeed, do we intend to condemn entire churches** that are either under the Roman Empire of the German nation or elsewhere. Rather, it has been our intention and desire in this way **to openly criticize and condemn** only the fanatical opinions and their stubborn and blasphemous teachers. (We judge that they should in no way be tolerated in our dominions, churches, and schools.) For these errors conflict with God's clear Word. They do so in such a way that they cannot be reconciled with the Word. We have written condemnations also for this reason: that all godly persons might be diligently warned to avoid these errors. For we have no doubt whatsoever that—**even in those churches that have not agreed with us in all things—many godly and by no means wicked people** are found. **They follow their own simplicity and do not correctly understand the matter itself. But in no way do they approve the blasphemies that are cast forth against the Holy Supper** as it is administered in our churches, according to Christ's institution. With the unanimous approval of all good people, the Lord's Supper is taught according to the words of Christ's testament itself.[19] We are also in great hope that, if these simple people would be taught correctly about all these things—the Spirit of the Lord

---

18   *Concordia*, 9 (Walther's emphasis). See also Müller, 16–17; *Triglot Concordia*, 19, 21.

19   See Matthew 26:28.

aiding them—they would agree with us, and with our churches and schools, to the infallible truth of God's Word.[20] And certainly, a duty is laid especially upon all the Church's theologians and ministers. With such fitting moderation,[21] they should also teach from God's Word those who have erred from the truth,[22] either from a certain simplicity or ignorance. They should teach about the peril of their salvation. They should fortify them against corruptions lest all may perish while the blind are leaders of the blind.[23]

Remember this passage well! If you meet with people who reproach you and say that the Lutheran Church claims to be the only church that saves, point them to this section of our Confessions!

While the Formula of Concord condemns Reformed **doctrine**, this condemnation does not refer to those who err in the simplicity of their hearts. It applies only to obstinate false teachers and blasphemers. These are people who admit that Christ said this or that, yet who refuse to believe. Such people who **speak shocking blasphemies against pure doctrine are not to be regarded as children of God.** They say things such as: "Christ says this or that, yet we choose to ignore it." These [people who follow the simplicity of their hearts] are people who have been reared from childhood in a certain error, but who nonetheless hold fast to their Savior. These are not wicked persons, even though they may immediately turn away a Lutheran who approaches them.

The preface [to the Book of Concord] continues:

Therefore, by our writing, we testify in the sight of almighty God and before the entire Church that it has never been our purpose, by means of this godly formula for union, to create trouble or danger to the godly who are suffering persecution today. We have already entered into the fellowship of grief[24] with them, moved by Christian love, so that we are shocked at the persecution and most painful tyranny that is used against these poor people with such severity. We sincerely detest it. In no way do we agree to the shedding of that innocent blood,[25] which undoubtedly will be required with great severity from the persecutors at the Lord's awful judgment and before Christ's court.[26] They

---

20   See John 17:17.
21   See Philippians 4:5.
22   See 2 Timothy 2:18.
23   See Matthew 15:14.
24   See Romans 12:15.
25   See Proverbs 6:17.
26   See Romans 14:10.

will then certainly render a most strict account[27] and suffer fearful punishment.[28]

Calvinists said, namely: "See, now they want to do in Germany what they did in France! Another St. Bartholomew's Night is sure to come!"[29] The Lutherans insist in this passage that they are not planning to persecute anybody. The blood of the Huguenots will be on only Papist hands. Lutherans condemn no one except those who condemn themselves![30]

Based on **Luther's** preface to the theses against indulgences published [before the Formula of Concord], we can see what a difficult task it was for him to work his way to the true knowledge. He writes (St. Louis Ed. 14:452f.):

> Of the many sufferings and trials through which I passed that first year and the year following, of the great humiliation that I had to undergo—and that was genuine and not put on, for it reached the degree of despair—of all these things little is known to these self-confident spirits who, after me, have attacked the majesty of the pope with great ranting and audacity. Still, with all their skill they would not have been able to harm a hair on the pope's head if Christ through me, His puny and unworthy instrument, had not previously caused [the pope] to suffer a deep, irreversible wound. Nevertheless, they carry off the glory and the honor as if they had done it—to which honor they are welcome, for all I care.

W² 14:452–53

But while they were looking on at my loneliness and jeopardy, I was not very cheerful, confident, and certain of my situation. For many things that I know now—God be praised!—I did not know at that time. For certain, I did not understand, nor did all the Papists together understand, the character of an indulgence; it was honored merely on account of long-established usage and custom. My object in inviting men to a disputation concerning it was not to reject it, but really to find out its effectiveness from others, since I knew absolutely nothing about it myself. Since the dead and dumb masters—I mean, the books of theologians and [canon] lawyers—could not give me enough information, I desired to seek counsel from the living and **to hear the Church of God itself**, asking such godly persons as might be

---

27 See 1 Peter 4:5.

28 *Concordia*, 9. See also Müller, 17; *Triglot Concordia*, 21.

29 See the entry for the St. Bartholomew's Day Massacre in the Luther to Walther timeline, page xxxvii. The Vatican would like the world to forget this event, so it has tried to acquire the medallions struck by Protestants in memory of the mass murder of many Huguenots in the name of Roman Catholicism. Concordia Historical Institute in St. Louis, Missouri, has one of these medallions in its collection.

30 The Dau text adds: "by resisting the known truth."

enlightened by the Holy Spirit regarding this matter to take pity on me—and not only on me but also on the entire Christian Church—and give us a true and trustworthy account of indulgences.

Many godly men were greatly pleased with my theses and thought highly of them. But I found it impossible to regard and acknowledge them as members of the Church, endowed with the Holy Spirit. **I only regarded the pope, the cardinals, bishops, theologians, [canon] lawyers, monks, and priests and was waiting for the Spirit from them.** So eagerly had I taken in their doctrine—or, I might say, devoured it and guzzled it—that I had been filled to bursting with it and was not sure whether I was awake or sleeping.

To this day, Papists try to keep the people within the Roman Catholic Church by teaching them: "You know that only *we* are the true church. No matter what the church teaches, if you want to be a true follower of Christ, you must hear the church. If the pope decrees that he is infallible, or that Mary was conceived without sin, or that the saints must be adored, you must accept these dogmas. Do not consult your reason. The true church has set up these dogmas, and it cannot err. If you fall away from the Roman Catholic Church, you fall away from the *true* church." This is the horrible bait with which they try to hook people.[31]

W² 14:453   Luther continues: "When I had disproved all the arguments against me with Scripture and thus overcome them, I scarcely succeeded, by the grace of Christ, in overcoming—with great anxiety, trouble, and work—this one final argument: that I must hear the Church."

Luther had already discovered that nearly every Papist teaching is on shaky ground, except for that one point that, as he says, troubled him greatly at the beginning and that kept him from becoming truly certain of the truth and being cheerful. The Papists had built the trap that they themselves later fell into. God's hour had come for revealing the Antichrist.

W² 14:453   For with all my heart I sincerely, reverently thought that the pope's church is the true Church—as opposed to these shameful and blasphemous twisters of the truth who are now opposing me boastfully and claim to have the pope's church backing them. If I had hated the pope as much as those people hate him who these days pretend to praise him highly with their lips, I would have been afraid that the earth would open up and devour me as it did Korah and his mob.[32]

---

31 Walther uses yet another fishing metaphor. Walther likely had an interest in fishing, particularly in fly fishing.

32 See Numbers 16:1–35.

May God keep you from becoming entangled with this false teaching regarding the Church, namely, that the Lutheran Church is the true visible Church of Jesus Christ *in the sense that you can be saved only in this church!* The Lutheran Church is indeed the true visible Church, however, only in the sense that it has the pure, untainted truth. As soon as you add the qualification "the only church that saves" to the Lutheran Church, you detract from the doctrine of justification by grace through faith in Jesus Christ and mingle Law and Gospel. May God keep you from this error for the sake of your own soul and those who will be entrusted to your care!

EDITOR'S NOTE: The thirty-second lecture was the last given in the 1884–85 academic year. Emilie Walther fell ill about six weeks after this lecture. Ferdinand Walther called in the family doctor, who prescribed opium to combat Emilie's increasing heart pain and difficulty breathing. The opium relieved the pain, but contributed to a high fever and progressive kidney failure that started on August 14. On Friday night, August 21, Emilie suffered a series of "attacks" that lasted into Saturday morning; her body was failing. Ferdinand heard his wife's confession and administered the Lord's Supper. Emilie slipped into a coma on Saturday evening and died Sunday afternoon, August 23, 1885. Ferdinand was at her side, weeping freely, and expressing his wish that he could have done more for her amid his busy schedule. He remembered the total devotion that she had for him, and he described as his "absolution" the selfless love in her eyes that she always had for him.

Walther gave the remainder of these lectures on Law and Gospel as a widower who had a poignant awareness of the shortness of this life and of the urgent need to properly discern Law and Gospel in preparation for the world to come. Walther began his thirty-third lecture with the opening of the 1885–86 academic year and with some introductory thoughts for his students. The following remarks will take on a deeper meaning in light of Walther's loss.

It goes without saying, my friends, that the first and the necessary qualification of a theologian is a complete, accurate, and clear knowledge of every single doctrine of divine revelation.

Thirty-third Evening Lecture:
Sept. 4, 1885

It would be contradictory to call any person a theologian who does not have this knowledge. As you know, theologians are to be caretakers of people's souls. A doctor must know, above all, the cures that nature provides for the healing of bodily ills. Similarly, the doctor of souls, that is, the theologian, must have a good knowledge of the spiritual cures that the Word of God provides for the ills of the soul. These spiritual cures, however, are nothing other than the doctrines that God has revealed for our salvation.

However, while an accurate, complete, and clear knowledge of every single doctrine of God's revelation to man is absolutely necessary for a theologian, this does not by any means define his entire need. There are mainly two additional requirements that he still needs.

What a pastor needs

First, he needs a good knowledge of how individual doctrines relate to one another. That will enable him to make the proper application of each doctrine. **Second**, he needs courage, love, and a liking for his theological calling. A doctor may know all sorts of medications that have healing properties, but by ignorantly mixing them in a wrong way he may neutralize their strengths. So, instead of curing the physical ailment of his patients, the doctor may actually be speeding up their death. Similarly, a theologian who does not know which doctrines he may combine and which doctrines he must carefully keep separate may easily do a soul more harm than good.

Lastly, a doctor will properly carry out his difficult duties only when he is motivated by love and a passion for his special work and is unconcerned about the filthy money that he may gain for his work. Even so, a theologian will be faithful in his calling only when he is filled with enthusiasm for it and finds his chief reward in the way God uses him to save souls, destroy the kingdom of Satan, build up the kingdom of God, and increase the number of those who are in heaven.

Purpose of the lectures

I have always considered it my sacred duty not only to present pure doctrine in my dogmatics lectures, according to the grace that God has given me, but also to find an hour at least once a week to gather the entire student body of our beloved Concordia and show them the importance, meaning, and the practical applications of the doctrines that are studied in dogmatics. Above all, however, I wish to cheer your hearts for your difficult calling.

We call these Friday evening lectures—which are also the conclusion of the week's instruction—"Luther Hours,"[33] chiefly because in these lectures I let our beloved Father Luther, the God-appointed reformer and our common teacher of the Church, speak to you.[34]

---

33   German: *Lutherstunden.*

34   Even though Walther was at the point in his career where he was most wary of the Church Fathers, nevertheless he always embraced the fact that God has provided true teachers of doctrine during every period of the Church's life. Walther always gives thanks when these

Until now, God has graciously blessed these lectures because my beloved students have gladly attended them, and many of them have solemnly assured me that they have benefited from them. Not only have they gained a clearer knowledge of Christian doctrine, but [they] have also been made more certain of the forgiveness of their sins, of their adoption by God as His dear children, and of their salvation.

I cherish the hope that God will also help our students who have just enrolled at Concordia, and whom we welcome tonight, to have the same helpful experiences. I pray to God that He would grant me grace to speak to you as I should and that what I say will be well received by you.

Keep in mind, however, that, if my prayer is to be heard, you will have to pray as well that you would receive His insight. For you are not here for the purpose of acquiring knowledge of secular sciences, but for the purpose of being taught how to become familiar with a doctrine that, in the first place, brings *you* salvation—and also to many others through your ministry.

Why you are here

This requires great earnestness. You will have to remove the shoes of your earthly, carnal mind and—just like Mary, [the sister of Martha]—sit down at Jesus' feet to hear from Him what the one thing is that is necessary.[35] May God grant this and let me be a helper to you for all time!

Based on twenty-five theses, last year we began discussing the distinction between Law and Gospel. We still have five theses left—and they are quite important.

We must wrap these up before taking up another subject. I hope that our first-year students—even though they will hear only a fragment of this topic—will nevertheless get some food for their spirits in these lectures. We pray that their faith would be strengthened, and that they would be encouraged to withdraw from the world and their service to sin, and that they would be drawn to Christ. For if we who are here assembled are not true Christians, then we are completely lost, and God cannot help but look down on us in anger. For what can be a more horrible prospect than not being a Christian and yet drawing pay for the time you serve as pastor of a congregation?

I hope that you are all true Christians or that the blessed Word of God has drawn you and that its divine power has made a deep and lasting impression on you. I hope that some day, when you leave this institution, you will go forth prepared not only with a fine foundation of theological knowledge but also with a heart burning with enthusiasm to proclaim the great things that the Lord has done for humanity.

---

teachers point to Scripture and teach it in all purity. Therefore, Walther is willing and proud to call Luther his father in the faith and hopes that his students will do so as well.

35 See Luke 10:38–42.

[At the same time,] I hope that our students who were here last year will not consider it tedious if I read all the theses that have already been discussed, so that our new friends may know what the discussion has been about and how important the remaining theses are.

(The first twenty theses were read, and some brief comments were made.)

Back to Thesis XX: True faith

True faith does not grow spontaneously out of any person. It is so firm that, even if the heavens were to cave in and hell were to open its jaws, we believers could cry out: "Let heaven fall down and hell open up! Who cares? I believe in Jesus Christ, true God, who has redeemed me, a lost and condemned creature, with His precious blood.[36] No devil and no hell can snatch this away from me." The faith of hypocrites, however, is like spring snow melting in the sun.

Some think that they are Bible Lutherans simply because they declare that only Lutherans can be saved. At any rate, they claim that people need to confess Lutheran doctrine, even if only on their deathbed—and if they do not, they will go to hell.

But in reality this claim stamps them not as genuine Lutherans but as *apostates* from Lutheranism. The Lutheran Church does not make such claims, but it does indeed teach people how to be justified and how to be saved by grace. But there are persons living among the sects who love the truth and may be better Christians than some Lutherans. Christ rules everywhere, even among His enemies.

---

36 The Dau text adds: "and secured him against the ravages of all the devils of hell." Compare with the explanation to the Second Article of the Apostles' Creed (*Concordia*, 329).

THESIS XXI

You are not rightly distinguishing Law and Gospel in the Word of God if you teach that the Sacraments save ex opere operato, *that is, merely by their outward performance.*

EDITOR's NOTE: In this thesis, Walther focuses on the Roman Catholic error that the Sacraments mechanically benefit a person. Apology XXIV 18 defines a sacrament as "a ceremony or work in which God presents to us what the promise of the ceremony offers."[1] Walther does not question the promise or the institution. Walther rejects the Donatist heresy that bases the promise on the moral character of the priest (AC VIII).[2] Echoing AC XIII, Walther condemns those who made *ex opere operato* into a false position on the beneficial aspect: "the Sacraments justify simply by the act of doing them."[3] As Walther shows, people receive the true Sacraments either to their judgment or to their benefit. An important part of the benefit received through Word and Sacrament includes "the Holy Spirit, putting the flesh to death, and new life" (Ap XXIV 39).[4]

Walther began to speak on this thesis only twelve days after his wife died. Here we supply footnotes to give context where Walther may leave it unstated. For example, Walther spoke of Baptism condemning anyone who does not receive it through faith. He did not mean a baby being baptized. He had in mind an adult who submits to the outward act of Baptism for selfish reasons.[5] We follow Walther's own direction to judge his words in light of Scripture and the Book of Concord.[6]

---

1 *Concordia*, 222. This is the original meaning of *ex opere operato* that was used against the Donatists. It affirms that the Word, together with the elements, really creates a sacrament and delivers the gift that God offers there. This happens regardless of the apparent holiness of the priest.

2 *Concordia*, 34. The Latin phrase for the Donatist position that considers the Gospel promises according to the one doing the work is *ex opere operantis*.

3 *Concordia*, 38.

4 *Concordia*, 227.

5 For example, the Prussian government gave preferred government jobs only to people who were baptized Christians. Those interested in such jobs often were baptized in the *Wilhelmskirche* in Berlin. The church is located near *Kaufhaus des Westens*, a department store similar in prestige to Harrod's in London or Macy's in New York City. Because the pastors of the *Wilhelmskirche* baptized any job-seeking civil servant as a formality, the church received the nickname *Taufhaus des Westens*, i.e., the "Baptism Emporium."

6 William Dallmann, *My Life* (St. Louis: Concordia, 1945), 30.

Sacraments not our work

A n extremely important thesis! It is a great error to say that the Sacraments are able to accomplish salvation based solely on the act being performed.[7] The Papists teach that. They say to people: "You will receive some benefit when you let yourself be baptized, even if you are not yet a believer, provided you are not actually living in mortal sin. The mere act of Baptism will bring you God's favor and make God gracious to you."

They say, "Every time someone attends a Mass, he will receive grace. Every time someone receives the Lord's Supper, he will receive grace simply because he goes to it." This is a godless and shameful teaching that directly contradicts the Word of God—in particular, the Gospel—which teaches that a person is justified before God and saved by grace alone and that he cannot perform any good work until he has been justified.[8]

Rom. 3:28

Romans 3:28: "For we hold that one is justified by faith apart from works of the law." But if I am justified and receive grace by submitting to Baptism or by going to the Lord's Supper, this would justify me by works—and miserable works at that! For when we view Baptism and Holy Communion as works that we do on our part, then those are meager works that barely need mentioning.

This is a horrible doctrine, completely contradicting the Bible, to claim that you receive divine grace if you merely use the Sacraments. The truth is your Baptism and your Holy Communion will damn you if you do not approach them in faith. They are Means of Grace only for the reason that a divine promise is attached to an external sign.[9]

By faith alone

You receive the promise of grace only by faith. If you do not believe, having water poured on you is of no benefit to you. Nor do you benefit by receiving blessed bread and blessed wine—despite the fact that in Holy Communion you are truly receiving the body and blood of the Lord. There is no benefit in all of this.[10] On the contrary, you are actually harming yourself by going to

---

7   Latin: *ex opere operato.*

8   Walther, following Philipp Melanchthon in the Apology, responds to the mechanical offer of grace as a reward for doing a work. Particularly helpful is Melanchthon's distinction in Ap XXIV between an atoning sacrifice and a eucharistic sacrifice (*Concordia*, 222–27).

9   The Latin word *signum* ("sign") is a technical term for the physical elements in the Sacraments. It does not suggest the "symbolic" meaning of the Sacraments that Ulrich Zwingli taught. A sign is God's "visible Word." The "Means of Grace" are the divinely instituted means by which God offers, gives, and seals to people forgiveness of sins, life, and salvation. Properly speaking, the Means of Grace is the Gospel of Christ (Romans 1:16–17). In the Sacraments, the Gospel appears as the visible Word (*verbum visibile*; Ap XIII 5 [*Concordia*, 184–85]; Augustine of Hippo, Tract 80 on John 15:3) in distinction from the audible Word (*verbum audibile*). The Means of Grace are where God offers the Gospel according to His gracious will: the Word and the Sacraments.

10   Walther is using classical terminology. "Benefit" comes from a Latin word that means "something that results in the good." In modern usage, when we say that something is of no use or of no benefit, we often dismiss the claim of truth behind the claim of benefit. Walther does not do that. He affirms the truth of the body and blood of Christ. That body and blood gives either grace or judgment (1 Corinthians 11:28–32). Lutherans practice

Communion without faith, because you become guilty of the body and blood of the Lord.

It all depends on the fact that I believe,[11] that I do not look primarily to the *water* in Baptism, but first to the *promise* that Christ has attached to the water. The water also belongs to the promise, for only to the water has the promise been attached.

The same applies to the Holy Supper. As someone approaches the Lord's Table, it is godless for him to think: "Now I have done yet one more work, one that God wants me to do, that He will have to credit to my account." The Lord says, "Take, eat; this is My body, **which is given for you**." "Drink of it, all of you; this cup is the new testament in My blood, **which is shed for you for the forgiveness of sins**."[12] These words open up a heaven full of divine grace to communicants, and to these words we must direct their faith.

The mere act of eating the bread with the body of Christ and of drinking the wine with the blood of Christ does not produce anything good in us. Grace does not operate in a chemical or mechanical manner, but only by the Word, by virtue of God continually saying, "Your sins are forgiven." It is to this word that you must cling by faith. If you do that, you can confidently meet God on the Last Day; and if He were preparing to condemn you, you could say to Him, "You cannot condemn me without making Yourself a liar. You have invited me to place my entire confidence in Your promise. That is exactly what I have done. For this reason You cannot condemn me—and You will not." So if God were to test the faith of His Christians even on the Last Day, all His saints would cry out: "It is impossible for us to go to hell. Here is Christ, our guarantor[13] and mediator. You must acknowledge, O God, the ransom that Your Son has given as payment in full for our sin and guilt."

Romans 14:23: *"For whatever does not proceed from faith is sin."* How can a person who uses the Sacraments without faith become acceptable to God by that act? How can he obtain God's grace by it, since he is committing a sin by doing something that does not come forth from faith? Rom. 14:23

Hebrews 4:12: "For the word of God is living and active, sharper than any two-edged sword, piercing to the division of soul and of spirit, of joints and of marrow, and discerning the thoughts and intentions of the heart." Even false teachers admit that preaching—if not received by faith—does not benefit the Heb. 4:12

---

closed Communion to care for those who would otherwise receive the Sacrament to their judgment.

11 German: *Alles kommt darauf an, daß ich glaube.* Walther does not refer to infant baptism here but only to an unbelieving adult in the Church who uses membership for selfish gain.

12 See the Service of the Sacrament (*LSB*, p. 162).

13 Traditionally, the word "bondsman" was used to describe Christ as the one who paid our ransom to the Father, but this word might be confused with "bail bondsman." Today's reader is more familiar with language such as co-signer and guarantor.

listeners. Rather, it increases the responsibility of the listeners. However, they claim that, with the Sacraments, it is a different matter, since they supposedly have this great advantage over the preached Word, namely, that God operates with His grace through them whenever people simply use them.

That is a godless doctrine, because the Sacraments are identical to the Word of God—attached to a physical element. Augustine beautifully calls them "the visible Word."[14] The Word of God does not benefit a person who does not believe. In the same way, an unbeliever benefits nothing by the act of being baptized.[15] When we urge people to believe in their Baptism, what we mean is that they are to believe their heavenly Father, who has attached such a glorious promise to Baptism. The idea that God is highly pleased when a person offers to have water sprinkled on his head is a shameful misuse of the visible Word. A Sacrament is the visible Word. As the Word only benefits a person who believes it, in the same way the Sacraments help only those who embrace them by faith.[16]

Therefore, the charge of the Enthusiasts[17] that Lutherans do not urge conversion is baseless. This charge rests on the assumption that Lutherans teach people to rely on the fact that they have been baptized and have received Holy Communion. But that is not at all what we teach. Rather, this is our doctrine: There is a certain promise of God attached to Baptism and the Lord's Supper, which you should embrace without doubting. Only people who have become poor sinners can do that. To say to a person, "You must take comfort in your Baptism," is the same as saying, "You must turn to Jesus Christ." So, while such people may imagine that they are believers, even the smallest affliction will put an end to their "faith." Only the Holy Spirit can give a person true faith.

---

14   Latin: *verbum visibile.*

15   German: *So wenig mir das Wort Gottes hilft, wenn ich nicht glaube, so wenig hilft es mir etwas, wenn ich getauft werde und ich glaube nicht.* Literally, "as little as the Word of God helps me when I do not believe, so to that same extent would Baptism help me if I were baptized and did not believe." In his prior lectures, Walther would make a broad statement like this and then qualify it (see, for example, Walther's use of the term *Gospel* in Thesis VII). In this thesis, Walther does not always supply qualifying statements. Walther allows part of the context to remain unstated, which is unusual for him. Here, he means a person who is being baptized for his own purposes and not the saving purpose that God intends. Walther is not attacking infant Baptism or questioning the promise in Baptism.

16   It is important to remember that God creates that faith and offers that faith through the Word and the Sacraments. The absence of faith is a human work, but the presence of faith is a divine work.

17   German: *Schwärmer.*

C urrently, anyone who insists that pure doctrine is a very important matter is immediately suspected of not having the right Christian spirit. The very term "pure doctrine" is considered taboo and is outlawed. Even contemporary theologians who regard themselves to be among the confessional Lutherans usually speak of pure doctrine only in scornful terms, treating it as the embodiment of "dead letter" theology. If anyone holds fast to pure teaching and attempts to fight against any false doctrine, he is put down as a heartless and unloving fanatic.

Why is that? First, unquestionably because "modern" [historical-critical][18] theologians know full well that they do not have the doctrine that has—in every age—been called pure doctrine and that truly *is* pure. Second, they even think that pure doctrine does not exist at all, that it is a dream world,[19] in the realm of ideals, in the Republic of Plato.

The era in which we live is what the apostle refers to when he says of false teachers that they are "always learning and never able to arrive at a knowledge of the truth." The spirit of our time is the same as in the era of Pilate, to whom the Lord had testified that He was the King of Truth in a kingdom of truth and who sneered, "What is truth?" Yet [Pilate] was not even interested in hearing an answer. That unhappy man was most likely thinking in his heart: "For thousands of years, the greatest of minds have tried uselessly to find the answer to the question 'What is truth?' yet they have not found it. Now You, a poor beggar, a worthless Nazarene, come along, making a fool of Yourself by claiming that, of all people, You are the King of Truth, and You are supposed to establish a kingdom of unquestionable and eternal truth."

To hate pure doctrine is to hate the truth, for pure doctrine is nothing but the pure Word of God—plain and simple. Truth is not, as some think, certain teachings that have been compressed into the dogmatics of the Church. Accordingly, when people hate pure doctrine, that is proof that we are living in a terribly miserable era. Just listen how the Scriptures themselves speak of God's Word and pure doctrine: In the prophecies of Jeremiah, chapter 23, we read: "Let the prophet who has a dream tell the dream, but let him who has

Thirty-fourth Evening Lecture: Sept. 11, 1885

2 Tim. 3:7; John 18:38

Jer. 23:28; Ps. 94:20; John 8:31–32

---

18   Walther uses the terms "modern theologians" (*die modernen Theologen*) or "Moderns" (*die Modernen*) to refer to theologians who use historical-critical methods. Walther rejected these theologians, as did Franz Pieper in the 1893 LCMS *Proceedings*, the source of the 1897 *Kurze Darstellung* and its translation, the 1932 *Brief Statement*, which still summarizes the position of the LCMS. For an extensive list of works in which the early LCMS shows historical-critical methods to be wrong, see Charles Schaum, "Biblical Hermeneutics in the Early Missouri Synod" (Master of Sacred Theology thesis, Concordia Seminary, 2008).

19   Walther uses the Latin *nonens*, a philosophical term used notably by Thomas Aquinas and others. The term comes from Greek philosophy via Parmenides and Plato. The *ens* is infinite mind, the One in All. The *finens* is limited intellect, such as human intellect. The *nonens* is the absence of meaning, the irrational. At the end of this list, Walther mentions Plato, again showing his debt to classical education.

My word speak My word faithfully. What has straw in common with wheat? declares the LORD." David addresses God Himself in the words of Psalm 94:20: "Can wicked rulers be allied with You, those who frame injustice by statute?" The word "statute" refers to the Word of God in general. What does our dear Lord Christ Himself say regarding this matter? In John 8:31–32, He says, "If you abide in My word, you are truly My disciples, and you will know the truth, and the truth will set you free." But it is horrible how German theologians are not ashamed to respond to this: "Bah! We seek the truth, but only a conceited, self-satisfied person would claim to have achieved it."

John 8:32; Jude 3   Such talk shows to what depths we have sunk. Does the Lord not say distinctly, "You **will know** the truth, and the truth **will** set you free"? The faithful apostle Jude writes in his Epistle (verse 3): "Beloved, although I was very eager to write to you about our common salvation, I found it necessary to write appealing to you **to contend for the faith that was once for all delivered to the saints**." The apostle is referring not to faith in a person's heart, but to objective faith, that is, to pure doctrine.

John, the beloved disciple, the spokesman of love, writes in 2 John 9–11:

2 John 9–11   Everyone who goes on ahead and does not abide in the teaching of Christ, does not have God. Whoever abides in the teaching has both the Father and the Son. If anyone comes to you and does not bring this teaching, do not receive him into your house or give him any greeting, for whoever greets him takes part in his wicked works.

The holy apostle Paul writes to Titus, [in chapter] 1, [verses] 9–11:

Titus 1:9–11   [A pastor] must hold firm to the trustworthy word as taught, so that he may be able to give instruction in sound doctrine and also to rebuke those who contradict it. For there are many who are insubordinate, empty talkers and deceivers, especially those of the circumcision party. They must be silenced, since they are upsetting whole families by teaching for shameful gain what they ought not to teach.

1 Tim. 4:16   In his First Epistle to Timothy (4:16), Paul writes: "Keep a close watch on yourself and on the teaching. Persist in this, for by so doing you will save both yourself and your hearers."

Gal. 5:7–9   Lastly, he writes to the Galatian congregation, after false teachers had made their way into their midst. Galatians 5:7–9: "You were running well. Who hindered you from obeying the truth? This persuasion is not from Him who calls you. A little leaven leavens the whole lump." He means to say that a single false teaching poisons the entire body of Christian doctrine, even as a little poison dropped into pure water produces a deadly potion.

Let us picture as vividly as we can the situation that would have arisen in the early Church after false teachers such as Arius, Nestorius, and Pelagius had surfaced—if men such as Athanasius, Cyril, and Augustine had not stood up against them. As early as the fourth and fifth centuries, the Church would have lost the primary article of the Christian faith. The foundation would have been removed from beneath it, and it would have had to collapse. That would indeed have been impossible in light of the eternal counsel of God concerning the Church. Nonetheless, *because* of that very counsel, God had to awaken tools such as those teachers.

True, while they were alive, they were hated and persecuted as evil disturbers of Christendom, but for more than a thousand years their names were beacons, great witnesses for the saving truth—and in eternity they will shine on as the brightness of the sky and the stars forever and ever.[20] Let no one, then, be discouraged from giving testimony on behalf of the truth just because someone mocks his "false spirit." Such claims come solely from unbelief.

Again, suppose that Luther had learned the truth, that he had indeed given witness to it among his immediate associates, but that he had not been drawn into the battle against the papacy and the horrors it had introduced into the Church. What would have happened? Christianity would have remained under the spiritual tyranny of the Roman Antichrist, and we would all still be subjected to it.

There is no question, then, but that both—yes, both—of these efforts are necessary: to defend the truth *and* to oppose every doctrinal error. To qualify you men for both tasks is one of the aims of these Friday evening lectures. May God send His blessing on the discussion of the subject before us tonight!

At our last meeting, we had barely begun to discuss the important contents of Thesis XXI, that is, that Law and Gospel are not properly distinguished when people claim that salvation can be received by the mere *act* of being baptized and going to Communion. This is a most horrible way of mingling Law and Gospel.

Back to Thesis XXI: Errors about *ex opere operato*

The Gospel simply states: "Believe . . . and you will be saved,"[21] while the Law issues the order: "Do this, and you will live."[22] Now, if the mere act of being baptized and partaking of Holy Communion brings grace to a person, then the Gospel has obviously been turned into Law, because salvation would then rest on a person's works. Moreover, this would turn the Law into Gospel because salvation would be promised to that poor, sinful person as a reward for his works.

Mark 16:16

You would indeed think it would be completely impossible for a Christian pastor to teach that the Sacraments save mechanically, *ex opere operato*. Still, that is exactly what happens over and over. The same men who wish to be

---

20   See Daniel 12:3.
21   See also John 3:18; Acts 16:31; Romans 10:9.
22   See Deuteronomy 30:16; Luke 10:28.

regarded as genuine, strict Lutherans teach this awful error every time they discuss the Sacraments. After they explain their version of the doctrine of Baptism, every listener would be under the impression that, in order to get to heaven, all they need to do is submit to the act of Baptism. Once these men finish their presentation of the doctrine of the Lord's Supper, the people are convinced that, to obtain the forgiveness of sins, all they have to do is step up to the altar and take Communion, because God has attached His grace to this external action.[23]

Scripture opposes *ex opere operato* effects   Last week I began to show you that this teaching is diametrically opposed to the doctrine of the Gospel. This is proved by all the passages that testify that the Gospel requires nothing but faith, that faith is the one condition. That being the case, how could anyone claim that this or that work would benefit a person?

If the Word that is preached will not benefit a person unless he believes it, then neither will being baptized and taking Communion benefit anyone who does not believe. Telling a person that he is saved by faith alone means nothing else than that he is saved by grace.

Rom. 4:16   But most people express it like this: "If you wish to be saved, you must perform this or that task. Oh, by the way, you have to **believe**. God requires that of you." In contrast to this idea, recall the precious text in Romans 4:16: "That is why it depends on **faith**, in order that the promise may rest on **grace**." Remember this most excellent passage! Any teaching contrary to this doctrine, that is, any teaching claiming that people are saved by their works, by scurrying about, or by any effort of their own, but that denies that we are saved by grace alone, is an error that subverts the foundation of Christian doctrine.

"You must believe" means "you must accept what is offered you." Our Father in heaven offers mankind forgiveness of sins, righteousness, life, and salvation. But what good is a present that is not accepted? Accepting a gift is not a work through which you earn the gift. Rather, it means taking hold of what is being offered. If you extend your hand with a gift to a beggar, you are not certain whether he is going to accept the gift, even though you are offering it to him in full sincerity. If he lets your gift fall to the ground, of course, he gets nothing.

---

23 Walther mentions these pastors by name at the end of this lecture. Books by Franz Delitzsch and Gottfried Thomasius probe the question of baptized Christians who fall away from faith. They wrongly suggest that the act of Baptism might yet save such people. On the one hand, Delitzsch and Thomasius affirm Baptism as a sort of natural process apart from faith. On the other hand, Pietism speaks of Baptism in a way that is subordinate to faith. Walther steers clear of both errors. Franz Pieper gives specific citations from Delitzsch (*Vier Bücher von der Kirche* [Dresden: Naumann, 1847], 43ff.) and Thomasius (*Dogmatik* 4:9). See Franz Pieper, *Christian Dogmatics* (St. Louis: Concordia, 1950), 3:265–66. See also Thomasius, *Christi Person und Werk* (Erlangen: Bläsing, 1853).

Consider well what the Lord has to say in Mark 16:16: "Whoever **believes** and is **baptized** will be saved." He does not say, "Whoever is baptized and believes," but the reverse. Faith is the most necessary thing, and Baptism is something to which faith clings. Moreover, the Lord continues: "But whoever does not believe will be condemned." This shows that even if a person were unable to be baptized, he is still saved, as long as he believes.[24]

In Acts 8:36–37 we read:

> And as they went along the road they came to some water, and the chamberlain said, "See, there is water! What prevents me from being baptized?" Philip said, however, "**If you believe with your whole heart, it may well be possible.**" He answered and said, "I believe that Jesus Christ is the Son of God."[25]

The only thing that Philip required was faith, as if he had said to the eunuch, "If you do not believe, being baptized will not benefit you at all." At our Baptism it is not we who are performing the work, but God.

Galatians 3:26–27: "For in Christ Jesus you are all sons of God, through faith. For as many of you as were baptized into Christ have put on Christ." This text shows that Christ is "put on" in Baptism only if a person believes. This is usually interpreted in the sense that **anyone** who is baptized has put on Christ. However, that is not what the apostle says. Rather, he says, "As many **of you**," namely, of you who are "the children of God by faith." Such people indeed put on Christ in Baptism. An unbeliever who receives Baptism does not put on Christ, but keeps on the spotted garment of his sinful flesh.

At the institution of the Holy Supper the Lord says, "Take, eat; this is My body, **which** is given **for you**. This do in remembrance of Me. Drink of it, all of you; this cup is the new testament in My blood, which is shed for you for the forgiveness of sins."[26] The Lord does not merely say, "This is My body," but He adds: "which is given for you." He does not merely say, "This is My blood," but He adds: "which is shed for you for the forgiveness of sins."

It is plain that He is saying this: "The key point is that you believe that this body was given **for you** and that this blood was shed for the forgiveness of **your** sins. That is what you must believe if you wish to receive the real blessing from this heavenly feast." By adding: "This do in remembrance of Me," Christ is implying: "Do this in faith." Surely He does not mean: "Think of Me when you partake of My body and blood—do not forget Me altogether!"

Mark 16:16

Acts 8:36–37
Luther

Gal. 3:26–27

---

24   Walther focuses on the harmful effects of unbelief. He does not speak here to the issue of infant Baptism; rather, he is speaking according to Scripture regarding faith and unbelief.

25   Acts 8:37 does not appear in the earliest Greek manuscripts.

26   See the Service of the Sacrament (*LSB*, p. 162, Walther's emphasis).

Whoever thinks that Christ merely warned His disciples not to forget Him altogether—he does not know the Savior. True remembrance of Christ means that the believing communicant would **believe** and reflect on the fact that "this body was given for me. This blood was shed for the forgiveness of my sins. This gives me confidence to approach the altar. I will cling to this truth by faith and honor my Savior's pledge very highly."

For when God adds a visible pledge to His Word, who would dare to doubt that His Word is truth and that His promise will certainly be fulfilled? Remember this for the good of your own soul and conscience. Whenever you go to Communion, let these words shine before your eyes: "Given for you." "Shed for you for the forgiveness of sins."

If you fail to do this, if you imagine that by going to Communion you have once again done your duty and that God will regard your performance favorably, then your going to Communion is a contemptible act that will land you in death and eternal damnation. Going to Communion and eating the body of Christ and drinking His blood with such a mind is disgraceful. But it is not disgraceful to hold fast to the word of His promise.[27]

Rom. 4:11
Romans 4:11: "[Abraham] received the sign of circumcision as a seal of the righteousness that he had by faith while he was still uncircumcised." Here we are told that Abraham believed before he was circumcised and that in his circumcision he merely received a seal of the righteousness of faith. Knowing how slow we are to believe—even after we have become believers—it is an act of great kindness on the part of God to add external signs to His Word and to attach His promise to them. For the Sacraments are connected with, and are understood in, God's Word. The shining star that glows is the Word.

People often claim that in our Church we teach that in Baptism we are mechanically adopted as children of God and that the Lord's Supper works the forgiveness of sins for us in a mechanical way.[28] Those false teachers beat this falsehood into people's heads and pretend it is Lutheran doctrine. If that *were* our doctrine, we should indeed not feel surprised if all true Christians were to shun us.[29] It would be horrible if we first stated: "People are not saved by works," but then added: "However, people can obtain forgiveness of their sins by doing these two unimportant works."

True, many Lutherans consult their calendars to determine whether it is time for them to go to Communion again. Why is that? Because they imagine

---

27   German: *Thun Sie das nicht und denken: „So, da hab ich auch wieder einmal meine Pflicht gethan! Dieses Werk wird Gott auch ansehen", so ist Ihr Abendmahlsgang ein verdammlicher Gang, der Ihnen Tod und Verdammniß bringt.* Walther's German here is quite specific to the case of the willful unbeliever.

28   Both instances of "mechanical" translate the Latin: *ex opere operato.*

29   A practice that arose notably among groups such as the Puritans, in which a person who was shunned was treated as an outcast.

that going to Communion is the **most important** work of Christians and they cannot afford to neglect [this work]. So they approach the altar and eat and drink death and damnation to themselves. No, what should urge a person to go to Communion is the promise of grace that God attaches to the visible signs in the Sacrament. If a person approaches the altar with faith in that promise, he will leave the Table of the Lord with a blessing in his heart.

It is a pity that many think and say, "I was reared to believe that it is my duty to go to Communion. And if I perform this duty, then I am sure of my salvation." And it is also true that the Lutheran Church speaks of the Sacraments with such high regard that the Enthusiasts[30] regard it as screeching in their ears. The Lutheran Church holds to the word of the Lord: "Whoever believes and is baptized will be saved." That is the reason it condemns all false teachers who say that Baptism is merely a ceremony through which a person is received into the Church. Rather, according to Lutheran teaching, Baptism "works forgiveness of sins, delivers from death and the devil, and gives eternal salvation to all who believe this, as the words and promises of God declare."[31] The Lutheran Church maintains that Baptism is "the washing of regeneration and renewing of the Holy Spirit"; that the water in Baptism, as St. Peter says, "saves you"; and that those who "were baptized into Christ have put on Christ."

As far as the Lord's Supper is concerned, the Lutheran Church—resisting all attempts to be misled—maintains the truth of the Lord's words when He says, "This is My body, which is given for you. This is My blood, which is shed for you."[32] The Lutheran Church regards the holy Sacraments as the most sacred, gracious, and precious treasures on earth and is firmly convinced that God is not a miserable master of ceremonies who decrees what rites we are to observe when receiving a person into our communion.[33] Christianity is not a

Mark 16:16;
SC IV;
Titus 3:5;
1 Pet. 3:21;
Gal. 3:27

---

30 German: *Schwärmer*.

31 *Concordia*, 339.

32 See Matthew 26:26–28; Mark 14:22–24; Luke 22:19; 1 Corinthians 11:24. In Luke 22:20 and 1 Corinthians 11:25, Jesus speaks of drinking of the "cup."

33 One speaks of church fellowship as a "communion" in a special manner. Normally, "communion" means a kind of consensus derived from the idea of oneness and "community" among people. In the life of the Church, however, God distinguishes between true communion (true oneness in Him, John 17:17–21) and membership in the world, whose prince is Satan (Ephesians 2:2). The oneness of the invisible Church as the Body of Christ is an article of faith, the "mystical union" (Latin: *unio mystica*). The oneness of the Church is expressed visibly by a church "communion" defined by a "symbol" of faith (Latin: *symbolum*) that defines a collection of beliefs taught according to Scripture. To breach church fellowship confuses Law and Gospel. The Law distinguishes Gentiles from believers (Matthew 18:15–18) in order to show both that they need to live in the Gospel and not in sin, lest they perish under the Law. The Gospel does not distinguish among believers (Galatians 3:28) once they have come to faith.

Masonic society.[34] When God commands a sacramental act, He commands something on which our salvation depends. **But when did the Lutheran Church at any time ever claim that people are saved by the mere external use of the Sacraments?** That is a teaching against which we have always raised our voice, something that we have always fought against and condemned.

Modern theology wrong; Lutheranism right

At this point, "modern"[35] [historical-critical] theologians once again reveal their Papist tendencies, which is strange for people who actually lean more toward Rationalism. These people declare that Baptism **is** regeneration, and based on this false statement, many draw a wrong conclusion as to what the Lutheran Church teaches. According to Lutheran teaching, Baptism **is not** regeneration. Rather, Baptism **effects** regeneration, it **produces** it. It is a **means** of regeneration. However, so you can see quite plainly that the Lutheran Church has nothing to do with the teaching of *ex opere operato* capabilities of the Sacraments, allow me to present a few testimonies from our Confessions.

SC IV;
1 Pet. 3:21

In the **Small Catechism of Luther**, we read: "How can water do such great things? Answer: It is not the water indeed that does them, but the Word of God which is in and with the water, and faith, which trusts this Word of God in the water."[36] When Peter says in 1 Peter 3:21, "Baptism . . . now saves you,"[37] he is speaking in synecdoche.[38] It is to the sacramental act of Holy Baptism that God has attached the great and glorious promise of grace.

Again, we read in the Sixth Chief Part of the catechism:

SC VI

How can bodily eating and drinking do such great things? Answer: It is not the eating and drinking, indeed, that does them, but the words, which are given here, "Given . . . and shed for you for the forgiveness of sins." These words are, beside the bodily eating and drinking, **the chief thing** in the Sacrament. The person who believes these words has what they say and express, namely, the forgiveness of sins.[39]

---

34 Freemasonry has its origins in the trade guilds of stonecutters and masons. Guilds helped to protect trade secrets and also helped masters in the craft establish standards of work that, in turn, allowed them to bargain for better wages. In the Enlightenment period, freemasonry and its inherent connections with mathematics and architecture helped to draw intellectuals steeped in Rationalism. Having pushed God aside, they adapted elements of the occult to create a false history and secret ceremonies as part of a quasi-religious gentleman's club. One had to pass through a series of rituals to enter the club and to pass into its inner circles. Important figures in England and the early United States were freemasons.

35 German: *die neueren Theologen*. The words *neu* and *modern* are synonyms.

36 *Concordia*, 340. See also Müller, 362; *Triglot Concordia*, 551.

37 The Dau edition adds: "the water in Baptism typified by the water of the Flood."

38 Synecdoche is a figure of speech in which a part substitutes for the whole or the whole for the parts. For example, one may refer to a sports car as "hot wheels."

39 *Concordia*, 343. See also Müller, 365; *Triglot Concordia*, 557.

As a rule, "modern" [historical-critical] theologians interpret the phrase "the chief thing in the Sacrament" to mean the Word of God that is recited in connection with the Sacrament and that they term, in dogmatic terminology, that which gives the Lord's Supper its proper form.[40] That is not at all what the catechism means. In this place, it discusses the **effect** of the Sacrament and declares that the chief thing, as far as its effect is concerned, is the words "Given for you" and "Shed for you."

In the **Augsburg Confession**, Article XIII,[41] we read:

> Our churches teach that the Sacraments were ordained, not only to be marks of profession among men, but even more, to be signs and testimonies of God's will toward us. They were instituted to **awaken and confirm faith in those who use them. Therefore, we must use the Sacraments in such a way that faith, which believes the promises offered** and set forth through the Sacraments, **is increased**.[42]

AC XIII 1–2

The purpose of the Sacraments is to awaken and strengthen our faith. The preaching of the Word should already strengthen a Christian's faith. But when he is told that, in addition to the Word, God has instituted a special sacred act to which His promise has been attached, the Christian must feel as if he were standing before the very gates of heaven. But this only happens if you cling to the promises of God. He wants to save us by His free grace. For that reason, it is idiotic to wonder: "What? Baptism is supposed to save me, just because I hold my head [over the font] and let someone pour water over it?" Indeed not. You can do nothing. Do not speculate about why God would prescribe for us to do something about which human reason would tell us: "That could not possibly work salvation for me." Yet the Enthusiasts[43] persuade people that this is our doctrine and that this teaching of ours is a remnant of Papist teaching. However, the mere mechanical performance of Baptism will result in nothing but damnation for a person if he does not also believe.[44] The truth of the matter is: God is so full of loving-kindness that He not only has certain men preach about His grace, but, in addition, He tells you to come to the Sacrament, where He seals to you the promise of grace. All you have to "do" is believe!

In the same way, a person who imagines that his sins would be forgiven by merely eating and drinking the Lord's Supper is under a delusion. The body

---

40 Latin: *forma sacrae coenae.*

41 *Concordia*, 38. See also Müller, 41; *Triglot Concordia*, 49.

42 See 2 Thessalonians 1:3.

43 German: *Schwärmer.*

44 Thus, in Matthew 28:19–20, baptizing is connected with teaching as Jesus instructs the eleven disciples.

of Christ does not produce anything in a physical manner, as the "Moderns"[45] claim when they say that it implants in humans the seed of immortality. That idea is nothing but a dream of human speculative theology.[46]

Lastly, our Confessions plainly condemn the teaching that the Sacraments have an *ex opere operato* effect. In the **Apology** of the Augsburg Confession, Article XIII, we read:

Ap XIII 3–5   If we call Sacraments "rites that have the command of God, and to which the promise of grace has been added," it is easy to decide what are true Sacraments. For ceremonies and external things instituted by human beings are not Sacraments according to this way of thinking. Men without [Christ's] mandate cannot promise grace. Therefore, signs established without God's command are not sure signs of grace, even though such signs, such as a painted cross, perhaps help children and coarse people remember [what they have been taught].

Rom. 10:17   Therefore, Baptism, the Lord's Supper, and Absolution are truly Sacraments. For these rites have God's mandate and the promise of grace, which properly belongs to the New Testament and is the New Testament. To that end, the external signs are established, that hearts are moved through them, simultaneously through the Word and the external signs. This happens when we are baptized, when we receive the Lord's body, in order that we believe that God will be truly gracious to us for Christ's sake, as Paul says, "Faith comes from hearing" (Romans 10:17).[47]

Ap XIII 5   Any so-called "sacrament" to which a promise of grace has not been added—we cannot accept that as a Sacrament. Thus the Apology: "But just as the Word enters the ears, in the same way the external signs are provided for the eyes, in order to stir up the heart and move it to faith."[48]

Moreover, even brand-new Christians know that, according to Scripture, the mere outward act of hearing the Word does not save anyone. Likewise, Scripture does not teach that the Sacraments save in this way. Just placing the mere signs before someone's eyes does not produce anything, though it does indicate what the Word proclaims. We baptize with water, and Baptism cleanses from sin, bringing about sanctification, regeneration, and renewal. The water signifies this. We *hear* in sermons what we can *see* in the external

---

45   Walther again means historical-critical theologians.

46   The Dau edition adds: "of which not a word is said in Scripture."

47   Müller, 202. For more on Walther's Book of Concord, see pages 467–68. See also *Concordia*, 184; *Triglot Concordia*, 309.

48   Müller, 202. See also *Concordia*, 184; *Triglot Concordia*, 309.

element of Baptism. And the Word and the Sacrament produce the same effect in the heart.

The "Moderns"[49] picture the situation like this: For various diseases God has ordained various cures. They do regard the Word as a cure, but they imagine that Baptism must be for a different purpose, namely, for the purpose of regenerating us. In the same way, they maintain that the Lord's Supper must be for still another purpose, namely, to unite us with the Body of Christ. But these are all human fabrications. Scripture does not say a single word about them. The Word produces faith, brings us forgiveness of sins, and gives us the grace of God and salvation. Baptism does the same, as does the Lord's Supper.

Now, a seal is of no benefit on its own. If I were to give you ten sheets with my seal affixed to them, you could not do business with them. When the apostle calls circumcision a seal, he indicates that all Sacraments are seals. What is the correlation between paper and Scripture? That is what God's Word is. God puts His Word in writing—on paper—and by means of the Sacrament He seals what is contained in His gracious promises. For this reason the Lord does not merely command us to baptize. Rather, He says, "Whoever **believes** and is baptized will be saved."

Mark 16:16

> The Word and the external sign work the same way in the heart, as Augustine said so well. He says that the Sacrament is a visible word.[50] For the external sign is received by the eyes and is a picture that means the same thing as the Word, that is preached through the Word. Therefore, the effect of both is the same.[51]

Ap XIII 5

In the pulpit the Word is audible. In the Sacraments it is visible. Further on, the *Apology* says:

> It is still more needful to debate and to understand **how the Sacraments are to be used**. Here we must entirely **condemn** the whole crowd of scholastic doctors, who teach that the Sacraments grant grace *ex opere operato* to those who merely use them without raising any particular obstacles, even when the heart has no good thoughts in it. This is absolutely a Jewish error that they maintain, that we become righteous and holy by a work and external ceremonies without faith and when the heart is not in it.

Ap XIII 18–22

> And yet this harmful opinion is preached and taught far and wide throughout the entire realm of the pope and in the church of the

---

49 Walther again refers to historical-critical theologians.

50 Latin: *verbum visibile*. German: *sichtlich Wort*.

51 Müller, 202–3. See also *Concordia*, 184–85; *Triglot Concordia*, 309.

pope.[52] Paul writes against [the idea] that Abraham was justified by circumcision.[53] He rather says that circumcision was a sign presented for the use and strengthening of faith. Thus we say that **faith belongs to the proper use of the Sacraments**, which should believe the divine promise and receive the promised grace that is offered in Sacrament and Word.

This is a certain and true use of the Sacraments, on which Christian hearts and consciences may risk heart and conscience. No one can take hold of the divine promise except through faith. But the Sacraments are the signs and seals of the promise. Therefore, faith belongs to the proper use of the Sacraments. When I receive the Lord's Supper, Christ clearly says, "That is the New Testament." For this reason I believe confidently I am offered grace and forgiveness of sins, which are promised in the New Testament. Thus may I receive this by faith and comfort my alarmed, silly conscience and stand with certainty on the fact that God's Word and promise do not fail,[54] but remain sure and still more certain than if God, by a new miracle, would declare from heaven that it was His will to grant forgiveness. But how would a miracle help at all, were faith not present?

And here we speak of faith where I myself believe, with certainty for me, that my sins are forgiven. [We do] not speak of general faith, where I believe that a god exists. This same proper use of the Sacrament truly comforts and enlivens consciences.

Moreover, no one can think enough, speak enough, or put enough in writing concerning the hateful, shameful, ungodly doctrine of *opera operatum*[55] that they have introduced as an abuse and an error. They teach that when I **use the Sacrament, the mere doing of the work makes me righteous before God and grants me grace**, even if the heart has no good thoughts along with that. From that has come the unspeakable, innumerable, horrible abuses[56] of the Mass. And they can show neither one book nor one letter of this in the ancient Fathers in order to prove the opinion of the scholastics. Indeed, Augustine

---

52   Here the word *Kirchen* is a dative singular.

53   See Romans 4:9.

54   German: *daß Gottes Wort und zusage nicht fehlen*. God introduces neither lies nor errors into His Word; it does not return to Him empty (Isaiah 55:11).

55   Works that are performed mechanically.

56   The German uses the singular as a collective noun, but it sounds better as a plural in English.

says the exact opposite: that faith in the Sacrament—and not the Sacrament itself—justifies.[57]

Errors of modern Lutherans

If you were to tell this to would-be orthodox Lutherans, they would say, "That is Calvinist. Baptism **is** regeneration, and the Lord's Supper works mysterious, but altogether gracious, things in us." Of course, those who know this declaration of the Apology would not dare to talk like this, but they certainly do think like this.

Kahnis[58] knew the doctrine of the Lutheran Church well enough. When I was visiting Germany, he gave me his book *The Doctrine of the Lord's Supper.*[59] In it he says, on page 328: "In general, the concept of sacraments has not been fully developed in the Lutheran Church. The fundamental concepts of the Word and faith have been attached to it too directly." He is saying that there is indeed a certain connection between the Word and faith, on the one hand, and the Sacraments, on the other. But it is wrong for the Lutheran Church to connect them so closely, he says, because the Sacraments operate directly—without the Word and without faith.

Thus Kahnis: "According to the Apology, a Sacrament is merely a qualified Word." That means the Lutheran Church really does regard Sacraments in the same way it regards the Word—the only difference being that the Sacraments have a sign[60] added to them. Page 200: "visible Word."[61] Page 267: "like a picture of the Word or a seal,[62] which, like the Word, has the power to forgive sins only by faith." He is faulting us for our beliefs! "In the presence of the Word the **specific blessing of salvation** of each Sacrament is hidden, just as its **specific saving effect** is hidden by faith." He declares the faith of the Lutheran Church—the faith that, from God's perspective, only the Word, and from man's perspective, only faith are necessary for salvation—he declares that to be worthless.

"No," Kahnis says, "one must make a great distinction between Word and Sacrament. Each Sacrament has its specific saving blessings and operations." He says, "A baptized person is regenerated and remains so until he dies. . . . The purpose of the Lord's Supper can be understood only from its essence. In the Lord's Supper we partake of the glorified body of Christ and, with Him, the Spirit and the life of Christ." This is the new teaching.

---

57 Müller, 204–5. See also *Concordia*, 186; *Triglot Concordia*, 313.

58 See Karl F. A. Kahnis in the Index of Persons and Groups, page 496. Walther and other Missouri Synod theologians often sparred with German theologians who were regarded as confessional Lutherans, yet whose doctrine was shaped more by contemporary philosophy than by Scripture.

59 Karl F. A. Kahnis, *Die Lehre vom Abendmahle* (Leipzig: Dörffling & Franke, 1853).

60 Again, "sign" refers to the visible elements in the Sacraments. See page 390 n. 9.

61 Latin: *verbum visibile.*

62 Latin: *quasi pictura Verbi seu sigillum.*

Delitzsch, whose Lutheran doctrine was once top-notch, also teaches falsely here. In his book *Four Books on the Church* (1847),[63] he writes on page 33:

> Anyone who is baptized and partakes of the Lord's Supper is a member of the Body of Christ. The Body of Christ is the totality of those who, "in one Spirit . . . were all baptized into one body—Jews or Greeks, slaves or free—and all were made to drink of one Spirit."[64] Whether you take Hengstenberg[65] or Wislicenus,[66] by virtue of the act of God, which faith does not produce nor which unbelief can frustrate, both are members of one and the same Body. Whether a person is Protestant or Roman Catholic, a Socinian or a Unitarian, by virtue of their Baptism they are all one in Christ.

Delitzsch even counts Unitarians as part of the visible Christian Church. Speaking of unbelieving and wicked persons who had been baptized as infants, on page 42 he says, "They may be parts, even organs, of the visible Church." But a member is only an organ through which life flows—life that flows through the whole body. According to Delitzsch, all these unbelieving, godless people are limbs of the Body of Christ, except for the fact that they are dead limbs. Yet they are not members of the Church, which is the Body of Christ. So what he is saying is that, in His own church, our Lord Jesus Christ is somehow a corpse!

"But they are not members of the Church, which is the Body of Christ." Now there [Delitzsch] speaks as the Church speaks—saying what our church teachers say. But Delitzsch [unfortunately] continues: "We cannot accept this distinction. Once a person is baptized, he is unalterably a member of Christ's Body."

If I no longer believe and have fallen from the faith, I need to build a new ship for myself. That is contrition and repentance.[67] But, according to

---

63   See the earlier note on Delitzsch and Thomasius, page 396 n 23.

64   1 Corinthians 12:13.

65   Walther comments on German Lutheran theologian Ernst Wilhelm Hengstenberg (1802–69) that, until just before his death, he "really was the prototype of orthodox teachers." Yet Hengstenberg also was a royalist who supported the persecution of Johann Scheibel and other anti-Union, confessional Lutherans in Prussian Silesia. See also the ndex of Persons and Groups, page 494, and the map of Saxony in the front of the book.

66   Walther adds concerning Gustav Adolf Wislicenus (1803–75): "a Freethinker." See also the Index of Persons and Groups, pages 493, 501.

67   When Walther says, "I need to build a new ship for myself," he paraphrases Ezekiel 27:9 from the pre-1912 Luther Bible. This is the lamentation over Tyre, which has parallels with the lament over Babylon in Revelation 18:11–19. A related verse is Genesis 6:14, where God comes to Noah, who responds to the divine proclamation of the flood by building the ark. Walther is saying that, just as God destroys Tyre and Babylon despite their wealth and power, so God will destroy the faithless, erstwhile Christian, regardless of Baptism. Walther builds on Luther in LC IV 80–82 (*Concordia*, 430–31). Luther criticizes Jerome's

Scripture, we say, "Your Baptism stands fast! God never takes away the Word He has given." If I fall into mortal sin after my Baptism, my Baptism does not help me one bit. But once I am back in my right mind, I can say, "I am not lost. I am baptized. God baptized me and said, 'I want you to be My child.' And God never takes back this Word." So, if I cling to my Baptism, that is, to God's promise, then I will regain all the benefits of my Baptism.

J esus says about Himself: "I am the way, and the truth, and the life. No one comes to the Father except through Me." Peter confirms this statement by declaring before the Jewish Sanhedrin: "And there is salvation in no one else, for there is no other name under heaven given among men by which we must be saved." And St. Paul adds his testimony by telling the Corinthians: "For I decided to know nothing among you except Jesus Christ and Him crucified." To be sure, then, it is a great and horrible sin not to draw to Jesus any soul entrusted to us for teaching, and not to tell that person over and over again what a treasure he has in the Lord Jesus, our Savior. To keep someone from believing in Christ is such an awful sin that words cannot express it.

Thirty-fifth Evening Lecture: Sept. 18, 1885

John 14:6; Acts 4:12; 1 Cor. 2:2

A preacher who would restrain a person from confidently laying hold of Christ is depriving that person of everlasting life—regardless of whether that preacher is doing it consciously or unconsciously, deliberately or out of blindness, through evil intent or as the result of a distorted passion for the salvation of souls. Instead of being a shepherd to that person, that preacher becomes a starving wolf. Instead of being a doctor of the soul, he becomes its murderer.[68] In fact, instead of being an angel of God, he becomes a devil to that person.

Alas, so many preachers have not realized until their dying day how many souls they have kept away from Christ by their unevangelical preaching. They alone are to blame that the souls entrusted to them will die of spiritual starvation. The result is that—on their deathbed—these unhappy preachers have to fight a severe spiritual battle to fend off self-accusations and despair. Quite a few of them have departed from this life without any consolation—in anguish, misery, and despair.

The worst offenders in this respect are Rationalist preachers, who with devilish audacity step up into their Christian pulpits and—instead of preaching Christ, the Savior, to all sinners—they recite their miserable moral

---

speaking of repentance as the "second plank" or ship, together with Baptism. Luther sees Baptism as the only ship, while repentance is the act of holding on to that same ship of Baptism after a Christian has fallen overboard into sin. Walther takes Jerome's statement and gives it Luther's meaning. Walther is not saying that one must build his own ship and sail to heaven under his own steam, which is how the Dau text understands it (thus in that edition, this section differs greatly).

68   Again, Walther offers a medical malpractice allusion after his wife's death.

regulations on how to lead a virtuous life. They fill the ears of the people with their empty blather.

Phil. 3:19;
Matt 23:13; 7:23

To these Rationalist mercenaries, whose "god is their belly," God addresses the terrible woe —even in our day—when He says, "But woe to you, scribes and Pharisees, hypocrites! For you shut the kingdom of heaven in people's faces. For you neither enter yourselves nor allow those who would enter to go in." What terror will seize these preachers who used to call themselves friends and adorers of Jesus Christ when they are forced to appear before His judgment seat and hear Him address them in words of flaming anger: "I never knew you; depart from Me, you workers of lawlessness."

No less coarse, however, is the offense of Papists in this respect. Neither do they draw people to Christ, who is the Savior and Friend of sinners. Rather, they describe Christ as a rigorous, tougher Lawgiver than even Moses, because they claim that He laid on people many more commandments—that are even more difficult to keep—than [those of] Moses.

Rev. 14:11

A poor sinner [who, in his anguish, comes] to a priest for advice is not directed to Christ, but to Mary, the so-called "Mother of Mercy." They teach people to be afraid of Christ, telling them that Mary must take them under her sheltering cloak. Or they direct them to some patron saint. For this horrible sin of directing poor souls away from Christ they will have to suffer the wrath of God, who will send them to the place where "the smoke of their torment goes up forever and ever." For failing to teach and proclaim Christ, telling people not to believe in Him, is as monstrous an offense as to blaspheme by branding Christ as a fanatic, as unbelievers do.

It is easy to avoid this coarse sin of keeping people away from Christ. I do not need to warn you against it. But it is difficult to avoid doing the same thing in a more refined manner. Countless preachers have imagined that they were preaching Christ and were proclaiming His doctrine until their eyes were opened and they saw that they had hidden Christ from the eyes of poor sinners. They had directed people *away* from Him rather than *to* Him. This more refined way of keeping people away from Christ is discussed in our twenty-second thesis.

THESIS XXII

You are not rightly distinguishing Law and Gospel in the Word of God if a false distinction is made between a person's being awakened and being converted; moreover, when a person's inability *to believe is mistaken for not being* permitted *to believe.*

EDITOR'S NOTE: In this thesis, Walther moves on to the errors of the Pietists, who take the focus off Christ in conversion and put it falsely on our works. Walther stresses the necessity to remain focused on Christ as the one thing needful for a poor, miserable sinner. It is from this position that one can properly read and interpret the Bible.

Errors about conversion

During the first half of the eighteenth century, the so-called "Pietists" were guilty of seriously mingling Law and Gospel. Among these were various theologians from Halle, including August Hermann Francke, [Joachim Justus] Breithaupt, Anastasius Freylinghausen, [Johann Jakob] Rambach, Joachim Lange, and those who had publicly adopted their views—such as [Karl Heinrich] Bogatzky, [Johann Philipp] Fresenius, and many others.

These men were guilty of a more refined way of mingling Law and Gospel, that is, of keeping people away from Christ. They did this by making a false separation between spiritual awakening and conversion. For they declared that, as far as the way of obtaining salvation is concerned, all people should be distinguished into three groups: (1) Those who are still unconverted. (2) Those who are already awakened but not yet converted. (3) Those who are already converted.

Even though these dear Pietists[1] were well-intentioned and by no means wished to depart from pure doctrine, nevertheless these three classifications were still completely wrong. They would have been correct if they had regarded people who are awakened to be people who are, in fact, occasionally very much impacted by God's Word—that is, by Law and Gospel—but who then quickly wipe away that impression so that there is no effect. If this had been their meaning, it would have been quite correct.

---

1   Walther does appreciate Pietists on some level. There was a time (1750–1817) when, if a Lutheran was not a Rationalist, he was likely a Pietist. Nevertheless, Walther opposes and corrects pietistic errors.

On the other hand, there are people who are tired of walking in their sinful, fleshly security yet who suppress that unease. This goes on until God hits them again with the hammer of the Law, after which they can taste the sweet sugar of the Gospel. But these awakened persons to whom the Pietists referred should no longer be regarded as being unconverted. According to Scripture, there are only two groups: those who are converted and those who are not.

Of course, there are people who, if [merely] compared [outwardly] to true Christians, could be described as "awakened," if they were not compared to the [examples given in] Holy Scripture. A great number of examples for such [seemingly "awakened"] people can be found in the Scriptures.[2] Herod Antipas was one of them. We are told that he used to listen to John the Baptist gladly because John preached many comforting sermons in which he pointed to the promised Messiah. Herod Antipas also occasionally asked John for advice and even followed it. Nevertheless, he remained the same Herod he had always been. By this king's order, John was decapitated to please a miserable dancing girl.[3]

Acts 24:25   Another example is Felix, the governor. Paul preached to him with great passion on righteousness, self-control, and the judgment to come. Paul's sermon struck home, and Felix's own conscience convicted him of being a condemned person. If Paul was preaching the truth (which, of course, he was), Felix knew he would be lost—fornicator, unjust judge, and adulterer that he was. But Felix stifled that belief immediately and dismissed Paul, saying, "Go away for the present. When I get an opportunity I will summon you." But Felix never did call for Paul because he was unwilling to hear that voice again.

Acts 26:24   A similar situation is that of Festus. When Paul thundered at him, preaching the Law to him, and then proclaimed the good tidings of the Gospel, Festus cried: "Paul, you are out of your mind; your great learning is driving you out of your mind." Despite the deep impression that the preaching of Paul had made on him, Festus declared Paul to be a fanatic.

Acts 26:28   Another instance is that of Agrippa, who even said to Paul, "In a short time would you persuade me to be a Christian?" What a powerful impression the apostle's address must have made on the king that it forced this public confession from him: that it would not take much to make him one of those despised and evil Christians! What was lacking that would have made him a Christian? Agrippa would have to stop his willful, stubborn resistance and allow the Lord to prevail over him. Yet Agrippa tried to defeat the Lord and

---

2   Again, in a manner that became more pronounced after his wife's death, Walther appears to speak faster than he can express the details. We have included the details in order to make things clearer.

3   See Matthew 14:1–12; Mark 6:14–29.

thus remained in his unconverted state. People like this must not be counted among the converted, nor should they be considered awakened. When Scripture speaks of awakening, it always means conversion.

You must bear this in mind when you read writings of Pietists, which contain a great deal of useful information. You must distinguish people into only two groups. The following passages will show you that by *awakening*, Scripture means conversion.

Ephesians 5:14: "Awake, O sleeper, and arise from the dead, and Christ will shine on you." This is evidently a call to genuine conversion and repentance. We are to wake up from our spiritual sleep and arise from spiritual death. Thus anyone who is awakened is awakened not from physical but from spiritual sleep. People who have been awakened in this way become alive, which means nothing other than that they have become Christians. **Eph. 5:14**

Ephesians 2:4–6: "But God, being rich in mercy, because of the great love with which He loved us, even when we were dead in our trespasses, made us alive together with Christ—by grace you have been saved—and raised us up with Him and seated us with Him in the heavenly places in Christ Jesus." Being awakened and being made alive are identical. Anyone who has been awakened is saved. These people are transferred into a heavenly life the moment they are awakened by the Holy Spirit. **Eph. 2:4–6**

Colossians 2:12: "Having been buried with Him in baptism, in which you were also raised with Him through faith in the powerful working of God, who raised Him from the dead." "Through faith!" The event described in this text took place "through faith." Accordingly, no one can be awakened unless they have faith. That means they must be Christians. **Col. 2:12**

However, Pietists object that any person who has not experienced genuine, thorough contrition in their heart is not yet converted—but merely awakened. By **thorough contrition** they mean contrition like that of David, who spent night after night crying and weeping in his bed, walking almost bent over with grief for days.[4] Anyone who has not passed through these experiences is only awakened and still unconverted. **Pietistic errors**

Because anyone who has not yet been sealed with the Holy Spirit and who is not quite certain of his state of grace and of salvation—anyone who is still wavering—such persons, Pietists claim, are certainly not Christians. They will be uncharitable. They will lack genuine patience and the proper willingness to serve their fellow human beings. But all of this is a false assumption.

Some people may have become true Christians without experiencing the great and terrible anguish of David. For though David really had these experiences, the Bible does not say that everyone must experience crises and suffer in the same degree. Regarding the sealing with the Holy Spirit, we read **Eph. 1:13**

---

4   See 2 Samuel 12:15–17.

in Ephesians 1:13: "In Him you also, when you heard the word of truth, the gospel of your salvation, and believed in Him, were sealed with the promised Holy Spirit."[5] First we must believe, though it may be a very weak faith, a faith that is constantly struggling with anxieties and doubts. God does not immediately grant everyone boldness of faith and heroic courage.

Acts 2:37–38, 42   That this is the pure, untainted truth can be seen in every record we have of people who were converted. For instance, take those present at the first Pentecost. We are told that these people were cut to the heart and asked the apostles, "Brothers, what shall we do?" The apostle does not say to them, "Wait a while. First you must go through a severe penitential struggle. You will have to wrestle with God and cry out to Him for a long time until the Holy Spirit gives you the inward assurance that you have obtained grace and are saved." No. The apostle merely says, "Repent and be baptized," and immediately they receive Baptism. "Repent" means: "Turn to your Lord Jesus, believe in Him, and—as a seal of your faith—receive Baptism. And all will be well." A bit further down we learn more about these new converts: "And they devoted themselves to the apostles' teaching and the fellowship, to the breaking of bread and the prayers." Thus they became truly converted in a few moments' time.

Acts 8:37 Luther   We can see this in the case of the Ethiopian court official. Philip merely says to him, "If you believe with all your heart, you may be baptized." When the court official answers, "I believe that Jesus Christ is the Son of God," Philip is fully satisfied. For he knows what the court official means by his confession, namely, that he now believes in the Messiah—true God and true man. After the official is baptized, they part and probably never see each other again. Philip is not the least bit worried whether the man is truly converted. He is quite certain of the man's conversion because he had declared: "I believe that Jesus Christ is the Son of God."

Acts 16:28, 30   Let us continue. The jailer at Philippi is in despair, not on account of his sins but because he fears that he will be executed for allowing all his prisoners to escape. Paul grabs the jailer by the arm, just as he is about to stab himself, and cries: "Do not harm yourself, for we are all here." The jailer is thunderstruck. He recalls the thoughts that had stirred his heart the previous night, when he had heard the prisoners—whom he had subjected to such cruel treatment—praising and glorifying God. Convicted of the wickedness of his heart and the severity of his sin, he falls at the apostles' feet, crying: "Sirs, what must I do to be saved?"

Acts 16:31   St. Paul does not say to him, "We can do nothing tonight. We first have to give you instruction and determine the condition of your heart. We admit that you have been awakened, but you are far from being converted." No. He

---

5   The Dau text adds: "The sealing presupposes faith."

simply says, "Believe in the Lord Jesus, and you will be saved, you and your household." The jailer believes and is filled with joy that he has become a believer. That is all that Paul and Silas do. They leave the jailer and, after their release, continue their journey.

Show me a single passage in Scripture where a prophet, apostle, or any other saint points people to a different way of conversion, telling them that they cannot expect to be converted speedily and that they must first experience this, that, and the other thing. On the contrary, they always preach in such a way as to terrify their listeners. As soon as their listeners realize that there is no refuge for them, as soon as they feel condemned, they cry, "Is there no help for us?" And the prophets and apostles tell them, "Believe in the Lord Jesus, and all will be well with you."

The Enthusiasts[6] declare that this is not the proper order of conversion. Indeed, it is not the fanatics' order, but it is God's order. As soon as the Gospel sounded in the ears of the people mentioned in the Bible (as related above), it shot straight into their hearts, and they became believers. For example, we read that after receiving Absolution, David still had to suffer a great deal of anguish. But, at the same time, his penitential psalms[7] are a confession of his assurance that God was gracious to him.

Suppose there is a person who has become alarmed over his sins. If the pastor is so slow in leading him that it may take months and years before that person can say, "Yes, I believe"—that is completely lost effort. A pastor such as that is a spiritual quack.[8] He has not led that person to Jesus, but rather to rely on his own works. And that is a great sin.

In a certain sense the Pietists were guilty of this awful sin. Overly enthusiastic pastors in particular are in danger of committing this great and serious sin. To be sure, they are sincere and mean well, but the only thing they accomplish is to martyr souls, and nothing more. Whenever a sinner becomes spiritually bankrupt and asks you, "What must I do to be saved?" you must say: "Very simple: believe in Jesus, your Savior, and all will be well."

Consider that—according to the Scriptures—it is not at all difficult to be converted. But to remain in a converted state—that is difficult. Accordingly, it is incorrect to interpret the words of the Savior: "Enter by the narrow gate," to mean repentance. Repentance is not a narrow gate through which a person has to squeeze. Repentance is something that God Himself must give to a

Truth about conversion; Matt. 7:13

---

6   German: *Schwärmer.*

7   Psalms 6, 32, 38, 51, 102, 130, and 143.

8   This is not simply a reference to the false claims of nineteenth-century medical quackery. References to false spiritual leaders as quacks or bad doctors occur in greater number after the death of Emilie Walther. This suggests that Walther was still coping with his grief by revisiting his thoughts about Emilie's medical care.

person. Any kind of repentance that we produce ourselves is false and God is disgusted by it.

We do not need to worry that we are unable to produce repentance in ourselves. All we need is to apply His forceful Word—and we have the first part of repentance. When the Gospel is presented to a person "straight," it will produce faith in him. All he has to do when he hears the Gospel is to accept it. **But here is where the struggle begins. The error of false teachers in this matter is that they claim this struggle takes place before conversion.** But there is no such thing as a spiritual struggle before conversion. The struggle takes place after conversion. And that is tough.

The narrow way is the cross that Christians have to bear, in that they have to kill their own flesh and suffer mocking, scorn, and the shame heaped on them by the world. They have to fight against the devil and renounce the world with its vanities, treasures, and pleasures. And all this is difficult. That is a task that causes many to fall away again soon after conversion and that causes them to lose their faith. Wherever the Word of God is proclaimed with the proof[9] of the Spirit and power of God, many more people are converted than we imagine.

If only we could look into the hearts of worshipers in a church where the Word is forcefully proclaimed in this way and [where] human works are not mingled with the teaching of saving grace. Then we would observe that many people—by the grace of God—resolve to become Christians. For they are convinced that the preacher is right. But many suppress these sensations the moment they leave the church. They kid themselves into thinking that they have been listening to some fanatic. Such people harden themselves, Sunday after Sunday, and work themselves into a most dangerous condition—where conversion is no longer possible.

The Savior Himself says that many receive the Word with joy[10] yet smother the bud as soon as tribulation[11] comes. This does not necessarily mean severe devilish afflictions, but, in general, spiritual boredom, sluggishness in prayer, negligence in hearing the Word of God, and the contempt that Christians must suffer at the hands of worldly people, and so on. Then, once again, that person's faith is lost entirely.[12]

Luke 8:13   In cases such as these, Pietists would say that the person had not been converted in the first place. But the Lord says, yes, "They **believe** for a while."

---

9 German: *Beweisung.*

10 See Matthew 13:20.

11 German: *Anfechtung.*

12 German: *Und nun ist alles wieder hin.* The person has returned to "square one" and stands under God's wrath. A similar statement would be "They are done for." The Dau text adds: "All these things may dissipate the impressions which had been made on the Christians' hearts."

This second group of listeners—people who quickly accept the Gospel—does begin to **believe**. However, they do not permit the Word to grow roots in their heart. Rather, when they are exposed to the next temptation, they once again surrender to the world and their own flesh, and all they had gained is again lost.

Beware, then, of the illusion that people may become secure if they are told how quickly they may be led to repentance and conversion. Rather, just concentrate on the greatness of God's grace. After a person has been converted, he must be told that, from that point forward, he will have to struggle daily and will have to focus on making spiritual progress day by day. He will have to exercise himself in love, patience, and meekness—and wrestle with sin.

That is a lesson for converted Christians who begin to cooperate with the divine grace in them. But the Enthusiasts put these spiritual conflicts **before** conversion. That is horrible—just horrible! This robs God of the honor owed to Him.

Our church declares in the *Formula of Concord*, Solid Declaration, Article II, paragraph 87:

> The conversion of our corrupt will, which is nothing other than restoring it back to life from spiritual death, is only and solely God's work (just as the restoration of life in the resurrection of the body must also be credited to God alone). This has been fully set forth above and proved by clear testimonies of Holy Scripture.[13]

FC SD II 87

Again, the same confession states:[14]

> In a word, what God's Son says remains eternally true, "For apart from Me you can do nothing."[15]

FC SD II 14

> Paul says, "For it is God who works in you, both to will and to work for His good pleasure."[16]

> **To all godly Christians who feel and experience in their hearts a small spark or longing for divine grace and eternal salvation this precious passage is very comforting. For they know that God has kindled in their hearts this beginning of true godliness.** He will further strengthen and help them in their great weakness to persevere in true faith unto the end.[17]

---

13 *Concordia*, 535. See also Müller, 609; *Triglot Concordia*, 913–15.

14 *Concordia*, 523, Walther's emphasis. See also Müller, 591; *Triglot Concordia*, 885.

15 John 15:5.

16 Philippians 2:13.

17 See 1 Peter 5:10.

Phil. 2:12–13

Where there is even a spark longing for grace, there is faith. For faith is nothing else than longing for mercy. A person in whom this takes place is not merely awakened in the false sense of the word, but converted. Note that in Philippians 2:12–13 the apostle says, first, "Work out your own salvation with fear and trembling," and then continues: "for it is **God** who works in you, both to will and to work for His good pleasure."

We need to work out our own salvation with fear and trembling for the very reason that our heavenly Father must do everything necessary for our salvation. That is what the apostle tells people who have been converted. A person who is hardened, blind, and dead cannot work out his own salvation. But a converted person can—and actually does—work out his own salvation. If he fails to do it, he is again stricken with spiritual blindness and relapses into spiritual death.

Decision theology an old error

Our opponents these days claim that God first awakens a person and thus gives him the power to decide whether he wants to be converted or not. That is simply a reworking of a false doctrine of long ago. It overlooks the fact that a person is either spiritually dead or spiritually alive. These people claim that a person must first be given a free will,[18] which means that he must be awakened before he can be converted.

From **Luther** we can see the necessary condition of people who need to come to the true faith. He says (St. Louis Ed. 18:1715):[19]

W² 18:1715
(cf. AE 33:61–62)

To begin with, God has given a sure promise to those who have been humbled, **that is, to those who grieve their sin and lose hope in their own efforts**. However, no person can thoroughly humble himself until he knows that—entirely apart from his own strength, counsel, striving, willing, and working—his salvation depends completely on the good pleasure (will), counsel, willing, and working of another, namely, of God alone.

These people must come to the point where they think: "I must surrender to God, whether it be to His grace or to His wrath. I cannot lift myself out of the slime of my sin." When they are in that condition, they are[20] the matter[21] that is to be converted. It is a waste of energy and robs God of His honor to urge people to rely on their own efforts toward conversion. Those who really, seriously mean it do this quite often.

---

18   Latin: *arbitrium liberatum*.

19   This is one of the few places in the original German text that has references to both the first and second Walch editions of Luther's works.

20   The Dau text adds: "in dogmatic terminology."

21   Latin: *materia*. Walther again makes reference to Aristotelian causality. Thought (*forma*) works through an agent to shape matter (*materia*). The matter thus receives the attributes of the form.

Luther continues:

For as long as a person is convinced that he has some ability—even
if only a little bit—to work out his salvation, he continues to trust in
himself and does not at all despair of his own efforts. Accordingly, he
does not humble himself before God, and he selects a certain place,
time, and work by which he hopes—or at least desires—to ultimately
obtain salvation. But a person who does not doubt whatsoever that
everything depends on the will of God completely loses hope in his
own effort. He does not choose God but expects God to **work** in him.
He **is closest to divine grace** and salvation.

Therefore, these things are publicly taught for the sake of the elect, in
order that they may be saved after being humbled and crushed in this
manner. The others resist this humbling. In fact, they reject the teaching that a person must despair of his own efforts. They demand that
there must be some ability remaining in them—no matter how small.
They remain secretly proud and are enemies of the grace of God. This
is, I say, the one reason [to teach this]: so that the godly who have been
humbled would know the promise of grace, pray for it, and accept it.

Unless a person is reduced to this condition, it is useless to preach the
Gospel to him. He is lost as long as he takes comfort in himself or thinks he
can help himself out of his difficulties. Accordingly, a pastor must first preach
with great force the thunder of the Law and—immediately after that—the
Gospel. These two should always be a pair. Otherwise, many a precious soul
may be led to despair and be damned. One day these souls will be demanded
of the pastor. For God will not let Himself be made fun of in this matter.

W² 18:1715
(cf. AE 33:62)

You would think that after our fall into sin and the absolute misery that
resulted from it, all people would accept the doctrine of Holy Scripture
with great joy. It states that a person is made righteous and saved by grace
alone, through faith in Jesus Christ. You would think that they would recognize from this very doctrine that the religion of the Bible must be the only
correct one, because it is exactly the religion that poor sinners like us need.
Unfortunately, that is not so.

In fact, the very opposite is true. To this very day, the world has been
stumbling over this again and again, offended precisely at this doctrine of
Holy Scripture, which the apostle Paul expressed in these words: "So then
it depends not on human will or exertion, but on God, who has mercy"
(Romans 9:16). Accordingly, even in his day the apostle had to testify: "But
we preach Christ crucified, a stumbling block to Jews and folly to Gentiles."

**Thirty-sixth
Evening Lecture:**
Sept. 25, 1885

**Law preferred;
Gospel rejected**

Rom. 9:16;
1 Cor. 1:23

Rom. 1:16   Yes, in the opinion of the whole world in those days it was actually a disgrace to proclaim this Gospel of the free grace of God in Christ Jesus. This is why the apostle had to declare: "For I am not ashamed of the gospel, for it is the power of God for salvation to everyone who believes, to the Jew first and also to the Greek." By nature, a blind, self-righteous Pharisee is hiding in every human being. Accordingly, all who have not been enlightened by God through the Holy Spirit imagine that the best and most trustworthy religion would be a religion that makes the most numerous and most serious demands on humans if they want to obtain salvation. Since salvation is something inexpressibly great, mankind would unquestionably have to achieve something exceedingly great to obtain it. Accordingly, when the old Adam inside of us observes that certain religions make salvation very difficult to achieve, we assume that these people must surely be on the straight road to heaven.

1 Kings 18:28   When the priests of Baal displayed such enthusiasm in the worship of their idol that they "cut themselves after their custom with swords and lances, until the blood gushed out upon them," the poor people who did not know the difference imagined that these men were the true prophets of God, and [they] challenged the real prophets to do likewise. This went on until the prophet Elijah, by a miracle, revealed the hypocrisy of the priests of Baal.

Similarly, in the days of Christ, the Pharisees and scribes taught the people that, in order to be saved, they had to fulfill the entire Law of Moses—down to the very last jot and tittle. So when the Pharisees demanded that the people had to keep the traditions of the elders as well, the poor undiscerning masses imagined that the religion of the Pharisees and scribes must surely be a better religion than that of Christ, who called to Himself even the filthiest and most shameful sinners and offered and promised them mercy.

Again, after false teachers had wormed their way into the congregations that the apostle Paul had founded in Galatia, they said to the members of those congregations: "Paul may be a powerful speaker, but he is showing you a way to salvation that is much too easy and too wide." They claimed that, in order to be a Christian, you had to, among other things, believe in Christ. But furthermore, they maintained that you also had to keep the Law of Moses if you wanted to be saved. In a short period of time, nearly all the congregations in Galatia fell away from Paul and his doctrine, deceived by the false glamour that those false teachers had spread about themselves.

It has always been this way. Why do so many millions of people remain under the papacy? Why do they stick around when the papacy has been revealed as antichristian? It is because of the false appeal of good works with which the Papists surround themselves. Why do so many people in this country fall for the preachers of fanatical sects? Because these sects cloak themselves with the phony appearance of great holiness. **Alas! Human beings**

regard the works of God as unimportant, yet they highly honor human works. That is one of the many results of the fall from grace.

If only this horrible mingling of Law and Gospel—and, in particular, this horrible leavening of the Gospel with the Law—occurred only in the papacy and among the fanatical sects! Sad to say, this takes place even in the pulpits of our dear Evangelical Lutheran Church. This error is nothing new—beginning in the days of the Reformation [and continuing] all the way to today, though not so obviously these days. This is the error we rejected in the second part of our twenty-second thesis and to which we will now turn our attention.

In their heyday the so-called Pietists were not the only people to make a false distinction between awakening and conversion. The preachers of the fanatical sects in our time do the same thing as well. Both groups refuse to regard those who have been awakened as Christians. They also confuse not being **able** to believe with not being **permitted** to believe.

When the Pietists had brought people to the point that they considered themselves to be poor, miserable sinners, unable to help themselves, the people asked their pastors, "Now what?" At that point, their pastors did not answer them as the apostles did by saying, "Believe in the Lord Jesus, and you will be saved." Rather, as a rule, the pastors told them the exact opposite. They warned them against believing too soon and thinking that, now that they had felt the effects of the Law, they should move on to believe that their sins had been forgiven.

The pastors told them that their contrition had to become more perfect, that they had to feel contrite—not so much because their sins would trigger God's anger and hurl them into complete destruction, but because they loved God. Unless they felt sorry for angering their merciful Father in heaven, their contrition was declared to be null and void. They were told that they had to *feel* that God was beginning to be merciful to them. They needed to move forward to the point where they could hear an inner voice telling them: "Be of good cheer. Your sins will be forgiven. God will be merciful to you." They were told to continue to struggle until their agony was over. Only after ridding themselves of the love of sin and only after being thoroughly converted would they start to feel comfort.

This is a truly horrible method. The truth is, we are not **first** converted and **then** believe. The feeling of having received grace does not come first. Rather—without feeling anything—we first believe that we have received grace, and after *that* we feel that we have received it. God distributes this to each of us according to His good pleasure.

Some people do not feel that grace for a long time. They see nothing but darkness surrounding them. They feel the hardness of their heart and the powerful stirring and raging of evil, sinful lust within themselves. Accordingly, if

Errors of Pietism and Holiness churches

Acts 16:31

you want to point someone to the way of salvation, it is not correct to tell him that he may not yet believe that he is saved, even if he regards himself to be a poor, lost sinner.

Prov. 27:7Of course, no one can produce faith in himself. God must do that. A person may be in such a state, such that he cannot believe and God is not willing to give faith to him. A person who still considers himself sound and righteous cannot believe. "One who is full loathes honey" (Proverbs 27:7). In the same way, the soul that is spiritually "satisfied" tramples on the honeycomb of the consoling Gospel.

Ability confused with permission; John 5:44

John 5:44: "How can you believe, when you receive glory from one another?" These words that the Lord addresses to the Jews are unquestionably directed chiefly against the Pharisees. As long as a person is greedy for honor, he cannot come to faith because seeking honor is a mortal sin. Using that statement, the Lord declares that a person who simply will not stop a certain sin **cannot** believe in Him. The Law must first crush the sinner's heart before the sweet comfort of the Gospel is applied.

But from this fact we must not draw the conclusion that the sinner **is not permitted to** believe. It is forever true that any person may believe at any time. Even when he has fallen into the most serious sin, he suddenly realizes that he has forsaken God. At that point, he can then get up with a crushed heart—and believe. Whoever would tell him that he is not yet permitted to believe is either a wicked person or someone who in this respect is still blind.

1 John 2:1–2 ESV; Luke 2:14 Luther

To tell a person that he **is not permitted to** believe is, in the first place, contrary to the perfect redemption of Christ from all sins, and [it is] contrary to the perfect reconciliation that [Christ] has accomplished. For in 1 John 2:1–2, John says, "If anyone does sin, we have an advocate with the Father, Jesus Christ the righteous. He is the propitiation for our sins, and not for ours only but also for the sins of the whole world." The entire world, then, has been reconciled. The wrath of God against the whole world has been removed. Through Jesus Christ, God has become every man's friend. That is the reason the holy angels sang even over His cradle: "Glory to God in the highest, peace on earth, **and to mankind, goodwill!**" In Christ, God shows His goodwill toward all people.

2 Cor. 5:14

Second Corinthians 5:14: *"One has died for all, therefore all have died."* A precious statement! The apostle is saying that, since Christ died, it is the same as if every person had suffered death for their sins, namely, the death that Christ died. It is the same as if all had atoned for their sins by their death. Now that the entire world has been redeemed and reconciled to God, is it not a horrible teaching to tell someone that he may not believe that he has been reconciled and redeemed and now has the forgiveness of sins? That doctrine shamefully denies the completeness of redemption and reconciliation with God.

Besides, this doctrine is contrary to the Gospel! After finishing the task of redemption and reconciliation, Christ said to His disciples, "Go into all the world and proclaim the gospel to the whole creation." To preach the Gospel means nothing else than to bring to all creatures the glad tidings that they have been redeemed, that heaven is opened to all, that all are made righteous, and that perfect righteousness has been brought to them by Christ. It means that we may enter only by the gate of Christ's righteousness, even as we will one day enter by the gate of eternal salvation.

Pietist teaching against the Gospel; Mark 16:15

Is it not horrible to tell people that they may not believe this? Everyone should know that the Gospel is for them, that God has brought His glad tidings to them. For what purpose? In order that they may believe the Gospel and take comfort in it. If they refuse to believe it, they are declaring God and all His prophets and apostles to be liars. Is it not horrible to tell people who have learned by experience that they are poor, lost sinners and are still stuck in sin that—even though God has indeed redeemed them—they still have to do much before they will be allowed to believe and be redeemed? According to this horrible teaching, sinners want to share with God in the work of their redemption. That is nothing short of blasphemy.

Nor does this harmonize with the fact that God has already declared in the presence of heaven and earth, of angels and men: "My Son has reconciled the world to Me. I have accepted His sacrifice. I am satisfied. He paid your warrant,[22] and I have set Him free. Therefore, rejoice because you have nothing of which to be afraid." By the resurrection of Jesus Christ from the dead, God has absolved the entire world of sinners from their sins. Is it not horrible for people to say that this is indeed a fact, but that a person may not yet believe it? Is that not charging God with lying—and denying the resurrection of Christ from the dead? This is dreadful!

Furthermore, this teaching is also contrary to the doctrine of Absolution. Christ says to His disciples in Matthew 18:18: "Whatever you bind on earth shall be bound in heaven, and whatever you loose on earth shall be loosed in heaven," and in John 20:23: "If you forgive the sins of any, they are forgiven them; if you withhold forgiveness from any, it is withheld." He is not speaking of certain qualities that people must have, but simply says, "If you forgive the sins of anyone, they are forgiven" and "Whatever you loose on earth shall be loosed in heaven." Who believes this? Only genuine Lutherans. For all sects, however, it is contemptible to hear.

Sects reject Absolution; Matt. 18:18; John 20:23

These people twist the precious words from the mouth of Truth, making them say something altogether different from what they really mean. It is the

---

22   See page 391 n. 13 regarding "bondsman" terminology.

Gospel truth, my dear friends: Jesus Christ has redeemed the entire world and has given His followers the power to forgive everyone's sins.

Some claim that the meaning of Christ is this: "When a pastor notices that a person is in the proper condition, he may persuade that person to believe that he has forgiveness of sins." But these are human thoughts. What the Lord is saying is simply this: "Your sins are forgiven."

Moreover, this statement can be readily understood by anyone who believes in the completeness of the redemption and reconciliation with God that Christ has accomplished. Here is an illustration: Suppose a king has declared that a rebellious town has been granted full amnesty and that no one needs to suffer for his rebellion. In a case such as that, anybody can say, "The king has crushed the rebellion. He has conquered you rebels. But you can be of good cheer, because he has pardoned you. I know this to be a fact because I personally heard the king say so." If the speaker were also to bring a document—signed and sealed by the king and containing the same state-ment—everybody would rejoice and begin to celebrate.

This situation is identical to the case we are now discussing. By the resur-rection of Christ, God has declared that He is reconciled with all mankind and does not intend to bring punishment on anyone. He has had this fact proclaimed in all the world by His Gospel and, in addition, has commanded every pastor of the Gospel to forgive people their sins, promising that He will do in heaven what the pastor is doing on earth. A pastor should not first look up to heaven to determine what God is doing. Rather, he should merely carry out God's orders on earth and forgive people's sins, relying on God's promise that He has forgiven them.

To the sects this looks like a horrible doctrine, but it is the most com-forting doctrine imaginable, firmly established in the blood of God, which is shed on the cross. Sin really has been forgiven, and everything God now does is so we would believe.

Truth and effect of Means of Grace We absolve people from their sins for no other purpose than for our parishioners to believe what is being proclaimed from the pulpit. Accordingly, none of them can say, "How can the pastor know the condition of my heart? What good is Absolution if I do not repent?" Answer: "Indeed, in this par-ticular case there is no benefit. But there is a benefit when you believe in your Absolution. But this is certain: you *are* absolved. And for this reason your eternal punishment would be all the more dreadful if you did not believe the Absolution that God Himself announced to all sinners and that He ordered His pastors to continue to announce to them."

This applies to the Sacraments as well. The water in Baptism saves us. When the Lord offers communicants the blessed bread and says, "This is My body, which is given for you," it is plain that He means to tell them that they must believe or His body would not benefit them. A person who believes that Christ, by sacrificing His body, has paid for the communicant's sins can leave the altar rejoicing and exulting. When the Lord offers the blessed cup and says, "This is My blood, which is shed for you for the forgiveness of sins," He emphasizes the words "for the forgiveness of sins." This causes every communicant who believes these words to shout with joy when he goes home from church after Communion.[23]

Lastly, when you confuse not being able to believe with not being permitted to believe, this is contrary to the practice of the apostles. Whenever someone demonstrated the attributes of a poor sinner, the apostles told him to believe in the Lord Jesus Christ. They never said, "Wait a bit for this and that to happen." At the first Pentecost, Peter told his listeners, "You used to hate Christ. But now believe in Him and be baptized."[24] Do not forget the example of the jailer at Philippi that I have mentioned so often.[25] The Enthusiasts would say, "Well, I cannot understand how the apostles dealt with this situation! How could they deal with it like this? I would have preached all of them into hell!"

Well, true enough, the blessed apostles also had the sad experience of seeing that hypocrites had wormed their way into their congregations. Just look at the example of Simon the sorcerer. We are told that, in the people's eyes, "even Simon himself believed," but he was later unmasked as a completely wicked man. Did that cause the apostles to become "more cautious" and to determine that they would not always invite people to believe in the Lord Jesus? We find no evidence to that effect because all the beautiful examples of the apostles urging people to admit that they were sinners and then to believe were *after* the account of Simon the sorcerer. | Acts 8:13

Likewise, it is very foolish to appeal to a person's good intentions. Pietists and many Enthusiast preachers have reasoned that, in order to make the conversion of their listeners complete, they must *not* allow them to take hold of what does not yet belong to them because that would prove a false comfort to them. But this reasoning is true fanaticism. They ought to consider that our heavenly Father is wiser than they are. He most certainly knows that if the consolation of the Gospel is imparted to every heart, many would imagine that they, too, can believe in it. But that is no reason to stifle this consolation. We must not starve children out of fear that the dogs would get some of the children's food, but [we] should cheerfully proclaim the universal grace of God freely and leave it up to God whether people will believe it or abuse it.

---

23 See the accounts of the institution of the Lord's Supper: Matthew 26:26–29; Mark 14:22–25; Luke 22:19–20. Compare with Paul's account in 1 Corinthians 11:23–25.

24 See Acts 2:37–41.

25 See Acts 16:25–34.

When a pit has been dug for the foundation for a very solid building, the pit must not be kept open too long, in case a rainstorm should fill it up and all the previous work be lost. A good builder immediately lays the foundation in the pit. In the same way, the digging of the foundation takes place spiritually when people are convicted of their sins. That is when you need to supply the Gospel immediately, pour it into their hearts, and build the entire structure of Christianity on that.

Or take another illustration. When a doctor lances a boil, he does not wait two weeks before applying a soothing ointment. He puts it on immediately, so the wound will not become dangerously infected and become deadly. When the boils of men's sins have been lanced, the soothing ointment of the Gospel must be applied immediately. That is the correct way to do it, whereas the "method" of the Methodists is wrong.

Let us now hear a few testimonies from **Luther's** writings on this matter. He writes (St. Louis Ed. 11:1141):

W² 11:1141   While the first kind of preaching—namely, that of the Law—is going on, people are filled with anxiety when they think of God and discover that they are condemned with all their doings. They do not know what to do. Their conscience becomes evil and timid, **and, if no one comes to their rescue speedily, they have to despair**.

Many a person might have been saved if the Gospel in all its fullness had been preached to them immediately. But since it was not preached to them, they either completely gave themselves over to despair, or they joined the world and decided that the Church was worthless.

Ps. 42:1–2   Therefore, the other kind of preaching must not be delayed for an extended period of time; the Gospel must be preached to them; they must be brought to Christ, whom the Father has given to us as our Mediator that we might be saved by Him out of pure grace and mercy, without any works and merits of our own. That is what makes the heart cheerful; it races to this grace like a thirsty deer to water. David felt that when, in Psalm 42:1–2, he wrote: "As a deer pants for flowing streams, so pants my soul for You, O God. My soul thirsts for God, for the living God. When shall I come and appear before God?"

In a sermon on Easter Sunday, **Luther** writes (St. Louis Ed. 12:1586):

W² 12:1586   Now, then, the benefit of the suffering and resurrection of Christ is this: He did not suffer these things on His own behalf, but on behalf of the entire world. He trampled underfoot the devil and my sin, which on Good Friday were suspended on the cross together with Him, and the devil must now run away at the mention of the name of Christ. If you wish to make use of these great treasures, look, **He has already**

given them to you as a gift. Do give Him the honor of receiving it with thanks.

The gift has already been made. All the sinner has to do is accept it. Again, **Luther** says in a sermon on Pentecost Monday (St. Louis Ed. 11:1104):

> It is none of our doing and cannot be earned by our works; **it has already been given to us as a gift and handed over to us.** All that is necessary is that you open your mouth—or, rather, your heart—wide and let God fill it, Psalm 81:10. That can be done in no other way than by your believing these words ["God so loved the world," etc.],[26] just as you are here told that faith is required for appropriating this treasure in its entirety.

W² 11:1104;
John 3:16

This is what is missing in all other church bodies: **They do not believe that redemption has been completely given as a gift to all people.** They imagine that the Gospel is merely a set of instructions as to what man must do in order to be reconciled with God after being reconciled by Christ. This is a self-contradiction.

Lastly, **Luther** writes (St. Louis Ed. 11:733f.):

> Accordingly, unbelief is nothing else than blasphemy and brands God a liar. For when I say to you, "Your sins are forgiven in the name of God," and you do not believe it, your action is just like saying, "Who knows whether it is true, whether God really means what He says?" If you do not believe, it would be better for you to be far removed from the Word of God. For God wants to have the preaching of His Word regarded as nothing other than His own preaching. Now, this is the authority that every Christian has as a gift from God. I have already spoken about this to a great extent; therefore, let this be enough.

W² 11:733–35

When they are being absolved, most people reason like this: "That is indeed very comforting, provided I know that I am in the proper condition to receive it." Well, that is not at all what God wants, because, now that redemption has been acquired, He wants this communicated to all. The situation is exactly as if God were standing before us, pronouncing Absolution to us. What would we do if God were to reveal Himself to us, standing before us with life and death in His hands, calling us by name and saying, "Your sins are forgiven"? With what joy would we depart from His presence and shout: "No devil will shake my faith in my salvation!"

Now, when a preacher absolves someone, **it is actually God absolving that person.** God does not want to deal with us immediately, that is, directly, but mediately, that is, through means. When they hear a Lutheran pastor

---

26 Walther supplied the words from John 3:16.

pronounce Absolution, the sects imagine that we Lutherans believe pastors, by means of their ordination, have received some kind of mysterious power, a unique ability to look into men's hearts.

However, that is not what we teach. Rather, we are absolving people whenever we preach the Gospel. Unfortunately, many people sitting in the pews before us do not believe our preaching and go home after the service as condemned and hardened sinners. But the children of God rejoice over the good sermon they have heard and go home feeling that the heavy load of their sins has been removed from their shoulders.

Thirty-seventh Evening Lecture:
Oct. 2, 1885

True pastoral passion

One of the most necessary and important qualities of a pastor, my friends, is for him to be filled with a sincere and burning passion to carry out his office properly and accomplish something of real value in the sight of God: that is to pluck from hell every soul that has been entrusted to him, lead it to God, make it truly godly, and bring it into heaven.

A faithful pastor must definitely have said good-bye to chasing after good times, money and possessions, honor and fame in this world. His supreme joy must be the assurance that his work in the Lord is not useless. That must be his most delightful reward for all his great and serious anxieties and concerns. Every day and every hour, the sigh, spoken by the aged and upright Pastor Neumann[27] in one of his beautiful morning hymns, must arise in his heart:

> O God, upon whose bread I feed,
> I wish, to You, I'd useful be![28]

---

27 The notes to Walther's lectures likely contain an error here, either in the shorthand or in the transcription. They render the name as "Lollmann," and it has so appeared since the German edition. Caspar Neumann (1648–1715) wrote the hymn that Walther cites. He was a beloved pastor and church leader who, in addition to a prayer book (*Kern aller Gebete* [Breslau, 1680]), wrote thirty hymns that became a treasured part of Lutheran hymnody in Breslau, Silesia, and other areas of Germany. It is unlikely that Walther misspoke Neumann's name because the hymn he cites was very dear to him (see note below). This is not the occasional confusion with Latin names that Walther had in later years. See also Ludwig Fürbringer, *Eighty Eventful Years* (St. Louis: Concordia, 1944), 85.

28 The hymn is translated here as "My God, Again Has Come the Morning" (*Mein Gott, nun ist es wieder Morgen*). The second stanza reads:
    Upon the earth I am still living,
    Where every day its trouble brings;
    Where, day by day, I'm only aging
    And heaping up misdeeds and sins.
    O God, upon whose bread I feed,
    I wish, to You, I'd useful be!
    This hymn was personally important to Walther. He used and mentioned this hymn when he was ill, depressed, or feeling frustrated. His use of this hymn in his lectures tells us that he was still in a period of deep grief over the death of his wife. After his lecture,

The greatest example of properly carrying out one's pastoral office is undoubtedly Paul, the great apostle to the Gentiles, who, in his great passion for the salvation of his brothers according to the flesh, went so far as to say that he wished he were himself accursed and cut off from Christ for their sake, for those with whom he had such friendship (Romans 9:3). **Luther** evaluates this passion in his *Church Postils*: "No reason can grasp this work.[29] It is much, much too high [a thought] that a preacher would rather be damned himself than to be the cause of the loss of any soul entrusted to him."[30]

However, while it is necessary and important to carry out one's pastoral office with great enthusiasm, this cannot be said regarding every kind of eagerness. There is also such a thing as false, ungodly, carnal enthusiasm that does not come from God and that is not produced by the Holy Spirit. Rather, it is rooted either in hostility against those who teach a different doctrine or in the selfish thought that a display of enthusiasm will bring the pastor honor—at least in certain congregations—or lead to fanaticism.

False enthusiasm

Oh, how enthusiastic in carrying out their office were the high priests at the time of Christ! With them also were the elders of the people, the scribes, and the Pharisees who opposed Christ. In order to direct their office against Him, they spared themselves no difficulty and allowed themselves no peace. Paul thus speaks concerning the Jews: "I bear them witness that they have a zeal for God, but not according to knowledge" (Romans 10:2).

Rom. 10:2

Look at the enthusiasm of the false teachers who tried to make the congregations in Galatia distrust the pure evangelical doctrine of St. Paul! They traveled over land and sea in their efforts! But the apostle says about them, "The one who is troubling you will bear the penalty, whoever he is" (Galatians 5:10). What he is saying is this: "No matter how highly you honor them as great heroes of faith, they have made you doubt the evangelical doctrine that you are saved by grace, through faith alone, for Christ's sake."

Gal. 5:10

What great enthusiasm the Anabaptists in Luther's time had! For the sake of their religion they gave up house and home, wife and children, and many of them preferred drowning to renouncing their doctrine.

Walther would have returned to his now-empty house, which was located behind the seminary. (The house was demolished around 1913; see also page 454.) Walther made his way through this trial by embracing Scripture and applying Law and Gospel. The Law dealt Walther a heavy blow by demanding the earthly life of his dear Emilie (Genesis 3:19). Yet the Gospel indeed pointed Walther to Christ, the Bread of Life, upon whom Ferdinand and Emilie fed in the Lord's Supper and whom Ferdinand and Emilie received as a guarantee of the resurrection and the life eternal (John 6:51; 11:25). See also D. H. Steffens, *Doctor Carl Ferdinand Wilhelm Walther* (Philadelphia: Lutheran Publication Society, 1917), 320.

29   The Dau edition translates this sentence as: "No reason can grasp what the apostle is doing."

30   Walther does not provide enough information that would further identify this citation.

But why cite these examples? All of church history proves—and our own experience in this country confirms—the declaration that false spirits and Enthusiasts demonstrate greater passion in thrusting their doctrine on people than orthodox teachers do in preaching the pure truth into people's hearts.

Why being a pastor is difficult

It is easy to explain why this is so. Preachers of false, man-made teachings are not restrained in their activity by their reason, by their flesh and blood. Rather, they are all the more fired up. In contrast, preachers of the pure doctrine of God's Word are continually restrained by their reason and their flesh and blood. That makes their task a thousand times more difficult. It is easy to speak from one's natural heart, but it is difficult to proclaim the truth on the basis of God's Word after earnestly searching the same, after passionate prayer, and after earnest struggles for enlightenment by the Holy Spirit. Why is this? Chiefly because it is so difficult to rightly distinguish the Word of truth or to separate properly Law from Gospel. It is easy to mingle these two doctrines, against which the apostle Paul warns every approved worker in the vineyard of God.[31] Case in point: our twenty-third thesis.

---

31 See 2 Timothy 2:15.

Thesis XXIII

You are not rightly distinguishing Law and Gospel in the Word of God if you use the demands, threats, or promises of the Law to try and force the unregenerate to put away their sins and engage in good works and thus become godly; and then, on the other hand, if you use the commands of the Law—rather than the admonitions of the Gospel—to urge the regenerate to do good.

Editor's Note: In this thesis, Walther argues against using the Law to make people "do good." The sinful nature of man desires to use the Law, but it also desires its own interpretations and exemptions as it "plays god." The true work of the Law is to destroy human self-reliance and reduce people to the state of complete dependence, at which point the Gospel takes over, and those who are broken receive grace, faith, and forgiveness and are healed. People only do good works after the Gospel has worked faith in them.

Walther sees the improper use of the Law to be common. Only with a broken and contrite heart can one truly understand the work of the Law and properly distinguish Law and Gospel according to Scripture.

The attempt to make men God-fearing by means of the Law and to encourage even those who already believe in Christ to do good by holding up the Law and issuing commands to them obviously mingles Law and Gospel. This is altogether contrary to the purpose that the Law is to serve after the fall. This will become apparent when we examine the following passages of Scripture, including Jeremiah 31:31–34:

Purpose of the Law

> Behold, the days are coming, declares the LORD, when I will make a new covenant with the house of Israel and the house of Judah, not like the covenant that I made with their fathers on the day when I took them by the hand to bring them out of the land of Egypt, My covenant that they broke, though I was their husband, declares the LORD. But this is the covenant that I will make with the house of Israel after those days, declares the LORD: I will put My law within them, and I will write it on their hearts. And I will be their God, and they shall be My

Jer. 31:31–34

people. And no longer shall each one teach his neighbor and each his brother, saying, "Know the LORD," for they shall all know Me, from the least of them to the greatest, declares the LORD. For I will forgive their iniquity, and I will remember their sin no more.

This beautiful and precious text is like the sun suddenly bursting forth out of the gray dawn of the Old Testament. We see from it that, while the Law was written on the hearts of [Adam and Eve] before the fall, it did not serve the purpose of making them God-fearing. For man had been created godly and righteous in the sight of God. The only reason [Adam and Eve] had the Law on their heart was that they might know what was pleasing to God. No special commandment was needed to inform them on that point. They simply willed whatever was God-pleasing. Their will was in perfect harmony with the will of God.

This situation changed after the fall. True, after the exodus of the Israelites from Egypt, God renewed the Law and reestablished a legal covenant with the Jews. However, what did the Lord tell them through the prophet Jeremiah? That the legal covenant had not improved their condition, because God had to force them to do His will—and forced obedience is simply no obedience.

Accordingly, He prophesies a time when He will make an entirely different arrangement. That does not mean that the new arrangement was not in force even in the time of the Old Testament, but since He had already established a covenant with the Israelites, it was legal and binding. Yet even during the time of this covenant the prophets were continually preaching the Gospel and pointing to the Messiah.

Regarding the new covenant that God would establish, He says that He would not issue any commandments, but that He would write the Law directly into their mind. He would give them a new and pure heart, so they would not need to be plagued with the Law and all kinds of commandments, saying, "You shall do this! You shall do that!" That would not help matters at all. That would not help people at all.

Jer. 31:34   We cannot fulfill the Law either. By nature we are carnal, and the Law cannot impose the Spirit on us. God says, "I will forgive their iniquity, and I will remember their sin no more." That is why the Law is written on our heart. This means nothing other than this: What the Law was not able to bring about is what the Gospel accomplishes, by the message of the forgiveness of sins. All who were saved in the Old Testament were, of course, saved in this way only, as Peter clearly declares at the first apostolic council.[1] Now, then, what are those doing who corrupt the Law in the time of the New Testament? They turn Christians into Jews, and not only that, but Jews of the

---

1   Acts 15:7–11.

worst kind who regard only the letter of the Law and not the promise of the Redeemer. Not only do they mingle the Law and Gospel, but they substitute the Law for the Gospel.

Romans 3:20: "For by works of the law no human being will be justified in His sight, since through the law comes knowledge of sin." This is the reason for this remarkable statement: Paul is saying that at the present time the sole purpose of the Law is to reveal people's sins, not to remove them. Instead of removing them, the Law increases sins. For when evil lust arises in our heart, the Law calls to us: "You shall not covet." That causes us to regard God as cruel for demanding what we are unable to accomplish. Thus the Law increases sin. It does not kill sin; rather, it makes it alive. Rom. 3:20; Exod. 20:17

Romans 7:7–13: "What then shall we say? That the law is sin? By no means! Yet if it had not been for the law, I would not have known sin. I would not have known what it is to covet if the law had not said, 'You shall not covet.'" This is the most horrifying feature of our condition: that by nature we do not recognize original sin in us. We imagine that when evil lusts arise in us—as long as we do not exactly delight in those lusts—God will not charge them to our account.[2] Rom. 7:7

However, the Law serves notice on us: "Evil lusts condemn us in the sight of God." "For sin, seizing an opportunity through the commandment, deceived me and through it killed me." Even pagans, such as godless Ovid, declared: "We desire the very things that are forbidden."[3] If they had not been forbidden, we might not desire them. What we are forbidden to do awakens our desire and triggers rebellious thoughts. We say to ourselves, "What? You want to deprive me of this?" Rom. 7:11

The fall of Adam proves this: It did not take the devil long to pull Eve over to his side when he said: "Did God actually say, 'You shall not eat of any tree in the garden'?" That was when our first parents fell from grace. "Apart from the law, sin lies dead." Gen. 3:1; Rom. 7:8

As long as we humans do not recognize the spiritual meaning of the Law, sin lies asleep in our heart, like a frozen serpent. We do not observe what a Rom. 7:9

---

2 Walther describes this false view of sin as a group of morally neutral or outwardly "good" shoppers looking at various sins displayed on store shelves. In this false view, the prospective "sinner" does not get charged with the deed until he does it. Doing the sin is like checking out.

3 Latin: *Nitimur in vetitum, semper cupimusque negata.* Walther has cited or made reference to this saying multiple times throughout these lectures (see also pages 19, 261). He also cites this phrase in the Baier *Compendium* (1:31). He rightly stresses the depth and depravity of human sin. In Walther's time, Methodism's claim that people can become holy provided a basis for literally dozens of sectarian Holiness groups that acted according to their own ideas instead of according to Scripture understood through Law and Gospel. Walther saw a related error of using the Law in the Roman Catholic Church, which he considered to be a system that fostered immorality under the guise of churchly holiness.

completely corrupt creature the serpent is. While this [dormant] condition lasts, [the serpent] does not break out so much.[4] But as soon as the Law is proclaimed to us in its spiritual meaning, we become mean and cry out: "What? You want to condemn me just because sin is stirring within me?" Yes, indeed; the Law condemns mankind. If we refuse to believe it, we will learn by experience that this is so. That is all the Law can do. "I was once alive apart from the law."

Paul is saying that he did not recognize the Law because he was so blind that he thought the Law did not apply to him. It is of no benefit, then, for people to know the Ten Commandments if they do not understand their spiritual meaning.

Rom. 7:9–13 But when the commandment came, sin came alive and I died. The very commandment that promised life proved to be death to me. For sin, seizing an opportunity through the commandment, deceived me and through it killed me. So the law is holy, and the commandment is holy and righteous and good. Did that which is good, then, bring death to me? By no means! It was sin, producing death in me through what is good, in order that sin might be shown to be sin, and through the commandment might become sinful beyond measure.

2 Cor. 3:6 Second Corinthians 3:6: "For the letter kills, but the Spirit gives life." If the Law kills, how can it make a person God-fearing? For these words do not mean: "The letter of the Holy Scriptures kills." That is usually the way Rationalists and also those in the Prussian Union interpret them. They say, "Do not cling to the letter." What these people are doing is twisting these words in an ungodly and shameful way! When you look at the context, you see that by the word "letter" the apostle means nothing else than the Law. It is the Law that kills and, therefore, cannot make anyone God-fearing. It may cause us to stop this or that vice, but it cannot change our heart.

Ps. 119:32 Psalm 119:32: "I will run in the way of Your commandments when You enlarge my heart!" The psalmist does not say: "When You strike me with the thunder of Your Law, I will run in the way of Your commandments. No, in that case I will not run. But when You comfort me so that my cramped heart is made large, I will cheerfully and willingly walk the straight and narrow way to heaven."

This is an experience that you probably have had personally. After a long season of being sluggish and lukewarm, a season during which you began to hate yourself because you saw no way to change your condition, you happened to hear a real Gospel sermon, and you left the church a changed man and rejoiced in the fact that you may believe and are a child of God. You

---

4 The Dau text adds: "in gross crimes."

suddenly become aware of the fact that it is not difficult to walk in the way of God's Commandments. You seem to walk in them of your own agreement.

How foolish, then, is a preacher who thinks: "Now I will let loose the thunder of the Law. I will describe hell in all its detail and paint them a real picture of damnation, and then they will shape up!" That will not improve the people at all. That has to happen in its own time, so that secure sinners are alarmed and become poor, contrite sinners. But the Law does not produce a change of heart, love of God, and love of one's fellow human being. If anyone is motivated by the Law to do certain good works, he does them only because he is forced, just as the Israelites had to be forced by the covenant of the Law.

Galatians 3:2: "Let me ask you only this: Did you receive the Spirit by works of the law or by hearing with faith?" The Galatians had let themselves be seduced into believing that Paul's preaching of salvation by faith through the grace of Christ alone was incomplete, to say the least. Therefore, they thought it was a dangerous doctrine by which a person might easily be led into damnation. Accordingly, they accepted the false prophets' doctrine of the Law. *Gal. 3:2*

With great sadness Paul learned that **these** congregations, which he had founded himself and which had flourished wonderfully, were being disrupted and devastated by false teachers. He asked them: "I would like to know this from you: Did you receive the Holy Spirit by works of the Law or by the preaching of faith?" He wanted to say, "Let me remind you about the sort of change that happened among you as I preached the Gospel of grace. Did you not receive the Spirit?" He meant the spirit of rest, of peace, of faith, and of joy. He asked them: "What, then, has become of the blessing you felt?"

In fact, he even says, "For I testify to you that, if possible, you would have gouged out your eyes and given them to me." They were so captivated and realized so vividly what a magnificent, heavenly, and precious teaching it was. They had been transformed in heart, soul, and mind. *Gal. 4:15*

The apostle asked them: "Did you receive this new, heavenly peace in your hearts, this spiritual joy, this exceedingly great confidence through the false teachers who dragged you back into bondage under the Law?" The apostle knew that the members of the congregations in Galatia went around sad and depressed, uncertain of their salvation. They were like people bewitched. They thought: "Since salvation is such a great treasure, one must do something great for it. That is also what our later teachers taught." They regarded their misery, their inability to do anything good, as something for which they had themselves to blame. They did not realize it was the false doctrine that had been put in their heart.

Remember what the apostle is saying in this text: If you want to revive your future congregations and cause the Spirit of peace, joy, faith, and confidence, a childlike spirit, and a restful Spirit to take up residence among the members of your congregation, do not, for God's sake, use the Law to bring that about. Even if you find your congregations to be in the worst condition imaginable, you must indeed preach the Law to them. But follow it up immediately with the Gospel. Do not give the Law to them today and then postpone preaching the Gospel to them until a later date. As soon as the Law has done its work, the Gospel must take its place.

Rationalists practice this shameful mingling of Law and Gospel in the crudest way. Believe it or not, there really are Rationalist preachers who think the Gospel is a dangerous doctrine. They think that the Gospel only makes people secure in their sins and that such people will not make the effort to become God-fearing because they always hear that we are made righteous and saved by faith alone. So to make people God-fearing, these Rationalist pastors preach ethics with great earnestness. What do they accomplish? The most passionate of them accomplish nothing more than that some of their listeners adopt a civil behavior to a certain extent, abstaining from crude, shameful vices and crimes. While these listeners do come to believe that they need a new heart, it would never cross their mind to love God and their neighbor.

In such a congregation, if someone were to stand up and declare with great joy that he loves God above all things and that God is his one and all, the others would think that person had lost his mind. Such people do not have the slightest idea that it is possible to love God above all things. They disregard the Second Table of the Law just as much as the First Table.[5]

What do members of so-called "free" congregations know of the Second Table, despite the enthusiastic preaching of virtue and piety by their pastor?[6] Nothing! They go home and cheat their neighbor until the cows come home. They go to church on Sunday, yet Monday they continue to cheat the money right out of people's pockets and call that "business." They may be up to their ears in sin and shame—and yet are still considered to be honorable people.

5　The First Table of the Law—the First, Second, and Third Commandments, according to the numbering used by Lutherans and Roman Catholics—focuses on love of God. The Second Table—the Fourth through the Tenth Commandments—focuses on love of neighbor. The Fourth Commandment connects divine authority in the First Commandment with that of parental and civil authority. It thus provides a framework for the remainder of the Second Table.

6　Walther does not mean "free" in the sense of a free church (*Freikirche*) separate from the state. He means something like an ethical society or the free-thinking sort of congregation that is Christian in name only. See also the entry on Freethinkers in the Index of Persons and Groups, pages 493–94.

On occasion they may be generous and even donate a hundred *Thaler*, but the next day they will cheat people out of a thousand *Thaler*.[7] Their motto is "Charity begins at home." When they are rebuked for not going about their business with the interests of their fellow human beings in mind but for the purpose of making a lot of money, they consider such a reproach to be fanaticism. So you see, by means of the Law we cannot raise anything better than miserable hypocrites.

The situation among the Papists is similar. They know nothing about the free grace of God in Jesus Christ. They continually preach ethics—mixed in with all sorts of references to Mary and the saints—but not a word of the Gospel. They do not direct the poor sinner to Christ, but say Christ is the Judge of the whole world. They urge people to seek help from the saints who will intercede for them with Christ and make Christ gracious toward them. That is the satanic teaching of the antichristian papacy.

What do [the Papists] accomplish? What is the fruit of their teaching? Read the reports from countries where Papists are in the majority and where Protestants are not keeping an eye on them. Conditions in those countries and in the lives of the priests are most shameful. The people know that their priest is the father of any number of illegitimate children, but since he has been ordained, they believe they can still obtain forgiveness of sins, life, and salvation from him.

And who are the most faithful Catholics here in America? The Irish, for example, are a coarse people.[8] They practice all kinds of villainy and go to confession at Easter, where they recite everything to the priest. He slaps a fine on them, or they have to fast, or they have to eat fish on this or that day—and their account is settled. Is that not hideous! Is that not dreadful?

However, this mingling of Law and Gospel occurs not only among Rationalists and Papists but also in many churches with pure doctrine. In the first place, it is common among pastors who themselves had to suffer through much struggle and anguish before they were certain of their state of grace. Some of them may have struggled for many years, refusing to be comforted, because they did not know pure doctrine. When these people

---

7   Walther mentions dollars earlier in his lectures. Here he uses the German *Thaler*. In many ways, Missouri Synod Lutherans of that time lived in two cultures and simultaneously felt "at home" in both while remaining alien to both. By 1917, the Missouri Synod and the Synodical Conference were doing mission work among many ethnic groups in the United States, including African Americans, American Indians, deaf-mutes, Finns, Italians, Jewish people, Persians (Iranians), Poles, Slovaks, and emigrants from the Baltic region of Latvia, Lithuania, and Estonia.

8   Walther shows a bias of his day that is unacceptable in ours. Certainly he was aware that others thought similarly about German immigrants in his time. Nevertheless, his point about Absolution is well-taken. Confession should lead to Absolution and turning over a new leaf. It should not be a revolving door for impenitent sinners.

start to proclaim pure doctrine, they always inject various remarks into their Gospel preaching. This motivates their listeners to say to themselves that this preacher must be a God-fearing man but that he does not know what poor people his listeners are. For they are certain they cannot meet the requirements laid down by the preacher. And these preachers are the best of the lot.

Second, this mingling of Law and Gospel also occurs when pastors become aware that all their Gospel preaching is useless because coarse sins of the flesh are still occurring among their listeners. There may be drunkards among the church members; some of them might get into fistfights, and so on. These people come to church occasionally but rarely go to Communion and refuse to contribute when a collection is taken up. In such cases, the preacher may say to himself, "Wait. I have preached too much Gospel to them. I have to take a different tack. I must be silent on the Gospel for a while and preach nothing but the Law, and conditions will improve."

But he is quite mistaken. There is no change in the people, except that they become very angry with their pastor for not permitting them to do what they love doing. A collection is taken up, and he gets twenty cents when he had expected twenty dollars.[9] He resolves to give these people hell and damnation next Sunday. This might increase the collection by ten or twenty dollars, but the offering is worthless in the sight of God, because it was made under duress.

Would a plantation owner be pleased with slaves whom he normally sees lounging about the plantation and who only jump at the crack of a whip?[10] Certainly not. Neither does God love service that is given only under coercion. Preachers who succeed in getting their people to stop certain evils by preaching the Law must not think that they have achieved something wonderful. But even the most corrupt congregation can be improved solely by preaching the Gospel in all its sweetness. The reason congregations are corrupt is always that their pastors have not preached the Gospel to the people enough. No wonder they have accomplished nothing. For the Law kills, but the Spirit—that is, the Gospel—makes alive.[11]

---

9 In today's money, that would be something like getting twenty dollars instead of two hundred.

10 Walther displays a bias during his lifetime that is unacceptable today. Walther did not support or encourage antebellum chattel slavery. Neither did he support abolitionism as being the exclusive will of God. He did argue, however, that the modern basis for human freedom has its roots in the autonomous, rational, self-aware individual. That Rationalist model from the Enlightenment period is inherently opposed to Scripture. See "Vorwort," *Lehre und Wehre* 9 (1863): 1–8, 33–46. For biblical perspectives on slavery, see *The Lutheran Study Bible* (St. Louis: Concordia, 2009), 2095, and John G. Nordling, *Philemon*, Concordia Commentary (St. Louis: Concordia, 2004).

11 See 2 Corinthians 3:6.

Let us take a look at **Luther's** comment on Romans 12:1, "I appeal to you therefore, brothers, by the mercies of God . . ." He writes (St. Louis. Ed. 12:318):

Rom. 12:1

> [Paul] does not say: I command you; for he is preaching to people who are already Christians and God-fearing by faith, in newness of life. They must not be coerced by means of commandments, but warned to do willingly what has to be done with the old sinful man in them. **For any person who does not do this willingly, in response to kind warnings, is not a Christian.**

W² 12:318

Is it not frightful to see a preacher do all he can to produce dead works and turn the members of his congregation into hypocrites in the sight of God? When people are forced to do good works by the threats or even by the promises of the Law, they are not good works. Good works are only those that a person does freely and from the heart. Everybody knows that. When a beggar approaches a person who does not have a lot of money and that person reluctantly gives the beggar something after thinking it over, his conscience tells him: "That was nothing! You were only pressured into doing it. You did not have your heart in it." Or if someone gives you a present and you notice that he does it only to receive a favor from you, you will not appreciate the present. You rejoice over a gift only when you know that it has been given out of love. Even the most beautiful present will put you off when not given out of love. In the same way, to our Father in heaven, forced gifts are repulsive.

Now, remember this important passage for the rest of your lives: "**And whoever wants to achieve this result by forcing those who are unwilling is not a Christian preacher or ruler, but a worldly jailer**." An enforcer of the Law—just like a jailer—does not care about the condition of the heart of the person with whom he has to deal. He is only interested in enforcing that person's obedience. He stands in front of the person in his custody with a whip and tells him that he will feel the whip on his back if he does not obey. The jailer does not think: "Oh, now you will become godly." The criminals, on the other hand—clapped in irons and chains and forced to obey—are secretly planning how to avoid being caught during their next theft. That is what a preacher of the Law does to the members of a Christian congregation: he puts them in irons and chains. Thus Luther:

W² 12:318

> A preacher of the Law comes down on people with threats and punishments. A preacher of divine grace coaxes and urges people by reminding them of the goodness and mercy God has shown them. This is because He does not want unwilling workers or cheerless service. He wants His people to be glad and cheerful in the service of God. Any person who will not permit himself to be coaxed and urged with sweet and pleasant words of God's mercy is worthless. These words bring us

W² 12:318

the mercy that God richly gave us in Christ, to do good joyfully and lovingly to the honor of God and for the benefit of our fellow people. All the work done for such people who reject these words is lost effort. If they do not melt and flow in the fire of heavenly love and grace, how can they be softened and made cheerful by laws and threats? It is not the mercy of fellow people, but the mercy of God that is given to us; and St. Paul wants us to consider this mercy in order that we may be stirred up and moved by it to serve God.

It would be wrong for a pastor to think that he must preach only the Law and proclaim the threats of God to people because preaching the Gospel to them would keep them from doing God's will. If that is all he does, he will only lead his people to hell. Rather than act as a policeman in his congregation, he ought to change the hearts of his members. In this way they would cheerfully do what pleases God.

A person who has a real understanding of the love of God in Christ Jesus is always amazed at its fire, which is able to melt anything in heaven and on earth. The moment people believe in His love, they cannot help but love God. They would do anything out of gratitude for their salvation, for love of God and for His glory.

It is useless to use the Law and threats to try and soften hearts that are not yet melted by love of God in Christ Jesus. The best preachers are those who do as Luther did. But those who preach only the Law accomplish nothing. The more often you present the Law in its spiritual meaning, the more often your listeners will sink into despair. Yet it will not make them willing to serve God.

Ps. 110:3 Luther   In conclusion, let me quote Luther on Palm 110:3, which reads: "After Your victory, Your people will offer sacrifices in holy adornments." What the prophet means to say is this: "At the present time, the people are not offering sacrifices to God willingly, but only out of fear and dread of hell. But once You have conquered, after the work of redemption has been completed, then the people will offer their sacrifices willingly." **Luther** writes (St. Louis Ed. 5:988f.):

W² 5:988–89   Furthermore, when the point is reached where [preachers] aim to
(cf. AE 13:288)   teach the people what God requires of us—that is, when they preach the Law or Ten Commandments with threats of punishment, and when they promise blessings and tempt people with good things if only they would keep the Law—it is possible that quite a few may be moved to try to be God-fearing. They serve God and exercise themselves diligently and earnestly in the works of the Law, as St. Paul did before he was converted and became a Christian.

Saul took his efforts quite seriously, but all his works were hypocritical. For the Law accomplishes nothing more than to make people perform
outward acts in which their heart does not cooperate. It leads people to a
pharisaical knowledge of the Law and to pharisaical activities.

However, all this is complete hypocrisy and mere external piety—
under constraint of the Law—and does not pass muster in the sight
of God. These people do not yet have any authentic love for the Law,
nor do they keep the Law with a cheerful heart. They have no genuine
inward obedience, fear, trust, or knowledge of God.

In fact, these people do not know or understand that the Law requires
perfect obedience of the heart. They do not recognize their sins and
disobedience. They view the Law only through a veil and continue in
their blindness, never understanding what God requires from them
and how far they are from offering it.

But at a certain point **the Law reaches its culmination** and does its
best work by bringing people to a clear knowledge and understanding
that God requires perfect, heartfelt obedience from them. At the same
time, they also understand that they cannot keep these requirements
and are not able to keep them.

At this point, **real, horrible disobedience against God begins to stir
in them**, and they realize the complete inability of their nature to offer
such obedience. They realize that they are not able to willfully obey
from the heart. Rather, the opposite is the case.

Because they are sentenced by the Law, subjected to the anger of God,
and condemned to hell, their nature begins to hate the Law. A horrible
anger and bitter hatred against God wells up in them. They become
extremely sinful and fall into blasphemy, despair, and eternal death—
if they are not rescued out of this condition by the Gospel of Christ.

W² 5:989
(cf. AE 13:288)

M any preachers—and some of them are quite good speakers—imagine
that they have accomplished a lot (in fact, that they have achieved their
goal) once they have awakened their listeners from their carnal security.
These preachers think they have reduced them to a point in which they doubt
that they are in a state of grace and are saved.

It is indeed necessary that every person who is to be saved be brought out
of a sense of false security, false comfort, false peace, and false hopes. They
must indeed be made to despair of their salvation and their present condition. But that is merely a preparatory stage through which they must pass. It

**Thirty-eighth
Evening Lecture:**
Oct. 23, 1885

is neither a matter of chief importance nor a chief goal. The key point is that they are fully certain of their state of grace and salvation, so that they can exult as pardoned sinners, singing along with the godly poet Woltersdorf:[12]

> I know it, I know, and shall always give witness:
> As sure as God's hands guide His realm in His goodness,
> As sure as His sun in the heavens does shine,
> So truly is pardon for sinners now mine.

There can be no doubt that this is the principal aim of an evangelical, Gospel-oriented pastor. For the pastor must preach the Gospel to those entrusted to him. He must bring them to faith in Christ, baptize them, and administer Absolution and the Lord's Supper to them.

However, preaching the Gospel means nothing less than telling people that they have been reconciled—perfectly reconciled—with God through Christ. Living, genuine faith of the heart is the divine assurance that they have the forgiveness of sins and that the gates of heaven are open to them.

Baptizing a person means taking him out of the world of lost sinners, by the command and in the name and in the place of God, and giving him the solemn assurance that God is gracious to him, that God is his Father, and that, after Baptism, he is God's child. Baptizing a person means that the Son of God is his Savior and that he is His child—and is already saved. It means that the Holy Spirit is his Comforter and that the Holy Spirit lives in him.

Administering Absolution to a person means saying to him by the command and in the name and place of Christ: "Your sins are forgiven." Administering Holy Communion means saying to him in the place of Jesus: "You, too, will share in the great achievement of redemption. To confirm your claim in it, this precious pledge is given to you, namely, the body and blood of Christ—the ransom with which He purchased the entire world."

Luke 10:20;
1 Cor. 6:11;
1 Pet. 2:25;
1 John 3:2

When you examine the Scriptures, you will find that the aim of every true pastor is to train his listeners so they can declare themselves to be children of God and heirs of salvation. When Christ said to His disciples, "Rejoice that your names are written in heaven," He was encouraging them to rejoice in the certainty of their salvation. Paul writes to the Corinthians: "But you were washed, you were sanctified, you were justified in the name of the Lord Jesus Christ and by the Spirit of our God." Peter writes to the Christians living in faraway lands: "For you were straying like sheep, but have now returned to the Shepherd and Overseer of your souls." Including himself in the statement, John says to his spiritual children, "Beloved, we are God's children now, and

---

12 Ernst Gottlieb Woltersdorf (1725–61) was a Lutheran pastor in Bunzlau, Silesia. This poem, *"Ich weiß es, ich weiß es und werd es behalten,"* appeared in many eighteenth-century hymnals.

what we will be has not yet appeared; but we know that when He appears we shall be like Him, because we shall see Him as He is."

Nowhere in the Holy Scriptures do we see the apostles treating the members of their congregations as if they were uncertain regarding the members' standing with God. The apostles imply that their members—despite their weaknesses and blemishes—are dear, beloved children of God.

These days, things are different. As a rule, even the best pastors are satisfied if they have taught their people to come to them occasionally and complain that they have no assurance of their salvation. These people are afraid they would go to hell if they were to die that night. Pastors who are not truly Gospel-oriented take this complaint as evidence that they have turned their listeners into good Christians. In reality, a complaint like this should alarm a truly Gospel-oriented pastor whose aim it is to get his listeners to profess: "I know that my Redeemer lives. I know in whom I believe."[13]

Why do so many people in our day and age live in uncertainty about being true Christians? The reason is that pastors, as a rule, mingle Law and Gospel and do not listen to the apostolic warning: "Do your best to present yourself to God as one approved, a worker who has no need to be ashamed, rightly handling the word of truth." For when the Gospel is preached mingled with Law, it is impossible for a listener to have faith in the forgiveness of his sins. On the other hand, when the Law is preached mingled with Gospel, it is impossible for a listener to arrive at the knowledge that he is a poor sinner in need of the forgiveness of sins.

2 Tim. 2:15

---

13   See Job 19:25.

Ferdinand and Emilie Walther await the resurrection at Concordia Cemetery. Located near the intersection of Bates and Morganford in South St. Louis, it is the second cemetery of the *Gesamtgemeinde*. Holy Cross sits on the original cemetery ground, and some saints still rest there. Image courtesy of Concordia Historical Institute.

THESIS XXIV

You are not rightly distinguishing Law and Gospel in the Word of God if you claim the unforgivable sin against the Holy Spirit cannot be forgiven because of its magnitude.

EDITOR'S NOTE: In this thesis, Walther addresses the sin against the Holy Spirit, which sin he sees pastors making mysterious, confusing, and threatening to Christians in their care. As Walther reads and applies the Bible concerning this sin, he makes the important point that you cannot "accidentally" commit the sin against the Holy Spirit. Nor can you struggle against the devil, the world, and your sinful flesh and, in the middle of that struggle, commit a sin that is "too great" for God to forgive. Those who have committed the unpardonable sin did so deliberately, with evil intent, publicly, and in a manner that shows no regret or worry.

These days, the way people describe the unpardonable sin is a horrible mingling of Law and Gospel. Only the Law condemns sin. Without exception, the Gospel absolves sinners from all sins. The prophet writes: "Though your sins are like scarlet, they shall be as white as snow; though they are red like crimson, they shall become like wool." The apostle Paul writes in Romans 5:20: "Now the law came in to increase the trespass, but where sin increased, grace abounded all the more." Accordingly, Luther sings out in a glorious strain:

> Though great our sins, yet greater still
> Is God's abundant favor;
> His hand of mercy never will
> Abandon us, nor waver.[1]

Now, then, what does Holy Scripture say regarding the sin against the Holy Spirit? Concerning this sin we have three parallel passages in the Synoptic Gospels,[2] a passage in the Epistle to the Hebrews, and one in the First Epistle of St. John. These passages provide the true doctrine regarding the sin against the Holy Spirit.

Isa. 1:18;
Rom. 5:20

Scripture on the unforgivable sin

---

1   These are the first four lines of the fifth stanza of Luther's hymn "From Depths of Woe I Cry to Thee." The translation is that of *LSB* 607.

2   The Synoptic Gospels are Matthew, Mark, and Luke. They have essentially the same structure as they present the life and work of Jesus Christ. John has a different structure that nevertheless complements the other Gospels.

Matthew 12:30–32:

Matt. 12:30–32

Whoever is not with Me is against Me, and whoever does not gather with Me scatters. Therefore I tell you, every sin and blasphemy will be forgiven people, but the blasphemy against the Spirit will not be forgiven. And whoever speaks a word against the Son of Man will be forgiven, but whoever speaks against the Holy Spirit will not be forgiven, either in this age or in the age to come.

This is the principal passage. To begin with, it states that every blasphemy against the Father and the Son will be forgiven. Only the blasphemy against the Holy Spirit will not be forgiven. Now, it is certain that the Holy Spirit is not a more glorious and exalted person than the Father and the Son. Rather, He is coequal with them. Accordingly, the meaning of this passage cannot be that the unforgivable sin is blasphemy against the person of the Holy Spirit. For blasphemy against the Father and the Son is exactly the same sin. The blasphemy to which our text refers is directed **against the office**, or operation, of the Holy Spirit. Thus whoever rejects the office of the Holy Spirit—that person's sin cannot be forgiven. The office of the Holy Spirit is to call people to Christ and to keep them with Him.[3]

The text mentions in particular that the person committing this sin "**speaks** against the Holy Spirit." This shows that the sin in question is not committed by blasphemous thoughts that arise in the heart. Quite often, good Christians imagine that they have committed this sin when they are plagued by horrid thoughts of which they cannot rid themselves. Our Lord Christ foresaw this, and for that reason He informed us that blasphemy against the Holy Spirit that is not forgiven must have been spoken by the mouth.

The devil shoots his fiery darts into the hearts of the best Christians, causing them to focus on the most horrible thoughts against their heavenly Father and against the Holy Spirit—albeit against their will. Sincere Christians sometimes complain that, while going to Communion, they have been harassed with the most horrible thoughts against the Holy Spirit. Such thoughts are the devil's filth.

When I am sitting in a beautiful room with the windows open and a rascal throws dung and filth into the room, how can I prevent that? In His wise providence, God permits His dear children to be annoyed day and night with such thoughts. The best preachers have met with such situations among the members of their congregations. But that is not a sin against the Holy

---

3   Walther stands squarely with the Lutheran dogmaticians. See "Theologische Axiome," *Lehre und Wehre* 7 (1861): 67. Walther's presentation here follows the sources used in that article. Here Walther engages Axiom 19 under the category of actual sin: "The sin against the Holy Spirit is not unforgivable [to the extent that it concerns] the person of the Holy Spirit but more so because [it concerns] His office and His beneficial work [of grace]."

Spirit, which consists in blasphemy that is pronounced orally. I once had to counsel a girl who even *spoke* thoughts of this kind, but at the same time fell on the ground, weeping and moaning to be delivered by God from her affliction. She did not find peace until she realized that it was not she who was speaking those thoughts. Satan had taken possession of her lips. Of course, "Modernists"[4] who deny such a power of the devil would call this explanation pure superstition.

Mark 3:28–30: "'Truly, I say to you, all sins will be forgiven the children of man, and whatever blasphemies they utter, but whoever blasphemes against the Holy Spirit never has forgiveness, but is guilty of an eternal sin'—for they were saying, 'He has an unclean spirit.'" Here we have the actual blasphemy against the Holy Spirit! When Christ—by the finger of God—cast out devils, the Pharisees who had come down from Jerusalem declared this work of the Holy Spirit to be a work of the devil. Inwardly, they were convinced that this was a divine work, but since the Savior had rebuked them for their hypocrisy and holier-than-thou attitude they were filled with deadly hatred against Christ. This stirred them up to blaspheme against the Holy Spirit. Mark 3:28–30

Here we have the explanation: to declare a **work** of the Holy Spirit to be a work of the devil even though you are convinced that it is a work of the Holy Spirit—*that* is blasphemy against the Spirit. This shows the seriousness of this matter. Every Christian occasionally resists the operations of divine grace and then tries to persuade himself that he is only chasing away gloomy thoughts. Can that mean anything else than that such thoughts are of the devil? This particular doctrine warns us that if we wish to be saved, we must yield immediately to the operation of the Holy Spirit as soon as we feel it. We should not resist it. For in the next step the person who resists may find himself saying, "This work is not of the Holy Spirit." The next step after that will be that he begins to hate the way God wants to lead him to salvation, and finally he will blaspheme Him in that way.

So let us be on our guard. Let us open the door to the Holy Spirit whenever He knocks and not think like worldly people who regard these sensations to be a symptom of melancholy.[5]

This is no laughing matter. Unless the Holy Spirit brings us to faith, we will never achieve it. Whoever rejects the Holy Spirit is beyond help—even by God. God wants the order maintained that He has ordained for our salvation. He brings no one into heaven by force.

---

4   Walther means historical-critical theologians.

5   See the note on temperaments, page 64 n. 17.

In one particular passage, Christ had just healed the man with the withered hand and had driven out the devil.[6] Everybody could see that the power of God was making inroads into the kingdom of Satan. But the unbelievers standing around said, "Ah! Beelzebub is inside this Jesus. That is why He is able to cast out lesser devils."[7] The very action that they had witnessed—the works and the words of Christ—demonstrated that He was against the devil and was destroying the devil's kingdom. It is completely illogical to imagine that the devil would help Christ in that work.

Luke 12:10   Luke 12:10: "And everyone who speaks a word against the Son of Man will be forgiven, but the one who blasphemes against the Holy Spirit will not be forgiven." Again, we see that the main point regarding the sin against the Holy Spirit is that the blasphemy is **spoken—knowingly and deliberately**.

There is a very important statement regarding this sin in Hebrews 6:4–8:

Heb. 6:4–8   For it is impossible, in the case of those who have once been enlightened, who have tasted the heavenly gift, and have shared in the Holy Spirit, and have tasted the goodness of the word of God and the powers of the age to come, and then have fallen away, to restore them again to repentance, since they are crucifying once again the Son of God to their own harm and holding Him up to contempt. For land that has drunk the rain that often falls on it, and produces a crop useful to those for whose sake it is cultivated, receives a blessing from God. But if it bears thorns and thistles, it is worthless and near to being cursed, and its end is to be burned.

This is a very important passage! The sin against the Holy Spirit has the characteristic that **the person who has committed it cannot be restored to repentance**. It is simply impossible. He cannot repent. It is not our dear Lord who puts people into this condition, but the sinner who by his own effort produces this state of permanent impenitence. Once this condition has reached a certain degree, God stops operating on that person. The curse has settled on him, and there is no further possibility for that person to be saved. Why? Because he is no longer able to repent. The soil of this person's heart has been finally cursed and is no longer enriched by the dew and rain of divine grace.

1 John 5:16   First John 5:16: "If anyone sees his brother committing a sin not leading to death, he shall ask, and God will give him life—to those who commit sins

---

6   See Mark 3:1–5. Compare with Matthew 12:9–14; Luke 6:6–11. Walther understands the healing of the man to happen immediately before the Pharisees' accusation against Jesus that He could cast out demons because He Himself was possessed by a demon (Mark 3:22). Even in the Bible histories of the LCMS, it was common to teach the Gospels as different aspects of a concrete history, not as independent literary works. The time sequence of this history, as understood through a harmonization of the Gospels, informed the time sequence of events in the individual Gospels.

7   See Mark 3:22. Compare with Matthew 9:32–34; Luke 11:14–16.

that do not lead to death. **There is sin that leads to death; I do not say that one should pray for that**." This passage contains important information for us, but we cannot act on it. For before a person's death we can say of no one whether he has committed the sin against the Holy Spirit.[8]

Even when a person's mouth speaks blasphemies, we do not know to what extent his heart is involved, or whether the phenomenon is perhaps the work of the devil, or whether he is acting in great blindness, or whether he may be renewed toward repentance. Christians in the days of the apostles had the gift to discern the spirits. Accordingly, John says here: "When you see that God has stopped being gracious to such or such an individual who has committed this sin, do not wish for God to be gracious to them. You should stop praying for them." Also, we cannot say to God, "Save those who have committed the sin against the Holy Spirit." Yet, as shocking as this statement may be, within it lies a greater comfort.

Someone may come up to you and say, "I am a wretched person—I have committed the sin against the Holy Spirit. I am quite certain of it." The afflicted person may tell you of the evil he has done, the evil he has **spoken**, and the evil he has thought. It may really look as if he has blasphemed the Holy Spirit. Now, remember the weapon that Hebrews 6 provides for dealing with a case such as this: That person is not at all rejoicing over what he tells you; it is all so awfully horrid to him. This shows that God has at least begun to lead this person to repentance. All he needs to do is to lay hold of the promise of the Gospel.

In this situation, ask the person whether he has been doing all those evil things intentionally—and in his state of fear he may even confirm it because Satan makes him say so. When you ask whether he wishes he had not done those evil things, he will answer, "Of course! These things are worrying me to death!" This is a sure sign that God has begun the work of repentance in that person. A case such as this is indeed not to be treated lightly. Since repentance is beginning to grow in him, show this poor person that he has clear proof that he has not committed the sin against the Holy Spirit.

In general, when preaching on this topic, the pastor must aim to convince his listeners that they have not committed this sin, rather than warning them not to commit it. To a person who has really committed this sin, preaching is of no benefit. If they are sorry for their sins and crave forgiveness, tell them that they are dear children of God but that they are passing through a terrible tribulation.

---

8   See "Theologische Axiome," 67. Here Walther uses Axiom 20 under the category of actual sin: "One should not rashly pronounce [that someone has committed] the sin against the Holy Spirit. Rather, only after the fact, only after [a person has been] impenitent unto death, can one make that judgment."

Acts 7:51, 60 In Acts 7:51, Stephen said to his listeners, "You stiff-necked people, uncircumcised in heart and ears, you always resist the Holy Spirit. As your fathers did, so do you." Had these people committed the sin against the Holy Spirit? No. For Stephen died praying for them: "Lord, do not hold this sin against them." This shows that, though the Jews had committed willful sins, they had not committed the sin against the Holy Spirit. Otherwise, the martyr would not have prayed for them. When praying for them, he was thinking that an hour might yet come when they would no longer resist the Holy Spirit.

Let us now hear **Luther's** comment on 1 John 5:16. He writes (St. Louis Ed. 9:1519):

W² 9:1519
(cf. AE 30:325)

I understand the heresy that these people set up in the place of the truth from the point of the "sin unto death." If they do not repent after the first and second warning,[9] their sin is a sin unto death. Indeed, in this group we may include people who sin out of stubbornness and defiance, like Judas, who had been given enough warning but, because of his hard-hearted, continual[10] wickedness, was beyond help. This group also includes Saul, who died in his sins because he would not trust in the Lord.[11] But the highest degree of hard-hearted resistance is found in those who insist on maintaining and defending their known error.

Rom. 5:20 This sin is not unpardonable because of its severity, for the apostle, as we heard, distinctly declared: "Where sin increased, grace abounded all the more." Rather, it is unpardonable because the person committing this sin rejects the only means by which he can be brought to repentance, faith, and steadfastness in faith. Here Luther is referring to people whose sin consists in that, in a hard-hearted manner, they defend an error that they have recognized as such—against their better knowledge and conscience.

W² 9:1519
(cf. AE 30:325);
Walther
disagrees
with Luther

Luther continues: "Of the same kind [within this group] is the sin against the Holy Spirit or the hardening against wickedness, the will to fight against the known truth, and those who are impenitent until death." It is doubtlessly incorrect to regard someone's impenitence until they die as the sin against the Holy Spirit, as Luther does, for in that case most people would have committed this sin. However, impenitence until the end is bound to this sin. The unique feature of this sin is that it opposes the **office**, that is, the work, of the Holy Spirit.

---

9 See Titus 3:10.

10 German: *Halsstarrigkeit*. Later we see its synonym, *hartnäckig*. Both refer to being "stiff-necked." This means someone who has shut out all advice, whose will has become like wood or stone, who resists all movement, who butts heads with everyone. This applies to the biblical example of Pharaoh in Exodus 7–12.

11 Saul committed suicide instead of dying heroically in battle like his sons (1 Samuel 31:1–6).

There is another kind of sin that is not unto death. This was the sin of Paul, to which he refers in 1 Timothy 1:13, saying, "Formerly I was a blasphemer, persecutor, and insolent opponent. But I received mercy because I had acted ignorantly in unbelief."

W² 9:1519
(cf. AE 30:325);
1 Tim. 1:13

Paul had committed the awful sin of blaspheming and trying to force Christians to blaspheme. But he was acting in horrible blindness. He had no idea that he was fighting against God.

Christ speaks of this sin in Matthew 12:32, saying, "Whoever speaks against the Son of Man will be forgiven." In the same way, the sin of the men who crucified Christ was not unto death, for St. Peter says to them: "And now, brothers, I know that you acted in ignorance," Acts 3:17. "If they had [understood it], they would not have crucified the Lord of glory," 1 Corinthians 2:8. However, this sin is unto death when it is defended after it has been adequately revealed and recognized as a sin, because it resists the grace of God, the Means of Grace, and the forgiveness of sin.

W² 9:1519
(cf. AE 30:325);
Matt. 12:32;
Acts 3:17;
1 Cor. 2:8

Let everyone take care not to resist the Holy Spirit. When a sin has been revealed to a person and his own heart affirms that it is a sin, do not let his mouth deny the fact. That may not yet be the sin against the Holy Spirit, but it may be a step in that direction. There are many people who admit that we all sin in many ways every day, but when they are rebuked, they claim that they never harmed a child.

Where there is no knowledge of sin, there is no forgiveness. For the forgiveness of sin is preached to those who feel their sin and are seeking the grace of God. **But these persons** [who have committed the sin against the Holy Spirit] **are not frightened by any scruples of conscience**, nor do they recognize or feel their sin.

W² 9:1519
(cf. AE 30:325)

Many of the people who claim that they are distressed because they think they have committed the sin against the Holy Spirit would not feel distressed if they really had committed that sin and were in that awful condition of heart. Rather, they would constantly delight in blaspheming the Gospel. However, these Christians in distress still have faith, and the Spirit of God is working in them; and if the Spirit of God is working in them, they have not committed the sin against the Holy Spirit.

An excellent explanation of this issue is found in **Baier.** In his *Compendium Theologiae Positivae*, he says in Part II, chapter III, paragraph 24:

The most serious of all actual sins, which is called the sin against the Holy Spirit,[a] consists[b] of a malicious renunciation[d] and a blasphemous[e] and obstinate[f] assault upon the heavenly truth that formerly was known[c] [by the person committing this sin].

> (Note a.) The manner of naming this sin comes from its object, which is the Holy Spirit. The term "Holy Spirit" in this place is understood *metonymically*; it is considered according to the office that the Holy Spirit carries out in converting the souls of people by the ministry of the Word. This meaning of the term is also found in 2 Corinthians 3:6. In order to be truly the sin against the Holy Spirit, a sin must be committed *against the office and ministry of the Holy Spirit and against the heavenly truth made known through that office and ministry.*[12]

To blaspheme the Holy Spirit means to blaspheme His office, to declare the work of the Holy Spirit to be the work of the devil, and to resist His office.

Baier continues: "It is also called a sin unto death. It is given this name according to the effect of this sin: quite definitely bringing about eternal death or damnation. 1 John 5:16." The phrase "sin unto death" must not be confused with "mortal sin."[13]

> (Note b.) The seat of doctrine [*sedes doctrinae*] for this sin is found in Matthew 12:30ff.; Mark 3:28; and Luke 12:10.

> (Note c.) That doctrine [of heavenly truth] may either have been approved [by the person in question] once upon a time with an assent of divine faith and by public profession, or it may only have been recognized so clearly that the heart [of the individual] was convinced and had no argument to set up against it. In the former manner the sin against the Holy Spirit is committed by those apostates[14] who renounce and insult the truth that they had once known and believed, such as the author of the Epistle to the Hebrews describes in chapter 6, verses 4ff. In the latter class belong the Pharisees and scribes, who never approved the doctrine of Christ by their [public] confession [of belief], though they were convinced of its truth in their heart by Scripture and the miracles of Christ, and [yet] had nothing but insults to set up against it.

There are Lutheran theologians who claim that only a person who is truly born again is able to commit this sin. But these men are going too far, because no one would believe that the Pharisees of old had been truly converted.

---

12   The italicized text in the last sentence is Walther's emphasis.

13   Here Walther recalls "Theologische Axiome," 65, Axiom 6 under actual sin: "Mortal sins are distinguished from sins that lead to death. The former kind deserves death. The latter kind actually brings about [physical or spiritual] death, without exception."

14   Apostates (from the Greek *apóstasis*) are those who once embraced and confessed the Christian faith, then fell away, and now publicly speak and act against the faith and the Church. The Dau edition mistakenly translates the Latin *apostatae* ("apostates") as "apostles."

Rather, they grew up in their evil nature. It is true that people who are born again are still able to commit this sin if they fall away from the faith—a point that the Calvinists call into question and where they err. It is quite probable that Judas was a believer. At the same time, it is hard to believe that the Savior would have called Judas if he had come under the wrath of God. But Judas did fall away, enabling Satan to snatch not only that wretched man's body but also his soul.

> (Note d.) In other words, the renunciation of, and assaults on, the heavenly doctrine must be made willfully, Hebrews 10:26, in such a manner that the source of this renunciation and assault is pure, downright evil intent and action. However, those who renounce their faith from ignorance or fear of danger are not on that account sinners against the Holy Spirit, but can obtain remission of their sin. See the examples of Paul in 1 Timothy 1:13 and of Peter in Matthew 26:70ff.

It is a horrible thing when you present God's Word clearly and precisely and then notice that it is making an impression on that person. He pauses, you can see his limbs start to shake, God is overpowering him, but then he still says, "No, I will not believe that! You are not interpreting Scripture correctly." While this is not yet the sin against the Holy Spirit, it is a preliminary step. Listen closely: a preliminary step! That person can climb that step, yet he can still turn around and be saved.

Peter climbed the first, second, and last preliminary steps—but they were still preliminary. He did not act out of hatred toward Christ, but out of fear. He thought: "If I admit that I am a disciple of Jesus, they will arrest me." That was Satan in the act of knocking down that strong pillar of Christ. But the Holy Spirit returned to him, and Peter repented of his sin.

> (Note e.) In the passages cited [in note b.], this sin is called "speaking a word against the Holy Spirit" or "blasphemy against the Holy Spirit." Accordingly, the form that this sin takes is insulting talk that is aimed against the office of the Holy Spirit, for instance, when His teaching and the miraculous works that were performed to confirm the teaching are attributed to the power and operation of Satan, as was done by the Pharisees.

> (Note f.) Therefore, it is in its very nature a sin of such a character that it cannot be forgiven—and never is forgiven to anyone, according to the passages cited from Matthew and Mark—because of itself and by its very nature it blocks the way to repentance. However, the reason final impenitence is so closely connected with this sin is that the people who commit it directly and with full evil intent and action oppose the means for their conversion and that God therefore withdraws His grace from them and gives them over to a reprobate mind.

A person who has committed the sin against the Holy Spirit is condemned—not so much because of that sin as because of unbelief. Unbelief is the general cause,[15] while evil and constant criticism of the truth is the particular cause[16] of damnation. However, these people do not reject Christ clearly and fully. Calvinists claim that such people cannot be saved because Christ had not suffered for them, had not done enough for them, and had not saved them. This is a devilish error.

There is a general agreement that a certain man named Spiera had committed the sin against the Holy Spirit. He had come to know the Gospel truth but had renounced it twice—the second time under oath. He slipped into an awful state of mind. Everyone could see that he was already suffering the torments of hell. Every attempt to comfort him failed. Paul Vergerius was at his sickbed and counseled him with the consolation of the Gospel. However, all our theologians hold that Spiera did not commit the sin against the Holy Spirit because he condemned that sin and was fully convinced that he deserved eternal damnation.

This was not the sin against the Holy Spirit. Rather, Spiera despaired of mercy. But despair is not the unforgivable sin against the Holy Spirit! The only reason Spiera renounced the truth was that he feared he would be burned by the Romanists. Quenstedt's account of Spiera is cited in Baier's *Compendium*, Part II, page 328.

The case of Spiera is an important, solemn warning for all time. It gave Vergerius the last push to finally leave the papacy because he saw what hellish agony a person had to suffer who had renounced the evangelical truth.

Thirty-ninth Evening Lecture:
Nov. 6, 1885

The world hates the ministry

There is not a single profession or calling, my friends, that has been scorned and hated as deeply as that of theologians or teachers of religion, which is basically the same thing. The world regards these men as the chief, if not the only, cause that delays the coming of the Golden Age. A hundred years ago, **Diderot**,[17] the notorious French encyclopedist, wrote: "Better times will not come for the world until the last king has been hanged by the guts of the last priest." Because of this and similar statements, the French government ordered that the writings of Diderot be burned and the author be put in prison. However, not only did his horrifying statement become the slogan of the French revolutionaries in 1789, but it has also been the slogan of all revolutionaries until the present day. We may expect, too, that this will be acted

---

15 Latin: *causa communis.*

16 Latin: *causa singularis.*

17 Denis Diderot (1713–84) was a French philosopher and the chief editor of the *Encyclopédie.* See also the Index of Persons and Groups, page 492.

on some day, for all signs are pointing in that direction. You may live to see this yet come true.

If only theologians and teachers of religion would not trigger so much hate and contempt by their own actions! Alas! This sad fact is recorded not only in the annals of church history, but it is also confirmed by our own experience. There are too many teachers of religion who misuse their sacred office, their sacred profession and calling, for the gratification of their worldly minds, their greed of money and glory, and their love of control. They repress and even continually deny the truth—partially because they are afraid of some people, partially from a desire to defer to others. Instead of preaching the pure Gospel, they proclaim the very opposite and spread lies and errors. Why, there is no vice too shameful, no crime too awful with which teachers of religion have not desecrated their office. Thus they have given the world offense—terrible beyond words. Will this fact stop you, my friends, from continuing your devotion to the study of theology?

Many bring shame on the office

God forbid! Consider, first, that our all-knowing God has foreseen these sad events and has nevertheless in His infinite wisdom adopted this order of administering the sacred office: not through holy angels who did not fall from their holy estate, but through fallen men who are subject to sin. May God keep us from taking offense at this arrangement! Rather, let us adore God for having made admirable provision that His Church shall not be overcome by hell, despite the fact that it is served by such poor and—at times—such shameful pastors.

The ministry remains valid and sure

Second, consider that—despite the contempt of the world—our great God has highly honored the office of teachers of religion and has exalted it above every other office. To begin with, in the days of His earthly ministry and while personally administering this office, from the very outset the Son of God encouraged the first teachers with these words: "The one who hears you hears Me, and the one who rejects you rejects Me, and the one who rejects Me rejects Him who sent Me." What glorious credentials He has given His pastors with these words—[preparing them] for their travels throughout the world!

Luke 10:16

Furthermore, the Word of God has revealed to us the fact that not only marriage unions but also unions between pastors and their congregations are sealed in heaven. What Scripture records concerning Jeremiah and St. Paul[18] applies to all true pastors: they are appointed not only in the present time, not only at their birth, but they also have been appointed by God from eternity to be His helpers for saving those who are entrusted to them.

Finally, no one has been given more glorious promises than teachers of the Gospel and pastors of the Word of God. Through the prophet Daniel, God

Dan. 12:3

---

18   Jeremiah 1:5; Acts 9:15–16.

says, "And those who are wise shall shine like the brightness of the sky above; and those who turn many to righteousness, like the stars forever and ever."

When the time comes that the worldly will gnash their teeth, they will witness all the elect and angels saying to God: "This man has been a faithful pastor and teacher. He has proclaimed the saving Word of God to a world of castaways. Down on earth he was despised, persecuted, and libeled, but he shines now as a star with imperishable luster." Truly, my dear friends, this fact should cheer us and keep us from becoming unfaithful to our God, who has called us into this office. Of course, what the prophet says applies only to true and faithful pastors.

Bearing this in mind, let us take up the final thesis in this series, which discusses the distinction between Law and Gospel and the mingling of these two doctrines. In studying this thesis, we will consider the chief and primary requirement of a true teacher of the Christian faith.

On May 7, 1887, to mark the home-going of C. F. W. Walther, black bunting draped the Walther home located across Texas Avenue from Holy Cross. Following Walther's death, Pastor K. Georg Stöckhardt was called to Walther's chair in exegesis at Concordia College and lived in this house until his death in 1913. The house was later demolished. Image courtesy of Concordia Historical Institute.

THESIS XXV

You are not rightly distinguishing Law and Gospel in the Word of God if you do not allow the Gospel to predominate in your teaching.

EDITOR'S NOTE: In this thesis, Walther offers concluding remarks that could just as easily introduce and even sum up the whole lecture series. Neither Walther nor others in the early Missouri Synod were trying to be mere lawgivers. On the one hand, early LCMS literature repeatedly speaks of a willingness to die for the truth revealed in God's Word. Yet this willingness does not arise from the fact that God's Word is true; rather, it comes from the fundamental principle that God's Word is *saving* truth. The stakes are eternal life and death.

As firm as they were in defending the truth, Walther, Franz Pieper, and their colleagues knew that Scripture is the source of all infallible testimony about everything that the Church does in its *saving* work. God's Word cannot die. Jesus, the Christ, did not remain dead. People made one in Him through Baptism, teaching, preaching, Absolution, and the Lord's Supper will one day say that they cannot die.

The Gospel will predominate entirely in the next world. Walther brings into the pulpit the reality of heavenly citizenship, of a life that continues and grows richer in eternal communion with God. It is finally for this reason that we read and interpret the Bible. Walther knew that he and his beloved Emilie would awaken one day, never to die again. May all who read this book, holding fast to the Bible as they distinguish Law and Gospel, join with them before God's everlasting throne.

Heavy on the Gospel

This is an exceedingly important subject that we are taking up in this, our concluding, study. This thesis tells us that Law and Gospel are mingled and corrupted for listeners of the Word when the Law predominates in a sermon. But this is also true when Law and Gospel, as a rule, are equally balanced and the Gospel does not predominate in a sermon. I have to say: as precious as this topic is, that makes me all the more afraid that I will spoil it for you. The longer I meditate on it, the less I can find the right words for it. What is presented here is simply too important! Let us now turn to Holy Scripture and convince ourselves that, in general, the Gospel must predominate.

Luke 2:10, 14
Luther

The first preacher who spoke immediately after Christ was born into this world gives us the first proof for this claim. Who was that? It was an angel. What did he preach? He preached to the shepherds who were terrified by his heavenly splendor, Luke 2:10: "Fear not; behold, I proclaim[1] to you great joy that will be to all people." Here we do not find the slightest bit of the Law, not a trace of commands, not a trace of demands that God makes on mankind. Rather, he preaches the exact opposite: about the goodwill and mercy of God to all people. He is joined by the heavenly host, who exult: "Glory to God in the highest, and on earth peace, and to people, goodwill!" Again, we hear nothing but a sweet, pleasant message of joy.

Our Father in heaven has had His honor restored to Him. He had created a race of humans of whom He knew that they would fall, yet He did everything possible to save them. The infant born in the stable at Bethlehem established peace between God and mankind. The only thing that God requires is that we humans be pleased with His arrangement for our salvation and take comfort and rejoice in this infant.

This heavenly preacher gave us an illustration of how we are to preach. True, we have to preach the Law too—but only as a preparation for the Gospel. Our ultimate aim when we preach the Law must be to preach the Gospel. Whoever does not adopt this aim is not a true servant of the Gospel.

Mark 16:15–16

Mark 16:15–16: "Go into all the world and proclaim the gospel to the whole creation. Whoever believes and is baptized will be saved, but whoever does not believe will be condemned." When these words were spoken, the time had arrived for Christ to proclaim in clear and distinct terms the basic facts of His religion. For He was about to ascend to heaven and now had to give His apostles instructions concerning how to continue His work. What did He say to them? He told them to go into the whole world and preach the Gospel to every creature. The very word *Gospel* made it clear that their message was to be a message of joy.

Mark 16:16

But so they would not think that this message was so big that no one would understand it, He immediately added these words: "Whoever believes and is baptized will be saved." This was to let them know that *this* was what He understands by the word *Gospel*. Then He added: "But whoever does not believe will be condemned." This, too, is a sweet word. He did not say, "Whoever has sinned much—over a long period of time—will be condemned." He states that unbelief is the only reason for condemnation.

Humanly speaking, you might say that these last words are the sweetest and most comforting. Think about the meaning of this statement: "But

---

1   Greek: *euangelízomai.*

whoever does not believe will be condemned." No matter what a person's character is and how badly he has sinned, nothing in his past will condemn him. But, of course, if a person refuses to believe the words—the message of Jesus—he has to go to hell. When the Lord terrifies [people] with hell, He does it only to bring people to heaven. So He does that here only to urge people to accept His gracious message and not to thrust it away from themselves.

These words of the Lord should not be read this way: "Whoever does **not** believe will be condemned," but rather: "Whoever does not **believe** will be condemned." What He is saying is this: "Your condemnation has already been removed from you. Your sin has been taken away. Hell has already been overcome for you. I have provided enough atonement for everything. It is now up to you to **believe** this, and you will be saved forevermore."

Second Timothy 4:5: "As for you, always be sober, endure suffering, **do the work of an evangelical preacher** [equals the work of an **evangelist**], fulfill your ministry."[2] Despite the fact that the word "evangelist" may refer to a special office, that does not weaken our argument. Those who were not apostles but [were] evangelists were such because they were to preach nothing but the Gospel, that is, only the doctrine by which they were to save their fellow human beings. 2 Tim. 4:5 Luther

True, if you meet people steeped in self-righteousness, in sins, [in] vices, and in carnal security, you must first crush their stony hearts. But that is merely preparatory work. The waters of grace cannot penetrate a stony heart. The Law is merely an auxiliary doctrine. It is not the real doctrine of Christ. "For the law was given through Moses; grace and truth came through Jesus Christ." Christ brought only grace, the Gospel, not a new Law, as the miserable, blind Papists claim. He preached the Law merely to prepare people for the sweet comfort that He had to offer them. John 1:17

Second Corinthians 3:5–6: "Not that we are sufficient in ourselves to claim anything as coming from us, but our sufficiency is from God, who has made us competent to be ministers of a new covenant, not of the letter but of the Spirit. For the letter kills, but the Spirit gives life." Here, the apostle speaks of himself as [being] an apostle. Preachers of our Christian era must remember that they are not Old Testament preachers but New Testament preachers. Why does the apostle say it? "The letter kills, but the Spirit gives life." *The letter* is the Law of God. A New Testament preacher as such should preach nothing else but the Gospel. He is really carrying out an alien function when he preaches the Law. It is a horrible blindness when the Papists state that the two doctrines that must be distinguished in Scripture are the Old Law and the Law of the **Gospel**. 2 Cor. 3:5–6

---

2 Walther speaks an "amplified" version of 2 Timothy 4:5. The Bible verse is rendered according to the German notes.

But "Law of the Gospel" is a contradiction in terms. How can there be any good news in the Law? Add to this the fact that the Antichrist claims that the Law of the Gospel is the more difficult of the two because the Mosaic Law had been satisfied by external obedience. He claims that the Law of the Gospel targets people's innermost heart.

1 Cor. 2:2   First Corinthians 2:2: "For I decided to know nothing among you except Jesus Christ and Him crucified." It is remarkable that during his stay at Corinth, day and night St. Paul wrestled with the problem of how to bring Christ into people's hearts and how to lay a solid foundation for their faith in Christ and their joy in Him. Jesus Christ was the marrow and substance of Paul's entire preaching, the golden thread that ran through all his sermons. He wrote down this fact for our benefit. So, when you say good-bye to your congregation, you can do so with a good conscience only if you also can say, "For I decided to know nothing among you except Jesus Christ and Him crucified." Woe to the preacher who preaches other things! Woe to him if, in order to make people God-fearing, he had preached the Law because he thought that the pure, untainted grace of God would not save them! If he has done that, he has been an unfaithful servant.

1 Cor. 15:3   First Corinthians 15:3: "For I delivered to you as **of first importance** what I also received: that Christ died for our sins in accordance with the Scriptures." The apostle says "of first importance."[3] He regarded all other matters as subordinate to his primary subject for preaching, namely, the Gospel concerning Christ.

Preach Gospel joy   Now, do not merely listen to this statement of the apostle, but think of the time when you will be the pastor of a congregation, and make a vow to God that you will adopt the apostle's method, that you will not stand in your pulpit with a sad face (as if you were asking people to come to a funeral), but like men who are wooing a bride or who are announcing a wedding.

If you do not mingle Law with the Gospel, you will always step up to your pulpit with joy. People will notice that you are filled with joy because you are bringing the blessed message of joy to your congregation. Furthermore, they will notice that wonderful things are happening among them. Alas! Many pastors do not experience these wonderful things. Their listeners remain sleepy; their parishioners remain stingy.

American Christians want to be in church   Why is that? They did not have enough Gospel preached to them. The people who go to church in America really want to hear the Word of God. We live in a free country, where it is nobody's concern whether you go to church or not. In accordance with God's will, it should be the preacher's goal to proclaim the Gospel to his listeners until their heart melts, until they give up their resistance and confess that the Lord is too strong for them and that from

---

3   Greek: *en prōtois*. Latin: *imprimis*.

that point forward they wish to remain with Jesus. It is not enough for you simply to be aware of your correct teaching and your ability to present pure doctrine correctly. These are indeed important matters. However, no one will benefit from them if you mingle Law and Gospel.

The most subversive way of mingling both occurs when the Gospel is preached **along with** the Law, but does not predominate in the sermon. That preacher may think that he has proclaimed the evangelical truth quite often. His listeners, however, only remember that on some occasions he preached quite comfortingly and told them to believe in Jesus Christ. But how should they believe if the preacher does not tell them how to have faith? As soon as you do not let the Gospel predominate, many of your listeners will die of spiritual starvation. They will be spiritually half-starved because the bread of life is not the Law, but the Gospel.

Second Corinthians 1:24: "Not that we lord it over your faith, but we work **2 Cor. 1:24** with you for your joy, for you stand firm in your faith." This is a fine text for your first sermon. Remember this word of the apostle well: When you become pastors, you become helpers of Christians' joy. Do not become pastors who irritate and torture people, filling them with uncertainty and causing them to go home from church heavyhearted. Write your sermons in such a way that you can say, "If anyone hears this sermon and is not converted, it is his own fault if he goes home from my church unconverted and hardened."

Do not worry; no harm will come to you if fanatics[4] come and say, "The pastor is still not yet converted; otherwise, he would let loose in a completely different way. He preaches his people straight into hell."[5] Let the fanatics judge you however they please. But you take comfort! This is nevertheless the correct way: Your job is to be assistants in bringing joy to Christians, not to subject them to the torture of the Law.

The longer you preach to your people in the way [Scripture describes **Why Missouri** above], the more they will praise God for giving them such a pastor. **If you Synod? should comb through all of church history—trust me on this—you will see that, despite its weaknesses and its defects, there are few church bodies**[6] **that have seen the successes that our synod has. That is not because of our cleverness. It is not because of our hard work. It is not because of our self- denial. No, the true reason is that we have preached the genuine Gospel to the people.**

4　German, here and following: *Schwärmer.* The Latin-based "fanatic" or even "fan" has the same root meaning as the Greek-based "enthusiast." The German word comes from the violent image of a person driven by a swarm of bees.

5　The Dau text adds: "you would come down on your people with the Law much more forcefully."

6　German: *Kirchengemeinschaften.*

As soon as a desire for God's grace and mercy bubbles up in the heart of listeners, when they think: "Yes! I, too, can still go to heaven," they are believers. Many remain stuck in their sins because they think: "I cannot get to the point where I can go to heaven. The pastor is such a godly man. I could never be that God-fearing." Do not hesitate to preach the Gospel of the grace of God in Christ Jesus frankly and cheerfully. Then such gloomy thoughts will vanish from the heart of your listeners.

Now, hear two quotations from the Book of Concord that show that our church, too, in its confessional writings has declared that the doctrine of the grace of God in Christ Jesus is a matter of primary importance.

Augsburg Confession, Article IV:

AC IV   Our churches teach that people cannot be justified before God by their own strength, merits, or works. People are freely justified for Christ's sake, through faith, when they believe that they are received into favor and that their sins are forgiven for Christ's sake. By His death, Christ made satisfaction for our sins. God counts this faith for righteousness in His sight (Romans 3 and 4 [3:21–26; 4:5]).[7]

Smalcald Articles, Part II, Article I:

SA II 1 5   Nothing of this article can be yielded or surrendered, even though heaven and earth and everything else falls.[8]

For there is no other name under heaven given among men by which we must be saved. (Acts 4:12)

And with His stripes we are healed. (Isaiah 53:5)

Upon this article everything that we teach and practice depends, in opposition to the pope, the devil, and the whole world. Therefore, we must be certain and not doubt this doctrine. Otherwise, all is lost, and the pope, the devil, and all adversaries win the victory and the right over us.[9]

W² 9:8
(cf. AE 27:145)   Now, hear a word from **Luther** that you should memorize and that you should use diligently. It is found in his *Preface to the Epistle to the Galatians* (St. Louis Ed. 9:8) and reads: "In my heart there reigns, and will ever reign, this one article, namely, faith in my dear Lord Christ. This alone is the beginning, middle, and end of all spiritual and godly thoughts that I may have at any time, day or night."

---

7   *Concordia*, 33. See also Müller, 39; *Triglot Concordia*, 45.

8   See Mark 13:31.

9   *Concordia*, 263. See also Müller, 300; *Triglot Concordia*, 461.

Luther might as well have said "in my sermons and writings," instead of "in my heart," for so it is indeed.[10] No one can preach the Gospel more sweetly and gloriously than our dear Luther.[11] Not only does he offer great comfort in his sermons, but he preaches in such a way as to lay hold of any doubting listener and drag him out of his doubts, compelling him to believe that he is a child of God and would die saved if he were to die that night.

Praise God, if only that testimony were given about you when you enter the ministry! Pray to God on your knees for His help in order that you may repeat Luther's confession. If only all pastors could repeat this confession, and—alas—I sadly must add: "all pastors in the Missouri Synod!" For even here [in our synod], pastors are not all alike. Some have a legalistic tendency, which does great harm to their own soul and those of their listeners. Some do not carry out their office with genuine cheerfulness and do not make their people cheerful Christians. But that is what you will have to do to achieve wonderful results. If you preach the Gospel abundantly, you need not fear that your people will leave your church for some spiritual snake oil salesman[12] who comes along and puts on a big show in his pulpit. Your people will say, "Our pastor gives us what we could not get anywhere else. He is a true Lutheran pastor and pours out a great treasure for us every Sunday."

"Old Missouri" was not perfect

Luther on John 17:10 (St. Louis Ed. 8:798):

Let everyone, then, see for himself how Christ is glorified in him. For there are many who boast of the Gospel and know how to talk a great deal about it. But having Christ glorified in yourself is not so common that it happens to everybody.

For, as we were told, glorifying Christ, or believing in Him, is nothing else than being certain that whoever has Him has the Father and all grace, divine blessings, and life eternal. The saints of this world, the pope, and the sectarian spirits cannot achieve that. For, though some talk about Christ and manage to speak words that He is the Son of God, that He has redeemed us, etc., they never learn by their own experience how a person must receive Him, use Him, seek Him, find Him, and hold fast to Him, and how to take hold of the Father in and

W² 8:798
(cf. AE 69:69–70)

---

10   The Dau text adds: "for his sermons and writings conform to the above rule."

11   The Dau text speaks of "our beloved Luther." As the Missouri Synod made the transition to English, professors and church officials began to translate the German adjective *lieb* as "beloved." Thus *unsere liebe Synode* became "our beloved Synod." "Our dear Luther" and "our dear Synod" are the appropriate translations for the present.

12   Walther's term is *Marktschreier*, something like a barker, hawker, or front man in an open-air market or on a carnival midway. "Snake oil salesman" is of that same genre, but it is more familiar. Think again of Walther's references to nineteenth-century quacks selling false cures off the back of their wagons at the farmers' market.

through Him.[13] Meanwhile, they soar up into the clouds and busy themselves with their own imaginations.

You can see this in some of our sectarian spirits, who have learned from us to speak of Christ and of faith. Yet **how rarely they promote**[14] **this doctrine, yes, how cold and inept they are** whenever they have to touch on **this chief point of doctrine**. How they rush over texts such as these and merely skim their surface, regarding this matter as an unimportant thing that everybody is able to do quite well.[15]

When you examine your sermons to see how much you used the Law and how much you used the comfort of the Gospel, you may find: "Oh, there is barely any room for the Gospel!" Now, [I say to] the preacher who steps out of his pulpit without having preached enough Gospel—so that some poor sinner who may have come to church for the first and the last time is not saved—woe to him! [That sinner's] blood will be required of [that preacher]!

W² 8:798
(cf. AE 69:70)

To sum up, these people are full of other thoughts, and even when they hit on something worthwhile, as will happen occasionally, they have no real understanding of it and immediately skip on to their dreams. **A true pastor, however, urges this article most of all, yes, without stopping**, since on it is based everything that pertains to the knowledge of God and our salvation, as you see in the Gospel of John and throughout the Epistles of Paul.

It is most important that your heart be full of this topic and that you speak of it from personal experience. When you reach this point in your sermons, you are forced to confess to your listeners that you cannot fully express all that you have experienced, that it frustrates all efforts to describe it in words, and that you can only stammer a few inadequate words about it. A preacher of this sort will soon notice that streams of the Holy Spirit are poured out on his congregation and that even the most hardened sinners are brought to Christ by the comforting preaching they have just heard.

We must not assume that saving knowledge is always produced in hearers by powerful preaching of the Law. Many people are convinced that they would go to hell if they were to die immediately. But when they hear a real Gospel

---

13   Compare this statement with LC II 66 (*Concordia*, 406). The statement has the same grammatical structure and makes a similar argument as the passage in the Large Catechism. This point is important for understanding both Luther and Walther as one properly distinguishes Law and Gospel. See also *One True God: Understanding Large Catechism II 66* (St. Louis: Concordia, 2006).

14   The German *treiben* can mean to treat or discuss in an applied sense. It can also have the sense of making the doctrine a part of one's life and practice. "Promote" is an umbrella word for these various interpretations.

15   This portion of Luther's sermons on John appears also in AE 69 (St. Louis: Concordia, 2009).

sermon, full of the richest consolation, it may readily happen that some of them are brought around to Christ.

Luther's *House Postil* on Psalm 68:18 (St. Louis Ed. 13:2014):[16]

What a King is this who has ascended on high, sat down above the clouds, at the right hand of Majesty in heaven, and has made captivity [itself] captive! While on earth, He was not engaged in child's play and busy work,[17] but captured an everlasting enemy and a great prison. Sin and the devil had made captive the entire world. He in turn made them captive. Even if sin and the devil are against me and want to torment me, nevertheless they cannot harm me in the least if I hold fast to Christ.

W² 13:2014–15

How foolish pastors are who preach for a long time without any success and then decide to preach nothing but the Law for a while, in order to awaken their people from their spiritual sleep! If they use that method, they will accomplish nothing.

This does not mean preached [in such a way] that the people become lazy and do no good works, as the Papists condemn us [of doing] and call us "sweet preachers."[18]

W² 13:2015

Luther would rather hear that he preaches too sweetly—sweetly preaching, that is, full of comfort—for that is the least of accusations. I would [also] happily bear this criticism. And if people were to say that my preaching prevents people from doing good works—well, it is just the opposite. I preach the very thing that alone can change their hearts so that they will do good works.

However, they would change their tone if they landed in *this* prison. When they stand at the left hand of the Judge, and anguish and terror get hold of them, they will experience what this prison means. Therefore, this is not a sermon for people's flesh and blood, as if they were given freedom to do according to their desires. But the point of Christ's ascension and His rule is to make sin captive, to prevent eternal death from putting us in shackles and keeping us there.

W² 13:2015

Now, if sin is to be made captive, I—a believer in Christ—must live in such a way that I am not overcome by hatred and envy of my

Ps. 68:18

---

16 This is the first sermon for Ascension Day on Acts 1:1–11. See also John Nicholas Lenker, ed., *Complete Sermons of Martin Luther*, trans. John Nicholas Lenker et al. (Grand Rapids: Baker, 1983, 2000), 6:121–22.

17 Literally, "child's play and crap [work]." German: *Kinderspiel und Dreck[werk]*. The first and second Walch editions handle Luther's earthiness with slight differences. Social standards and sensibilities differed in Luther's time. In Walther's time, sensibilities were already changing. Luther's language is not appropriate today.

18 In Luther's time, as in Shakespeare's, to call a man "nice" or "sweet" would be like calling him a "fairy."

fellow humans or by other sins. Rather, I must fight against sin and say: "Listen, sin! You want to stir me up to become angry, to envy, to commit adultery, to steal, to be unfaithful, etc. This I will not do." Likewise, if sin wants to assault me from another angle and fill me with terror, I must say: "No, sin. You are my servant, and I am your lord. Have you never heard what David sang about my Lord Jesus Christ: 'You ascended on high,' etc.? Until now, you have been a hangman and a devil to me. You have taken me prisoner. But now I believe in Christ, and you will be my hangman no longer. I will not permit you to accuse me, for you are a prisoner of my Lord and King, who has put you in the stocks and cast you beneath my feet."

Understand this matter correctly: By His ascension and by the preaching of faith, Christ does not mean to rear lazy and sluggish Christians who say, "We will now live according to our pleasure, not doing good works, remaining sinners, and following sin like captive slaves." **People who talk in this way do not have a right understanding of the preaching of faith.** Christ and His mercy are not preached so that people should remain in their sins. On the contrary, this is what Christian doctrine proclaims: The prison should release you—not so you may do whatever you desire, but so that you will sin no more.

Luther is telling us to preach the real Gospel with its comfort without hesitation, and not to fear that we would preach people into hell with the Gospel. True, some may take carnal comfort from our Gospel preaching, but we must not think that they will have an easy death with their false comfort. In the presence of death their comfort will vanish like snow in a March sun. We are not responsible for any false comfort that a listener might draw from our preaching. Such listeners live in security and imagine that they are not so awfully wicked, that they have many good traits. Even though they drink occasionally and curse, these are merely bad habits that still cling to them, etc. They will undoubtedly go to heaven, so they think. Such people have never received into their hearts the Gospel that was preached to them.

Mark 16:15   Do not allow occurrences of this kind to disturb you. You must cheerfully preach the Gospel, since Christ commanded His disciples to "go into all the world and proclaim the gospel to the whole creation."

Sometimes all hope seems to vanish from those who have lived in false comfort because they had imagined that they were basing their confidence on what their faithful pastor had preached. A pastor may have an awful time with such people when he prepares them for their departure from this world; they seem to despair of salvation. **God grant that someday people may say about you that you are preaching well, but much too sweetly!** Do not spend too much time on the Law. Let the Gospel follow immediately. When the Law has made the iron red hot, immediately apply the Gospel and shape it into a proper form. Because once the iron has cooled, you can do nothing with it.

Lastly, **Luther** writes in his *House Postil* (St. Louis Ed. 13:800ff.):[19]

Luther has the last word;
W² 13:800–801;
Matt. 7:16

Now this is the second rule that the Lord gives: we are to let go of external appearances and look for fruits. He says, "You will recognize them by their fruits." He offers a parable to show this.[20] No one among you is so foolish as to go into a field full of thorns and thistles and look for grapes and figs. Such fruit we seek on a different plant, which is not so prickly and thorny. The same thing happens in our gardens. When they see a tree full of apples or pears, everybody exclaims: "Ah, what a fine tree that is!" Again, where a tree bears no fruit or when the fruit is worm-eaten, cracked, and misshaped, everybody would say, "That tree is worthless, good for nothing except to be cut down and thrown into the oven so that a better tree may be planted in its place." The Lord says that if you apply these same principles to the false prophets, you will not make a mistake—no matter how good their appearance may be. Even if a wolf puts on twenty sheepskins, you still need to recognize that he is a wolf, so he will not deceive you.

Now, what is the fruit of a true prophet or preacher by which we can know that he is not a wolf, but a good sheep? It is not his way of living, his title and office, nor his special gifts and graces. For our Lord Himself testifies, along with what our experience teaches, that people are often duped and deceived by these external marks. The genuine fruit—as the Lord states at the end of His parable—is doing the will of the Father in heaven.[21]

Note here that the Lord is not speaking of Christians in general, but of prophets. But, of course, *all* Christians are to do the will of the Father and are to be saved by doing it.

Matt. 7:21

We are frequently misunderstood. People imagine they can recognize a true prophet by the fruit of his godly life and by his great success in the ministry. But Christ says, "Not everyone who says to Me, 'Lord, Lord,' will enter the kingdom of heaven, but the one who does the will of My Father who is in heaven."

---

19   This is the sermon on Matthew 7:15–23 for the Eighth Sunday after Trinity. This version does not appear in John Nicholas Lenker, ed., *Complete Sermons of Martin Luther*, trans. John Nicholas Lenker et al. (Grand Rapids: Baker, 1983, 2000).

20   See Matthew 7:15–20.

21   See Matthew 7:19–20.

W² 13:801–2;
John 6:40

Now, "doing the will of the Father" refers not only to the will that one does in the Ten Commandments, of which God requires obedience. Since we cannot do this will of God completely in the present life, it would be impossible for us to glory in having done the will of the Father. Therefore, we could not go to heaven. But the Father's will [also] means what Christ says in John 6:40: "For this is the will of My Father, that everyone who looks on the Son and believes in Him should have eternal life, and I will raise him up on the last day." That is the only way in which we all, preachers and listeners, are to walk if we are to be saved. Now, in this passage the Lord speaks, in particular, of preachers or prophets, whose real and proper fruit is nothing else than this: that they diligently proclaim this will of God to the people. They should teach them that God is gracious and merciful and has no pleasure in the death of sinners, but wants them to live. Moreover, they should teach that God has revealed His mercy by having His only-begotten Son become man.

Now, whoever receives Him and believes in Him, that is, whoever takes comfort in the fact that, for the sake of His Son, God will be merciful to them, will forgive their sins, and grant them eternal salvation, etc.—**whoever is engaged in this preaching of the pure Gospel and thus directs people to Christ, the only mediator between God and people, he, as a preacher, is doing the will of God.** That is the genuine fruit by which no one is deceived or duped. For even if the devil himself were to preach this truth, this preaching would not be false or made up of lies—and a person believing it would have what it promises.

After **this fruit**, which is **the principal and most trustworthy one** and which cannot deceive, there follow in the course of time other fruits, namely, a life in beautiful harmony with this doctrine and in no way contrary to it. But these fruits should **be regarded as genuine fruits only where** the **first** fruit, namely, **the doctrine** of Christ, already exists.

WALTHER'S BOOK OF CONCORD

Until the middle of the nineteenth century, the Evangelical Lutheran Church determined its confessional position based on the 1580 German text and 1584 Latin text of the *Book of Concord*. (See, for example, the 1851 English edition of the *Book of Concord* by S. D. Henkel and his brothers.) Toward the latter part of the nineteenth century, Johann Tobias Müller's edition of the Lutheran Confessions became the standard reference work. The Müller edition would form the basis for all modern editions.

The influence of Müller includes the 1880 Anniversary Edition of the 1580 German *Book of Concord* printed by Concordia Publishing House. This edition and its revised print run in 1881 included page references to Müller in the margins. Yet Walther and the Missouri Synod followed only the German text of Müller. Walther preferred the German text of the 1580 *Book of Concord*, of which Walther had an original copy. In its Articles of Incorporation from 1894 to the present, the Missouri Synod has declared the 1580 German text to be its confessional standard.[1]

Henry E. Jacobs produced both scholarly and lay English editions of the *Book of Concord* in 1911 based on Müller with additional research.

In 1917, Concordia Publishing House published the *Triglot Concordia*, a Latin-German-English edition based on a corrected eleventh Müller edition. Its Latin title is also well-known: *Concordia Triglotta*. Unlike the 1880 edition, the *Triglot Concordia* uses both the Latin text and the German text where its editors, William H. T. Dau and G. Friedrich Bente, believe such use to be important. *Concordia: The Lutheran Confessions*, a reader's edition of the Lutheran Confessions published in 2006 by Concordia Publishing House, is based on the *Triglot*.

In 1930, the Müller edition was replaced by the *Bekenntnisschriften*, which in turn was revised in 1952 and has been reprinted since as a standard critical edition. Other editions based on the *Bekenntnisschriften* include the 1959 edition edited by Theodore Tappert and the edition edited by Robert Kolb and Timothy J. Wengert that was published in 2000.

Concordia: The Lutheran Confessions has a conscious awareness of the 1580 German text, though it is based on *Triglot Concordia*. English texts of the *Book of Concord*—from the Jacobs and *Triglot* editions to that of Kolb and Wengert—have taken various positions on what Latin or German editions to translate. The result is that the Dau translation of Walther's *Law and Gospel*,

---

1   See, for example, the 1924 *Synodalhandbuch*, 99; and the 2007 *Handbook*, 202.

because it picks up the English text from the *Triglot*, sometimes uses Latin texts where Walther uses the German. This does not change much in terms of meaning, but it can make the text sound awkward. Where possible, the choice for this edition of *Law and Gospel* is to cite *Concordia: The Lutheran Confessions*. When that conflicts with Walther's language, a translation has been made of Walther's German text.

APPENDIX TWO

WALTHER AND THE CHURCH FATHERS

The first lecture in Walther's series on Law and Gospel was delivered on September 12, 1884, which followed shortly after Walther presented an essay at the 1884 assembly of the Evangelical Lutheran Synodical Conference of North America. In the essay, Walther rejects entirely the notion of deriving doctrine from the Church Fathers and takes aim at the popular Anglo-American idea of "common sense," the idea that people are basically good when given enough freedom.[1] Walther used the English phrase in his German text.

The presentation given at the Synodical Conference is important because it explains why there are few quotes in the Law and Gospel lectures from any Lutherans other than Luther himself. Walther occasionally includes material from Johann Gerhard and Martin Chemnitz, but from few others. Yet Walther includes a greater proportion of quotes from various Lutherans and other Church Fathers in the 1875 edition of *Church and Ministry*.

The more extensive use of the Church Fathers in Walther's mid-career work on church and ministry reflects his changing attitude regarding the Church Fathers. At the start of his career, he uses only the citations of the Church Fathers included in the Book of Concord. Later, Walther was encouraged by the works of orthodox Lutheran authors to study the Church Fathers more extensively.[2] However, beginning in 1881, because the antagonists of the Missouri Synod claimed that Walther was using the Church Fathers instead of Scripture as a source of doctrine, Walther became sharply critical of using their works. That criticism emerges at several points in the Law and Gospel lectures.

---

1 Several English and French philosophers helped form the idea that people, left in their natural state, tend to be good. That premise helps to form American political identity.

2 In the pages of *Lehre und Wehre*, F. A. Crämer translated the 1605 *Compendium of Patristic Theology* by Heinrich Eckhardt from Latin into German. This translation ran serially from 1875 to 1883. It was never finished. It shows that the Missouri Synod viewed the Church Fathers through a Lutheran lens.

APPENDIX THREE

OTHER PRIMARY SOURCES

Walther wrote several articles published in *Lehre und Wehre* that oppose both pietistic and rationalist positions. These articles include "Is It Really Lutheran Doctrine, That the Salvation of Mankind Finally Rests on Man's Own, Free Decision," which ran from July to December 1872.[1] From 1875 through 1878, an unsigned article in *Lehre und Wehre*, "What About the Progress of Modern Lutheran Theology in Doctrine?" sparred mainly with the theologians of the University of Erlangen to show how their theology may sound Lutheran but differs from that of Luther, Chemnitz, and other orthodox Lutherans.[2]

Johann A. Hügli dealt with related issues involving the "analogy of faith" in the Northern District *Proceedings* of 1876 and 1877. Walther confronted the issue in his 1877 book on the Formula of Concord.[3] In 1880, Walther published another article in *Lehre und Wehre* about "The History of Dogma Concerning the Doctrine of the Relationship of Faith to Predestination."[4]

Walther includes in his lectures on Law and Gospel a number of arguments made in these and other sources, including Walther's 1881 pamphlet, *Dispute Concerning the Doctrine of Predestination, That Is, Simple, Proven Advice for Pious Christians That Would Greatly Desire to Know Who, in the Current Controversy Over the Doctrine of Predestination, Teaches in a Lutheran Manner and in an Un-Lutheran Manner.*[5] Other materials published in 1881 by Walther through Concordia Publishing House include: *The Doctrine of Predestination in Question and Answer Drawn from the Eleventh Article of the Formula of Concord of the Evangelical Lutheran Church* and the essay *Illumination of Stellhorn's Tract on the Dispute Concerning Predestination.*[6]

---

1   "Ist es wirklich lutherische Lehre: daß die Seligkeit des Menschen im letzten Grunde auf des Menschen freier, eigener Entscheidung beruhe?"

2   "Was ist es um den Fortschritt der modernen lutherischen Theologie in der Lehre?"

3   *Der Concordienformel: Kern und Stern* (St. Louis: M. C. Barthel, 1877).

4   "Dogmengeschichtliches über das Verhältniß des Glaubens zur Gnadenwahl."

5   C. F. W. Walther, *Gnadenwahlslehrstreit, das ist, einfacher, bewährter Rath für gottselige Christen, welche gern wissen möchten, wer in dem jetzigen Gnadenwahlslehrstreit lutherisch und wer unlutherisch lehre* (St. Louis: Concordia, 1881).

6   Two sources include *Die Lehre von der Gnadenwahl in Frage und Antwort dargestellt aus dem elften Artikel der Concordienformel der evangelisch-lutherischen Kirche* and *Beleuchtung des Stellhorn'schen Tractats über den Gnadenwahlslehrstreit.*

Later publications include Carl Manthey Zorn's presentation in two parts about conversion and election and Franz A. O. Pieper's book on finding unity amid the opposing positions concerning predistination.[7]

---

7   Carl Manthey Zorn, *Bekehrung und Gnadenwahl*, 2 vols. (St. Louis: Concordia, 1902); Franz A. O. Pieper, *Zur Einigung der amerikanisch-lutherischen Kirche in der Lehre von der Bekehrung und Gnadenwahl* (St. Louis: Concordia, 1913).

READING KEY
FOR *GOD'S NO AND GOD'S YES*

G od's No and God's Yes (hereafter *No and Yes*) was a student edition of
Walther's Law and Gospel lectures in greatly condensed format. It was
published by Concordia Publishing House in 1973. The table below provides
a reading key for those who want to use this reader's edition in a classroom
setting in which *No and Yes* might previously have been assigned reading.

The introduction to *No and Yes* on page 6 describes the condensed text as
"hazardous," yet the intent was to make Walther's lectures accessible to a wider
audience. This reader's edition offers some of the same helpful approaches as
No and Yes without condensation. *No and Yes* says that it deletes "the extensive quotes from the Lutheran Confessions, Martin Luther, and the dogmaticians," yet it also deletes Scripture texts that Walther used and refers to only
a few Bible passages, sometimes without quoting them. In contrast, both the
original German notes and the Dau translation show that Walther intended
to speak *with the very words* of Scripture, the Book of Concord, Luther, and
the writers of the Lutheran dogmatic tradition.

The reader and teacher using *No and Yes* will notice that Walther uses the
pronoun "I" in places where this edition uses "you." That occurs as a result
of Walther's particular literary device of setting himself on the same level
as his students with respect to Law and Gospel. Walther was trying to communicate to his hearers that he, like they, was a sinner who needed the pure
proclamation of Law and Gospel. For Walther, "I" plus "you" equals "we."
Since Walther has passed on, it is often clearer to render this dialectic, this
wechselseitige Redensart, as "you" except where Walther specifically makes
the point that he needs to stand under both Law and Gospel.

This reading key will enable students and professors to use this reader's
edition of Law and Gospel in the same helpful manner as *No and Yes* without
the drawbacks of the condensed text.

Section	*No and Yes*	*Law and Gospel: How to Read and Apply the Bible*
Walther's Introduction	page 13	pages 9–10
Theses Listing	pages 7–11	pages 2–5
Thesis I	pages 15–18	pages 11–12, 14–16, 18–22

Thesis II	page 19	pages 35–37, 45
Thesis III	pages 20–23	pages 49–53, 58–64
Thesis IV	pages 24–25	pages 69–70, 74–75
Thesis V	pages 26–28	pages 79–84
Thesis VI	pages 29–31	pages 89–93
Thesis VII	pages 32–34	pages 101–5
Thesis VIII	pages 35–40	pages 113–16, 127–32
Thesis IX	pages 41–53	pages 143–53, 167–69, 174–76, 184–87, 206–7, 212–14, 217–20, 225
Thesis X	pages 54–57	pages 229–33, 239–40, 243–47
Thesis XI	pages 58–61	pages 259–64, 270–71
Thesis XII	pages 62–66	pages 275–81
Thesis XIII	pages 67–69	pages 287–89
Thesis XIV	pages 70–71	pages 297–99
Thesis XV	pages 72–75	pages 309–11, 319–20, 326–28
Thesis XVI	pages 76–78	pages 333–37
Thesis XVII	pages 79–82	pages 343–46, 348–51
Thesis XVIII	pages 83–84	pages 355–58
Thesis XIX	pages 85–88	pages 363–68, 370–71
Thesis XX	pages 89–93	pages 375–81
Thesis XXI	pages 94–99	pages 389–92, 395–400, 402–3
Thesis XXII	pages 100–108	pages 409–16, 419–23
Thesis XXIII	pages 109–12	pages 429–36, 438
Thesis XXIV	pages 113–16	pages 443–52
Thesis XXV	pages 117–18	pages 455–59

Glossary

Absolution, Lutheran history of. In accord with AC XI (*Concordia*, 35–37), the Lutheran Church retained private confession and Absolution until around 1670. The rise of Pietism and Rationalism dealt a blow to the practice, but because of the confessional renewal efforts of Claus Harms and J. K. Wilhelm Löhe, Absolution experienced a resurgence in the nineteenth century. Walther did not favor private confession and Absolution, yet he did not oppose it, as the LCMS *Proceedings* of 1848 and section 16 of Walther's *Pastoraltheologie* indicate. The issue emerged again in the 1860 *Proceedings* of the LCMS. The 1875 *Proceedings* of the old Northwestern District (Wisconsin and Minnesota) have a Waltherian congregational model for generally public confession and Absolution, while the 1880 *Proceedings* of the Eastern District use Löhe's model and require pastors to teach and retain private confession and Absolution. From 1880–85, an article by G. Gößwein in *Lehre und Wehre* and the 1885 Nebraska District *Proceedings* appear to have settled the issue by finding a basis in Scripture and the Lutheran Confessions for both approaches. Practical concerns related to the topic concerned the Office of the Holy Ministry. Already in the LCMS *Proceedings* of 1847, the pastors and laity sent by Löhe approached issues with a general attitude of trust for the pastoral office, while the Saxon pastors and laity show a general mistrust of fallible human pastors in the wake of Martin Stephan's moral collapse. The LCMS did not divide during this fifty-year debate because all involved, while earnestly committed to Scripture and the Lutheran Confessions, understood the benefits of a united synod and therefore extended to each other a full measure of patience and Christian love as they carefully worked through the theological issues. See also **absolve; confession**.

absolve. To set free from sin. By virtue of his office, in the name and stead of Christ, a pastor absolves those who have confessed their sins, affirmed their faith in Christ, and promised to amend their lives (Matthew 16:19; 18:18; John 20:19–23). The Lutheran Church retains private confession and Absolution as "the very voice of the Gospel," declaring that it would be impious to abolish it (AC XI; Ap XI 2; SA III VIII; SC V).

Absolution may be called a Sacrament (Ap XIII 4). See also **Absolution, Lutheran history of; confession**.

accident. In philosophy, an attribute or property that may or may not belong to the subject of reference without affecting its substance. For example, the colors of a person's eyes, hair, and skin are "accidents" because they do not make that person any more or less human than all other people. They do help make that particular individual the special person that God intended. In theology, original sin is a prime example of an accident (see FC Ep I 23; FC SD I 31, 54). See also **substance**.

administer, administration. To faithfully deliver God's Word and Sacraments to the intended recipients.

anathema. From the Greek word for "cursed." In the New Testament and in Church terminology a solemn curse, pronounced in God's name on heretics and the ungodly (Galatians 1:8–9; 1 Corinthians 16:22). Designates eternal separation from God (Romans 9:3).

Anfechtung. This German word means much more than simply being afraid. In Luther's usage, *Anfechtung* is the all-consuming fear for one's life and salvation in light of God's right to condemn all sinners and in light of the unceasing attacks of the devil, the world, and the sinful flesh. Without the Gospel, someone experiencing this fear has no way of escape from certain doom and no hope.

Antinomianism. From Greek for "against the law." Adherents maintained that a Christian is free from all moral law and that the Gospel causes knowledge of sin and repentance. Some in this movement denied the third use of the Law and the role of the Law in good works. See also **Antinomians** (p. 489).

anxious bench. Seat near the speaker at some revivals. Designated specifically for those who are concerned about their spiritual condition. Also called "anxious seat" and "mourner's bench." See also **revival**.

apology. A public defense or clarification of stated belief.

apostasy. From Greek for "departing from a former state." A total lapsing from principles or faith. The New Testament mentions as causes of apostasy: the putting away of faith and a good conscience (1 Timothy 1:19–20), listening to seducing spirits and doctrines of devils (1 Timothy 4:1; 2 Timothy 4:4), shallowness (Luke 8:13), lack of spiritual insight (John 6:63–65), and love of the world (2 Timothy 4:10; Matthew 19:22). The Old Testament gives, among others, the following reasons: absence of spiritual leaders (Exodus 32:1), evil company (1 Kings 11:4), worldly success (Psalm 78:57; Hosea 6:4; Zephaniah 1:6).

apostle. One of the Twelve, or St. Paul, who was chosen by Jesus to guide the mission of the early Church.

Arianism. See **Arians** (p. 489); **Arius** (p. 489).

Arminianism. Term embracing in general the teachings of Jacobus Arminius, a minister in Amsterdam in the late sixteenth century. His theological views are: (1) From all eternity, God predestined to eternal life those whom He foresaw would remain steadfast in faith to their end. (2) Christ died for all mankind, not only for the elect. (3) Man cooperates in his conversion by free will. (4) Man may resist divine grace. (5) Man may fall from divine grace. The 1618–19 Synod of Dordrecht condemned Arminian doctrines, but the new view spread rapidly, moving into the Church of England and into French Calvinist theology. Much of what passed for Arminianism was in fact Pelagianism—synergism in some form. A modified Arminianism arose again in England in the Wesleyan Reformation of the seventeenth century; its ablest expositions may be found in the works of John Wesley and others. See also **Methodism**.

atheism. Denial of the existence of God. In its widest sense, it denotes the opposite of *theism* (the belief in a personal God) and includes *pantheism* (God is in and throughout creation) and *Deism* (an impersonal God that drives natural phenomena). In a more restricted sense, it denotes the denial of the Deity above and outside of the physical universe. In the most commonly accepted sense, it is a denial of anything that may be called "God." The materialism of the eighteenth and nineteenth centuries, together with Charles Darwin's theory of evolution by natural selection, have given strong impetus to atheistic trends of thought. In France, the eighteenth century produced many writers opposed to the idea of a personal God, among them the encyclopedists Denis Diderot and Voltaire. The nineteenth-century German materialists—among them Karl Marx—were equally outspoken. Of the great religions of the world, Buddhism, Jainism, and a strain of Brahman philosophy deny the existence of a personal God. Despite claims to the contrary, no amount of reasoning can erase from the human heart the God-given conviction that there is a Supreme Being; those who theoretically deny God's existence replace Him with something else. Likewise, no people group has ever been found entirely devoid of religious belief. See also **encyclopedists** (p. 492).

atonement. Consider the word: *at-one-ment*. It properly reflects a mutual exchange or a drawing together of parties previously separated. From the Old Testament sacrifices to the cross, the sins of God's people were laid on a blameless victim who took their place and bore God's wrath. God's action of obedience and sacrifice in Christ to forgive sin restored the relationship between Himself and His fallen creatures.

attrition. Term used by Roman theologians. Hatred of sin arising from love of the offended God is called "perfect *contrition*," while other motives—such as fear of hell and of punishment, or realization of the heinousness of sin—are called *attrition*. The Roman Church teaches that attrition alone does not justify, but that it prepares the penitent to receive grace and that if people properly receive the sacrament of penance, they are justified. See also **contrition**.

audible Word. See under **Means of Grace; Word of God**.

Calvinism. See **Calvin, John** (p. 491)

carnal. Of the body; earthly, fleshly, sinful, temporal, worldly. This word often has a negative meaning of following the temptations of the sinful flesh in the present world.

catechism. Primarily a manual of religious instruction, often published in question-and-answer format. For example, see *Concordia*, 307–48.

catechumen. A person receiving instruction and examination in the basics of the Christian faith and life, leading either to Baptism and/or confirmation.

cause. A Greek philosophical term used in scholastic theology also used during the period of Lutheran orthodoxy. A system of cause and effect describes how the world changes and remains the same. Tangible matter is the passive, *material cause* that an agent or subject (*efficient cause*) shapes through the structure of his thought (*formal cause*) toward a specific goal (*final cause*). For example, when speaking of the operation of the Holy Spirit through Scripture to create faith, the *material cause* is Scripture: human words written down. Yet those words do not come from human agents but are the inspired Word of God (*formal cause*) flowing from the Holy Spirit (*efficient cause*) in order to create faith and new life in a Christian (*final cause*). For an English explanation of the Latin terms, see also Richard A. Muller, *A Dictionary of Latin and Greek Theological Terms* (Grand Rapids: Baker, 1995).

chrism. In Roman Catholicism, this mixture of olive oil and balm is applied after Baptism, at confirmation, and at the conferring of holy orders.

Christology, kenotic. Along with Gottfried Thomasius, Karl Kahnis believed that Jesus Christ emptied Himself of such operative, or relative, divine attributes as omnipotence, omniscience, and omnipresence. Johann C. K. von Hofmann, as well as W. H. C. F. Gess, went further to say that Christ emptied Himself of all divine attributes or that a human personality replaced the divine.

church. In the simplest modern sense, a building in which believers gather for worship. The basic sense in the New Testament is an assembly of people. It can refer to a local congregation and to the universal Church (Ephesians 1:22). In combination, the word "church" carries much theological meaning. The Church is the Body of Christ created and sustained by God (1 Corinthians 12), the new Israel (Galatians 6:16). Because of human sin, Lutherans speak of the *invisible* Church as all true believers that God sees to be part of the Body of Christ as compared with the *visible* church—those whom people see as calling themselves Christians but whose true heart, whether believing or hypocritical, remains hidden. One may also refer to "church" with respect to a given place or time.

Many speak of the Church Militant that is still engaged in fighting the powers of this world (Ephesians 6:12) and the Church Triumphant, those who rest from their labors and celebrate their victory in Christ before the throne of God in heaven (Revelation 14:13).

closed Communion. Biblical practice (Matthew 18:15–20; 1 Corinthians 11:18–34) of administration of the Sacrament whereby Communion fellowship is limited to members of a common confession of faith, usually a synod or denomination, including also groupings of denominations that formally recognize their common faith. Part of that confession is the loving pastoral practice of keeping willful sinners and those having false beliefs regarding the Lord's Supper from receiving it to their judgment.

concupiscence. The material element of original sin (AC II 4), which seeks and loves carnal things (not only sinful lusts of the body but also carnal wisdom and righteousness), ignores and despises God, lacks fear and trust in Him, hates His judgment and flees it, is angry at Him, despairs of His mercy, and trusts in temporal things (Romans 7:7, 23; 1 Corinthians 2:14; Ap II). The Roman Church regards concupiscence as the tendency to sin, but not itself to be actual sin.

condign merit. According to Roman Church teaching, the reward people gain for themselves by grace. This kind of merit is rewarded for a good deed that fulfills its goal. Its premise is that God rewards the actions of believers out of a sense of justice, as holding a debt, for the work performed. The Roman Church teaches that extra amounts of goodness produced by works having condign merit flow into a treasury that can be tapped by, for example, indulgences. The Lutheran Confessions reject the distinctions of condignity and congruity as screens for Pelagianism (Ap IV 19), robbing Christ of His honor, giving it to people (Ap V 195–97), and leading eventually to doubt and despair (Ap V 200). See also **congruent merit; indulgences**.

confession. Has two general meanings: (1) Acknowledgment, admission, or disclosure of one's own sins. Confession is beneficial and should be embraced as an opportunity to renew the rejection of Satan made at Baptism and to receive forgiveness in Christ through the Gospel. Confession is necessary when a believer has committed a coarse, premeditated sin (see the discussion in Thesis X, pp. 229–42). The Lutheran Confessions reject both the requirement and even the possibility of enumerating all sins in confession (AC XI; Ap XI; SA III III) but insist on retaining private confession, though they grant that it is a human establishment of the Church. The Absolution that follows confession is the "living voice of the Gospel" (Ap XI; SC V). (2) Speaking in unity with others of the same faith (John 9:22; Romans 10:9; Philippians 2:11; 1 Timothy 3:16; 1 John 4:3; 2 John 7; Revelation 3:5). See also **confession, history of**.

confession, history of. In the Old Testament, confession of sin is both formal (Leviticus 5:5; Numbers 5:6–8) and personal, private, or spontaneous (Psalm 32; 51). In the New Testament, confession of sins is prominent in the ministry of John the Baptist (Matthew 3:6), as well as in the early Church (Acts 19:18; James 5:16; 1 John 1:9). The mode of confession or the person to receive it is not dictated in the New Testament or in the writings of the early Church. We do, however, see both a private and a public element of opportunities to confess sin (Leviticus 16:21; 26:40; Numbers 5:7; Matthew 18:15–17; James 5:16; 1 John 1:8–9). Tertullian and Cyprian associated acts of reparation with the act of confessing mortal sins—notably murder, idolatry or apostasy, and coarse sexual offenses. That became part of the basis for the threefold Roman Catholic sacrament of penance: heartfelt contrition, oral confession, and satisfaction of works. The Western Church tended to focus on satisfaction and restitution by the offender to the one offended (cf. Numbers 5:7). The Eastern Church tended to focus on healing between the sinner and God (cf. Psalm 32:5). In the Western Church, private confession of sins before a priest replaced public discipline of coarse offenders. In modern Roman Catholicism, confession usually refers to the sacrament of penance. Roman Catholicism and Anglicanism normally speak of the sacrament of penance. Eastern Orthodoxy speaks of the mystery of reconciliation. Lutheranism can refer to Absolution as a sacrament. Other Christians see confession as merely symbolic. See also **Absolution, Lutheran history of**.

Confessions, Lutheran. Statements of faith gathered in the 1580 *Book of Concord* that are intended for public use and that set forth with authority certain articles of belief. The documents identified by the catch-all phrase "Lutheran Confessions" or, simply, "the Confessions" include: the Augsburg Confession, the Apology of the Augsburg Confession, the Smalcald Articles, the Treatise on the Power and Primacy of the Pope, the Small Catechism, the Large Catechism, and the Formula of Concord. Lutherans consider these documents to be expositions of the Bible passages that pertain to articles of belief. Thus while Lutherans refer to the Confessions for doctrinal positions, the true source of these positions is always God's Word.

confessor. A pastor who hears private confession and pronounces Absolution. See also **Absolution, Lutheran history of; absolve; confession**.

congruent merit. According to Roman Church teaching, the reward people gain for themselves by their own power, even if the work of merit does not succeed in its goal. Similar to an "E" for effort, this merit is based on the understanding that God rewards the actions of believers on the basis of His own liberality. See also **condign merit**.

consistory. An administrative board consisting entirely, or chiefly, of clergy.

contrition. Movement of the heart prior to conversion, namely, "that the heart perceive sin, [and] dread God's wrath" (FC SD II 70). Scripture teaches two truths about contrition: (1) Contrition always precedes genuine conversion (FC SD II 70). Fear of God's wrath and damnation always precedes faith (Joel 2:12; Mark 1:15; Luke 15:18; 18:13; 24:47; Acts 2:37; 16:29; FC SD II 54, 70). True contrition is not active, that is, fabricated remorse, but passive, that is, true sorrow of the heart, suffering, and pain of death (SA III III 2). It should not be concluded from this that contrition is a cause of forgiveness (Romans 3:28). (2) Contrition in no way brings about, implements, or occasions justification through faith (FC SD II 30–31). See also **attrition**.

conversion. In the wider sense, this term designates the entire process whereby man is transferred from his carnal state into a spiritual state of faith and grace and then enters, and under the continued influence of the Holy Spirit continues in, a state of faith and spiritual life. Conversion in the narrower sense is essentially the bestowal of faith in God's promise of salvation for Christ's sake. It takes place in the heart and consists in this: that a heart, broken and contrite because of sin, comes to faith in Christ and trusts in Christ for grace and forgiveness (Acts 11:21). It takes place when the Holy Spirit engenders faith in the hearts of penitents through the Word of God (Law and Gospel) and the Sacraments (Isaiah 55:10–11; John 1:45–50; 6:63; Acts 8:34–38; 16:13–34; Romans 1:16; 10:17).

Council of Trent. See **Trent, Council of**.

decision theology. Belief that one must make a conscious decision to accept Christ. Stands in contrast to the biblical teaching about sin and faith affirmed by the Council of Ephesus in 431. Augustine, Luther, and Calvin all rejected forms of decision theology like the ideas of Pelagius, who spoke of faith as a decision to unlock a path of righteous works that leads to God. Evangelical and Fundamentalist Protestant preachers, such as Billy Graham, have popularized the altar call, a moment of decision based on confrontation with one's sin and need for salvation. It is thus a form of Arminian theology that affirms cooperation between man's free will and the grace of God in salvation. It opposes the doctrine of regeneration that says the Holy Spirit must first kindle faith in the heart of sinful man. Infant Baptism tends to be neglected by believers of decision theology. See also **Arminianism**.

Diet. The legislative assembly composed of lay and clerical leaders of the major constituent states and free cities of the Holy Roman Empire. These semiautonomous states, in turn, had territories and cities under their representation and administration. The organizational model is similar to the states' rights model of viewing the United States Constitution. The Diet, or Imperial Congress, moved to different cities as necessary until it was permanently located at Regensburg in 1663. Among its members were the Electoral College, the group of four lay princes and three prince-bishops who elected the king of Germany, who in turn could be consecrated as emperor by the pope or remain "emperor-elect." Charles V was the last consecrated Holy Roman emperor of the German nation. His successors were content with the title "emperor-elect."

Divine Service. The worship opportunity to be forgiven by God for sin. At the time of the Lutheran Confessions until around 1670, the Divine Service (German: *Gottesdienst*) included the celebration of the Mass or Lord's Supper at least every Sunday (Ap XV 40; XXIV 1). Pietism reduced the celebration of the Lord's Supper to about four times per year. The Divine Service in the Lutheran tradition normally includes confession and Absolution, the reading of Scripture, the sermon that properly distinguishes and applies Law and Gospel, prayer, and the Lord's Supper.

doctrine. The teachings, principles, or tenets held and spread by a group.

dogma. A doctrine or doctrines (usually of the Church) considered authoritative on their own merits.

Donatism. A fourth-century movement that believed persecution was a mark of the Church and that sin is a disease that is passed from one infected person to another. By this thinking, Sacraments administered by a priest who fell away from faith or deserved excommunication were invalid. A church failing to excommunicate such leaders ceased to be the true Church, and its Baptism became invalid. See also **Donatists** (p. 492).

Dordrecht, Synods of. Gatherings of the Reformed churches of Holland and Zeeland (now the Netherlands). The first meeting was in 1574 and established church structure and doctrine, specifically determining that ministers and teachers would subscribe only the Belgic Confession and use only the Heidelberg Catechism. Adherence to the Belgic Confession and the Heidelberg Catechism were reiterated at the subsequent gathering in 1578 and in the assembly that met from November 13, 1618, to May 1619. This latter synod also rejected Arminianism. See also **Arminianism**.

Dort, Synod of. See **Dordrecht, Synods of.**

ecclesiastical. Having to do with the Church, its leadership, ritual, or members.

efficient cause. See under **cause**.

elder. Term derived from the Old and New Testaments (Exodus 3:16; Luke 7:3). The Greek word *presbyteros*, "elder," is a synonym for *episkopos*, "bishop" (Acts 20:17, 28), "ruler" (1 Timothy 5:17), and "pastor" (1 Peter 5:1–4). Large congregations had a number of presbyters or elders (James 5:14; Acts 15:4, 6, 23; 20:17, 28; 21:18). At least some elders preached and taught (1 Timothy 5:17).

elect, the. In theological terms, those whom God knew from eternity as His chosen saints who will live forever with Him in the new heaven and earth. This election does not presuppose the fall, nor is it based on any merit or faith of the saints. It is the purely gracious act of God toward humanity.

Election Controversy. In Lutheran history, at least two events with this name occurred. The first controversy occurred from 1592–94 when Wittenberg professor Samuel Huber taught that a Christian must make his eternal election certain by repentance and faith. He was opposed by Wittenberg professor Aegidius Hunnius. A second controversy began to escalate from the early 1870s until it reached a climax between 1880 and 1910. It began to subside until 1928. The question involved the pietistic view that faith is confirmed by ethical deeds. Some—such as several Norwegian groups, the Ohio Synod, and the Iowa Synod—saw Baptism as an entry to the covenant relationship that is repeatedly confirmed by a righteous life. They did not take the position of decision theology that practically excludes Baptism, but they confused Law and Gospel by making it necessary for people to confirm God's free, gracious act of election. Walther and the remainder of the Synodical Conference stood firmly opposed to the popular views of Pietism on this matter.

ens. From Greek philosophy, this Latin term refers to infinite intellect, a kind of divine mind, the One in All. See also ***finens; nonens***.

Enthusiasm. Belief that Christians should expect special revelations or experiences from the Holy Spirit. Enthusiasts expect God to draw, enlighten, justify, and save them without the Means of Grace (Word and Sacraments). See also **Fanaticism; *Schwärmer***.

Epicureanism. A movement founded by the Greek philosopher Epicurus (ca. 341 BC–ca. 270 BC), who followed the materialism of Democritus. The goal of this philosophy is the absence of pain and the attainment of tranquility with modest pleasure. Classified as a restrained form of *hedonism*, Epicureans believe that physical pleasure is the greatest good. Adherents opposed Platonism, Stoicism, and Christianity, and the movement was considered heretical by Christians and Jews in the Middle Ages. Its popularity surged in the Enlightenment among French and English Rationalists. Thomas Jefferson considered himself to be an Epicurean.

ethics. (1) A discipline with such concepts as good, bad, duty, and obligation. (2) A set of moral principles or values. (3) The philosophical study of behavior and principles of conduct.

ex opere operato. Latin: "for the sake of the work performed." In the Roman Church, sacraments, simply based on their technical performance, confer grace so long as the recipient does not put an obstacle (usually mortal sin) in the way. According to this view, faith in the heart of the recipient is not required.

faith. (1) The body of truth found in creeds (objective). (2) The human response to divine activity (subjective); the personal appropriation of divine truth (itself a "gift," not a "work," Ephesians 2:8–9).

Fanaticism. Irrational zeal that prevents deliberation or consideration on the basis of either Scripture or reason (see Luke 9:53; John 19:15; Acts 7:57; 9:1). See also **Enthusiasm; *Schwärmer***.

fides formata, fides informis. Roman Catholics distinguish between *fides informis* (mere faith, dead faith, unformed faith, faith that lacks life because it lacks works, especially love) and *fides caritate formata* (faith permeated by formative love, faith with works).

final cause. See under **cause**.

finens. From Greek philosophy, this Latin term refers to finite intellect, such as the kind that human beings possess. See also ***ens; nonens***.

formal cause. See under **cause**.

Gnesio-. From the Greek for "genuine." Lutherans used the term for those "genuine" Lutheran pastors and laypeople who did not accept the changes that Melanchthon and his followers adopted, both before and after Luther's death. Those changes, for example, allowed for understandings of the Lord's Supper and of the human will that contradicted Scripture. The great achievement of Gnesio-Lutheran theology is the Formula of Concord.

Gnosticism. From Greek *gnosis*, "knowledge." This religious movement has its roots in pre-Christian times, though it flowered during the second and third century AD and has experienced a modern revival after discoveries at Nag Hammadi, Egypt. Gnosticism draws on many ancient traditions and often emphasizes occult lore, magic words, and secret names so that adherents may be redeemed from the material world and escape into the *pleroma*, the fullness of God. See also **Gnostics** (p. 494).

Gospel. (1) The Gospel of Jesus Christ, in its proper and narrow sense, is the glad tidings of forgiveness, peace, life, and joy; the eternal divine counsel of redemption, of which Christ Himself ever was, is, and will be the living center, the very heart and soul. The Gospel (a) imparts the forgiveness of sin; (b) produces true joy and the zeal to do good works; and (c) destroys sin both outwardly and inwardly. (2) In the broad sense, the term *Gospel* may also refer to the sum of Christian teaching, including both Law and Gospel.

grace. God's goodwill and favor in Christ toward sinners who can plead no merit. Grace implies mercy or compassion for one who has by every right forfeited his or her claim to love. God's grace to the sinner is "free" because it is not grounded in any worthiness of mankind (Romans 11:6). In the Roman Church, grace is more of a power given by God to do good works ("infused grace") so as to earn righteousness. In Christian theology, saving grace has been distinguished in its various operations as *prevenient*, inasmuch as by means of outward circumstances and associations, particularly through the outward hearing of the Word, the Holy Spirit would prepare the heart for conversion; as *operative*, inasmuch as it generates faith; as *cooperative*, inasmuch as it is active in the Christian, jointly with the regenerated will, to produce good works.

heresy. Stubborn error in an article of faith in opposition to Scripture.

heterodox. From the Greek for "other teaching," the term describes in the Christian context those who claim to be a part of the Church, yet whose teachings depart from the teachings revealed by God in Scripture. Opposite of orthodox.

historical criticism. Term used to designate a variety of methods using rationalist assumptions to guide historical research. Instead of believing that the Scriptures are the inspired, inerrant, and normative Word of God, which reveals objective, unchanging, and eternal truths, such methods presume that the Scriptures are the result of human communities that wrote

about their religious ideas and experiences. As a result, historical-critical methods consider Scripture to be subjective and relative. Instead of focusing on the existing text, critical scholars attempt to reconstruct the supposed history of the text, including the life of the religious community and the literary sources, forms, and editorial activity that they assume were part of the production of the text. Enlightenment-era rationalists regarded Scripture as a kind of fairy-tale used for moral application. The nineteenth and twentieth centuries saw archaeology confirm many details formerly dismissed as false. In reaction, some historical critics sought to affirm the psychological value of Scripture while setting aside the discussion of whether the events in the text, such as miracles, really happened. They spoke of a text whose symbolic language of miracle and mystery created a psychological, religious event that was central to the community. This approach still rejected the Scriptures as the factual Word of God and replaced biblical truth with human psychology and sociology, where any sort of "good news" could serve as a religious moment. That kind of religion cannot save.

imputation. Synonym of "credit" used by some dogmaticians with reference to Adam's sin and Christ's righteousness. Adam's sin is credited by God to every person, so that his sin becomes each person's own and makes him guilty in the eyes of God. Additionally, each person embraces this original, "alien sin" in his natural state and proceeds to make it his actual, "proper sin." The righteousness of Christ is similarly credited to a believer as his own; it justifies him. The Christian, so converted and reborn, follows in that righteousness by doing good works.

indulgences. Roots of the Roman doctrine of indulgences reach back to the ancient practice of penitential discipline. As the Crusades helped the Roman sacrament of penance to evolve, penance changed from an expression of sorrow for sin or a kind of restitution to the offended to an act of merit that is pleasing to God, a payment for sin. People were offered merits of indulgence either by going on a crusade or by supporting crusaders with money and acts of piety and charity. This concept developed into merit that could remove, by degree, a portion of that temporal punishment (chiefly purgatory) that could not be removed by absolution. Indulgences became commutations of divine punishment gained by giving money to churches and monasteries, by pilgrimages, and sometimes by direct payment to the priest. Contrition, or at least attrition, was in theory necessary to gain indulgence. See also **attrition; contrition**.

infused grace. See under **grace**.

Interim. The provisional agreement in religious matters until the next Church council.

Islam. Arabic for "submission." This religious movement arose in seventh-century Arabia under the leadership of Muhammad (570–632). Originally peaceful, it became warlike after Muhammad fled from Mecca to Medina in 622. Islam separates the world into the "domain of Islam" and the "domain of war" and emphasizes submission to God (Allah). One who submits to God is called a Muslim. The sacred book of Islam is the Qur'an, which is regarded as God's revelation through Muhammad. Unlike the Bible, the Qur'an was not written by a prophet or an apostle but was compiled at least twenty years after Muhammad's death. Unlike the Bible, the Qur'an contains only sparse historical references. By 732, Islam had spread throughout North Africa, Spain, and France to claim half of the former Roman Empire. Later, Islam spread toward India and the Far East. It destroyed the Byzantine Empire in 1453 and threatened Vienna in Luther's lifetime.

Judaism. This religion is based on the Pentateuch, the five books of Moses, which adherents interpret as a record of how God made Israel His people and how He gave ordinances for faith and life. After the return from Babylon, the Pharisees added many legalistic regulations. The name "Jew" comes from this period and means "one from Judah or Judea." The Sadducees opposed the Pharisees and embraced Greek and Roman culture. Sadducees were more liberal in matters of sexuality (Mark 6:16–21) and rejected core beliefs such as the resurrection of the dead (Acts 23:6–8). The conquest of Jerusalem and the destruction of the temple by the Romans in AD 70 marked the rise of the Talmud. In the twelfth century, Maimonides helped codify the previously disorganized teachings of Judaism under thirteen principles. Modern Judaism has three main groups: Orthodox Judaism tries to hold on to tradition. Conservative Jews respect the Torah and traditional laws of Judaism but

have made some changes. Reform Judaism has its basis in German Rationalism and largely departs from historic Judaism.

justification. Judicial act of God where He charges our sin to Christ and credits Christ's righteousness to us. This justification is received through the gift of faith. The Lutheran Confessions call the doctrine of justification the most important teaching of divine revelation (Ap IV 2, 3; FC SD III 6). Justification is both objective (won by Christ for all people) and subjective (applied personally through the Means of Grace).

Keys. The peculiar, special, unique spiritual authority given by Christ to the whole Church to forgive the sins of repentant sinners but to withhold forgiveness from the unrepentant as long as they do not repent (John 20:22–23; Matthew 16:19; 18:15–20; Revelation 1:18). In particular, the Office of the Keys, administered by pastors (AC V) by the call of the Church (AC XIV), is the office Christ has given to His Church to administer forgiveness and discipline by rightly distinguishing Law and Gospel. The Christian congregation, by the command of Christ, calls pastors to carry out the Office of the Keys publicly in His name and on behalf of the congregation.

Law. God's will, which shows people how they should live in order to please God (e.g., the Ten Commandments), condemns their failure to fulfill His will (sin), and threatens God's wrath because of sin. The preaching of the Law is the cause of contrition. Although the ceremonial laws of the Old Testament have been abolished (Colossians 2:16–17), the moral Law (the Ten Commandments) is in force until the end of time (Matthew 5:18).

lectionary. Book containing Scripture readings as lessons for the church year.

loci/locus. From the Latin word for "topic." A standard category that helps gather passages of Scripture in order to help people better understand a subject or word in Scripture. Theological works entitled *Loci* were produced in the sixteenth and seventeenth centuries by Philipp Melanchthon, Martin Chemnitz, Johann Gerhard, and others. Over time, the phrase *loci communes* ("common places [or topics]") came to mean any summary of Christian doctrine, while the phrase *loci theologici* ("theological topics") came to denote the content, and thus the main passages of Scripture as included in individual loci.

Manichaeism. This dualistic religious movement blended religious elements into a system of light and darkness in which good and evil were in perpetual war. Respective powers supposedly led each side. Within humans, the body was said to be evil and the soul good. Manichaeism became popular in the Roman Empire and a threat to Christianity in the third century. See also **Mani** (p. 496).

Marburg Colloquy. As the political situation encompassing the princes and territories of Germany deteriorated in the early years of the Reformation, Evangelical princes, led by Philip of Hesse, tried to build political alliances between the Swiss and the Saxons. This brought about a colloquy, or theological discussion, between Ulrich Zwingli (leader of the Reformation in Switzerland) and Luther to resolve disagreements between the two camps. At this gathering in 1529 at the Marburg Castle, Luther gave Zwingli and his followers "the hand of peace and charity" and found agreement with them in fourteen points of controversy, but he could not agree with them on the question of the sacramental union in the Lord's Supper. As a result, confessional Lutherans continue to believe that unity and fellowship must be based on agreement in all points of doctrine—not just a majority.

Mass. An older name for the Lord's Supper, which in the Middle Ages became the most common name for the Divine Service in the Western Church. The name comes from the dismissal after the distribution of the Eucharist: *Ite, missa est* ("Go, [you are] dismissed"). Lutherans kept the Mass, though purified from certain abuses (AC XXIV 1, 40; Ap XXIV 1).

material. Having to do with matter or physical substance; not spiritual.

material cause. See under **cause**.

materialism. Theory originating in Greek philosophy that regards matter as the original cause of all, even psychic, phenomena. Asserting that all psychic processes are caused by changes of material molecules, it denies the existence of the soul. Developed by French encyclopedists, this philosophy became prominent in Germany in the nineteenth century.

Means of Grace. This term denotes the divinely instituted means by which God offers, bestows, and seals to people forgiveness of sins, life, and salvation. Properly speaking, there is only one Means of Grace: the Gospel of Christ (Romans 1:16–17), but because in the Sacraments the Gospel appears as the *visible Word* (Ap XIII 5; Augustine of Hippo, Tract 80 on John 15:3) in distinction from the *audible Word*, it is rightly said that the Means of Grace are the Gospel and the Sacraments. The Sacraments have the same effect as the spoken or written Word because they are nothing else than the visible Word, that is, the Gospel applied in sacred action in connection with the visible signs. There are Means of Grace because there is, first, Christ's objective justification or reconciliation (2 Corinthians 5:19–21) and, second, Christ's institution. In other words, there is forgiveness for all through Christ's active and passive obedience. Christ wants this forgiveness to be offered and conveyed to all people through the Gospel and the Sacraments (Matthew 28:19–20; Mark 16:15; AC V, VIII). The Means of Grace have an offering or conferring power—by which God offers to all people forgiveness of sins, life, and salvation (Matthew 18:20; 26:28; Acts 2:38; 20:24; FC SD II 57)—and an operative or effective power, by which the Holy Spirit works, strengthens, and preserves saving faith (Romans 1:16; 10:17; 1 Corinthians 4:15; 2 Corinthians 2:14–17; 3:5–6; 1 Thessalonians 2:13; 1 Peter 1:23; FC SD II 56). See also **sacrament**.

Methodism. Grew from the religious experiences of John Wesley, Charles Wesley, and their co-workers through the Holy Club at Oxford (1729 onward). Their personal piety contrasted with the indifference in Anglicanism of the time. Their missionary activity resulted in the first Great Awakening in England and America. Methodism had its greatest expansion in the United States and was tied closely to Revivalism. Wesley stressed Christian perfection. He rejected Calvin's double predestination, saying that Christ died for all. He held that all who are obedient to the Gospel according to their individual ability are in God's kingdom. Wesley spoke of a free decision to accept salvation and the direct communication of the Holy Spirit. This led, on the one hand, to Holiness churches and, on the other, to the adoption of Rationalism and the Social Gospel. See also **Holiness churches** (p. 495).

morganatic marriage. Latin: *matrimonium ad morganaticum.* A second marriage to a spouse of lower social rank in which the offspring of the union has no legal right of dowry or inheritance beyond any specific gifts of (usually) the husband to the wife. A morganatic union technically does not violate bigamy laws because of the inequity of social status, but it does forbid subsequent breaking of the marriage vows. While English law has forbidden all such unions, the practice was most common in Germanic countries, though France allowed the practice of the "openly secret" marriage. Such practices by European nobility reflect the centuries-old tendency to violate the biblical doctrine of marriage. Regardless of long-standing tradition and even churchly "approval," morganatic marriage displeases God.

nonens. Also written *non-ens.* From Greek philosophy, this Latin term refers to the absence of intellect, the irrational world of dreams at the edge of existence. See also ***ens; finens.***

office. A particular position or area of responsibility having certain prescribed duties.

Office of the Holy Ministry. An office established by God (Matthew 28:16–20; John 20:21–23) to proclaim and teach the Word of God, specifically the Gospel, and to administer the Sacraments. This office does not exist apart from the Church. It exists to serve the Church, as Christ became a servant (John 13:1–20; Philippians 2:5–11). In doing so, holders of this office are worthy of double honor (1 Timothy 5:17), not because of their personal attributes but because of the Gospel and of Christ.

Office of the Keys. See **Keys**.

omnipotence. An attribute of God by reason of which He can and does perform whatever He pleases (Psalm 115:3)

omniscience. An attribute of God by which He exhibits an ever-present knowledge, one that directly knows things that exist and come to pass; not progressive knowledge, but total and perfect knowledge (Psalm 139:1–4; John 21:17). He and His knowledge had no beginning (Psalm 90:2; Ephesians 1:4).

ordination. Solemn public rite whereby the Church confirms the call of God that is extended to a man to serve in the Office of the Holy Ministry in a given location. Ordination itself comes from the example of Christ (John 20:22) and the apostles (1 Timothy 4:14; 5:22; Hebrews 6:2). The laying on of hands is also connected with Baptism and the gift of the Spirit (Acts 8:17–19; 19:6). There is no specific mandate from Christ to lay on hands in the rite of ordination. Yet, beginning with the Eleven onward, some form of ordination has accompanied the call as an affirmation of God's will (Acts 6:6; 1 Timothy 4:14; 5:22).

orthodox. Implies conformity to a certain standard; used especially in a religious sense of correct doctrine and worship.

pagan. A religion, or nonreligious person, opposed to Christianity.

pantheism. Religious and philosophical view that God and the universe are one. This belief denies the personality of God and ascribes to Him only an existence that is woven throughout the fabric of the universe, identifying Him with it. Besides destroying the personality of God and reducing Him to a lower object of worship, pantheism destroys the individuality and personality of man, who becomes merely a part of the whole. Individual responsibility and the moral world order are destroyed. Pantheism does not explain the existence of evil or it embraces the eternal duality of good and evil as necessary opposites. According to this belief, Christ's redemptive work becomes an illusion.

papacy. The office of the Roman pope. Having to do with the pope, his authority, or the Roman Church in general.

Papists. In light of Scripture and its truth, those who support the false teachings of the papacy.

Peasants' War. This uprising of German peasants in 1525 was brought on by the oppression of powerful landowners. Luther first sided with the peasants, but when they refused to refrain from violence and murder, he called on the rulers to suppress the peasants. The authorities violently overreacted, disregarding Luther's admonition for mercy toward innocent peasants. This war deepened Luther's understanding of the sinner-saint and caused him to depart from an earlier idea (ca. 1523) that the Gospel could cause a person to stop sinning.

Pelagianism. In this religious system attributed to Pelagius and his followers, man's nature is not depraved since the fall but is still in its original state of moral indifference and depends on the individual will to develop the moral germ of his nature and be saved. Irresistible grace and absolute predestination do not fit this system. But according to the view of Pelagius, neither was grace or salvation by Christ necessary (a view incompatible with the essence of Christianity). Positions that affirm some ability of man to refrain from sin or respond on his own to grace have been called Pelagian or semi-Pelagian. Modern Roman Catholicism, Eastern Orthodoxy, decision theology, Methodism, and Holiness churches related to Pentecostalism all contain elements of Pelagianism.

penance. See **confession, history of.**

Pietism. This religious movement developed after the Thirty Years' War (1618–48). At the University of Halle, Philipp Jakob Spener helped form the following central points of this movement that was then carried on by August Hermann Francke and Johann Jakob Rambach: (1) Church based on small-group Bible studies. (2) Governing right of the universal priesthood of believers. (3) Essential requirement of both Christian knowledge and its practice. (4) Sympathetic attitude to those adhering to false doctrine. (5) Centrality of the devotional life in Christian university training. (6) Preaching style that emphasized conversion, implanting doctrine into the new man, and reaping the fruit of faith. The positive results of this movement include stress on the role of biblical interpretation and the proper rules used to interpret a passage. Among its negative results are a confusion of justification and sanctification, the dominance of individualism, and a legalistic emphasis on ethics. Nikolaus Ludwig von Zinzendorf and other nobles helped finance Pietism. It in turn helped to pave the way for Rationalism and the Enlightenment.

piety. Conforming to a certain belief or standard of conduct, especially in religious matters.

postil. A sermon based on an annual cycle of Bible readings. The name comes from medieval Scripture notes where one sees: "the text affixed to this word" (Latin: *post illa verbum textus*). These notes became the basis for sermons organized on Scripture readings instead of those based on themes. Luther produced both a series of church *postils* and of house *postils*. Walther published two volumes of *postils*—one based on

the Gospel readings and one on the Epistle texts. They were a beloved pair of books in the early Missouri Synod.

Predestinarian Controversy. See **Election Controversy.**

predestination. The doctrine that God, before the foundation of the world, chose us in His Son, Jesus Christ, out of the mass of sinful mankind unto faith, the adoption of sons, and everlasting life (Ephesians 1:4; 3:11; 2 Thessalonians 2:13; 2 Timothy 1:9). This election is not based on any good quality or act of the elect (those predestined), nor was it made in view of those who eventually would come to faith. Rather, our predestination in Christ is based solely on God's grace, the good pleasure of His will in Christ Jesus. While the Bible does teach the predestination of the elect, it does not (as opposed to Calvin) teach the predestination of the damned, nor does it solve the problem of the human intellect seeking to understand universal grace and predestination (see FC Ep XI 5–7; FC SD XI 14–23). See also **Election Controversy.**

presbyter. See **elder.**

prevenient grace. See under **grace.**

purgatory. In Roman Catholic teaching, all who have not been thoroughly perfected in this life will be "purged" by fire in an intermediate state of existence between earth and heaven. Masses, prayers, and good works by the living aid those suffering in purgatory and reduce its sentence. Those who die with mortal sin unconfessed and unabsolved do not enter purgatory, but hell.

Rationalism. This philosophical-religious movement went beyond supranaturalism by seeing no reason for a supernatural order. It interpreted the universe through the reasoning individual. In England and France, empirical philosophy produced English Deism and a French cult of reason that set aside traditional belief and established a system of natural law and religion based on analytical philosophy. Thomas Jefferson and Benjamin Franklin promoted this sort of thinking. The Reign of Terror in France (1793–94) produced a reaction in German and other Continental thought that tried to preserve traditional language about religion and other institutions but introduce modern philosophical meanings. Because of the work of Friedrich D. E. Schleiermacher (1768–1834), this stream has formed much of mainline Christian thought today. See also **supranaturalism**.

real presence. Term applied to the Lord's Supper. It was first used in the thirteenth century to claim the ongoing presence of the body of Christ in the consecrated wafer held in the monstrance and carried about in the *Corpus Christi* procession. Anglican clergy used it to argue against Luther's doctrine of the Lord's Supper. American Lutherans started using the term around the 1820s to make a clear statement in support of the scriptural doctrine of the sacramental union held by Lutherans. This was partly in response to the American Reformed environment that stressed the symbolic and spiritualizing interpretations of the Eucharist almost to the point of absence. The term then traveled back to European Lutherans. It is not an improper way to speak, but its different meaning among different groups makes careful definition necessary. Lutherans have always spoken of the sacramental union between the elements and the body and blood of Christ. See also **sacramental union**.

repentance. In a wide sense, change from a rebellious state to one of harmony with God's will, from trusting in human merit to trusting in Christ's merit. Embraces contrition and justifying faith; sometimes the fruit of repentance are included (Ap XII 28). In the narrow sense, faith and fruit are not included. The means to repentance is God's Word (see Jeremiah 31:18; Acts 5:31). Sometimes taken as an equivalent to penance and penitence. See also **confession, history of**.

revival. The phrase "revivals of religion" commonly indicates renewed interest in religious subjects or, more generally, religious awakenings. In its best sense it may be applied to the work of Christ and the apostles and to the sixteenth-century Reformation. But the term is often applied also to enthusiastic outbursts of religious emotion. The term "revival" is most often associated with an increase of spiritual activity in English-speaking Protestant churches. In the American context, there was a revival at Northampton, Massachusetts, beginning in 1734 and throughout New England in the early 1740s (most famously led by Jonathan Edwards the Elder). Another period of revival in the United States occurred at the turn of the nineteenth century, when Lyman Beecher and Timothy Dwight began their remarkable work. Other revivalists include Asahel Nettleton (1783–1844), Charles Grandison Finney (1792–1875), and Dwight L. Moody (1837–99). Modern revivals have been led most notably by Billy Graham. A similar kind of radio preaching occurred with preachers such as Billy Sunday. See also **anxious bench**.

righteousness. God's righteousness is the essential perfection of His nature. The term "righteousness" is applied to Christ not only in view of His essential righteousness but also in view of the righteousness that He gained for mankind (Jeremiah 23:6; see also **justification**). The righteousness of the Law is the obedience that the Law requires (see **Gospel; Law**). The righteousness of the Christian is the righteousness of faith (see **faith; justification**).

sacrament. A sacrament is a sacred act instituted by God in which God Himself has joined His Word of promise to a visible element, and by which He offers, gives, and seals the forgiveness of sins earned by Christ. By this definition, there are two sacraments: Holy Baptism and the Lord's Supper. Sometimes Holy Absolution is counted as a third sacrament, even though it has no divinely instituted element (LC IV 74; Ap XIII 4). See also **Means of Grace**.

sacramental grace. Grace received when one receives the Sacraments. Zwingli argued that a person who desires to receive a Sacrament already possesses grace and that the Sacraments are just an outward sign of what the Holy Spirit has worked in the heart of that person. Against that position is 1 Peter 3:21: "Baptism now saves you." See also **grace**.

sacramental union. The Lord's words (Matthew 26:26–29; Mark 14:22–25; Luke 22:19–20; 1 Corinthians 11:24–25) unite His body and blood with bread and wine for the purpose of distribution to Christians who can examine themselves with regard to their need for the Sacrament, their contrition, and their resolve to live in accord with the body and blood that they receive spiritually and into which they are incorporated.

sanctification. In a wide sense, sanctification includes all effects of God's Word (Acts 26:18; Ephesians 5:26; 2 Thessalonians 2:13; Hebrews 10:14; 1 Peter 1:2). In a narrow sense, sanctification is the spiritual growth (1 Corinthians 3:9; 9:24; Ephesians 4:15; Philippians 3:12) that follows justification (Matthew 7:16–18; John

3:6; Ephesians 2:10). By God's grace (Galatians 5:22–23; Philippians 2:13), a Christian cooperates in this work (2 Corinthians 6:1; 7:1; Philippians 2:12; 1 Timothy 4:14; FC SD II 65–66). Through the Holy Spirit's work, faith is increased daily, love strengthened, and the image of God renewed but not perfected in this life.

satisfaction. According to Roman Church teaching, temporal punishments (justly due because of sin) can be paid through works of penance, the third component of the Roman Catholic sacrament of penance. See also **confession, history of.**

schism. From Greek; the *ch* is silent or pronounced like *k*. Used of divergent opinions (John 7:43; Acts 14:4). The Church uses the term in the sense of dissension, division, or discord (1 Corinthians 1:10; 11:18; 12:25). Schismatics disrupt Church harmony and unity.

Scholasticism. This movement became dominant in the later Middle Ages and lasted into the Renaissance (1100–1500). It was a tool that built on ancient attempts to harmonize theology and Greek philosophy. The influence of Aristotle became stronger than that of Plato in the thirteenth century, as did the use of deductive arguments based on an accepted body of first principles. Islamic, Jewish, and Christian philosophical influences mingled in their interpretation of ancient Greek texts on religion, mathematics, logic, and other sources. A result, especially among the Dominican monks, was that dialectics and speculation was used to discuss, comprehend, harmonize, and prove doctrines rationally. The Renaissance emphasis on returning to the source texts and Luther's application of that emphasis by going back to Scripture posed a strong challenge to the deductive approach.

Schwärmer. Related to the English word *swarm*, in the Middle Ages, *Schwärmer* could mean someone who lives wildly, without self-control—imagine a person chased by a swarm of bees. Luther applied this word to those who follow false teachers and then become wrapped up in an extremely emotional, even violent, way of living.

security, carnal. The belief regarding oneself that "I am not really a bad person." Accompanies a lack of terror when confronted with the Law. A person in such a state can receive no good from the Gospel because the Law must first cause contrition. See also **contrition.**

sign. From Latin *signum*. Technical term for a physical element, such as water, bread, and wine, to which a divine word of Scripture attaches a gracious, Gospel promise, such as the affixed seal of the name of God, the sacramental union of the body and blood of Christ, and the promise of sin forgiven, salvation, strengthening of faith, and eternal life. The sign is thus a visible Word, a concrete instance of the promise. See also **Word of God.**

sin. The breaking of God's Law (Romans 4:15; 1 John 3:4). Sin may be divided into *original* sin (the inherited tendency to sin and God's resultant condemnation) and *actual* sin. Actual sin (every thought, emotion, word, or act conflicting with God's Law) may be involuntary or may be done ignorantly (Acts 17:30) and includes *sins of commission* (Matthew 15:19; James 1:15) and *sins of omission* (James 4:17). Sin arouses God's righteous wrath and deserves His punishment. Willful sin sears the conscience; repeated, it hardens the heart and may lead to, but is not identical with, the unpardonable sin against the Holy Spirit.

sin, mortal and venial. The Lutheran Confessions speak of sin that is deadly, that is, irreconcilable with faith (Ap IV 48, 64, 109, 115). When believers fall into open sin, faith has departed (SA III III 43–44). One who obeys his lusts does not retain faith (Ap IV 144). Original sin is mortal; it brings eternal death on those who are not born again (AC II 2 [Latin]). One who is dead in sin is insensitive to sin (LC V 77–78). Sins remain in believers (SA III III 40; FC SD II 34). In harmony with Scripture, Lutherans believe that all actual sin is *mortal*, deserving of death, until it is made *venial* by the washing of Christ's blood that is offered through the Means of Grace (SA III III 36–38; Matthew 5:18–19; Galatians 3:10; James 2:10; Ezekiel 18:4; Romans 6:23; 8:1; 1 John 1:7, 9; 2:1–2). Lutherans also teach that premeditated sin is *mortal* sin because the planning and doing of a sinful act is, in fact, a rejection of the Gospel and an active participation. Scripture does not class sin by degree of evil in terms of how God sees sin; rather, Scripture speaks of sin according to its ability to sever one from faith and the Gospel. Departing from Scripture, Roman Catholic theology views mortal and venial sin as differing by degree. A *mortal* sin is said to deprive the soul of sanctifying grace and supernatural life (thus causing death to the soul). By its degree of evil, one claims that a mortal sin makes a person an enemy of God, takes away the merit of all good works, deprives one of everlasting happiness in heaven, and makes one deserving of hell. It is an intentionally evil thought, word, and deed, or an intentional failure to do good. *Venial* sins are said to be less evil and do not deprive one of sanctifying grace. Based on Genesis 3, Scripture clearly shows this view to be false. All sin is infinitely evil because it offends an infinitely good God. Yet some sins have worse temporal effects than others.

Socinianism. A forerunner of modern Unitarianism, this sect denies the deity of Christ and His vicarious atonement, original sin, and the resurrection of the flesh. Adherents also reject the doctrine of hell and believe that the wicked will be annihilated. They reject Baptism and Holy Communion and believe that people save themselves. This movement became fashionable among the Polish aristocracy and also among some in England. It served as the forerunner of Rationalist Christianity. See also **Socinians** (p. 499); **Sozini, Fausto Paulo** (p. 499); **Sozini, Lelio** (p. 499).

sophistry. Subtle reasoning or argumentation designed to deceive.

substance. The essential nature of a thing; that which exists by itself essentially. The created human nature is a "substance" defined as the human body and a rational soul (FC Ep I 23: FC SD I 21, 54). See also **accident**.

supranaturalism (also "supernaturalism"). Term that came into prominence especially in England and Germany between 1780 and 1830 in theological discussions arising especially from the tensions created by Deism and Rationalism. Supranaturalists held that the authenticity of divine revelation is attested, in part, by prophecies and miracles. After Immanuel Kant and Georg W. F. Hegel, the term "supernaturalist" was applied to those who held the absolute transcendence of God; later, the name supernaturalism was applied to many systems within Christianity that rejected reason as an absolute norm and held authoritarian, inner, emotional, or other criteria.

synecdoche. A figure of speech in which a part substitutes for the whole or the whole for a part. For example, one may refer to a sports car as "hot wheels."

synod. From the Greek word for "gathering together." The term arose among caravan traders whose beasts and drivers stretched out in long lines during the day, yet gathered together for mutual support and protection at night. The early Church adopted this language to mean a conference where an important point of doctrine needed to be discussed for the mutual benefit and protection of believers. Issues discussed include questions affecting the faith and discipline of the Church. In Lutheran teaching, the theological basis for synods is found in Acts 15. In the modern Lutheran understanding of the term "synod" (developed during the confessional Lutheran renewal in the nineteenth century), either pastors by themselves or pastors and representatives of congregations meet according to a system of jurisdiction in order to converse with one another about the doctrine and the business of that jurisdiction. They strive to find a scriptural basis for unity in doctrine, order, and life. The authority of synods derives from the activity of the Holy Spirit, yet that authority always stands under Scripture and the Lutheran Confessions.

Synoptic Gospels. The Gospels according to Matthew, Mark, and Luke.

Tetrapolitan Confession. Consisting of twenty-three articles, this confession is the oldest Reformed symbol in Germany. Martin Bucer, Wolfgang Capito, Caspar Hedio, and Jakob Sturm prepared the document quickly in 1530 for the Diet of Augsburg. Presented at the Diet by representatives from Konstanz, Lindau, Memmingen, and Strasbourg, the Tetrapolitan Confession tried to effect a compromise between Lutherans and the Reformed, especially concerning the Lord's Supper.

theocracy. A form of government, such as that of ancient Israel or modern Iran, in which either God or those claiming divine authority govern the nation.

theologian. From the Greek word for "one who speaks about God" or "one who speaks the words of God." John was called "the Theologian" because he wrote about the divine mysteries in a simple yet profound way that penetrated beyond reason into the revelatory unveiling of God. Those who study or practice theology may be called theologians, yet they must be held accountable to Scripture.

theology. Includes the words that God reveals about Himself in Scripture and the words that we use to teach and confess Him to others. Traditionally, theology is divided into four general categories. The interpretation of the Bible is called *exegetical* theology. *Historical* theology studies the people, places, developments of thought, and other aspects of the Church's life and work through the ages. *Practical* theology speaks to how one goes about doing the actual work of the Church. *Dogmatic* theology engages the dogmas of the Church that gather Scripture passages together around principal proof texts called "seats of doctrine" (Latin: *sedes doctrinae*). Walther opposed the "modern" approach of using philosophical systems to organize the Church's teachings as "systematic theology." In *Lehre und Wehre*, Walther referred to people who reduced theology to human systems of thought as being wrong to the point of getting it all backward (German: *verkehrt*).

Trent, Council of. This council met in reaction to some of the issues raised by Luther and the other sixteenth-century reformers with the specific intent of restoring order to the Roman Church. Church leaders gathered three times over an eighteen-year period in the Italian city of Trent to discuss topics as far-ranging as the canonical Scriptures, original sin, justification, sacraments, purgatory, and indulgences. The council enacted various reforms, the most prominent of which concerned the education of the clergy, the conferring of benefices, and the administration of property.

tribulations. See *Anfechtung*.

unionism. Religious unionism consists in joint worship and work of those not united in doctrine. Its essence is an agreement to disagree. In effect, it denies the doctrine of the clearness of Scripture.

Unitarianism. Belief that God has only one person and essence. Ancient forms include modalism. Modern forms arose among Anabaptists, Socinians, and other radical sects. See also **Socinianism.**

visible Word. See under **Means of Grace; Word of God.**

Word of God. In the general sense, this is synonymous with Holy Scripture because the formal content of Scripture consists of the actual words that the Holy Spirit inspired through the chosen human authors of Scripture. In particular, one may speak of the *audible* Word, the word that one reads or hears, and the *visible* Word that is united to a sign and produces a sacrament. The power or efficacy of the Word of God is categorized into three main senses: the *representative* power, the *excitative* power, and the *exhibitive* or *collative* power. The representative power deals with Scripture's ability to speak clearly about God, to teach divine matters. The excitative power is motivational; it "excites" people to hear and to do what Scripture says. The collative power is associated with the distinction between Law and Gospel. It refers to Scripture's ability to exhibit and deliver what it says to its hearers and readers. Scripture delivers both the sting of the Law and the refreshment of the Gospel. See also **sign.**

INDEX OF PERSONS AND GROUPS

NOTE TO THE READER: This index focuses on the persons and groups that Walther mentions in his lectures. It does not attempt to treat exhaustively all potential persons and groups that the discussions might engage. Additional resources that can be helpful include *Concordia: The Lutheran Confessions—A Readers Edition of the Book of Concord* and *Christian Cyclopedia* (http://www.lcms.org/ca/www/cyclopedia/02/).

Agricola, Johann. See **Antinomians**.

Albrechtsbrüder. See **Evangelical Church**.

Albrechtsleute. See **Evangelical Church**.

Anabaptists. From Greek for "rebaptize." Beginning in the fourth century, this term designated groups that rebaptized (a) people baptized by heretics and (b) people baptized by clergy who later fell from faith during persecution. During the Reformation, this name of reproach was applied to groups that insisted on rebaptism of people baptized as infants. Anabaptists were most influential from Switzerland down the Rhine River to Holland. Modern Anabaptist groups include Mennonites, Amish, Swiss Brethren, and others.

Antichrist. This term was used in the New Testament (a) of all false teachers (1 John 2:18; 4:3) and (b) of one outstanding adversary of Christ (1 John 2:18). Characteristics of Antichrist are taken from Daniel 7; 8; 11:31–38; Revelation 11; 13; 17; 18; writings of John; and especially 2 Thessalonians 2:3–12. The Apology shows that the papacy has marks of Antichrist as depicted by Daniel (Ap VII–VIII 24; XV 19; XXIII 25; XXIV 51) and by Paul (Ap VII–VIII 4). It speaks of the papacy as part of the kingdom of Antichrist (Ap XV 18). The Treatise (paragraphs 39–44; *Concordia*, 300–301) offers several proofs that the pope is the Antichrist. The Smalcald Articles (II IV; *Concordia*, 269) maintain that the pope, by his doctrine and practice, has clearly shown his office as Antichrist since it exceeds even the Turks and Tatars in keeping people from their Savior.

Antinomians. From Greek for "against the law." Those who maintain that a Christian is free from all moral law, a position first promoted by Johann Agricola (1492–1566) in 1527 against Melanchthon, who stressed the Law to counter the abuse of free grace. Agricola argued that the Gospel causes knowledge of sin and repentance. In 1556, followers of Melanchthon denied the third use of the Law and the role of the Law in good works. See also **Antinomianism** (p. 474).

Arians. Followers of the early Church heretic Arius. The most radical Arians (after 357) rejected any likeness in substance between the Father and the Son and used the slippery term "similar" (Greek: *homoíos*). Moderate Arians preferred the term "of similar substance" (Greek: *homoioúsios*). Radical Arians became too extreme, thus helping orthodox Eastern theologians to convince moderate Arians to accept the term "of the same substance" (Greek: *homooúsios*), which has been used since that time to describe what Scripture says regarding Christ. Today, Jehovah's Witnesses hold to Arian beliefs by considering Jesus divine but not equal to the one God. See also **Arius**.

Arius (ca. 280–336). A priest in a suburb of Alexandria, Egypt, this arch-heretic in the early Church taught that Jesus was divine but not equal to God the Father. Arius argued that the Son of God must have a beginning if He is "begotten" of the Father. The Council of Nicaea (325) refuted and rejected the heresy of Arius and his followers in the Nicene Creed, but the aftermath of the controversy troubled Christendom for two centuries. See also **Arians**.

Athanasius (ca. 296–373). This attendee of the Council of Nicaea (325) became bishop of Alexandria, Egypt, in 328. Against the heresy of Arius, Athanasius adopted the formula that Christ was of the same substance (Greek: *homooúsios*) with the Father. His efforts united Greek and Latin theologians regarding the three persons and the one essence of God and led to the present form of the Nicene Creed, which was adopted at the Council of Constantinople in 381. He did not write the Athanasian Creed, but it is based on his teaching. See also **Arians; Arius**.

Augustine (Aurelius Augustinus; 354–430). Influenced by Ambrose, bishop of Milan, this renowned North African teacher and philosopher converted to Christianity in 386 during study of the Book of Romans. Baptized the following year, Augustine returned to North Africa, sold his family inheritance, and founded a monastery with a clerical school. He served as bishop of Hippo Regius, near Carthage (396), and vigorously fought the heresies of Pelagius, the Donatists, and others. His writings were the basis of Western theology until overshadowed by Scholasticism. Augustine taught justification by grace, but only for the elect. Luther studied Augustine's writings, but broke with him to emphasize Scripture alone. Augustine's views on predestination greatly influenced Calvin and Reformed theology. See also **Calvin, John; Donatists; Pelagius**.

Baier, Johann Wilhelm (1647–95). Born in Nürnberg; died in Weimar. Professor and rector at Jena and Halle; general superintendent, court preacher, and city pastor at Weimar. His chief work, *Compendium theologiae positivae*, went through many editions; that of Walther (1879) included a rich collection of extracts from earlier Lutheran theologians and served as the scholarly dogmatics text of the LCMS.

Bellarmine, Robert (1542–1621). An Italian Jesuit, cardinal of the Roman Catholic Church, and prominent participant in the Counter-Reformation, Bellarmine was an able scholar and controversialist. His chief work, the *Disputationes* (1581–93), is a systematic apology for the Roman Catholic position and one of the earliest systematic responses to Protestantism. It emphasizes the necessity of the papacy and church hierarchy to teach the faith and interpret tradition. The Lutheran response included

the equally significant *Loci Theologici* of Johann Gerhard. See also **Gerhard, Johann**.

Bogatzky, Karl Heinrich von (1690–1774). Born in Silesia, Bogatzky studied law at Jena, then theology at Halle under August Hermann Francke. Poor health limited his activities to writing. He spent the last twenty-eight years of his life at the Halle orphanage. His writing included pietistic meditative and devotional works, as well as hymn texts.

Breithaupt, Joachim Justus (1658–1732). Professor of theology at Halle; later, general superintendent in Magdeburg; a colleague of August Hermann Francke and a leading Pietist.

Bucer, Martin (1491–1551). German Protestant reformer. Born in Sélestat, Alsace, Bucer studied at Heidelberg and came under the influence of Erasmus and Luther. He introduced the Reformation at Strassburg in 1523, but after 1525 sought Protestant unity by avoiding specific language in doctrinal statements and refusing to take sides. Although he generally agreed with the Augsburg Confession, Bucer helped draw up the Tetrapolitan Confession among the Zwinglians. He also worked with Johann Bugenhagen and Luther, eventually agreeing on the 1536 Wittenberg Concord. After refusing to sign the Interim (1548), he was invited by Archbishop Thomas Cranmer to teach theology at Cambridge, where Bucer influenced the *Book of Common Prayer*. He died in Cambridge. See also **Tetrapolitan Confession** (p. 487).

Bugenhagen, Johann (1485–1558). After becoming a follower of Luther in 1520, Bugenhagen served as Luther's pastor in Wittenberg from 1522–28. He then served in Pomerania, Denmark, and as general superintendent of the church in Saxony. He organized Lutheran churches throughout northern Germany and, with Melanchthon, made great contributions to education. As Luther's pastor, Bugenhagen heard Luther's confession.

Calixt, Georg (Calixtus; Callisen; 1586–1656). This professor in Helmstedt was influenced by humanism, Melanchthon, and his study of the Church Fathers. He tried to revive the unity of the ancient Church by distinguishing fundamental and nonfundamental doctrines. Calixt incorporated ideas from Calvin and Nicolaus Hunnius (son of Aegidius). He influenced liberal Anglican theology. In the name of compromise, Calixt rejected the Formula of Concord and combined some Reformed positions with Lutheran ones, thus he came under the charge of syncretism. Johann Hülsemann, Johann Konrad Dannhauer, and Abraham Calov all regarded his positions as heresy, based on Scripture and the Lutheran Confessions.

Calov, Abraham (Calovius; 1612–86). Born in East Prussia and educated in Königsberg and Rostock, Calov served as professor and pastor in Königsberg, as well as superintendent of schools and churches. He shepherded churches in Danzig and Wittenberg, where he also served as general superintendent and head professor and dean of faculty at Wittenberg. In addition to his administrative and writing talents, Calov wrote prolifically on every area of theology. His greatest work, the *Biblia illustrata* (1672–76), is a commentary.

Calvin, John (1509–64). Influenced by humanism, by 1533 Calvin had joined the Reformation in France, but he had to escape to Basel, Switzerland. The early editions of his *Institutes of the Christian Religion* (first published in 1536) show great affinity to Luther's theology. Calvin reformed Geneva in 1536, but was exiled to Strassburg in 1538 before returning to Geneva (1541–64). His legalistic approach to Christianity emphasized God's sovereignty, honor, and glory. Other key features of his theology include accepting only Christ's spiritual presence in the Lord's Supper and the belief that God chose some people for heaven but others for hell (double predestination).

Carthusians. Strict order of reclusive monks that grew out of a community of hermits in the Chartreuse Mountains in France founded by Bruno of Cologne in 1084. Their life blends Western monastic tradition with the solitude and self-denial of the older Egyptian hermitic style of monasticism.

Chemnitz, Martin (1522–86). A student of Melanchthon, Chemnitz stressed the importance of the proper distinction between Law and Gospel. Ordained in 1554 by Johann Bugenhagen, Chemnitz tried to bring peace between the Philippists and Gnesio-Lutherans. He worked closely with other "second-generation" Lutherans, such as Jacob Andreae and Nicholas Selnecker, and was the driving force behind the theological precision of the Formula

of Concord. His writings include *Concerning the Lord's Supper* (1560), *Examination of the Council of Trent* (1565–73), *Concerning the Two Natures in Christ* (1570), and his posthumous *Loci Theologici* (1591).

Chrysostom (John; ca. 347–407). This Greek title, which means "Golden-mouth," was given to John after his death in recognition of his gift for preaching. John came from a rich family but led a life of poverty. He served as bishop of Antioch, then patriarch of Constantinople (398). He initiated a reform program in the clergy that stressed helping the poor and attacked luxury.

Clement of Alexandria (ca. 150–ca. 215). As leader of the catechetical school of Alexandria, Clement united Greek philosophical traditions with Christian doctrine and helped to create a Christian form of Platonism. He mentored Origen.

Cordatus, Conrad (ca. 1476–1546). Educated in Vienna and Ferrara, later deposed and repeatedly imprisoned for evangelical preaching in Hungary, Cordatus spent some time in Wittenberg and became a teacher, pastor, and eventually superintendent in Stendal (1540). He gathered a collection of Luther's table talks and opposed Melanchthon and his followers on the issue of human cooperation with grace, rejecting the false belief of human cooperation held by the Philippists. Nicknamed "Blockhead" (*Quadratus*) by Melanchthon.

Crell, Paul (Crellius; Krell; 1531–79). Pastor in Meissen and Wittenberg; also taught at Wittenberg. With Paul Eber he rejected the ubiquity of Christ but still taught the sacramental union of Christ with the elements in the Lord's Supper. He participated in the development of the Torgau Book, which led to the Formula of Concord. He took a middle position between Philippists and Gnesio-Lutherans, causing him difficulty from both sides.

Cromwell, Oliver (1599–1658). An "Independent" Puritan, Cromwell advocated local congregationalism against church hierarchy and opposed the English monarchy with force. He supported the 1649 execution of King Charles I and became lord protector (1653–58) of the Commonwealth of England.

Cruciger, Caspar (the Younger; Creutziger; 1525–97). Born in Wittenberg, Cruciger embraced Antinomianism, writing that the Gospel has a stronger terrifying force than even the Law, a position similar to the Roman Catholic view of the Evangelical Counsels. Imprisoned and eventually banished from Saxony as a Philippist, Cruciger became a Reformed pastor and president of the consistory in Kassel, near the Rhine valley.

Dallmann, Charles Frederick William (1862–1952). Born in Neu Damerow, Pomerania (Prussia), Dallmann came to the United States in 1868. He graduated from Concordia Seminary in 1886 and served parishes in Missouri, Maryland, New York City, and Wisconsin. He was president (1899–1901) and vice president (1901–5) of the English Evangelical Lutheran Synod of Missouri and Other States and first vice president of the LCMS (1926–32). In addition to his administrative and missionary efforts, Dallmann was a prolific writer and served as editor of *The Lutheran Witness* (1891–95).

Dannhauer, Johann Konrad (1603–66). Born in Köndringen, Germany, and educated in Strassburg, Marburg, Altdorf, and Jena, this theologian of the Lutheran orthodox tradition served as professor in Strassburg. He opposed Roman Catholic and Reformed theology and rejected the theology of GeorgCalixt as syncretism. He influenced Philipp Jakob Spener.

Dau, William Henry Theodore (1864–1944). Born in Lauenburg, Pomerania, Dau came to the United States in 1881. He graduated from Concordia Seminary in 1886 and served as a pastor in Tennessee and Indiana, as well as president of Concordia College, Conover, North Carolina; professor at Concordia Seminary, St. Louis; and president of Valparaiso University. Dau also served as editor of *The Lutheran Witness* and three other LCMS periodicals, coeditor of *Triglot Concordia*, translator of *The Proper Distinction Between Law and Gospel*, and wrote or edited numerous other projects.

Delitzsch, Franz (1813–90). Born in Leipzig, this prominent theologian of the Erlangen school served as professor at Rostock, Erlangen, and Leipzig. An enthusiastic Lutheran, Delitzsch was acquainted with the founders of the LCMS. Later, he fell under the influence of modern scientific theology and opposed a literalistic use of the Formula of Concord. His specialty was exegesis and his works include commentaries on Old Testament books (with Johann F. K. Keil).

Diderot, Denis (1713–84). This Rationalist Enlightenment philosopher was educated at the Jesuit-run Lycée Louis-le-Grand in Paris, an elite French school. He alienated many by his independent course during the Enlightenment as a writer and art critic. Diderot passed from Roman Catholicism through Deism to pantheistic naturalism. Most noted as the editor of the French *Encyclopédie*, he was supported by Catherine II of Russia, who was sympathetic to the Enlightenment, the spirit of which Diderot helped to define.

Dietrich, Veit (1506–49). Luther's secretary (1527) who attended the reformer at Marburg (1529) and at Coburg (1530). During his lifetime, Dietrich served as a private instructor, a member of the Wittenberg faculty, a pastor in Nürnberg, and as an active participant in the political side of the Reformation.

Donatists. This fourth-century sectarian group was led by one of two possible North African leaders: Donatus of Casae Nigrae or Donatus of Carthage. The sect formed after protests against the consecration of Caecilian as bishop of Carthage (311). Donatists held that only they were the true Church. The sect was destroyed by Islam in the seventh century AD. See also **Donatism** (p. 478).

Donatus. See under **Donatists**.

encyclopedists. People who have written or edited encyclopedias. Walther would have been referring to encyclopedias of the eighteenth century, specifically the *Cyclopedia* of Ephraim Chambers, which appeared in England and encouraged the publication of the French *Encyclopédie* edited by Denis Diderot and Jean le Rond d'Alembert. The *Encyclopédie* received contributions from Voltaire (François Marie Arouet), Jean Jacques Rousseau, and Charles-Louis de Secondat, Baron de Montesquieu. These philosophers formed the soul of French Rationalism and Enlightenment thought.

Enthusiast. From Greek for "one possessed by a god." The Latin term is "fanatic." The word describes a person so taken by his views that he uses violence or radical separation from society to enforce those views—actions typical of religious cults. The Lutheran Confessions use the word to describe fanatics who believed that God spoke to them directly without Holy Scripture and would save them without the Means of Grace.

Erasmus, Desiderius (ca. 1467–1536). This great Christian humanist scholar produced editions of the New Testament in Greek and Latin. Luther used Erasmus's second Greek New Testament (1519) for his German translation. Although sympathetic toward Luther, Erasmus considered the reformers to be too extreme. Among his many books are *In Praise of Folly* and *On the Freedom of the Will*. Luther responded to the latter with *On the Bondage of the Will* (1525). Erasmus drew the anger of both Roman Catholics and Protestants, thus his reputation declined after the Reformation, though it rose again with the Enlightenment.

Eutyches (ca. 378–ca. 454). Although he opposed Nestorius (who denied the communion of the two natures in Christ), Eutyches taught that Christ's human nature was swallowed up in the divine after the incarnation. Eutyches was condemned at the Council of Chalcedon (451). See also **Nestorius**.

Evangelical Church. Also known as *Albrechtsbrüder* or *Albrechtsleute*, this group arose in 1803 from the work of Jacob Albrecht (Albright) of Pottstown, Pennsylvania. Of German Lutheran origin, Albrecht converted to Methodism. Language and cultural issues kept his German-speaking group from merging with English-speaking Methodists. The Evangelical Church spread as its members began to speak English, and it eventually joined the United Methodist Church.

Evangelical Synod of North America. As members of the Prussian Union immigrated to the United States, they organized in Gravois Settlement, near St. Louis, Missouri (also near the present location of Eden Seminary in Webster Groves, Missouri). The name Evangelical Synod of North America was adopted in 1877, and in 1959 the group merged into the United Church of Christ.

Fanatic. See **Enthusiast**.

Flacius, Matthias (1520–75). A star pupil of Luther and Melanchthon, Flacius stressed the natural depravity of man by making sin part of the *substance* of human nature since the fall into sin. This position must conclude that God and sin join in Christ because no component of a substance may be removed without the substance

being destroyed or changing completely into something else. If Christ cannot have a human nature like us, we cannot be saved. Article I of the Formula of Concord (*Concordia*, 474–77) rejects this error. Nevertheless, Flacius helped fundamentally to shape the study of church history and biblical hermeneutics with the *Magdeburg Centuries* and the *Clavis*.

Francke, August Hermann (1663–1727). Born in Lübeck, Germany, Francke was a philanthropist, preacher, educator, and the leader of Pietism. He studied philosophy, theology, and languages, especially Hebrew. In 1686 he co-founded an association devoted to closer, devotional Bible study. Through Philipp Jakob Spener's influence, Francke became a professor at Halle in 1692 and the guiding spirit of Pietism after Spener's death. Francke's school for poor children, founded in 1695, expanded into a cluster of educational and charitable institutions. Under his leadership, Halle became the center of the Danish-Halle mission to India, which became connected with Zinzendorf and, through him, the Moravians at Herrnhut.

Frederick William III (Friedrich Wilhelm; 1770–1840). King of Prussia, 1797–1840. After suffering repeated defeats at the hands of Napoleon, Frederick lost his kingdom in 1807, though Prussia was restored by victory in 1813–15. Frederick joined the Holy Alliance that emerged as the first modern international peacekeeping organization. Its task was to uphold the 1815 Congress of Vienna. He used Pietism and unionism to create social unity in Prussia. After decreeing the use of a common church agenda in 1798, Frederick promulgated the Prussian Union and the takeover of Wittenberg by Halle in 1817. He persecuted those who opposed his religious programs.

Frederick William IV (Friedrich Wilhelm; 1795–1861). King of Prussia, 1840–61. Forced by the 1848 socialist revolutions to grant a constitution, Frederick was more tolerant than his father. On July 23, 1845, he issued the *Generalkonzession*, which permitted Lutherans who remained separate from the Prussian Union to organize free churches, though they were prohibited from displaying any public likeness to a church. These "old Lutherans" did not gain equal rights until 1930.

Freethinkers. People who recognize no other authority in religion than their own reason. In England the term was applied to deists. French freethinkers (e.g., Rousseau, Voltaire, and other encyclopedists) were usually pantheists, agnostics, or atheists. German Enlightenment thought led to the organization of *Freie Gemeinden* (Free Congregations). Free thought is reflected in the 1789 *Declaration of the Rights of Man and of the Citizen*, which held that no one should be interfered with because of his views, also in religion, provided these views do not lead to disturbance of public order. Famous freethinkers include Charles Darwin, Denis Diderot, Thomas Paine, Anthony Ashley Cooper (third Earl of Shaftesbury), and Herbert Spencer. Closely associated with them are Benjamin Franklin and Thomas Jefferson.

Fresenius, Johann Philipp (1705–61). A student of theology at Strassburg, Fresenius clashed with Jesuit Johann Nikolaus Weislinger, resulting in flight to Darmstadt in 1731. Called by Landgrave Ernst-Ludwig of Hessen-Darmstadt to be castle preacher in Giessen, Fresenius was given an administrative post in Darmstadt and a professorship in Giessen. In 1743 he became the *senior* and consistorial director in Frankfurt am Main. He opposed the Moravians and was respected by Goethe.

Freylinghausen, Johann Anastasius (1670–1739). Theologian, composer, and poet, Freylinghausen was born in Gandersheim, Brunswick, and educated at Jena, Erfurt, and Halle. He became August Hermann Francke's pastoral assistant, married Francke's daughter, and (with brother-in-law G. A. Francke) headed institutions founded by Francke. Freylinghausen edited collections of hymns and composed several hymn tunes.

Gerhard, Johann (1582–1637). Severe illness and depression at the age of fifteen shaped the later theology of this native of Quedlinburg, Germany. Johann Arnd, a forerunner of Pietism, urged Gerhard to study theology, and he received his doctorate from Jena in 1606 before being ordained and made superintendent at Heldburg. Gerhard later served as general superintendent of Coburg, as a professor at Jena, and as a political advisor. One of the most influential Lutheran theologians of his time, Gerhard participated in the broad intellectual renewal of Aristotelian thought around 1600 that coincided with the rise of the Counter-Reformation and the need for a common intellectual framework in German universities. His careful study of the Church Fathers influenced many later Protestant theologians. His *Loci theologici* are cited in this volume.

Gnesio-Lutherans ("Genuine Lutherans"). After the death of Luther, so-called genuine Lutheranism was represented by men such as Nikolaus von Amsdorf, Matthias Flacius, Wigand, Gallus, Judex, Mörlin, Hesshus, Timan, Westphal of Hamburg, Aegidius Hunnius, Poach, and E. Sarcerius. This group was based at Jena beginning in 1557. Their opponents were called Philippists. Based on Scripture, the Gnesio-Lutherans rejected the tendency to seek compromise on fundamental doctrines with Roman Catholics and the Interim, on one hand, and with Calvinists regarding the Lord's Supper, on the other hand. Some members, such as Flacius, became too extreme in their opposition and themselves fell into error.

Gnostics. From Greek *gnosis*, "knowledge." These followers of Gnosticism adopted a matter/spirit dualism of good and evil. Some believed that the "savior" is a spirit that possessed Jesus of Nazareth from His birth to shortly before His death. This reduces Jesus to a legalistic teacher of secret knowledge. The Gnostic ethical system based on this dualism tried to destroy the flesh either by rejecting all worldly comfort or by engaging in extreme depravity.

Grabau, Johannes Andreas August (1804–79). Born in Olvenstedt, near Magdeburg, Germany, Grabau studied theology at Halle and served as pastor at St. Andreas, Erfurt. Imprisoned twice for refusal to use the official *Agenda* (because he opposed its Reformed tendencies), Grabau was permitted to emigrate with supportive Prussian Lutherans in 1839. Grabau and his group settled in the region of Buffalo, New York, where he served as pastor for about forty years. He founded Martin Luther College in Buffalo and the Synod of the Lutheran Church Emigrated from Prussia (the Buffalo Synod).

Harms, Claus (1778–1855). Born in Fahrstedt, Schleswig-Holstein, Germany, Harms was educated in Meldorf and Kiel. Impressed by J. F. Kleuker, a Pietist professor who believed in supranaturalism, and influenced by Friedrich D. E. Schleiermacher's *Speeches on Religion*

(*Reden Über die Religion*), Harms eventually turned from rationalism to Lutheranism at Kiel. He served as a deacon, archdeacon, chief pastor and provost, and counselor of the high consistory. In 1817, Harms issued Martin Luther's Ninety-five Theses together with ninety-five of his own against rationalism and the Prussian Union. Thus Harms sparked the Lutheran confessional awakening of the nineteenth century and is considered to be the father of all modern confessional Lutheran churches.

heavenly prophets. See **Zwickau prophets**.

Heerbrand, Jakob (1521–1600). Born in Giengen, Germany, and educated in Tübingen and Wittenberg, Heebrand served as deacon in Tübingen and pastor at Herrenberg. A signer of the Württemberg Confession in 1551, he was selected by Christoph of Württemberg as a delegate to the Council of Trent. Heebrand participated in the process that generated the Formula of Concord.

Hegel, Georg Wilhelm Friedrich (1770–1831). The philosophical system of this Berlin professor (1818–31) rests on the triad: Idea-Nature-Spirit. Idea (God) properly exists when it passes into Nature (the antithesis of Idea). Nature passes into Spirit as mind awakens to the idea of Self as the unity of Idea (logic) and Nature (space). This occurs as history. Hegel thus builds on earlier ideas to speak of process theology, the idea that mankind is where the truth of God is developing and emerging. This evolutionary motif underlies the leftist ideologies of socialism and communism. It also stands behind fascism on the right. Hegel's thought influences much secular opposition to Christianity and its witness to unchanging divine truth in Scripture.

Hengstenberg, Ernst Wilhelm (1802–69). Born in Fröndenberg, Westphalia, Germany, the son of a Reformed pastor, Hengstenberg was educated in Bonn. Through private study he found Christ in the Bible and became Lutheran. He opposed rationalism, unionism, and the "mediating theology" of Friedrich D. E. Schleiermacher and his followers. The founder of *Evangelische Kirchen-Zeitung* (1827), Hengstenberg also authored numerous Bible commentaries.

Herrnhuters. See **Moravians**.

Holiness churches. After the United States Civil War, many Methodists and others began a general holiness movement. Evangelistic societies were formed to promote the doctrine of complete perfection and related views. This movement spawned dozens of church bodies, including the Church of God, Church of God in Christ, Church of the Nazarene, various Pentecostal bodies, and the Wesleyan Church. Holiness bodies differ greatly on biblical interpretation. Some believe all forms of luxury to be sin. Others require a manifestation of their understanding of the charismatic gifts, such as speaking in tongues and miraculous healing. All are millennialists. Their common Arminian beliefs include free will, human responsibility, and the ability to reach perfection—all of which rest on false teaching about the nature of sin and the requirements of the Law. See also **Arminianism** (p. 475).

Huber, Samuel (ca. 1547–1624). In 1586, this Reformed pastor rejected the Calvinist doctrine of double predestination at the Colloquy of Montbéliard (Mömpelgart). Deposed in 1588, he subscribed to the Formula of Concord at Tübingen in the same year. In 1592 he became a professor at Wittenberg and taught that man must make his eternal election sure by repentance and faith. He was deposed again in 1594 and exiled in 1595. See also **Hunnius, Aegidius**.

Hülsemann, Johann (1602–61). Born in Esens, Ostfriesland, Germany, this Wittenberg professor represented Lutheranism at the Colloquy of Thorn in 1645, where he opposed Calixt and syncretism.

Hunnius, Aegidius (1550–1603). Born in Winnenden, Württemberg, Germany, and educated at Tübingen, Hunnius served as an assistant pastor and as a professor. He tried unsuccessfully to win support for the Formula of Concord in the University of Marburg and the territorial church of Hesse. He opposed Calvinism and sparred with Samuel Huber, who insisted that a person makes his election sure through repentance and faith. The predestinarian controversy that Huber created caused his rejection by both Reformed and Lutherans. Hunnius was the main Protestant spokesman at the 1601 Regensburg Colloquy, where the Jesuit Adam Tanner defeated him. Hunnius helped compose the Saxon Visitation Articles.

Hus, John (Jan; 1369–1415). This Czech reformer and forerunner of the Reformation taught the sole authority of Scripture and held that the

Church is the body of the elect. Although he preached Christ as Savior, he confused Law and Gospel and mixed justification with sanctification. Hus suffered martyrdom at the Council of Constance (1415).

Hutter, Leonhard (1563–1616). Born in Nellingen, near Ulm, Germany, Hutter was educated at Strassburg, Leipzig, Heidelberg, and Jena and served as a professor in Wittenberg. This champion of Lutheran orthodoxy was called *redonatus Lutherus* (Latin: "Luther given back"), an anagram of "Leonardus Hutterus." His works include *Compendium locorum theologicorum*, a standard textbook in Saxony until shortly before Walther's birth. He also authored *Concordia concors*, referred to by Walther.

Jerome (Sophronius Eusebius Hieronymus: ca. 345–420). A rhetorician and philosopher, Jerome was baptized in Rome and, after traveling, settled in Bethlehem and turned to theology. He served as secretary to Pope Damasus I of Rome. Jerome's works include the revision of the Latin Bible (the Vulgate), as well as commentaries on books of the Bible. For his work on the Vulgate, Jerome used the Hebrew Old Testament instead of the Greek (the *Septuagint*), which caused an outcry in the Church regarding the use of the Psalms in worship. Jerome seems never to have clearly understood Christ's redemptive work.

Jesuits. See **Jesus, Society of**.

Jesus, Society of. Founded in 1534 by Ignatius of Loyola and six companions, this Roman Catholic order of clerks regular is better known as the Jesuits. Members of the order, which emphasizes obedience (including special obedience to the pope), typically focus on education (especially higher education) and missions. Recognized officially by the pope in 1540, the Jesuits had a prominent role in the Counter-Reformation, especially in western Europe. By 1773, however, the order had been suppressed everywhere but in Russia; it was not restored until 1814.

Kahnis, Karl Friedrich August (1814–88). Born in Greiz, Germany, and educated at Halle, Kahnis taught at Berlin, Breslau, and Leipzig. At first he defended confessional Lutheranism—even joining the Old Lutherans in 1848. Later, he adopted a subordinationist view that Jesus Christ was not equal to the Father as touching

His divinity. He also developed different views on Scripture and the Lord's Supper.

Keil, Johann Friedrich Karl. See under **Delitzsch, Franz.**

Keyl, Ernst Gerhard Wilhelm (1804–72). Born and educated in Leipzig, Keyl served as a pastor in Saxony before joining the emigrant society of Martin Stephan. Upon arriving in the United States in 1839, Keyl shepherded churches in Missouri, Wisconsin, Maryland, and Ohio. He wrote a four-volume commentary on Luther's Small Catechism that served the LCMS for fifty years.

Kinner, Samuel (1603–68). Born in Breslau, Germany, Kinner was court physician of the duke of Liegnitz-Brieg. He wrote the hymn "*Herr Jesu Christ, du hast bereit*'" (English: "Lord Jesus Christ, You Have Prepared"), which was cited by Walther.

Kromayer, Hieronymus (1610–70). Born in Zeitz, Germany, Kromayer was educated in the orthodox Lutheran centers of Leipzig, Wittenberg, and Jena. These institutions sought to maintain the confessional integrity of Lutheranism. During Kromayer's lifetime, the theologians mentored by Georg Calixt at Helmstedt argued for a Lutheranism effectively cut loose from the Lutheran Confessions, especially the Formula of Concord.

Lange, Joachim (1670–1744). Born in Gardelegen, Altmark, Germany, this professor at Halle was a prominent Pietist and controversialist who opposed orthodox Lutherans, especially Valentin Ernst Löscher, who saw in Pietism the encroachment of the Enlightenment. Lange also opposed rationalists, including Gottfried Thomasius and Christian Wolff, forerunners of Immanuel Kant. Lange stood against the Wertheim Bible, a version of the Pentateuch that was edited on the basis of coarse Enlightenment rationalism that was more extreme than historical-critical thought.

Luthardt, Christoph Ernst (1823–1902). Born in Maroldsweisach, Lower Franconia, Germany, and educated at Erlangen and Berlin. Luthardt taught at the *Gymnasium* at Munich 1847–51, at Erlangen 1851–54. He became a professor at Marburg 1854–56 and at Leipzig 1856–1902. He belonged to the so-called Erlangen School, whose criteria were Scripture, the Lutheran Confessions, and personal experience. He edited the *Allgemeine Evangelisch-Lutherische Kirchenzeitung*; other works include books on dogmatics, ethics, and apologetics.

Manes. See **Mani**.

Mani (Manes; Manichaeus; ca. 216–276). Born in Persia (modern Iran), Mani allegedly received divine revelations; claimed to be the last and highest prophet; and traveled probably to India and perhaps China. He became acquainted with Buddhism, returned to Persia, and perhaps suffered a cruel death in prison. See also **Manichaeism** (p. 481).

Melanchthon, Philip (Schwartzerd; 1497–1560). Born in Bretten, Lower Palatinate (Baden), Germany; educated at Heidelberg and Tübingen in classics. He became known as a humanist, published a Greek grammar (1518), and was recommended by Johannes Reuchlin for a professorship at the University of Wittenberg. He arrived on August 25, 1518, and Luther encouraged him to study theology. The rise of the Zwickau prophets and the Peasants' War in the 1520s emphasized the need for an education program to implement the Lutheran Reformation. Melanchthon planned an educational process using classical languages and philosophy as the basis for specialized vocational studies. His reforms eventually were promoted throughout Germany, which garnered him the title *Praeceptor Germaniae*, "the teacher of Germany." Melanchthon was prominent in the preparation of the Saxon Visitation Articles, but his later theological career was clouded in controversy. See also **Antinomians; Philippists**.

Methodists. See **Methodism** (p. 482).

Moravians (*Herrnhuter*). This group has roots in the Czech movement sparked by the execution of John Hus. In 1433, victorious followers of Hus were permitted to receive Communion in both kinds. Moderate Utraquists, from Latin for "both-kinders," helped Roman Catholics to suppress Hus's radical followers. In 1457, the Unity of Brethren (Latin: *Unitas Fratrum*) arose from this conflict and eventually influenced early Lutheranism. The Brethren later fell under Calvinist influence and helped to form the Moravian Church, in which Lutheran and Reformed doctrine often coexist. Through the support of Nikolaus Ludwig von Zinzendorf, the Moravians established ties with pietistic Lutherans and expanded into Pennsylvania.

Current Moravian beliefs generally correspond to Calvinism.

Münzer, Thomas (ca. 1489–1525). This German Enthusiast was born in Stolberg, Saxony, and educated in Leipzig and Frankfurt an der Oder. A preacher in Zwickau in 1520, Münzer tried to surpass Luther as a reformer, but he became a fanatical ascetic Anabaptist. He built his religion on direct revelation and claimed enlightenment by inner light through visions, dreams, etc. A leader in the Peasants' War, Münzer was defeated at Frankenhausen and beheaded.

Muslims. See **Islam** (p. 480).

Naogeorg, Thomas (Kirchmeyer; 1508–63). A playwright, Protestant theologian, and pamphleteer, Naogeorg became a Lutheran pastor and was at first on good terms with the Wittenberg faculty. In 1544, Luther and Melanchthon refused him permission to print his commentary on 1 John because he believed that the elect retain the Holy Spirit despite their coarse sins. After Luther's death, Naogeorg developed problems in his doctrine of the Lord's Supper. Defrocked, he remained a popular author who wrote against the papacy.

Nestorius (ca. 381–451). A monk who studied in Antioch, Nestorius became patriarch of Constantinople in 428—though he was sent back to the monastery at Antioch and in 436 banished to Upper Egypt. The Council of Ephesus condemned him in 431 for denying the communion of the divine and human natures in Christ. For Nestorius, Mary was only the mother of a human Christ, not the mother of God (Greek: *Theotokos*), and Christ is only God by adoption according to His human nature. See also **Eutyches**.

Neumann, Kaspar (Caspar; 1648–1715). This Lutheran hymnist was born in Breslau, Germany, and educated at Jena. Among other positions, he served as court preacher at Altenburg and as a professor at Breslau. His hymn "*Mein Gott, nun ist es wieder Morgen*" was a favorite of Walther's in difficult times.

Origen (ca. 185–ca. 254). The successor of Clement of Alexandria as head of the school for catechumens (202), Origen sought to set forth all the science of the time from the Christian point of view and to elevate Christianity to a theory of the universe compatible with Hellenism. In this context he interpreted Scripture in an allegorical manner. His commentaries are marred by his highly fanciful interpretations. The Fifth Ecumenical Council of Constantinople condemned Origen as a heretic in 553.

Osiander, Andreas (the Elder; ca. 1496–1552). This co-worker of Luther introduced the Reformation to Nürnberg and sided with Luther against Zwingli. He supported Luther at Augsburg in 1530 and reformed many areas of Germany. Later, Osiander taught that being declared righteous for Christ's sake in the Gospel (forensic justification) was overemphasized. He claimed that God makes the sinner to be just not by crediting the righteousness and obedience of Christ to the sinner, but by sending Christ to dwell in the sinner. He also claimed that Christ is our righteousness only according to the divine nature and that God does not judge sin. Article III of the Formula of Concord rejects Osiander's positions.

Pelagians. See **Pelagianism** (p. 483).

Pelagius (354–420). This educated layman led a life of poverty. After fleeing the sack of Rome by Alaric's Goths in 410, Pelagius arrived in Carthage, where his teaching that man has free will to refrain from sin flourished. He was opposed by Augustine. See also **Pelagianism** (p. 483).

Pezel, Cristoph (1539–1604). Born in Plauen, Germany, and educated in Jena and Wittenberg, Pezel was a professor and preacher in Wittenberg. He was banished in 1576 for Crypto-Calvinism (claiming to be Lutheran while holding to the teachings of John Calvin). Pezel openly accepted Calvinism after 1577.

Pharisees. See under **Judaism** (p. 481).

Philippists. The later editions of Melanchthon's *Loci Communes* increasingly reflected his growing synergism. The Colloquy of Worms (1540) revealed Melanchthon's tendency to make concession. His alterations of the Augsburg Confession in 1540 generated controversy over the Lord's Supper, especially after Melanchthon's death in 1560. His most harmful compromise was his personal involvement in preparing and supporting the Leipzig Interim (1548). Calvinists felt comfortable with the Augsburg Confession according to the changes made by Melanchthon. Those who espoused these alterations, in addition to those who rejected the third use of the Law and those who

allowed a Calvinist understanding of the Lord's Supper, were later called "Philippists."

Pieper, August Otto Wilhelm (1857–1946). Brother of Franz and Reinhold Pieper, he received the same education as Franz. He shepherded congregations in Wisconsin before becoming a professor at the Wisconsin Synod seminary in Wauwatosa, Wisconsin, in 1902.

Pieper, Franz August Otto (1852–1931). Born in Carwitz, Pomerania, Prussia, Pieper came to the United States in 1870 with his mother and brothers (August and Reinhold) after his father's death He was educated at Northwestern University, Watertown, and Concordia Seminary, St. Louis. Pieper's clear, concise defense of Scripture during the Election Controversy made him the premier theologian of the LCMS. He followed Walther as president of Concordia Seminary (1887–1931) and as president of the Missouri Synod (1899–1911). His book *Christliche Dogmatik*, posthumously translated as *Christian Dogmatics*, shaped Missouri Synod doctrine in the twentieth century.

Pieper, Reinhold (1850–1920). Brother of August and Franz Pieper, he received the same education as Franz. He served as pastor in Wisconsin and Illinois, and as president of Concordia Seminary, Springfield, Illinois (1891–1914).

Pietists. See **Pietism** (p. 483).

Propst, Jakob (Praepositus; 1486–1562). Born in Ypres, Belgium, Propst was prior of the Augustinian monastery in Antwerp. After studying in Wittenberg in 1521, he returned to Antwerp and preached against indulgences. In 1522, he was imprisoned and recanted. He resumed evangelical preaching, was arrested again, escaped, and ended up in Wittenberg in 1523. A friend of Luther, Propst served as a pastor and later as superintendent of Bremen, replaced by Tilemann Hesshus.

Protestants, Society of. In 1863 the *Protestantenverein* was formed in Germany to promote the union and progress of established Protestant churches on the basis of a "culture over Christ" approach. A number of clergy and lay leaders founded the organization in Frankfurt am Main. It represented liberal parties of the various German Lutheran and Reformed churches. It addressed the problem of the increasingly conservative nature of Germany following the exodus of

German liberals to the United States and elsewhere after 1848. The society's interests suffered defeat in a number of church elections. Nevertheless, the society continued to exist as a liberal German Protestant organization.

Rambach, Johann Jakob (1693–1735). Born in Halle, Germany, and educated in Halle and Jena, Rambach was a Pietist who taught at Halle and Giessen. Influenced by English theologians and philosophers, Rambach helped create an understanding of the "heart" that would do the right thing, given the chance. He believed in supranaturalism and the harmony between the natural and the supernatural order. He authored books on hermeneutics and ethics that influenced both Walther and those whom Walther opposed. He also translated the hymn "Baptized into Your Name Most Holy."

Rationalists. See **Rationalism** (p. 484).

Reformed. The beginnings of Reformed churches may be traced to Switzerland, France, Holland, Scotland, and England. The name "Reformed" came into general use by the end of the sixteenth century in reference to followers of Calvin, Zwingli, Martin Bucer, Johann Heinrich Bullinger, and Johannes Oecolampadius. Followers of Luther were called Lutheran especially after the Colloquy of Marburg (1529). Reformed churches divided into Calvinist and Arminian groups (see **Arminianism** [p. 475]; **Calvin, John; Holiness churches**). Today, the word "Reformed" is used commonly of Calvinists and rarely of Arminians. Calvinists in England and Scotland tend to be Presbyterian. In its strictest sense, "Reformed" refers to Calvinist churches on the European continent. The main difference between Presbyterian and Reformed churches is their polity (human organization) and related nomenclature.

Sacramentarians. During the Reformation, this term identified those who rejected both transubstantiation and the sacramental union of the body and blood of Christ with the elements of bread and wine. It was applied especially to Zwingli and his followers. The position of the followers of Wolfgang Capito, Andreas Bodenstein von Karlstadt, and Martin Bucer eventually drew closer to the Lutheran position. The term has been used for the Reformed in general. It has recently been used by those with a symbolic or spiritualizing view of the Lord's Supper to disparage those with a "high" view of the Eucharist, such as Lutherans, Roman Catholics, and Eastern Orthodox.

Sadducees. See under **Judaism** (p. 481).

Schaff, Philip (1819–93). This prominent Swiss-German scholar and professor at Mercersburg, Pennsylvania, and Union Theological Seminary in New York helped translate the *Realencyklopädie für protestantische Theologie und Kirche* as the *Schaff-Herzog Encyclopedia of Religious Knowledge*. He also wrote *Creeds of Christendom* and *History of the Christian Church* and edited the series *Nicene and Post-Nicene Fathers*. Schaff and others of like mind founded the Evangelical Union, a forerunner of the Ecumenical Movement.

Smets, Wilhelm (1796–1848). Born during the brief marriage of Johann von Ehrenstein, a criminal judge in Bonn who became an actor, and his second wife, Sophie, an actress, Smets endured a turbulent childhood before embarking on a brief military career and ending up as an author and teacher. He studied Roman Catholic theology and was ordained in 1822. Much of his remaining career involved publishing.

Socinians. These followers of two members of the Sozini family rejected the doctrine of the Trinity; denied the deity of Christ and His vicarious atonement, original sin, and the resurrection of the flesh; rejected the doctrine of hell and believed that the wicked would be annihilated; rejected Baptism and Holy Communion; and believed that people save themselves.

Socinus. See **Sozini, Fausto Paulo; Sozini, Lelio**.

Sozini, Fausto Paulo (1539–1604). The nephew of Lelio Sozini, Fausto became firmly established in Antitrinitarianism while studying theology. He held court positions at Florence, Italy, lived in Basel, Switzerland; went to Transylvania in 1578, but left amid theological turmoil and an outbreak of the plague. Fausto ended up in Poland, where he freed scattered Antitrinitarians from Anabaptists and chiliastic groups and organized them. He lived mainly in Krakow, under abuse and opposition, until driven from the city in 1598.

Sozini, Lelio (1525–62). A student of theology, Lelio came to doubt the Trinity and other doctrines that reason rejects. He traveled widely in

Reformation lands and became acquainted with Melanchthon and Calvin.

Spalatin, Georg (Georg Burckhardt; 1482–1545). Born in Spalt, near Nürnberg, Spalatin, like Luther, studied at the University of Erfurt. Johann von Laasphe ordained both Spalatin and Luther. Spalatin served as the tutor of future elector John Frederick, then as tutor to the nephews of Frederick III. He also was librarian, court chaplain, and secretary. He lived at the Saxon court in Torgau from 1511 until the death of Frederick III in 1525. Spalatin then lived in Altenburg and administered the doctrinal government of Lutheran churches in Saxony.

Spangenberg, Cyriacus (1528–1604). This pastor and hymnist lost his vocation in 1575 because he supported the heretical position of Matthias Flacius regarding original sin. Spangenberg also taught that sin corrupts essential parts of the human nature, thus making it impossible for Christ to be without sin.

Spener, Philipp Jakob (1635–1705). Influenced by reformist voices in Lutheranism and an emphasis in practical theology that he received in Strassburg and Geneva, Spener helped to form Pietism. He alienated orthodox theologians in Wittenberg, Dresden, and Leipzig, but was warmly received in the rationalist atmosphere of Berlin in Prussia. In 1694, Spener helped found the University of Halle as a center of Pietist learning. His 1675 *Pia Desideria* emphasized central points of Pietism.

Spurgeon, Charles Haddon (1834–92). Born in Kelvedon, Essex, England, Spurgeon joined the Baptists in 1851. He served as a pastor in England and established a preachers' college. He rejected the doctrine of baptismal regeneration and withdrew from the Baptist Union (1887), though he remained a nonconformist Baptist.

Starck, Johann Friedrich (1680–1756). Born in Hildesheim, Germany, and educated in Giessen, Starck was a preacher and pastor. Unlike many other Pietists, he believed that Baptism does have divine power. His version of Pietism embraced historic Lutheran doctrine that the Enlightenment rejected, which made his prayer book and book of devotions universally popular among believing Lutherans. His devotional books continue to shape Lutheranism today.

Staupitz, Johann von (ca. 1468–1524). The head of the German Congregation of Augustinians from 1503–20, Staupitz received his doctorate from Tübingen and was a charter faculty member of the University of Wittenberg. He guided Luther into an academic career and in 1518 released Luther from his monastic vows, simultaneously protecting the Augustinian order and freeing Luther to act on his reforming ideas. Staupitz retired to Salzburg, became a Benedictine monk, and repudiated the Protestant Reformation.

Stephan, Martin, Sr. (1777–1846). Born in Stramberg, Moravia; studied theology at Halle and Leipzig. Stephan became a pastor in Haber, Bohemia (today: Czech Republic) in 1809 and Dresden, Germany 1810–37. He opposed rationalism and was widely known as a spiritual adviser. Stephan resolved in the 1830s to emigrate to the US with his followers. He was placed under temporary suspension in 1837 and led the Saxon emigration to Missouri in 1838/39. He was deposed for maladministration and scandalous behavior. Stephan was taken to Illinois in 1839. By 1841 he was living in or near Kaskaskia, Illinois, and preaching there in the courthouse every 2 weeks. He served a congregation at Horse Prairie, southeast of Red Bud, Illinois, 1845–46.

Stephan, Martin, Jr. (1823–1884). Born in Dresden, Germany, he came to Missouri with his father while his mother and siblings were left behind in Germany. He then studied architecture in Dresden, later traveling to New York City in 1847 where he worked for a lithographer until 1849. He was a private tutor in Brattleboro, Vermont, in 1849. He then moved to St. Louis, where he designed the first building of Concordia College. The younger Stephan became a student of Walther, a parish pastor 1853–84, and also designed the teacher's seminary at Addison, Illinois, in 1864.

Stiemke, Timotheus (1847–1908). Stiemke served as a pastor in Texas, Louisiana, and Maryland, as well as president of the Southern District (1882–88).

Storch, Nicholas (Nikolaus; d. 1525) A weaver by profession, Storch claimed prophetic power. He influenced especially Andreas Bodenstein von Karlstadt. See also **Zwickau prophets**.

Stubner, Markus. See **Zwickau prophets**.

Thomasius, Gottfried (1802–75). This Lutheran theologian was born in Egenhausen, Middle Franconia, Germany, and educated in Erlangen, Halle, and Berlin. He was a pastor, professor at Erlangen, and university preacher. He adopted a form of kenotic Christology that said Christ not only regularly refrained from using His divine attributes during His state of humiliation but also that He emptied Himself altogether of some divine attributes. Similar to the historical-critical desire to affirm Jesus' full humanity while retaining something intelligible of His divinity, Thomasius and others helped to develop a new theory of interpretation according to "the whole of Scripture" and not to any particular passage, lest critics disprove that passage using rationalist methods. The result was a psychological religion that Franz Pieper strongly rebuts in *Christian Dogmatics.*

Turks. See **Islam** (p. 480).

Wislicenus, Gustav Adolf (1803–1875). After studying at Halle, Wislicenus became a pastor. He joined "Friends of the Light" (*Lichtfreunde*) in 1844 and attacked the authority of the Bible, which led to his defrocking in 1846. He continued to publish as a preacher of the Free Congregation in Halle, though in 1853 he was sentenced to two years in prison for aggravated idolatry. Wislicenus fled to the United States to avoid prison, but returned to Europe and settled near Zurich. He continued to publish rationalist interpretations of the Bible. See also **Freethinkers**.

Woltersdorf, Ernst Gottlieb (1725–61). A Lutheran pastor in Bunzlau, Silesia, Woltersdorf founded and directed an orphanage designed according to the model of the orphanage in Halle. A tireless worker with young people, Woltersdorf also wrote many poems and hymns in the pietistic style.

Zinzendorf, Nikolaus Ludwig von (1700–1760). After studying at Halle and Wittenberg, in 1722 Zinzendorf allowed persecuted members of the Moravian or Bohemian Brethren to build the Herrnhut community on part of his Berthelsdorf estate. He supported the printing of many pietistic books and tracts and the sending of missionaries through connections with the Danish crown. He broke with the Lutheran Church and was consecrated as a Moravian bishop in 1737, though he continued to present himself as a Lutheran in his bid for unionism. During his journey in the United States, Henry Melchior Muhlenberg opposed him. He died in 1760.

Zoroaster (Hellenistic name of Zarathustra). The founder of Zoroastrianism and alleged author of Zend-Avesta, Zoroaster lived before the sixth century BC in Persia. He claimed revelations from Ahura Mazdah regarding a new monotheism that he was to preach in opposition to contemporary polytheism. After eleven years of failure, he converted King Vishtaspa (ca. 618 BC), through whose influence the new religion spread. Zoroaster spoke of both an eternally good spirit, Ahura Mazdah, and an eternally evil spirit, Angra Mainyu or Ahriman. Between these two spirits are human beings, who have a free will to choose between good and evil and who will be rewarded or punished accordingly. Characteristic of the system is a well-developed doctrine of angels and the afterlife.

Zwickau prophets (heavenly prophets; *Bilderstürmer*). This name was given to a group of radical Anabaptists from Zwickau, Saxony, led by Nicholas Storch. The group stressed rigid conformity to New Testament rules; advocated separation of a believer from an unbelieving spouse; and rejected infant Baptism, the use of oaths, use of civil power, and military service. Some members of the group destroyed statues, paintings, and other images. Storch and others came to Wittenberg in December 1521, influenced Andreas Bodenstein von Karlstadt and even Melanchthon for a time, and caused Luther to return to Wittenberg from the Wartburg in March 1522.

Zwingli, Ulrich (Huldrych; 1484–1531). This Swiss theologian denied God's work through means and focused on divine providence and the direct communication of the Holy Spirit with man. Zwingli also said that the elements in the Sacraments were merely symbols. Luther opposed Zwingli by defending God's work through means and maintaining the sacramental union in the Lord's Supper between the elements and the body and blood of Christ. Luther affirmed that the personal union of Christ allows His human nature to have the attributes of the divine, such as being present where the divine is present or being present in the Lord's Supper. Zwingli rejected this view and limited Christ's human nature to a physical body present at a fixed location. Luther saw this limitation as rejecting the union of natures in Christ. Thus Luther believed that Zwingli was not truly Christian.

RESOURCES

The following resources by C. F. W. Walther are available at www.cph.org

Church and Ministry (Kirche und Amt). Translated by John T. Mueller. St. Louis: Concordia, 1987.

God Grant It. Compiled by August Crull. Translated by Gerhard Grabenhofer. St. Louis: Concordia, 2005.

God's No and God's Yes. Condensed by Walter Pieper. St. Louis: Concordia, 1972.

Selected Writings of C. F. W. Walther. Edited by August R. Suelflow. St. Louis: Concordia, 1981. Volumes in the series are:

> *Convention Essays*
>
> *Editorials from "Lehre und Wehre"*
>
> *Law and Gospel*
>
> *Letters*
>
> *Sermons*
>
> *Walther on the Church*

The Proper Distinction Between Law and Gospel. Translated by William H. T. Dau. St. Louis: Concordia, 1986.

The True Visible Church and the Form of a Christian Congregation. Translated by John T. Mueller. St .Louis: Concordia, 2005.

Walther Speaks to the Church. Edited by Carl S. Meyer. St. Louis: Concordia, 1973.

The following resources about C. F. W. Walther and the early Missouri Synod are available at www.cph.org

C. F. W. Walther: The American Luther. Edited by Arthur H. Drevlow. 1987.

Church and Ministry. By Eugene F. A. Klug. St. Louis: Concordia, 1993.

Government in the Missouri Synod. By Carl S. Mundinger. St. Louis: Concordia, 1947.

Handling the Word of Truth. By John T. Pless. St. Louis: Concordia, 2004.

Moving Frontiers. Edited by Carl S. Meyer. St. Louis: Concordia, 1964.

Servant of the Word. By August R. Suelflow. St. Louis: Concordia, 2000.

Zion on the Mississippi. By Walter O. Forster. St. Louis: Concordia, 1990.

Scripture Index

SUBJECT AND PERSONS INDEX